Praise for *A Military History of India since 1972*

"In combination with Arjun Subramaniam's earlier volume on 1947–1971, this book is a much-needed survey of India's military history since independence. As a retired air vice marshal of the Indian Air Force, the author brings an important triservice perspective to the topic. The paucity of available official sources means that the real strength of the work is the interviews and correspondence with senior commanders in all three Indian armed forces. It is a major contribution to the contemporary military history of India."

—**Alan Jeffreys**, author of *Approach to Battle: Training the Indian Army during the Second World War*

"A worthy successor to his first volume, Subramaniam continues his deeply researched and sweeping account of modern Indian military history. Strategy, technology, operations, mobilization systems: it's all here. Simply indispensable for anyone trying to understand India's history and its place in modern global security dynamics."

—**Wayne E. Lee**, Bruce W. Carney Distinguished Professor of History, University of North Carolina

"A sequel to *India's Wars: A Military History, 1947–1971,* this book examines the wars and conflicts India has fought since 1972. With a deft hand and the perspective of a military professional, Subramaniam provides a detailed yet vivid and insightful account of the operations of India's armed forces. Anyone interested in India's role in the world should read this book."

—**M. Taylor Fravel**, Arthur and Ruth Sloan Professor of Political Science and director, Security Studies Program, Massachusetts Institute of Technology

"Air Vice Marshal Arjun Subramaniam, a career Indian Air Force fighter pilot and accomplished scholar of international security affairs, has followed his earlier magisterial *India's Wars: A Military History, 1947–1971,* with this richly documented sequel that expands on India's continued combat experiences as the country has steadily matured into an emerging twenty-first-century heavyweight. Along the way his riveting account reads almost like a war novel at times as it inserts the reader directly into the flow of often fast-paced events and explores the steady gains that have been registered throughout the past four decades in the ever closer and more synergistic integration among India's three uniformed services. In a commendably balanced and fair-minded way, he offers an informed appreciation of their experiences under the varying stresses of combat across the conflict spectrum—all conveyed with a degree of intimate familiarity with the relevant political, strategic, and tactical-level details that only a warrior-scholar of his background and upbringing can capture with such authority."

—**Benjamin S. Lambeth**, nonresident senior fellow, Center for Strategic and Budgetary Assessments, and author of *Airpower in the War against ISIS*

"*A Military History of India since 1972* is well written, well researched, and provides excellent critical insights into the Indian military and its role in South Asian security."

—**James S. Corum**, coauthor of *Airpower in Small Wars: Fighting Insurgents and Terrorists*

"As one of India's important military historians, Air Marshal Arjun Subramaniam masterfully brings the reader on a vivid journey through India's evolving military doctrine as the country's global stature and influence continues to rise. *A Military History of India since 1972: Full Spectrum Operations and the Changing Contours of Modern Conflict* provides a meticulous historical understanding of India's military positions and current conflicts through the author's firsthand experience as an Indian Air Force fighter pilot and personal accounts shared by many of India's top military leaders."

—**William S. Cohen,** United States Secretary of Defense (1997–2001)

"A sweeping landscape of war and conflict in contemporary India, *A Military History of India since 1972* is a must-read for those who believe that India will be a leading power in the twenty-frist century."

—**Admiral James G. Stavridis,** United States Navy, Supreme Allied Commander at NATO (2009–2013)

"Since 1947 the Indian armed forces have been involved in many varied operations. In the second part of his military history of India, Arjun Subramaniam picks up the story from 1972. He includes a range of campaigns: counterinsurgency against the Nagas, the troubled peacekeeping operation in Sri Lanka, and the high-intensity Kargil conflict. As before he brings to the subject not only extensive research but also an insider's recollections and insights."

—**Sir Lawrence Freedman,** emeritus professor of war studies, King's College London, and author of *The Future of War: A History*

"Arjun Subramaniam has done it again. Through meticulous research he has uncovered telling details that vivify the familiar story of India's post-1971 conflicts in a new history that does justice—and honor—to all of India's armed forces. Both scholars and policymakers will benefit greatly from this intimate window into modern India's military operations."

—**Ashley J. Tellis,** Tata Chair for Strategic Affairs, Carnegie Endowment for International Peace

"Arjun Subramaniam's *A Military History of India since 1972* is a clear, comprehensive, and intriguing account of the conflicts that the Indian state has coped with both on domestic and external fronts. He not only has made deft use of the extant literature but also has drawn on a range of interviews with senior military and civilian defense personnel. This work will be of considerable interest to journalists, analysts, and academics concerned with the evolution of India's security policies since 1972."

—**Sumit Ganguly,** Rabindranath Tagore Professor of Political Science, Indiana University Bloomington, and coauthor of *Ascending India and Its State Capacity: Extraction, Violence, and Legitimacy*

A MILITARY HISTORY
OF INDIA SINCE 1972

A MILITARY HISTORY
OF INDIA SINCE 1972

Full Spectrum Operations and
the Changing Contours
of Modern Conflict

Arjun Subramaniam

University Press of Kansas

Published by the University Press of Kansas (Lawrence, Kansas 66045),
which was organized by the Kansas Board of Regents and is operated
and funded by Emporia State University, Fort Hays State University,
Kansas State University, Pittsburg State University, the University of
Kansas, and Wichita State University

Library of Congress Cataloging-in-Publication Data

Names: Subramaniam, Arjun, author.
Title: A military history of India since 1972 : full spectrum operations
and the changing contours of modern conflict / Arjun Subramaniam.
Other titles: Full spectrum operations and the changing contours
of modern conflict
Description: Lawrence : University Press of Kansas, 2021 | Series:
Modern war studies | Includes bibliographical references and index.
Identifiers: LCCN 2020048509
ISBN 9780700631988 (cloth)
ISBN 9780700631995 (ebook)
Subjects: LCSH: India—History, Military—20th century. | India—History,
Military—21st century. | Military art and science—India—History—20th
century. | Military art and science—India—History—21st century.
Classification: LCC DS442.6 .S836 2021 | DDC 355.020954—dc23
LC record available at https://lccn.loc.gov/2020048509.

British Library Cataloguing-in-Publication Data is available.

Printed in the United States of America

10 9 8 7 6 5 4 3 2 1

The paper used in this publication is acid free and meets the minimum
requirements of the American National Standard for Permanence of
Paper for Printed Library Materials Z39.48-1992.

FOR MY FATHER,
WHO HELPED ME REALIZE THE POWER
OF THE WRITTEN WORD

CONTENTS

A photo gallery follows page 212.

ACKNOWLEDGMENTS

This was a tough book to write—largely because it was a sequel to a book that had no expectations. It was written under pressure and a sense of dislocation following a premature retirement from the Indian Air Force to pursue teaching and writing and take advantage of two prestigious fellowships at Harvard and Oxford. The no-strings-attached financial support from the Tata Education Trust and the British Ministry of Defence enabled me to pursue my dreams. I owe gratitude to several unnamed well-wishers who helped me obtain the Tata support, and Brigadier Mark Goldsack, defense attaché at the British High Commission, a former a student of mine, ensured that I got to Oxford.

Professor Sugata Bose recommended me for the fellowship at the Harvard Asia Center and was a mentor during my stay there. I am also deeply indebted to the Changing Character of War Program at Oxford University and its director, Professor Rob Johnson, for giving me the space to write and receive feedback from the program's diverse participants.

Teaching a course titled War and Conflict in Contemporary South Asia at the Fletcher School of International Law and Diplomacy in the fall of 2018 allowed me to share ideas with the faculty, students, and US military fellows. I am grateful to Admiral Stavridis and Professor Richard Shultz for welcoming me into the International Security Studies Program and to Professor Ian Johnstone for his continued support. Professor Raj Echambadi from Northeastern University supported my writing in Boston by offering me a concurrent fellowship at the D'Amore McKim School of Business.

Mahesh Rangarajan, Srinath Raghavan, Rudra Chaudhuri, and Sreeram Chaulia were all responsible for ensuring that I had flexible teaching assignments at Ashoka University and the Jindal School of International Affairs in 2019. I was able to finish my manuscript in peace because of that consideration. General Rawat, India's current chief of defense staff, and Air Chief Marshal Dhanoa, the previous air chief, were particularly supportive of my endeavor during the last phase of research and writing in 2019. They spent quality hours with me recounting their operational experiences and offering critical senior leadership perspectives.

I am deeply indebted to the scores of battle-hardened military veterans and serving officers from all three services who infused credibility and context into my narrative by spending long hours being interviewed by me and engaging in subsequent email exchanges and telephone conversations. Several former chiefs of the three services were especially frank in their recollections of their operational careers, and I am lucky to have spoken with them. A number of colleagues, classmates, students, friends, and military history enthusiasts who believed in my mission offered assistance whenever I asked. I cannot name everyone here, but I am grateful to them all. The National Defence College, my springboard to a second career, remains close to the heart of this endeavor, with piles of books from its library strewn across my study.

Professor Paul Springer from the Air Command and Staff College offered several suggestions to refine the manuscript, and I am grateful for his careful critique. I am also grateful to several anonymous reviewers who helped me refine my narrative and cautioned me wherever I had engaged in overreach. Joyce Harrison and Bill Allison were patient, enthusiastic, and encouraging during my first foray into the tough university press circuit in the United States. Mike Kehoe and Colin Tripp were great to work with on the last lap of the book, and I hope to meet all of them soon. Ramneek Singh, a young graphic designer from New Delhi, did great work on the maps, as always. Thank you, folks!

My wife, Mowthika, has sacrificed much for me to write these books and has acted as a sounding board for my ideas as they emerged. Shruti and Meghna, our two daughters, have been tolerant of my eccentric behavior and erratic parenting over the years. My parents will always be an inspiration in any intellectual endeavor—particularly my father, a brilliant academic who did not get an opportunity to read any of my writing. This book is for all of them.

ABBREVIATIONS

AFSPA	Armed Forces Special Powers Act
AGPL	actual ground position line
AISSF	All India Sikh Students Federation
AWACS	Airborne Warning and Control System
BBC	British Broadcasting Corporation
BDCA	Border Defense Cooperation Agreement
BSF	Border Security Force
BVR	beyond visual range
CIA	Central Intelligence Agency
CNDP	National Congress for the Defense of the People
CRPF	Central Reserve Police Force
DGP	director-general of police
DRC	Democratic Republic of Congo
EBO	effects-based operations
EPRLF	Eelam People's Revolutionary Liberation Front
EROS	Eelam Revolutionary Organization of Students
FARDC	Armed Forces of the Democratic Republic of Congo
FCNA	Force Command Northern Areas
FDLR	Democratic Forces for the Liberation of Rwanda
FLB	forward logistics base
GDP	gross domestic product
HM	Hizbul Mujahideen
HQ	headquarters
HuA	Harkat-ul-Ansar
HuM	Harkat-ul-Mujahideen
IAF	Indian Air Force
ICV	infantry combat vehicle
IED	improvised explosive device
IGAR	Inspector General Assam Rifles
INA	Indian National Army
IPKF	Indian Peacekeeping Force
IRBM	intermediate-range ballistic missile
ISI	Inter-Services Intelligence
ISLA	Indo–Sri Lanka Accord
J&K	Jammu and Kashmir
JeM	Jaish-e-Mohammad

JKLF	Jammu and Kashmir Liberation Front
JVP	Janathā Vimukthi Peramuna
LAC	line of actual control
LeT	Lashkar-e-Taiba
LOP	limits of patrolling
LTTE	Liberation Tigers of Tamil Eelam
MARCOS	Marine Commandos
MNF	Mizo National Front
NATO	North Atlantic Treaty Organization
NEFA	North Eastern Frontier Agency
NFG	Naga Federal Government
NFU	no first use
NLF	National Liberation Front
NLI	Northern Light Infantry
NNA	Naga National Army
NNC	Naga National Council
NNRC	Neutral Nations Repatriation Committee
NSCN	National Socialist Council of Nagaland
NSG	National Security Guard
ONUC	Organization des Nations Unies au Congo
OODA	observe, orient, decide, and act
OP	observation post
PAK	Pakistan Air Force
PLA	People's Liberation Army
PLOTE	People's Liberation Organization of Tamil Eelam
PoK	Pakistan-occupied Kashmir
R&AW	Research and Analysis Wing
RAPID	Reorganized Army Plains Infantry Division
RGN	Revolutionary Government of Nagaland
R2P	responsibility to protect
RUF	Revolutionary United Front
SAM	surface-to-air missile
SAS	Special Air Service
SFF	Special Frontier Force
SIB	Subsidiary Intelligence Bureau
SRBM	short-range ballistic missile
SSG	Special Service Group
SSW	Subsector West
TELO	Tamil Eelam Liberation Organization
UN	United Nations
VDC	Village Defense Committee

Introduction

Our own generation is unique, but sadly so, in producing a school of thinkers who are allegedly experts in military strategy and who are certainly specialists in military studies (also called Strategic Studies by some) but who know virtually nothing of military history, and who do not seem to care about their ignorance.
—Bernard Brodie in Carl von Clausewitz, *On War*

A Military History of India since 1972 is the second part of a holistic attempt to understand war and conflict in contemporary India. The first part, *India's Wars: A Military History, 1947–1971*,[1] set the stage for a sequel, not unlike a fighter aircraft making a second pass over a target area.

A second pass is carried out to ensure that the target is destroyed, assuming that there is ammunition left. However, if the first pass was not good enough, this move is fraught with danger because the element of surprise is lost. Unless a new attack pattern or an unpredictable flight profile is adopted before the second attack, the enemy could be lying in wait with interceptor aircraft and ack-ack (military slang for antiaircraft guns) or surface-to-air missiles (SAMs). The first kills achieved by the Indian Air Force in the 1971 war with Pakistan were the result of a four-aircraft Pakistani Sabre aircraft formation carrying out repeated passes in a predictable pattern over an Indian Army brigade in the Boyra Sector of erstwhile East Pakistan. It was this careless bit of tactical flying that allowed the Indian Gnat aircraft (affectionately called the "last real fighter" by the pilots who flew them) to pounce on them from above. The Sabres paid a heavy price for their complacency.[2]

As fighter pilots pull out of an attack and reposition for a second pass, most do a quick recap of the previous attack. They first try to assess the damage they caused while simultaneously checking their radar warning receiver for any lock-on from airborne fire-control radar or the tracking radar of a SAM. A deep breath and a check of engine and weapon parameters follow. In the meantime, if the attack was controlled by a ground-based forward air controller, pilots wait for feedback on the previous attack. All this typically takes thirty to forty-five seconds before the next attack commences. Everything happens in a blur at speeds of 700 to 850 kilometers per hour.

The second pass is done rapidly, and all ammunition is expended. The pilots then duck down to treetop level and head home after regrouping with other formation members. There is no relaxing until they cross the border and hear the calming voice of a friendly radar controller, who guides the formation back to base. After landing, the adrenaline is still pumping, knees are wobbly, and overalls are invariably drenched with sweat. One of the most important factors for an effective second pass is the speed at which the pilots assess any changes in the environment, the impact of their first attack, and the configuration of the next one—whether they should stick to the same pattern or do something different. *A Military History of India since 1972* is much like a consistent second pass. It adheres to an applied military history narrative that weaves the strategic and operational dimensions of war and conflict in contemporary India with tactical vignettes and credible personal perspectives to create a coherent mosaic of contemporary Indian military history.

All conflicts that India fought before 1971 were mostly conventional wars that could be sequenced chronologically. The only departures were the two insurgencies in the northeastern states of Nagaland and Mizoram and the India–China skirmishes at Nathu La and Cho La in 1967, which I could not cover in the first book. I have respected reader feedback and included them in this volume, along with a few United Nations peacekeeping operations in the 1950s and 1960s as part of a larger examination of India's combat experiences in pursuit of global peace in troubled lands.

As was the case with *India's Wars,* this volume retains a practitioner's flavor and is reinforced with scholarly rigor. The credibility of the narrative rests on three pillars: triangulation of facts and authenticity derived from the available primary sources (mainly regimental archives, official doctrines, personal papers, and interviews), deep mining of secondary sources and existing literature, and a practitioner-scholar's unique perspective on war and conflict. This is so because much of the actual fine print regarding how the Indian state has conducted military operations is still shrouded in secrecy and has not been declassified. Unrestricted access to Lieutenant General Rostum Nanavatty's meticulously preserved diaries and recollections provided the much-needed primary sources to dissect operations in those sectors and construct my narrative. Interviews and conversations with more than a hundred serving and retired officers and men, some of whom wished to remain anonymous—including former chiefs from all three armed forces—served as highly credible primary sources for land, air, and naval operations.

The Indian Army has over 1.2 million personnel, the Indian Navy has more than 100 front-line combat ships, and the Indian Air Force has more than 50 squadrons and 800 aircraft. These large forces have been in a state of near-constant readiness and have seen much action. I have made every effort to write a representative and running history that does justice to all

three services without fear or favor. I reiterate my deepest respect for all
the regiments, fleets, and squadrons of India's armed forces, and any omis-
sions are the result of space limitations: I simply could not fit in everything I
wanted to write about. Some warriors emerge as larger-than-life characters,
but that does not suggest that others stood on the sidelines and watched.
This is essentially a book about India's contemporary soldiers, sailors, and
airmen, and I wanted them to occupy the pole position in this book. Writing
about war and conflict, especially when one has witnessed success and failure from the inside, can be perilous. Many of the protagonists I write about
are battle-hardened professionals and practitioners, and my contextual and
measured criticism in hindsight may appear harsh at times. All I can do is
seek their indulgence and magnanimity.

This book is also about how the Indian nation-state and its armed forces
have coped with the changing contours of modern conflict in the decades
since 1972. During this period, India's democracy has flourished, surmount-
ing many challenges even as multiple geopolitical fractures have plagued
the world. One need look no further than the Soviet Union, the Balkans,
western Asia, and the Caucasus to situate India's predicament and progress
in the right strategic context. I ask the same questions, but from an Indian
perspective, that Sir Lawrence Freedman asked in the introductory chapter
of *War,* a 1994 compilation of essays: "What are the causes of War? How
have they been fought and what are the prospects for the future? Are there
basic principles which should shape the conduct of war if it is to be successfully prosecuted?"[3]

The narrative also offers a changing perspective of India's approach to the
conduct of war and conflict in contemporary times. These include the 2016
"surgical" or cross-border strikes by the Indian Army's Special Forces across
the line of control with Pakistan, the face-off with the Chinese at Doklam in
2017, the preemptive punitive strikes by the Indian Air Force against terrorist camps in Pakistan in 2019, and the large-scale aerial engagement between
the Indian Air Force and the Pakistan Air Force the following day. The
structure of the book offers readers a choice: they can embark on a comprehensive and chronological examination of war and conflict in contemporary
India, or they can base their reading on specific timelines or campaigns. A
chapter on the development of India's nuclear capabilities has been included
because nuclear posturing in the India–Pakistan context has given the United
States much to worry about in South Asia. Space and cybercapabilities are
still fledgling areas and remain predominantly in the highly classified domain, so they have no place in what is primarily a historical narrative. India's Central Armed Police Forces and Paramilitary Forces, particularly the
Assam Rifles, Border Security Force, Central Reserve Police Force, and Indo-

Tibetan Border Police, have done a sterling job in complementing India's armed forces in a wide range of operations. I could not possibly do justice to their exploits in this volume.

This book is a tribute to the soldiers standing vigil through the night at lonely outposts, not knowing when an enemy sniper might bring them down, while the rest of the country celebrates Diwali, Guru Purab, Eid, or Christmas (festivals celebrated in secular India). It is an ode to the unsung helicopter and transport pilots who snake through narrow valleys in poor weather to drop sacks of flour and potatoes or to deliver bagfuls of letters, which are then read by soldiers within the confines of their thermal tents at 19,000 feet. And it is a salute to the sailors helping the captain navigate their frigate through a stomach-churning storm on the high seas while on an antipiracy mission. I hope this book fulfills its primary objective of serving as a historical narrative of war and conflict in contemporary India, one that appeals to a wide spectrum of readers in India and elsewhere.

I

Chameleon Wars

She [Indira Gandhi] defended Indian interests and security when threatened. For that the nation must be grateful to her. In her ability to anticipate security problems . . . and the need to build up Indian power she truly reflected the Indian intelligentsia.

—K. Subrahmanyam, *Security in a Changing World*

INDIAN PERSPECTIVES ON CONTEMPORARY CONFLICT

Thinking about large-scale conventional war is now back in fashion, given the emerging military rivalry between the United States and China and a resurgence in Russian military posturing. It is equally clear that limited wars and subconventional conflicts in varied terrain, including the vast maritime spaces, will constitute the main template for conflict in the twenty-first century.[1] This will all take place under the nuclear shadow looming large over the India-Pakistan security relationship. These scenarios remain a distinct possibility because of India's adversarial relationship with its two powerful neighbors—a rising China and a revisionist, failing Pakistan. Adding to the complexities of contemporary conflict is the COVID-19 pandemic and its likely impact on warfare in general.

Subconventional conflict, irregular warfare, fourth-generation warfare, and even fifth-generation warfare are merely generic terms encompassing armed conflict and noncontact warfare. These conflicts are above the level of peaceful coexistence and below the threshold of conventional or structured war between nation-states.[2] Hybrid war, cyberwar, proxy war, border skirmishes, armed militancy, insurgency, and terrorism are contemporary manifestations of such conflicts. These wars are characterized by asymmetric force levels between the regular state forces and the irregulars, wherein the force applied and the violence generated depend on the motivation, intent, and capabilities of the combatants. The modus operandi of nonstate actors is often marked by irrationality, indiscrimination, unpredictability, and ruthlessly destructive behavior, while states respond with restraint or ruthless force, depending on the state architecture (democracy, dictatorship, majoritarian, or communist) and the laws that govern the actions of its armed forces.

5

I support the "realist" argument that India's emergence as a potential global power will be dictated not only by its economic rise and the exercise of "soft power" but also by its calibrated exploitation of force as a visible and potent tool of statecraft. India's conventional war-fighting strategy in the post-1971 era has revolved around deterrence by limited coercive and punitive action, primarily to protect its geographic boundaries and sovereignty. An example was the limited high-altitude campaign during the Pakistan-initiated Kargil Conflict in 1999. The large-scale deployment of conventional forces along its northern and western frontiers against powerful, unfriendly neighbors has become an inescapable imperative. Force employment and application strategies against insurgencies and secessionist movements have been markedly restrained and calibrated, even in the presence of clear evidence of external abetment. The performance and conduct of the Indian Army in the troubled areas of the northeast and Jammu and Kashmir (J&K) reflect this strategic maturity and restraint.[3]

What this means in simple terms is that India's armed forces must constantly be prepared for what is commonly termed full-spectrum operations. It is important to understand the basic characteristics of these genres of conflict if one wants to comprehend the complexities and ambiguities of modern warfare. None of these forms are new—they have been practiced for millennia in one form or another. For example, Oxford historian Sir Hew Strachan argues that "all war is potentially asymmetric, in that an intelligent opponent should try to maximize the enemy's vulnerability rather than play to their strength." He goes on to speculate whether "hybrid wars are those which occupy some middle point in the spectrum between regular and irregular, or whether they are characterized by simultaneous activity on both ends of that spectrum."[4]

CONVENTIONAL CONFLICT IN CONTEMPORARY INDIA

Conventional conflict generally denotes a conflict between the standing armed forces of two nation-states. It is invariably caused by the failure of political negotiations and diplomacy. India's experience with conventional conflict since independence has been varied. It has a large standing army, navy, and air force that were initially trained to fight conventional wars across varied terrain. It has two acknowledged adversaries: Pakistan and China. It has fought four wars with the former since 1947, while the 1962 war remains the only conflict with the latter. These wars have been fought over territorial and sovereignty issues that are deep rooted and highly emotive, making a negotiated resolution very difficult to achieve over the years.

Three of India's major wars with Pakistan were fought on multiple fronts (1947–1948, 1965, and 1971). It also fought a limited but high-intensity conflict in Kargil (1999). The conflict in Kargil was interwoven with the ongoing high-altitude slugfest in Siachen, continued infiltration along the line of control, and the covert war Pakistan has been waging against India in J&K since 1947. The two-front conventional war with China in 1962 has not been repeated, but it has resulted in a protracted cat-and-mouse game of deterrence that has effectively prevented conflict between the two nations. Embedded in this tension have been interludes of posturing in the form of numerous skirmishes, face-offs, and encounters, with the latest one in Ladakh showing signs of escalating into a limited conflict. Confounding many security analysts is the astounding fact that not a single shot was fired across the line of actual control with China since the last major firefight at Nathu La in 1967 and a patrol skirmish in 1975,[5] until the recent violent clash in the Galwan Valley of Ladakh on 15 June 2020. Pushing and shoving are commonplace at numerous border posts. All these events are moves on a complex strategic chessboard and are fascinating examples of the ambiguities of the India–China conundrum.

What are the significant takeaways from India's experience in conventional conflict? Despite being dragged into war barely months after independence, the Indian Army and the Indian Air Force leveraged their experience gained from World War II and thwarted the larger Pakistani objective of wresting away the entire state of Kashmir. Large tracts of territory remained under Pakistan's control, however, as Pakistan-occupied Kashmir.[6] The performance of conventional forces in battle depends largely on the synergy between the political leadership and the armed forces as instruments of statecraft. When there is abject neglect of this tool, defeat is almost always inevitable, as was the case in the 1962 war with China.[7] The buildup of conventional forces is a long, drawn-out process that takes decades to translate into effectiveness on the battlefield. The 1965 war was an example of such a process, wherein a strategically nimble Pakistan sought to leverage its conventional superiority on the ground and in the air to achieve the stated political objective of redrawing historical boundaries.

It is a testimony to India's resilience that it turned an operational stalemate into a strategic advantage by successfully focusing on intangibles such as leadership, morale, and political will. Even though Pakistan had reached the limits of its war-fighting potential, the Indian military was reluctant to go for the jugular.[8] Likewise, political diffidence during crunch-time negotiations failed to convert operational gains into decisive strategic outcomes.

The deft synergizing of all instruments of statecraft—and a final blow delivered by conventional military forces across multiple fronts—saw the dismemberment of Pakistan and the creation of Bangladesh in December 1971.[9] However, the Shimla talks in 1972 saw India's prime minister Indira Gandhi being outmaneuvered by her wily Pakistani counterpart, Zulfiqar Ali Bhutto. Convinced by Bhutto's assurances that he would come up with a mutually acceptable plan to resolve the Kashmir problem, she failed to convert India's decisive military victory and its 93,000 prisoners of war into tangible geopolitical gains. India would pay a heavy price over the years for this indecisiveness—a fact that has been deliberately underplayed in contemporary Indian strategic discourse. Realizing its inability to achieve any strategic objectives through a conventional war across wide fronts, Pakistan came up with a limited war option by initiating the Kargil Conflict in 1999, forcing its more powerful adversary to limit the application of its combat capabilities to a small area. When that too failed to deliver desirable strategic outcomes, Pakistan realized that a limited war with conventional forces against an exponentially more powerful adversary like India was a nonstarter. It would have to employ other means to wage war against a nation that it saw as an existential threat to its survival.

ORCHESTRATING THE BIG BATTLE

Operational plans for conventional conflict are generally made well in advance and disseminated to field formations, which then develop tactics and drills that are assiduously practiced in exercises and sand-model discussions.[10] When hostilities are imminent, defenses are strengthened, and offensive formations are moved closer to the border. When diplomatic parleys fail, the nimbler and more aggressive protagonist invariably makes the first move by launching a preemptive strike that signals the commencement of hostilities. These strikes could be land based, aerial, or maritime, depending on which offers the greatest element of surprise and the greatest chance of destroying enemy combat potential. Air strikes have often been the first choice for preemption, as seen in the 1967 Arab–Israeli war and the India–Pakistan wars of 1965 and 1971. The land option has also been exercised, such as when the Egyptians crossed the Bar-Lev Line on Yom Kippur in 1973. Conventional conflict generally involves set-piece moves, where speed, surprise, firepower, maneuver, and destruction of the adversary's combat potential hold the key to conflict termination.

Three concepts in modern conventional warfare have interested the Indian military in recent decades: the air-land concept of joint operations propagated by the United States in the late 1970s and early 1980s,[11] sequential military operations,[12] and parallel operations.[13] The air-land battle concept or doctrine was first articulated in the United States in the late 1970s as *Field Manual 100-5*. Its stated objectives were to meet the challenges of a possible conflict on the plains of Europe between North Atlantic Treaty Organization (NATO) members and Warsaw Pact countries. It also sought to address two weaknesses that plagued the US armed forces, which had emerged as the predominant bulwark against the mighty Soviet war machine that constantly threatened to steamroll across Europe. These weaknesses were the large deployment distances for US surface and maritime forces and the overwhelming numerical superiority of Warsaw Pact mechanized forces. The doctrine also had to rethink existing US war-fighting strategies in the aftermath of the Vietnam debacle. This it did by advocating maneuver, leveraging the emerging technology revolution to drive tactics and creating synergies between the army and the air force to maximize their fighting potential. Finally, it needed a strategy to combat the overwhelming might of the Soviet army and its amassed armor and artillery in the tactical battle area. By advocating the concept of "deep battle," it sought to use airpower to punch holes in enemy defenses, interdict follow-on forces, and create space for maneuver, which would then be exploited by a combined-arms assault. The doctrine was an effective deterrent against conventional Soviet military strategy as it opened offensive windows for NATO.

Both India and Pakistan were quick to draw lessons from *Field Manual 100-5*. The Indians acted first under General K. Sundarji, their talismanic army chief in the mid-1980s, but Pakistan soon evolved its own version based on its traditional preemptive philosophy. Sundarji, who was attending a course at the US Army War College in the 1970s when the air-land battle concept was being debated, saw it as an opportunity to change the stagnant mind-set that had taken root in the Indian military. He knew that on India's western front, its military top brass was more comfortable with attrition warfare and fighting a "holding battle" while waiting for suitable opportunities to launch limited offensives. During his tenure as chief, he sought to drive home the importance of maneuver and offensive action and the need for the Indian Air Force to commit more resources to winning the land battle.[14]

Complementing Sundarji's views on offensive action was another brilliant military mind from the Indian Air Force, Air Commodore Jasjit Singh. Although Singh preferred to view airpower through the lens of the "big battle"—with deep strategic strikes and air dominance being the key determinants of the employment of airpower—he was also among the first to acknowledge the necessity of supporting the army in the tactical battle area either directly or by interdicting reinforcements before they joined the battle.[15]

A follow-up of the air-land battle was what militaries across the world termed "sequential operations," which sought to systematically degrade and destroy the enemy's combat potential. Sequential war fighting relied heavily on what came to be known as effects-based operations (EBO).[16] EBO used military power to systematically and speedily destroy target systems, with a debilitating impact on an adversary's capacity to sustain military operations. Airpower emerged as a key element of this style of war fighting and was used to good effect during Operation Desert Storm in 1991. The Indian Air Force embraced this concept in the 1990s and tried unsuccessfully to convince the Indian Army that ground forces could be effective only if they allowed the air force to win the air battle before launching an offensive with its own strike elements.

Experiences during the early decades of the twenty-first century suggest that long conventional wars are a phenomenon of the past. Militaries must now plan and execute military campaigns that offer speedy conflict termination to satisfy political leaders. Parallel operations offered such an option, wherein land, sea, and air operations were no longer sequenced but were applied simultaneously to create overwhelming pressure on adversaries and force them to capitulate without necessarily suffering heavy casualties. US military operations in Iraq in 2003 delivered one such template by mounting combined land and air assaults during Operation Iraqi Freedom, which led to the collapse of Saddam Hussein's forces.[17] Following the Indian Army's inability to mobilize rapidly after the suicide attack on India's parliament by Pakistan-sponsored terrorists of Lashkar-e-Taiba and Jaish-e-Mohammad in December 2001, it had to recalibrate its strategy based on mobility and logistics on the western front. The Indian Army now embraces some elements of an orchestrated and synergized application of combat power, bolstered by the significant power of the Indian Navy and Air Force.[18] More about this strategy emerges in chapter 18.

UNDERSTANDING THE STRATEGIC MILIEU

The end of the Cold War saw the emergence of a fragmented world dotted with numerous localized but seemingly intractable conflicts arising from fundamental differences related to religion and ethnicity.[19] Terrorists, insurgents, and freedom fighters found remarkably new ways of combating the coercive capabilities of established states and coalitions. While powerful nations such as the United States, Russia, India, and Israel have been building full-spectrum military capabilities to calibrate escalation and prevent extended conventional wars, their opponents have been employing sophisticated tools and techniques of limited hybrid war that gradually nibble away at the fabric of the state. These types of warfare have existed in some form for millennia, but they have now emerged as effective asymmetric counters to coercion, and the tools are unlike those of conventional coercion, be it diplomatic or military. Mao's peasants and Tito's guerrillas waged limited wars against stronger adversaries and achieved asymmetric outcomes.

In recent times, limited wars have become the focus of the study of war and conflict. By the end of the twentieth century, several military historians in the West had declared the death of large-scale conventional conflict and questioned the need for big-ticket military acquisitions, particularly in the air and maritime domains. India, however, has never had the space to reflect on and debate the need to limit the development of full-spectrum capabilities. Until there is clear political and strategic guidance in a post-COVID-19 world that India should discount the possibility of waging conventional conflict on multiple fronts, it can ill afford to go easy on developing robust conventional capabilities to deter its neighbors' aggressive strategic designs. Concurrently, India has the ability to tackle the entire range of conventional and subconventional threats to national security.

THE PARADOX OF SUBCONVENTIONAL CONFLICT

It is easy to be confused by the plethora of definitions of the various conflicts below the level of conventional conflict. Some academics—such as Dan Stoker, a former professor of strategy at the US Naval Postgraduate School at Monterey—like to group everything that is not total war under the heading "limited war." Other Americans like the terms "small war," "irregular war," "operations other than war," and "fourth-generation warfare." India prefers the terms "subconventional conflict," "low-intensity conflict," and "proxy war." "Hybrid war" has also gained some traction in recent doctrinal pronouncements. A scan of these definitions offers insight into the ambiguities and uncertainties that dog contemporary conflict and the challenges faced by countries like India.

The Indian Army doctrine defines subconventional operations as "armed conflicts that are above the level of peaceful coexistence amongst states and below the threshold of war. These include militancy, insurgency, proxy war and terrorism either employed as part of an insurrectionist movement or independently."[20] It expands the definition used by the United States and NATO and defines insurgency as: "Armed rebellion by a section of the population against the legally constituted Government, with the support or sympathy of the local population, obtained voluntarily or by coercion. It covers the full spectrum of conflict from subversion to full-scale guerrilla war, including the emergence of guerrilla bands into regular units."[21] Taking the debate a step further, the Indian Army doctrine states:

> Low-intensity conflict encompasses a variety of violent and low-level conflict situations. In most cases, such conflicts fall under the category of "politico-military confrontation" between contending states or groups. Such conflicts are at a much lower scale than conventional war but are above the routine and peaceful competitions among states. One of the parties to the conflict may not be a state, as in an insurgency situation. It frequently involves protracted struggle of competing principles and ideologies. Low-intensity conflict ranges from high-grade internal-struggle situations to extensive employment of the armed forces in counterinsurgency operations. It is waged by a combination of means, employing political, economic, informational and military instruments. It includes terrorism but excludes purely criminal acts.[22]

Finally, terrorism is distinct from insurgency and relies on coercion rather than popular support. It shares similarities with violent and organized crime and is defined in a variety of ways, depending on interpretation, focus, and perspective. The Indian Ministry of Defense defines terrorism in its glossary of terms as "the wanton killing of persons or involvement in violence or in the disruption of services or means of communications essential to the community or in damaging property with a view to putting the public or any section of the public in fear; or affecting adversely the harmony between different religious, racial and language groups or overawing the sovereignty and integrity of a nation."[23]

A more nuanced explanation is offered in the Indian Army's subconventional doctrine, which is similar to the one offered by the US Department of Defense: "Terrorism is the unlawful use or the threatened use of force or violence against people or property to terrorize, coerce or intimidate governments or societies; this is most often resorted to with the aim of achieving political, religious, or ideological objectives."[24]

Praveen Swami, one of India's most accomplished journalist-scholars, has been studying and writing about the ongoing proxy war and terrorism in J&K for almost three decades. His interpretation of the terms "terrorist," "insurgent," and "militant" is relevant, as they are used indiscriminately and interchangeably in South Asia. He writes: "I define terrorism to mean a political strategy that involves the use of violence to coerce civil society into submission to the ideological agenda of its adherents. Armed groups in J&K and Punjab have principally directed their violence at civilians, hence the term 'terrorists.'"[25] Based on this definition, Lashkar-e-Taiba, Jaish-e-Mohammad, and Hizbul-Mujahedin are all terrorist groups, regardless of whether they fight the Indian Army or kill innocent civilians, because their aim is to wage jihad on the Indian state and force the secession of J&K.

The bottom line is that India is familiar with terror. In the northeastern states of Assam, Manipur, and Nagaland, insurgencies have demonstrated chameleon-like characteristics and left a window open for terrorism to enter and take root. Terrorism has occasionally reared its ugly head and demonstrated subnational, communal, and ethnic overtones. The Indian state, however, has managed to control it. In central India, left-wing extremism is an example of terrorism being used as an instrument for social and economic reform. Punjab in the 1980s and J&K after the 1990s remain the most emphatic examples of terrorism faced by the Indian state. J&K will continue to be the subject of a covert war for the foreseeable future, with tools changing from insurgency to terrorism. Finally, Pakistan will likely continue to employ terrorism as an instrument of state policy to destabilize India until a black swan event forces it to abandon the strategy.[26]

COVERT, PROXY, AND HYBRID WARS

Further complicating conflict genres for countries like India are two other derivatives of limited conflict: proxy war and hybrid war. It is important to understand the finer nuances of the two, as the proxy element usually facilitates the hybrid means. Very rarely are low-intensity conflicts decided in a few months. Most often, these conflicts last for years or even decades, as we have seen in Malaysia, Vietnam, Northern Ireland, Sri Lanka, J&K, Nagaland, Iraq, Afghanistan, Syria, and so on. Involvement of proxies can have a significant impact on the outcome of such conflicts, as they provide additional resources, military heft, and international recognition, as well as more ways to pressure opponents and reduce their effectiveness. These proxies could be governments, nongovernment organizations, or individuals with resources and personal influence. They have varying motives, but they can prolong the conflict, change the outcome, or even become contestants themselves.

Independent India's tryst with covert war began in 1947, when Pakistan hatched a plan to sever Kashmir from the Indian Union by aiding and supporting raiders backed by an armed militia. This plan was repeated in 1965, shelved for a while, and then revived in the early 1990s as a strategy for a protracted armed struggle in J&K. Pakistan's proxy war in Kashmir is merely a sophisticated derivative of covert war that uses the instrument of terrorism to sap India's growing power by "bleeding it with a thousand cuts."[27] When China joined the fray as part of Pakistan's security strategy, India had no choice but to be alarmed. It does not have the luxury of letting up on building its military capability.

The term "hybrid" is derived from the Latin *hibrida*, meaning the "offspring of a mixed union." Hybrid warfare is a combination of two or more dissimilar elements from conventional, asymmetric, irregular, information, nonlinear, or fourth-generation warfare.[28] The first step in the transition to a hybrid conflict is escalating an insurgency or a covert war with external ideological support, a supply of sophisticated weaponry and finances, and training. It gives the nonstate actor the wherewithal to scale up the conflict to levels that resemble conventional conflict in many ways, yet retain the flexibility and ambiguity unavailable to regular state forces. Frank Hoffman explains the nuances of hybrid warfare and argues: "A distinctive feature of hybrid warfare is that it blends the lethal nature of conventional force employed by the state with the fanatical and protracted fervor of irregular warfare."[29]

The most recent examples of hybrid wars were the conflicts in Lebanon, Georgia, Crimea, and Syria. Offering a practitioner's perspective of hybrid war, David Kilcullen suggests in his seminal work, *The Accidental Guerrilla*, that "the tendency towards hybrid forms of warfare combining terrorism, insurgency, propaganda and economic warfare to sidestep Western conventional capability is not only an Arab or Muslim phenomenon."[30]

In 1999 two colonels from the People's Liberation Army (PLA) wrote a book entitled *Chao Xian Zhan* (Unrestricted Warfare).[31] It directly countered the dominant Western way of war fighting by introducing the disruptive maxim "no rules and nothing is forbidden."[32] These diffused forms of warfare lead to cognitive dissonance and nontraditional means of waging war, such as information warfare and even biological warfare. When embedded in conventional strategic thinking, this drives military leaders into "fighting the war they wanted to be fighting, rather than the war they actually were fighting."[33]

IMPORTANCE OF THE OBSERVE, ORIENT, DECIDE, AND ACT LOOP

Among the most important elements of war fighting in the contemporary world of unstructured warfare is the observe, orient, decide, and act (OODA) loop.[34] Its impact has been so pervasive that it is now discussed not only in war studies courses and military operations rooms around the world but also in corporate boardrooms as part of business strategy. The OODA loop emerged as a key operational concept in modern warfare in the early 1980s, thanks to a maverick US Air Force fighter pilot, Colonel John Boyd. Boyd argued that split-second decision making during air combat was dependent on four main sensory actions that he attractively packaged as the OODA loop.

A pilot who observed the enemy first and analyzed the combat environment in all its complexity—either with the help of radar or with his own eyes—and then oriented himself in time and space more quickly than the adversary gained a few extra seconds to decide how to act. This advantage invariably resulted in an action that marked the difference between victory and defeat or even life and death. Boyd argued that the OODA loop could be shortened by complementing human ingenuity and reflexes with training and advances in technology. He also suggested that organizational lethargy and a lack of imagination could lengthen the loop and allow nimble adversaries to seize the advantage. The OODA loop has turned modern warfare on its head and offered a level playing field to decision makers across the full spectrum of conflict, allowing them to operate inside one another's loops and gain disproportionate advantages.

CONSTITUTIONAL MANDATES AND CODES OF CONDUCT

The Indian Constitution has clear provisions for the employment of India's armed forces in various contingencies and eventualities. However, its founding fathers had little inkling of how the nature of both internal and external conflicts would evolve. Although there have been periodic amendments and modifications, there is a disturbing disconnect among the judiciary, the executive, the legislature, the military, the media, and civil society when it comes to the application of force as an instrument of statecraft. There is also a widespread lack of understanding of the difference between deploying the armed forces to maintain law and order during civil disturbances and deploying them to combat internal armed conflict. While the former is mandated under the strangely worded Criminal Procedure Code of 1973, the latter is governed by the Armed Forces Special Powers Act (AFSPA).

The AFSPA was first passed in 1958 to declare the Naga Hill districts of Assam a "disturbed area," and it was later imposed in several other areas.[35] Despite Pakistan's attempts to wrest Kashmir from India in 1947 and 1965, the AFSPA provisions dealing with J&K were promulgated only in 1990, when violence there necessitated large-scale deployment of the Indian Army to counter the externally abetted armed rebellion.[36] The debate about whether to declare an insurgency-ridden area a "disturbed area" to empower security forces is often shrill and uninformed, and it can have an adverse impact on national security.

A perusal of the AFSPA as it relates to J&K is instructive. Paragraph 3 clearly states that it will be considered a disturbed area:

If, in relation to the State of Jammu and Kashmir, the Governor of that State or the Central Government, is of opinion that the whole or any part of the State is in such a disturbed and dangerous condition that the use of armed forces in aid of the civil power is necessary to prevent—activities involving terrorist acts directed towards overawing the Government, or striking terror in the people or any section of the people, or alienating any section of the people or adversely affecting the harmony amongst different sections of the people. . . . It also includes activities directed towards disclaiming, questioning or disrupting the sovereignty and territorial integrity of India or bringing about cession of a part of the territory of India or secession of a part of the territory of India from the Union or causing insult to the Indian National Flag, the Indian National Anthem and the Constitution of India.[37]

Activists such as Sanjoy Hazarika have been highly critical of the Indian state's continued reliance on the AFSPA and argue that it is time to reexamine its relevance in the northeastern parts of India where peace and normalcy are fast returning.[38] However, in J&K, even a cursory glance at the conditions that have forced the government of India to invoke the AFSPA in twelve of the twenty-two districts, along with the existing patterns of violence, indicates how difficult it is to review its relevance by district.[39]

Lieutenant General Rostum Nanavatty urges caution when labeling genres of contemporary conflict. In his academically robust book Internal Armed Conflict in India, he argues that "indiscriminate use of terminologies does little to foster comprehension of the new forms of conflict."[40] Finally, Clausewitz too recognized that war and conflict are governed by both continuity and change.[41] This reflects India's struggle to define the limits of war and conflict as an instrument of statecraft in contemporary times.

2

India's Military Renaissance

We have become a very soft people and we must realize that nations are not built through soft options, nor are the country's frontiers secured by a soft line.
—Indian defense minister George Fernandes, *New York Times*

THE INITIAL BEAR HUG

The Indo-Soviet Treaty of Friendship and Cooperation of August 1971 formalized almost a decade of close defense cooperation between India and the Soviet Union, even though the former steadfastly refused to align itself politically with Soviet Russia. It also opened the floodgates for the licensed production of Soviet military equipment (not to be confused with technology transfer), which was supposedly designed to boost the indigenization of India's military-industrial complex and industrial infrastructure. The first Indo-Soviet military deal was based on a $140 million loan from Russia to be repaid over ten years, at a measly interest rate of 2 percent per annum. After the United States refused to supply C-130 Hercules transport aircraft and additional Bell helicopters in the late 1950s, the Indian Air Force became the initial beneficiary of the India–Soviet military cooperation.

It was the Russian IL-14 and An-12 transport aircraft and Mi-4 helicopters that sustained and resupplied the Indian Army during the 1962 war, along with American C-119 Packets and a few Bell helicopters acquired in the 1950s. After the initial MiG-21s were inducted in 1963 and used very sporadically in the1965 war with Pakistan, additional MiG-21 squadrons were quickly raised, along with a few squadrons of Sukhoi-7 fighter ground-attack squadrons. Finally, one of the most impactful acquisitions from the Russians in the early 1970s was a hardy helicopter, the Mi-8, which would continue in service for more than four decades and served as forerunner to the Mi-17/25/35 class of helicopters. The Indian Navy soon got its share of the pie too, with the induction of the Foxtrot-class diesel submarines in 1967 and the Osa-class missile boats in 1970.[1]

Although the Indian Army received large numbers of Soviet T-54 and T-55 tanks, India's armored divisions preferred the more reliable Centurion tank and the new and indigenous Vijayanta tank. The only Russian tank that

17

made a difference in the eastern sector during the 1971 India–Pakistan war was the PT-76, which was lighter and smaller and had significant amphibious capability.[2] One of the biggest impediments to effective maneuvering on the ground for the Indian Army, as experienced in the 1971 war, was the lack of infantry combat vehicles (ICVs). The Indian Army had a few Czech Topaz ICVs in 1971, but not until the mid-1970s was the highly effective Soviet BMP-1, with a lethal 57mm gun and antitank missiles, inducted. These were followed in the early 1980s by the potent T-72 tank and the BMP-II ICVs, which would form the mainstay of the Indian Army's mechanized punch and mobility for almost three decades, until the former was replaced by the T-90 main battle tank. The foundations of India's ground-based air defense systems were laid through the 1970s with surface-to-air missiles (SAMs)—the medium-range (fifteen to forty kilometers) SAM-2 and the short-range (two to fifteen kilometers) SAM-3—the ZSU-23 self-propelled antiaircraft guns, and a mobile SAM-6 variant with its launchers mounted on a BMP-1 called Kvadrat.

THE STAGNANT 1970S

In 1973 India's armed forces were just under 1 million strong, and the national population was approximately 600 million. The Indian defense budget of $2.4 billion was approximately 3.75 percent of gross domestic product (GDP); it rose more than 50 percent by the end of the decade in real terms, to $3.72 billion, but marginally declined as a percentage of GDP (3.5 percent). The Indian Army's offensive punch comprised one armored division, with a second one being raised a few years later; five independent armored brigades were largely assigned to standard infantry divisions as their maneuver arms in the plains. Near-obsolete Soviet T-54s and T-55s made up more than 50 percent of the inventory, while the equally aged British Centurion and French AMX-13 constituted almost 30 percent of the force. This meant that the 500 indigenous Vijayanta medium tanks were the spearhead of India's armored corps.[3] Although this tank was much appreciated by India's tank crews, and almost 900 had been built by the end of the 1970s—mainly to replace the Centurions and T-54s—it had too many flaws, such as light armor and a suspect engine, to be developed into a tank of the future.[4]

The Indian Army's artillery arm had thousands of obsolete towed and self-propelled 25-pounders and Abbot 105mm guns of British origin. Along with several hundred Russian 100mm and 130mm guns, they constituted the main fire support element for both attacking and defensive formations. Complementing these guns were Russian recoilless antitank weapons and obsolete air defense artillery guns, which were bolstered by the end of the decade with the highly effective Russian radar-controlled ZSU-23 air defense guns.[5]

The vanguard of the Indian Army had only marginally increased from fourteen to sixteen infantry divisions, along with the eleven mountain divisions that made up a force equivalent to eight to nine corps.[6] Two corps were deployed in the eastern theater, and the rest arrayed against Pakistan along the disturbed western and northern frontiers. Interestingly, although several divisions manned the contested frontier with China on the eastern front, only one division defended the entire line of actual control with China in eastern Ladakh. The primary infantry weapons were 7.62mm self-loading rifles and a variety of near-obsolete light and medium machine guns.

The successes achieved by the Indian Navy in 1971 acted as a catalyst for its expansion. In the early 1970s the aircraft carrier INS *Vikrant*, a few near-obsolete British destroyers and frigates, two modern Indian-designed Nilgiri-class frigates, the efficient but aging Soviet Petya-class light destroyer escorts, the Osa-class missile boats with Styx missiles, and four Foxtrot-class submarines constituted the primary combat fleet. These were complemented by patrol boats, minesweepers, and landing craft of World War II and 1950s vintage. By the end of the 1970s, the transformation of the Indian Navy was well under way. Two additional modern Nilgiri-class frigates and four Foxtrot-class submarines joined the fleet, along with several smaller ships (Soviet minesweepers, missile boats, and corvettes), boosting the strength of the western and eastern fleets. The Soviet influence on naval aviation had not yet begun, and British Seahawks and French Alizes continued to be the main carrier-based fighters, with the aging American Super Constellation constituting the fixed component of maritime reconnaissance. Modern British Sea King maritime reconnaissance and antisubmarine warfare helicopters and French-design Chetak helicopters (an Indian derivative of the Alloutte-III) formed the rotary-wing component.[7]

The Indian Air Force (IAF) fleet of the 1970s comprised mainly Soviet and British aircraft. The Indian element petered out by the end of the 1970s because Hindustan Aeronautics Limited (HAL) could not address the deficiencies in the indigenously designed and manufactured HF-24 (Marut), which had performed creditably in the desert sector during the 1971 India–Pakistan conflict.[8] Although HAL was able to scale up production, manufacturing more than a hundred aircraft instead of the initial figure of seventy, it was able to equip only three squadrons and delivered the last aircraft to the IAF in the mid-1970s. The Marut remained operational into the early 1980s, but it was always an aircraft that failed to deliver on its promises. This was primarily due to HAL's inability to develop or reverse-engineer a suitable engine to replace the underperforming Orpheus engine.[9]

Driven by necessity and aging platforms, the IAF looked to employ many of its fighter and bomber platforms in multiple roles. The obsolescent but reliable and battle-proven Canberra bomber continued to be the only offensive-cum-reconnaissance (recce) platform that could fly reasonably deep (over 400 kilometers) into enemy territory, while the Hunter MK 56A and MiG-21 FL took on multiple roles. The Sukhoi-7 and HF-24 remained tactical ground-attack aircraft, with the Gnat Mk 1 and the MiG-21 FL assigned to air defense roles. However, by the end of the 1970s, the ground-attack variant of the MiG-21, called the MiG-21 M or T-96, had also been inducted. Acquisition of the multirole MiG-21 Bis, MiG-23 BN strike aircraft, MiG-23 MF interceptor, and MiG-25 strategic recce aircraft meant that Soviet fighter aircraft formed the mainstay of the IAF combat fleet (around thirty-six squadrons). The IAF's airlift capability was in serious trouble in the 1970s, with obsolete and aging American C-119 Packets and Dakotas, British Avros, and Soviet An-12s making up the twelve squadrons that struggled to cope with multiple requirements. Soviet Mi-4 and Mi-8 helicopters, complemented by Chetak light communication helicopters, were the mainstays of the IAF's twelve helicopter units.[10] An overall assessment reveals that the IAF had a hybrid mix of Western and Soviet platforms, flown by operationally proficient pilots with a penchant for employing Western aerial tactics on Soviet platforms.[11]

The 1970s were marked by economic stagnation, but the security landscape in the subcontinent and South Asia evolved quite rapidly after the Soviet invasion of Afghanistan in 1979. The arming of Pakistan as a frontline and proxy state by the United States was a Cold War strategy that resulted in its military dictator, President Zia-ul-Haq, leveraging much of that capability against India. Consequently, India was forced to embark on a rapid military buildup. Across the Himalayas, a resurgent China realized that it risked failing in its quest to emerge as a global power by the end of the twentieth century unless it built a credible military capability.

THE MUSCULAR 1980S

India faced its most diverse security challenges between 1984 and 1990, and it can be argued that there was little justification to cut defense spending. Strangely, that is exactly what happened: the defense budget declined from 3.79 percent of GDP in 1980 to 3.28 percent in 1989, even as the GDP grew almost threefold—from $100 billion in 1980 to almost $280 billion in 1989.[12] Despite serious structural problems that necessitated defense budget cuts late in the decade, speedy and pragmatic acquisitions were made between 1980 and 1987. Driven by rising foreign exchange holdings and the political backing of the military as a critical instrument of statecraft under Prime Minister Indira Gandhi and her son and successor Rajiv Gandhi, the Indian armed forces acquired the necessary muscle before the slump of the 1990s.[13]

Under Deng Xiaoping, China embarked on a reform process in the People's Liberation Army (PLA) in the 1980s, with defense budgets varying from a low of $12 billion to a high of $20 billion, or between 3.0 and 5.25 percent of GDP.[14] Revisiting this comparison in 2000, 2010, and 2016 reveals the emerging nonlinear asymmetry in military modernization between India and its principal adversary. For the first time, the total of India's armed forces crossed the million mark, with the Indian Army accounting for more than 80 percent of this strength. There was some force restructuring because of the counterinsurgency and counterterrorist operations in Punjab, Sri Lanka, and Nagaland, and larger maneuver forces were created in the form of mechanized infantry regiments and the Reorganized Army Plains Infantry Divisions (RAPIDs). The latter was the brainchild of the farsighted General Sundarji, army chief from 1985 to 1987. These divisions were raised to support offensive operations in the plains against a rapidly modernizing Pakistan Army. Older infantry battalions from all major regiments were converted into mechanized units, a move that caused some distress within the traditional infantry constituency.[15]

Sundarji also expanded the army's integral air arm and formed the Army Aviation Corps by convincing the IAF to part with its attack helicopter fleet of Mi-25s and giving the Indian Army's strike corps operational control over them. The major acquisition for the Indian Army in the 1980s was the Russian T-72 tank, which replaced the obsolete T-55s and the Vijayanta as its main battle tank. By the end of the decade, the Indian Army had 700 of these tanks as its main offensive force. The acquisition of large numbers of BMP-II ICVs and the addition of the versatile 155mm FH-77B Bofors artillery gun significantly enhanced the strike corps' ability to conduct offensive operations in conventional conflict scenarios.

The 1980s also saw the emergence of a robust maritime discourse within India's strategic establishment, as scholars such as K. Subrahmanyam and Raja Menon emphasized the Indian Ocean as a maritime space of great relevance if India wanted to emerge as a power of consequence in the years ahead.[16] The Indian Navy rapidly expanded in both the surface and subsurface domains. With the induction of the refurbished INS *Viraat* (formerly HMS *Hermes*) of Falklands vintage, the Indian Navy could deploy an aircraft carrier–based fleet on both its eastern and western seaboards. Replacing the Seahawks and Alizes with the battle-proven British-made Sea Harrier jump jets was a major step toward the expansion of naval aviation.

With eight indigenously designed Nilgiri-class frigates, three Godavari-class frigates, and five new Kashin-class destroyers, the Indian Navy's surface fleet was in fine fettle. Its capabilities now more than outmatched those of both the Pakistan Navy and the PLA Navy. However, the Indian Navy's submarine fleet was in danger of being outclassed by Pakistani and Chinese submarines, so the old Foxtrots were replaced by eight Kilo-class and four silent German HDW type-1500 submarines, along with the leased nuclear-powered Charlie-class Soviet submarine INS *Chakra*. Maritime reconnaissance got a fillip with the induction of the huge four-engine Tu-142 and the reliable Il-38 aircraft, in addition to the expansion of the Sea King fleet for tactical reconnaissance and antisubmarine warfare.[17]

Building on the impetus given to airpower by Air Chief Marshal P. C. Lal during the 1971 war, the IAF emerged as an independent arm of war fighting and a critical enabler in joint operations. This was forcefully asserted by Air Commodore Jasjit Singh, a self-taught practitioner-scholar and protégé of K. Subrahmanyam, who was arguably the preeminent security strategist of independent India.[18] Acquisition of the British Jaguar deep-penetration strike aircraft in large numbers from the late 1970s through the 1980s, along with variants of the MiG-23 and MiG-27 aircraft, strengthened the IAF's offensive punch. Procurement of MiG-25s for strategic reconnaissance, MiG-29s for air superiority, and Mirage-2000s as fourth-generation multirole combat aircraft transformed the IAF into the most advanced third-world air force.

Induction of the heavy-lift Il-76 aircraft and the medium-lift An-32 aircraft gave the air mobility fleet inter- and intratheater capability, and the introduction of medium-lift Mi-17 and Mi-25 attack helicopters provided significant rotary-wing flexibility and enhanced air maintenance support to the Indian Army in remote deployments along the line of control and line of actual control. The IAF's tactics and combat development establishment—which was formed before the 1971 war and came up with some innovative tactics during that conflict[19]—expanded its repertoire significantly.

More impactful in the 1980s, though, was the attempt by Indira Gandhi and Rajiv Gandhi to proactively leverage this transformed military capability to support an aggressive foreign policy, albeit with mixed results. However, the sudden flurry of military actions from 1984 onward shook the Indian military out of its post-1971 slumber. A mix of successes and failures prompted a recalibration of both equipment profiles and operational strategies. The successes included occupation of the Siachen Glacier in 1984 (Operation Meghdoot); Exercise Brasstacks, a massive air-land exercise; the thwarting of China's impending move in Arunachal Pradesh in 1986–1987 (Exercise Falcon); and the air-land operation in Maldives in 1988 (Operation Cactus). But the disastrous storming of the Golden Temple in 1984

(Operation Blue Star) and the failure of the extended military intervention in Sri Lanka from 1987 to 1990 (Operation Pawan) had greater strategic and national fallout.

THE 1990S AND BEYOND

Plagued by an economic crisis and a lethargic national security apparatus, India experienced a negative nonlinear growth in defense expenditures in the 1990s, which reflected an apathy toward building hard power as an element of Indian statecraft. From 1990 to 1998, while India's GDP increased from just under $300 billion to around $420 billion (an increase of around 40 percent in real terms), the defense budget rose from $9.25 billion to just $10 billion, a measly increase of 7.5 percent. The Kargil crisis finally precipitated a much-needed 20 percent boost in the defense budget in 1999. Yet defense spending as a percentage of GDP hovered between 2.5 and 2.8 percent, compared with 3.7 to 4 percent in the previous decade. Even Japan spent more on defense in the 1990s. For the first time, the official Chinese defense budget surpassed that of India, even though it was widely known that PLA spending remained completely opaque until the first decade of the twenty-first century.[20]

Following the breakup of the Soviet Union, replacing and even maintaining the Soviet inventory became problematic, as India shopped around for spare MiG and An-32 aircraft and T-72 tanks in Russia, Ukraine, and Romania, among other countries.[21] India's inability to reverse-engineer systems and components, and slow progress in its indigenous fighter aircraft and tank programs, meant that India would have to rely on its Soviet inventory for longer than it could be logistically supported.

Faced with a covert proxy war of terrorism in Kashmir since the early 1990s, the Indian Army raised a counterinsurgency force in 1990 called the Rashtriya Rifles, which was initially deployed in Punjab. General B. C. Joshi, the army chief in 1993–1994, played an important role in expanding the Rashtriya Rifles to thirty-six battalions and assigning it specific areas in both South and North Kashmir.[22] Its role gradually expanded to counterterrorist operations in Jammu and Kashmir (J&K). General Joshi's son, Akshay Joshi—a former lieutenant commander in the Indian Navy and now a joint secretary in the National Security Council Secretariat—recollects that his father was one of the first military leaders to liken Pakistan's support for the violent secessionist movement in J&K to a proxy war. Because proxy war was a form of warfare, the general argued, the army was the right instrument of the state to combat it.[23] He believed that terrorism in J&K differed from terrorism as experienced elsewhere in the world. Arguing forcefully that this was a "legitimate task" for the army, he suggested restructuring the force to fight this menace more effectively.[24] That is why General Joshi spent so much time and effort to make the Rashtriya Rifles an effective counterinsurgency and counterterrorism force in the Kashmir Valley.

The force was designed to ensure a constant and uninterrupted flow of intelligence and a superior knowledge of terrain and capabilities of all arms and services of the Indian Army, rather than using only the infantry to fight insurgency. According to a former defense minister, "The Rashtriya Rifles has provided the requisite continuity in the low-intensity conflict/internal security grid and allowed the army to retain a strategic reserve for other border [conflict] variants."[25] By the end of the 1990s, Rashtriya Rifles had grown to over fifty battalions divided among four counterinsurgency forces identified as Victor, Kilo, Delta, and Romeo. While the Victor and Kilo Forces operated in the Kashmir Valley north of the Pir Panjal range, the Delta and Romeo Forces were responsible for the area south of the range, comprising the regions of Doda, Rajouri, and Poonch. The army would add one more division-sized force, called Uniform Force, in the 2000s for Udhampur. The army also raised an additional strike corps headquarters (HQ) and a corps HQ in the northeast during the 1990s.

The main equipment acquisitions by the Indian Army during the 1990s were the Pinaka multibarrel rocket launchers, an entire range of surface-to-air missile systems for air defense of the tactical battle area (SAM-6, SAM-8, and SAM-13), and battlefield surveillance radar for monitoring the extremely active and volatile line of control in Kashmir. After the interservice recriminations following the Kargil Conflict, the Indian Army would also get its own Searcher unmanned aerial vehicles from Israel.

The Indian Navy continued its dual acquisition spree as it modernized its surface fleet with indigenous and Russian-built frigates and destroyers and added two Kilo-class submarines to its subsurface fleet. The navy fleet comprised twenty-six principal surface combatants (aircraft carriers, destroyers, frigates, and large corvettes), fifteen submarines of three classes, and thirty-eight patrol and coastal combatants (small corvettes, mine-warfare ships, coastal patrol boats, and amphibious support ships).

The IAF made few major purchases in the 1990s apart from the first Su-30 squadron equipped with the Russian Su-30K, which was obtained in 1999. Other minor acquisitions included a few VIP and electronic warfare Boeing aircraft, Mi-35s to replace the Mi-25 attack helicopters, an upgrade of the Jaguar fleet, and the completion of deliveries in all other fleets. Its combat fleet increased to forty squadrons, close to the authorized limit of forty-two. The acquisition of six Il-78 aerial tankers enhanced the combat reach of the IAF's fighter fleet and addressed its major operational weakness—lack of a robust ground-based air defense network comparable to the Pakistan Air Force's well-networked system, which linked multiple tiers of radars to provide a composite picture.

According to Air Marshal Patney, former commander in chief of Western Air Command (the IAF's largest), the one thing he was immensely satisfied with in the 1990s was the improvement of the IAF's air defense network.[26] Using high-frequency radio to integrate multiple radar pictures onto one screen, known as the Tactical Air Defense Integrated Display System (TADIDS), helped operationalize the control and reporting center concept. This allowed multiple radars to be networked with adequate redundancy (satellite, radio, and visual reporting). As the IAF slowly embraced networks involving the fusion of data, it caught up with the Pakistan Air Force in the realm of air defense. Fusing these networks with fourth-generation aircraft such as the Mirage-2000, MiG-29, and SU-30 gave a significant fillip to India's lagging capabilities in air defense.

ENTERING THE NEW MILLENNIUM: CHINA LOOMS LARGE

By the beginning of the 2000s, India's strategic establishment was over its obsession with Pakistan and realized that India's major strategic and security challenge would be a resurgent China. Voicing his concern openly for the first time in 1998, India's combative defense minister George Fernandes declared that "China and not Pakistan was India's principal adversary." Highlighting one of India's major concerns about the possibility of collusion between the two, he added, "China has provided Pakistan with both missile as well as nuclear knowhow. We have become a very soft people and we must realize that nations are not built through soft options, nor are the country's frontiers secured by a soft line."[27]

When Deng handed over power to his successor Jiang Zemin in the early 1990s, the modernization of the Chinese military was on an upward trajectory. In 1990 China had a reported defense budget of $6.13 billion (which, in reality, could have been twice that amount), versus India's reported defense budget of about $9 billion. Relying heavily on its nuclear arsenal, its mass, and a manpower-intensive army for deterrence, the only area where China was both qualitatively and quantitatively better positioned than India was in the realm of rocket units and submarines. Supported by a galloping economy that had grown to three times the size of the Indian economy by 2000, China's defense budget had increased from $12.6 billion in 1999 to $14 billion to $15 billion in 2000.[28] Chinese defense spending remained nontransparent, and official accounts substantially understated real military expenditures, which were estimated at more than $40 billion in 1999—three times the official figure. In contrast, India's defense budget remained relatively stagnant at around $12 billion.

By 2010, China's armed forces had showcased its accelerating military modernization and caught the world's attention. The comprehensive military capabilities on display at events commemorating the sixtieth anniversary of the founding of the People's Republic of China put the world on notice that a powerful China was ready to take its place on the global stage. China's defense budget had skyrocketed to what most defense analysts agreed was at least twice the officially stated figure of $70 billion—almost four times India's officially stated figure of $35 billion. The PLA, PLA Air Force, and PLA Navy had modernized at a startling pace, with an eye toward closing the gap with the United States, even as China jostled for clear leadership in Asia.

India, in contrast, seemed content to build military capability primarily for deterrence and to protect its interests. By 2016, China's official defense budget had more than doubled over the preceding six years to $145 billion, keeping pace with the growth in GDP; in comparison, the Indian budget of $51 billion had increased by only 37 percent, despite a GDP growth rate that almost matched China's.[29] Even if the actual Chinese defense budget is assumed to be only 1.5 times the official figure, it is still four times the Indian defense budget.

The modernization of the Chinese military has resulted in sweeping top-down organizational changes to ensure that the PLA is now part of integrated theater commands and shares leadership space with the much smaller PLA Air Force, PLA Navy, and PLA Rocket Force. In India, integration is still a work in progress, hampered by turf battles among the three armed forces and other stakeholders in national security. Some movement toward better synergy is visible on the horizon, with a slew of reforms announced by the Modi government and the appointment of a chief of defense staff. However, it is too early to assess its impact on operational capability. Much of the asymmetry that has emerged between India and China in land warfare capability can be attributed to the rapid expansion of the conventional element of the PLA Rocket Force—formerly known as the Second Artillery—which forms part of China's first-strike capability. India has no force to match this capability, other than its meager inventory of Prithvi and Brahmos cruise missiles. Artillery has been another area of stark asymmetry, but the Indian Army has finally addressed this shortcoming by inducting two highly mobile guns—the US-built M777 howitzer, a 155mm 39-caliber towed gun, and the heavier K-9 Vajra, a 155mm 52-caliber towed gun. The former is being assembled in India by Mahindra Defense Systems; the latter was developed by

Samsung Techwin of South Korea and is being manufactured by the Indian engineering giant Larsen and Toubro.[30] With 245 of these guns scheduled to be produced within the next three years, the Indian Army can be more confident of its ability to respond with adequate firepower to a rocket or artillery assault—the PLA's preferred option.

The PLA Navy has undergone the most aggressive expansion, reflecting China's renewed interest in increasing its maritime influence.[31] Protecting its naval lines of communication and ensuring the safety of its expanding infrastructure in the form of the Belt Road Initiative (to connect Tibet and Xinjiang Province with the Arabian Sea at the port of Gwadar) seem to be the focus of this expansion. The PLA Navy has grown into a modern force with one operational aircraft carrier, about sixty-five submarines of different classes and capabilities, eighty principal combatants, and 450 to 500 support vessels comprising coastal defense, amphibious craft, and logistics support ships. Apart from its traditional watch areas in the East and South China Seas, a confident and resurgent PLA Navy now makes regular forays and deploys into areas that converge with the Indian Navy's areas of interest, influence, and deployment—the entire Indian Ocean region.

In contrast, force levels in the Indian Navy have remained relatively static over the last decade, with one aircraft carrier, fourteen to sixteen submarines, forty-five to fifty combatants, and ninety to a hundred support vessels. Despite having a vibrant indigenous manufacturing program that has resulted in the induction of Delhi-class destroyers, Brahmaputra and Shivalik-class frigates, and Arihant-class nuclear submarines, the Indian Navy's share of the defense budget has remained within the narrow range of 14 to 17 percent over the last decade. This does not support the conversion of doctrine into capability. If there is one area of strength that India can build on, it is in the realm of maritime surveillance and antisubmarine warfare. With eight aircraft, the Indian Navy operates the world's second-largest fleet of Boeing P-8 Orion maritime reconnaissance aircraft.

For a long time, the IAF was sanguine in its conviction that it was superior to the PLA Air Force on every parameter except numbers. In the last two decades, however, the PLA Air Force has acquired indigenously manufactured (mostly reverse-engineered) fourth- and fifth-generation fighters, Airborne Warning and Control System (AWACS) platforms, aerial refuelers, highly sophisticated and reverse-engineered missile systems, long-range air-launched weapons, significant airlift capability, and high- and medium-altitude long-endurance unmanned aerial vehicles. During the same period, the IAF has seen a significant decrease in the number of fighter squadrons—without any replacements—and a sluggish indigenization of aircraft, weapons, and sensors.[32] Though the IAF's competitive advantage seems to be fast eroding, the recent crisis in Ladakh has galvanized the Indian government to speed up indigenization and the development of a fifth-generation fighter aircraft.

The impending induction of two state-of-the-art squadrons of the French-built Rafale multirole fighters and the ongoing induction of the indigenously designed and built Tejas light combat aircraft are likely to stem the IAF's slide. In addition, the IAF is in good shape for decades to come in the air mobility domain. With the induction of C-17 and C-130J aircraft, Mi-17 V5 and Chinook helicopters, and, most recently, Apache attack helicopters, the air mobility component of joint operations is more than comparable with whatever the PLA Air Force has to offer. However, more needs to be done if the Indian Air Force hopes to match up overall to the PLA Air Force in the years ahead.

One area in which all three arms of the Indian military are significantly better placed than the PLA is actual battle experience across the spectrum of conflict. Lessons learned from friends and strategic partners during the extensive joint exercises held since the early 1990s have added significant value to India's fighting potential. President Xi Jinping's purpose in committing Chinese troops to United Nations operations and increasing the number of exercises with allies such as Pakistan over the last decade has been to give the PLA vital overseas operational experience.

Having provided an overview of how the Indian military has coped with the rapidly transforming global and regional landscape of war and conflict, it is now time to dive headlong into the heart of the book—the various conflicts India has participated in, beginning with the Naga insurgency in the steamy jungles of northeastern India.

3

The Naga Rebellion

India's stand on the Naga question is based on the honest conviction that the
Nagas are as much part of the Indian nation as the Assamese or the Manipuris.
—D. R. Mankekar, *On the Slippery Slope in Nagaland*

BACKGROUND

Northeastern India comprises the seven distinct states of Assam, Meghalaya,
Arunachal Pradesh, Nagaland, Tripura, Mizoram, and Manipur, colloqui-
ally known as the Seven Sisters. Sikkim became part of the group after it
joined the Indian Union in 1975. Except for Meghalaya and Sikkim, which
have been relatively peaceful, these states have witnessed strife of varying
intensity and duration. While the common thread across the region is a
governance deficit and neglect by successive governments in New Delhi, it
is the secessionist, cultural, religious, ethnic, immigrant, and demographic
fault lines that have given rise to internal armed conflict of various kinds.

The Naga insurgency continues to be the wellspring of much of the unrest
along India's northeastern frontiers, warranting the use of force by the state.
In all subsequent insurgencies in the region—such as the Mizo uprising, rebellion in Tripura, tribal strife in Manipur, and ethnic strife in Assam—the
state governments have sought the help of the Indian Army and Air Force
to counter the protracted violence. For paucity of space, I focus on the joint
operations in Nagaland and Mizoram.

I have served in and frequently visited the northeast—as a fighter pilot
posted to Tezpur in the state of Assam on two occasions, as a student officer
and faculty member at war college, and on numerous trips to Arunachal
Pradesh, Nagaland, Meghalaya, and Tripura and to the extremities of the
frontier at the junction of India, China, and Myanmar at Kibithoo. I have
trekked in the Dirang Valley and spent time with my army and air force
comrades at Imphal, Zunehboto, Mukokchong, and Chakabama. My experiences in the northeast are nothing compared with the hardships faced by
the uniformed personnel posted there for years and the civilians who invariably get caught in the crossfire of internal conflict. What they have given me,
however, are perspective, empathy, and an understanding that goes beyond
mere historical analysis. I often refer to Indian forces as "security forces"

because operations in the northeast over the last six decades have involved troops from the Indian Army, Assam Rifles, and state police forces.

RUMBLINGS OF DISSENT IN THE NORTH EASTERN FRONTIER AGENCY

Operation Mop was conceived in the early 1950s and executed by Major Bob Khathing, administrator of the erstwhile North Eastern Frontier Agency (NEFA). The operation aimed at amalgamating the tribal areas of the region into the Indian Union before China could execute its creeping strategy of co-opting Tawang and large parts of NEFA as "Southern Tibet."[1] Khathing was a Manipuri Naga who had assisted Field Marshal Slim's XIV Army during the Burma Campaign of World War II as part of Victor Force, a small, covert unit that provided information and intelligence on the Japanese advance. He was subsequently commissioned as an officer in the Kumaon and Assam Regiments of the Indian Army. Khathing retired from the army after independence to steer NEFA's integration into the Indian Union. He was later appointed India's high commissioner to Burma (renamed Myanmar in 1989) and is one of independent India's lesser-known nationalists.[2]

Before contending with the Chinese, however, the Indian state had to deal with the Thagins, a tribe in the Siang Frontier Division, which lay south of the McMahon Line astride the Subansiri, one of the Brahmaputra's major tributaries. In the years following independence, the Thagins had fiercely resisted any attempts by the Assam Rifles—India's first paramilitary force—to bring them under control and even inflicted some casualties on the force. The tipping point was the massacre of a large column of Assam Rifles—including an officer and some local government officials—by a raiding party of Thagins, who ransacked the Aching Mori outpost on 22 October 1953 and took a few hostages. Alarmed at this turn of events, the NEFA administration swung into action and ordered the Assam Rifles to raise a strong force and send it into the area to free the hostages and maintain the peace.[3]

A battalion of the Assam Rifles—with troops from the Indian Army and officials of the political department—advanced on Aching Mori, with direct offensive air support provided by the Spitfires and Harvard aircraft of Fourteenth and Seventeenth Squadrons, respectively. Five Dakotas from Eleventh Squadron based at Jorhat, an Indian Air Force (IAF) airfield in Assam, dropped paratroopers near the troubled area, where they helped construct an advance landing ground by 14 November. Additional troops were then flown in from army formations around Jorhat and other places in the northeast. Clearly, there had been much joint planning to ensure the success of this operation.[4] The mandate of the force as it converged on

Aching Mori was not to kill or lay waste to the land but to threaten, deter, and finally coerce the more belligerent tribals into submission. Before and during the approach march, troops demonstrated their firepower so that the more recalcitrant among the tribes would be duly cautioned, while the friendlies would be reassured. Airpower demonstrations were also staged at selected spots. The targets were unpopulated areas such as hilltops and other prominent natural features. Spitfire Mk XVIIIs from Fourteenth Squadron, which were deployed at Jorhat airfield in Assam, attacked these targets with rockets, bombs, and 20mm cannon in a show of force.[5]

But these measures did not always have the desired effect. Interestingly, local witch doctors cashed in on these "near misses" by the IAF, claiming that their charms had kept the rain of bombs away from the villages. The slow-moving Harvards dropped leaflets over both hostile and friendly villages, highlighting government initiatives and proposed welfare schemes. There was some exchange of fire as the hostiles ambushed patrols and made one determined bid using rifles and Sten guns to dislodge troops from their positions on the night of 15 December. The column returned fire with mortars and light machine guns, followed by low early-morning passes and strafing by the Spitfires and Harvards. This blunted the attack, and the security forces soon had the tribals on the run. By the end of December 1953, they had ceased to offer any resistance. This was the Spitfire's last operational task in the IAF before it flew into the sunset of its glorious existence.[6] In January 1972 NEFA became the union territory of Arunachal Pradesh and was declared a federated state of India in 1987. Barring a few stray instances of Naga violence that spilled over into the state, it has remained peaceful and stood steadfast as a northeastern bastion, defying the territorial aspirations of a revisionist China.

THE LONGEST INSURGENCY

More than six decades ago, two companies of the Seventeenth Battalion of the Rajput Regiment marched through nearly 250 kilometers of unfamiliar jungle and mountain terrain in Nagaland, marking the beginning of independent India's first prolonged counterinsurgency operation. In April 1955 the small force set out from Amguri—a sleepy town on the border between Assam and what is now the state of Nagaland—and headed east. Marching to Mokokchung and Aghunato through Naga territory—inhabited mostly by the Ao and Sema tribes—it swung north and headed into Tuensang province, the wild and uncharted area bordering Burma and home to the fierce Konyak tribe.[7]

Tucked away in the extreme northeastern part of the Indian subcontinent,

where the sun rises many hours before the rest of India wakes, lies a pristine
and beautiful land. The rolling hills rise to a maximum of 10,000 feet, while
verdant and lush subtropical forests offer a breathtaking variety of flora
and fauna. The terrain is dotted with evergreen forests that are denser in
the north, along the India–Myanmar border. The hills pose a military challenge in terms of their broken contours, frequent crests, and densely forested
slopes. The defining feature of this land is its people, the Nagas. Their diversity is astounding, with no fewer than seventeen tribes in Nagaland; six of
them—Konyaks, Aos, Semas, Angamis, Chakesangs, and Lothas—constitute
almost 70 percent of the total population of Nagaland.[8] Tribal loyalties, distinct customs, and fierce territorial possessiveness were the prime reasons for
the lack of cohesion among the Nagas during the nineteenth and twentieth
centuries. Their relative isolation from development and modernity resulted
in a feudal and violent system of decision making and conflict resolution.
Head-hunting was prevalent until the early part of last century, particularly
among the Konyaks, who inhabited North Tsuensang in the northeastern
corner of the state.

It was in this rather inaccessible and remote part of northeastern India
that the first organized and sustained rebellion against the Indian government gained momentum. Organized loosely under the leadership of A. Z.
Phizo,[9] a slippery and ambitious Naga separatist from the Angami tribe, it
was supported over the years by both Pakistan and China and would tie up
tens of thousands of Indian Army troops for years. *Time* magazine described
the rebellion as follows:

> A Mau Mau–like war of terrorism against villages and Indian government
> posts, wielding their razor-sharp daos (axe-like knives) or shooting off Japa-
> nese and British arms pilfered from World War II caches. They were led by
> one A. Z. Phizo (who, lacking a Christian name, took the first and last letters
> of the alphabet). Phizo, 56, a mission-educated Naga, guided his warriors on
> ruthless raids in which they slaughtered hundreds of villagers and Indians, then
> retreated into the jungles and pathless mountain terrain. Afraid that the Naga
> revolt may spread to other tribes and give Red China an opening to step in on
> the disputed Indo–Tibet border, Prime Minister Nehru last week called on the
> Indian army to join Assam's armed police in an offensive operation against the
> rebels. Next day Naga terrorists kidnapped seven pro-government villagers in
> broad daylight, and beheaded four of them.[10]

The robust response of the Indian state during the early years of this rebellion must be judged based on this perspective, not solely through the lens of
regional media that selectively reported the heavy-handedness of the Indian

Army while ignoring the violence perpetrated by the Phizo's band of secessionist insurgents.

COLONIAL RULE

The late-medieval history of the Naga people is closely linked with the rise and fall of the great Ahom Dynasty, which ruled over Assam and most parts of northeastern India for almost six centuries until its collapse in the early nineteenth century.[11] For much of this period, the Nagas were remotely subjugated by the Ahoms and paid tribute in return for noninterference in their animistic and tribal way of life. The collapse of the Ahom dynasty around 1830—and the subsequent conquest of Assam by the British—marked the eastward expansion of the British Empire. The British made their first military foray into the region around 1840, establishing a few strong outposts across the Naga hills as they attempted to subjugate the tribes as a precursor to establishing political dominance.[12] By the turn of the century, much of the southern and central Naga hill regions were under British control. Only a few tribes—such as the Konyaks and the Changs—remained in the northern regions that bordered Burma and extended northward toward the trijunction of India, China, and Burma (Myanmar).

With the advent of Christianity by around 1850, the Naga society slowly opened itself to education and the Western way of life. Dedicated Christian missionaries combined their religious zeal with a genuine attempt to usher in some form of development in the region. This gained traction with the arrival of American Baptist missionaries in the 1870s. Although the number of Christian converts was a mere 579 in 1901,[13] the 1961 census revealed that more than 200,000 Nagas—or nearly 50 percent of the total population—had converted to Christianity.[14] Interestingly, the British encouraged these missionaries to go into tribal areas to protect the tea business. It proved to be a cheaper method of preventing attacks on the tea plantations than deploying the police or Assam Rifles.

By the Indian yardstick, Nagaland is a small state—occupying an area of 17,000 square kilometers and extending about 450 kilometers from the trijunction in the north to the border with Manipur in the south. It is approximately 325 kilometers from the border with Assam in the west to the international boundary with Myanmar in the east. Although the tribal solidarity movement in the northeast started as early as 1900 in what is now the Indian state of Meghalaya, the first armed uprising took place in the Naga hills. Until the outbreak of World War II, the British viewed areas east of Assam as merely a frontier that must be monitored. The relentless advance of Japanese divisions through Burma had them knocking on the Crown's frontiers by early 1944 and forced the British to reinforce the garrisons of Imphal and Kohima. This brought the Nagas into contact with other Indians for the first time, as tens of thousands of Indian troops streamed into the region as part of Field Marshal Slim's XIV Army.

However, a select group of Nagas had already been recruited by Subhas Chandra Bose, a breakaway Indian nationalist freedom fighter, for his Indian National Army (INA), which had allied itself with the Japanese. Among them were the young Phizo and his brother, who had escaped to Rangoon after committing a few transgressions in Kohima.[15] They provided intelligence to the INA about British troop deployments in Nagaland. In April 1944 some of the bloodiest battles were fought around Kohima as the Second Indian Division of Slim's mighty XIV Army pushed the Japanese and the INA out of India in one of the greatest battles of the war. At the other end of the spectrum were the exploits of Naga soldiers and officers such as Major Bob Khathing, who, as part of Slim's Victor Force, conducted covert operations behind Japanese lines.[16] Phizo was briefly imprisoned after the war for collaborating with the Japanese and remained in Burma for a few months after his release. In deciding whether to lead the Naga freedom struggle on a communist platform or to retain the tribal, ethnic, and Christian flavor of the movement, he chose the latter. Returning to Nagaland, he led a secessionist movement that would trouble the Indian state for more than six decades.

BEGINNINGS OF INSURGENCY

The winds of freedom that swept across the Indian subcontinent in 1947 blew in Nagaland too. An opportunistic Phizo—with very little sense of history, geography, or nationhood—sought independence from colonial rule for his motley bunch of tribes, professing that "historically Nagaland has no connection with India."[17] He was emboldened by a meeting with Mahatma Gandhi—who empathized with the Nagas and promised to help them achieve their aspirations without endorsing their cry for freedom—and issued a slew of petitions to the British. He went on to form the Naga National Council (NNC) in early 1947 and declared an independent Nagaland on 14 August 1947.

The declaration of independence was a nonstarter, given that the British had amalgamated large parts of Nagaland into the administered state of Assam. The new Indian government also deemed that Naga territory was part of the state of Assam and not an area that could exercise self-determination outside the Indian Constitution. Mainstream India's political administration was too preoccupied with the horrors of Partition—the ongoing conflict with Pakistan over Kashmir—and a host of other problems in the princely states of Hyderabad, Travancore, and Junagadh to pay any attention to the Nagas. Sir Akbar Hydari, the suave governor of Assam, extended an olive branch to Phizo in the form of a nine-point agreement that offered to review the Nagas' status ten years after the NNC agreed to amalgamate with the Indian Union.[18]

When Sir Hydari passed away in 1948, Phizo used this opportunity to interpret the agreement on his own terms and convert his struggle into a popular movement. He had the active help of the church, in the complete absence of any government machinery or capability in the region. Phizo and his charismatic deputy, Sakhrie, sensed that the collective mood of the Naga tribes favored self-determination, and they sought a referendum. This rattled New Delhi, and in a contentious meeting with Phizo in 1951, a brusque Prime Minister Nehru clearly stated that he was not prepared to accept any referendum that endorsed a break from the Indian Union. Phizo nonetheless went ahead and held a dubious referendum in 1952, in which 99 percent of the Nagas voted for independence. Phizo then appealed to the international community to intervene. When that move did not yield any results, Phizo decided that an armed struggle was the next logical step. It was a move that would bring untold misery to the people of Nagaland for the next six decades.

The various tribes of Nagaland have always been valiant fighters, skilled in archery and spear throwing. It was customary for warring head-hunting tribes and factions to settle disputes through violence. So, only a spark was needed to set this tinderbox aflame. That spark was provided by a charged Phizo and his initial band of insurgents, who were committed to the idea of an independent Nagaland. They included an erudite and articulate Sakhrie, who had written an impassioned letter to Mahatma Gandhi; a young Kaito Sema, who would become one of the most feared and wanted guerrilla leaders in the Naga hills; and Scato Swu, who was the moderate voice of the Naga struggle from the 1960s onward. Waiting in the wings were young student leaders such as Muivah and Mowu Angami, who would give up their promising academic careers to join the secessionist guerrilla movement. Alarmed by Phizo's rise, the Indian intelligence agencies tracked him closely as he repeatedly crossed over into Burma in the 1950s to organize the armed struggle and garner help from Naga outfits that had rallied together under the Eastern Naga Revolutionary Council. Tipped off by intelligence from Burma, Phizo was arrested by the Indian government in late 1952 for a second time.[19] However, he was released the following year on compassionate grounds when his wife met with a terrible accident.

Nehru's conciliatory visit to Kohima in 1953, accompanied by Burmese prime minister U Nu, went awry when he was booed by thousands of bot-tom-smacking Nagas for turning up late at a public meeting where he was supposed to explain the government's stand on the Naga issue. A humiliated Nehru would never forget this slight.[20] Following Nehru's visit, Phizo melted away into the jungles of northern Nagaland and Burma to build the most formidable insurgent outfit the Indian Army would face for decades. The legend of Phizo unfolded over the next few years as the newly formed Naga National Army (NNA) and its invisible headquarters (or Oking) caused im-measurable attrition among the Assam Rifles, which was tasked with border security and management.

The years 1953 to 1956 brought an escalation in violence as Phizo's NNA held sway all over Nagaland, including in the capital, Kohima. Scholars within the movement—such as Sakhrie—were among the first to realize the futility of waging an armed struggle against the mighty Indian state and raised their voices, calling for reason and peace. Crying treason, Phizo had Sakhrie assassinated in early 1956, sparking the first of many internecine killings among competing Naga groups. Tensions began to simmer between the Angamis, Semas, and Tangkhuls—Naga fighters on the Indian side—and the Konyaks and Aos—Nagas from Burma. In 1955, sensing an opportunity to exploit the intra-Naga strife, the Indian Army moved into the region in large numbers.

THE INDIAN ARMY MOVES IN

What about the military dimension of the Naga insurgency? A review of the forces ranged against each other reveals a typical counterinsurgency profile that is now easy to analyze. A few thousand well-armed and well-trained insurgents, who knew the terrain intimately and used the land and its people as both a logistics chain and a shield, were ranged against a perceived oc-cupier with nascent counterinsurgency capabilities. The Indian Army in the 1950s had a peacetime cantonment culture and severe budgetary constraints that seriously impacted its operational capabilities. It was an army trained to fight on the borders, not against militias and insurgents embedded in the civilian population. Moving into such a situation at short notice and without any specialized training or indoctrination was a momentous decision by the Indian government, one that the Indian Army obeyed without fully realizing the magnitude of the task.

During the initial years of the insurgency, the insurgents possessed a huge stockpile of World War II–vintage rifles, light machine guns, and mortars. These had been recovered from abandoned and dispersed caches of Allied and Japanese weapons in the jungles of Burma and Nagaland. Although devoid of any formal military training or inclination, Phizo had studied the mechanics of revolutionary warfare as conducted by Mao and had closely observed Japanese jungle warfare tactics. Deeply impressed by Phizo's revolutionary zeal, hundreds of Naga youths joined the movement across the state. Led by young commanders such as Zekheto Sema (Phizo's intelligence chief), Thungti Chang (head of the military wing), Kaito Sema (a ruthless front-line commander), and Mowu Angami, the force expanded into an imposing cadre of fighters, intelligence operatives, guides, and trackers numbering over 15,000.[21] By July 1955, the Naga insurgency had reached a point of no return. The modus operandi for violence followed a predictable pattern: Naga villagers in remote areas refused to pay taxes, the local administration sent police or paramilitary forces to investigate the issue, and these forces were waylaid by insurgents and brutally killed. Despite the beefing up of paramilitary forces in the Naga hills, the raids and ambushes continued unabated.[22]

The governor of Assam, Jairamdas Daulatram, finally had to call on the army, invoking its constitutional duty to aid civil authorities. The easternmost bastion of the Indian Army in the early 1950s was the 181st Independent Infantry Brigade at Shillong. It was this formation that shed one of its battalions in the middle of the monsoon of 1955 and rushed it to the Naga hills to douse the fire of rebellion. Marching through Mokokchung to the troubled district of Tsuensang and the central Naga hills, the Seventeenth Battalion of the Rajput Regiment attempted to restore normalcy, with the help of the already deployed Assam Rifles battalions. The battalion's mandate was outlined by General Shrinagesh, the army chief of staff:

> You must remember that all the people in the area where you are operating are fellow Indians. They have a different religion and may pursue a different way of life, but they are Indians. The very fact that they are different and yet part of India reflects India's greatness. Some of these people are misguided and have taken to arms against their own people and are disrupting the peace of the area. You are to protect the mass of the people from these disruptive elements. You are not there to fight the people in the area but to protect them. You are fighting only those who threaten the people and those who are a danger to the lives and properties of the people. You must, therefore, do everything possible to win their confidence and respect to help them feel that they belong to India.[23]

This is one of the earliest official pronouncements by the Indian Army on what became an enduring principle of counterinsurgency operations across the post–World War II world. This later came to be known as the "winning hearts and minds" strategy (WHAM).

It soon became clear that a single battalion was woefully inadequate to tackle the determined Naga resistance, so three more battalions were sent into Nagaland by mid-1956, pulled from forces under the command of the general officer in the Assam area. By early 1957, there were two un-dermanned brigades in the region based at Kohima and Mokokchung.[24] Skirmishes continued, and the Indian Army took heavy casualties, despite destroying several camps. The violence escalated after the brutal execution of Sakhrie under the noses of the Indian Army, and the situation was exac-erbated by the unfortunate killing of a respected citizen, Dr. Haralu, by the Indian Army during enforcement of a curfew.[25] Encounters became fiercer, and rules of engagement were cast aside.

Despite claims by the Naga insurgents that they had killed numerous In-dian Army personnel by early 1956, Indian Army records indicate that it lost its first soldier in February 1956 when a young lieutenant colonel was killed in an ambush near Kohima.[26] In June 1956 Kaito's fighters ambushed a payroll convoy and fatally injured the commanding officer of an infantry battalion that had stormed one of Kaito's hideouts and killed numerous insurgents. The gloves were now off, and Kohima was virtually under siege. The Indian Army found it difficult to differentiate between common citizens and insurgents, as Phizo and his cadres roamed the streets wrapped in col-orful red and black shawls, spreading the stern message that whoever sup-ported the Indian security forces would meet Sakhrie's fate.

Sensing that it was only a matter of time before the Indian Army tightened its noose, Phizo decided it was time to leave the area and scout for interna-tional assistance from India's adversaries and those sympathetic to the Naga cause. Despite the Indian Army's dragnet around Kohima, Phizo made a remarkable escape. He headed southeast toward the Cachar hills of Assam via Dimapur, ending up in the extreme northeastern parts of East Pakistan's Sylhet district. He was a prize catch for the Pakistani government, which welcomed him with glee and saw Phizo as a proxy to wage war against India. Phizo was followed into East Pakistan by a few NNA leaders such as Mowu Angami, who were trained, armed, and routed back into Naga ter-ritory to escalate the conflict against the Indian Army. After two agonizing years of indecision and strategizing in East Pakistan, Phizo fled westward in early 1960. He first went to Zurich and then to London, where he set up the Naga Revolutionary Council in exile. He was assisted in this westward transition by a Christian missionary, the Reverend Michael Scott. Scott was taken in by the movement and saw himself as the conscience of the Naga people—until he was deported for anti-India activities in the late 1960s.[27]

In a setback for Phizo, Mowu Angami was captured in 1957 by Indian security forces, as a parallel movement for peaceful reconciliation with the

Indian government gathered momentum. A general amnesty was later announced for all insurgents, including Mowu Angami. In New Delhi, there was misplaced confidence that a political resolution was right around the corner. That assessment was off-target, as the Indian government had not reckoned with the military capability of Phizo's other commanders—led by the enigmatic Kaito and the elusive Zunheto Sema—who remained at large and continued to inflict heavy casualties on the Indian Army.

The hard truth was that, in almost eighteen months of counterinsurgency operations, the situation had not stabilized. The Indian Army was beginning to realize that it was up against a bold and innovative adversary that had the support of the local populace. The absence of any government machinery to support military operations made matters worse. This hampered the achievement of the overarching political objective of integrating the Nagas into the Indian Union.

JOINT OPERATIONS

Guerrillas and insurgents around the world are largely prepared to live and die by the sword. When the battlegrounds and sanctuaries span international borders, the risks are even greater, and Phizo's commanders understood this. They constantly flirted with danger as they shuttled between the Naga hills and sanctuaries in East Pakistan and Burma. It was during one such crossing in August 1958 that Zekheto Sema and Thungti Chang were killed in an encounter with the Assam police following a tip-off. It was a body blow to the insurgents and infuriated Kaito. He immediately stepped up operations against the army, and suspected informers were dealt with brutally whenever they were caught.

In 1959 the Indian Army responded to the growing ferocity of combat by increasing its troop density to more than three brigades. It also revived the famous Twenty-Third Indian Division from World War II, appointing Major General D. C. Mishra as its first commander post independence.[28] At that point, the Naga insurgents had never attacked the strongholds of either the Indian Army or the Assam Rifles. Instead, they resorted to ambushes and classic hit-and-run guerrilla tactics, inflicting asymmetric casualties and significantly eroding the morale of army troops. The siege of Purr (now traceable as Phor on Google Maps, very close to the India–Myanmar border) signaled a change in strategy. Purr was located on high ground in the northern part of a mountain range east of Kohima. The post was occupied by two platoons of Assam Rifles and supported by two other posts in the vicinity. In late August 1960, in a well-executed pincer and isolating operation, a large force of almost 500 Naga insurgents comprising Semas, Angamis, and Tangkhuls cut off the post by destroying a linking bridge and then laid siege to it for four days, until the post ran out of ammunition and supplies.[29]

The IAF—which up to that point had not joined the fight beyond providing routine air maintenance—responded to a call for help from division headquarters (HQ) and sent two DC-3 Dakotas of World War II vintage from Forty-Third Squadron to drop essential supplies and ammunition at Purr on 28 August 1960. Flying extremely low, the Dakotas had mixed success and then had to take evasive action as more than a hundred insurgents opened fire with rifles and light machine guns. One of the Dakotas was badly hit, but miraculously, the other managed to get back to base. The damaged Dakota lost both its engines and crash-landed a few miles south of Purr in hostile territory. The aircraft was captained by Flight Lieutenant Singha, with Flying Officer Raphael as copilot and Flight Lieutenant Chandrasekhar Misra as navigator. There were six others on board—a navigator in training, a flight signaler, and a dropping crew of four Indian Army soldiers. The entire crew survived the crash. They were taken prisoner by a large group of hostiles under the command of Zuheto Sema and held captive for 617 days deep in the jungles of Burma before being released sometime in mid-1962.[30]

Numerous search-and-rescue sorties were undertaken over several months by all kinds of aircraft in an effort to locate Singha—a high-profile captive because he was the brother-in-law of Dev Anand, a Bollywood superstar. It is alleged that the pilot was released after Anand paid a ransom to Phizo in London.[31] Though the experience was harrowing and took a psychological toll on the crew, Misra acknowledged that they were treated well and suffered mainly from boredom and the weather. More than anything, the episode boosted the reputation of the Nagas, as numerous attempts to rescue the hostages failed.

Following these events, there was a hardening of resolve in New Delhi. Offensive airpower was now used against Naga insurgents in sparsely inhabited areas. There is very little official information available, but many IAF fighter pilots who served in the region—at bases such as Tezpur, Kumbhigram, and Jorhat—confirmed that they were often flown by helicopter to brigade HQ at Mukokchong and briefed by the army on possible hideouts and rebel locations.[32] Two fighter squadrons based at Tezpur began operations in late 1960, with a third joining the fray in 1961. Toofanis (the Indian name for the French Ouragan fighter) and Vampire jet trainers were the main aircraft deployed, and a slow-moving Harvard trainer was used for visual reconnaissance.[33] Major General D. K. Palit, an accomplished soldier-scholar, writes: "The IAF was brought into action in a tactical role, bombing and strafing rebel oppositions."[34] Highlighting the close cooperation between the army's Twenty-Third Infantry Division and Eastern Air Command, the operational record book of Twenty-Ninth Squadron for the quarters ending December 1961 and March 1962 records numerous air strikes on rebel locations. Indian troops reported extensive explosions and damage to rebel positions, and several casualties were evacuated in an easterly direction, possibly into the thick jungles of Burma.[35] Innovative tactics were employed, such as using the Harvard propeller aircraft as target locaters and pathfinders, with additional assistance from ground troops via radio links. Locations of these targets were ascertained based on 1961 Indian Army grid references converted into coordinates. When extrapolated on Google Maps, they seem to be accurate.[36]

Twenty-Ninth Squadron had moved from Kumbhigram in southern Assam to Tezpur in northern Assam for two reasons. First, Tezpur was the air base closest to the Tawang area, where the India–China crisis was brewing; second, it was also close to central and northern Nagaland, where most of the fighting between the Indian Army and the Naga insurgents took place. Some key observations from the operational record book make interesting reading. On the twelfth night (12 December 1961), the air force approved Twenty-Third Infantry Division's request for an air strike on a hostile camp consisting of one large *basha* (tent) and five small ones.[37] The strike was carried out the next morning by seven Toofanis and five Vampires of 101st Squadron. A total of 1,500 rounds and nineteen T/10 rockets were expended. The target was seen to be on fire, and hostile casualties were estimated at sixty killed.[38] Follow-up attacks, coordinated with ground troops, were carried out six days later against larger camps that were closer to the India–Burma border.

Jottings in the operational record book reveal that attacks were carried out on Target Alpha, which had eight *bashas*, and on Target Bravo, which had seven *bashas*. A slow-moving Harvard aircraft acted as a spotter and mission director and proved very useful. Target Alpha was reportedly destroyed, with sixty-eighty hostile casualties. An interesting feature of the strike was the good air-to-ground communication, which helped pinpoint and strike the targets.[39] Slow-moving De Havilland Otters of Forty-First Squadron were modified and converted into mini gunships to carry rocket pods and cabin-mounted machine guns. These gunships escorted the Mi-4 helicopters and Dakotas that dropped supplies to garrisons under siege in the Naga hills.[40] As war clouds loomed on India's northern border with China, the Twenty-Third Mountain Division left Nagaland and headed for NEFA. Phizo cleverly used this time to recoup and reorganize his forces and to orchestrate events from London.

SEARCHING FOR A SOLUTION

The first group of Naga insurgents that entered East Pakistan in 1958 were trained in a camp in the Sylhet region.[41] After 1962, there was a hardening of militant Naga nationalism and increased training support from East Pakistan. Formal military training in these camps empowered the Naga insurgents to go beyond ambushes and frontal engagement with the Indian Army, adopting tactics such as bombing trains and planting explosive devices to create panic among the civilian populace. Alarmed by the formation of a Naga Federal Government (NFG), the Indian Army wasted no time and sent its battle-weary units back into action in the hills of Nagaland, despite the bruising it received at the hands of the People's Liberation Army in 1962.

Rostum Nanavatty, a former commander of the Indian Army's Northern Command, retired as a lieutenant general in 2002. He is unarguably one of the most operationally accomplished, articulate, and scholarly Indian generals of recent times. My six-year engagement with him took me from his flat in Pune to the sylvan surroundings of his home in Dehradun, aptly named "Saltoro" after the daunting Saltoro Range that flanks the Siachen Glacier, where he commanded a brigade from late 1988 to 1990. Nanavatty was commissioned into the Second Battalion of the Eighth Gorkha Rifles as it retreated on orders from Walong during the 1962 war with China.[42] Early in his career, he was thrust into leadership roles in the Naga hills that he never imagined he would have to assume. His battalion, along with two others, was among the first to return to Nagaland between December 1962 and January 1963. He reminisces:

> We trucked from Dinjan (the army cantonment near the town of Dibrugarh on the eastern tip of Assam) to Dimapur, where we received our new commanding officer—the previous one had been killed in action during the Battle of Walong. We then distributed web equipment, boots, raincapes, and mackintoshes to our stoic Gorkhas and set out on foot to Tamenglang along the Kohima–Imphal highway. Having established a grid to intercept Naga gangs which had slipped into East Pakistan for training and recuperation, a ten-man section from the unit had its first scrap with an approximately thirty-strong gang in Tamenglang. Outnumbered, we pulled back and ran into another gang. This time around, the Nagas melted away into the jungles, avoiding a firefight. We were then ordered to march to Zunehboto in the Sema heartland, where I was put in charge of a double company post. We experienced constant skirmishes, which included the stealing of weapons from under our noses. The Nagas were constantly needling us, and we had to ensure that every man remained on duty or patrol all the time. After a year in the Satakha-Zunehboto area, the battalion relocated closer to the Myanmar border, to the town of Mukokchong.[43]

FOREVER IN OPERATIONS

In 1963 the Indian Army HQ swung into action under General J. N. Chaudhuri and took steps to consolidate its state presence and improve the command-and-control structure of its forces in the northeast. It deployed the newly raised Eighth Mountain Division with three brigades in Nagaland under Major General K. P. Candeth. Candeth had seen success as a commander during Operation Vijay, undertaken for the liberation of Goa in December 1961.[44] One of the best narratives of the operations of an Indian Army division after independence is that penned by Colonel R. D. Palsokar, an infantryman who won a Military Cross in World War II as a young lieutenant in the Burma theater. Titled *Forever in Operations*, the book tracks the sterling exploits of Eighth Mountain Division during its early years in Nagaland and during the 1971 war in the eastern theater.[45] The division returned to counterinsurgency operations in Nagaland, Manipur, and Tripura after the 1971 war to stem insurgencies that showed signs of revival, abetted in no small measure by an interfering China. Redeployed in the Kashmir Valley in early 1990, where the insurgency had intensified with active Pakistani support, the elite division also played a role in the Kargil Conflict of 1999.

The period between 1965 and 1970 saw pitched battles between units of Eighth Mountain Division and Naga gangs, who described themselves as battalions of the Naga Army. After its initial formation, the division settled down at its HQ at Zakhama, with three brigades at Zunehboto, Dimapur, and Ukhrul. In addition, several battalions of the Assam Rifles, the Central Reserve Police Force, the Railway Protection Force, and even a Kerala police battalion had been moved there during the 1962 conflict. Their principal adversaries were Naga gangs, whose regional commanders were under the unified political leadership of Phizo. These gangs had a clear division of political and military responsibilities, which Indian intelligence attributed to the training they had received in East Pakistan and China.[46]

Between 1963 and 1968, the central government made several attempts to hold elections. Interlocutors attempted to broker cease-fires and peace, but all these efforts failed in the face of increased insurgent activity. Making matters worse was the breakdown in Naga unity, which led to the creation of splinter groups: an Angami faction that was pro-Phizo and pro-NFG, and an anti-Phizo Sema faction led by Kaito Sema. The latter called itself the Revolutionary Government of Nagaland (RGN), and it vied for the support of the Naga people and external entities such as Pakistan and China. By 1969, the journey across Burma to China was becoming extremely hazardous for Naga insurgents. When the self-styled NFG commander in chief Mowu Angami attempted to return to Nagaland through Burma with a

600-strong gang, he met determined opposition from the locals and reportedly lost about half his gang in a series of battles. Tia Ao, the son of NFG elder statesman Imkongmeren Ao, was killed in this encounter. At the same time, NFG cadres looted the two towns of Tiddim and Falam.

When the NFG insurgents reached the border of Nagaland, they found their access routes blocked by the Indian Army. RGN scouts apparently contacted General Mowu and his band and persuaded them to take "sanctuary" in the RGN camp, which was protected by a cease-fire agreement. Although the full story has not been told, it appears that Indian authorities learned of the arrival of General Mowu and his 162 men and orchestrated their capture with minimal resistance, aided in no small measure by the treachery of the RGN. Shortly afterward, eighty-three members of a second contingent of China-trained Naga cadres were captured, but their leader, Issac Swu, eluded security forces and managed to slip into Manipur with about a hundred of his men. The capture of large contingents of NFG insurgents substantially altered the balance in Naga politics. Morale in the NFG dipped to a new low, enabling the RGN to recruit NFG defectors.

RGN leaders—who desperately wanted peace talks to resume—soon discovered that the Indian government under Indira Gandhi saw no reason to negotiate. Even as storm clouds gathered in East Pakistan, a hopelessly fragmented Naga secessionist movement resulted in an improved security situation in Nagaland. Instead of exploiting the situation, Indira Gandhi procrastinated. The Indian prime minister may well have lost a golden opportunity to transform concerted military action into a lasting political solution.

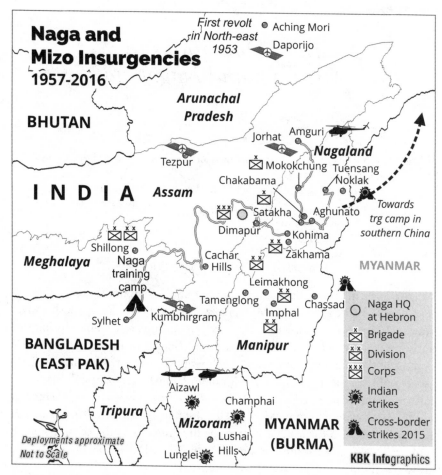

Map 1. Naga and Mizo Insurgencies

4

Joint Operations in Mizoram and Nagaland

The Mizo Accord so far remains the only successful peace accord of its kind in Independent India's history.
> —Sushil Kumar Sharma, "Lessons from Mizoram Insurgency and Peace Accord 1986"

INSURGENCY IN MIZORAM

Mizoram is a hilly state flanked by Manipur and Assam to the north, Tripura and Bangladesh to the west, Myanmar to the east, and Bangladesh to the south. Unlike Nagaland, Mizoram was demographically stable during the early years after independence. The Lushai tribe constituted more than 60 percent of the total population, and no other tribe accounted for more than 8 percent of the residents.[1] When the Mautam famine swept through the Mizo Hills in 1959, it caused great distress. Government apathy led to the emergence of the Mizo National Front (MNF) as the militant voice of the Mizo people.[2] Led by Laldenga, a former *havildar* in the Indian Army (a noncommissioned rank equivalent to a corporal in the US Army), the MNF would challenge the army's might after the 1965 war with Pakistan.

Indira Gandhi had taken over as prime minister of India following the death of Lal Bahadur Shastri during the Tashkent peace talks. Seeking to seize the initiative in the wake of political uncertainty in New Delhi, and riding on the wave of Naga turbulence, the MNF sounded the bugle for an armed revolt on the night of 28 February 1966. It declared independence, seized the treasury in Aizawl, and laid siege to the Assam Rifles garrison located next to it. Armed cadres simultaneously moved into other important towns such as Lunglei and Champhai, in what the rebels called Operation Jericho, and they overwhelmed the Assam Rifles companies located there. Border Security Force (BSF) posts in other towns were also overrun, as the MNF saw the rebellion as the first step in creating the state of Greater Mizoram, which sought to include parts of the neighboring states of Assam, Tripura, and Manipur.[3] Prime Minister Gandhi reacted promptly and flew into the area with her defense minister, the experienced Y. B. Chavan. Accompanying them were the home secretary and the chiefs of the army and air force. Lieutenant General S. H. F. J. (Sam) Manekshaw, head of Eastern Army Command, advocated a swift and hard response during discussions with the prime minister and her team. New Delhi was rattled by the MNF operation, which had taken Indian intelligence agencies by surprise. To the prime minister's credit, she did not hesitate to use force to quell the rebellion. She reportedly established an immediate rapport with the no-nonsense Manekshaw, a relationship that would yield rich dividends during the 1971 war with Pakistan.

Manekshaw entrusted the operation to 101st Communication Zone, a division-sized force that oversaw operations in the region. Sixty-First Mountain Brigade was promptly ordered to undertake a helicopter-landed operation to relieve the siege and retake the treasury. The 105th and 110th Helicopter Units—equipped with Mi-4 helicopters—were tasked to fly in two companies of the Eighth Battalion of the Sikh Regiment and two companies of the Fifth Battalion of the Parachute Regiment in several waves to relieve and reinforce the Aizawl garrison. The first waves flew in on 5 March 1966, but the helicopters had to return to base when they were fired on by more than a hundred Pakistan-trained Mizo insurgents and Indian Army deserters who had joined the MNF. The insurgents had surrounded the treasury and five other posts nearby, even firing at and damaging a Caribou transport aircraft carrying senior army and air force officers for a recce mission over Aizwal.

Lieutenant General Mathew Thomas, who would go on to command the Indian Army's only parachute brigade in the 1971 war, was a lieutenant colonel in 1966 and in command of the Fifth Battalion of the Parachute Regiment. Disappointed that he had been unable to participate in the 1965 war, he saw this as an opportunity to give his troops a battle inoculation. He was surprised by the response from the MNF cadres, who had "planned well, executed the plans swiftly, and fought cleverly."[4] Given that the Indian Air Force (IAF) had conducted extensive offensive operations against Naga camps in the early 1960s, it did not take long for Manekshaw to reach out to his counterpart in Eastern Air Command, who readily agreed to provide offensive air cover for another attempt at the helicopter landings and paradropping of ammunition and supplies at Aizawl.

Air Commodore D. J. Sarma, who commanded the IAF's Thirty-Third Squadron and Air Force Station Guwahati in later years, was flying Dakotas with Forty-Ninth Squadron at the time. He joined the six-aircraft detachment at Kumbhigram soon after the first abortive landing attempt. He recollects that they had a "predawn briefing by hurricane lamps in the bamboo gazebo with glasses of tea." They were "airborne by dawn to drop ammo and provisions onto the drop-zone at the camp under siege. On the final run-in, two Toofanis flew abreast of the Dakotas and slightly ahead, firing their guns as protective fire."[5]

While Toofani fighters from Kumbhigram escorted the heliborne force and the Dakotas, Hunters from Seventeenth Squadron based at Jorhat carried out their first strikes on Aizwal on 6 March 1966. Air Marshal Teshter Master, who retired as the IAF's director-general of inspection and flight safety, was a flight lieutenant at the time. He recounts:

> We were briefed that air support/supply by helicopter and Dakota aircraft had been met by small-arms fire from the rebels. The Assam Rifles unit was in danger of suffering casualties and needed close air support. The unit was in barracks with a clear area around them the size of a few football fields. It was decided to use rockets and guns to attack the rebels and provide relief to the surrounded troops. The army unit would put markings on the ground to indicate the target. The markings comprised an arrow to show the direction of the target and strips laid diagonally below the arrow to indicate distance. If I remember right, the baseline was 1,000 yards and each strip was plus 100 or 200 yards. So, if there were two strips below the arrow, the target was 1,200 or 1,400 yards in that direction.[6]

Master's logbook confirms that he flew two strikes on 6 March and used rockets and guns to strafe the designated area, identified as a rebel camp. Seventeenth Squadron also carried out armed reconnaissance along the main highway leading to Aizwal to interdict vehicular movement, but found no targets. The squadron received messages that its missions had been successful and that the besieged army unit had been relieved. These operations intercepted MNF cadres on the move and introduced an element of speed and urgency.[7]

Air Marshal Bharat Kumar, an accomplished airpower historian and fighter pilot who was part of a squadron based in the eastern sector, recollects, "The situation at that time was really grim. Not only did the Mizos want to announce their 'own government,' there was real danger to the local army and police as well as some civil servants who were surrounded—it was feared they [would] be massacred. It was a difficult decision, but the Mizo struggle frittered away immediately after the air attacks and the talks started soon after."[8] There is no official record of any civilian or rebel casualties during the air attacks, but locals insist there were several, although they cannot provide any evidence of how many.[9] Colonel Vivek Chadha interviewed several locals during research for his book *Low Intensity Conflicts in South Asia*, including Brigadier Sailo, the son of Laldenga and later a chief minister.[10] Apart from feelings of hurt and indignation, there is little to suggest that there was much collateral damage. In the final analysis, the gravity of the situation forced Manekshaw to use all means available to ensure that the troops under his command were not massacred by the Mizo rebels, who were disorganized, angry, and liable to engage in indiscriminate killing.

By 7 March, additional troops had linked up with those landed by helicopter and relieved the siege at Aizawl. Troops from the Gorkha Rifles and Bihar Regiment then moved toward the towns of Champhai and Lunglei, while paratroopers secured the areas around the border with East Pakistan the following day.[11] By 17 March, intense military operations in Mizoram had ended, although limited operations would continue until military resistance by the MNF ended almost a decade later, and it would take years for peace to be restored in Mizoram. Laldenga escaped first to East Pakistan and then westward to London, where he remained in exile for almost two decades. After the low-grade insurgency petered out in the face of a resolute Indian Army, a proactive church convinced the MNF to lay down arms and join the mainstream political process. Laldenga became the first chief minister of Mizoram after signing a historic accord with the Rajiv Gandhi government on 30 June 1986.[12] Mizoram has been largely peaceful since then, barring stray occurrences of infiltration, drug running, and arms smuggling.[13]

THE CHINA FACTOR IN NAGALAND

Emboldened by their military victory over India in 1962, and seeing the ease with which Naga insurgents slipped into East Pakistan and returned to Nagaland after military training, the Chinese saw an opportunity to deliver a double whammy to India. They offered to train the Nagas in camps in the southern Yunan Province. Along with providing military training, the People's Liberation Army tried to indoctrinate senior Naga leadership in Maoist ideology. Kaito Sema, Mowu Angami, and Thunglang Muivah were taken to Beijing, where they interacted with Chinese government officials and leaders of the Vietcong in North Vietnam. For more than two decades, this policy of aiding the Naga insurgency waxed and waned as China attempted to make inroads into the various secessionist movements that sprang up along India's northeastern border. After the crushing of the armed rebellion in Mizoram and the eventual birth of Bangladesh, training grounds in erstwhile East Pakistan dried up, and the Naga movement looked to China for help sustaining the armed struggle.

Based at Chabua Airfield, 105th Helicopter Unit was given the twin tasks of maintaining army units on the frontier with China and supporting counterinsurgency operations in Nagaland. Equipped with Mi-4s, the unit maintained a large detachment alongside Eighty-First Mountain Brigade at Chakabama, which was located on the northern fringes of Eighth Mountain Division's operational area. A senior IAF group captain was colocated at Eighth Mountain Division headquarters (HQ) in Zakhama, where he was the air force liaison officer and coordinated the assignment of complex daily tasks. Pilots such as Harry Ahluwalia and Anil Bendre spent weeks at Chakabama, performing several risky missions over insurgent-infested areas. On 20 May 1974 the new division commander, Major General Girish Narain Sinha, was severely injured when rebels shot at a Mi-4 helicopter piloted by Bendre as they were flying low in the Zunhebuto Valley. One bullet brushed Bendre's helmet, while another pierced Sinha's arm and exited through his back. More bullets damaged the communication box. Luckily, none hit the engine, and Bendre was able to bank sharply and get out of the valley. Sinha was rushed to division HQ, where he underwent surgery immediately. As a result, he had to hand over command to Major General G. S. "Ganjoo" Rawat. Later, it was discovered that they had flown right through the area of a well-trained unit of Sema fighters who had just returned from China.

Rawat was a proactive commander who liked to take the battle to the enemy. During his tenure (1974–1976), several rebel gangs attempted to sneak through a well-established counterinsurgency grid as they returned from training in Yunan. He aggressively employed the IAF's Mi-4 helicopters for aerial reconnaissance and for troop deployment to cut off routes to and from Burma.[14] The IAF got more involved in operations in the Naga hills after the Mi-8 helicopters were inducted in the mid-1970s. The 118th Helicopter Unit operating out of Guwahati was employed for reconnaissance and troop insertion, and it played an important role in blocking egress routes and logistically sustaining small teams engaged in missions behind rebel lines. As hectic operations continued through the late 1970s, another Bollywood connection was made in Nagaland when Major General Ashoke Dutt—younger brother of renowned character actor Utpal Dutt—assumed command of Eighth Mountain Division.

RECONCILIATION, FACTIONALISM, AND REVIVAL

Moderate elements within the Naga National Council (NNC) were tired of the two-decade-long insurgency and the relentless action by the Indian Army, and they had become disillusioned with Phizo's remote leadership. As a result, they signed the Shillong Accord with the Indian government on 11 November 1975. Led by Zashei Huire and driven by a dominant Indira Gandhi, the accord offered much promise, but it did not translate into peace and stability for two principal reasons: the Indian government's inability to usher in good governance and spur development in the region, and the Naga people's inability to rise above tribal and ethnic loyalties. The chaos that followed the emergency of 1975—Prime Minister Indira Gandhi's crackdown on the political opposition—led to her ouster in 1977. Thereafter, a series of weak coalition governments failed to convert the Shillong Accord into something permanent and stalled the peace process, leading to the return of widespread violence in Nagaland. When Gandhi returned to power in 1980, she failed to revive the Naga peace process due to the emergence of other internal security issues, such as the Sikh separatist movement in Punjab (see chapter 5).

Prior to the signing of the Shillong Accord, the Indian government announced that 800 guerrillas had surrendered between October 1968 and March 1969 and that another 2,316 guerrillas had surrendered over the two-year period ending 16 December 1969.[15] Almost 2,000 of the surrendered rebels were inducted into three battalions of the BSF between 1969 and 1973. It was a move that promised much but failed to make a dent in the combat potential of the various Naga groups. The 111th Battalion of the BSF, located near Zunehboto, has more than eighty former insurgents who are still serving at older than seventy years of age.[16] A major split took place within the Naga movement in 1980, when dissatisfied militants of the NNC broke away to form the National Socialist Council of Nagaland (NSCN), with Phizo's blessing. Led by Thuingaleng Muivah, Isaac Swu, and S. S. Khaplang, the NSCN was emboldened by limited support from China. This marked the next phase of the armed struggle between the Nagas and the Indian Army. All factions of the NSCN gave the Indian Army a hard time with their sophisticated guerrilla tactics and significant firepower. The violence would last almost two decades, until the next comprehensive cease-fire in 1997.

Lieutenant General Narasimhan, a hardy infantryman from the Madras Regiment, retired in 2016 as the director-general of military intelligence and is now the director-general of a government-sponsored think tank on China. He was one of the few officers in the Indian Army to serve a ten-year stretch in his first battalion, the Twenty-Fifth Battalion of the Madras Regiment. Narasimhan served as company commander and commanding officer as the unit moved between various insurgency-prone areas. He also served in the Counter Insurgency and Jungle Warfare School and has deep insight into the thinking and the operational philosophies of the numerous militant groups in Nagaland and Manipur. Narasimhan clearly recollects that, after Phizo's death in 1990, the NNC—which represented the political face of the secessionist movement—no longer enjoyed the confidence of the Naga people, and the original cause of an independent Nagaland faded away. Reminiscing about his early tenure in Nagaland, particularly in the Chakabama and Tsuensang areas, Narasimhan recalls that Naga insurgents—unlike the local and foreign terrorists in Jammu and Kashmir (J&K)—adhered to a battle code of conduct. They issued warnings before attacking and respected fallen soldiers.[17]

Factional rivalries, tribal loyalties, and a reduction in support from China caused rifts in the NSCN. After a series of deadly strikes by the Khaplang-led group made up of Konyaks, Aos, and Burmese Nagas against the Tanghkul and Sema groups led by Thuingaleng Muivah and Isaac Swu, the NSCN splintered into the Khaplang (K) faction and the Isaac and Muivah (I&M) faction in April 1988. India's intelligence agencies also played a part by undertaking a disinformation campaign that sowed the seeds of doubt in the minds of competing groups. The main operational areas of the NSCN (K) were restricted to the northern parts of Nagaland (Tsuensang and Mon) and the overlapping Naga-inhabited areas of Myanmar and Arunachal Pradesh. The NSCN (I&M) group dominated the larger swath of territory in the Sema and Tanghkul areas spanning the hill districts of the adjoining state of Manipur. More than anything else, this split precipitated a violent reaction from indigenous Manipuris (Meiteis), making Manipur another hot spot in the northeast.[18]

The splintering of the NSCN based on tribal loyalties was accompanied by an ideological vacuum as the Chinese—who had invested heavily in the insurgency as a means of maintaining pressure on India's eastern frontiers—stopped their large-scale assistance. This was more out of a desire to cut their losses rather than any altruistic design to appease India. Running camps for Naga rebels in Yunan was proving to be an expensive proposition without any tangible payoff. As external funding dried up, the Naga factions turned to extortion, illegal taxation, and drug trafficking to generate money. This gradually eroded their credibility. Feeling the heat of sustained Indian Army pressure in the early 1990s, Khaplang fled to Myanmar, while Isaac and Muivah escaped to Thailand.

In 1989 the Congress Party made inroads into Nagaland by convincing local parties such as the Progressive United Democratic Front to merge with it. S. C. Jamir and Hokishe Sema were at the forefront of the political process. They dominated the political stage as chief ministers of Congress Party–led coalition governments until Hokishe Sema joined the Bharatiya Janata Party in 1999, following differences with Jamir. When Jamir aligned himself with the NSCN (K), Hokishe Sema had no choice but to support the NSCN (I&M). It was clear by now that local politicians and political parties had little interest in fulfilling the aspirations of the Naga people. They were more interested in consorting with insurgent groups for personal gain, while the national parties invested little in the political process. Consequently, the security situation remained stressed, and the army continued to be involved in stability operations in the absence of robust policing and internal security structures.

THIRD CORPS AND THE LONG ROAD TO PEACE

When Eighth Mountain Division celebrated its twenty-fifth anniversary in 1988, it was the Indian Army's most experienced counterinsurgency force. Its services were soon requisitioned in another hot spot: Jammu and Kashmir. Consequently, even as Indian Army HQ decided to move the division to J&K in late 1989, it assigned Third Corps, which had its HQ at Dimapur on the border between Nagaland and Manipur, with the task of fighting insurgencies in the northeast. This formation would emerge as the largest corps in the Indian Army with the dual responsibility of countering insurgency and defending large portions of the line of actual control in Arunachal Pradesh.

Third Corps was initially formed with two divisions at Dinjan and Zakhama—Second and Fifty-Seventh Mountain Divisions—to manage insurgencies in Nagaland, Manipur, and parts of Assam. Its first commander was Lieutenant General B. Joginder Singh. The corps soon expanded to include one additional division—Fifty-Sixth Mountain Division—to oversee operations in eastern Arunachal Pradesh, as well as a division-sized complement of Assam Rifles to defend the border with Myanmar and conduct counterinsurgency operations in Nagaland and Manipur. This was a huge area extending from the central parts of Arunachal Pradesh to the Lohit division in the east at the trijunction of India, China, and Myanmar, covering the states of Nagaland, Manipur, Tripura, and Meghalaya and areas of Assam south of the Brahmaputra.

Operations across the Naga hills and into the Kohima plains are now run by Inspector General Assam Rifles (IGAR) (North), who commands a large division-sized force of the Assam Rifles. Similarly, IGAR (South) is located close to Imphal to combat the ongoing insurgency in Manipur, along with IGAR (East), another recently formed division-strength force. Sitting in New Delhi, it is easy for armchair critics to question the need for such large forces in this region. But considering the several security fault lines in the region, these elements of state power are essential not only to conduct counterinsurgency operations but also to help maintain law and order and prevent the outbreak of violence in the absence of effective policing and governance.

Facing immense pressure from a well-established counterinsurgency grid—much like in the period preceding the 1975 Shillong Accord and during the split in the NSCN—the NSCN (I&M) entered into a cease-fire agreement with Prime Minister Atal Bihari Vajpayee's government in 1997 and claimed leadership of the Naga movement. Third Corps, however, continued its operations against the NSCN (K), much to the ire of Nagaland's chief minister, S. C. Jamir, who was an Ao himself and had failed to rise above sectarian loyalties. Commanding Third Corps from September 1997 to June 2000 as a lieutenant general, Rostum Nanavatty recalls that Jamir pressured him to "go easy" on the Khaplang faction. He also remembers meeting Hokishe Sema, who represented the political aspirations of the NSCN (I&M), and found him to be more balanced than Jamir.

Characterizing instances of human rights violations by the Indian Army against civilians in the northeast as "unfortunate and unacceptable," Nanavatty was emphatic about the broader restraint shown by the army. He said:

> Our record is nothing to be ashamed of. We do not now use offensive airpower, tanks, or heavy weapons in our operations anymore and are paying one hell of a price for this restraint. The Indian Army does its best to punish human rights violations, and I personally recollect numerous instances where I had to severely punish officers because of a variety of transgressions. I recognized that large organizations, including armies, do tend to "cover up" and have a "hota hai" (it happens) attitude, and came down quite heavily whenever aberrations came to my notice.[19]

He then recalled an incident that took place in 1997:

> A classic example of "regular force retaliation" after suffering significant casualties was when, on 27 December 1997, a unit under my command lost their commanding officer in an ambush and firefight with insurgents of the Naga army and the attackers then slipped away into the [surrounding] villages. A disproportionate response from the unit followed, which caused several civilian casualties. This is the ambiguity and the fog of war in counterinsurgency operations that every professional army in the world has had problems dealing with. The Indian Army has been no different.[20]

Acknowledging that he had trouble dealing with transgressions in the northeast because of societal differences, Nanavatty emphasized that it was essential for any commander to display fairness and firmness as part of an overall strategy, even if it involved sacking officers with outstanding operational records. He remembered one occasion when village elders asked the commanding officer of a battalion in his corps to reduce the punishment meted out to a soldier who had been accused of groping a woman at a road opening point.[21]

ALMOST THE END

On 5 June 2015, as a convoy of the Indian Army's Dogra Regiment wound its way through a densely forested road at Chandel—close to the border between the states of Manipur and Nagaland—it was ambushed by insurgents from three diverse rebel groups: the NSCN (K), the Manipur-based Kangleipak Communist Party, and the Kanglei Yawol Kanna Lup, also based in Manipur. Eighteen Dogra soldiers lost their lives in the murderous ambush. Little did anyone realize that they would become the catalysts for the possible resolution of the longest insurgency in the post–World War II era. The incident unleashed a chain of events that would lead to swift retaliation and a recalibration of the way the Indian state considered punitive action in subconventional warfare.

While the NSCN (K) represented the Naga secessionist movement, the other two groups involved in the attack represented the Manipuri Meitei elements of a defensive movement that sought to protect its adherents from Naga and Kuki insurgents. The political dynamics of these groups indicated their desperation to remain relevant in the increasingly fractured Naga polity that had emerged after the signing of the Naga Framework Agreement between the government of India and the dominant Naga group, NSCN (I&M), in August 2015.[22] The NSCN (I&M) had progressively diluted its secessionist stand over the years and replaced it with a demand to integrate all Naga-dominated areas of northeastern India—including parts of Manipur, Assam, and Arunachal Pradesh—into a Greater Nagalim. Marginalized in this discourse, the NSCN (K)—comprising primarily Nagas from northern Nagaland and adjoining parts of Myanmar—refused to endorse the agreement and joined with Manipuri and Assamese insurgent groups to disrupt the fragile peace in the region.

General Bipin Rawat—the current chief of India's Defense Staff and commander of Third Corps at the time—had reservations about the robustness of the loosely worded cease-fire and discussed his concerns with the central government interlocutor.[23] His worry was that no clear lines had been laid down for the rebels, who flaunted their weapons with impunity and imposed ridiculous restrictions, such as declaring a no-fly zone over their base at Hebron, barely twenty kilometers from Rawat's HQ. Ignoring this restriction, Rawat deliberately flew over Hebron every time he visited one of his formations. When the rebels complained that he was flouting the cease-fire agreement and warned that he ran the risk of drawing fire, Rawat dared them to shoot at him.

In a wide-ranging interview, Rawat recalled being uneasy about the regrouping of various Naga rebel factions months before the 2015 attack.

Adding to the tension was the groups' ongoing extortion within their respective areas of influence. The tipping point came when the NSCN (K) attacked an Indian Army Signals Corps convoy and a post of the Assam Rifles in the heart of Kohima in May 2015, killing several soldiers. Realizing that many units had been lulled into a false sense of complacency, Rawat directed the northern division of IGAR (North) in Kohima to launch an informer-guided and intelligence-driven operation against an NSCN (K) camp in a nearby forest. The operation had to be aborted when the informer chickened out barely 500 meters from the camp and fled, indicating that an ambush was highly likely. Concurrently, Rawat commenced planning a punitive operation and identified six or seven rebel camps along the border with Myanmar as likely targets. He reckoned that he would have launched a punitive strike even if the Chandel ambush had not taken place.[24]

Determined not to fritter away the advantage gained from the various peace initiatives, the Indian Army planned a swift operation to hunt down the perpetrators of the Chandel ambush. Several options were considered. These included hitting selected NSCN (K) camps with attack helicopters and then following up with special heliborne operations. Rawat was given a free hand by his superiors, and he worked closely with Air Marshal Kler, the senior air staff officer at HQ Eastern Air Command in Shillong, who ensured that Mi-35 attack helicopters were speedily sent to Third Corps' zone from their home base at Pathankot. Operating from Imphal, Kohima, Leimakhong, and other helipads built to support such operations, they carried out reconnaissance missions and live firing practice.

However, the two days spent mulling over the various options gave the rebel groups time to disperse and melt away across the border. Drawing on extensive human intelligence and other reliable aerial and space-based recce assets, Indian forces were able to pinpoint two major rebel camps for targeting. Situated less than ten kilometers across the Myanmar border with Manipur and Nagaland, the camps were said to be buzzing with insurgent activity. The northern camp lay opposite the town of Noklak in the district of Tsuensang, and the southern camp had sprung up across from the town of Chassad in Manipur. Once the targeting was complete, the attack helicopters continued to operate normally to instill a sense of status quo. The rebels assumed the search missions would continue without crossing the border, as had been the norm in previous decades, even when the provocation had been grave.

Rawat chose the night of 6 June to attack the camps after receiving the requisite clearance from all levels, including the national security adviser and the prime minister. However, he had to postpone the attack by one day for operational reasons. At the tactical level, there was never any doubt that the operation would be entrusted to teams from the two Special Forces units under Rawat's command. One of the units had honed its fighting skills over decades in the northeast, but the other had only recently taken on the role and was hungry for action.[25]

Two teams of around sixty men each were selected for the mission. Each team's main aim was to assault the camps from a distance with mortars and rocket launchers, while performing various supporting roles such as setting up blocks and ambushes and supporting exfiltration. The idea of a fire assault did not appeal to Lieutenant Colonel Nectar Sanjeban, the tough second in command of one of the units leading the southern prong of the mission. The target was a large camp with many insurgents from the Manipur-based groups that had combined with the NSCN (K) for the Chandel ambush. Rawat recalled that when he briefed Nectar, the colonel said, "Sir, what is the point of Special Forces doing a fire assault from a standoff distance, you may as well use mortars or artillery from here. I will go in close and hit them with surprise and stealth." Rawat had been ordered to carry out a fire assault because the risk of taking casualties from close combat was too high. However, he respected Nectar's opinion and told him, "Go ahead, but ensure no casualties are left behind in the adversary's territory." Their agreement was that Nectar would ignore orders and Rawat would back him up if something went wrong.

After getting the go-ahead from the prime minister on the evening of 7 June and a call from the national security adviser confirming the green light, the mission was launched with complete radio silence. All contingencies were in place, including helicopter support for casualty evacuation and extrication. Even though the southern camp was barely four kilometers from the India–Myanmar border, Nectar and his team detoured through some high ground that gave them good visibility of the camp and allowed them to retain the element of surprise. Setting out at 7:00 p.m. on 7 June, the group encountered two local hunters and their dogs. They tied up the men and muzzled the dogs and left four men to guard them. Once they were in visual contact with the camp, the group settled down for the night in the dense foliage, covering themselves with repellent to keep away the snakes, leeches, and insects. But according to Rawat, all the men were covered with boils and insect bites when they returned. The lead recce party found the forward sentry huts empty but detected two sentries in trees. They were promptly taken down with silenced Israeli sniper rifles.

It was 6:00 a.m. on 8 June by the time the assault group entered the camp, which still appeared deserted. This prompted Nectar to alert Rawat that things might not be going their way: "The camp is empty, sir. I am going in deeper." Rawat replied, "You guys will get us into trouble." Nectar responded before signing off: "Don't worry, sir—no casualty will be left behind." A trifle apprehensive about the turn of events, Rawat alerted the IAF attack helicopters, Army Aviation's advance light helicopters, and the extrication team to be ready for any contingency. As the commandos crept closer, they heard the clatter of utensils and saw a single guard outside what seemed to be a large dining hall. Nectar assessed that about thirty to forty insurgents had gathered for their morning meal. Silencing the guard with a knife, the assault group surprised the insurgents by firing their weapons and then picked them off as they fled. Rawat reckons the firefight was over in minutes. Still, instead of heading straight back, the team perceptively chose to take the longer route to avoid running into villagers or other insurgents. The return journey was uneventful; the more fatigued among the force were extricated by the army's light helicopters, and the others just trekked back. Nectar's force suffered no casualties, and after a Bara Khana (a traditional celebratory meal) that included some very welcome rum and whiskey, it was business as usual the following day.

The northern group had a longer but uneventful walk to the high ground where the fire assault was to be carried out. The lead assault group's reconnaissance discovered only two guards, who were neutralized. There were just a few women at the camp, so the assault team concluded that the insurgents either had fled after being tipped off or were out collecting firewood. After a brief wait, the team leader realized that discretion was needed, and he called off the mission. The group headed back to base with no casualties. When asked how he felt about the northern group's lack of success, Rawat was fully supportive of the decision by the man on the spot to abort the mission. As far as he was concerned, the operation was more about demonstrating intent and serious political posturing. Lieutenant Colonel Nectar Sanjeban was awarded the Kirti Chakra (the second-highest gallantry award during peacetime operations), and six others received awards for their exploits during the operation.[26]

Following the success of the cross-border strikes of 2015, there was no letup in the pursuit of rebel groups that threatened the region's fragile peace. Adding heft to this strategy was the Indian government's ability to assist the Myanmar Army in a series of joint operations that destroyed camps belonging to the Kachin Army, a rebel group that has been a thorn in Myanmar's side for decades. Acting on credible intelligence that the Kachin Army was looking to link up with anti-India insurgent and terrorist groups such as the NSCN (K) and attack infrastructure projects along the Kaladan Multi-Nodal Transit Corridor, the Indian Army launched Operation Sunrise in early March 2019.[27] Indian Special Forces, Ghatak (specialized commando) Platoons from Third Corps, and advance light helicopters from the Army

Aviation Corps were involved in the operation, demonstrating the Indian Army's commitment to military diplomacy in an environment with great economic and geopolitical promise.

Furthering India's ambitious Act East policy—which seeks to enhance its economic and geopolitical relationship with countries on its eastern frontier, such as Myanmar and Bangladesh—the operation was executed jointly with the Myanmar Army. The Indian Army preempted attacks by rebels along the corridor connecting the Indian port of Kolkata with Sittwe, a port in eastern Myanmar.[28] When queried how this operation differed from the one in 2015, General Rawat said: "This time around, the Myanmar Army was fully on board as we too supported operations against insurgents who were suspected of attacking the Myanmar Army. We also supplied and sustained many units of the Myanmar Army through the winter rains as they combed the jungles for insurgent camps."[29]

PEACE AND LESSONS

At the politico-strategic level, it is ironic that the cause of the Naga tragedy was the inability of Nehru and Phizo to understand each other. Both were men on a mission. Nehru had the power of the state, and Phizo had a myopic and messianic view of Naga sovereignty. Many believe the Naga struggle might have taken a different course had Phizo not left his homeland, but others argue that sooner or later he would have either been incarcerated by the Indian government or realized the futility of waging an armed struggle.

The Naga insurgency lost its separatist sting in the late 1990s following the split in the NSCN and the marginalization of the NNC after Phizo's death in the United Kingdom on 30 April 1990.[30] The idea of "Nagalim" resurfaced after the breakup of the NSCN in 1988 and the emergence of the NSCN (I&M) as the preeminent group. Isaac and Muivah channeled the aspirations of Naga communities across northeastern India and Myanmar to push for a "Greater Nagalim" comprising "all contiguous Naga-inhabited areas." In addition to Nagaland, this included several districts in Assam, Arunachal Pradesh, and Manipur, as well as a large tract of Myanmar. This unrealistic aspiration—periodically endorsed by the Nagaland Assembly—sought to expand the footprint of Nagaland from the current 16,527 square kilometers to about 120,000 square kilometers.[31]

As the movement degenerated into a criminal and terrorist movement, New Delhi failed to seize the initiative and let it drift aimlessly for almost two decades, despite some good work during the tenures of prime ministers Narasimha Rao and Atal Bihari Vajpayee. Vajpayee provided some much-needed balm in 2003, when he became the first prime minister to visit

Nagaland since Nehru was booed away in 1960. Speaking at a public reception in Kohima, Vajpayee warmed the hearts of the Nagas when he spoke to them in the local language: "*Ami laga bhai aru boyni-khan, aami Nagaland-te matiye karone besi khusi paise dei* [My dear brothers and sisters, I am very happy to be amid you on the soil of Nagaland]."[32] Unfortunately, the lack of follow-up by subsequent governments and the extension of the 1997 cease-fire into Manipur allowed the insurgencies in Nagaland, Manipur, and Assam to combine.

Lieutenant General D. S. Hooda, who retired in 2016 as the Northern Army commander, was the commander of Fifty-Seventh Mountain Division under Third Corps in 2009–2010. Operating out of the town of Leimakhong in Manipur, he witnessed the exacerbation of existing fault lines in that state. The NSCN (I&M) joined hands with the pro-Naga groups in Manipur—which dominated the hilly areas around the plains of Imphal—to exert pressure on the Meiteis, who held political power and claimed to be the rightful and original inhabitants of Manipur. Meitei groups in turn aligned with the NSCN (K) and insurgent groups from Assam, such as the United Liberation Front of Assam, to fight the Indian security forces and counter the expansionist concept of Nagalim.[33] Years of extortion and terror continued as pro-Nagalim and Meitei groups clashed with each other as well as with Indian security forces.

When speaking of the fractured polity in Nagaland during his tenure as commander of Third Corps in 2015–2016, General Rawat highlighted the near absence of the rule of law and structured governance. He was shocked to find that even civil servants and men serving with the National Cadet Corps were paying 10 percent tax to whichever NSCN faction dominated an area. The division of these spoils was based on tribal domination. Extortion from transport contractors and trucks plying the lucrative Myanmar–Kohima route was rampant. The NSCN (K) set up a base of operations in Ukhrul, Manipur, to intercept these convoys, exploiting ambiguities in the peace accord. The Semas of the NSCN (I&M) controlled Dimapur and the outskirts of Kohima, the Aos of the NSCN (K) dominated the town of Kohima, and the areas from Peren to Mon were under a conglomerate that called itself the Eastern Peoples Naga tribes.

Prime Minister Narendra Modi's government made some bold moves in 2015, initiating a settlement that promises to bring peace to the region—despite some stonewalling by the disgruntled Naga and Manipuri rebel groups.[34] The success of India's Act East policy depends on extinguishing the last embers of rebellion in the region. The challenge for the Modi government will be to dismantle the proposition of Greater Nagalim, rein in the NSCN (K), and usher lasting peace and prosperity into the region.

India's counterinsurgency strategy in Nagaland has evolved gradually and in several phases. The Indian Army—which initially had little to no intelligence regarding the area or the people—was shocked by its attrition at the hands of surprisingly skillful Naga insurgents. The first few units retaliated by pursuing a scorched-earth policy, wherein entire villages were burned down and reprisals were ruthless.[35] Indian troops and convoys were frequently ambushed and never even saw their attackers. This led to the establishment of road-opening parties tasked with sanitizing stretches of road and protecting the convoys that traversed them. A structured counterinsurgency grid was established following the formation of Eighth Mountain Division in the early 1960s and Third Corps in the late 1980s. This allowed the Indian Army to implement a dual strategy that sought to weaken the military component of the insurgency and win the hearts and minds of the local people.

Tactically, the Naga fighters excelled in marksmanship and ambushes, and they often disengaged to fight another day during the initial decades of the insurgency. However, their fighting skills declined with the criminalization of the insurgency. Gradually, the Indian state has worn down the Naga insurgency with a calibrated mix of what Shekhar Gupta calls "the force, persuasion, and concession strategy," which finally seems to be working.[36] Finally, the Nagas themselves have apparently realized that they are missing out on much of India's spectacular growth and development and that they need to seek a resolution that meets the requirements of all stakeholders. Namrata Goswami argues that "a counterinsurgency strategy of trust and nurture based on democratic political culture, measured military methods, special counterinsurgency forces, local social and cultural awareness and an integrative nation-building approach will result in positive handling of India's various internal security problems."[37]

It would be reasonable to hope that with the death of Isaac Swu in 2016 and the squeezing of the NSCN (K) by security forces from both India and Myanmar, the insurgency is in its final phase. However, tribal and ethnic loyalties are still deeply rooted and will be the biggest stumbling blocks to developing a cohesive Naga identity and reaping the benefits of economic prosperity. Contrary to the public perception that China no longer looms large on the northeastern horizon with its support for the Naga secessionist movement, there is still a free flow of arms from southern China into Nagaland and Manipur. Bibhu Prasad Routray, a security analyst who tracks terror and insurgent networks, argues that Beijing could be "gradually unveiling a grand design to revive the battered (northeast) insurgencies." He cautions, "Provision of safe houses, supply of weapons and even playing a more prominent role in directing attacks on security forces could be emerging as Beijing's instrumentalities to disturb peace in the fragile northeast."[38] Clearly, Indian security forces cannot let their guards down.

On a more positive note, and reflecting the mood of the populace in the region, Colonel Sanjeev Hazarika explains why this is an opportune moment to take the peace process forward:

> After having faced the brunt of insurgency for seventy years, the public is yearning for peace. Incidents of public outrage against militants are on the rise and offers opportunity for mobilizing them against militants by effective psychological operations and deft handling. The dynamics of ceasefire with the militant groups and the political process that is in progress cannot be underrated. However, at the tactical level, security forces must cater for contingencies, build up intelligence and ensure a high state of operational preparedness always.[39]

5

Operation Blue Star
Ours Is Not to Question Why

Operation Blue Star can perhaps be classified as one of the most traumatic, sensitive and thankless missions ever undertaken by any army in the world.
—Lieutenant General K. S. Brar, *Operation Blue Star: The True Story*

BREWING CRISIS

It was the autumn of 1981, and Lieutenant General S. K. Sinha had come a long way. As a major, he had coordinated the aerial move of the First Battalion of the Sikh Regiment from Palam airfield to Srinagar in the early days of the first India–Pakistan war of 1947–1948. Sinha was now commander of Western Army Command, the Indian Army's largest.[1] He was facing a crisis of sorts because Darbara Singh, the chief minister of Punjab, wanted him to dispatch troops to arrest a violent and troublesome Sikh preacher named Jarnail Singh Bhindranwale. Bhindranwale—the head of the Damdami Taksal, a fundamentalist Sikh religious organization[2]—was holed up in a *gurudwara* (Sikh place of worship) at Mehta Chowk, some fifty kilometers from Amritsar, Punjab. He was accused of masterminding the killing of Lala Jagat Narain, a Hindu newspaper editor in Jalandhar who had exposed the preacher's divisive and sectarian politics.

In addition to targeting Hindus, Bhindranwale had allegedly killed a rival Sikh preacher of the Nirankari sect, whose adherents were considered nonconformists and heretics.[3] Bhindranwale and his ragtag group of armed followers had escaped from a guest house in the neighboring state of Haryana minutes before the Punjab police arrived to arrest him. Frustrated by the police force's inability to take Bhindranwale into custody or control the hostile crowd that had gathered at Mehta Chowk, Darbara Singh turned to Sinha for assistance and requested armored escort vehicles from the Indian Army. Rightly deeming this to be highly inappropriate, Sinha politely refused, arguing that the military must intervene in internal security operations only if the state's primary instrument of law and order—the police—failed to execute its mandate.

Darbara Singh appealed to Delhi, and a day later, Sinha received a directive from the vice chief of the army staff to plan a military operation to arrest Bhindranwale. Sinha stuck to his guns and impressed upon his chief, General Krishna Rao, that such an action would be detrimental to the image of the Indian Army and must be carefully thought through. To his credit, Krishna Rao conveyed the same message to Prime Minister Indira Gandhi, who abandoned the idea.[4]

Bereft of any operational plan, the Punjab police waited for forty-eight hours as 30,000 followers gathered outside the *gurudwara*. The cult leader then triumphantly surrendered in full view of the restive crowd. This became a defining moment, and Bhindranwale was released within a couple of days—allegedly under instructions from Delhi, and much to the chagrin of Darbara Singh. He was the first Congress Party politician to recognize the ominous threat Bhindranwale posed to the security landscape in Punjab. Sadly, his warnings went unheeded by Delhi, and one can only wonder whether events would have panned out differently had Indira Gandhi recognized the danger sooner. Some years later, Sinha rightly assessed that even if the army had arrested him in 1981, Bhindranwale would have been released, given the vitiated and fractured political environment.

Indira Gandhi was shaken and rattled by her political decline and crushing electoral loss following the infamous emergency of 1975. But she stormed back to power in 1980 after five years of misrule by a series of coalition governments. Among the early political challenges in her second tenure was to ensure the primacy of the Congress Party over the Akali Dal, a Punjabi regional party that was rallying Sikhs around a largely sectarian narrative that sought to create a separate Sikh state. After the passing away of Akali leaders such as Master Tara Singh and Sant Fateh Singh, the Akalis feared a marginalization of the Sikh ethos in Punjab. This feeling was strengthened after the state of Haryana was carved out of Punjab in 1966. Responding to the changing political and demographic dynamics, the Akalis passed the Anandpur Sahib Resolution in 1973, which marked a shift in strategy. Fundamentalism began to erode the traditional values of harmony and tolerance and set in motion a polarization process to wean the Sikhs away from Congress Party influence.[5]

Wary and fearful of the Sikhs' increasingly militant behavior, the Jan Sangh—a predominantly Hindu party—also began mobilizing cadres in Punjab. Adding to the prime minister's woes were two rival heavyweight Sikh leaders within the Punjab Congress: Darbara Singh, chief minister of Punjab, and Zail Singh, home minister in the central government. Zail Singh would soon become the president of India, and he was a close confidant of the prime minster and her powerful son, Youth Congress leader Sanjay Gandhi. This combination of Zail Singh and Sanjay Gandhi emboldened

Bhindranwale to counter both the Akalis and Darbara Singh. They encouraged Bhindranwale to peddle his inflammatory and muscularly separatist narrative as an alternative to the emerging Akali narrative, which was more restrained and based on the Anandpur Sahib Resolution.[6] The resolution in its original form was no more than an expression of Sikh angst and identity politics to encourage Sikhs to overcome other constituencies in the region made up of Hindus, lower castes, and the migrant population. The Akalis and the Congress Party had sowed the seeds of separatism and terrorism and would soon reap a whirlwind.

DEFILING THE SANCTUM

Emboldened by his release from custody, Bhindranwale realized that he had an opportunity to seize a leadership role in the fragmented political space. Consequently, as debate and discussion exited the scene, rhetoric, coercion, violence, and religion became the framework of a new discourse that Brigadier R. K. Chopra termed a "plain vanilla secessionist movement demanding a separate state for the Sikhs."[7]

Unleashing a reign of terror from within the confines of the Guru Nanak Niwas—a rest home on the periphery of the Golden Temple in Amritsar—Bhindranwale assassinated several prominent Sikh and Hindu activists who spoke or wrote against him. Among the 192 civilians killed were H. S. Manchanda, a Sikh leader of the Congress Party in Delhi; Ramesh Chander, the fearless editor of the *Hind Samachar*; and Summan Singh, the editor of another Punjabi magazine.[8] The hijacking of an Indian Airlines plane to Lahore in September 1981 by Sikh separatists owing allegiance to the Dal Khalsa, Bhindranwale's primary terrorist outfit, allowed Pakistan to enter the Punjab terrorist movement even as it sentenced the hijackers to life imprisonment.[9]

The growing movement for an independent Sikh state of Khalistan started to gather overseas support, particularly from United Kingdom–based separatists such as Jagjit Singh Chouhan, who had established strong links with Pakistan's Inter-Services Intelligence (ISI).[10] The hijackers, Tajinder Pal Singh and Satnam Singh, were released from prison in 2000 and deported to India, where they faced additional charges for a variety of offenses. As the violence spread in Punjab in the wake of Bhindranwale's incendiary speeches and an abysmal lack of counternarratives from either the Punjab government or the central government, the secessionist flavor began to permeate government organizations. The Punjab police were eventually proved complicit in covering up the terrorist-military buildup within the Golden Temple complex that Bhindranwale had commenced in mid-1983.

According to Praveen Swami, much of the pre-1984 help from Pakistan was in the form of low-grade weapons.[11] Heavy weapons reinforced the arsenal only when an illustrious but disillusioned war veteran, Major General Shahbeg Singh, joined Bhindranwale. The South Asia Terrorism Portal estimates that the number of fatalities between 1981 and 1984—during the first round of the "Khalistan war"—totaled about 650, which includes a conservative estimate of the deaths following operations in the Golden Temple in June 1984.[12] This figure would be contested by the media and the Sikh community, although the numbers closely match those provided by the Indian Army.

BLOWOUT

Having succumbed to the political machinations of her son Sanjay on numerous occasions, Indira Gandhi realized that she was staring at rebellion by the end of May 1984. Following the spate of killings and a complete breakdown of law and order in Punjab, the shaken prime minister directed her army chief, General Arun Vaidya, to flush Bhindranwale out of the Golden Temple. She had little choice but to assign the task to the Indian Army because, at the time, India did not have a dedicated counterterrorism force that could undertake such a complex mission.

Deferring to the prime minister's orders without first consulting his principal staff officers at Indian Army headquarters or mulling over the consequences, Vaidya immediately assigned the task to Western Army Command under Lieutenant General Krishnaswamy Sundarji. Sundarji obviously wanted to micromanage the operation, as evidenced by his choice of commanders and formations. Instead of assigning the commander of Jalandhar-based Eleventh Corps to oversee the operation, he chose his chief of staff, Lieutenant General Ranjit Singh Dayal. Also inexplicable was the decision to give Meerut-based Ninth Infantry Division the task of storming the Golden Temple—instead of Amritsar-based Fifteenth Infantry Division—and recalling its commander, Major General K. S. Brar, back from leave to execute the mission. Fifteenth Infantry Division was tasked with sealing Amritsar off from the rest of Punjab and preventing any infiltrations from across the international border. Because both his trusted lieutenants were Sikhs, Sundarji was confident that their plan would be viable.[13]

Recollecting events on the day prior to the storming of the Golden Temple, Mark Tully wrote in the *Telegraph*:

> The next morning, I found the Golden Temple complex surrounded by the
> Bihar Regiment. Bhindranwale held a defiant press conference in the Akal Takht

at which he promised to give the army a fitting reply. I could see how heavily
fortified it was, and thought that there was bound to be a bloody battle unless Bhindranwale cracked. The army was in too much of a hurry to bother
about public relations, so all the journalists were then bundled out of Punjab.
As we drove through Amritsar, we heard intermittent small-arms fire and the
occasional whoof of a mortar. The government had clamped a strict curfew on
the whole state. Frequent army check posts insured that there was no traffic on
Kipling's Grand Trunk Road.[14]

Brar had roughly two brigades for the operations, and he assigned the
task of storming the temple to four infantry battalions—Ninth and Fifteenth
Battalions of the Kumaon Regiment, Twenty-Sixth Battalion of the Madras
Regiment, and Tenth Battalion of the Regiment of the Guards—as well as a
paracommando battalion (First Parachute Battalion), and the Special Group
from the Special Frontier Force (SFF).[15] Reinforcing this assault force was
an infantry battalion of the Bihar Regiment, which threw an outer cordon
around the temple; a battalion from the Garhwal Regiment; and select Central Reserve Police Force (CRPF) and Border Security Force (BSF) companies
to assist in storming selected locations on the perimeter.[16] The paracommandos and Special Group were to breach the Akal Takht (seat of power),
where Bhindranwale and his core group were manning defenses, and ensure
the safety of two senior Akali leaders, Harcharan Singh Longowal and Gur-
charan Singh Tohra, who were holed up in a wing adjoining the Akal Takht.
Keeping these leaders alive was considered essential for postconflict negotiations, as they represented the moderate face of emerging Sikh separatism.
  Led by Tenth Guards, First Parachute Battalion (First Para) and the Special Group were to follow closely behind during the first attack and assault
the main temple complex from the northern entrance. They had multiple objectives, including to clear the Parikrama (the walkway around the Harmandir Sahib, the main sanctum in the center of the temple complex that housed
the Sikhs' sacred scriptures), capture the Darshini Deori (the entrance to the
sanctum), secure the Harmandir Sahib, and clear the Akal Takht of all terrorists. The last objective would prove most difficult to achieve, as it was the
defenders' main center of gravity and the command-and-control center. It
was also where Bhindranwale and his military commander, Shahbeg Singh,
were controlling the battle, along with more than a hundred heavily armed
fighters.
  The southern and eastern assault force comprised Twenty-Sixth Madras
and Ninth Kumaon, which were later reinforced by Fifteenth Kumaon, armored personnel carriers, and Vijayanta tanks when the assault floundered.
Their objectives were to clear the hostel complex and capture the Akali lead-

ership, enter the Parikrama, secure its eastern and southern flanks without damaging the library, and support the force assaulting the Akal Takht. The main operation was to commence at around 10:00 p.m. on 5 June and end by daybreak on 6 June, a period of six to eight hours.

FORMIDABLE ENEMY

After his deployment in Nagaland, Major Katoch was back with his battalion, First Para, in Nahan, a cantonment in the picturesque state of Himachal Pradesh. But it was not long before he was back in action, as First Para was told to move to Amritsar without any preliminary briefing on the night of 2 June—forty-eight hours after the decision to storm the temple.[17] Heading to Amritsar in a convoy with three tons of explosives, the commandos were prepared to blast their way into the target area rather than engage the enemy in a frontal assault. More than one-quarter of First Para's troops were Sikhs, and the unit moved with its *granthi* (priest) to Amritsar. Along the way, the officers took great pains to explain to their Sikh troops what was happening and what to expect in the days ahead.

Upon their arrival in Amritsar the next day (3 June), the commanding officer and Katoch (who was second in command) were shown a hazy photograph of the Golden Temple complex that was marked "Secret"—but as Katoch recalls, there was nothing secret about it. Only after walking around the periphery of the complex did the paracommandos understand that they would be facing a well-prepared and tactically proficient enemy who had dug in with sandbags and fortified the watchtowers around the complex with light machine guns and other weaponry. Later, Katoch realized how lucky they had been not to get shot during their walk—no one had briefed them about the seven CRPF soldiers who had been shot at a couple of days earlier during a recce of the periphery. Perhaps the terrorists had been instructed not to target the Indian Army until it initiated combat operations.

Given the heavy fortifications, it was clear to the paracommandos that the only way to get Bhindranwale was to blast their way into the Akal Takht from the rear. This, they reckoned, would surprise the defenders and leave them rudderless once their leadership was eliminated. Katoch was surprised when their plan was rejected by Brar on the evening of 3 June. Instead, they were directed to take part in a frontal assault on the Akal Takht via the main north entrance along with Tenth Guards and the Special Group. Members of the Special Group surprised Brar by declaring that they had briefed the prime minister about a plan to storm the Akal Takht using gas canisters to immobilize the defenders. What they had not factored in was the wind direction and the limited availability of gas masks to protect the accompanying assault troops. Most importantly, the SFF had not realized that the Akal Takht would be sealed. Luckily for the paracommandos, a consignment of masks arrived on 5 June, and they were distributed among the paracommandos and Tenth Guards who would be in the vicinity during the gas attack.

What about the military pedigree of the defenders? Some angst within the Sikh community emerged after the 1982 Asian Games at New Delhi, when several decorated war veterans and accomplished senior officers were randomly stopped and frisked. Much displeasure was expressed during a meeting of Sikh ex-servicemen at the Golden Temple in October 1982 in the presence of Bhindranwale. Although there was general disagreement when Bhindranwale proposed direct armed confrontation, his belligerent posturing attracted two senior retired paratroopers, Major Generals Jaswant Singh Bhullar and Shahbeg Singh. Bhullar left Bhindranwale's flock before the final showdown, but Shahbeg stayed on. An ex-paratrooper, Shahbeg had an excellent reputation as a combat soldier and tactician. He had also trained and commanded the Mukti Bahini forces in Bangladesh.[18] Angry and bitter at being sacked from the military for the petty misappropriation of funds, he was drawn to the secessionist movement and emerged as one of Bhindranwale's most radicalized lieutenants. Bhindranwale had found his military strategist, one who would prepare him to challenge the might of the Indian Army.[19]

The fifth of June was a hot and cloudless day that saw the Indian Army closing in on the target area, much like a conventional operation in a built-up area. There was absolutely no element of surprise element, as loudspeakers warned civilians to exit the temple while they had time, and outer-ring targets were being engaged by the paramilitary forces. By the evening, Shahbeg's reinforced and well-armed watchtowers—on top of two minarets and a water tank that offered excellent views of the temple complex and the surrounding areas—had been reduced to rubble by 106mm recoilless launchers and howitzers. By all parameters, Brar thought he had the operation under control.

The final assault commenced at 10:30 p.m. with Tenth Guards attempting to breach the Parikrama and having to withdraw when met with well-directed fire from multiple directions and levels as they climbed the stairs of the main entrance. Captain Jasbir Raina—a young Sikh officer who led the assault and had carried out a daring reconnaissance of the temple defenses the previous morning—was the first officer casualty. He was followed by many others. They were evacuated by a team of First Para that followed onto the Parikrama. The paracommandos and the Special Group met with a similar fate as casualties mounted, but the gritty soldiers made their way to the Akal Takht and Darshini Deori along a closed veranda and the riskier open Parikrama. Here, well-placed snipers from the Harmandir Sahib and

Akal Takht picked off troops in the moonlight. Katoch recalled that some of his divers had been alerted that they would have to swim across the Sarovar (water tank) and secure the Harmandir Sahib, a proposition that seemed preposterous as the battle unfolded.

Staying alive was now the primary task for Katoch's men as they absorbed the initial blast of Shahbeg's defensive plan. As the battle progressed and the Indian troops advanced with their cumbersome 7.62mm self-loading rifles, they encountered fire from light and medium machine guns and AK-47s. Katoch fell in the early hours of 6 June as he approached the Darshini Deori, a vantage point from which both the Akal Takht and Harmandir Sahib could be engaged. After taking two bullets in his right shoulder, he was quickly evacuated by his men out of the temple complex and taken to Amritsar General Hospital. He lay there for the next thirty-six hours before being moved to the Jalandhar military hospital, where he underwent surgery. There was no medical evacuation plan, and Katoch recalled that as the battle progressed, there was chaos in the hospitals and clinics in Amritsar, which had not been warned to expect casualties by either the army or the local administration. Katoch wryly remarked that he had to salute Indira Gandhi with his left hand when she visited the unit afterward.[20]

The paratroopers had taken thirteen casualties in the initial assault, with Tenth Guards bearing the brunt. The SFF would take heavy casualties too as it attempted to assault the Akal Takht soon after. Several soldiers were cut down by shots fired at knee level from holes cut in the marble as they ran up the stairs. A conventional assault was being torn to shreds by a clever and tactically proficient enemy who had been grossly underestimated by the Indian Army leadership. The other frontal assaults from the southern and eastern wings by troops from the Kumaon and Madras Regiments faced similar fire from concealed positions. Initially, there were strict orders that no rocket launchers—such as the highly effective Carl Gustaf—would be used and that armored personnel carriers would not be permitted to provide covering fire, as they would damage the marble stairs and walkway. Sundarji had assumed that the early capture of Harmandir Sahib would be a symbolic victory that would hasten the capitulation of Bhindranwale and his terrorist fighters. But the plan to capture the Harmandir Sahib using paracommandos—who were expected to swim across the water tank with flippers and light weapons and take the defenders by surprise—was shelved as the early battle went awry.

DAWN BREAKS

As Brar's plan of clearing the temple by daybreak faltered in the face of a determined enemy, he had a dilemma. His troops were scattered around

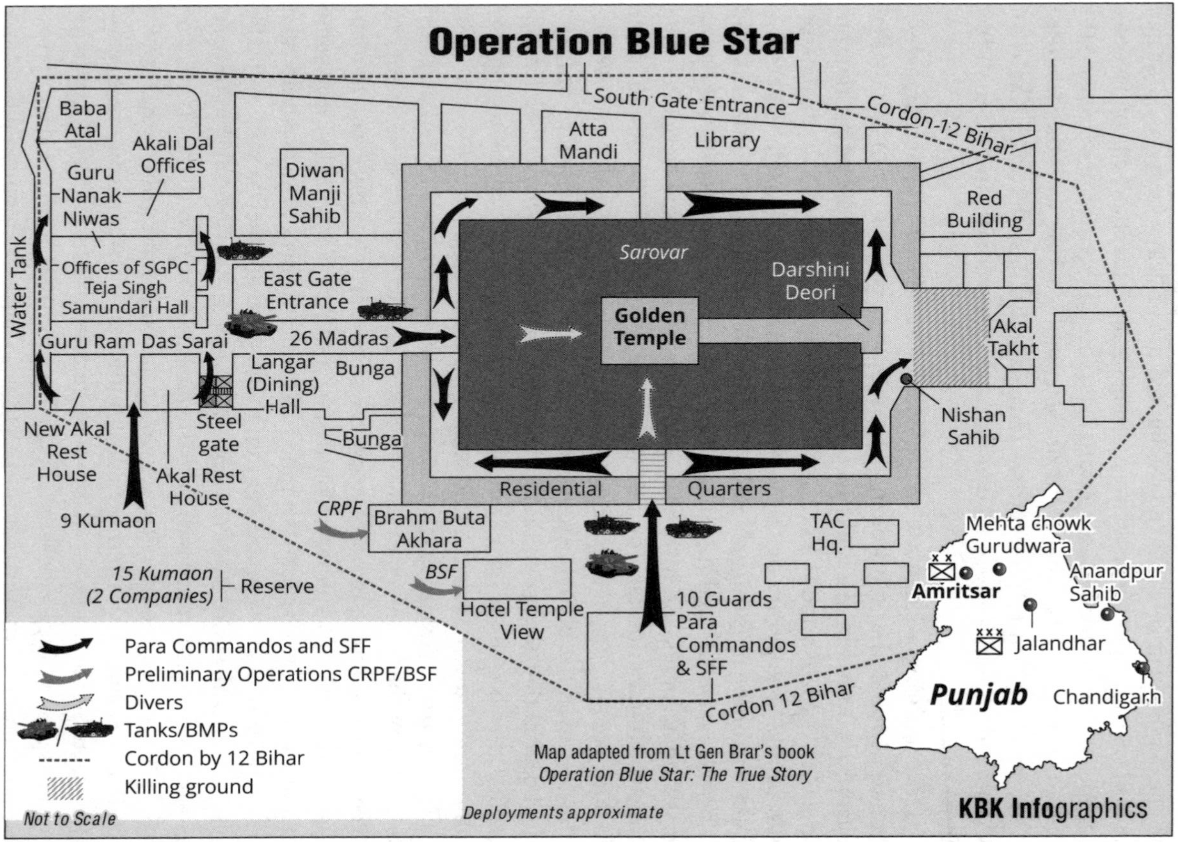

Map 2. Operations around the Golden Temple

Operation Blue Star

Cordon-12 Bihar

Red Building

Akal Takht

Nishan Sahib

South Gate Entrance

Library

Sarovar

Darshini Deori

Golden Temple

Atta Mandi

Quarters

TAC Hq.

Residential

10 Guards
Para Commandos & SFF

Cordon 12 Bihar

Diwan Manji Sahib

East Gate Entrance

26 Madras

Bunga

Langar (Dining) Hall

Bunga

Brahm Buta Akhara

BSF

Hotel Temple View

CRPF

Akali Dal Offices

Baba Atal

Guru Nanak Niwas

Offices of SGPC Teja Singh Samundari Hall

Guru Ram Das Sarai

Steel gate

Akal Rest House

New Akal Rest House

9 Kumaon

Water Tank

Legend:
- Para Commandos and SFF
- Preliminary Operations CRPF/BSF
- Divers
- Tanks/BMPs
- Cordon by 12 Bihar
- Killing ground

15 Kumaon (2 Companies) | Reserve

Not to Scale

Punjab map:
Mehta chowk Gurudwara
Anandpur Sahib
Chandigarh
Jalandhar
Amritsar

KBK Infographics

Map adapted from Lt Gen Brar's book *Operation Blue Star: The True Story*

Deployments approximate

the Parikrama—some in the covered veranda and others out in the open—
and they would be easy targets for Shahbeg's well-concealed fighters. Withdrawal was one option, but that would have meant a humiliating defeat for
the mighty Indian Army. Brar was determined to accomplish his mission,
even if it meant a fight to the finish. Getting clearance from Sundarji, Brar
deployed a few infantry combat vehicles (ICVs) and Vijayanta tanks to provide covering fire to troops as they advanced toward the Akal Takht. Prior
to the deployment of tanks and the limited use of heavy weapons, Brar had
announced a temporary cessation of firing to allow the hundreds of devotees
trapped inside the temple complex to exit the area. Seeing the writing on the
wall, many terrorists slipped out of the complex along with the devotees.
They would go on to join various terrorist outfits, such as the Khalistan
Commando Force, and would continue their secessionist struggle for a few
more years.[21]

Once the heavy weapons were deployed, it was the end for Bhindranwale.
Sundarji would later tell students at the College of Combat in Mhow that
every round fired by the tanks had been personally authorized by him, but
in reality, the tanks and ICVs provided fire support based on the situation on
the ground. The library on the southern wing of the Parikrama might have
been one of the unfortunate victims. Although several Sikh chroniclers and
historians have accused the Indian Army of intentionally burning it down,
firsthand accounts and interviews note that several snipers were operating
from the library and targeting the troops of Twenty-Sixth Madras and the
brigade commander. The prolonged battle likely started the fire that eventually destroyed the library. An injured Sikh tank commander told Katoch in
the hospital that he had in fact fired in the direction of the library. Katoch
replied that he would have done the same in a Hindu temple to support
comrades who were being cut down.

Troops from Twenty-Sixth Madras finally approached the Akal Takht
from the southern wing at around 7:00 a.m. and were the first to attempt to
silence the machine gun posts below the staircases. The entire assault team
was cut down, and a junior commissioned officer was killed in gruesome
fashion when the terrorists strapped dynamite to his body. It would take
a few more rounds from the Vijayanta tanks and another assault to finally
silence the Akal Takht. By 11:00 a.m. on 6 June, the battle seemed to be over,
as many terrorists jumped into the Sarovar and swam toward the Harmandir
Sahib. They were promptly cut down. At the same time, good progress was
made in clearing the eastern wings of militants.[22] Troops from the Special
Group and First Para were the first to enter the Akal Takht shortly after
noon, and what they saw there shocked them. Apart from the dead terrorists—including Bhindranwale and Shahbeg Singh—the commandos found

several bodies of women and some skeletons in the rubble. Clearly, Bhindranwale and his men had converted the sacred temple into a den of iniquity and vice.[23]

Katoch lamented that media access to the operation was denied, which meant there was no one to provide a real-time narrative. A few reporters who managed to remain within the Golden Temple complex fell for the information provided by the extremists, which focused on alleged atrocities committed by the security forces. The killing of cornered terrorists or those attempting to escape cannot be discounted, nor can the deaths of civilians caught in the crossfire or buried in the debris caused by tank shells. However, most officers—both Sikh and non-Sikh—are quite emphatic that there was no spontaneous execution of civilians after the Indian Army took over the temple, as some have suggested.[24] Sporadic fighting continued throughout the day at places such as the *langar* (dining area), until it dawned on the terrorists that their leaders were dead. Many terrorists slipped out through tunnels, while others surrendered. Mopping-up operations continued through 9 June.

The president of India visited the temple on 8 June; it was a solemn moment that signaled the end of the battle. However, President Giani Zail Singh—a Sikh himself and commander in chief of India's armed forces—may well have been one of the chief architects of the disaster that was Operation Blue Star. According to the Indian government's white paper on the Punjab agitation, Indian security forces suffered significant casualties, losing 83 killed and 248 injured. However, with 493 terrorists killed and another 592 apprehended, the terrorist movement experienced a significant setback. Others, such as journalist Harminder Kaur, insist that the casualties on both sides were much higher.[25]

OPERATIONAL POSTSCRIPT

My first opportunity to explore the dark corridors of Operation Blue Star at the military level occurred in the most unlikely of places—the Defence Services Staff College at Wellington, in the salubrious Nilgiri hills. It was the summer of 1993, and I was attending a military education course for majors in the army and equivalent ranks in the air force (squadron leader) and navy (lieutenant commander). General Krishnaswamy Sundarji, the former army chief, had settled there after retirement in a bungalow dubbed "Alcatraz" by students. Eloquent as always, Sundarji had just released his book *Blind Men of Hindoostan*, but he rarely entertained visitors, except for groups of student officers who wished to engage with him intellectually. Most comfortable when asked to expound on maneuver warfare, nuclear strategy, and the integrated application of firepower, he turned reflective when asked about

Operation Blue Star and Operation Pawan, the Indian peacekeeping mission–turned–military intervention in Sri Lanka.

Looking around his large, walled compound protected by concertina barbed wire and security towers, he said to us one morning, "The government says that I need all this to insulate me from the Khalistanis and the LTTE [Liberation Tigers of Tamil Elam, the Sri Lankan terrorist group]. Unfortunately, after what happened to Indira Gandhi, Arun [General Arun Vaidya], and Rajiv Gandhi, I have no choice in the matter." The first two were assassinated by Sikhs in 1984 and 1986, respectively. Rajiv Gandhi was blown up by an LTTE suicide bomber in 1991. I was part of a study group on insurgencies and terrorism in South Asia and wanted to hear Sundarji's views on the storming of the Golden Temple, as he had been the head of Western Army Command at the time. To Sundarji's credit, he stuck to his guns and said that, as an operational field commander, it had been his mandate to execute the difficult task assigned to him.

When asked whether he had had any doubts about succeeding in the Indian Army's first real experience with dense urban warfare, he replied in the affirmative but said the conservative soldier in him had pushed those doubts away. He emphasized that those had been troubled times, the likes of which the Indian state had not experienced before, and even though numerous moral and ethical dilemmas had crossed his mind as operations were being planned, the sheer brutality of Bhindranwale's cadres and the impunity with which they challenged the writ of the state overshadowed those dilemmas. What remained with me, though, were his parting words: "I hope no Indian field commander is ever asked to execute such an operation again." Little did Sundarji anticipate that much of the warfare waged by India's armed forces in the decades ahead would involve decisions and dilemmas like those faced at the gates of the Golden Temple—albeit with varying intensity.

Several officers who were thrust into action on those fateful days in June 1984 are critical of General Vaidya's acquiescence to Indira Gandhi's panicky decision to storm the Golden Temple without adequate planning and preparation. They point out, "General Vaidya had three choices when ordered to flush Bhindranwale out—say yes, say no, or ask for more time to shape the environment in a manner of his choosing." In hindsight—and these officers acknowledge the ease of reflecting on military actions in hindsight—the last option would have been best, given that the Indian Army had never been involved in a major operation in urban terrain and that, in a less-than-war situation, there would be no clear rules of engagement. Many suggest that a few weeks—or even a few months—of concentrated military strategizing on how to defang Bhindranwale would have been more likely to succeed than a force-on-force engagement that ran the risk of alienating the Sikhs. Moving beyond the strategy of laying a long siege to the Golden Temple, they argue that embedding Sikh volunteers in Bhindranwale's force to assess the impact of Shahbeg's shrewd military mind, or even planning a covert operation to eliminate the leadership, may have yielded better outcomes. Dwelling on command-and-control issues, Vaidya may have erred in delegating the entire operation to Sundarji, who had assured him that it would be over in hours. Both men were the operational products of the "big battle," and however competent they may have been, this was uncharted territory for the Indian Army leadership.[26]

According to Katoch, the only man who could have infused some caution into the plan was the chief of staff, Lieutenant General Ranjit Singh Dayal, a hero of the 1965 war. That he did not do so, even with all the ominous bits of intelligence trickling in between 3 and 5 June, reflected the operational hubris within the Indian Army at the time. Brar too had built up a reputation as a cool and competent commander. One wonders whether he ever contemplated going back to Sundarji and asking for more time, either after the initial recce reports indicated well-concealed fortifications or when the initial assault met with unexpectedly heavy fire. One aspect of the Indian military leadership that merits attention is the fear and stigma of command failure, which prompts leaders to persist with suboptimal operational plans. Had Brar asked Sundarji for more time, most reckon that Sundarji would have sacked him and brought in another commander to continue with the operation. For Sundarji, there was no going back.

Retired Lieutenant General Ghei, a Sikh paratrooper of some accomplishment, is scathing in his indictment of Operation Blue Star thirty-five years after the operation:

> It was a political blunder but was possibly a hasty reaction from the government after the intelligence agencies had lost a senior officer [Deputy Inspector General Atwal] at the gates of the Temple. The timing was totally wrong—the day was the celebration of the birth (Gurpurab) of the 5th Sikh guru, because of which there were many peasant devotees inside the Temple when the assault was launched. One cannot understand the urgency. There was no justification for that, nor for the use of artillery and tank main guns. They [meaning the army chief] should have told the prime minister to wait till they had a correct assessment and a better plan to execute the mission. The military hierarchy from the chief downwards did not display professional prudence.[27]

General Brar has been very honest in his analysis of the operational lessons from Operation Blue Star. There were three army divisions in the area: Fifteenth Infantry Division was located at Amritsar, Ninth Infantry Division was at Meerut, and Seventh Infantry Division was at Ferozepur. Why Ninth Division was chosen to execute a task that could have been assigned to another division that knew the area better (Fifteenth Division) has baffled many. It may have been a result of General Sundarji's personal preference to have Major General Brar lead the operation. As the planning process morphed into an operational plan, it barely conformed to existing army principles on fighting in built-up areas. There was no study of the Indian Army's operations in 1973 to put down the Provincial Armed Constabulary revolts in the Uttar Pradesh towns of Bareilly, Meerut, and Agra.[28] Comfortable with classic semiurban cordon-and-search operations, the trio of Sundarji, Dayal, and Brar seemingly ignored all available intelligence that indicated heavily fortified defenses and well-trained and radicalized terrorists who were prepared to fight to the last man.

Hoping to clear the temple in six to eight hours, as envisaged by Sundarji, was certainly overly optimistic. Thirty-five years later, Katoch emphatically claimed that the best strategy would have been to cut off the water and electricity for a few days, given that it was the peak of summer. Then, having sapped the will of the fighters, the commandos could have blasted their way into the Akal Takht from the rear, while Tenth Guards created killing grounds along the Parikrama and the corridors if the terrorists attempted to flee. Instead of entering simultaneously from multiple directions, the operation could have been commenced with the sole objective of eliminating the adversary's principal center of gravity—its core leadership led by Bhindranwale. Once that had been achieved, a combination of psychological warfare through loudspeaker announcements and selective assaults would have resulted in the speedy capitulation of the remaining terrorists.

Over the years, there has been speculation in the media that Indira Gandhi sought British prime minister Margaret Thatcher's assistance and that British Special Air Service experts helped plan the operation.[29] Responding to these claims, Katoch said, "I was in the thick of planning in Amritsar from 3 June and did not see any British operatives. If they were around, it could only have been to advise the S[pecial] G[roup] at their home base before the balloon went up."[30] In any case, this is more of a political issue in Britain, where the Sikhs are one the largest immigrant groups. They have a significant voting bloc and include a small seditious element that sparked the Khalistan movement after Operation Blue Star.[31]

MUTINY

The Sikhs are courageous fighters, emotional and easily provoked. As news of the storming of the Golden Temple filtered out of Amritsar, there were ripples of dissent among the large complement of Sikh troops in the Indian Army. Although they were mostly distributed between two exclusive regiments—the Sikh Regiment and the Sikh Light Infantry Regiment—there were Sikhs in many other regiments as well, but it was mainly in the Sikh Regiment that trouble brewed. Ganganagar in Rajasthan was home to the Ninth Battalion of the Sikh Regiment, and it was there that the first major mutiny broke out. Troops ransacked the armory on 7 June, and large numbers set out in convoys toward Delhi. Some may have found their way to Pakistan.[32]

In the absence of any official communication from the officers to the troops about what had happened at Amritsar, it is possible that rumors of atrocities committed by the Indian Army infuriated the soldiers. It was not too long before the rebellious Sikh soldiers were disarmed and rounded up by other regiments of the Indian Army, without much shooting or loss of life. News of the mutiny traveled slowly, and on 9 June a second major mutiny broke out in Ramgarh, Bihar, where the regimental center of the Sikh Regiment was located. It was here that the Indian Army faced its sternest internal threat since independence, as almost a thousand young recruits led by a radicalized soldier looted the armory, killed the commandant, and injured a few others in a shoot-out. Setting out in a large convoy toward Amritsar, they were engaged along the way by artillery and effectively stopped by several roadblocks. According to official figures, at least thirty-five mutineers were killed.[33] The official court of inquiry attributed the mutiny to poor leadership and inadequate sensitization, rather than any seditious or externally abetted rebellion. A few other combat regiments of the Indian Army—particularly the Punjab Regiment—also saw sporadic uprisings that were speedily put down.

Official records related to Operation Blue Star are unavailable, with the exception of a hastily written white paper released in July 1984. Thus, narratives of the operation have been varied. Arguably, one of the most objective academic studies of the causes and consequences of Operation Blue Star is by Professor Apurba Kundu, currently an acting dean at East Anglia University in Cambridge.[34] Kundu asked a group of ninety-six officers, comprising non-Sikhs and Sikhs in a ratio of five to one, three fundamental questions: Was the military action justified? Were the means employed the most optimal ones? Why did the postoperation mutiny by Sikh troops take place, and did it damage the ethos of the Indian Army? To the first question, all non-Sikh respondents and one Sikh respondent answered in the affirmative. The second question was more contentious—only a few non-Sikh officers approved of the direct military action, while most of the others were critical of the means employed and the haste with which the operation unfolded. The third question elicited the most interesting response. Most respondents concurred that the mutiny was the result of poor leadership and had no long-term adverse impact on the ethos of the Indian Army. One Sikh respondent emphatically stated, "The role of the Sikhs in the military is not compromised."[35] The declining Sikh enrollment in the Indian Army is a result of societal and economic factors, such as filling vacancies based on each state's recruitable male population, rather than any disillusionment with the institution.

AFTERMATH

Although Operation Blue Star left Bhindranwale's secessionist movement in disarray, the army action made a deep impression on the psyche of the masses. The assassination of Indira Gandhi by her Sikh bodyguards on 31 October 1984 galvanized the extremist struggle and turned it into a global movement that would trouble the Indian state for several more years. The resurgence of extremism in Punjab took a while to manifest and peaked around mid-1986, almost a year after an Akali government supported by the Congress Party came to power and the Rajiv Gandhi–Longowal Accord failed to strike a chord with either the people or the secessionists.[36] The accord, which sought to address most of the Akalis' long-standing demands, was sabotaged by extremists and hard-liners within the Akali Dal, leading to the assassination of Longowal in August 1985 by Sikh terrorists. The Sikh extremists—initially led by the All India Sikh Students Federation (AISSF)—had regrouped with Pakistani help. Other groups that emerged later or rejuvenated themselves were the Khalistan Commando Force, Khalistan Liberation Force, Dashmesh Regiment, Babbar Khalsa, and United Sikh Army. Wasan Singh Zafarwal and Labh Singh stood out among the 350 to 400 hard-core terrorists identified by the Punjab government in 1985–1986.

The main weapons used by these groups were semiautomatic rifles, Sten guns, pistols, and crude homemade weapons. They concealed their weapons under *chadars* or shawls and carried out daring motorcycle and scooter attacks in broad daylight. Sympathizers and sanctuaries in both rural and urban areas allowed the attackers to escape and hide. A five-member Panthic Committee was formed to coordinate the move toward the creation of Khalistan, which reflected a firm intent on the part of the secessionists. They banned any dialogue with a government that did not have Khalistan on its agenda and gradually made the Akali government irrelevant. The rise of Hindu groups such as the Rashtriya Swayam Sewak Sangh and Shiv Sena across Punjab, particularly in the urban areas of Amritsar, Jullundur, Hoshiarpur, Batala, and Gurdaspur, exacerbated matters.[37]

Pakistan's military dictator General Zia-ul-Haq was pleased to have a

ready-made hunting ground for his policy of "bleeding India with a thousand cuts." He adopted a four-pronged strategy to wage a covert war against
India in Punjab, which remained in effect until his death in 1988. The first
prong was to provide safe havens to hundreds of disgruntled Sikh youths
and Bhindranwale's remaining terrorists and set up camps to provide basic
training in small arms, explosives, and subversion techniques. The second
prong was to create and spread a narrative in rural Punjab that revolved
around Bhindranwale's legacy and the atrocities committed by Indian security forces inside the Golden Temple. The third prong was to support
infiltration by trained Sikh terrorists along the porous international border,
particularly in Rajasthan. The terrorists would then carry out bombings and
other terrorist acts, targeting the Hindu community in Punjab to exacerbate
the communal divide. The last prong was to support the Khalistan movement globally by providing financial and propaganda support to Sikh secessionists in Europe, Canada, and the United States.

External support was provided by wealthy and influential Sikhs such as
Jagjit Singh Chohan in the United Kingdom and Ganga Singh Dhillon, an
influential US-based Khalistan ideologue. The ubiquitous ISI was the con-
duit through which the strategy of creating a mass movement was to be executed.[38] Consequently, it sponsored the Lahore-based Akal Federation and
helped the Babbar Khalsa and Damdami Taksal (Bhindranwale's original
outfit) set up training camps in Sialkot and Narowal in Pakistan for about
700 Sikh youths and a few disgruntled army men who had crossed over after
Operation Blue Star. Matters finally came to a head in March 1986 when
fierce clashes erupted between Sikh terrorists and Hindu social groups across
the state of Punjab, with the latter bearing the brunt of organized killings
by AISSF-led mobs.

According to *India Today*, fifty-three civilians lost their lives that month.[39]
Thousands of Sikh farmers laid siege to the industrial town of Batala for
more than a week until security forces dispersed them, but not before eleven
Hindus were killed on the outskirts. The Akali government was a mute
spectator to this violence. This emboldened the Panthic Committee to raise
its war cry of secession by formally declaring the formation of Khalistan on
29 April 1986. Attacks on civilians (mainly Hindus and dissenting Sikhs) increased, despite the presence of a weakened and dysfunctional Punjab police
force. In a clear revenge killing, two motorcycle-riding terrorists of the Khalistan Commando Force shot the retired army chief, General Arun Vaidya,
as he was driving home in Pune on 10 August 1986. By the time Prime
Minister Rajiv Gandhi declared president's rule in Punjab in May 1987,
more than 800 civilians had lost their lives since January. Brigadier Chopra
was scathing in his assessment of why Punjab continued to simmer: "The

Government and its policies towards solving the Punjab problem are, so far, like rowing a rudderless boat. It has failed to provide protection, neutralize terror networks and create public awareness."[40]

Punjab limped back to normalcy in the late 1980s and early 1990s and did not go the way of Kashmir. Here, the role of two outstanding police officers, Julio Ribeiro and K. P. S. Gill, cannot be overlooked. Ribeiro was brought in by the central government in 1986 as director-general of police (DGP) in Punjab; he was elevated to the post of adviser to the governor in 1987, after surviving an assassination attempt. Gill then took on the operational role of DGP, transforming the demoralized Punjab police force into an effective semiurban counterterrorist and counterinsurgency force. Countering terror with terror and using hard-line methods to persuade the civilian populace to stop aiding Sikh terrorists, Gill had eliminated hundreds of cadres and driven a large number of them into Pakistan by the end of 1988.[41] Some, however, decided to make a last stand at the Golden Temple in Amritsar, which had been off the government radar since the 1984 debacle. As a result, extremist and AISSF leaders used the Golden Temple as a hideout under the very noses of the Akali government and the Punjab police in 1986 and 1987.[42]

May 1988 saw the government swing into action as the Golden Temple was once again turned into a fortress. This time, the recently formed National Security Guard (NSG) and elite commandos of the Punjab police were entrusted with the task of clearing the temple complex in Operation Black Thunder.[43] Within the NSG, Fifty-First Special Action Group—made up of army commandos led by Major General Naresh Kumar—executed the operation over ten days. It was an intelligence-driven process, with the Special Action Group planting an operative inside the temple for two days and gathering vital information on defensive dispositions and approximate terrorist strength. Intelligence was complemented by political patience, a whole-government approach, snipers, and psychological warfare. Periodically, the terrorists were offered the opportunity to surrender, and trapped devotees were allowed to leave the temple safely. Restraint was the hallmark of the operation, which was monitored by Prime Minister Rajiv Gandhi and the director-general of the NSG, Ved Marwah.

In his book *Uncivil Wars*, Marwah puts the operation into perspective: "The most important difference between the two operations (Blue Star and Black Thunder) was that the former was conceived in haste, underestimating the militants' determination and capacity to fight, and the latter was meticulously planned with inputs from all concerned (including the IAF, which sent in clear recce photographs)."[44] Despite the extremely effective strong-arm tactics of Gill and the Punjab police during the post–Operation Black Thunder phase, the terrorist movement did not lose steam. The security forces' offensive action was not complemented by good governance and political stability on the ground. Making matters worse was the complete absence of effective communication directed at weaning the patriotic and nationalistic nonurban Sikhs from the secessionist narrative. With Rajiv Gandhi preoccupied with Sri Lanka, it would take a few years for the Khalistan movement to lose steam.

Pakistan reignited the covert war in Jammu and Kashmir after realizing that it would be unable to sustain the Khalistan struggle. Quitting while the going was good was an excellent move by the ISI. The Sikh religious elders also gradually came to shun the Panthic Committee. The BSF's sealing and patrolling of more than 600 kilometers of the border from Hussainiwala to Chhamb Jaurian, and the gradual success of the campaign to win the people's hearts and minds, led to peace in Punjab. Prime Minister Narasimha Rao's government empowered and supported a strong Punjab state government led by Beant Singh in the early 1990s.[45] A two-pronged strategy was implemented to bring peace to Punjab: cracking down on terrorism, and convincing the people of Punjab that they risked being left out of Delhi's ongoing economic liberalization program. It proved to be a winning strategy. By the mid-1990s, Punjab was back on track.

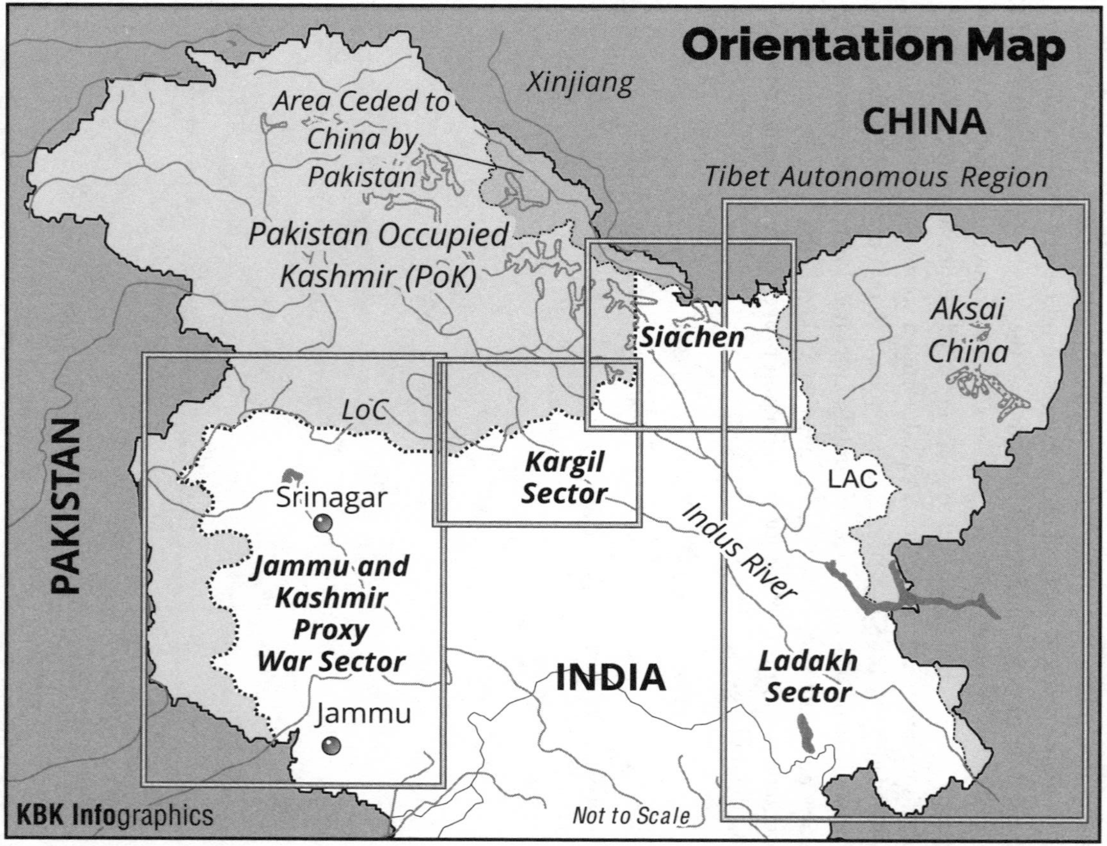

Map 3: Orientation
Map of India's Northern
Conflict Zones

Orientation Map

CHINA

PAKISTAN

INDIA

Xinjiang

Tibet Autonomous Region

Aksai China

LAC

Area Ceded to China by Pakistan

Pakistan Occupied Kashmir (PoK)

Siachen

Indus River

Ladakh Sector

Kargil Sector

LoC

Srinagar

Jammu and Kashmir Proxy War Sector

Jammu

Not to Scale

KBK Infographics

6

Siachen
An Icy Battleground

Fighting and dying at breathtaking altitudes, Indians and Pakistanis are locked
in an icy stalemate over a disputed Himalayan boundary. Who will compromise?
—Edward Desmond, "War on High Ground"

CARTOGRAPHIC DISPUTE

The Russian tundra is a most unforgiving battleground for armies. Hitler's
defeat at Stalingrad in the bleak winter of 1942—his Panzer divisions destroyed by the hardy and acclimatized Russian forces—was one of the critical turning points of World War II. The battles fought by Major General
Thimayya's Sri Division (later, Nineteenth Infantry Division) against invad-
ers from Skardu and Gilgit across the snowbound passes of Jammu and
Kashmir (J&K) and Ladakh in the early summer of 1948 are all standout
examples of endurance and courage. So are the battles fought by the Indian
Army in 1965 and 1999 in the Kargil Sector at altitudes of 13,000 to 15,000
feet—where every breath is an effort. These examples, however, pale in comparison to the India–Pakistan face-off on the Siachen Glacier, where even the
soaring Himalayan eagle does not dare to venture.

Averaging 15,000 to 17,000 feet above mean sea level, the Siachen Glacier
was discovered in 1821 by British explorer William Moorcraft. The parts of
the glacier from the snout northward were first surveyed in 1909 by another
Englishman, Dr. Tom Longstaff, when he climbed to the Bilafond La, a pass
in the Saltoro Range that would see much action in the years ahead.[1] And
it was Professor Giotto Dainelli, an Italian geographer and naturalist, who
mapped the glacier to its northernmost point in 1930.[2]

In the local language, "Siachen" means "the land with an abundance of
roses." The Siachen Glacier drains into the Nubra River, which goes on
to join the Shyok River, a major tributary of the Indus. It lies between the
Saltoro Range on the west, the Karakoram Range to the north and east, and
the Shaksgam Valley to the northwest. Interestingly, Shaksgam was part of
the erstwhile state of J&K before Pakistan ceded it to China in 1963.

The Saltoro Range is dominated by the towering Saltoro Kangri, which rises to more than 25,000 feet. There are many other peaks above 23,000 feet, the most relevant ones being the Sia Kangri and Sherpi Kangri. The Indra Col, Sia La, Bilafond La, and Gyong La—at heights of 18,000 to 22,000 feet—are the most prominent passes. The Saltoro Range flanks the glacier, shielding it from Pakistan-occupied J&K to the west, and it joins the Eastern Karakoram Range at Indra Col. It then runs in a southeasterly direction until it reaches the Karakoram Pass. The southern tip of this range is a geographic grid square designated NJ 9842.

In the cease-fire agreement signed on 27 July 1949 after the first India–Pakistan war, the cease-fire line was demarcated on maps up to grid NJ 9842.[3] The agreement then went on to state, rather ambiguously, that the cease-fire line would continue "thence north to the glaciers." In 1972, prior to the signing of the Shimla Agreement between India and Pakistan, the cease-fire line was redrawn—with both sides retaining the areas they had captured on either side of the line—and designated the line of control. The vague description beyond NJ 9842 remained unchanged and lent itself to differing interpretations by the two sides, causing problems several years later. Had some care been taken to extend this line northward along the Saltoro Ridge, the Siachen Conflict might have been avoided.[4]

The Indian claim was based on the universally accepted watershed principle of demarcation. In India's view, the line of control (now known as the actual ground position line, or AGPL) ran northward from NJ 9842 for almost 110 kilometers along the Saltoro Range ridgeline, that is, the watershed of the Dansam and Nubra Rivers. Pakistan, however, asserted that the line of control should continue in a northeasterly direction as the crow flies, up to the Karakoram Pass. As a result, the Pakistanis claimed the Saltoro Ridge, the Siachen Glacier, and the magnificent climbing areas surrounding it. Pakistan began to allow foreign expeditions to trek in the area in the late 1970s. These expeditions climbed the Saltoro Kangri and Teram Kangri and then explored the glacier by descending through the various passes.[5] In an article in *Pakistan Horizon*—a journal published by the Pakistan Institute for International Affairs—Dr. Omer Farook Zain reinforced the glacier's Islamic connection when he claimed that a Muslim saint, Syed Ali Hamadani, had traveled along the glacier from Kashmir to Kashgar, spreading the message of Islam and constructing mosques.[6]

OPERATION MEGHDOOT UNFOLDS

Lieutenant General M. L. Chibber, the Northern Army commander in 1983–1984, is widely considered to be the brain behind Operation Meghdoot,[7] the Indian Army's stunning high-altitude attempt to occupy the Saltoro Ridge and the Siachen Glacier. He became interested in the area in September 1978, when Colonel "Bull" Narinder Kumar led an expedition to Teram Kangri, a 24,000-foot-high peak on the northeastern flank of the Siachen Glacier. Chibber then set in motion a chain of events that would alter the way the world looked at high-altitude combat.[8]

At the time, Flying Officer (later Air Vice Marshal) Manmohan Bahadur was posted to the 114th Helicopter Unit. Called the Siachen Pioneers after moving to Leh, it is the Indian Air Force's most decorated helicopter unit and has been equipped over the years with a fleet of Chetaks, Cheetahs, and Cheetals.[9] Little did Bahadur imagine that on 26 September 1978 he would be part of the first crew to land on the glacier as Bull Kumar's expedition traversed it.[10] For the next few weeks, Bahadur served as copilot to three experienced squadron leaders, carrying supplies and mail for the team as it made its way past Camp 1, Camp 2, and Camp 3. Since the Chetaks did not have skis, they had to fly low, hover over the glacier, and roll out the supplies. In response to a call for help, on 6 October 1978 the Chetak picked up two casualties from the northern tip of the glacier after a long sortie (two hours and fifty minutes, according to Bahadur's logbook) and evacuated them to Thoise airfield, where they were admitted to a forward base hospital. Bahadur went on to become an accomplished test pilot and commanded 114th Helicopter Unit from 1994 to 1997.

Following the expedition, Bull Kumar recommended that India immediately occupy some of the heights to preempt the Pakistanis' attempt to do the same. The plan was considered but shelved—as it was rightly assessed that the posts would be unsupportable in winter—although regular summer patrols were authorized. Kumar was revered by the Indian mountaineering community, particularly its members in the Indian Army. However, the mere mention of his name raised the temperatures of Pakistani military officers who participated in the early years of the operation. Kevin Fedarko, an American photographer and high-altitude trekker–cum–journalist, met one such officer at a Pakistani post on the western slopes of the Saltoro Ridge in 2002, who fumed, "Colonel Kumar is the man who started all this, I have no wish to meet him—that bastard."[11]

Things remained quiet until Chibber returned to the region five years later as the Northern Army commander. He had hardly settled in when he was alerted to a protest from Pakistan regarding Indian patrols in the Siachen area. This was followed by another one in August 1983, which was a trifle alarming: "Request instruct your troops to withdraw beyond Line of Control south of line joining NJ 9842 and Karakoram Pass. Any delay in vacating our territory will create a serious situation."[12] A few days later, another protest followed, clearly laying claim to the entire Siachen Glacier and reiterating that the line joining NJ 9842 and the Karakoram Pass should be treated as the de facto line of control. A few months later, when intelligence reports indicated that the Pakistan Army was seriously scouting around for high-altitude equipment from European manufacturers, Chibber realized that something was cooking. German intelligence alerted India's military attaché in Bonn that India's large order for mountaineering equipment was being hijacked by the Pakistanis at exorbitant rates. Given a free hand by the army chief, General Arun Vaidya, Chibber—along with Lieutenant General P. N. Hoon, commander of Fifteenth Corps in Srinagar—brainstormed a preemptive plan to occupy the 100-kilometer-long Saltoro Ridge overlooking the Siachen Glacier.

Pakistan displayed tactical nimbleness and dispatched a small force with machine guns and mortars in the winter of 1983 to occupy Bilafond La and Sia La, two of the highest passes in the Northern Sector of the glacier. However, it apparently had to turn back due to inclement weather and a logistical inability to support the force.[13] Had this plan succeeded, Pakistan might have succeeded in occupying the entire Saltoro Ridge, as access from the west was easier than from the east. India's attempt from there would come a few months later.

MAKING MILITARY SENSE OF THE SIACHEN GLACIER

Many believe that the Siachen Glacier is one long, menacing stretch of snow that is separated from Pakistan by the Saltoro Range and that both armies can assault the ridge from their own sides. However, mountain ranges do not spring up—they gradually unfold. A few kilometers north of the snout of the glacier, the glacier floor rises from around 11,000 feet to 15,000 feet, until it abruptly ends at a point where it branches out in a forklike feature. One prong leads to the Sia La, and the other heads toward Indra Col, where the Saltoro Range blends with the Eastern Karakoram Range. Along the way, it is joined by subsidiary glaciers emanating from the Saltoro Range. All Indian posts are approached via these subsidiary glaciers—known as G-1, G-2, Lolofond, and G-3—from north via the Central Glacier and farther south via the Gyong Glacier. Of greater relevance from a military perspective are the glaciers to the west of the AGPL in Pakistani territory: the Kondus Glacier, Dong Dong Glacier, Bilafond La Glacier, and Chumik Glacier. It was from these glaciers that the Pakistan Army launched attacks between 1984 and 2003 to displace Indian troops from the heights along the Saltoro Ridge. A peak on the Saltoro Ridge appears close as one walks along the main glacier, but reaching it on foot is possible only via a subsidiary glacier.

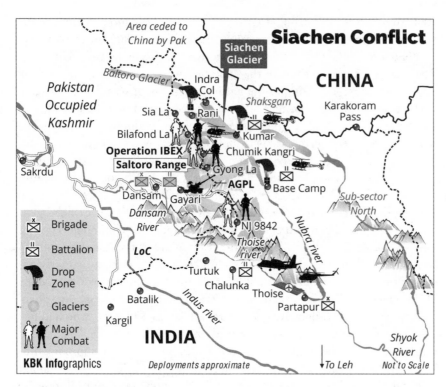

Map 4. The Siachen Conflict

The winter of 1983 witnessed hectic parleys between Chibber and New Delhi on how to prevent Pakistan from physically occupying the Siachen Glacier and the major passes around it without escalating the situation beyond a localized conflict. After extensive war-gaming, it was determined that the only way to ensure control over the region was to occupy the two pivotal passes of Sia La and Bilafond La in the northern section of the Saltoro Ridge. A decisive Indira Gandhi gave the go-ahead sometime in early 1984, and thus began Operation Meghdoot.

ASSAULT AND WHITEOUT

The essence of a sound military plan is its simplicity, surprise, sustainability, and clarity of purpose in terms of likely strategic and operational outcomes. From these emerge other operational imperatives such as force levels, contingency plans, and costs—both human and material. Chibber reckoned that the element of surprise was essential for capturing Bilafond La and Sia La, as it would give India a lead time of about two weeks to beat back any Pakistani attack, however strong it was. This would allow Indian troops to dig in, stock themselves, and create a logistics base for resupply. Deployment by helicopter right to the pass was the only way to make this plan work. There were many who thought the operation was doomed and that such an audacious attempt to combat the natural elements of weather and terrain was too risky. Chibber thought otherwise and believed that these challenges could be overcome with adequate preparation and training, especially when there was no enemy firing at his troops. He drew on history to validate his proposition—citing the accomplishments of mountaineers and Arctic explorers—and reinforced the idea that this move would spook the Pakistanis, who were not used to such aggression from the Indians.

Brigadier Vijay Channa, commander of Twenty-Sixth Sector headquartered at Turtok, also had the Siachen Glacier under his command. His two units—Fourth Kumaon and the Karakoram Wing of the Ladakh Scouts— were well acclimatized and familiar with the region, having regularly patrolled the area up to Sia La and Bilafond La in the summer of 1983. Many of the officers and men in these units were accomplished mountaineers, including Major A. N. Bahuguna and Captain Sanjay Kulkarni, who had just climbed Stok Kangri, a 20,000-foot peak on the Saltoro Ridge. Channa did not know about the plan until March 1984, when he was summoned to Fifteenth Corps headquarters (HQ) in Srinagar and briefed by Lieutenant General Hoon. The commanders of the helicopter units and pilots were briefed a couple of weeks later at the high-altitude warfare school in Gulmarg. It was left to Channa to choose his teams and the date of the assault, within a window between 1 and 30 April. Channa chose 13 April because it was Baisakhi—a holiday celebrated in both Punjab and Pakistan—which he reckoned would provide the element of surprise.

It was also determined that there would be no chance to undertake a helicopter reconnaissance of likely landing spots close to the passes without forfeiting the element of surprise. Channa reckoned that landing spots would be available on the firm snow during March and April. He agreed to the plan to land almost sixty troops of the Fourth Battalion of the Kumaon Regiment and the Ladakh Scouts on Bilafond La and Sia La, respectively. Squadron leader Rohit Rai was among the handful of pilots chosen for the helicopter task force that was put together from four units: 114th Helicopter Unit, 131st Forward Air Controller, and 662nd and 663rd Air Observation Posts. The last two units were manned principally by army pilots and were employed for surveillance and artillery direction. The helicopter task force at Thoise, comprising six to eight Cheetah helicopters and thirteen to fifteen pilots, was led by Wing Commander C. S. Sandhu, with Colonel G. S. Ghuman, the most senior army pilot on the task force, acting as the force commander.[14]

It is possible that only Ghuman and Sandhu knew the detailed plan in the first week of April. On 10 April all the helicopters moved to Thoise from their respective locations in Jammu and Udhampur and Srinagar. Though several of the captains and copilots had flown in the Nubra and Shyok Valleys and in the northern subsector of eastern Ladakh, the Siachen Glacier and the Saltoro Ridge were unfamiliar airspace for all of them. It was only on 12 April that Rohit Rai caught a glimpse of possible landing areas around Bilafond La and Sia La, along with officers from Fourth Kumaon and the Ladakh Scouts, during a reconnaissance sortie. Captain Kulkarni led the first wave onto Bilafond La with his company from Fourth Kumaon.[15] It would take a herculean effort of about forty sorties over several days to land the men and their basic equipment and supplies on the two passes.

In an interview with Nitin Gokhale, Kulkarni highlighted the importance of being well-equipped for such an operation. He remembered that the special winter clothing and allied equipment "arrived on 12 April evening, barely hours before we were being launched into Operation Meghdoot. Thermal coats, thermal pants, very nice balaclavas, excellent tents, ice axes, goggles, the works were bought from Europe. The weapons however remained the basic Indian Army 7.62mm SLR [self-loading rifle]. Of course, we had mortars, MMG [medium machine guns], missiles, Grad P rockets. Some of the weapons came by air, some came through porters."[16] Soon after being landed at Bilafond La by helicopter, Kulkarni and his team were cut off from the rest of the world by a blizzard and experienced whiteout conditions for four days. Almost immediately, they lost a soldier to frostbite, and their radio operator had to be evacuated on the first day, which meant that they lost radio contact with the rest of the force. Had they not been so well equipped and familiar with the terrain, it is unlikely that many would have survived. By the time the weather cleared on 18 April and reinforcements and medical help arrived, twenty-one of the remaining twenty-eight men had suffered some degree of frostbite. Only when Kulkarni radioed for the evacuation of a fallen comrade did the Pakistanis discover that the heights they coveted had already been occupied.

Exploiting the good weather, Bahuguna and his company from the Ladakh Scouts landed on Sia La and a lower camp on the same day. Joining the effort that day were two Mi-8 helicopters that carried supplies and ammunition from Thoise. After occupying Sia La, the rest of the force linked up at the forward logistics base (FLB) on the glacier and set up two more camps that would support both the Bilafond La and Sia La locations. The Kumar FLB—as it came to be known—also emerged as HQ for the Northern Glacier Battalion. It remained so until it was relocated, along with the logistics base, a few kilometers east, away from the glacier floor and out of range of Pakistani artillery. In view of the increasing Pakistan Air Force activity, Kumar FLB was reinforced with towed antiaircraft guns (ZU-23)—the first such guns on the main glacier. Some posts higher up were given SAM-7 shoulder-fired missiles too. The years ahead would see a variety of guns in action on both sides.

As units of the Indian Army settled into a routine, the life-threatening physiological effects of the climate, the hazardous terrain, and enemy action all took a toll. The lack of oxygen degraded psychomotor performance and induced altitude sickness, also called high-altitude pulmonary edema. Frostbite and gangrene set in rapidly following exposure to temperatures in the range of −15 to −40 degrees Celsius. Blizzards, fog, and whiteouts disoriented both soldiers on the ground and aviators. Threats from the terrain included avalanches, rockfalls, crevasses, ice falls, and ice walls. The typical routine at such posts involved patrolling, manning observation posts, sentry duty, and evacuating casualties. The last task was challenging in the early days, as it involved carrying casualties to a lower post or helipad, often in inclement weather. Regular camp activities included attending to personal health and hygiene, heating water, and maintaining weapons and critical equipment. The relief and rotation of manpower at high-altitude posts was carried out every fifteen days.

NARRATIVES AND COUNTERATTACK

In his book *Fangs of Ice*, Lieutenant Colonel Syed Ishfaq Ali gives a Pakistani perspective that is typically jingoistic and Kashmir-centric: "The Siachen dispute is basically a manifestation of Hindu hegemonic design and has now become a complicated affair and a sedimentation of various unsettled issues like the Kashmir problem."[17] He then goes on to deftly add a China and Soviet perspective to India's preemptive move by arguing rather fancifully:

> It is commonly believed that one reason of Indian presence in Siachen is to ultimately pose a threat to the Karakoram Highway. Taken at its face value it appears rather preposterous because there are over 155 miles over inaccessible glaciated mountain ranges that no army can cover in any manner. Thus, the Indian move on Siachen was a flanking maneuver meant to pave the way towards a future cutting off Pakistan's strategic lifeline to China. Moscow, motivated by much the same concerns as its military ally, is obviously well placed in the Wakhan Corridor to facilitate Indian designs.[18]

Adding Soviet designs to India's occupation of Siachen at a time when the Soviets were entrenched in Afghanistan was a masterstroke that drew US scholars into the Siachen debate.

Even as Chibber was planning his operation, President Zia-ul-Haq, Pakistan's military dictator, had assembled a battalion-sized force at Skardu. The Burzil Force was named after the Burzil Mountains that separate the Gilgit and Baltistan provinces of Pakistan-occupied Kashmir from the Kashmir Valley. Comprising Special Service Group (SSG) commandos and a sprinkling of soldiers from the Northern Light Infantry (NLI) who possessed specialized knowledge of the region, the force commenced training for high-altitude and glacier operations in early 1984. The final assault was planned for April or May of that year. Frustratingly for Zia, the Indians beat him to the Saltoro Ridge. The first probing counterattack from the Burzil Force came at Bilafond La on 24 April, and it was beaten back easily. Realizing that a frontal assault was next to impossible, the force was expanded over the next few days and split into company-sized groups with names such as Asghar Force, Hafeez Force, and Shahbaz Force. Despite extremely spirited attempts, these too were repulsed by the entrenched Indians.

By the end of August 1984, the Burzil Force realized that it would be better off occupying the lower ridgelines of the Saltoro Range and a few higher posts. Located some distance from the glacier, these posts would enable partial observation of Indian activity in the region and support periodic attacks whenever the opportunity presented itself. With brigade HQ at Dansam, the force had to first establish routes of ingress and set up suitable logistics hubs and camps along the Chumik and Bilafond Glaciers. In 1984 the Bilafond Glacier became the center of action. Consequently, Gayari—at the snout of the two glaciers—was chosen as the FLB to support ingress on both routes, while Naram was an intermediate camp en route to Ali Braganza at approximately 16,000 feet. From here, the final assaults would be launched to capture either unoccupied posts on the Saltoro Ridge or some vital Indian posts. After multiple attacks failed to dislodge the Indians from the heights, a Pakistani general reflected, "When we saw the Indians at those heights, we knew they came to stay."[19]

Both sides spent much of 1984 and 1985 consolidating their positions, enhancing force levels up to that of a large mountain brigade, getting artillery guns into position, and engaging in localized firefights. On the Indian side, Twenty-Sixth Sector was converted into 102nd Infantry Brigade, and Brigadier Jal Master took over command in May 1985. Pakistan formed 323rd Infantry Brigade to look after Siachen operations along with the SSG, complementing the infantry battalions in all the assault operations. The first pilot casualty in Operation Meghdoot was Major S. K. Gadhiok, who died on 30 August 1985. Gadhiok was shot in the head by a Pakistani sniper as he was directing artillery fire on Pakistani posts from his Cheetah helicopter in the Central Glacier. The copilot, Captain Guleria, flew back to base camp with Gadhiok slumped forward in the captain's seat.

The Indian Army divided the glacier into the Northern, Central, and Southern Sectors. The Northern Sector—which saw most of the action during the initial years of the conflict—comprised the Sia La complex, Bilafond La complex, and G-1 complex, all named after subsidiary glaciers. In the Indian military lexicon, a complex signifies a cluster of posts. Subsidiary posts are located to protect approaches to the main posts, while observation posts (OPs) may be located at vantage points that can accommodate only a few people and are difficult to access. A large post typically accommodates a maximum of twelve men and has a helipad that can receive a light helicopter, while a subsidiary post is large enough to house six to ten men. OPs generally have dug-in shelters to accommodate four to six men and are occupied during fair weather, when the visibility is good and it is possible to observe enemy movements or direct artillery fire.

Prominent posts in this area were Sia La, Bilafond La, Kumar, Sonam, Bhim, and Bana, along with a few subsidiary OPs on the northern shoulder of Bilafond La. Cheekily, the Indians called a drop zone on the glacier floor Benazir, probably because Benazir Bhutto came to power on the back of a political campaign that castigated President Zia-ul-Haq for losing Siachen to India. Benazir serviced the Sia La complex—including Tiger Saddle, the northernmost Indian post in the complex—and was later renamed Rani after Bhutto was voted out of office in 1997. The HQ of the Northern Sector Battalion, along with its complement of artillery support, was located at Kumar for almost two decades before it moved eastward in 2001. While the Indian brigade had infantry battalions that cut across regions—the Sikh, Dogra, Garhwal, Gorkha, and Madras Regiments, to name a few—the Pakistani brigade drew most of its personnel from the NLI, which was made up of various sects from the Gilgit and Baltistan region. There has been an attempt to widen this base over the years and ensure that all units of the Pakistan Army serve on the glacier and in the Kargil Sector, but the Punjabi-dominated military establishment of Pakistan has often been accused of putting the NLI in the line of fire.

Among the most significant achievements of the Pakistan Army during the early years of the conflict was the occupation of Quaid Post (at approximately 22,000 feet) in April 1986. Measuring no more than sixteen feet in radius and towering over the Indian posts in the Bilafond La complex, Quaid Post permitted the Pakistanis to observe parts of Kumar FLB and the surface routes to the forward posts of Bilafond La over the Lolofond Glacier. Based on these observations, the Pakistan Army could direct effective artillery fire; up to that point, most of the Pakistani artillery fire had been speculative.

Quaid Post emerged as an irritant for the Indians, and its capture was high on the list of objectives for Brigadier Chandan Singh Nugyal, commander of 102nd Infantry Brigade.

COURAGE ON UNCHARTED HEIGHTS

In early 1986, almost two years after the likes of Kulkarni and Channa had established Indian dominance over the Saltoro Range, the Ladakh Scouts, in a daring but completely unsustainable operation, attempted to establish posts on the lower slopes (over 20,000 feet) of the Saltoro Kangri massif that formed part of the Northern Sector. Captain Navkiran Singh Ghei, a young paratrooper, had been posted to the Ladakh Scouts after finishing his tenure as an instructor at the National Defence Academy. Ghei went on to command a battalion and the Indian Army's only parachute brigade, a division engaged in counterinsurgency operations in the northeast, and a corps in Punjab before ending his illustrious career with a three-year stint as commandant of the National Defence College.

Ghei had to open a small post at 20,000 feet and maintain it for over six months with hardly any backup or logistics support, along with five "Nunnus" (as troops from the Ladakh Scouts are affectionately called). By then, ideas about how to dominate the entire glacier were flowing thick and fast from both the Northern Command and Indian Army HQ. It was considered important to establish more posts in the Northern Sector, as that would enhance visibility of the communication lines that extended toward the Pakistani posts in the Central Sector and on Saltoro and Baltoro Ridges and improve the direction of artillery fire. The site chosen overlooked Indian posts on the northern shoulder of Bilafond La and offered visibility of the Pakistani logistics line that ran up the Bilafond Glacier on the western slopes of the Saltoro Range toward Quaid Post.

At the time, the Ladakh Scouts had its HQ in Leh and was divided into two forces of eight to ten companies each. These were known as the Karakoram Force and the Indus Force, after the areas they patrolled and defended. After a period of acclimatization at base camp and Kumar FLB,[20] Ghei and his platoon—platoon commander Subedar Sonam and four Ladakhi troops—set out on an arduous climb from 15,000 to 20,000 feet. At around 8:00 p.m. on 26 February 1986, they reached their intended summit of Point 6135 (20,245 feet). They pitched their three-man arctic tents and burrowed in for the night, not realizing they would have to endure whiteout conditions and appalling weather for the next three days. Ghei recalled that they could not see beyond a couple of feet and had to make do "without a pee or a crap for days." It was a surreal experience for the six men as they huddled in their small tents and wondered how they were going to survive a week, let alone a couple of months. Realizing that they had bitten off more than they could chew, Ghei radioed for assistance and asked for a larger tent, some supplies, and reinforcements.[21]

Once the weather cleared, the team established camp for the long haul and hoped they would be rotated every few weeks. Unfortunately, Ghei's replacement was struck down by acute mountain sickness and had to be evacuated to the base camp and then to the military hospital at Thoise. This meant that Ghei had to remain on station. On a clear day, the team had a good view of Pakistani supply lines along the Bilafond Glacier and directed artillery to fire on these lines. The rarefied atmosphere posed significant challenges for the Indian gunners, as the lower air density meant that the shells encountered less drag. They often overshot the target by miles, as there were no calibration charts for these altitudes. Ghei often radioed the artillery posts to "drop 300 meters" or "drop 500 meters," advising the gunners to aim much shorter. The gunners invariably responded that the firing picture indicated an impact point in friendly territory, sometimes even coinciding with Ghei's own location. It was virgin territory for India's gunners, but eventually, the ballistics were worked out to ensure acceptable levels of accuracy.

One month turned into two and then almost six. Ghei and his team continued to man the post, but they were like zombies. When asked how they managed to endure, he said the Ladakhis were amazing survivors, and they gave him the courage to lead from the front. Deprived of sleep, suffering from periodic hallucinations, and surviving on milk powder and the odd paratha (Indian bread) the Nunnus made for him, Ghei lost a lot of weight and was suffering from partial memory loss by the time his six-month vigil on Point 6135 ended. After the team returned and reported the conditions there, the post was abandoned and never manned again.

VERTICAL ASSAULT AND COURAGEOUS DEFENSE

Major General Chandan Singh Nugyal of the Sikh Regiment is a Pahadi (a person from the hills, in colloquial Hindi) and one of the most decorated officers in the Indian Army. A fine mountaineer and an outstanding leader, he was commander of the Siachen Brigade during the fiercest fighting in the Northern Sector (1986–1987). Although the most talked about operation during his tenure was the capture of Bana Post, the fierceness of the other battles across the Bilafond La complex in the summer and autumn of 1987 tested Nugyal's leadership skills to the maximum. Access to the complex from the Bilafond Glacier was easier from the Pakistani side than from Kumar FLB via the Lolofond Glacier.

The capture of Quaid Post by a five-member team of the Eighth Battalion of the Jammu and Kashmir Light Infantry under Naib Subedar Bana Singh and its defense by an equally worthy opponent are elements of a well-chronicled saga of sheer bravery and close combat in icy conditions. Bana Singh's exploits during the operation—which lasted three days, from 23 to 26 June 1987—have made him a legend. Now almost seventy years old and happily retired, he still patiently recounts details of the operation to anyone who asks. Of all the narratives of his exploits, the most riveting is by Major General Raj Mehta, written in 2013 for the Centre for Land Warfare Studies in Delhi.[22] Equally interesting is an interview given by Bana and published in the *Illustrated Weekly of India*.[23] The narrative that follows draws heavily on both these sources, as well as unit diaries.

After a month of preparation and preliminary probing attacks, Lieutenant Colonel A. K. Rai—the commanding officer of Eighth J&K Light Infantry—chose three teams of thirty men for the assault. Major Virender Singh was the leader of the mission, and Bana was one of the section commanders. Armed with only light machine guns, 9mm SAF carbines, and grenades, the teams commenced the attack on 23 June 1987. After a couple of failed night assaults that involved climbing near-vertical ice walls and the loss of a few men to enemy fire, the force had already spent more than thirty-six hours in assault mode. Desperate times call for desperate measures, so, in a move that could have decimated Bana and his team, Rai ordered an assault in broad daylight.

Still recovering from two successive night assaults, the eight defenders on Quaid Top—300 meters above Quaid Base—were not expecting a daytime assault. Naib Subedar Atta Mohammad of the SSG, commanding Quaid Post and its subsidiary OP, was supremely confident of beating back any attack because he had reinforced the post with four SSG commandos a week before the assault. Quaid OP—where all eight SSG commandos had dug in—was accessible from only one direction. Mohammad knew that an attack was imminent because there had been continuous artillery bombardment for days, albeit with limited accuracy. His commander, Major Irshad, had alerted him on 20 June to prepare for a final battle.[24]

Biting cold and a raging blizzard sapped their energy as the SSG commandos took turns shoveling snow and keeping the areas around their igloo navigable and combat ready once the weather improved. Making matters worse were the Indian howitzers and guns that were attempting to soften Quaid OP and block any reinforcements that Irshad might send up. The commandos suffered their first casualty even before the assault began, and Mohammad was left with only six men to ward off the repeated attacks. By the time the second attack took place, Indian artillery fire had taken out another commando. Despite the Pakistani artillery's success in pinning down the Indian attack, the relentless Indian fire made it appear that a much larger force was assaulting the top.

When Bana led his section for the final assault on 23 June 1987 in what was supposed to be broad daylight, the sky turned murky, and the operation commenced in virtual darkness at noon. Bana recalled the appalling weather and the lack of clarity whether to follow standard operating procedures for day or night operations, given the ambient light conditions. Also, given the sustained artillery shelling, he realized that the Pakistanis knew something was going on. Bana led his men through an extremely difficult and hazardous route, climbing in near darkness in a snowstorm and reaching the single deep bunker at the top after a two-hour firefight. The defenders were quiet until Bana and his five-man team assaulted the bunker with grenades and single-shot light machine guns. They overcame some spirited resistance from Mohammad and his remaining commandos in an intense close-quarters battle. It lasted only a few minutes, but it must have seemed like an eternity for Mohammad and his doomed comrades.[25]

The Pakistani narrative alludes to the possibility of Mohammad being the sole survivor and battling Bana's men alone when they stormed the bunker. It also claims that the assaulting troops numbered in the hundreds and suffered well over thirty casualties.[26] However, according to the Indian narrative, it was a firefight with more than one defender and a dozen Indian casualties. Numbers really lose their significance in such battles, and even seasoned soldiers marvel at the sheer courage required to attack and defend at such altitudes. The satisfaction of victory did not dent the battle ethics of fair play and chivalry, and Eighth J&K Light Infantry "handed over the body of each *shaheed* (martyr) after giving it a military salute."[27]

If there was one difference between the Pakistani defenders and the Indian attackers, it was leadership. Why was there no officer at this highest and toughest post, even though the Pakistanis knew that an attack was imminent? Although Bana led the final assault, the presence of two officers in the assault teams was a significant force multiplier. Bana recollected that it was the "roaring voice of Major Varinder Singh and Captain Anil Sharma encouraging us along which gave us strength and hope."[28] The capture of Quaid Post came at a heavy price, as Eighth J&K Light Infantry lost a young second lieutenant, a junior commissioned officer, and eight other men in the various assaults. Even today, it is the most highly decorated unit that has seen action on the glacier. Bana Singh was awarded the Param Vir Chakra (India's highest wartime gallantry award), and Major Varinder Singh and eight others were decorated with Vir Chakras (the third highest wartime gallantry award). Naib Subedar Atta Mohammad was awarded Pakistan's highest peacetime gallantry award, the Sitara-i-Jurrat. Quaid OP was renamed Bana Top, and Quaid Post became Bana Base.

The Pakistan Army's riposte for the loss of Quaid Post came fast and strong. In September 1987 it attacked two Indian posts on the northern shoulder of Bilafond La while an overstretched and battle-weary Eighth J&K Light Infantry, long overdue for relief, was handing off to the Third Battalion of Fourth Gorkha Rifles. One of the attacks was beaten back after fierce hand-to-hand fighting. Major Krishna Gopal Chatterjee, a company commander, was awarded the Maha Vir Chakra (India's second highest war-time gallantry award) after the attack. Chatterjee recalled the action in a conversation with Rostum Nanavatty when the two met in Delhi prior to the latter assuming command of 102nd Infantry Brigade. Chatterjee saw the unmistakable signs of an attack developing, so he told his men that if any-one was not up for the fight, this was his chance to leave quietly. Not a man flinched. During the fighting, a Pakistani soldier clambered onto the post and managed to fell Chatterjee with a body blow before one of Chatterjee's fellow Gorkhas cut him down with a *khukri* (dagger). Despite taking heavy casualties, the Pakistanis continued to engage the Indians with sporadic at-tacks and artillery fire. Interestingly, the Pakistani brigade commander at the time was Brigadier Parvez Musharraf, the future army chief and Pakistani president. On that day, Musharraf came out second best in his duel with Chandan Singh Nugyal.

HOLDING FIRM

Brigadier Rostum Nanavatty assumed command of the Siachen Brigade from Nugyal in late 1987. He recollects that while the Sia La complex in the Northern Sector remained quiet, fighting on the northern shoulders of Bilafond La continued unabated. He flew to all the posts in the area—which were now manned by a battalion of the Garhwal Rifles—and saw for himself how difficult it was to survive on those icy heights, let alone defend them. It was during an intrusive aerial recce of Conway Saddle—a Pakistani post opposite Tiger Saddle (the Indian Army's northernmost post in the Sia La complex)—that Nanavatty witnessed aerial activity on the Pakistani side that remains etched in his memory: "We had a Pakistan Army medium-lift chopper hovering directly below us over the Conway Saddle helipad just as two [Pakistan Air Force] fighters streaked westward over their high-altitude training camp in the Baltoro Glacier area—a magnificent sight."[29]

Nanavatty adopted an aggressive approach right from the start. He wanted to test the effectiveness of the SAM-7 shoulder-fired missile at extremely high altitudes and ordered a post to engage an enemy helicopter should it come too close. Although the missile missed, it did send a message to the enemy. However, Major General V. R. Raghavan, Nanavatty's division commander, was not amused. Nanavatty recalled, "General Raghavan admonished me because he thought my action ill-considered. He believed it could escalate matters and adversely impact our air logistics support. Considering our greater dependence on air support, this would be to our disadvantage."[30]

Nanavatty communicated simple tactical objectives for his battalions. "By occupying the extreme high ground on the Saltoro Ridge, we were paying a high price in terms of casualties from terrain and weather as well as air logistics support," he said. "It was imperative therefore that we exploit our tactical advantage to completely dominate the enemy by fire and observation. The rules of engagement were simple—interdict all observed enemy activity within range by direct and indirect fires. The authority to open fire was suitably delegated."[31] He was at a forward OP for the first successful Bofors firing by the Thirty-Sixth Maratha Medium Regiment, which had a battery at the base camp.

Brigadier Devender Kumar was a captain posted to the Seventh Battalion of the Brigade of the Guards in mid-1988, after completing his officer's course. The battalion was entrusted with watching over the Northern Sector. After a customary period of acclimatization, Devender found himself serving as the post commander at Sonam, which, at almost 20,000 feet, was the highest Indian post with a helipad. Typical tenures on these posts varied from forty-five to sixty days, followed by a period of rest, recuperation, and continued training at base camp. Seventh Guards caused significant attrition to the enemy, though Devender admits losing twenty men during their six months on the glacier. Some perished during enemy firing, but most were lost to the weather, altitude, and terrain.

The Central Sector assumed great operational importance in 1988 following Pakistan's failure to dislodge the Indian Army from any posts in the Northern Sector. Desperate for an effective strategy of interdiction, the Pakistan Army established two posts to the south of the Bilafond La Ridge on the higher slopes of the Chumik Glacier. These posts—designated North OP and South OP by the Indian Army—allowed the Pakistanis to contest the Indian Army's domination and direct effective harassing fire. This area emerged as the next hot spot on the glacier and saw maximum fighting from 1988 to 1995.

The major posts in the Central Sector were K, D, J, G3, and C.[32] Battalion HQ was located at the base camp (11,600 feet), along with the HQ of an artillery regiment. Most of these posts had small helipads that could accommodate only the smaller Cheetah helicopters, but they were able to receive drops from Mi-17 helicopters. The force multiplier in this sector was a troop of Bofors guns located at the base camp; these guns had the range to engage targets across the Saltoro Range and along the length of the glacier. Supplementing the Bofors were other medium artillery guns. The loss of life on both sides during operational engagements was largely caused by artillery fire, not close combat engagements. Broadly speaking, posts in the Northern and Central Sectors were at heights between 16,000 and 18,000 feet, while a few higher posts were located above 20,000 feet.

The Southern Sector to the west of the Nubra Valley included NJ 9842 and had a set of heights that enabled observation of the line of control in the Turtok Sector. R, B, and G were the prominent posts in this sector, with large helipads that could accommodate the Mi-17 helicopters. Chalunkha served as the base camp, logistics hub, and battalion HQ for this sector. Chulung La was the southernmost pass held by India along the AGPL, and the western approaches to the glacier were along the Shyok River. Chorbat La (16,700 feet) was not part of the Southern Sector, but it has seen much action over the years, as both India and Pakistan have repeatedly made attempts to alter the line of control in this area.

On the Indian side, one major road ran eastward from Turtok and Chalunkha, connecting the brigade HQ of Partapur to the base camp. The road network on the Pakistan side was far more elaborate because of the lower heights and extended to the town of Gayari at the base of the Bilafond and Chumik Glaciers. This meant that Indian posts had to be maintained by the medium-lift Mi-17 helicopters, which carried loads from the base camp or Thoise to the FLBs. At some FLBs, such as Kumar, Sonam, and B, loads were taken up by foot, snow scooters, or smaller Cheetah helicopters. The 129th and 130th Helicopter Units were the two Mi-17 units supporting Siachen operations from a detachment at Thoise. Generous in his praise for these units, Nanavatty recalled some daring Mi-17 helicopter drops in the Southern Sector undertaken to reduce the load on the Cheetahs. Specifically, he recalled one valley-hugging sortie to the B helipad and drop zone. Staying low in the valleys was the only way to avoid detection by the enemy, which held the western slopes.

OPERATION IBEX

The highlights of Nugyal's tenure as brigade commander were the capture of the Quaid complex and the Indian Army's complete domination over the Northern Sector with aggressive action. However, during Nanavatty's tenure, Operation Ibex (April–May 1989) in the Central Sector was triggered because of a misunderstanding. The catalyst for the operation was an uncorroborated intelligence assessment of an impending Pakistani operation and Pakistan's desperate attempt to secure a foothold on the Saltoro Range prior to the upcoming diplomatic talks.[33] The central section of the Saltoro Ridge has two prominent glaciers that dominate access to the various heights occupied by the two sides. The Gyong Glacier led to the Gyong La Pass occupied by the Indians, from which they could thwart any northward move. The Chumik Glacier allowed the Pakistanis to set up camps that could serve as springboards for taking control of the few unoccupied heights. This posed a threat to the Indian Army's logistics line from base camp to both the Northern and Central Sectors.

In early 1989 the Pakistan Army took over two unoccupied OPs—called Victor and Sher by the Pakistanis and South and North by the Indians—on a ridgeline overlooking Indian posts. Colonel J. K. Sharma, the acting brigade commander in Nanavatty's absence (he was on leave), reckoned that the Pakistanis' next move would be to seize a prominent unoccupied height known as Point 6400 (21,000 feet) and consolidate their position in the area.[34] He assessed that this position could dominate the lower Indian posts D and K and disrupt support to the Gyong La subsector.[35] As a morale-boosting ploy, the Pakistan Army called these posts Baniya (Trader) and Sadhu (Mendicant) to highlight the Indian Army's nonmartial profile. Major General Jamshed Ayaz Khan, commander of the Pakistan Army's Force Command Northern Areas, had directed his forces to dig in at these posts. This hinted at a prolonged occupation, which did not augur well for the Indians.[36]

In the absence of Nanavatty, Major General Raghavan and the commander of Fifteenth Corps approved an operation proposed by Colonel Sharma to disrupt the Pakistani camp with occasional artillery bombardment. These attempts, however, failed to prevent the buildup. By mid-March, there were reports that the SSG was being brought into the region. On Sharma's advice, Raghavan took steps to preempt the likely Pakistani move to capture Point 6400. Leading this assault was a fresh battalion from the Dogra Regiment, which had been in the sector for just a few weeks. Complementing the inexperienced Dogras were about twenty-five seasoned mountain warriors from the Ladakh Scouts and a few instructors from the Siachen Battle School. In support were two 81mm mortar platoons, a battery with 105mm and 130mm medium guns, and a few Bofors guns. Assisting the force were Cheetah helicopters from the Army Air OP Squadron and Mi-17s from the Indian Air Force.[37]

The month-long operation had three objectives. The first was to occupy the highest point on the same ridge (Point 6400) to negate the advantage gained when the Pakistan Army set up Victor and Sher. Capturing Point 6400, located on a difficult ridgeline, would demand the best mountaineering and survival skills. The second objective was to protect the two main Indian posts, K and D, which could become easy targets should Pakistan get to Point 6400. The last objective was to evict the Pakistanis from South and North OPs and destroy the Chumik camp with sustained artillery bombardment directed from Point 6400. When Nanavatty returned from leave, he was presented with a fait accompli.

What this operation demanded of the officers and men is reflected in the citation Nanavatty wrote for Second Lieutenant Deepak Thapa, a tough young Dogra who attempted to keep the supply lines to Point 6400 open for almost a week:

> For his inexhaustible strength, stamina and endurance; his outstanding military mountaineering skills; his professionalism and organizational ability and leadership in the task of organizing the defence of Point 6400; in opening the hazardous route from Kaman to Support Base; and in establishing line communications and ferrying vital stores to Point 6400 under the harshest imaginable conditions of combat, I recommend Second Lieutenant Deepak Thapa for the award of Yudh Seva Medal (YSM).[38]

The motley group of Dogras, Sikhs, and Ladakhis led by Captain Vijayant Singh first made their way to the Kaman Post, climbing and clawing over sheer ice walls and crevices. Avalanches buried seven of their comrades, whose bodies were never recovered. Then they traversed an uncharted southern approach to the ridgeline to establish a support point at Thapa Base (named after Deepak Thapa), where they could assault Point 6400 unobserved by the two posts set up by Pakistan's 323rd Infantry Brigade. By mid-April, following a series of risky helicopter insertions and a treacherous eight-hour climb from Thapa Base, they had succeeded in ensuring a section strength of six to fifteen personnel, which included three officers.

Sustained mainly from Thapa Base via Cheetah landings at a lower helipad in good weather, the post managed to beat back repeated attacks by the Pakistanis from the north and the west while continuing to direct intense artillery fire onto all Pakistani posts through the last week of April and into early May. This forced both brigade commanders to call for a local cease-fire, followed by three meetings at Kargil between Nanavatty and his Pakistani counterpart from 323rd Infantry Brigade.[39] In addition to several citations for Second Dogra, which included a Vir Chakra for Captain Vijayant Singh, Nanavatty awarded eight citations for gallantry to the Karakoram Wing of the Ladakh Scouts. Captain Singh vividly recalls the recovery of a Cheetah helicopter from Point 6400 after it developed engine problems.[40] Nanavatty called this a stupendous task and said it matched the recovery of another Cheetah from Amar helipad in the Northern Sector.

The Pakistani narrative is different, as is to be expected. In an account of

Operation Chumik, as it was called in Pakistan, Lieutenant Colonel Syed Ashfaq Ali narrates a tale of equal courage and daring in three chapters: "The Razor's Edge," "The Overreachers," and "Crowning Triumph." This includes setting up Victor and Sher, helicopter assaults on Naveed Top (a post slightly below Point 6400), and uncorroborated firefights that forced the Indians down from Point 6400.[41] According to Kevin Fedarko—the first Westerner to gain access to both Pakistani and Indian posts—three teams of Pakistani soldiers attempted to reach the summit to thwart the Indian operation, but failed: one team was wiped out by an avalanche, and the others were halted by cornices (overhanging ridges of ice). A last-minute decision was made to airlift troops to a point just below the mountaintop (22,185 feet) by French Lama helicopters that were modified to fly no higher than 21,000 feet (like the Indian Cheetah helicopters). The air was so thin that the pilots feared they would crash if they attempted to hover.[42]

Nanavatty contests the Pakistani claims with great clarity:

> The truth is that our patrol held Point 6400 from the time we occupied it until the time it was decided at the 3rd Flag Meeting to disengage and revert to the status quo, i.e., the previously held positions in the subsector. Apart from the continuous pounding by enemy artillery, the only direct attempt made by the enemy to occupy the position was after the brave and innovative heli-insertion of the Pakistani patrol on a feature to the west of Point 6400 (presumably Naveed Top). This attempt was thwarted by Captain Vijayant Singh and a small team using the 84mm Carl Gustav at close ranges. There was no other close-quarter battle. The earlier attempt made by the enemy to approach Point 6400 along the ridgeline from the direction of their South OP had stalled because of terrain difficulties at least 1,500 m[eters] away from the objective. On my first recce the morning after my return, I flew over this enemy column and drew small-arms fire. I realized that they posed no threat—they were going nowhere but down where they came from.

To explain the rationale for the speedy de-escalation, he added:

> Multiple avalanches caused by the heavy artillery exchanges had by this time obliterated Thapa Base, causing casualties and completely disrupting the tenuous surface routes of communication. Even resupply using helicopters was proving very difficult. One helicopter had malfunctioned and had to be recovered after repairs in situ. A question mark hung over our ability to sustain the patrol logistically. In my mind was just one thought—it simply was not worth sacrificing the lives of our men for an overreach on our part. This [is] what I conveyed to the army commander on his first visit after my return.[43]

WEAPONS AND GUNNERS

Most early commanders on the glacier bet on the Carl Gustav rocket launchers as the most effective close-range weapons at those altitudes and temperatures. They rarely malfunctioned, and they caused significant damage during assaults and close-range fighting. The Grad P rocket launchers were also particularly effective at medium range and caused great damage from 500 to 1,000 meters. The main personal weapons were the 9mm SAF Sten carbines and 7.62 self-loading rifles. The former came in handy only at close range, and the latter jammed frequently and had to be kept warm by placing them either next to a stove or inside a sleeping bag. After repeated complaints, the 7.62 self-loading rifles were replaced by a limited number of AK-47s. Light and medium machine guns functioned well, and 81mm mortars were frequently used for harassment fire, causing significant damage to igloos and personnel.

Artillery was the prime means of destruction and dislocation for both sides on the glacier, but the role of gunners has often been underplayed in comparison to the raw and primordial nature of close-quarters combat. Nothing can be more demoralizing than to see an igloo or a bunker shattered by a single shell or to see a comrade suddenly lose a limb to a sudden burst of artillery fire from across the crest line. Much like the impact of airpower, the physical and psychological shock of artillery fire proved to be a decisive force multiplier for the Indian Army in Operation Meghdoot.

The 155mm Bofors gun was the most effective and reliable weapon on the glacier. The maximum range of these guns at high altitudes varies between thirty and thirty-five kilometers, and they can effectively clear all the crest tops. In mid-1988 one battery (six guns) was airlifted to Thoise for deployment in support of operations on the Siachen Glacier.[44] The 130mm medium guns were normally deployed at Chalunkha to support operations in the Southern Sector and at the base camp to supplement the Bofors. The field guns that proved to be most mobile were the 75/24 howitzers, which were used initially, along with the 120mm and 105mm Indian field guns. The 105mm gun has good loft characteristics to negotiate the heights. It has a range of ten to twelve kilometers and can be broken down into three or four modules for transport. Artillery support has always posed a challenge, as the guns were delivered in dismantled condition and had to be assembled.

Brigadier V. K. Sharma was a captain in 1988 when six 105mm field guns were flown in by Mi-17s of 129th Helicopter Unit and dropped at a partially prepared post later named Sehjra (17,000 feet). The ground was determined to be unfit for landing by the large Mi-17 helicopters, so the dismantled guns were dropped from a low altitude. Of the six, only three could be assembled, as the others were lost in crevasses or damaged on impact.

Maintenance of these guns was also a tremendous challenge. The moment things quieted down in the area, the guns were withdrawn to Kumar FLB, which also served as the battalion and battery HQ.[45] In 1989 the entire post and its complement of personnel were buried by an avalanche following a shoot. There were no survivors, and Sehjra was abandoned. However, the guns were later recovered. Located even higher were the ZSU-23 antiaircraft guns and SAM-7 shoulder-fired missiles, which Nanavatty positioned after noticing increased enemy air activity in the area. Adapting to the situation, the ZSU-23 guns would also be used against surface targets.

Artillery engagements on the glacier consisted of several types: punitive, counterbombardment, speculative, or deterrent. Punitive engagements cause maximum destruction to the enemy's combat potential, while counterbombardment engagements target the enemy's gun positions. Speculative engagements are undertaken when target observation is absent, in which case targets are based on OP reports. Deterrent engagements precede an ongoing ground operation or large-scale aerial resupply operation. A typical shoot involved an OP report of troop or logistics movement, along with calculated coordinates. During the initial months of the conflict, there was an attempt to place an artillery officer in most OPs, but later, most infantry officers and even junior commissioned officers were trained to direct artillery shoots. On clear days, Cheetah helicopters directed shoots too. Through a continuous method of trial and error, enemy posts would be registered and then engaged, often with deadly effect. Edward Desmond reported a conversation he had with an Indian officer: "The rules of engagement are clear-cut on both sides: if there is a target, fire. Artillery observers posted on peaks and ridgelines keep watch day and night with night-vision equipment after dark for the other side's patrols and supply columns. We wait for them to be well out in the open where they cannot run for cover."[46]

The fiercest artillery battles on the glacier—particularly in the Bilafond La complex (Northern Sector), K and D Posts (Central Sector), and R Post (Southern Sector)—took place in 1989 and 1990. For example, in 1990 there were approximately 190 exchanges of small-arms fire and more than 400 exchanges of artillery fire in the Bilafond La complex. The Indians fired more than 5,000 rounds, and the Pakistanis retaliated with more than 6,000 rounds—not because the Pakistanis were more aggressive but because they had a larger number of Indian posts to engage.[47]

LIFELINE PROVIDERS

Engineers are always a critical combat support arm, particularly in hostile terrain such as deserts or mountains. Never had engineers from the Indian

Army had to cut their way through glaciers, ice, and crevasses as they did in Operation Meghdoot. They had no doubt opened the Baltal–Zoji La axis in 1948 and facilitated the defense of Leh, but this was a different ballgame. Brigadier A. K. Ramesh, a former chief engineer at Fourteenth Corps in Leh, is a soft-spoken and articulate sapper who highlighted some of the major engineering tasks that can make or break operations on the icy heights—the toughest being what he described as "lifeline and survival tasks" to facilitate mobility, connectivity, and life itself.[48] These included providing crossings over crevices spanning more than eighty feet, constructing helipads at extremely high altitudes, and fabricating living and observation shelters with the ingenuity and intelligence that India's sappers have displayed since World War II. In the early years, the engineers used extendable aluminum ladders with fabricated sockets, perforated steel plate sheets, and empty jerry cans, as well as natural shelters, fiberglass sheets, and drop parachutes, to supplement the insulated arctic tents as they built "homes" for the boys in olive green. Apart from their many routine tasks, the engineers maintained the snow scooters that are indispensable on the glaciers.

Supporting the Indian Army's resolve and dogged determination were the air warriors of the Indian Air Force and the Indian Army's Aviation Corps. Flying in and out of Siachen is hazardous in the extreme. Appreciating the challenges faced by aviators on the glacier, Nanavatty is effusive in his praise for them: "Air operations call for nerve, courage, and exceptional flying skill. There is no margin for error and even less hope of recovery. Routinely pushing man and machine beyond all known limits, they really are 'our magnificent men in their flying machines.'"[49]

7

Flyboys over the Glacier

For the men confined to the white wilderness, the characteristic shrill whine of the single-engine Cheetah and the flutter of its rotors as it comes in to land is as soothing as a mother's heartbeat is to her infant child. The base camp helipad notches up as many as seventy landings and take-offs, making it the busiest helipad in the country, if not in the world.

—W. P. S. Sidhu, "Tenuous Lifeline"

ANGELS FROM THE SKIES

There was much action in the early 1990s in the Central and Southern Sectors of the Siachen Glacier.[1] The Indian Army had established several helipads across the glacier, and there was hectic flying by the Cheetah helicopters of 114th Helicopter Unit, several Mi-17 helicopter units of the Indian Air Force (IAF), and 666th Air Observation Post Squadron from the army's aviation arm. It is a matter of great pride for any helicopter pilot to be posted to these units, as the assignment is one of the most challenging in the world. By 1984, 114th Helicopter Unit had been reequipped with the Cheetah light utility helicopter, a variant of the Chetak with skis. It could land on tiny makeshift helipads at dizzying heights of over 21,000 feet, which even the manufacturer considered well beyond its capabilities.

Air Commodore Shashank Mishra was a young flying officer with the Siachen Pioneers (114th Helicopter Unit) between 1990 and 1992. He recollects that new pilots were whisked straight to the station's sick quarters, where a mandatory examination by the friendly doctor was followed by three days of restful acclimatization.[2] Mild diarrhea and headache were common because of hypoxia (lack of oxygen). Meals consisted of small portions of packaged food that included powdered eggs and precooked chapatis (flat breads), with regular treats awaiting the pilots when they landed at the army helipads. Usually most of the unit flew off early in the morning, leaving behind three or four pilots who were either recuperating from illness or had flown the maximum of sixty hours a month. Very rarely was anyone who was fit and available found on the "not on program" list.

FLYING ON THE GLACIER

There were three approaches to the Siachen Glacier for the flyboys. The Nubra Valley ended at the base camp and enabled access to the Northern Sector. The highest posts in the glacier at heights between 18,000 and 21,000 feet lay there—Amar, Sonam, Gyong La, Bilafond La, Sehjra, Sia La, and Camp V, among many others. Immediately west of the base camp was access to the valleys leading to the Central Sector. Major helipads there were at J, C, and G-3 posts. Then there was a narrow valley leading steeply to Z helipad, the highest in the sector at 18,000 feet. There was also a southern approach to the glacier through Shyok Valley from Thoise, which is a critical air base near Partapur, at the head of the Shyok River, and headquarters (HQ) of the Siachen Brigade. Halts were made en route at Chalunkha, which served as the logistics base for this sector for support through the valleys leading to the important posts of G, B, and R, all of which were at heights of 14,000 to 15,000 feet.

The first sortie to the glacier had to be earned, but outfitting the pilots came first. The North Atlantic Treaty Organization (NATO) suit—so called because it was procured from Europe—was the standard cold-weather uniform for NATO air forces. However, these were in short supply, so IAF pilots usually inherited a used jacket, along with the trousers and the inner layer. These items usually had to be altered and repaired before use. Buying shoes for cold-weather operations at Chandigarh was the next step. The pilots then underwent a period of general handling of the aircraft to get used to the aerodynamics and engine characteristics at high altitudes and low temperatures. Then the pilots began the process of earning the coveted title of "glacier captain." It started with 100 hours of flying over the glacier as a copilot, assisting the captain with safety procedures and power management, monitoring load cards for various helipads, and closing doors. If they got lucky, a magnanimous captain would hand them the controls for a while, which did wonders for their confidence. It was tough going, and copilots had to earn the confidence of their captains before they were certified to fly in tough weather and terrain conditions. The glacier overawes most pilots with its unforgiving, dangerous, and gaping blue ice crevasses. The sensation of whiteout is common, and it takes some getting used to.

In the early days, army helipads were made of flattened cardboard cartons and marked with embedded coffee powder, which stood out in the snow. They could barely accommodate the skids of a Cheetah helicopter. Helipads were often elevated with "gullies" on the sides, where the waiting troops could protect themselves from the icy downwash of the rotors during landing and takeoff. The approaches and takeoffs were tricky, and any unplanned variation could have catastrophic consequences. These were discussed at length during preflight emergency sessions. Young pilots dreaded these sessions because one wrong simulated action would incur the wrath of the flight commander.

In winter, pilots were woken at around 4:30 a.m. by an orderly with a steaming cup of *solja* (a local tea) and an effervescent greeting of "*Jullay saab le*" (Good morning, sir). While the *saab* tried to muster the courage to emerge from his heavy quilt and into the freezing room, orderlies would light up the *bukhari* (a traditional Kashmiri wood heater). The orderlies would then give the pilots their first weather briefing, which was generally as accurate as the official briefing that followed. While walking to the briefing hall, pilots tried to guess the prevailing temperature based on the amount of pain in their limbs. Anything lower than -15 degrees Celsius meant more pain. The preflight briefing at 5:30 a.m. was followed by a quick meal, a hot cup of tea, and a concurrent sortie briefing before heading out for the day. The unit's engineering officer, warrant officer, and early-morning ground crew started their day an hour before the pilots arrived to complete their preflight servicing and checks in the numbing cold.

Usually a four-ship formation would be readied for departure: the commanding officer and flight commander (numbers 1 and 3), with younger captains as wingmen (numbers 2 and 4). Rookies were generally copilots. The first challenge was negotiating the steep ascent over Khardung La, which lay sixteen kilometers east of Leh and had to be crossed at 18,500 feet. This was followed by a descent and a relatively comfortable ride down to the Nubra Valley. Along the way, an air traffic controller in a mobile station at Thoise would exchange a few pleasantries and some banter before his voice faded away as the helicopters entered the Nubra Valley.

An hour later, the helicopters would land at the base camp at an elevation of 11,500 feet. Since 114th Helicopter Unit also kept two or three helicopters at Thoise, it had a lead time of about an hour over the Leh formation. As the Leh formation approached the base camp, those pilots often saw their comrades disappearing into the mouth of the glacier for their first mission to Amar and Sonam. These two highest helipads could not be negotiated easily after 11:00 a.m., so the small window that opened at dawn had to be exploited. The helicopters from Leh followed, making four to five approaches to Amar and Sonam.[3] The late breakfast served at the base camp between missions was unique. An igloo was used as the crew room–cum–cafeteria, and the troops on duty made the pilots a scrumptious Maggi (noodle) omelet.

PUSHING THE ENVELOPE

Each battalion on the glacier had a loadmaster, usually a junior commissioned officer who was an expert in prioritizing loads and estimating the weight of each bag by sight. He had an eye for detail and could easily juggle loads to ensure that the odd soldier could be accommodated on board. These little things made him everyone's best friend. Mishra recalled:

> One morning, while landing in whiteout conditions, an army captain who was the post commander had tears rolling down his cheeks and insisted that I accept a bag of cashews as a gift. This was a helipad where perhaps a sortie landed a few times a week. Troops would look forward to mail from home and it was heartrending looking at bleeding lips and faces covered in black polish to ward off UV [ultraviolet] rays while we were clad in NATO suits and shaven fresh as daisies. We were grateful that we served those who defended the borders in such difficult conditions, and they for the little conveniences we offered in terms of an occasional pickup to the base camp—saving days of treacherous treks—or simply a letter or a cake delivered just in time.[4]

Maintaining radio silence while flying led to the development of a unique system that warned of enemy shelling at an intended destination. Helicopters approached for landing from below the helipad, gradually climbing until the pilots could barely discern the surface of the helipad. Then they would fly in and hover before landing. One of the copilot's secondary tasks was to count the black marks left by artillery shells on the white snow around the helipads. If there were several, it indicated that the area was unsafe, and the approach would be terminated. As backup, the troops at the post would place a red flag in the center of the helipad as a warning, in case the copilots missed the black marks. They would then radio the base camp for artillery support from the Bofors or 130mm guns to silence the enemy guns and ensure that the helicopters could land safely. Most of the enemy gun positions were registered, so the enemy knew what was about to happen. In a way, it was like a silly comedy.

The Cheetah squadron's capacity to carry loads was rather limited and could be compared to ants going about their business with grit and determination. The Cheetahs delivered about forty tonnes of supplies each month to posts that could not be sustained by the heavier Mi-17 helicopters. They were truly a lifeline for these higher posts. Mishra lived through some dangerous moments on 3 June 1990, when an IAF Cheetah was hit by a burst of enemy ground fire, experienced engine failure, and was forced to land at the Amar helipad (19,500 feet). Troops of the Eleventh Battalion of the Sikh

Light Infantry and an IAF maintenance crew changed the engine at those hostile altitudes and made the aircraft airworthy within days.[5] It was able to be flown out, just as 666th Air Observation Post had done from Point 6400 (approximately 21,000 feet) the previous year, during the final phase of Operation Ibex.

A couple of years later, in early August 1992, Indian fire brought down a Pakistan Army Lama light-utility helicopter with Brigadier Masood Anwari, the 323rd Infantry Brigade commander, on board. Expecting an escalation of hostilities after the incident, both sides stopped flying over the glacier for a while. This caused great hardship and forced the two countries' director-generals of military operations to discuss de-escalation. Flying was resumed on 14 August 1992, after both sides realized that it would be prudent to de-escalate to avoid losing men at their air-maintained posts. The Southern Sector also witnessed intense action over unoccupied heights and ridgelines that dominated the approaches to Indian posts B, G, and R. On 26 August 1996 the occupation of one of these ridgelines by Pakistani troops resulted in the shooting down of an IAF Mi-17 that was on a supply mission to one of these posts. It is suspected that another Indian Cheetah helicopter crashed in the same sector on 2 July 1997 due to enemy fire.[6]

THE WORKHORSES OF SIACHEN

The versatile Russian Mi-17 helicopters proved to be an excellent replacement for the Mi-8 helicopters in 1986. The Mi-8s had done a wonderful job up to that time, but they had started to develop serious engine problems and other issues because of their age. Three Mi-17 helicopter units initially took on air maintenance duties on the glacier from the late 1980s onward: 127th Helicopter Unit commanded by Wing Commander Fali Major, the first helicopter pilot to become chief of air staff; 128th Helicopter Unit commanded by Wing Commander Mike Dutt; and 129th Helicopter Unit, with Group Captain Harpal "Harry" Ahluwalia at the helm. These units maintained detachments at Thoise in a rotation comprising a group of very senior pilots who had combat experience in Mi-4 and Mi-8 helicopters. Ahluwalia and Major were almost permanent members of the Thoise detachment, preferring the adrenaline rush of flying on the glacier to the urban environment of the air force station at Hindon near Delhi, where the units were based.

The typical load for an Mi-17 parachute or free drop was 1.8 tons of ammunition boxes, dismantled artillery pieces, and dry rations. All drop zones were on the glacier floor except at J and G-3, which were on subsidiary glaciers in the Central Sector. All the valleys were narrow, and loads had to be transported to higher posts such as Amar and Sonam on snow scooters because they did not have helipads or drop zones. This exercise demanded exceptional skill, and Mi-17 crews were fascinated to watch the scooters reduced to specks in the white landscape as they disappeared up the subsidiary glaciers. According to Ahluwalia, 1988 and 1989 were particularly tough years at the base camp, as Pakistani artillery periodically targeted it from gun positions on the Chumik Glacier. In response, Colonel K. S. Jamwal, commander of Thirty-Sixth Maratha Medium Regiment—the Bofors unit at the base camp—let loose six rounds of rationed ammunition across the actual ground position line (AGPL) to welcome Ahluwalia when he landed there. Enemy mortars commenced firing the moment the Pakistanis heard the helicopters heading toward the valleys close to Amar and Sonam, which were key posts in the Bilafond La complex. This forced the helicopters to take a different route every day. When asked about Brigadiers Nugyal and Nanavatty, Ahluwalia replied, "They were tough guys, great soldiers."[7]

The winter of 1988 brought terrible flying weather, creating a tremendous backlog in missions. As soon as the weather improved, there was a frenzy to catch up. To support Operation Ibex in the Central Sector, the posts at Kaman and Thapa Base had to be reinforced. These were lifelines to the isolated section on Point 6400. On 22 April 1989 Ahluwalia flew thirteen sorties. He remarked:

> We loved it—flying, switching off, refuelling, loading, dropping and back again. We made up for the winter shortfall that month. Along the way, we were once buzzed by fighter aircraft, albeit accidentally, when an IAF MiG-23 from Air Force Station Adampur, piloted by one of the commanding officers on a routine reconnaissance, decided to descend and see what it meant to streak across the glacier floor at 800 kilometers an hour as we were on a dropping mission. It was a narrow shave but all's well that ends well. At the end of Operation Ibex, Air Marshal M. M. Singh, the Air Officer Commanding-in-Chief (AOC-in-C) of Western Air Command, and Lieutenant General B. C. Nanda, the Northern Army Commander, flew in to Thoise to congratulate the unit on some stupendous flying. The AOC-in-C even wrote me a nice letter.[8]

THE FIXED-WING HEROES

The IAF's heavy-lift transport aircraft, the IL-76, was the mainstay of the Indian Army's continuous troop movements onto the glacier. The versatile An-32s complemented the Mi-17 helicopters in air maintenance operations. They delivered various loads at the drop zones at the base camp, the Kumar forward logistics base (supporting the Bilafond La complex), and the northernmost Rani (supporting the Sia La complex). Group Captain K. S. Lamba recently commanded Forty-Eighth Squadron (the Camels), which is equipped with An-32 aircraft. An old glacier hand, Lamba routinely woke up bleary-eyed at 4:00 on cold winter mornings to make a 5:00 briefing and a 6:00 takeoff for a drop sortie over the glacier.[9] Arising two hours before their commanding officer, the technical crew prepared the aircraft for flight even as the loadmaster and the logistics team from the army loaded the aircraft. From a fixed-wing aviator's perspective, the Siachen Glacier was not as difficult to negotiate as the narrow and misty valleys in the northeast. However, the loss of power or some other emergency were everyday risks. As one squadron pilot put it, "Every risk we faced in our pressurized cockpit paled in front of the existential threat to life that officers and men of the Indian Army face on the glacier."[10]

The main logistics lifeline for the Leh-based Fourteenth Corps is the Srinagar–Leh National Highway 1A, but it is complemented extensively by air maintenance from Chandigarh, where a major portion of the IAF's air transport assets are located. This base is home to one of the heavy-lift IL-76 aircraft squadrons, the only heavy-lift Mi-26 helicopter unit, and the ever-reliable and recently upgraded An-32 medium-lift transport aircraft. Life- and mission-sustaining loads are prepared there for delivery to Siachen and the desolate areas of eastern Ladakh, even as troops assemble there for the move to Thoise. A regular day for the Camels begins at 3:00 a.m., as the aircraft are prepared for forward-area drop missions. The operations room is active by 4:00 a.m., with a never-ending flow of coffee, tea, and sandwiches. As the crew is prepared and briefed for the mission, dozens of army trucks position their loads on the huge tarmac. The loading process is both manual and mechanical, demanding good teamwork from the flight engineer–cum– loadmaster and his army counterparts. By 5:00 a.m., all the briefings and weather reports have been assessed, and the aircrew is set for takeoff as the first rays of sunlight filter through the gray sky.

A normal flying day involves two waves of four to five aircraft each, as the squadron attempts to beat the weather, which normally starts to deteriorate by noon. Climbing to almost 30,000 feet, the An-32s cross the breathtaking Zanskar and Ladakh Ranges in a northeasterly direction, turning north at Leh and crossing the Khardung La Pass. Then they descend to fly over Partapur, Thoise, and the base camp at speeds of 550 kilometers an hour at 1,000 feet above the glacier floor. Along the way, they cross the mountain passes of Rohtang La, Kunzum La, Chang La, and Khardung La; the winding Satluj and Chandra Rivers; and the scenic Spiti, Indus, and Nubra Valleys. The lakes of Kartso and Tso Morari are an equally enchanting sight. The crew, however, seldom has time to take in these views. Instead, crew members compete with one another to assign peculiar names to landmarks to allow easy identification while flying. These come in handy during emergencies. For instance, IAF crews may identify certain landmark peaks and mountains as an ice cream cone, a temple, a tiger, or an elephant.

The activity level picks up as the aircraft approaches the drop zone. The captain initiates a quick review of escape routes in case of engine failure or emergency decompression. In the event of such contingencies, the aircraft would have to descend below the hills and make a crash-landing. Sighting ground features beyond a certain distance is therefore mandatory for the crew, and this visual acquisition also determines the feasibility of the drop. Weather, wind, and air traffic determine the drop plan. There is another quick briefing in the air by the captain while the loadmaster gets busy preparing the load. Troops at the posts and the drop zone keep their ears open for the sound of an An-32 engine. The drop zones are marked with an orange "T," and smoke is blown to help the aircrew assess wind speed. Strong winds at such altitudes are the norm, and even a small difference in wind speed can drastically affect the precision of the drop. This activity requires a lot of skill, coordination, and composure.

When the cargo ramp door is open, the entire crew must use oxygen. Severe turbulence close to the ground and deteriorating weather in the afternoon present significant challenges as the captain makes his final alignment. The countdown to the drop zone is called out aloud in the cockpit as the aircraft is held steady in a gradual descent with the cargo ramp fully open and the load skids raring to go. As the load exits the aircraft, the orange and white parachutes deploy—there is no better sight for the troops waiting below than seeing them land in sequence in the designated drop zone. The route back is equally tricky, and the aircrew cannot afford to let their guard down until they clear the Zoji La Pass. By 9:00 a.m., the steel birds touch down at their home base. The machines are prepared for the next mission, while the crews use this time for a quick bite before their second sortie of the day. An-32 operations on the glacier epitomize the spirit of "jointmanship" that is so strong at the tactical and operational levels. Jointmanship is "a term exclusively used within the Indian armed forces to highlight synergy and interoperability between the three services."[11]

RARE ATMOSPHERE—IAF FIGHTERS PITCH IN

There is a misconception that only the helicopter and transport fleets of the IAF and the helicopters of the Army Aviation Corps participated in the Siachen Conflict and the ongoing tension along the line of control in the area. During my tenure (1983–1985) in 108th Squadron, a MiG-21 squadron in

Adampur (an air base near the town of Jalandhar in Punjab), we shared the base with 223rd and 224th Squadrons, the two MiG-23 MF squadrons. At the time, they were the IAF's main air defense fighters, as neither the MiG-29 nor the Mirage-2000 had been inducted yet. They used to call themselves the first "air superiority fighters" in the IAF—which evoked much mirth when the Mirage-2000s and MiG-29s came in.

The MiG-23 MF was a brute of a machine, weighing a monstrous fifteen tons and having an engine that generated a thrust of almost thirteen tons. It was a formidable platform at high altitudes because of its powerful engine and ability to vary the lift. It had a variable geometry wing—that is, the wing could be swept to fourteen, forty-five, or seventy-two degrees, depending on maneuverability requirements. For example, the aircraft could achieve top speeds only when the wings were swept back to seventy-two degrees. It was, however, most maneuverable when the wings were swept forward to four-teen degrees, and it cruised best at a forty-five-degree sweep angle. During the mid-1980s the MiG-23 MF was the only IAF fighter that could face the significantly more advanced F-16 that had recently been inducted into the Pakistan Air Force (PAF).

Several of my contemporaries spent their formative years flying the MiG-23 MF at Adampur and performing missions about which they had very little prior knowledge. For example, the evening before, they would be told only that they were to escort a Canberra bomber–turned–reconnaissance platform on a mission "up north." One morning in April 1988, Wing Commander "Cheech" Brar and his number 2, who is still serving in the IAF, took off from Adampur to carry out an aerial rendezvous with a single Canberra well before crossing the line of control. Climbing to 26,000 feet, they headed north over the Burzil Range that separates the Kashmir Valley from the Gilgit and Baltistan areas of Pakistan-occupied Kashmir. Using the Nun Kun peak as a navigational aid, they ducked down to 500 feet above the ground as soon as they crossed the range, to avoid radar detection. Skardu, their destination, is less than 150 kilometers away from the closest point on the line of control, and it takes barely ten minutes to reach it at 850 kilometers an hour—the optimal speed for fighter jets at low level. This time, however, the MiG-23s had to match the slower speeds of the Canberra; as a result, the formation had to intrude into hostile airspace at around 700 kilometers an hour.

The plan was for the Canberra to carry out a high-speed run over Skardu, photograph some newly added infrastructure, and then head southward at top speed. The MiG-23s would form a defensive shield against the possibility of being intercepted by PAF F-16s—which, according to intelligence reports, were occasionally deployed in Skardu. Unbeknownst to Brar, there was another formation on a similar mission from the other squadron on base. They were streaking toward Skardu, along with another Canberra from the same squadron, but along a different run-in direction. After flying along the Nubra Valley into the Siachen Glacier area, the second formation crossed the Kumar forward logistics base, turned west, crossed the Bilafond La complex, and ducked down as low as possible to head for Skardu airfield. Brar's number 2 was the first to spot a glint in the east and was tempted to radio his leader about the likely threat emanating from the right. He decided to wait a couple of seconds and soon recognized the MiG-23s. Just to be safe, Brar asked the Canberra to turn back. The PAF was not amused, but it rarely interfered with these missions because it had insufficient radar cover to prevent such intrusions.[12]

On another occasion, a MiG-23 pilot saw two F-16s parked on the tarmac at Skardu airfield. They were part of small detachment the PAF maintained at Skardu during good weather. In the 1980s the strike version of the MiG-23—the MiG-23 BN—buzzed Skardu occasionally. MiG-23 MFs also escorted the MiG-25 high-speed and high-altitude reconnaissance aircraft on photo runs over the glacier and during intrusive missions toward Skardu and Gilgit. In later years, MiG-21 and MiG-29 squadrons regularly entered the Siachen Glacier area and flew along the Nubra Valley to familiarize themselves with the terrain; these were known as "milk runs" because of the absence of any action in the air. The IAF fighter fleet thus acquired some high-altitude operational experience during Operation Meghdoot, albeit without engaging in combat or attacking ground targets. This would later be useful when the IAF was called on to help the Indian Army evict Pakistani troops from the Kargil heights, not far from Siachen.

THE STORM SUBSIDES: POINT 5770 FALLS

Thirteen years after Operation Blue Star, Lieutenant General Prakash Katoch found himself commanding the Siachen Brigade at a time when the Northern and Central Sectors were relatively stable. The action had shifted to the Southern and Chorbat La Sectors.[13] Katoch's tenure from late 1997 to November 1999 coincided with General Musharraf's attempts to create an arc of instability from the Mushkoh Valley in the west to the Southern Sector of the Siachen Glacier. This would cost the Indians dearly and culminate in the Kargil Conflict of 1999. Katoch got his first glimpse of the glacier in 1990. Interacting with Nanavatty—the Siachen Brigade commander—inspired the combat-proven paratrooper to set his sights on command of this elite formation. Seven years later, in July 1997, Katoch volunteered to command the brigade and found himself at the helm, replacing Brigadier Randhir Singh.

Katoch determined that the Southern Sector merited attention and foresaw that it would emerge as an extended battlefront if the Indian Army neglected it. In his initial operational assessment, he identified two areas as particularly vulnerable. The first was Point 5770 and the ridgelines that ran west, south, and north. The second was the underpatrolled forty-kilometer gap at Chorbat La, between the western limits of 102nd Infantry Brigade's area of responsibility and the eastern limits of the Kargil Brigade. Making matters more difficult was the temporary cessation of IAF operations in the sector in 1997. The IAF had been forced to do so after Pakistan shot down an Indian Mi-17 helicopter during a supply drop sortie to B and G posts in retaliation for the loss of a brigade commander. This meant that, for months, the Southern Sector had to be maintained on foot and by the occasional Cheetah sortie.

It soon became clear to Katoch that Point 5770 stood like a sentinel in the area, and if the Pakistanis crept to the top, they would be able to dominate several Indian posts and logistics routes by directing effective fire onto the area. Anticipating this, he assembled an assault task force composed of the Twenty-Seventh Battalion of the Rajput Regiment, the Ladakh Scouts, a team of high-altitude warfare school instructors, and Fifth Parachute Battalion. This task force advanced on Point 5770 via its southern and northern shoulders. Throughout 1998 the Indians made concerted attempts to reach Point 5770 but failed because of the challenges posed by terrain and weather. Instead, the teams managed to set up small posts along the route as launchpads for further assaults. Katoch, however, was not done with Point 5770, particularly when the Pakistanis set up a post 600 meters west of it in mid-1999 as the Kargil Conflict raged.

Colonel K. H. Singh, the commanding officer of Twenty-Seventh Rajput, reported to Katoch a few weeks after commencement of the Kargil Conflict that the Pakistanis indeed may have reached Point 5770. This galvanized Katoch into action. He decided that the only way to surprise the enemy was a vertical assault from the east with a small team during the summer. After obtaining speedy approval for an assault from division HQ, Katoch and Singh put together a crack assault team made up of Major Navdeep Singh Cheema (Twenty-Seventh Rajput), Captain Shyamal Sinha (Kumaon Regiment), Havildar Dola Ram (First Parachute Battalion), and six or seven additional men. Their instructions were clear: launch a vertical assault in broad daylight from the east, where the enemy least expected them.

The assault team climbed for seven hours in full combat gear carrying AK-47s and carbines. They reached the post at 2:00 p.m. and took the defenders by surprise. Eleven defenders were killed in close combat. The attackers found communication lines and *sangars* (rock shelters) a short distance from the summit. Among those killed was Captain Taimur Malik, the grandson of a Pakistani politician and the brother of Pakistan's defense attaché in Washington. Three letters were found on his person. One was from his father, who had fought the Indians in Bangladesh and taken up arms as a jihadi after his retirement from the Pakistan Army. The father exhorted his son to continue fighting the Indians. The second letter was from Malik's mother, inquiring about his health and well-being. The third had been written by Malik himself and stated, "We have reached the top and are going to give them hell." At the Pakistanis' request, Katoch transported the bodies of the dead to Kargil, where they were handed over during a flag meeting. While the Kargil Conflict was still raging, Cheema and Sinha were awarded Vir Chakras, and other members of the team were given Sena medals. Colonel K. H. Singh was awarded a Yudh Seva medal for his inspiring leadership of Twenty-Seventh Rajput.

Discussions of joint operations and synergy with the IAF evoked a mixed response from Katoch. From his perspective, and based on his experience, it was clear that the trajectory of jointmanship, whether in peace or in conflict, was determined by individuals and not by inbuilt mechanisms. In contrast, Air Chief Marshal Fali Major has fond memories of his time spent with the army as base commander at Leh:

> With regards to interservice relations, I had an excellent tie-up with Fourteenth Corps, Third Mountain Division, and the Batalik and Siachen Brigades. With army stalwarts like Rostum Nanavatty, Katoch, Panag, and Arjun Ray, it was great going and I really enjoyed my association with them. My previous experience of commanding two Mi-17 units and operating in the same area of my responsibility now was an added benefit and no one could poodle-fake me! I spent three winters there![14]

Colonel A. Jayaram is a seasoned army aviator and rotary-wing test pilot. He was the commander of 666th Air Observation Post Squadron at Partapur and saw much action during Katoch's tenure as brigade commander. Although the unit's area of responsibility extended from Batalik Sector eastward across the Siachen Glacier into subsector north in eastern Ladakh, almost 70 percent of its flying was in support of the Siachen Brigade. When asked about Katoch, Jayaram said, "He was always on the move and wanted to be where the troops were. He visited almost all posts and would fly out to an accessible helipad. Then he'd walk up to inaccessible posts to see for himself how his men were doing. I recollect that he even spent a few days at Sonam, one of the highest posts in the Northern Sector."[15]

According to Jayaram, the most challenging missions were casualty evacuations in inclement weather and during twilight. He explained, "The stakes were high—those were course mates with whom we have broken bread, stayed on our haunches and rolled together as cadets at the National Defence Academy and the Indian Military Academy; regimental colleagues, bodies lying in the same bunker and much more." Highlighting some of the risky missions undertaken by his unit during Katoch's tenure, Jayaram reflected, "We continued to selectively break existing peacetime rules and launched missions even late in the afternoon. We would then come in to land at Partapur in the dark with an improvised electrical flare-path and not kerosene lamp goosenecks, as the wind speed was too high and we ran the risk of starting a fire. It was action all the way and immensely satisfying."[16]

TRAINING

Led over the years by some of India's hardiest and most courageous officers from all over the country, the 102nd Infantry Brigade remains a prestigious and coveted command even today. A survey of the units deployed on the glacier between December 1989 and February 1993 reveals a mix of ten regiments with a truly Pan-Indian flavor.[17] Brigadier V. M. B. Krishnan, a recent commander of the brigade, spoke about the travails of commanding troops on the icy heights of the Saltoro Ridge and Siachen Glacier. He emphasized, "The key to survival and efficiency on the glacier were fitness, mental agility, and situational awareness." He added, "Upper-body strength and oxygen retention capability were more important than classical endurance. Coping with contingencies brought about by the weather and medical emergencies were the ultimate tests of mental agility, even more than facing fire. On the glacier, every man had to extract that extra bit all the time, to survive the three to six months that constitutes a normal tenure."[18]

Thoise remains the gateway to the glacier as the aerial maintenance hub. A steady stream of IL-76, An-32, and, more recently, heavy-lift C-17 aircraft and Chinook helicopters arrives loaded with troops, guns, rations, and letters from Chandigarh to sustain life and operations on the glacier. Today, Partapur is a bustling military camp at the confluence of the Nubra and Shyok Rivers and remains the HQ of India's Siachen Brigade. Long convoys line the road from Partapur to the base camp. A similar scenario unfolds at Dansam, across the line of control, where Pakistan's 323rd Brigade is located. Convoys head to Gayari, a battalion HQ and the major logistics hub on the Pakistanis' side of the war zone.

On the Indian side, new units of soldiers and officers eagerly make their way to the Siachen Battle School, a short distance away on the upper reaches of the base camp, for a three-week high-altitude inoculation module. Every soldier takes this program seriously because he knows his life depends on it. Failure to complete the module is a stigma that is hard to shake off. The school was set up by Brigadier Nugyal and expanded by Brigadier Nanavatty. Major Basil Hobkirk from the Brigade of the Guards was its first commanding officer. The scope of the training program is wide. The initial focus is on mountain awareness, ice craft, and rock climbing, followed by survival training, weapons and equipment training, and high-altitude leadership and administrative training for officers and junior commissioned officers. Then it is time for tactical training on reading the battle, situational awareness, setting up posts, night operations, and directing artillery fire. The preinduction training process for an infantry battalion commences with a three-week program for instructors, including the firing of all specialized infantry weapons such as medium machine guns, heavy machine guns, 81mm mortars, 120mm Grad P launchers, 84mm rocket launchers, and sniper rifles. This group is then responsible for training the rest of the battalion in the second phase of preinduction training. Artillery units have their own training program. After the completion of two weeks of standard training, there are specialized modules for manning gun positions, snowmobile operations, and managing helicopter operations. The whole process of inducting an infantry battalion or artillery regiment takes about two months from the start of acclimatization until the unit disperses to its posts.[19]

Over the years, the Indian Special Forces have gained significant low-temperature, high-altitude fighting experience on the glacier. Nanavatty played a part here, too, translating his experience in the United Kingdom into standard operating procedures for the Indian armed forces. Posted to the United Kingdom in 1985 as Indian Army liaison officer, but with no clear charter, Nanavatty concentrated on understanding how the Royal Marine commandos and the elite British Special Boa Service (SBS) trained and fought, particularly in the mountains and in the Arctic. Spending two weeks in Norway with the SBS in the middle of winter was nowhere close to the conditions in Siachen, but it was an eye-opener nevertheless. Nanavatty was impressed with the British training regimen, situational awareness, and fighting skills, as well as the easy understanding and familiarity within units and the outstanding leadership skills displayed by noncommissioned officers, who shouldered great responsibility. Developing the leadership skills of junior officers has been among the most challenging tasks for every Siachen Brigade commander.

LEADERSHIP AND MOTIVATION

The main leadership challenge on the glacier was keeping the troops motivated to fight fear, isolation, monotony, superstition, passivity, and foolhardiness. Subedar Major (the highest-ranked junior commissioned officer) Satheesan from the Madras Regiment was initially enrolled in the Assam Regiment in 1988 and served on the glacier in 1992. He was awarded the Shaurya Chakra for the gallantry he displayed in the Kashmir Valley during counterterrorism operations in 1996. Satheesan boarded an aircraft for the first time in his life at Chandigarh as his battalion was inducted into Thoise and then sent to the base camp for acclimatization. He spent a month at Hathi Post (19,588 feet), along with eight other soldiers, and then another two months at a post that was maintained by air and where firing was random and sudden. Being better educated than some of his comrades, Satheesan was assigned the task of overseeing daily letter-writing and -reading sessions to maintain morale by sharing family and village happenings. Another *havildar* was responsible for ensuring that no one went hungry, despite the frequent loss of appetite. Dry fruits were a vital source of energy. According to Satheesan, there was a superstition that the spirits on the glacier shaved two years off the lives of those who dared to live there. Whenever morale slipped, men drew strength by remembering the exploits of the soldiers who, with nothing but grit and determination, had secured the heights they now occupied. Evacuation by foot or ropeway was dreaded, particularly in adverse weather conditions, and whenever sections were relieved for rest and recovery, the first stop after the descent to base camp was the unit's place of worship.[20]

Other than basic survival training and maintaining morale, building professional pride was a challenge. It was achieved through alertness, self-discipline, and controlled aggression, along with the courage and will to win. Junior and senior leaders on the glacier had no choice but to set a personal example in terms of physical fitness, mental agility, and the robustness to plan, organize, and execute in a such a way that "your men will follow you to hell and back."[21] Also required was the ability to empathize and show genuine concern for the soldiers' welfare. Echoing Napoleon, Nanavatty said, "On the glacier, there are no good or bad battalions, only good or bad officers."[22]

A PRICE TO PAY

The Indian Army—and the IAF, to a lesser extent—has paid a heavy price for domination of the Siachen Glacier. The Indian Army has lost more than 850 officers and men, and others are still suffering the ill effects of their time on the glacier. Most of those lives were lost not to enemy fire but to the unforgiving elements of nature—primarily avalanches, crevices, blizzards, and whiteouts. Soldiers have experienced high-altitude pulmonary edema, hypoxia, frostbite, hypothermia, altitude sickness, and deep vein thrombosis. Between 1984 and 1990 the Indian Army lost 433 personnel; another 1,787 were injured by a combination of enemy action, terrain accidents, and climatic conditions. Of these, only 102 were killed and 195 wounded by enemy action. Reflecting the ethos of the Indian Army, officers led from the front and put themselves in the line of fire. Eleven officers lost their lives, and another hundred were injured. The latest figures compiled by the *Times of India*—based on various sources, including figures reported to the Indian Parliament and from reliable Pakistani sources—put the total number of Indian soldiers killed as of 2016 at 869, including 33 officers and 55 junior commissioned officers. Pakistan lost an average of three to four more personnel per year.[23]

Although there was a sharp decline in the number of deaths between 2014 and 2015 (with only one loss of life in 2015), an avalanche in 2016 left a battalion of the Madras Regiment mourning the loss of more than ten soldiers. Miraculously, Lance Naik Hanumanthappa was rescued after being buried in the snow for six days, but he succumbed to multiorgan failure a few days later. His death sensitized the nation to the perils of serving on the glacier and revived the debate about the futility of holding on to it. In addition, the numerous amputations necessitated by frostbite and gangrene have left hundreds of soldiers maimed for life. Many are also dealing with the psychological disorders that are inevitable in such unforgiving conditions.

Much of the modern survival equipment to ensure soldier comfort and efficiency was bought during George Fernandes's tenure as defense minister from 1998 to 2004. He stated in Parliament that the cost of sustaining operations in Siachen was 3 crore per day. Various reports have estimated that three decades of conflict on the glacier have cost more than 15,000 crore. The current costs of maintaining existing force levels are 700 to 800 crore per year,[24] although other estimates have pegged the annual costs at around 2,000 crore during the peak years of conflict. The environmental degradation caused by occupation of the glacier has been precipitous, despite the army's laudable attempts to minimize it. However, anyone who flies over the glacier during the summer can clearly see the extent of the destruction in this once pristine area. It is safe to assume that Pakistan faces similar challenges and tribulations.

RESOLVING THE SIACHEN IMBROGLIO

Following the loss of about 150 Pakistani soldiers and civilians in an avalanche in the Gayari Glacier area in 2012, the Pakistani military establishment, led by General Kayani, put forward a proposal to demilitarize the glacier. But the proposal failed to take India's views on the position of the line of control into account.[25] Before this massive number of casualties, Pakistan's position had always been that it would be doing India a favor by agreeing to discuss resolution of the Siachen imbroglio. It invariably linked Siachen to the larger issue of Kashmir, a proposition that has always been unacceptable to India. Interestingly, Kayani was the director-general of military operations when the historic cease-fire along the international boundary between India and Pakistan was declared in November 2003 but never formalized in writing. Kayani's 2012 proposal was no different from what had transpired in the eight rounds of talks held between 1989 and 1998. The deadlock was strikingly similar every time: before delimiting the line of control beyond NJ 9842, Pakistan wanted India to vacate the heights; it refused to share maps and wanted to go back to the 1971 deployment. Pakistan's view of de-escalation relied solely on an Indian pullout, which the Indians' saw as preposterous.[26]

Katoch has shared some interesting vignettes about India's and Pakistan's efforts to diffuse tensions on the glacier. One such narrative revolved around a 1998 visit to the area by Indian defense secretary Ajit Kumar and a team of officers from the Ministry of External Affairs and Indian Army HQ. At the time, the Americans were trying to get involved as interlocutors, and coincidentally, the US chairman of the Joint Chiefs of Staff was visiting Leh at the same time. During the briefing, the defense secretary asked whether the Indian Army could vacate the Saltoro Ridge, and he got diverse opinions. Katoch was asked to give his views and explained that the entire sector could be enveloped from the west and south by Pakistan and from the east by China, putting Leh within artillery range. "Withdraw this brigade," Katoch warned, "and you will barely have one battalion from Chorbatla to Khardungla against two Chinese divisions in eastern Ladakh."[27]

Katoch was also quite dismissive of the "Mountain of Peace" initiative suggested when Manmohan Singh was prime minister. Katoch described it as a meaningless initiative involving people who had never served on or even been to the glacier. This hard-line view has largely dominated the discourse in the years after the 2003 cease-fire. Former Indian foreign secretary Shyam Saran made a rather startling disclosure in his book *How India Sees the World*, revealing that during the brief India–Pakistan entente (2003–2008), the Manmohan Singh–led Congress Party government almost succeeded in sealing a deal with Pakistan to vacate the Siachen Glacier as part of a larger "peace process."[28] The deal was scuttled following "realistic" inputs based on reports by field commanders and objections from Indian national security adviser M. K. Narayanan.[29] Barring a few incidents, the glacier has been quiet since 2003. However, a permanent solution is still nowhere in sight.

China is accelerating its "dream project" of the Belt Road Initiative, which seeks to connect Tibet and Xinjiang Province with the Arabian Sea at the port of Gwadar. This road will run through the Baltistan region of Pakistan-occupied Kashmir as part of the China–Pakistan Economic Corridor. Pakistan currently holds a few posts on the western slopes of the Saltoro Range ridgeline that are extremely vulnerable to both fire and avalanches. India's position is almost impregnable, as it holds the four highest passes along the entire Saltoro Ridge, as well as numerous other positions along the eastern ridges.

Glacial modeling has revealed the formation and deepening of glacial lakes in the region. One such lake on the Rimo Glacier—which feeds the Shyok River—merits close monitoring. With both the Nubra and Shyok Rivers prone to flash flooding, much of the Indian Army's infrastructure in areas such as Partapur and the base camp is in danger of being washed away. Twenty-three soldiers of a Bihar regiment were lost during the Leh floods of 2010. Although these floods were not directly linked to the melting of the Siachen or any other glacier, they indicate that the region is vulnerable to the effects of climate change and global warming. The lake on the Rimo Glacier could be a disaster waiting to happen, because even a minor earthquake or heavy rainfall could lead to a flash flood.[30] Will the gods finally intervene?

Is there a solution to the problem? In a hard-hitting article published in *Indian Defence Review* in May 2014, Brigadier Karan Kharb reckons that the presence of Indian posts in the vicinity will be a deterrent to China's ambitions to connect Aksai Chin to Baltistan through the Karakoram Pass and Shaksgam Valley.[31] Nanavatty argues that real distances debunk the theory that the heights of the Saltoro Ridge offer a great tactical advantage in terms of visibility into the Shaksgam Valley or the ability to watch over the Karakoram highway. He maintains that agreement on Siachen cannot be reached in isolation, nor can it be based on altruistic aspirations.[32] General Hooda highlights that India–Pakistan negotiations on de-escalation continued until 2007 but stopped when the Indians realized that no headway was being made on the mutual mapping of existing posts and the agreement to use them as the AGPL. This, he argued, was the first step, which could then be followed by an extension and demarcation of the line of control. Only then could troop withdrawals be discussed, given that access to the Saltoro Ridge is much easier from the Pakistan-controlled western slopes.[33]

Brigadier Javed Hassan, a commando from the Pakistan Army's Special Service Group, argues that "the only way out of this morass is to demilitarize this area with the UN acting as the guarantor."[34] This proposition irks the Indians, who see it as a bilateral dispute with no room for any kind of international mediation. The broad consensus in India is that unless there are dramatic concessions from Pakistan and reasonable guarantees from

China, the current Indian government led by Narendra Modi will not yield any space on the desolate battleground. Giving teeth to India's determination to hold on to the Saltoro Ridge is the hectic construction activity by the People's Liberation Army in the Shaksgam Valley abutting the glacier—an area ceded to China by Pakistan in 1963.[35] Even though the proposed road does not lead toward the Saltoro Ridge or the Siachen Glacier, it is provocative action because it runs through disputed territory. However, the sheer absurdity of the conflict demands a resolution and a closing argument.

Nanavatty notes that "the conflict is essentially over preserving territorial integrity and upholding national military pride. It is an irrational conflict in subhuman conditions with significant costs and little prospect of military solution. Its perpetuation does no credit to political and military leadership at the highest levels in both countries." He goes on to suggest that "India's approach to a final settlement should be based on demilitarization of a limited, well-defined and mutually agreed area following a political agreement. There should be a lasting cease-fire, delimiting, demarcation, disengagement, redeployment, verification, and joint monitoring and administration. The bottom line is that peaceful resolution of India–Pakistan disputes is only possible when the two countries cease to view each other as military adversaries."[36]

In contrast, an intransigent and jingoistic Pakistani perspective is offered by Omer Farook Zain: "Particularly, Indians are paying a heavy price for enjoying the beautiful landscape of Siachen. For Pakistan, Siachen glacier is worth the blood spilled over it, and to give it up would be nothing short of giving up its coat of arms."[37] The deterioration in India–Pakistan relations in recent years—and Pakistan's enhanced support of the secessionist movement in Jammu and Kashmir—has ensured that the Siachen issue remains unresolved, despite the cease-fire. Indian and Pakistani soldiers will continue to patrol the glacier, and the best the two countries can hope to do at this juncture is to minimize the human price paid on the glacier. Many of those who have served on the icy heights laugh at this proposition and say, "You have to live there to realize that for those few weeks and months, you have no choice but to draw on all your reserves with a constant prayer on your lips."

8

Standing Up to the Dragon

Operation Falcon was to occupy a forward position in the Tawang Sector to prevent intrusion, improve defensive positions and assert our claim on the Mc-Mahon line. It increased the risk of a war with China.
—Email correspondence, Lieutenant General J. M. Singh, commander, Fifth Mountain Division, during Operation Falcon, 15 June 2019

RISING TENSION

Lieutenant General S. H. F. J. Manekshaw moved to the Western Army Command in November 1963 as its commander in chief. Defense Minister Y. B. Chavan was impressed with Manekshaw's understanding of the ongoing Chinese threat and asked him to move to the eastern theater in late 1964. Manekshaw was entrusted with the task of deterring China from opening a second front should India and Pakistan head for another conflict. Some civilian narratives suggest that Manekshaw was moved out after troops from Western Command were deployed in Delhi to control crowds after Nehru's death, alarming some within the security establishment.[1] Had there been any truth to that theory, Indira Gandhi surely would not have chosen Manekshaw to lead the Indian Army a few years later. Manekshaw had two corps and two divisions under his command. Fourth Corps in Tezpur was entrusted with the defense of the North Eastern Frontier Agency (present-day Arunachal Pradesh) and parts of Assam, and Eighth Mountain Division and 101st Communication Zone controlled counterinsurgency operations in Nagaland and Mizoram and maintained vigil along the international border with East Pakistan. Thirty-Third Corps had Seventeenth and Twenty-Seventh Mountain Divisions under it to control operations in the Sikkim Sector, which included the vulnerable Chumbi Valley.

Prior to the outbreak of the India–Pakistan conflict of 1965, Lieutenant General Bewoor was in command of Thirty-Third Corps, while Major Generals Sagat Singh and Harcharan Singh were in command of Seventeenth and Twenty-Seventh Mountain Divisions, respectively. It was Manekshaw who assessed that a swift Chinese operation through the Chumbi Valley had the potential to sever communications between eastern India and the rest of the country. Following China's demands in 1965 that India vacate Nathu

Map 5. Nathu La and Cho La Skirmishes

La and Jelep La and other passes on the Sikkim–Tibet border, the Indian Army increased its vigil along the line of actual control (LAC). In a largely unknown and unchronicled episode that was subsumed by the unfolding crisis on the western front that led to war, sustained pressure on the Indian defenses forced Twenty-Seventh Mountain Division to vacate Jelep La and withdraw some distance south of the watershed.

Sagat, however, refused to vacate Nathu La and comply with his corps commander's operational strategy of fighting a defensive battle along a line south of the watershed. This surprised the People's Liberation Army (PLA), which had by then amassed forces along the LAC in Sikkim and forced it to desist from attempting to crack the Indian defenses along the line. A few skirmishes and firefights took place between September and December 1965, but Sagat had planted a seed of doubt in the PLA's mind about the firmness of India's defensive resolve.[2]

NATHU LA SKIRMISH

In September 1967 clashes between the PLA and the Indian Army across two high-altitude passes in Sikkim—Nathu La and Cho La (15,000 feet)—left hundreds of dead on both sides. It was the first time since the 1962 war that the two nations had exchanged artillery fire, and it remains the most recent exchange of fire in the intriguing military standoff between China and India. There has been continued hostility and recurring face-offs without bloodshed across what is probably one of the most inhospitable stretches of frontier on this planet. It was a peculiar calibration of conflict between two rising powers.

The likely trigger for the Nathu La and Cho La clashes was the political situation in Sikkim at the time. The state visit of Sikkim's *chogyal* and his American wife to India in September 1967 led the Chinese to believe that the unpopular monarch had decided to cozy up to the Indians in an effort to consolidate his position in return for abdicating more power to the Indian state. Given the typical Chinese ambiguity and the lack of any official accounts, it is still difficult to ascertain whether the skirmishes took place because two aggressive local commanders were responding to an evolving tactical situation on the ground or because aggression was part of Mao's coercive signaling strategy. Inder Malhotra, one of India's most respected political commentators, thought the Chinese intended to use the incident to warn Sikkim.[3]

By then, Lieutenant General Jagjit Singh Aurora, a calm and phlegmatic soldier, had taken over command of Thirty-Third Corps from Bewoor. The aggressive Sagat Singh continued to command Seventeenth Mountain Division and knew his area of operation like the back of his hand. The latter was entrusted with the defense of the Nathu La complex comprising Nathu La, Cho La, and Sabu La. The entire complex was under 112th Mountain Brigade, which was commanded by Brigadier M. M. S. Bakshi, an armored corps officer awarded the Maha Vir Chakra in the 1965 war. Nathu La was defended by the Second Battalion of the Grenadiers Regiment under the command of Lieutenant Colonel Rai Singh, while Cho La was held by the Seventh Battalion of the Eleventh Gorkha Rifles, commanded by Lieutenant Colonel K. B. Joshi.[4] Across the border opposite Seventeenth Division was the PLA's Eleventh Division. PLA intrusions increased in late July 1967, prompting the Eighteenth Battalion of the Rajput Regiment to be moved to Nathu La in August.

In an article in *Indian Defence Review*, Major General Sheru Thapliyal— then a second lieutenant—wrote that as things began to heat up in early September 1967, Bakshi decided to fence the area south from Nathu La toward

Sabu La along the LAC.[5] This decision was precipitated by a series of heated exchanges between the English-speaking political commissar of the PLA and Rai. The tipping point came on 11 September when the commissar was allegedly roughed up by some Indian soldiers. The PLA quietly withdrew after the scuffle, and the Indian fence-laying party from Seventieth Engineer Regiment continued its operation, along with Eighteenth Rajput. Soon thereafter, the PLA opened fire with medium machine guns, accompanied by mortar and artillery fire, inflicting about forty casualties on the Indians. Rai was injured, and two young officers were killed while rallying the troops. It took a while for the Indians to calibrate a suitable response. In the ensuing riposte, scores of PLA soldiers were apparently killed by well-directed Indian artillery fire, which blasted the Chinese bunkers and silenced the machine guns in a display of outstanding gunnery.[6] Clearly, the PLA—which had stunned and shocked the Indians' forward defensive line in all sectors in 1962—had been given a taste of its own medicine.

P. K. Roy, an Indian reporter for the *Baltimore Sun*, wrote quite disparagingly about the fitness and preparedness of the PLA soldiers as compared with their Indian adversaries. He observed that although the Chinese Eleventh Division was stationed near Nathu La, most of the Chinese soldiers seemed to be less acclimatized to the high altitude than the Indians, as they had been seen gasping for breath while climbing.[7] The impact of good leadership, fitness, and morale of the Indian troops at Nathu La was telling, as was the decision to surprise the Chinese with artillery fire.

On 12 September the PLA rejected an Indian overture for a cease-fire, and fierce artillery duels raged for the next two days. When the Indian Army did not back off or blink, the PLA stopped firing on 14 September and sought a flag meeting to diffuse the tension. Two weeks later, in a concerted effort to hit back after the reverse at Nathu La, the PLA attempted to overrun another Indian position at Cho La—the highest pass on the Sikkim–Tibet border at more than 15,000 feet. By then, the Indian Army had reinforced its defensive positions with crack paratroopers who, along with the determined Gorkhas, pushed the PLA three kilometers back. Brigadier Vivek Sapatnekar, who commanded India's parachute brigade in the mid-1980s, was a young officer at Cho La during the skirmish. He recalled that the Indian Army used its positional advantage to blunt the Chinese attack and once again effectively used mortars and field artillery.[8]

In a telling assessment of the larger strategic picture, Joseph Lelyveld (best known for *Great Soul*, his controversial biography of Mahatma Gandhi) praised India for its firm stand at Nathu La in what he described as a Himalayan street fight. He wrote in the *New York Times* that, in their military and diplomatic posture, the Indians sought to reflect firmness and restraint.

Emphasizing this point, he noted, "This was not just posturing. In 1962, when they were woefully underprepared to meet the Chinese, they engaged in a good deal of braggadocio; the Chinese ruthlessly made them eat their words. This time, after five years of building up their Himalayan defenses, the Indians felt no need for brave words."[9]

India's politico-military leadership demonstrated great self-assurance during these skirmishes. As the firing peaked on 14 September, Manekshaw, Aurora, and Sagat Singh visited the scene of battle. This cheered and gave confidence to the Indian troops, whose morale had remained high despite the loss of two officers and the wounding of a battalion commander. Prime Minister Indira Gandhi made her first major public statement only after the Cho La incident on 1 October. In Mumbai, she said she "hoped that it would only prove to be a local affair like the previous exchange at Nathu La."[10] She went ahead with her plans to visit Ceylon (now Sri Lanka), even as Defense Minister Swaran Singh and the Chief of Army Staff, General P. P. Kumaramangalam, continued their official visits to Moscow and France, respectively. Clearly, they all had immense confidence in Manekshaw.

The Chinese threat to bring the PLA Air Force into the fray was completely discounted by India's operational planners because the military airfields in Tibet could not support the launch and recovery of fighters and bombers with the ability to interdict Indian positions. However, Indian fighters (MiG-21s and Gnats) and fighter-bombers (Hunters) could easily operate from the Bagdogra airfield in West Bengal. They could reach their target areas around Nathu La within thirteen to fifteen minutes to provide air defense or to attack PLA positions. An Indian Air Force (IAF) Canberra photo reconnaissance aircraft from 106th Squadron in Agra carried out a few missions over the area to ascertain the Chinese buildup. Though there is no archival record in either the PLA Air Force or the IAF to suggest that any kind of aerial flare-up was expected, IAF fighter squadrons were ready to intervene if the need arose.

Notwithstanding the robust response, an all-around analysis of India's defense preparedness was undertaken within its military and strategic establishment. There was a realization that India would never be able to confront the Chinese on equal terms if it had to defend a border with too many forward positions. From division headquarters (HQ) at Gangtok (6,000 feet), it was an arduous drive of several hours followed by a climb of 8,000 feet to reach Nathu La. The PLA faced no such challenges, as its division HQ opposite Nathu La was located on a plateau and connected to forward locations by a network of steel-top roads. However, the Indian positions in the Nathu La Sector were well fortified and had adequate fire support; they were also logistically well stocked and proved to be more than a numerical match for

PLA forces. Indian commanders realized that the PLA did not have the requisite force ratio of five to one to overrun the strong Indian positions. Leadership at all levels was resolute, and officers at the battalion level led from
the front. A less-explored consequence of the showdown is the analysis from
Washington, DC, that China's belligerence may have prompted a cornered
India to accelerate its attempts to acquire nuclear weapons capability.[11]

JOINT RESPONSE AT SUMDORONG CHU

Almost two decades after the Nathu La incident, China was irked by the
certainty that the Union Territory of Arunachal Pradesh—which the Chinese
claimed large portions of—would become the twenty-fourth state of the
Indian Union. Chinese troops encroached on Indian territory in Arunachal
Pradesh in late June 1986 and set up camp.[12] The area of dispute was a grazing ground north of Tawang at Wangdung on the Sumdorong Chu rivulet. It
was a remote and inaccessible valley not far from the infamous 1962 Battle
of Namka Chu.[13] Wangdung was literally a "no-go" area for the Indian
Army, as patrolling there constituted a provocation.[14]

Angered that Indians were using Wangdung during the summer, the Chinese rapidly built a post in the area and, for the first time, used helicopters
to stock it. India's response was swift and deliberate under the leadership
of its army chief, General Sundarji, and two exceptional field commanders—Lieutenant General N. S. Narahari, commander of Fourth Corps, and
Major General J. M. "Jimmy" Singh, commander of Fifth Mountain Division at Tenga. Jimmy Singh's recollections of the face-off are remarkable.[15]
He clearly remembers that the limits of patrolling (LOP) laid down for the
Indian Army in the early 1980s stopped short of all disputed areas. He
also recalls that the winds of change started blowing in 1982, when Indira
Gandhi gave the go-ahead for Operation Faulad in the Tawang Sector. That
operation was a modestly calibrated move to build adequate infrastructure
to support a limited forward posture by the Indian Army against Chinese
attempts to make inroads into disputed areas along the LAC.

Fifth Mountain Division was still defending the main ingress route employed by the PLA in 1962—from Bum La to Tawang. It also held the
Tawang Garrison with one mountain brigade. Construction of permanent
defenses for deployment of the remaining division at Tenga began in 1983;
it continued during 1984 and 1985 and was ongoing when Jimmy Singh
took over command of the division. He recalls that the Sumdorong Chu
Valley, which lay forward of the LOP, was "disputed" at the time and unin-
habited. However, Chinese patrols had been visiting Wangdung every year
since 1980, as yak ranchers from both sides used several grazing grounds in

the valley. In 1982, after a team of Indian surveyors confirmed that Wangdung was on the Indian side of the LAC, a seasonal Subsidiary Intelligence Bureau (SIB) was set up in the summer of 1984 to watch, inform, and run a covert transborder network of sources. In the summer of 1986 the SIB's role in alerting the Indian Army to an increased Chinese presence would prove timely and critical.

PROACTIVE DEFENSE OF TAWANG

Jimmy Singh spent the first two months of his command walking the division's entire sector, as there were no roads beyond Tawang except for an operational track to Bum La. He immediately realized that his defenses were weak and vulnerable to being overcome by Chinese forces. After General Narahari took over Fourth Corps, Jimmy advised him of the need to adopt a genuine forward position in the Tawang Sector. It was critical to move one of the brigades occupying defenses on the western flank of Tawang northward to the Hathung La–Kyhpo Ridge astride the Zimthang Valley. He reckoned that the move would give depth to the Tawang Garrison, but it would be possible only with secure logistics lines, artillery support, adequate air mobility, and the assurance of close air support. While Narahari agreed to the proposal, the Eastern Army Command and Indian Army HQ were tentative about this forward posture.

Irritated by the earlier presence of the SIB, the Chinese increased their patrols in May–June 1986. They commenced some track-building activity in the Sumdorong Chu Valley before the seasonal SIB post was set up. Not wanting to provoke the Chinese unnecessarily, the SIB—which was not under Jimmy's command—did not revive its Wangdung post in 1986. Alerted by some local grazers and the SIB, the Indian Army also discovered telltale signs of Chinese patrols around Lungro La, a pass that offered access to the Sumdorong Chu Valley from the Indian side. This was alarming, as Lungro La's ingress routes could threaten Tawang's defenses from the northwest, an area that was not defended because it was beyond the LOP. The saving grace was that Khypo—a high feature overlooking Lungro La—was defended by the Assam Rifles. Wangdung lay at the bottom of a steep approach to the Sumdorong Chu Valley and would be tactically indefensible if the surrounding slopes were held by the Chinese.

On 23 June, when the Indian Army still had not moved forward, the SIB reported that the Chinese were establishing a large camp at Wangdung. Even though the information was unverified, Jimmy immediately ordered the occupation of Lungro La by a protective patrol and gave the patrol commander discretion to open fire with small arms if the Chinese approached the pass. He also ordered the deployment of 81mm infantry mortars to provide fire support. He readied one infantry battalion to move to Lungro La—which was fifteen kilometers from the nearest road head—but a track to facilitate the deployment of field artillery guns still needed to be laid. Work commenced in early July without the approval of command HQ in Kolkata. Infantrymen doubled as porters, and mule convoys were used to ferry building materials. An army officer was embedded with the Assam Rifles at Khypo to act as the division's forward intelligence input. As anticipated, a Chinese patrol soon approached Lungro La but retreated when challenged by the Indian troops deployed there.

In August 1986 the surveillance officer at Khypo reported a stream of Chinese helicopters flying into Wangdung, despite inclement weather. Jimmy was unaware of the existence of a helipad at Wangdung, and after grilling the officer and other witnesses on the telephone, he accepted the information as verified. General Narahari was on leave, and everyone up the chain of command was dithering over what immediate action should be taken, so Jimmy ordered an acclimatized infantry company to reinforce Lungro La, supported by fighting porters and mules. They were deployed within twelve hours.

Jimmy assumed responsibility for deploying troops across the LOP (called Laxman Rekha by the troops) because his operational orders directed that he defend Indian territory and Tawang. He was convinced that he would be failing in this task if he did not take timely action to prevent the Chinese from occupying the tactical ground that extended from Lungro La to Khypo— even if it meant marginally transgressing the LOP. "History was staring at me in the face," he said, "and I had to cater for a worst-case scenario that could lead again to the capture of Tawang."[16] Narahari's operational orientation had the hallmark of his engineering expertise, and Jimmy leveraged this to the fullest extent. Within three months, a thirteen-kilometer-long class 9 (capable of supporting a nine-ton vehicle) operational track to the base of Lungro La was complete. Engineering expertise and explosives were used to construct tracks, with the infantry performing the manual work. A battery of 105mm Indian field guns was also deployed.

Instead of commending the initiative shown by their field commanders, the reaction from higher authorities was not encouraging. Narahari and Jimmy were advised not to provoke the Chinese, cross the LAC, or open fire. Existing orders authorized the division commander to use only small arms, machine guns, and infantry mortars, while the corps commander had the authority to use artillery. This mandate remained unchanged, despite the gravity of the situation. Despite the operational diffidence displayed by higher formations, Jimmy wanted to firm up his operational strategy before winter set in, and he and Narahari visited the entire deployment before the snows came. Narahari then sent a personal message to Sundarji, who visited Tawang in the first week of October for a briefing and operational discussion.

Jimmy commenced the most important briefing of his career by emphasizing that despite Operation Faulad, only one of his three mountain brigades was garrisoned at Tawang, and another battalion covered the Bumla axis. That battalion was modestly supported by short-range artillery guns, a company of engineers, and signal and logistic components. With forward defenses coming up very slowly, the rest of the division was at Tenga. The existing operational philosophy was to establish a first line of robust defense along the Sela Ridge, well to the south of Tawang. Jimmy argued that he might not be able to defend Tawang with the existing positions, and Sundarji responded by saying, "Then I will sack you." Narahari asked Sundarji to hear Jimmy out, who continued by outlining the aims of the division: to prevent intrusion, improve defenses in case of a full-scale war, and assert India's claim along the McMahon Line. Sundarji said, "You are the divisional commander. Who is stopping you? Why don't you go forward?" Jimmy replied, "I do not have any roads. I would require more than 1,200 mules just to maintain the force level, and also longer-range artillery to support Zimithang Sector. I will not deploy troops in a forward position unless I can provide them with artillery support." Narhari added that this would take a long time to achieve, to which Sundarji responded, "Why are we talking about mules in this era? Let's talk about helicopters."[17] So they discussed transporting guns, ammunition, supplies, and water by helicopter, and Sundarji assured Jimmy that the newly inducted Mi-17s had just arrived in India and would be made available. All the issues raised and resources sought by Narahari and Jimmy were approved by the chief, including a fourth mountain brigade, additional artillery guns, close air support, air defense guns, and additional signal resources for command and control. Also approved was the quick conversion of the first 155mm Bofors medium regiment, which was then allotted to Fifth Division.

Soon after, Air Chief Marshal Denis La Fontaine, chief of the air staff, visited Tawang. La Fontaine was pleased to see that Jimmy had started building an aviation fuel supply chain and the requisite infrastructure for helicopter operations. Ordering the immediate deployment of forward air controllers,[18] La Fontaine assured Narahari and Jimmy of logistics and close air support. Jimmy was told that six Mi-8s and Mi-17s would be arriving the following day, but he had to request a weeklong delay so that he could build up refueling stocks and get the forward maintenance base organized.

General V. N. Sharma, who would replace Sundarji as army chief, was

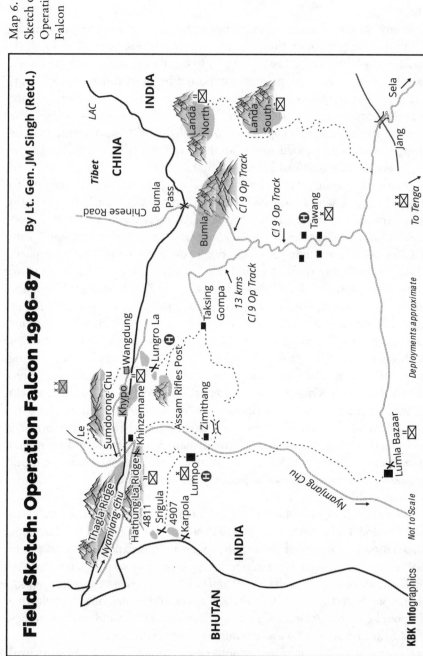

Map 6. Field
Sketch of
Operation
Falcon

commandant of the College of Combat in Mhow at the time. He recollects flying down to the area and reconnoitering it as a precursor to an exercise he was planning at Mhow. Clearly supportive of the initiative taken by Jimmy and Narahari, he advised them to hold firm. Little did he know that he would soon be army commander of Eastern Command and would oversee the final phase of the crisis.[19]

THE FALCON TAKES OFF

The fine print of Operation Falcon speedily emerged, and it was deemed to be a tough but doable strategy of proactive deterrence. This strategy essentially involved the adequate deployment of infantry and firepower based on a minimum force level. Infantry deployment had to be accompanied by a rapid logistics buildup of artillery, ammunition, mines, supplies, water, and stores to build defenses. The construction of helipads, mule and foot tracks, and extensive landline communications was important to ensure that forces did not get cut off and isolated. The robust and responsive organization headed by Jimmy's deputy had representatives from all the services—air maintenance, artillery, engineers, signals, and transport companies. Operation Falcon commenced on 8 October 1986 with the occupation of Lungro La by an infantry battalion. This was followed by the integration of the Khypo and Lungro La defenses and their extension down the slopes and spurs leading to Wangdung. On 31 October the Chinese reacted by attempting to establish posts on the lower slopes overlooking their camp at Wangdung, moving up the slopes toward Lungro La. On 8 November the Indians opened a burst of dissuasive small-arms fire on the Chinese troops creeping up the slopes, compelling them to remain on the lower slopes.

Jimmy then ordered the brigade commander to aggressively patrol and establish defended localities overlooking the Chinese posts. Despite clearance from Sundarji, there was skepticism in army and command HQ about this aggressive posturing. In addition, the China Study Group—supported by the Ministry of External Affairs—was pushing for détente with the Chinese. In November the Chinese made a final attempt to occupy an unnamed rocky feature that dominated Lungro La. A platoon led by a young Indian officer preempted the Chinese with a daring display of rock climbing and occupied this feature. Thereafter the Chinese remained pinned to the bottom of the Sumdorong Chu Valley.

Not satisfied with occupying the Lungro La–Khypo Ridge, Jimmy shifted his attention to the Zimithang Sector. He had another battalion occupy the Hathung La Ridge overlooking the Namka Chu Valley, where Indian posts had been destroyed by the Chinese in 1962. This was followed by aggressive patrolling of the Namka Chu Valley and blocking of the southern approaches by another infantry battalion. All forward deployments in the area were carried out on foot on a manpack basis, and Mi-17 helipads were constructed within twenty-four hours to enable air-landed buildup. Maintenance by paradrops and free drops from helicopters was retained as a standby option. The Mi-8s and Mi-17s landed on the quickly built helipads made of corrugated sheets of galvanized iron. Mule tracks were then developed for routine maintenance and water supply, which freed up the helicopters for more important tasks such as moving dismantled artillery guns, mortars, and ammunition stocks.

Lumpo was developed as an aerial hub with a main helipad that could accommodate the giant Mi-26 helicopter and a large drop zone for An-32s. Later, another battalion was tasked to cover the western approaches to Tawang. This difficult and daring operation was carried out in November to occupy Point 4811 and Point 4907 (about 16,000 feet). It was intended to block approaches from the west through Sirgu La, Gorgyi La, and Karpo La, the high passes used by yak grazers. This high ridge provided direct observation over the Lumpo helipad, the drop zone, gun areas, brigade HQ, and the Indian Army's maintenance area, and it could enable the Chinese to outflank the Hathung La defenses and disrupt the rear areas. The infantry battalion deployed to protect Lumpo cut its way through snow and ice to occupy Point 4907 and Point 4811 and even built small helipads close to the heights.

At Jimmy's request, the *rimpoche* (chief priest) of Tawang Monastery directed every family in the Tawang area to send three members to help build the maintenance lifeline. The sturdy Monpas (local inhabitants) ferried loads for more than a month to Point 4907, surviving prolonged exposure to the harsh conditions and spending their evenings praying in the local *gompa* (Buddhist temple). They lived and worked on faith and refused Jimmy's offer to provide them with high-altitude clothing and snow boots because they did not want to deprive the fighting troops of their clothing. They were the unsung heroes of Operation Falcon, and Jimmy had to persuade them to accept payment for their services once the crisis blew over.

By the onset of winter, Seventy-Seventh Mountain Brigade was entrenched in the Zimithang Sector. The troops were on the heights, on the slopes, and in the valleys, ready to take on whatever the Chinese threw at them. Jimmy usually spent half the day visiting forward formations down to local companies. These visits provided him with vital input for decision making and enabled him to fine-tune the orchestration of logistics. Daily induction tables were reviewed and crosschecked with the receiving formations after the last air maintenance sortie. The next day's induction table would invariably be finalized around midnight, after approval from Jimmy. Last-minute changes were made after speaking to commanders and catering to their priorities.

Jimmy's overall assessment of the first phase of Operation Falcon reflects a quiet sense of pride at what was accomplished. The swift induction of troops on foot, followed by a rapid buildup, took the Chinese by surprise, and their only reaction was "a feeble attempt at probing gaps in our defenses."[20]

REALIZING THE IAF'S POTENTIAL

The IAF's support for the operation was measured and swift. All of Fifth Mountain Division's demands were met by the air maintenance unit at Jorhat—the IAF's largest transport base in the east. The An-32 was the latest medium-lift transport aircraft, designed by the Russians to meet the IAF's requirements for air maintenance in the mountains. Mi-8 helicopters were initially rushed into the sector from three units in Assam, and some were even co-opted from the VIP squadron at Delhi to bolster the numbers.

Raju Srinivasan was a flight lieutenant posted to the 110th Helicopter Unit at Kumbhigram. He was among the first group of pilots briefed on the ongoing operation by Narahari at Fourth Corps HQ in Tezpur. Srinivasan reflected on his experience flying in support of Operation Falcon:

> We were tasked to carry ammunitions to the forward helipads at Hathung La, Lungro La and in the depth of the Bum La and Landa sectors. It was a melee in the valleys as helicopters from 118, 105 and 110 Helicopter Units crisscrossed in the sky. I recollect around ten Mi-8s during the peak build-up period apart from the giant Mi-26 that came in for a trial landing but was not used subsequently. We flew in field artillery to the Zimithang and Landa sectors. I was there for three weeks and it was a wonder that there were no accidents, because every Mi-8 exceeded their flying limits in some respects.[21]

While the Mi-8s operated from Tezpur and Guwahati, it was not long before the newly inducted Mi-17s joined the party, as promised by Sundarji and La Fontaine. With its more powerful engine and better high-altitude capability, it was the perfect machine to operate from Tawang—where 127th Helicopter Unit maintained a regular detachment for almost a year.

Air Chief Marshal Fali Major fondly recalls those hectic times when he commanded and operationalized the first Mi-17 unit of the IAF. "While our main task was in support of Operation Meghdoot in the Siachen glacier, the unit was also inducted into the Tawang sector in support of Operation Falcon. This dual tasking . . . was because of the envisaged high-altitude operations in Tawang and the Mi-8's payload restrictions at these altitudes."

The IAF had ten brand-new Mi-17s but only a few qualified pilots, and it was an onerous task to maintain two detachments of three Mi-17s each at Thoise and Tawang. Each pilot in the unit averaged almost a hundred hours a month initially, switching between Thoise and Tawang, with a couple days of rest and recuperation at Hindon. Fali added, "The good part of this deployment was that my pilots were battle-inoculated in almost warlike operations on a new type [of aircraft] almost immediately after the induction. I was indeed very fortunate to have a fine team."[22]

Jimmy Singh greatly appreciated the IAF's contribution, and in fact, the system worked so smoothly that he never bothered to find out who controlled the air effort. He meticulously recorded events and stored data, so he was able to provide load statistics and flow patterns of the air maintenance activity during the various phases of the operation. During the initial induction and buildup in Seventy-Seventh Mountain Brigade's sector, 605 tons were carried by mules, 1,838 tons were lifted by helicopters, and 1,027 tons were dropped by An-32s. In the Zimithang Sector, Lumpo was developed as the brigade maintenance area. All stores dispatched by An-32s from Jorhat and by Mi-8s and Mi-17s from Tawang were received at the drop zone or the helipad at Lumpo. Thereafter, they were sent by mules to the forward infantry battalions. Extra stocks were maintained at both Tawang and Lumpo to provide irregular aerial deliveries and make up for losses due to inaccurate drops. Such losses became fewer as the crews gained experience, and the fast-track construction of storage sheds ensured logistical redundancy to cope with bad weather and the onset of winter.

According to Jimmy, helicopter operations started at dawn, with Mi-8s delivering both landing and drop loads of 600 kilograms. The Mi-17s operated at altitudes above 3.7 kilometers, landing 200 kilograms and dropping 1,600 kilograms. Load tables for each sortie had to be carefully adjusted to create the desired mix of dropping and landing loads. Cheetahs, Mi-8s, Mi-17s, and An-32s were all flying and dropping in the Zimithang Valley in the morning hours. However, the skies were well managed by the Tawang air traffic control center, and there were no accidents. Jimmy recalls, "Jointmanship was evident at each level. No mission was ever refused, and risks were taken during the induction and buildup phases to land with priority loads at forward helipads hastily hewn out of the mountains. I always felt that the air force crew were a part of my division."[23]

CONTOURS OF A NEW FORWARD POSTURE

As Operation Falcon stabilized, Fifth Mountain Division's forward position improved significantly compared with the haphazard deployment in

1962. Fifth Mountain Division had three brigades deployed in "hot war" locations ahead of Tawang by the beginning of 1987. The earlier focus of the Tawang Brigade in the Central Sector had been to defend the Bum La axis and Tawang. Now it moved an infantry battalion forward to occupy defenses at Lungro La and Khypo—overlooking Wangdung and Sumdorong Chu—to block any Chinese attempts to climb up. It had an operational class 9 track with ready defenses and artillery support.

One infantry battalion held the Bum La axis with a well-established logistics setup that relied on a combination of vehicles and mules. Another one was deployed on the same axis to offer a layered defense. The main challenge in this sector was to cover Bum La and the new deployments overlooking Wangdung by improving the operational track and building additional feeder tracks to the Lungro La maintenance base and the main gun areas. With 120 guns deployed in this sector, and with 300 rounds per gun, it was an enormous task to strip the guns and load them into vehicles. Two tractors were then employed in tandem, and the guns were winched up the slopes. Finally, they were put into emplacements by the soldiers.

In the flanking Western Sector, Seventy-Seventh Mountain Brigade was moved forward to the Hathung La Ridge and then to the critical Zimithang Valley to cover the western approaches to Tawang. It merged its defenses with an Assam Rifles battalion located at Khinzemane, the last border post in the Zimithang Valley. Although the Zimithang Sector was accessible by mule track, the turnaround time was six days, and operationally, it was most vulnerable to a possible Chinese incursion. The IAF, together with Narahari and Jimmy Singh, implemented a template for a brigade maintained and supported by air. They built a large helipad and drop zone at Lumpo, along with additional Mi-8 and Mi-17 helipads constructed at forward locations.

The Eastern Sector under Eleventh Mountain Brigade still had no roads. It was served by a supply chain that relied on mule transport and good mule tracks. It was further constrained by only partially ready defenses constructed during Operation Faulad. The concept of logistics in this sector was to pre-dump ammunition and supplies, create buffer stocks and storage, and build helipads prior to the induction of troops, who walked to the posts. The artillery guns and ammunition were moved partly by helicopter and partly by mules. Seventy-two artillery guns were deployed in this tough sector, with 300 rounds per gun.

Later, during the consolidation stage, the Khypo–Lungro La area was brought under Seventy-Seventh Mountain Brigade to ensure a single command over the Zimithang and Sumdorong Chu Valleys. The relieved infantry battalion was reverted to the Tawang Brigade, its parent formation.[24] When Jimmy handed over command in early 1987, the division had adequate artillery—including the newly inducted Bofors 155mm guns—to support both offensive and defensive operations. Major V. K. Ahluwalia led a battery of Bofors guns to Tawang through Misamari, Tezpur, Bomdilla, and Se La to support operations planned in the sector. It was the first time these heavy guns (the gun train weighed approximately thirty-one tons) were moved in such difficult mountainous terrain.[25]

The guns were installed at a place midway between Tawang and Bum La, along the central axis of the sector. The guns' excellent range meant they could support operations along the western and eastern axes too. The rarefied atmosphere at 11,000 feet resulted in extended firing ranges of up to thirty-five kilometers. Command and control of the guns necessitated a good second tier of command, with additional fire direction centers. An additional 697 kilometers of communication cables were laid during the induction phase for this purpose. Radio communications had to be boosted for defensive fire tasks, and infantry officers were trained to fill in as observers to direct artillery fire from their remote locations. Linking helipads with regimental aid posts enabled the speedy evacuation of critically injured casualties to the military hospital at Tezpur and then on to the command hospital at Kolkata. There were only a few cold-related and altitude-related injuries per month—remarkable statistics, considering that there were nearly 16,000 personnel in the division.[26]

LEADERS AND POSSIBILITIES

After the flawed Operation Blue Star, General Sundarji seized the opportunity to support empowered subordinate commanders. Jimmy Singh shared some of his recollections of both Sundarji and Narahari. "In many ways both the generals were alike—professional, upright, well-read, knowledgeable, open to new ideas, clear thinkers with courage of conviction and great team makers." He added:

> I first met General Sundarji when he was commanding 33 Corps and I was posted under him to command 164 Mountain Brigade in 27 Mountain Division on the Sikkim border. Always willing to question established norms, he expected a high standard of professional conduct and serious application of mind, and backed ideas and subordinates to the hilt. Witty and a good conversationalist, he loved to socialize, and was a friend when off-duty.

Though Narahari was a contemporary, Jimmy had immense respect for his corps commander: "Narahari served with me when both of us were commanding officers in the same division. I found him to be an unassuming and capable soldier who was well-informed and had an enquiring mind. Narahari's clear thinking, determination and courage of conviction were behind the success of Operation Falcon. Throughout the operation he supported me, but never intruded into my command."[27]

Building on the success of their proactive defensive positions, Narahari and Jimmy designed a limited offensive action to evict the Chinese from Wangdung and secure the Thag La Ridge. Sundarji agreed with this plan and moved one brigade from Shillong, placing it under Jimmy's command to carry out counterattacks. Jimmy had 100 guns in support of his initial offensive, with a total of thirty-seven fire units (222 guns) and 1,200 tons of ammunition available for a sustained operation. However, when the Chinese did not persist with their provocative moves, the operation was shelved. Sundarji firmly supported Narhari and Jimmy when they promoted the concept of sustained helicopter-based maintenance in the mountains, and he provided enough resources to make it a success. Although defensive operations provided significant validation of this concept, the duo was unable to test it in a limited offensive because New Delhi was reluctant to needlessly provoke Deng Xiaoping, who had emerged as Mao's successor and was someone the Indian government felt it could negotiate with.

In the summer of 1987 Lieutenant General V. N. Sharma, the new Eastern Army commander, hosted Prime Minister Rajiv Gandhi at Tawang. The prime minister had flown in to see the situation for himself and interact with the troops. De-escalation took place a few months later, after India demonstrated a firmness in negotiations that had not been seen earlier. Local Indian commanders laughed off threats that the Chinese would use tactical nuclear weapons if the Indians failed to pull back, telling their Chinese counterparts that the prevailing winds would carry the radiation into Chinese-held areas.

THE BIG PICTURE

It has never been determined whether the initial intrusions into Wangdung occurred with Beijing's approval or whether they were the handiwork of an aggressive local commander. In any case, the Chinese did not expect escalation by the Indian side, which triggered a disproportionate response by the PLA as it rapidly moved two underprepared divisions onto the eastern Tibetan plateau. However, Deng Xiaoping had just started his strategy of modernizing China and did not want a flare-up with India. India's armed forces were bold, motivated, and well trained, and Deng rightly realized that the Indians would be no pushovers in a limited high-altitude engagement. He therefore took advantage of the first opportunity to de-escalate, once India demonstrated a willingness to negotiate a mutual pullback. The

meeting between Deng and Rajiv Gandhi during the latter's 1988 visit to
Beijing was positive, and there appeared to be a willingness on both sides to
move forward on the border issue.[28] There was clearly a newfound respect
for Indian resolve and capability, and better border management followed
Operation Falcon.

India seized the initiative and deployed in strength around Wangdung
after correctly assessing that the PLA was not about to launch a major attack; it was merely testing Indian resolve while showing solidarity with its
strategic ally Pakistan. Building on the success of Operation Falcon, Sundarji
expanded the debate on how to counter China militarily by conducting an
exercise (called Chequer Board) in the Eastern Army Command with the
assistance of its commander, Lieutenant General V. N. Sharma. It was essentially an operational and tactical brainstorming exercise based on an earlier
exercise conducted by Sharma at the Army War College. Jimmy Singh—who
had relinquished command of his division—was chief of staff at Eastern
Command and was chosen to role-play the Chinese Army commander in
Tibet.

The methodology and impact of the exercise were absorbed across the
Indian Army's war colleges and can rightly be considered the wellspring
of India's contemporary military strategy against the PLA in Tibet. Jimmy
considered it an opportune moment to brainstorm contingencies and possible scenarios along the LAC against the backdrop of a possible revival of
a more robust forward policy.[29] At the time, the Chinese in Tibet were not
prepared. Their border defenses were neglected, their units had many unwilling soldiers of Tibetan origin, and logistical support was poor. In addition,
Chinese troops were fed mostly dry rations. "In the Wangdung sector, the
Chinese sentry was just a few meters away from our forward post," Jimmy
recalled. "The smell of curries cooking in our camp drove them nuts. When
no one was watching, the sentry accepted hot food offered by our troops.
Finally, we had upstaged the Chinese in a sector from where we were driven
out in 1962, and restored the confidence of our troops." Ruminating on the
possibility of limited and shallow offensive thrusts across roadless terrain
in Tibet, Jimmy noted that several things were essential to shape such an
environment: the use of helicopters to move infantry and artillery guns, and
logistics supported by gunships and airpower to gain air superiority, provide
close air support, and interdict rail and road links in Tibet. "The key to
tackling the Chinese in Tibet," he concluded, "is airpower."[30]

The concept of a reorganized army mountain infantry division emerged
from Operation Falcon.[31] Three decades later, such ideas still reverberate
in debates about how to militarily manage the Dragon (China). The idea
of a strike corps and integrated battle groups in the mountains stems from

Sundarji's concept of an offensive formation in the mountains. The success of Exercise HimVijay in Arunachal Pradesh in October 2019, which was conducted to test the efficacy of integrated battle groups, is testimony to that vision.

Operation Falcon was undoubtedly one of Sundarji's successes as Indian Army chief. Its clearly specified aims were to take a forward position in the Tawang Sector to prevent Chinese intrusion, strengthen India's defensive positions, and assert India's claim on the McMahon Line. Fulfilling these aims risked provoking a war with China. But if it had flared up into a localized conflict, the PLA would have received a bloody nose—if not across the entire LAC, then certainly in the Tawang Sector. Rajiv Gandhi's visit to Beijing was followed by ongoing negotiations to maintain peace and tranquility along the LAC through simple mechanisms such as imposing a no-fly zone of ten kilometers for military aircraft and apprising each other of scheduled military exercises. It can be argued that the Indian Army's actions at Sumdorong Chu led to a newfound respect for the Indian military from its principal adversary. On the flip side, it shook the Chinese and precipitated a concerted military buildup in Tibet that would leave the Indians far behind and constantly playing catch-up for the next three decades.

9

Peacekeeping in Sri Lanka
Was India Prepared?

Tamils in Sri Lanka are a minority fighting a majority domination that is of relatively recent origin.
—Channa Wickremesekara, *The Tamil Separatist War in Sri Lanka*

BACKGROUND

When India decided to intervene militarily in Sri Lanka, it perceived all the Sri Lankan Tamil secessionist groups as insurgent groups. However, from a Sri Lankan perspective, the Liberation Tigers of Tamil Eelam (LTTE) had clearly emerged as a terrorist group by the mid-1980s. India did not recognize the LTTE as a terrorist group until 1992, a year after former prime minister Rajiv Gandhi was assassinated by an LTTE suicide bomber. The Indian Army, however, experienced the group's transformation into a deadly terrorist outfit during three years of bitter fighting, and several of its soldiers were brutally killed by the LTTE after being captured. It is in this context that the LTTE is termed a terrorist organization throughout this chapter. Other groups involved in the secessionist struggle are referred to as insurgents.[1]

SEEDS OF CONFLICT

Operation Pawan—the military intervention in Sri Lanka by the Indian Peacekeeping Force (IPKF) between August 1987 and March 1990—marks an important moment in the ethnic conflict between the LTTE and the Sri Lankan government. It was one of the longest ethnic conflicts of contemporary times and came to a bloody end in May 2009. The conflict started in the decades after Ceylon (Sri Lanka from 1972 onward) gained independence from British colonial rule in 1948. It was caused by the Sinhala's majoritarian behavior and the perceived and actual neglect of the aspirations of the Tamil minority. The Tamil liberation movement was centered mainly in northern and eastern Sri Lanka, comprising the Jaffna Peninsula, Killinochchi, Mannar, Vavuniya, Trincomalee, and Batticaloa. The conflict was exacerbated by the Sinhala majority's misplaced fear that they would be overwhelmed by the minority Tamils with the overt and covert support of India.

The Sinhala majority of Sri Lanka claims descent from King Vijaya, who fled the Indian province of Kalinga (the modern Indian state of Orissa) with hundreds of his followers and settled in the central part of the island.[2] The influx of Tamils into Sri Lanka began between the tenth and thirteenth centuries, following the arrival of the Chola and Pandyan rulers of southern India into the areas around modern-day Anuradhapura. The kingdom of Jaffna was carved out of these Tamil conquests. The Tamil rulers of Jaffna resisted Sinhala attempts to recover their lost territory in a series of battles over the centuries. Colonial settlers—Portuguese, Dutch, and British—arrived in the seventeenth century, followed by the East India Company in 1815.[3] Cinnamon, rubber, tea, and coffee plantations sprang up in the north and east, accompanied by an inflow of cheap Tamil migrant labor from southern India, altering the demography of the island. Sri Lanka measures no more than 330 kilometers from north to south and 218 kilometers from east to west, and the Indian Tamils created an ethnic divide in the tiny island nation.[4] A collision between the cultures was inevitable.

Tamils constituted almost 30 percent of the population of Ceylon at independence. The initial secular character of the Ceylonese government ensured peace in the 1950s and 1960s, and Tamils held key positions in government, business, and civil society. However, the emergence of the Janathā Vimukthi Peramuṇa (JVP)—a radical, leftist, militant political party with distinctly Sinhala characteristics—changed the political discourse.[5] In the 1950s and 1960s the differences between the Tamil minority and the government triggered a slew of civilized and legitimate demands for greater autonomy for the northern and eastern provinces. The Tamils, led by S. J. V. Chelvanayakan, repeatedly won elections in Jaffna and united the Sri Lankan Tamils and the Tamils of Indian origin to take on the Sinhala political parties. Chelvanayakan's failure to convince the government in Colombo to initiate reforms led to demonstrations and violent protests in Tamil-dominated areas across Sri Lanka.

The younger sections of the Tamil diaspora, led by Kandipan and Vellupalai Prabhakaran, took up arms in the early 1970s. The assassination of the Tamil mayor of Jaffna in 1975 led to sporadic violence, and it was symptomatic of more to come. In a prescient cable dated 23 November 1976, Donald Camp of the US embassy in Colombo wrote: "Both the adamancy of the Sinhalese on the language issue and the poor economic and employment prospects will contribute to continued ill-feeling between the two communities and may lead to a gradual shifting of Tamil opinion toward the more extreme solution of separatism for their problems."[6]

In 1977 security personnel burned down the Jaffna Library, along with thousands of rare Tamil books and manuscripts, sparking a violent response from the Tamils.[7] The insurgency gradually expanded over the next few years as cadres from various Tamil organizations started attacking small Sri Lankan Army camps in the Jaffna Peninsula. They progressively eroded the writ of the state and declared *eelam* (independence) as their goal. Among the major insurgent groups were the LTTE led by Vellupillai Prabhakaran, the Tamil Eelam Liberation Organization (TELO) led by Sri Sabaratnam, the People's Liberation Organization of Tamil Eelam (PLOTE) led by Uma Maheswaran, the Eelam Revolutionary Organization of Students (EROS) led by Velupillai Balakumar, and the Eelam People's Revolutionary Liberation Front (EPRLF) led by Padmanabha.[8]

LTTE RISES—INDIA GETS SUCKED IN

By the mid-1980s, the LTTE had assumed leadership of the struggle for Tamil self-determination in Sri Lanka, even though other groups were jostling for power and influence. The struggle flared up into a full-scale military conflict in July 1983, when the LTTE officially declared war against the Sri Lankan state by ambushing a Sri Lanka Army night patrol in the heart of Jaffna.[9] Thirteen Sri Lankan soldiers were mowed down in a vicious ambush by the LTTE insurgents. This sparked Sri Lankan security forces to unleash a disproportionate response against Tamils in Colombo, which resulted in widespread killing, arson, and rape and led to the Tamils' complete alienation. "Black July," as this period was termed, could well be considered the beginning of the First Eelam War. The Second, Third, and Fourth Eelam Wars would come in the bloody decades that followed, until the LTTE was finally defeated in 2009.

India was drawn into the conflict because of the proximity of northern Sri Lanka—comprising the Jaffna Peninsula and Mannar—to the southern Indian state of Tamil Nadu. The Sri Lankan security forces' violence against Tamils across the Sinhala-dominated areas around Colombo and the central highlands led to an influx of refugees and insurgents into Tamil Nadu. The targeting of Tamils gradually expanded northward in what many termed "ethnic cleansing." New Delhi and Colombo disagreed about how to resolve the crisis without further bloodshed.

The Sri Lanka armed forces were poorly trained and equipped and had no answers for the hit-and-run tactics of the terrorists and insurgents. However, they revived between 1983 and 1986 under Lalith Athulathamudali, the dynamic minister for national security. According to Indian journalist Shekhar Gupta, who has a deep understanding of war and reported from the conflict zone in Sri Lanka for several years, Athulathamudali was a "rising star in Sri Lankan politics and one of the most brilliant and articulate politicians" he had ever met.[10] Under Athulathamudali's leadership, the Sri Lankans searched the world for arms and equipment and acquired assault rifles and rocket-propelled guns from China, recoilless guns and mortars from Pakistan, light attack aircraft from Italy, and Bell helicopters armed with medium machine guns. The navy was reinforced with warships and Israeli patrol boats armed with powerful 20mm cannons.[11] India watched these developments with concern and was genuinely worried that Sri Lanka was preparing for a protracted and ruthless war against the Tamils. The Sri Lankans received military and intelligence training from Israel, acquired sophisticated weaponry from all over the world, and created a special task force to counter the armed secessionist movement.[12]

This escalated the conflict and created serious security problems for India as it grappled with the 200,000 Tamils in refugee camps across Tamil Nadu. The influx of ten million refugees from East Pakistan in 1971 was still fresh in the minds of India's strategic planners, and New Delhi realized that it had to act before the situation got out of hand. A stable Sri Lanka has always been vital for India's maritime security around its southern flank. Any instability there without a suitable response from India would invite the attention of regional and global players such as Pakistan, China, and the United States. This was something India wanted to avoid at all costs. A friendly or even neutral Sri Lanka was what India needed. When the LTTE took on the Sri Lanka armed forces with some success in the mid-1980s, this created extreme instability in the region. The likelihood of Sri Lanka approaching Pakistan, China, or the United States for help in containing the expanding secessionist movement caused some unease in India and may have been the reason it stepped in.

EVENTS IN TAMIL NADU

After India's independence, the Dravida Munetra Kazhagam emerged as the main political party in Tamil Nadu. It was later challenged by the All India Anna Dravida Munetra Kazhagam, a breakaway faction led by the immensely popular cinema star M. G. Ramachandran, which became more prominent in the 1970s. The two parties competed to be the symbol of Tamil identity. The Tamil refugee crisis and struggle for *eelam* crystalized in 1983 after the first thousand refugees landed on the shores of Tamil Nadu. This became a powerful catalyst for the revival of Tamil chauvinism, albeit in a neighboring country. Tamil Nadu's involvement in the struggle for *eelam* in northern and eastern Sri Lanka must be seen through this prism.

In three superb pieces written for the *Indian Express*, Shekhar Gupta provides a clear picture of what happened in the state of Tamil Nadu during the crucial years from 1984 to 1987. The first piece—which incurred the wrath of Prime Minister Indira Gandhi—was particularly interesting. Gupta wrote about the overt presence of insurgents from several Tamil groups in training camps across Tamil Nadu and the involvement of the Indian intelligence agency's Research and Analysis Wing (R&AW) in training them.[13] R&AW had successfully trained the Mukti Bahini during the 1971 war that led to the creation of Bangladesh, under the stewardship of the same prime minister. Indira Gandhi was convinced that covert operations were a powerful tool of statecraft, and to further this strategy, plans were put in place to build up the Tamils' militant capability. The aim was to prevent Sri Lanka from involving external powers in the region as a counterbalance to India's growing geopolitical clout.

As various outfits jostled for leadership of the Tamil struggle, they scouted the refugee camps in India to recruit cadres. According to the *Hindu* newspaper, Kolathur—located close to the Mettur Dam in the district of Salem—was the largest training camp for the LTTE.[14] The same newspaper reported the existence of several other training and refugee camps in the adjoining state of Karnataka and even in the northern state of Uttar Pradesh. As stories of persecutions and killings filtered into these camps from Sri Lanka, the number of volunteers rose dramatically. By 1985, the LTTE was ready to take on the increasingly belligerent Sri Lankan armed forces in what would be a fight to the finish.

The Prabhakaran-led LTTE was the preeminent group in the Jaffna area and had already executed many spectacular strikes against government forces. However, India's intelligence agencies also trained and expanded other insurgent groups such as EROS, TELO, and PLOTE. Prabhakaran had left Sri Lanka in 1983 to orchestrate the insurgency from Tamil Nadu and spearhead its conversion into a full-blown terror campaign against all who opposed the secessionist struggle. His unyielding belief in the concept of *eelam* was at odds with India's long-term objective of brokering a peace between the Tamils and the Sri Lankan government. The Indian intelligence agencies thought that TELO and PLOTE were more malleable and would be better outfits to train and arm. Too arrogant to play second fiddle to his Indian trainers, Prabhakaran would never forget this slight.

M. R. Narayanswamy—Prabhakaran's biographer and one of the most perceptive Tamil journalists writing on the ethnic conflict in Sri Lanka—posits that the main reason for the sudden escalation was India's covert involvement, which dramatically altered the dynamics of the separatist movement. Formerly a ragtag band of loosely trained rebels, the organization had begun to acquire a cutting-edge focus.[15] Indira Gandhi had used the issue of Tamil refugees to strengthen her political base in Tamil Nadu, which had been weakened after the 1975 emergency. Thus, she had no choice but to align with one of the power centers in Tamil Nadu to ensure adequate support in Parliament. This was undoubtedly the main political reason for endorsing Tamil militancy and providing central assistance and training to the Tamil insurgents.

Indira Gandhi was still highly suspicious of and antagonistic toward the United States—which she never forgave for its support for Pakistan. She viewed US attempts to gain a foothold on the east coast of Sri Lanka—by building oil storage tanks at Trincomalee—as a threat to India's maritime interests. Australian maritime researcher David Brewster links India's intervention in Sri Lanka to this development:

> After 1947, India effectively withdrew to the Indian subcontinent and asserted what has been called "India's Monroe Doctrine" according to which India would not permit any intervention by any "external" power in India's immediate neighbours in South Asia and related islands. While India's attempts to exclude other powers from South Asia had only limited success, India's Monroe Doctrine was used to justify military interventions in Sri Lanka and Maldives in the 1980s.[16]

The assassination of Indira Gandhi in October 1984 was a setback for India's strategic maneuvering in Sri Lanka. Had she lived a while longer, an India–Sri Lanka accord might have secured adequate autonomy for the Tamils, before Sri Lanka spiraled into chaos.

CYCLE OF VIOLENCE

It is believed that Junius Jayewardene, the second-longest-serving head of state in Sri Lanka, initiated the tough military response against the Tamil armed secessionist struggle. Jayewardene told J. N. Dixit—India's high commissioner to Colombo during the fateful years of the IPKF operation—that had Indira Gandhi survived, she would have ensured the breakup of Sri Lanka. She may not have managed a breakup, but she surely would have orchestrated something dramatic. It was common knowledge that Jayewardene disliked Gandhi for several reasons—the main one being her closeness to his main political rival in Sri Lanka, Sirimavo Bandaranaike.

The escalation of violence in Sri Lanka can be attributed to the hardening stance of Jayewardene's United National Party, which was driven by two ruthless politicians: Premadasa and Athulathamudali. The year 1984 saw the cold-blooded killing of forty Tamils in the eastern province of Mullaitivu by security forces. This led to a brutal reprisal by the LTTE, which killed sixty-two Sinhala convict-settlers in two large communes in the same area. The LTTE also struck a police station at Chavakacheri on the Jaffna–Kandy highway and killed twenty-four policemen. The situation worsened in early 1985, when thirty-nine Sinhala and Tamil passengers on a Colombo-bound bus from Jaffna were targeted. This was followed by a deadly bombing at Anuradhapura, the spiritual seat of Sinhala Buddhism, in May.

The increasing violence and belligerence of the LTTE resulted in the declaration of a state of emergency in Sri Lanka in 1985. An abortive truce and lull lasted for a few months, which only allowed both sides to regroup for renewed conflict in 1986. Remotely directing his forces around Jaffna from Tamil Nadu, Prabhakaran proceeded to systematically eliminate rival groups, such as TELO and PLOTE, in the humid jungles of Jaffna, Trincomalee, and elsewhere in the eastern province. By March 1986, many of these rival groups had fled to India, leaving just one group standing in the Jaffna Peninsula: LTTE. This may have been the turning point when the LTTE ceased to be an insurgent outfit and became a deadly terrorist group.

Attacks against LTTE strongholds escalated in February 1986 when the Sri Lanka Air Force assaulted terrorist positions in the city of Jaffna with its newly acquired Machetti trainer aircraft and Bell 212 armed helicopters.[17] Drums filled with explosives and incendiary chemicals were dropped from Avro medium-lift transport aircraft, causing much collateral damage to both people and property. LTTE retaliation followed. An explosion at Colombo airport on 21 May 1986 killed sixteen, and a nearly simultaneous attack on a post office resulted in eleven fatalities. One of the tactics the Jayewardene government employed to counter the rising Tamil terrorist movement was the creation of buffer zones between the northern and eastern provinces. This was combined with a Sinhala push northward into the eastern province. Many villages were cleared of their ethnic Tamil populations (both Sri Lankan and Indian Tamils) and replaced with large communes of Sinhala convicts, who cleared the jungles and created agricultural land. This was expected to pave the way for a gradual influx of Sinhalese in search of meaningful livelihoods, breaking the contiguity of the northern and eastern provinces and preventing their likely merger.

It was estimated that by 1985, more than 300,000 Sinhalese had resettled in a 2,000-square-kilometer area that had once been inhabited by Tamils. Four or five of these large settlements, called *oyas*, were created in the areas around Mullaitivu, Vavuniya, and Trincomalee, displacing tens of thousands of Tamils, who were forced to relocate or flee to India. It was in Weli Oya that the Sri Lanka Army allegedly massacred innocent Tamils in 1984. In retaliation, the LTTE waylaid a convoy of buses on their way from Aluth Oya to Colombo on Good Friday 1987 and massacred more than 120 people in broad daylight. This was followed by a bus station bombing in Colombo that killed 110. Sri Lankan security forces then launched a multipronged offensive in the Jaffna Peninsula. Clearly, both sides were going at each other hammer and tongs, unmindful of the collateral damage they were causing.

Sensing that the time was ripe, Prabhakaran decided to assume direct military leadership of the struggle. According to Narayanswamy, in five years, Prabhakaran had been transformed into "one of the world's most dreaded guerrilla leaders and one who held the key to peace in Sri Lanka."[18] By the time Prabhakaran returned to India in late July 1987, he had become the unchallenged leader of the armed struggle against the Sri Lankan state.

The Sri Lanka Army launched an offensive against Jaffna in May 1987 as part of Operation Liberation. Jaffna and its suburbs were besieged for almost two weeks, and although the LTTE took significant casualties, the operation also left hundreds of civilians dead.[19] The primary objective was to capture the thin strip of land called Vadamarachchi, which was the gateway to Jaffna and connected the Elephant Pass to the Jaffna Peninsula. Located northwest of the strip were the two important towns of Point Pedro and Velvithurai, Prabhakaran's hometown. Sri Lankan intelligence indicated that Prabhakaran was in the area, and the capture of this strip would mean a significant victory for the Sri Lankan armed forces. Should this operation succeed, the second phase would be the capture of Jaffna. Vadamarachchi fell within a week, and it was only a matter of time before the three Sri Lankan brigades closed in on Jaffna. The battle lines had clearly been drawn, and the citizens of Jaffna braced themselves for a torrid time. This was when a concerned India stepped in.

A SUBMARINER'S TALE

Not satisfied with orchestrating covert operations on land, India's intelligence agencies were keeping an eye on Sri Lanka's coast. In the background was the fact that the United States had shown interest in Trincomalee as a potential offshore base and oil farm sometime in 1986. Commander Vinayak Agashe, who served in the Indian Navy for thirty-six years, was commanding INS *Vagli*, a Foxtrot-class diesel-electric submarine. He received verbal orders to conduct an innocuous operational patrol off the east coast of Sri Lanka between Mullaitivu and Batticaloa. "Operational patrol" was a euphemism for the clandestine gathering of technical intelligence of every kind. *Vagli*'s mission was to snoop around for a few days and get as close to the shore as possible. It was to remain submerged, as usual, and operate with extreme caution.

Ordered to rendezvous with a fishing boat abeam the lighthouse at Madras (later Chennai), Agashe was surprised when the director of naval operations came aboard and briefed him on the mission, code-named Operation Amethyst. *Vagli* was tasked with monitoring natural changes in oceanography and access to harbors, recording acoustic and magnetic signatures of ships of every kind, intercepting radio and radar signals, and infiltrating or exfiltrating intelligence operatives. *Vagli* set sail from the port of Visakhapatnam and was escorted into the operational area by the frigate INS *Vindhyagiri*. With Captain Arun Prakash (Indian naval chief, 2004–2006) at the helm, *Vindhyagiri* and its onboard complement of Chetak and Sea King helicopters would provide *Vagli* with a protective surface umbrella and evacuate *Vagli*'s divers should things go awry. Entering the operational area silently at a depth of a hundred meters, *Vagli* took up a position at the boundary of the territorial waters before sunset. During the night, *Vagli* would rise to a depth of fifty meters for its foray along the coastline. Since the continental shelf was steep, the water depth shown on the navigational chart of the target area was "bottomless," or more than 1,000 meters.[20]

On board *Vagli* were four Gemini inflatable boats with divers. They were clandestinely launched in the dead of night, close to preselected beachheads, to reconnoiter water depth at the shoreline; soil conditions; tides; presence of habitation, pickets, or military patrols; inland obstacles; and the like. They were launched and retrieved uneventfully for two nights, and after completing its mission, *Vagli* headed for the open sea. Once it was back in international waters and away from shipping lanes, Agashe radioed the code word for successful completion of the mission. *Vagli* was escorted back into territorial waters by *Vindhyagiri*, where it surfaced and sailed the final stretch to its home base at Vishakhapatnam, headquarters (HQ) of the Indian Navy's Eastern Fleet. Arun Prakash recollects that *Vindhyagiri* masqueraded as a British naval ship during this operation and shared its pennant number of F-42 with HMS *Phoebe*, a Royal Navy Leander-class frigate. When challenged one night by a patrol boat of the Sri Lanka Navy, they managed to stay clear of any suspicion.[21]

What has come to light only recently is that the mission almost ended in disaster when the submarine got caught in an underwater volcanic eruption, followed by a mini tsunami. This resulted in rapid changes in seawater depth and triggered all kinds of alarms as *Vagli* nearly breached the surface and then plunged to crushing depths. According to Agashe, "this would have led to the crew achieving Nirvana at the bottom of the ocean." Thanks to good leadership, teamwork, following procedures, and luck, catastrophe was averted. A subsequent inquiry into the incident revealed the existence of deep-sea volcanic activity and unpredictable oceanographic characteristics in the area where *Vagli* was operating. Many years later, in 2004, similar deep-sea volcanic activity—not far from Sri Lanka's east coast—would trigger a catastrophic tsunami in the region.[22]

INDIA RESPONDS

It had been a tough few years for India's young prime minister, Rajiv Gandhi, as he attempted to fill the shoes of his illustrious mother. Hassled by terrorism in Punjab and preoccupied with Exercise Brasstacks on the western front, Operation Falcon on the eastern front, and the ongoing slugfest between India and Pakistan over Siachen Glacier, Gandhi did not have Sri Lanka on his radar. Matters came to a head in March 1987, when India's intelligence agencies reported that their insurgents were giving the Sri Lankan security forces a tough time. These agencies recommended that the time was ripe to push President Jayewardene toward a viable peace plan. A couple of months of procrastination by the Indian side was all it took to pass the initiative to the Sri Lankan security forces. They used this time to plan and execute Operation Liberation (of Jaffna). After the fall of Vadamarachchi in June 1987, the Sri Lanka Army tightened its noose around Jaffna. A blockade was imposed around the peninsula in preparation for what would have been a final assault on the LTTE bastion. However, Jayewardene balked when it came to allocating a follow-on division, much to the disappointment of General Cyril Ranatunga, who led the Sri Lankan security forces during this operation.

Ranatunga had been at the forefront of the military action to crush the JVP rebellion in the 1970s. In 1985 Jayewardane pulled him out of retirement, promoted him to the rank of lieutenant general, and gave him a clear mandate to crush the Sri Lankan Tamil secessionist movement. Three reasons prevented Jayewardene from going the full distance and making the final push into Jaffna. First was the increasing criticism from the West regarding collateral damage and ethnic cleansing by Sri Lankan troops in captured areas. Second was the fear of a coup by the JVP should the troop concentration in Colombo thin out. Third, and most pervasive, was the constant pressure from India to halt the offensive. The pause after securing Elephant Pass and capturing the vital Vadamarachchi strip broke the momentum of General Ranatunga's offensive. He writes in his autobiography that had Jayewardene stood firm, the First Eelam War would have been the first and last war with the LTTE.[23] Rohan Gunaratna, a stridently anti-Indian Sri Lankan academic and counterterrorism expert, blames India's intelligence agencies for beginning a secret war in Sri Lanka. He argues that, by covertly training thousands of Tamil refugees and strengthening Sri Lankan Tamil terrorist and insurgent groups, India prevented "the Sri Lankan security forces from achieving a military victory."[24]

The pause in the Sri Lankan offensive shifted the spotlight to India. Rajiv Gandhi issued a veiled warning to Colombo to stop the offensive in Jaffna or face the consequences of an Indian military intervention. Not getting the desired response, India dispatched a flotilla of relief ships on an essentially humanitarian mission to relieve the siege of Jaffna. It was escorted by a lightly armed Indian Coast Guard ship, *Vikram*. The flotilla was intercepted by the Sri Lanka Navy on 4 June 1987 and forced to turn back. Why India failed to adopt a more muscular approach is baffling, as it indicated the Indians' tentativeness about intervening. In his book *Assignment Colombo*, J. N. Dixit argues in favor of India's strategic dillydallying, stating that adhering to absolute principles of morality is the safest and most noncontroversial stance in foreign relations.[25] This policy, however, rarely serves any purpose in the inherently amoral nature of international relations. A young and inexperienced Rajiv Gandhi floundered at a critical moment in the initial days of the siege of Jaffna.

As a backup plan, the Indian Air Force (IAF) was asked to plan an aerial operation to drop supply and relief materials in Jaffna, called Operation Poomalai ("garden of flowers" in Tamil). There was palpable excitement at the air force stations in Agra and Gwalior—the parent bases of the An-32 and Mirage-2000 aircraft, respectively. Bangalore was chosen as the launch base because there was enough support there to load and launch the mission. Moreover, the distance of 425 kilometers to Jaffna was well within the radius of action of the Mirage-2000.[26] The An-32, a twin-engine turboprop aircraft, was inducted into the IAF in 1984. It has medium-lift capability and carries around five tons of payload or a complement of forty paratroopers with light equipment. It has a rear ramp that opens to facilitate equipment drops and acts as a smooth exit point for two rows of paratroopers. The Mirage-2000 was procured from France in 1985. It was the first fourth-generation multirole combat aircraft acquired by the IAF and formed the vanguard of its fighter fleet.

The broad plan for Operation Poomalai was to send five An-32s escorted by four Mirage-2000s and drop supplies over Jaffna in broad daylight. No aerial opposition was expected from the Sri Lanka Air Force, and the Sri Lankans had been warned not to fire on the aircraft. The An-32 formation was led by Group Captain B. K. "Bunty" Sunder, one of the IAF's most accomplished transport pilots; the Mirage formation was led by Wing Commander Ajit Bhavnani, commander of Seventh Squadron, also called the Battle Axes.

When the sea relief mission failed to break the siege of Jaffna, India's strategic establishment was jolted into action. This time around, there was no hesitation in ordering supplies air-dropped into Jaffna. On 4 June 1987 the aircraft proceeded serenely toward Jaffna and dropped more than twenty tons of supplies, including food. There were loud cheers in Jaffna as the parachutes floated down from the sky. The world community saw the successful airdrop as the action of a responsible power that was ready to assume leadership of the region. However, it drew predictable criticism from Sri Lanka and Pakistan—particularly from the latter, which was providing military assistance and training to the increasingly aggressive Sri Lankan armed forces.[27]

THE INDO–SRI LANKA PEACE ACCORD

The success of the airdrop and the temporary reining in of Prabhakaran emboldened India. Sri Lanka was pressured to declare a cease-fire and initiate talks with the various Tamil factions. An overconfident Rajiv Gandhi and his somewhat overbearing foreign secretary, Romesh Bhandari, were sure they could stitch together a watertight peace accord and saw no need to draw up contingency plans. It was quite clear that in early July 1987 Rajiv Gandhi was not considering any kind of large military intervention and believed that, with just a little arm-twisting, both Prabhakaran and Jayewardene could be made to see reason.

At the end of the hectic negotiations, the Indian government had convinced all the Tamil insurgent groups—except the LTTE—to accept the blueprint for a settlement. Rajiv Gandhi then summoned the egotistic Prabhakaran from Jaffna to Delhi to try to cajole or coerce him into endorsing the peace accord. However, anyone who knew Prabhakaran sensed that he had no intention of honoring any commitment. On the Sri Lankan side, Prime Minister Premadasa and Defense Minister Athulathamudali were bitterly against calling a halt to Operation Liberation just when they were at the gates of Jaffna. They fell in line only because of the immense pressure exerted by India. However, they would continue to sabotage the accord in the years ahead.

Group Captain "Harry" Ahluwalia was selected in July 1987 to command 129th Helicopter Unit, a new unit raised in Jodhpur. After being reequipped with Russian Mi-17 helicopters, the unit was relocated to Hindon, an air base on the outskirts of Delhi.[28] On the morning of 22 July 1987, Air Marshal Raghavendran, the vice chief of air staff, told Ahluwalia to take three helicopters and head for Sulur—an air base close to Coimbatore in Tamil Nadu—for a secret mission. It was already 2:00 p.m. by the time Ahluwalia and his formation took off from Hindon in peak monsoon conditions, so they headed for Nagpur (850 kilometers away), where they spent the night. Luckily, the formation was able to refuel at Khajuraho, even though the airfield there was closed. Upon seeing the helicopters land, the Indian Oil representative had rushed out to the airfield, thinking a consignment of rum had arrived.

The following day, Ahluwalia and his group reached Sulur, only to be told to head for Thanjavur with no further information. To their surprise, they were met there by the commander in chief of the IAF's Southern Air Command, Air Marshal R. S. Naidu. He was accompanied by a wiry Tamil gentleman who was fidgeting nervously. Sen announced, "Ahluwalia, you have to head to Jaffna immediately and get Prabhakaran and his family out of there. We only know the coordinates of some temple to the north of Jaffna and no other details—this guy is an LTTE chap and he will guide you to the proposed pickup zone." As the formation entered the Jaffna area, Ahluwalia found, to his horror, that his LTTE guide was disoriented and blabbering away in Tamil, which no one understood. The failure to provide an interpreter reflects the completely ad hoc nature of the operation. Luckily, the coordinates of the temple were correct. As the formation approached it, they saw a convoy of cars in a cloud of dust. Prabhakaran was there, in the flesh. Ahluwalia described Prabhakaran as short, with a menacing demeanor; he seemed fidgety and insecure, his eyes constantly darting from side to side. Also on board were Prabhakaran's wife and two sons and a few aides and bodyguards. The return sortie to Trichy was uneventful. Prabhakaran then headed to Delhi via Chennai in a waiting An-32. He met Rajiv Gandhi after paying a courtesy call to his benefactor and covert supporter—M. G. Ramachandran, the chief minister of Tamil Nadu.

Having seemingly convinced Prabhakaran—who was being kept under soft detention at an undisclosed location in northern India—to accept the peace accord, Rajiv Gandhi flew to Colombo. On 29 July the Indo–Sri Lanka Accord (ISLA) was signed by the Indian prime minister and Sri Lankan president, with Dixit looking on.[29] Gandhi had a narrow escape while in Colombo when he was assaulted by a Sri Lankan sailor the next day during a Guard of Honor. Not having Prabhakaran as a signatory to the accord was a mistake—although it can be argued that he was neither the accepted leader of a united separatist movement nor an elected representative of the Tamil people.

The agreement focused on the following goals:

- Preventing any forces detrimental to India's strategic interests from acquiring bases and gaining a foothold in Sri Lanka.
- Neutralizing the forces that were gaining impetus in Tamil Nadu in the wake of the ethnic conflict.

- Withdrawing the Sri Lankan armed forces and the LTTE to pre-1987 positions.
- Implementing and enforcing a cease-fire within twenty-four hours of signing the accord. This required the LTTE to surrender its weapons within seventy-two hours.

Preserving the sovereignty and integrity of Sri Lanka was as essential as protecting Indian interests, and recognizing Sri Lanka as a multiethnic and multilingual society was key to the ultimate success of the peace process. Within this overarching template came the complex process of ensuring that the aspirations of the Tamil minority were met, taking into account geographic realities, historical tensions, and the majoritarian tendencies of Sinhala society. The accord assumed the emergence of the northern and eastern provinces as a contiguous province with reasonable autonomy that balanced Tamil aspirations with Sinhala insecurities and state sovereignty.

PLANNING FOR OPERATIONS

In May 1987 the Indian Army and the various intelligence agencies had yet to receive any directives on military operations against Sri Lankan Tamil terrorist and insurgent groups. It had been six months since a small military intelligence unit had been set up in Chennai to establish a relationship with the LTTE and other Tamil insurgent groups based in the city. The unit comprised Tamil-speaking operatives of various ranks, including a young Tamil army officer hereafter identified as X. It established contact with high-profile Tamil separatist ideologues and military commanders such as Anton Balasingam and Lawrence Thilagar (LTTE), Uma Maheswaran (PLOTE), Varadaraja Perumal (EPRLF), and Balakumar (EROS).

Lieutenant General Depinder Singh, the Southern Army commander, called for a briefing on all the insurgent and terrorist groups from the officer in charge of the unit.[30] This was the first detailed information made available to the Indian Army's senior leadership. Soon thereafter, Depinder invited all the separatist leaders to have tea with him at the officers' mess in Chennai; they all accepted except for the LTTE. This was the Indian Army's first opportunity to assess the dissonance within the separatist movement. But because the LTTE representative did not attend, the army could not assess its motives and was unable to advise the political leadership of the futility of any accord without first defanging the LTTE.

Up to that point, the Indian armed forces' experience with irregular or subconventional warfare had been limited to counterinsurgency operations in the northeast against Naga and Mizo groups and semiurban counterter-

rorism operations in conjunction with state police forces against groups in
Punjab. This time around, India's armed forces came up against a well-
armed, well-trained terrorist group that was tactically proficient in guerrilla warfare. There is no evidence that the Indian Army studied the LTTE;
nor had it war-gamed the prevailing situation in Sri Lanka on any operational templates. Beyond a few operational briefings at Indian Army HQ
and Southern Command HQ, there had been little discussion of what was
unfolding in Sri Lanka. According to several field commanders from the
IPKF, there were serious flaws in Sundarji's operational orientation in such
scenarios.[31] Known more for his contribution to maneuver warfare in conventional operations, Sundarji was not interested in low-intensity and subconventional conflict.

The successes of Exercise Brasstacks (chapter 18) and Operation Falcon
(chapter 8) convinced Sundarji that the days of the "big battle" were not
over. When queried by Rajiv Gandhi about the LTTE's military capability,
a dismissive Sundarji indicated that it would take the Indian Army no more
than two weeks to neutralize the LTTE. Because this vignette is taken from
Dixit's book,[32] one is tempted to brush it off as his attempt to deflect attention from his own mistakes. But several senior commanders—including
Brigadier R. R. Palsokar, who commanded a brigade in the Vavuniya and
Mullaitivu Sectors—have confirmed Sundarji's inadequate understanding of
the operational environment in Sri Lanka and the military potential of the
LTTE.[33] In an attempt to defend Sundarji, many argue that much of the
Indian Army's senior leadership was unprepared for the "vicious and dirty
fighting" unfolding in Sri Lanka.[34]

General V. P. Malik, a future army chief, had a ringside view of the planning prior to Operation Pawan as part of the army's military operations
directorate. He revealed that Sundarji had initially earmarked Fifty-Fourth
Infantry Division for a conventional operation against the Sri Lanka Army
if it refused to halt its advance on Jaffna. Malik, who was preoccupied with
Exercise Chequer Board when ISLA was signed, rushed into the operations
room to alert Sundarji of ongoing developments and the ramifications of
Fifty-Fourth Infantry Division's mission. Sundarji remained unperturbed
and decided that Fifty-Fourth Division would become a peacekeeping force
instead.[35]

Within the Indian Army and the IAF there is no record of any discussion
of joint operations in a counterinsurgency or counterterrorist environment.[36]
Browsing through the operational record books and diaries of the battalions
and helicopter units that were eventually inducted into the various theaters
of operations, one finds no account of officers being sent for counterinsurgency training nor any discussions at the unit level on the nature of the

enemy or the terrain.[37] The IAF was ill equipped to deal with insurgencies and terrorism, as it was preoccupied with large-scale cross-border operations involving hundreds of aircraft. Recently inducted attack and armed helicopters had not yet operated jointly with army formations, and casualty evacuation capabilities had not been tested since the India–China war of 1962.

Like the IAF, the Indian Navy was surprised when it was asked to support the counterinsurgency-counterterrorism campaign, and it was underequipped and undertrained to do so. The navy's first direct involvement was when INS *Vindhyagiri*, with Captain Arun Prakash in command, was deployed off the coast of Colombo during the signing of ISLA. According to Prakash, there was little discussion of the Indian Navy's role in case the accord failed or of any possible peacekeeping mission. Prakash confirmed that at no time prior to Operation Pawan was there any major joint planning.[38] Rear Admiral Kapil Gupta, *Vindhyagiri*'s navigation officer, noted, "We were deployed off Colombo and watched live on Sri Lankan TV as Rajiv Gandhi was attacked by a Sri Lankan sailor whilst reviewing a guard of honor at Colombo" on 30 July 1987. Gupta continued, "We had a unit of the 1 PARA on board our ship. Their mission was to extricate President Jayewardene from his residence in case there was an attack on him."[39]

It is evident that in the prelude to Operation Pawan, synergy was missing at all levels. At the strategic level, the political establishment did not find it necessary to keep the chiefs of the Indian armed forces in the loop while brainstorming the contours of the accord and its ramifications for national security. Of the three chiefs, only Sundarji enjoyed the confidence of Rajiv Gandhi and Arun Singh, the influential minister of state for defense. The armed forces were on completely different pages when military intervention was discussed in the run-up to the signing of ISLA. They looked at the operation in Sri Lanka as an extension of their regional commands and not as an integrated or expeditionary operation, as it should have been.

The army operation was handed over to Southern Command, where Depinder Singh took over as overall force commander. A tactical HQ was set up at Fort St. George in Chennai. Lieutenant General A. S. Kalkat was appointed commander of the IPKF, reporting to Depinder Singh and to New Delhi. Inexplicably, Kalkat too was stationed at Chennai instead of directing operations from Sri Lanka. Air support was to be provided by the fledgling Southern Air Command in Thiruvananthapuram, without any divestment of command and control. Air detachments at places such as Palaly (Jaffna), Trincomalee, and Batticaloa reported to Southern Air Command rather than to a central force commander. The naval component was to be controlled

by Southern Naval Command based at Kochi. During the early days of the
IPKF operation, it was treated as a purely peacetime deployment. Leave rotation continued as usual, and soldiers, sailors, and airmen told their families
that they were heading out on temporary duty and would be back in a few
weeks—possibly with a Panasonic TV or a Sony music system bought at the
cheap markets in Jaffna and Trincomalee.

DEPLOYMENT OF THE IPKF

Major General Harkirat Singh was surprised when his Secunderabad-based
Fifty-Fourth Infantry Division was chosen to spearhead the implementa-
tion of ISLA.[40] The division had performed well during the 1971 war with
Pakistan under Major General W. A. G. Pinto,[41] and it was part of one of
India's two strike corps. At the time, the two divisions with active counterinsurgency experience were Eighth and Fifty-Seventh Mountain Divisions,
both of which were deployed in the northeast. Harkirat Singh thought those
divisions would be better suited than his infantry division for the initial
induction into Sri Lanka. However, geography and command-and-control
convenience were prioritized over expertise. His division was under the army's Southern Command for peacetime administrative purposes and was
thus the easiest formation to deploy.

Harkirat's mandate was clear: implement ISLA by separating the bel-
ligerents, ensure that the Sri Lankan armed forces withdrew to mutually
agreed positions, supervise the laying down of arms by the various insurgent
groups, clear the minefields and booby traps, and create a favorable environment for provincial elections. Sundarji told him the army was going in as a
peacekeeping force, and nowhere in this initial directive was there an even
oblique reference to combat.[42] The strategic hubris and overconfidence in
Delhi were such that not one of the officers at Indian Army HQ cautioned
the chief about the need to be prepared for combat. Instead, the force was
prepared for a United Nations–style peacekeeping operation.

The initial induction of the IPKF commenced by air and sea on the night
of 29 July 1987.[43] The IAF placed thirty-six An-32, five An-12, and three
IL-76 aircraft at the army's disposal at several air bases. Simultaneously, the
Indian Navy readied a small fleet of amphibious landing craft and offshore
patrol vehicles. Airfields at Chennai and Hyderabad were the mounting
bases for aerial induction, and Vizag and Chennai were the ports from which
troops embarked for their sea journey. They would head to Kankesanturai, a
port on the northern tip of the Jaffna Peninsula, and to Trincomalee on the
east coast of Sri Lanka. The IAF had also positioned several standby aircraft
at Bangalore, Hyderabad, Coimbatore, and Thanjavur.[44] Palaly air base—

located a few kilometers southeast of Kankesanturai—was the sole airfield on the Jaffna Peninsula, and it had been identified as an ideal location for the operational HQ of Fifty-Fourth Infantry Division.

Strangely, the IPKF HQ remained at Chennai, against all tenets of operational wisdom. It ought to have been relocated to Palaly when the going got tough a few weeks into the deployment. Either Depinder Singh had too much on his plate or Indian Army HQ had grossly underestimated the magnitude of the task. By 4 August, a depleted Fifty-Fourth Infantry Division—with three brigades and a little more than 8,000 troops—had been deployed across a vast area that stretched from the Jaffna Peninsula to Vavuniya and Trincomalee. The distance from Jaffna to Vavuniya is about 140 kilometers, and Trincomalee is 95 kilometers further east of Vavuniya, across inhospitable terrain dotted by jungles and lagoons. A single arterial road–cum–rail link ran from Jaffna to Anuradhapura, the largest city in the central province. Soon, the IPKF realized that the operational area needed to be extended southward to Batticaloa, as that area had also become an LTTE bastion.

The induction of troops and their supporting logistics by sea from Chennai proceeded smoothly through August 1987. A few shallow-draft inshore patrol vessels belonging to the Indian Coast Guard were placed under the navy's control and were used to patrol Palk Bay, which separated India from Sri Lanka. The coast guard's F27 aircraft, operating from Madras, carried out air surveillance extending a hundred miles seaward off the east coast of Sri Lanka. To ensure the smooth induction of forces, Indian Navy liaison teams were positioned at Trincomalee, Palaly, Kankesanturai, and Karainagar.[45] An ad hoc IAF base commander was appointed at Palaly, with limited helicopter assets. Fifty-Fourth Division consolidated its presence by mid-August, with one undermanned infantry brigade at Jaffna (Ninety-First), Vavuniya (Forty-Seventh), and Trincomalee (Seventy-Sixth). However, the area demanded a force that was three times as large.[46] Two more brigades were inducted into Sri Lanka over the next two months, along with some supporting tanks, armored personnel carriers, artillery, and engineers.

DECEPTIVE WELCOME

The IPKF got a mixed reception in the Jaffna Peninsula. Many of the early inductees were welcomed with placards and banners. The citizens of Jaffna had high expectations that their "big brothers" from India would usher in peace in no time. Even the Sri Lankan security forces were cordial and welcomed the first wave of the IPKF in the right spirit. However, the IPKF was banned from entering LTTE areas. Soon there were massive demonstrations and protests orchestrated by LTTE cadres demanding the release of their leader. A line of control ran from Kankesanturai (port) and Palaly (airfield) southward to the town of Jaffna, east of which was designated LTTE territory. The IPKF needed to find a way to penetrate LTTE areas and obtain intelligence.

The anonymous covert operative mentioned earlier—X—masqueraded as a journalist sympathetic to the LTTE cause and managed to slip behind "enemy" lines. He survived an elaborate vetting process by multiple tiers of LTTE operatives that included the new Jaffna commander, Kumarappa. X was allowed an audience with Mahattaya, Prabhakaran's deputy, who had to be convinced that X was indeed an LTTE sympathizer and that he was there to report the actual situation on the ground. X was heckled by a large Tamil crowd during his escorted visit around the areas of Jaffna held by the LTTE and manhandled by a group of Tamil women, despite speaking fluent Tamil and commiserating with them.

X spent the night with the family of one of the LTTE cadres, who turned out to be wonderful hosts. Expecting to turn in early after an exhausting day, he was instead confronted by six to eight girls in their late teens and early twenties who barged into the house. "They started arguing with me about the accord and how India had stabbed them by holding their leader under detention in Delhi," X recalled. "After trying to make them understand the situation, I realized they were not like other normal people who had discussed the issue with me that day—they were totally brainwashed cadres of the LTTE. I promised that I would take their grievances to the right quarters." X was dropped off the next day at the same spot where he had been picked up, and he immediately briefed the army commander about his experiences.[47]

At the strategic level, the wily Prabhakaran outthought Rajiv Gandhi. He managed to return to lead his cadres only days after ISLA was signed, thereby seizing the initiative. It is believed that once Prabhakaran had been convinced to back the accord and issue a statement of support, he was held at an Indian intelligence base in western Uttar Pradesh. The plan was to allow him to return to Sri Lanka only after the Tamil rebel groups had laid down their arms and a modicum of peace had been restored. However, he reportedly convinced Rajiv Gandhi to allow him to return immediately after the accord was signed. Much to the annoyance of India's intelligence agencies, he managed to establish a coercive presence in the Jaffna area.

There was intense competition between J. N. Dixit and Harkirat Singh to claim credit for whatever was unfolding in Jaffna, whether it was the Tamil insurgents laying down their arms, the Sri Lanka Army returning to its barracks, or the political process being restored. Much has been written about the farcical and unnecessarily ceremonial twist given to the surrendering of arms by the LTTE and other Tamil insurgent groups. Harikarat boasts about his helicopter trip to meet Prabhakaran at Jaffna University before the arms surrender ceremony, but he conveniently avoids mentioning that Prabhakaran did not attend the ceremony—a fact highlighted by Narayanswamy in his biography of the LTTE commander.[48] Instead, his deputy, Yogi, marked the occasion by dramatically giving up his Mauser weapon. In reality, the LTTE surrendered barely 10 to 15 percent of its arsenal.

On 4 August Prabhakaran delivered an inflammatory speech to a crowd of 40,000 Tamils in the presence of senior Indian military officers. He thundered, "Let me make it clear to you beyond the shadow of a doubt that I will continue to fight for the objective of attaining Tamil Eelam . . . the Liberation Tigers yearn for the motherland of Tamil Eelam. I do not think that this agreement will bring a permanent solution to the Tamil question. The time is not far off when the monster of Sinhala racism will devour this agreement."[49]

The simmering rivalry between the LTTE and groups such as EROS, EPRLF, and PLOTE—and the disruptive role played by R&AW in this rivalry—added to the uncertainty. By early 1987, the intelligence agency had mistakenly assessed that it could marginalize Prabhakaran and the LTTE by training and arming rival groups independently—without keeping the Indian Army in the loop. Colonel R. Hariharan was head of the Indian Army's intelligence operations in Sri Lanka from 1987 to 1990. He argues that, unlike in Bangladesh—where the Indian Army had been at the forefront of training the Mukti Bahini and built a rapport with them—R&AW took up the military training of Tamil insurgents on its own and sought only limited assistance from the army.[50] This backfired, as Prabhakaran saw through this strategy.

Despite being isolated and ignored by R&AW in the run-up to ISLA, Prabhakaran exploited the lack of synergy between R&AW and the Indian Army in the months after the accord was signed. This allowed him to consolidate power across the Tamil-dominated belt from Batticaloa in the southeast to Trincomalee in the east.[51] The Indian Army had no clue about the LTTE's strategic and operational prowess, and Hariharan and his band of military intelligence operatives were left to put the pieces together once the IPKF arrived in Sri Lanka.[52]

THE SITUATION WORSENS

Meanwahile, Fifty-Fourth Infantry Division was striving to restore normalcy in parts of the Jaffna Peninsula with an undermanned brigade. Expecting the IPKF to check the rise of the LTTE and concurrently restore peace in Jaffna,

Trincomalee, Vavuniya, and Batticaloa with just three undermanned brigades demonstrated a complete lack of foresight and planning. Adding to the IPKF's woes was the peacetime ethos that prevailed within the senior leadership, as well as the traditional turf battles over the allocation of resources. In his book, Depinder Singh laments the lack of synergy between the IPKF's overall force commander and Southern Air Command over the allocation of transport and helicopter resources.[53] Similarly, the IAF repeatedly complained that it was kept out of the initial planning process and thus would respond to requests for air support from the IPKF on a case-to-case basis. Air Marshal Bharat Kumar claims that Harkirat gave no respect to the air force commander at Palaly and wanted all air assets "under command."[54] There was hardly a war-zone environment in division HQ at Palaly. Sitdown lunches were the norm, and senior newcomers and high-profile visitors were entertained at the commander's high table, where there was little operational discussion.[55]

In addition to scuttling the election process in September, the LTTE embarked on a killing spree in Batticaloa and Trincomalee. More than a hundred cadres of the EPRLF and PLOTE were killed in a coordinated strike by Mahattaya right under the noses of the IPKF and the Sri Lankan police. A young LTTE commander called Thileepan threatened to fast until several Sri Lankan Tamil political prisoners were released—a prerequisite for the resumption of any political dialogue. Matters worsened after Thileepan died on 26 September.

Gunrunning across the Palk Strait was a common LTTE activity. On 3 October, during one of these missions, seventeen men—including two top LTTE commanders, Pulendran and Kumarappa—were apprehended by the Sri Lanka Navy off the coast of Point Pedro. Shrewdly taking advantage of the existing amnesty arrangement, the LTTE demanded that the insurgents be released. The navy, unwilling to cede to these demands and claiming that the amnesty did not extend to the waters around Sri Lanka, detained the men at the IPKF-controlled Palaly air base to await a flight to Colombo to stand trial. Some people believed that the capture was a result of a tipoff from the diabolical Prabhakaran to test the IPKF's resolve.[56] Dixit and Major Sheonan Singh—who was entrusted with the detainees' security—advised Harkirat Singh that handing over the LTTE men to the Sri Lanka Army would be disastrous. However, Harkirat decided to wait for instructions from Indian Army HQ. New Delhi first instructed him to hand over the prisoners; then, when Dixit tried to intervene, it rescinded the order. By then, it was too late. After a scuffle with their Sri Lankan captors, the prisoners had bitten into cyanide pills. Twelve of the seventeen, including Pulendran and Kumarappa, died despite doctors' desperate attempts to revive them.[57]

X was with a friend in the Nallur area of Jaffna when he saw the bodies of the LTTE men being taken for cremation. The ceremony was telecast live on the LTTE TV channel Nidharsanam. The event sparked off riots against Sinhala in Batticaloa and Trincomalee. The next morning was even worse. X witnessed several Sinhala being killed as burning tires were placed around their necks. Realizing that things were getting bad, X managed to get a cab to Palaly. Hardly thirty minutes later, the curtains were drawn on any hope for peace.

Lieutenant General S. Pattabhiraman, from the Corps of Engineers, was a major posted in the directorate of military operations during the planning and induction of the IPKF. He was privy to the operational culture prevalent at the time and faults the entire top army leadership for misreading the situation on the ground and the LTTE's motivation. He says that during both the Thileepan incident and the handing over of the LTTE gunrunners to the Sri Lankans, Indian Army HQ delayed making a decision about the situation and failed to understand its ramifications.[58] One possibility is that Prabhakaran was furious that his men were being handed over to the Sri Lanka Army, and as a result, Tamil emotions ran high against the IPKF. However, it is also likely that Prabhakaran realized that the IPKF commander was unsure and indecisive and knew it was time to strike.

On 7 October 1987 the LTTE carried out its first terrorist-style attack on the IPKF, capturing and killing five commandos in Jaffna by placing burning rubber tires around their necks. This gruesome act jolted the entire Indian establishment. There was an immediate flurry of visits to Sri Lanka— including one by Sundarji—to assess the IPKF's operational preparedness and reinforce it with additional brigades. Sundarji ordered Harkirat to launch operations to take Jaffna, break the back of the LTTE, and capture Prabhakaran. "How many days to Jaffna?" Sundarji asked, and Harkirat told him it would take no more than three or four days to get things under control. It was 10 October 1987, and the die was cast for a conflict that India was completely unprepared for.

10

Into the Tiger's Lair

Absence or amorphousness of strategy in war on foreign soil is singularly un-
professional . . . in insurgency it is strategy which is so much more important
than tactics.
                              —Lieutenant General S. C. Sardeshpande, *Assignment Jaffna*

BATTLE FOR JAFFNA

Early October 1987 saw the decision to go on the offensive against the
Liberation Tigers of Tamil Eelam (LTTE). Fifty-Fourth Infantry Division
was hastily reinforced with two more undermanned infantry brigades—
Eighteenth and Seventy-Second—within five days. This ensured that the beleaguered Major General Harkirat Singh had sufficient forces to launch a
three-pronged offensive on Jaffna. As the battle progressed and Indian Army
headquarters (HQ) became desperate for a quick victory, Forty-First Brigade
and 115th Brigade were also flown in between 15 and 17 October. They
went into battle with hardly any training and education.

The LTTE defenses around Jaffna were a combination of reinforced
military-style positions and positions embedded in the local population.
These defenses met the Indian Peacekeeping Force (IPKF) head-on and
allowed the cadres to slip into civilian areas if necessary. Joanne Richards
has tracked the evolution of the LTTE and calls it "arguably one of the most
sophisticated non-state armed groups ever assembled." Ironically, India
played a significant role in the development of its fighting abilities. Richards
states that between 1983 and 1987, the Research and Analysis Wing (R&AW)
trained "an estimated 1,200 Tamils in the use of automatic and semiautomatic weapons, self-loading rifles and 84mm rocket launchers."
They were also trained in mine laying, map reading, guerrilla warfare,
mountaineering, demolitions, and antitank warfare.[1]

Surprised by the casualties to his force, Harkirat sent in his tanks and
attack helicopters to break the LTTE's resistance. Mi-25 attack helicopters
were first used for close air support in the final days of the assault on Jaffna
town. Two helicopters attacked LTTE positions with rocket and cannon fire
at Chavakacheri bus station, thirty-two kilometers east of Jaffna. The most

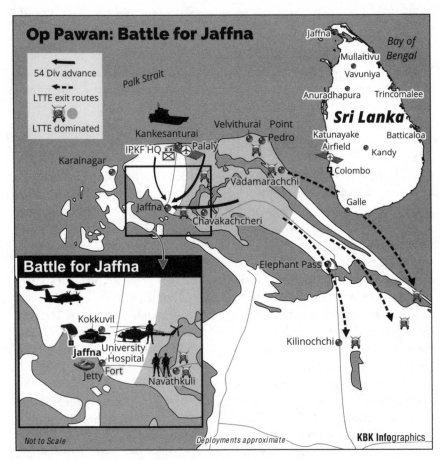

Map 7. Operation Pawan and the Battle for Jaffna

effective resistance faced by the Indian Army during the Battle of Jaffna came from LTTE snipers.[2] Maximum casualties were caused by the systematic detonation of mines, most of which had been laid by the LTTE under the IPKF's very nose in the two months preceding the offensive. After more than two weeks of bloody fighting, the LTTE finally abandoned Jaffna on 26 October—but not before making the IPKF pay a heavy price.

Official estimates provided by the Indian Army in December 1987 stated IPKF casualties in the Jaffna sector as 214 dead, more than 800 injured, and at least 40 missing. The LTTE reportedly lost more than 800 fighters—although the number was impossible to ascertain, as the LTTE never left its dead and wounded behind.[3] Around 90 militants were captured by the IPKF, but at least 1,500 experienced fighters managed to slip away into the jungles of Vanni, Trincomalee, and Batticaloa. Shekhar Gupta and Dilip

Bobb—journalists who covered the battle—provide the most accurate accounts.[4] Many of Gupta's observations were confirmed by numerous soldiers involved in the action, including the adverse impact of casualties on the troops' morale.[5] Writing about collateral damage during the battle, Bobb stated that the ferocity of the action meant that civilian deaths were impossible to avoid.[6]

DISASTROUS HELIBORNE OPERATION

On the night of 11 October 1987 a bold attempt was made to capture or eliminate the LTTE leadership. However, the attempt was doomed from the start, as the essential elements for the success of such an operation were cast aside.[7] Official details of the operation are still classified, but it is possible that Depinder Singh and General Kalkat got the idea for a heliborne operation after meeting Prabhakaran a couple of days earlier. To assume that Prabhakaran had not considered this possibility is preposterous, but to plan such a major operation within three days is even more so. It demonstrated a "cowboy" approach that completely underestimated the enemy. The mission had been vetted and cleared by staff at various levels—including at HQ Fiftieth (Independent) Parachute Brigade—indicating the hubris and overconfidence that prevailed at every level of planning.

The plan envisaged using Mi-8 medium-lift helicopters to land more than 300 paracommandos from Tenth Parachute Battalion (Para) and regular infantrymen from the Thirteenth Battalion of the Sikh Light Infantry Regiment in multiple waves on the University of Jaffna's sports grounds. The landing site was chosen by Kalkat and Depinder. The first group of troops would ensure that the landing zone was adequately sanitized and insulated from enemy interference to facilitate subsequent landings. The landing ground was very close to the presumed LTTE HQ at Kokuvil, and it was chosen because it offered a high probability of hitting the LTTE's top leadership, including Prabhakaran. There was no information regarding either the number of terrorists in the area or their weaponry. It was suicidal to expect Thirteenth Battalion—inducted into Jaffna barely a day prior to the operation—to carry out the specialized task of hitting an unfamiliar urban target.

Only four Indian Air Force (IAF) Mi-8s were available for the operation, and there was no mock-up of the target area to brief the force. The experienced paracommandos were expected to get the job done while the infantry held off any counterattack by the LTTE. The operation was a disaster from the outset. The paracommandos made their way into the target complex under the command of Major Sheonan Singh. But instead of 200 soldiers, only 30 men from Thirteenth Battalion were landed. There were several reasons:

the battalion arrived late at the airport, the second wave of helicopters missed the landing area, and the helicopters were severely damaged in the first two attempts. This forced the IAF to cancel further sorties.[8] At 2:00 a.m. on 12 October, about a hundred paracommandos and the thirty infantrymen were scattered around the sports grounds of the University of Jaffna. They had lost communication with their HQ and had no means of knowing there would be no more sorties. Come daylight, LTTE snipers picked out the infantrymen one by one. Despite a valiant fight—including close combat with bayonets—the infantrymen were taken down by the experienced LTTE terrorists. Only one of them survived to tell his story.

Meanwhile, Sheonan and the paracommandos had headed for the building where the LTTE leadership was holed up. Unable to identify the building, they found themselves in the streets of Kokuvil waiting for the inevitable to happen. They drew heavy fire from multiple directions and soon realized they were hopelessly outnumbered. All they could do was fight their way into a maze of houses and streets and hope that a large backup force would arrive. The backup force comprised two companies of Fourth Battalion of the Fifth Gorkha Rifles and tanks from Sixty-Fifth Armored Regiment. Colonel Dalvir Singh, the commanding officer of Tenth Para, led the rescue force as it attempted to fight past tough LTTE defenses. It was joined by the soldiers of Thirteenth Battalion who had not landed at the University of Jaffna the previous night. By midnight, the Gorkhas had lost three men, including their commander, in fierce fighting. When the force reached the outskirts of Kokuvil at dawn, a volley of fire hit one of the tanks, causing more casualties.

By then, Sheonan and his paracommandos had been fighting for more than twenty-four hours and had lost six men. However, they had also caused severe attrition among the LTTE, as it is estimated that at least fifty LTTE cadres died in the fighting. The paracommandos walked six kilometers to the Urelu temple, where they finally linked up with the rescue force. They were taken to the Palaly airfield by truck after thirty-six hours of fighting. They had managed to keep casualties at six killed and fourteen wounded in a professional display of courageous fighting against overwhelming odds. Even though the helicopter pilots—Wing Commander Sapre, Squadron Leaders Vinay Raj and Doraiswami, and Flight Lieutenant Prakash—had performed admirably in the circumstances, an irate Harkirat accused them of landing the Sikh troops in the wrong field and exposing them to murderous fire. However, Sheonan came to their defense, confirming that they had done a good job and the landing had been accurate. Sheonan, Dalvir, Sapre, Raj, Doraiswami, and Prakash would later be awarded Vir Chakras for bravery under fire. In what was a disastrous joint operation, much was learned about the "lungi-clad fighters," as some Indian generals derogatorily described the LTTE terrorists.[9] Despite inflicting heavy losses on the IPKF, the LTTE's forced withdrawal from the town of Jaffna into the jungles of Killinochchi, Vavuniya, and Mullaitivu was a big humiliation for Prabhakaran.

SHIFT IN THE CENTER OF GRAVITY

There was much optimism in Colombo, New Delhi, and IPKF HQ after the LTTE's withdrawal from Jaffna. It was widely believed that the time was ripe to push ahead with the political process. Winning the hearts and minds of the people of Jaffna was the first step toward that objective. This was necessitated in part by the LTTE's highly effective propaganda regarding the excesses committed by the IPKF, which had to be countered with an alternative narrative. Chosen to spearhead that initiative was Major General S. C. Sardeshpande, who replaced a fatigued Harkirat in January 1988 as the commander of Fifty-Fourth Infantry Division. Sardeshpande appointed Brigadier Kahlon as the town commandant in Jaffna. Roads were repaired, schools reopened, and hospitals made functional. Life in the area limped back to normalcy. However, it is rather perplexing that during this entire period (November 1987 to March 1988), everyone, including Indian Army HQ and R&AW, wrote off the LTTE and started to prop up a rival militant group—the Eelam People's Revolutionary Liberation Front (EPRLF)—to align with the Tamil United Liberation Front, the political arm of the moderate Tamil groups.

While the Indian politico-military establishment was congratulating itself on freeing Jaffna from the clutches of the LTTE, more than 5,000 LTTE cadres were busy regrouping and consolidating their position in the sparsely populated and densely forested Vanni region. Farther south, the Indian-trained and -supported EPRLF dominated the Trincomalee and Batticaloa region. The IPKF commanders hoped they would soon be able to turn the EPRLF against the LTTE and bring about a military collapse of the latter. The Indian Army recognized the need for more boots on the ground after Fifty-Fourth Infantry Division failed to block the escape of the LTTE cadres and leadership from the Jaffna Peninsula. It progressively inducted three additional divisions into Sri Lanka to bolster the thin deployment in Vanni, Trincomalee, and Batticaloa. This allowed Fifty-Fourth Infantry Division to consolidate Indian domination of the Jaffna Peninsula and create conditions conducive to holding elections, thereby achieving the objectives of the Indo–Sri Lanka Accord (ISLA). However, Sardeshpande was scathing in his indictment of Delhi for inferring that conflict termination in Jaffna would automatically lead to conflict resolution across the island. He argues that there was no blended military, psychological, economic, reconstruction, and rehabilitation strategy to supplement ISLA and consolidate the "notional victory that New Delhi claimed in Jaffna."[10]

By the end of February 1988, the three additional divisions were in place: Thirty-Sixth Infantry Division commanded by Major General Jameel Mahmood at Trincomalee, Fifty-Seventh Mountain Division commanded by Major General T. P. Singh at Batticaloa, and Fourth Infantry Division commanded by Major General J. N. Goel in the Vanni region. Except for Fifty-Seventh Mountain Division—which had moved in from insurgency-ridden Nagaland—these divisions lacked adequate personnel and training to undertake classic counterinsurgency and counterterrorist operations in jungle, lagoon, and semiurban terrain. Particularly hard-pressed was Fourth Division's Seventh Infantry Brigade, which had moved piecemeal into Sri Lanka during the final stages of the battle for Jaffna in October 1987. It finally found a hostile home in the Vanni area in December 1987. Vanni turned out to be the toughest battlefield, as the LTTE had consolidated its forces, logistics caches, and armories in the area. Seventh Infantry Brigade would emerge as one of the longest-serving and least-recognized IPKF brigades, remaining in Sri Lanka until December 1989.

OVERSTRETCHED BRIGADE

Brigadier Palsokar is probably the only IPKF brigade commander to write a detailed account of operations against the LTTE during 1988–1989—in his book titled *Ours Not to Reason Why*.[11] There is an element of personal angst in the book, which is to be expected from someone who commanded an underprepared brigade with little support from higher formations in conditions that were completely alien to the Indian Army at the time. However, that is overshadowed by his meticulous retelling of events as they unfolded without covering up the failures—including his own. Palsokar is unsparing in his indictment of the senior leadership and the disconnect with operations at division level and above, particularly in his sector. This objectivity makes his account a good reference when describing operations in the Vanni region.

Palsokar's brigade was totally unprepared for the missions assigned to it. Adding to the confusion was that Palsokar assumed command of the brigade in Sri Lanka in December 1987 without any fresh orders or directives that spelled out its objectives in the rapidly changing combat environment. Trained for classic infantry warfare that envisaged force-on-force defensive and offensive operations, the brigade had to reorient itself to combat with an unseen enemy who was mastering the art of guerrilla warfare. Operating in the middle of a contiguous battle space dominated by forests and lagoons

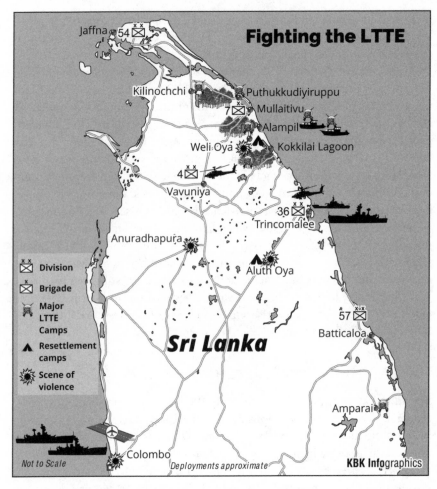

Map 8. Fighting the Liberation Tigers of Tamil Eelam (LTTE) across Sri Lanka

that extended from Killinochchi in the north to Batticaloa in the east, Palsokar's brigade needed time to come to grips with the fighting. Xerxes Adrianwalla, Palsokar's brigade major (later a brigadier), recounted the brigade's principal tasks:

> Our major tasks were to dominate the LTTE, conduct search and cordon operations and man multiple Road Opening Parties (ROPs). Some of our peripheral tasks were to manage the tension between the Tamils and Sinhala settlers in areas where the two lived close to one another. Making matters worse was the continuing internecine conflict between the LTTE and rival Tamil groups and the emerging collusion between the Sri Lanka Army and the LTTE.[12]

After the LTTE retreated from Jaffna, it built its first bastion in the jungles immediately northwest of Mullaitivu. Seventh Infantry Brigade had some early successes in this area, despite taking heavy losses during the first six months of its deployment, mainly from ambushes and improvised explosive devices (IEDs). But even so, it failed to prevent the LTTE from withdrawing south toward the dense forests—called Alampil and Nittikaikulam—around the Nayaru lagoon. These forests proved to be the nemesis of the IPKF and Seventh Brigade for two main reasons: first, because the brigade was very thinly deployed, despite reinforcements from Thirty-Sixth Infantry Division at Trincomalee; and second, because the wide range of competencies and specialized troops required were hard to come by.

The exception was several instances in which the Special Forces reinforced Palsokar's brigade, such as the extrication of a trapped company in the forests around Alampil in May 1988 and a larger operation in August and September 1988 called Checkmate IV. The former involved rescuing Eleventh Battalion of the Garhwal Rifles as it was returning from a patrol along the coastal areas of the Nayaru lagoon and Alampil forest.[13] The latter was a concerted attempt by the IPKF to close in on Prabhakaran at a large camp in the Nittikkaikulam forest. Checkmate IV commenced in Palsokar's absence, and he reckons that, given the number of casualties and the destruction of a helicopter within the forward-deployed tactical HQ perimeter, he would have been sacked if he had been there. "Only after this operation did Kalkat realize what it meant to operate in the jungle in my sector," he said. "Many claims were made by IPKF HQ about the successes achieved by Checkmate IV, but these were hollow and without substance, as by then, both the army and the LTTE were opposed to the ISLA."[14]

Though the fighting subsided in early 1989, the brigade got a respite from sustained operations only in September 1989—when a cease-fire was formally declared and New Delhi decided to pull the IPKF out. By December 1989, Seventh Infantry Brigade had been decommissioned after two tough years in the jungles of Mullaitivu. Embedded within Palsokar's narrative are vignettes of resilience, personal courage, and loyalty under fire by soldiers of the Garhwal, Rajput, Sikh, Gorkha, and Rajputana Rifles and the paracommandos who operated in the brigade's sector. He also acknowledges the risky exploits of the armed Ranjit helicopters operated by the Army Aviation Corps and the IAF's Mi-17 helicopters that sustained his brigade from Vavuniya.[15]

THE ALLIGATOR STRIKES

If there was one weapon system that put the fear of God in the LTTE, it was the IAF's Mi-25 Akbar helicopter gunship. Referred to as *Mutalai* ("alligator" in Tamil) by the LTTE, the Mi-25 had a formidable armament load of two 250-kilogram bombs, 256 rockets, and 1,200 rounds of heavy-caliber cannons. After repeated requests from the brigades involved in the Jaffna offensive, they were finally permitted to employ offensive airpower against the LTTE. The 125th Helicopter Unit commanded by Wing Commander S. C. Malhan came in to Palaly with four aircraft and commenced operations on 25 October. Initial missions flown by Malhan and other senior crew members included attacks on LTTE ammunition dumps and retreating vehicles.[16]

Palaly was a busy airfield throughout Operation Pawan. Despite heavy security and constant patrolling, there was random sniper fire from the surrounding coconut groves, particularly at dusk. This was quite frustrating, and occasionally, when the likely direction of fire could be ascertained, an Mi-25 would be ordered to get airborne and fire at the trees. This brought down a hail of coconuts but hardly ever a sniper. Flight Lieutenant Rajnish Malhotra was one of the several MiG-21 pilots who flew the Mi-25 prior to Operation Pawan. He was present at Palaly during those tumultuous times and noted that even if a couple of snipers were brought down by a fusillade of heavy-caliber fire, there would always be an LTTE party waiting to remove the bodies.

The Mi-25s were initially employed to interdict the movement of insurgents and terrorists on the Jaffna Peninsula and the neighboring islands and mainland of Sri Lanka. This was intended to prevent the LTTE from bringing in reinforcements of personnel and supplies and from exfiltrating its cadres from Jaffna. In the initial weeks, several LTTE fighters were caught in the open by the Mi-25s. Additionally, Mi-25s were used in the lagoons to destroy LTTE boats and vehicles. On 27 October 1987 an Mi-25 piloted by Flight Lieutenant Atanu Guru of 125th Squadron fired on five LTTE heavy transports carrying massive quantities of ammunition and explosives on the old Karaitivu causeway. More than a hundred LTTE terrorists were killed, and the resulting explosions could be heard thirty kilometers away.[17]

As the conflict expanded toward Mullaitivu, Trincomalee, and Batticaloa, the four Mi-25s were split into three detachments. There were two at Palaly and one each at Vavuniya (Fourth Infantry Division) and Trincomalee (Thirty-Sixth Infantry Division). However, the rest of the squadron was based at Pathankot—testimony to India's preoccupation with its western front and Pakistan. Pilots recall that operations were chaotic, fluid, and devoid of hard intelligence. Photo intelligence was almost nonexistent until the later stages of the conflict, even though the IAF launched a few Jaguar missions with infrared line scan pods designed to see through foliage and forest cover. Sometimes the air intelligence was inaccurate, such as the time the pods detected telltale signs of terrorist camp activity that turned out to be the remnants of cooking fires at an abandoned camp.[18]

A typical day began with a dawn search-and-strike mission in a large area to see whether any LTTE cadres could be spotted as they cooked their meals. Malhotra recalled that after taking off from Vavuniya, they would land at Seventh Brigade HQ at Mullaitivu. During his briefing, Major Adrianwalla would stab his fingers on a grid on the map and say, "Here"—sending the pilots off on another search-and-strike mission. Even the slightest movement in the area would prompt the Mi-25 gunship to pull up to about 800 meters and commence its attack, first dropping bombs and then firing rockets in two passes. For those few minutes, the jungles absorbed the pounding as the LTTE terrorists took cover until the Mutalais left the area.

The Mi-25s were proficient at night attacks too, and several junior pilots received their training in night gunnery over the jungles of Mullaitivu. Coping with ground fire at night was a harrowing experience, as tracers whizzed past. But the sheer exhilaration of spotting the location and then firing 1,200 rounds of heavy-duty ammunition was an experience the pilots would never forget. Although the Mi-25s flew tirelessly in Sri Lanka and were always in the thick of battle, their operational impact was modest. Much like "jungle bashing" in Vietnam, firepower came off second best against a largely invisible enemy.

BAPTISM BY FIRE: YOUNG OFFICERS REFLECT

Sri Lanka was a bitterly chastening experience for the hundreds of young officers whose baptism by fire took place in the semiurban combat milieu of Jaffna, the steamy jungles of Mullaitivu, or the treacherous lagoons around Trincomalee and Batticaloa. Many of them are now senior commanders in the Indian military who have seen action and commanded units and formations in Jammu and Kashmir, the northeast, and Siachen. They are justifiably proud of their accomplishments. But mention Sri Lanka, and they can only remember how inept they were made to look by "guerrilla fighters with unmatched motivation, sophisticated communications, and a fanatic streak."[19]

One brilliant officer from the Corps of Engineers who spent two years in Sri Lanka after the fall of Jaffna recounts his tenure with sadness, disbelief, and some sardonic humor directed at the organizational apathy. His unit was rushed from a cantonment in Uttar Pradesh to Chennai on "white-hot" priority. There were "eight to ten generals huddled around a tourist map and trying to make sense of what was going on in the Vavuniya, Mullaitivu, Trincomalee, and Batticaloa sectors."[20] When he joined the engineer unit attached to Seventh Infantry Brigade in Vanni in the early months of 1988, there was complete chaos, as the brigade was still adjusting to the move into a hot operational area and was taking heavy casualties. Because this officer was proficient in Tamil, the brigade commander asked him to monitor LTTE radio chatter. Quick to understand the LTTE's tactics, techniques, and procedures, he observed that many units of the Indian Army just burned any LTTE camps they came across, without bothering to collect material that could help them better understand their adversary. He recollects there being pamphlets on how to build a campsite and inspirational military videos such as *Omar Mukhtar* and *Lawrence of Arabia*. LTTE writings revealed very high levels of intelligence and analysis. For example, one LTTE tactic was to hit a BMP-1 (the Indian Army's infantry combat vehicle) on the side—where its armor plating was weakest. Though severely injured during an operation, this young officer survived and rose to the upper echelons of the army leadership.

Another young officer from the Garhwal Rifles recalled his first posting. He disembarked at Trincomalee, utterly ignorant of the location of his battalion until someone at the transit camp told him it was at Vavuniya. Once he arrived in Vavuniya, he was told that the battalion had moved to Mullaitivu. The situation was so grim that convoys were led by infantry combat vehicles, followed by troops on foot; trucks and jeeps trailed at the end because of the threat of mines and the fear of crossfire. The young officer walked almost sixty kilometers under the constant threat of an ambush. He noted the tremendous fire discipline of the LTTE. An LTTE ambush commenced with a single shot targeting the officers, followed by a volley of fire even before the Indian troops could pinpoint where it was coming from.[21]

PARACOMMANDOS IN ACTION

Among the few sound decisions made by the military operations directorate in the early months of Operation Pawan was the progressive introduction of three paracommando battalions (Special Forces). First and Tenth Parachute Battalions were initially deployed at Palaly. Part of the former was also positioned in Colombo and off the coast on board INS *Vindhyagiri*, disguised in naval uniforms and plain clothes. The commandos' deployment on a naval warship was undertaken at the behest of the Prime Minister Rajiv Gandhi to ensure the security of President Jayewardene, who had expressed concern about a possible army coup in a private conversation with Gandhi.[22] Complementing First and Tenth was Ninth Parachute Battalion, which was seconded to Fourth and Thirty-Sixth Infantry Divisions toward the middle of 1988 as the fighting spread southward and eastward into the Vanni jungles and Mullaitivu.

After the fiasco at the University of Jaffna and the battle that followed, Colonel Rustom Nanavatty was sent to Jaffna as commander of the Paracommando Task Force with operational control. He is full of praise for the performance of the paracommando units in battle, calling it one of the few success stories amid the pall of gloom that permeated the IPKF. Prakash Katoch took over command of First Para after his predecessor had serious differences with division commander Harkirat Singh over operational issues. Unfortunately, the unit had also recently lost three officers in an ambush in Vavuniya. According to Katoch, the dispersed deployment of his battalion was a major impediment to operations. Motivating his teams and maintaining their morale were the main challenges, and he was often asked questions such as "Why are we here?"[23]

Weapons and personal equipment were a major issue for small teams, and Katoch demanded AK-47 assault rifles for his unit from the IPKF leadership. In response, he was given 120 rifles out of the 100,000 imported by the Indian Army. He also requested better maps, radio sets, and interpreters and started training extensively with Mi-8 helicopters in the jungles of Vavuniya. In August 1988 the Indian Army planned a major offensive against the LTTE in the forests of Alampil and Nittikaikulam, where it had identified a large camp with multiple security rings, suggesting Prabhakaran's presence. Both First and Ninth Parachute Battalions saw maximum action and took maximum casualties before and during these operations.

The paracommandos worked with units of Seventh Infantry Brigade and Thirty-Sixth Infantry Division, and their presence reassured the infantry battalions. The commandos would have preferred to take out the camps differently, but they had no choice in the matter, as Kalkat chose the conventional philosophy of cordon, clear, and move. It took First Para and a Gorkha unit three days to build a cordon. When they finally reached the camps, they found food still on the fire and claymore mines in the trees with trip wires laid all around. However, the large LTTE force—including Prabhakaran—had disappeared into the jungle. The two units took eleven casualties from the overhead mines, which were well camouflaged by the foliage. Seven other battalions converged on the camps in a futile show of strength.

Katoch is still indignant about the completely wrong way the IPKF fought the LTTE in the jungles. "We should have inserted multiple small teams after adequate deep reconnaissance," he laments. "Everyone wanted to use the paracommandos, but no one wanted to listen to them."[24] Concerned with the number of casualties, First Para had to reassess its tactics, training, and procedures as the conflict progressed. Despite Katoch's honest assessment of what went wrong, others had good things to say about the paracommando battalions. Nanavatty, who interacted mainly with Ninth and Tenth Parachute Battalions, says that Ninth Para performed brilliantly, was very well trained, and fought cleverly and stealthily. Tenth Para was a tough unit that went forward regardless of casualties in a show of valor.[25] These units contributed significantly to the few operations in which the Indian Army inflicted heavy casualties on the LTTE.

MARINE COMMANDOS IN ACTION

Commodore Arvind Singh and Captain Prakash Chandavarkar are among the pioneers of the Indian Marine Special Forces—later called the Marine Commandos (MARCOS)—which saw action throughout the IPKF's deployment. Before setting up the naval element of India's Special Forces, Arvind Singh had trained with the US Navy Seals and Chandavarkar with the Royal Marine Commando Force in the United Kingdom. The new force was trained in India by the Special Protection Group at Sarsawa in Uttar Pradesh, and in 1986 it moved to its base: INS *Abhimanyu*. It was not long before a handful of marines were pressed into action. The Indian Navy realized that the waters around Jaffna needed protection, and it was an ideal opportunity to give the fledgling force some battle experience.

Chandavarkar remembers operating alongside Ninth and Tenth Parachute Battalions, wearing the same uniform and absorbing their fighting skills. This was a tremendous learning experience for the MARCOS. By the beginning of 1988, they had moved to the port of Kanakesanturai, which was the hub of Indian naval activity. Supplies and personnel were off-loaded there daily. Following reports that the shallow approach waters had been mined by the LTTE, the MARCOS ventured into LTTE-dominated areas. They lay in wait in their armed Gemini inflatable boats and intercepted LTTE fishing boats and trawlers as they ferried cadres across the lagoons. The unit sank many such vessels in 1988. Arvind Singh and Chandavarkar were decorated with the Mahavir Chakra and Vir Chakra, respectively, for several of these hazardous operations.[26]

GETTING IT RIGHT IN BATTICALOA

The town of Batticaloa is located on a thin coastal strip in the eastern province, bounded by the Bay of Bengal to the east and a forty-kilometer-long lagoon to the west. The thickly forested Amparai—located about seventy kilometers southwest of Batticaloa—was the southernmost area dominated by the LTTE during Operation Pawan. It abutted the central province and was used primarily as a haven to control Batticaloa and keep watch on developments in the adjoining Sinhala-dominated central and north-central provinces. Part of the heterogeneous eastern province, Amparai was populated by Sri Lankan Tamils and many Sinhala settlers. The LTTE's hold in the area depended on the local cadre—as the terrorist outfit grew in strength, so did its recruitment in Batticaloa, gaining members from other insurgent groups and from among local youths. As the battle in Vanni intensified, Prabhakaran moved large cadres from the south into the Vanni jungles, replacing them in Batticaloa with cadres from the north, who were fatigued and needed a rest.

Fifty-Seventh Mountain Division proved effective in Batticaloa and Amparai, as it could function more cohesively in a smaller area. Commanded by Major General T. P. Singh, the division had gained counterinsurgency experience in India's northeastern jungles, where the terrain was similar. It took the division two months to induct its three brigades, and it was ready for operations by the end of February 1988. The brigades' primary tasks were to seal off Batticaloa from LTTE influence, destroy the LTTE's lines of communication through the jungles and lagoons, and create an environment for the peaceful conduct of provincial elections in November 1988.[27] Proficient in cordon-and-search operations, the division had soon sanitized Batticaloa and the villages around it.

Within months of commencing operations, the division had scored major successes in terms of capturing or eliminating LTTE cadres or convincing them to surrender. Like other divisions, Fifty-Seventh Infantry Division suffered major casualties from IED attacks and ambushes. One of the few encouraging reports from Sri Lanka came from Batticaloa in June 1988. Anita Pratap of *India Today* wrote that IPKF operations in and around Batticaloa had been a major success.[28] Taking over command of the division in mid-1988, Major General Ashoke Mehta continued the good work of his predecessor. He consolidated the strategy of winning hearts and minds with concurrent operations against the LTTE. Unfortunately for India and Fifty-Seventh Infantry Division, much of this effort was in vain. The LTTE made a startling comeback when Ranasinghe Premadasa became president of Sri Lanka, followed by the gradual collapse of ISLA.

STUTTERING ELECTIONS, FAILED MANDATE, AND WITHDRAWAL

The IPKF consolidated its presence in the northern and eastern provinces and squeezed the LTTE but failed to deliver the final punch to finish it off. In October 1988 the force launched Operation Mahan Kartavya to ensure a peaceful environment for three sets of elections: provincial elections in the northern and eastern provinces in November 1988, the presidential election in December 1988 that brought Premadasa to power, and parliamentary elections in February 1989. Akin to a stability operation that relied on a show of strength accompanied by an effective communication strategy, Operation Mahan Kartavya was designed to insulate the eastern province from the LTTE-dominated northern province while trying to convince the latter to join the electoral process. Voters in Jaffna boycotted the provincial election when the LTTE refused to join the electoral fray. Elections in the eastern provinces (Amparai, Trincomalee, and Batticaloa) saw the EPRLF emerge as the single largest insurgent group willing to abide by the terms of ISLA. The India-backed EPRLF—led by Vardaraja Perumal, with K. Padmanabha as its military commander—formed the provincial government after decisively winning the November 1988 election.

Prematurely elated that the tide finally seemed to be turning in the direction of peace, India's intelligence agencies and strategic leadership did not pick up the ominous signs of the growing understanding between the LTTE and Premadasa. Premadasa, leader of the nationalist United National Party, had scored a thumping victory over the more moderate and pro-India Sirimavo Bandaranaike in the December 1988 election. This set the stage for the gradual undermining of ISLA. There was an emerging confidence within the United National Party that it was time to send the Indians home and sort out matters domestically with the LTTE.[29] In the parliamentary elections in February 1989, the LTTE-backed Eelam Revolutionary Organization of Students (EROS) emerged as the clear winner in the northern province, revealing a completely fragmented Tamil separatist movement.

The politico-military landscape in March 1989, after all the elections were over, was dominated by an emboldened and hard-line government in Colombo led by the hawkish and anti-India Premadasa. Across the Palk Strait, Rajiv Gandhi faced increasing domestic flak over the intervention in Sri Lanka. A fatigued IPKF had no clear direction: should it go after Prabhakaran or let the LTTE survive? Rohan Gunaratna highlights this confusion by suggesting that Indian generals told their troops, "This war was not to destroy your adversary but to guide him in the right direction," or, "You must realize that your adversary is not your enemy."[30] In such a strategic milieu, the informal cease-fire declared by the IPKF in the run-up to the elections allowed the LTTE to initiate direct negotiations with both Indian intelligence agencies and the new Sri Lankan government.

Despite protests by IPKF field commanders that the LTTE was playing a double game, New Delhi did not want to close the door on the LTTE. It would pay a heavy price for this decision, as the LTTE used this opportunity to build up its arsenal via the sea route from India. The new army chief, General V. N. Sharma, had many run-ins with his civilian intelligence counterparts regarding their new strategy of cultivating the LTTE.[31] He consistently argued that the LTTE had suffered heavily at the hands of the IPKF through 1988, and it was time to deliver the final blow. X agrees with General Sharma's assessment and says that the new government led by Premadasa, sensing a weakening of the LTTE, made its first move in June 1989. Premadasa offered the LTTE a false hand of friendship, which Prabhakaran accepted because it was better than getting destroyed by an increasingly battle-hardened Indian Army. Premadasa then fired his first salvo on the eve of the South Asian Association Regional Conference summit by telling the Indians to withdraw the IPKF. Rajiv Gandhi refused, but the die had been cast.

Soon thereafter, in November 1989, Rajiv Gandhi was forced to resign following his defeat in the general elections. The weak interim National Front government led by the new prime minister, V. P. Singh, decided to withdraw the IPKF. Meanwhile, Premadasa kept hounding Dixit to advise the Indian government to hasten the IPKF's exit. Dixit went so far as to secretly procure forty Czech revolvers and told General Sharma to organize self-defense training for the high commission staff.[32] Sharma claimed he had convinced Premadasa not to do anything that would jeopardize the safety of the IPKF.

OPERATION JUPITER

While the Indian Army readied an extra infantry division and its paracommando brigade as part of a contingency plan to cover the IPKF's withdrawal, the Indian Navy sailed the aircraft carrier INS *Viraat* into the waters off the Kerala coast in mid-July 1989. Code-named Operation Jupiter, this was a backup plan in case the Premadasa government crossed the line by completely undermining ISLA and openly aligning itself with the LTTE to hasten the IPKF's departure. *Viraat* would also assist in evacuating the staff at the Indian high commission in Colombo should the situation get rough. Commanding *Viraat* was Captain Madhavendra Singh, a future chief of naval staff. Those momentous events commenced with a brief order on 17 July to sail south. Madhavendra was told that he had "twelve hours for steam," which in naval parlance meant twelve hours to get to full operational readiness from his current position, anchored barely two miles off Mumbai harbor.[33]

As they passed Goa, the Sea Harriers embarked from their base on INS *Hansa*, complementing the Sea King 42 C (commando carriers) and the Cheetah light helicopters as *Viraat*'s aerial component. Choppy seas prevented the loading of missiles, ammunition, and other aviation equipment.

This meant that *Viraat* had to stop at Cochin to pick them up. Off Cochin, Madhavendra was informed that he would have company on board— Seventh Battalion of the Garhwal Rifles Regiment. Commanded by Colonel (later Lieutenant General) Mohan Bhandari, Seventh Garhwal Rifles was airlifted from Bareilly into Trivandrum by the IAF's IL-76 aircraft and transported by road to the Cochin airfield. In a commendable operation that took place on 26 July 1989, approximately 400 officers and men, along with all their equipment, were airlifted to *Viraat* in five and a half hours. *Viraat*'s Sea King and Cheetah helicopters flew seventy-six sorties in a stupendous display of flying in monsoon conditions. Originally a commando carrier with the Royal Navy in the post–World War II era, *Viraat* had adequate space to accommodate the 400 Garhwalis, with spare beds for the high commission staff should an evacuation be necessary.

According to Madhavendra, this operation provided good experience in planning and preparing for out-of-area contingency operations. *Viraat* and its Sea King and Cheetah crews spent quality training time with Seventh Garhwal Rifles for almost two weeks as they waited in Indian international waters, out of sight of the Sri Lanka Navy.[34] After the operation was called off, Madhavendra overheard the Garhwalis talking among themselves in Hindi as they disembarked. About *Viraat* they said: "*Arey Yaar, yeh kamal ki cheez hai—mini shahar hai*" (this is a wonder—just like a mini city).

The IPKF's withdrawal commenced in December 1989 and was completed by March 1990. By several yardsticks, the intervention was a failure, despite some commanders and foreign policy practitioners who argued that there were several positive takeaways from the two-year intervention.[35]

LESSONS FROM SRI LANKA

David Brewster, a maritime security expert at Australian National University, is among the few researchers who has tracked what he calls "India's coercive strategies." He has written extensively about India's strategy with regard to Sri Lanka and the emergence of an "Indira Doctrine on the lines of the Monroe Doctrine."[36] Rajiv Gandhi chose the less risky option of attempting a "peacekeeping intervention" rather than a muscular unilateral military intervention. He cannot be faulted for his strategic intent. Where he faltered was in his timing and in the inability to assess whether India had the operational capability to achieve a favorable strategic outcome. Also, the prime minister was not cautioned by his foreign secretary, army chief, or high commissioner about the possibility of a peacekeeping operation turning into a bloody and prolonged counterinsurgency and counterterrorism campaign. Adding to the confusion were the unprepared armed forces and the poor intelligence acquisition and dissemination by the intelligence agencies. These contributed significantly to the failure of the campaign.

Intelligence

Colonel Hariharan served in military intelligence for nearly three decades and worked closely with all of India's intelligence agencies. His interactions with R&AW and the Intelligence Bureau were particularly robust. One of the few officers in the Indian Army with both staff and field experience in counterinsurgency operations, he was a natural choice to head the military intelligence effort in Sri Lanka. More important, however, was his ability to speak Tamil, which was imperative for operations in northern Sri Lanka. Hariharan identifies two main reasons for the lack of a comprehensive intelligence mosaic. First was the suboptimal synergy between R&AW and military intelligence; second was the shocking and complete misjudgment at every level about the LTTE's capabilities. R&AW resources were focused on meeting the Indian government's aims, which were largely political. Military intelligence was practically the only agency collecting daily intelligence on the LTTE for operational exploitation. According to Hariharan, the LTTE remained neutral and aloof from the IPKF, unlike the other militant groups, which were quite friendly. Military intelligence never considered Prabhakaran a freedom fighter and was intensely skeptical of his vaguely worded acceptance of ISLA—an apprehension that was not taken seriously by either Indian Army HQ or the political establishment.[37]

X remarks that, at the operational and tactical levels of intelligence, intelligence units cannot be expected to simply plug in and start providing input. Capability has to be slowly built up, and "all the units did an excellent job, be it networking, operating sources, or interrogation." He also mentions the fate of LTTE detainees in IPKF detention camps in Kankesanturai, Vavuniya, and Trincomalee prior to the IPKF's departure. Although some IPKF commanders were inclined to hand over these detainees, there was concern that they might be killed by Sri Lankan forces. X argues that since the Sri Lankan government had helped the LTTE with arms and ammunition, it "had to share the blame for many IPKF deaths and had no moral right to stand in judgment and decide the fate of detainees held by the IPKF."[38] It is a pity that undercover agents such as X have gone unrecognized over the years.

Operational Glitches

The initial euphoria with which the IPKF was received in Sri Lanka soon faded because of the LTTE's reluctance to lay down arms and the Sri Lankan forces' hesitation to comply with the terms of ISLA. The altered military objectives of the IPKF from peacekeeping to peace enforcement did not go down very well with the LTTE. Moreover, the IPKF did not have the ability to either coerce or compel its principal adversary to do its bidding. There was poor operational synergy, and the successes, if any, can be attributed to individual acts of initiative and courage. General Sundarji failed to involve his fellow chiefs in any of the strategic discussions with Rajiv Gandhi, and there was no attempt to set up a joint task force. Consequently, the army units were controlled from Pune and Chennai, the air force from Trivandrum, and the navy from Cochin. Synergy improved when General V. N. Sharma took over as army chief, but it was too late by then. Some pin the failure of Operation Pawan on the inability to make the transition from peacekeeping to peace enforcement and counterterrorism in varied terrain. Sundarji had a brilliant mind, but he did not anticipate the vicious turn of events and the "dirty fighting." Harkirat was completely out of his depth and not in sync with the reality of the unfolding landscape.[39] Major General Ashoke Mehta says that although the "LTTE varied its strategy from 'confrontation' to 'avoidance of contact,' 'hit and run' remained the mainstay of its tactics. The IPKF on the other hand could not shed its psyche of a conventional force, though it effectively engaged in small-scale counterinsurgency operations." He adds, "It was unable to engineer a change in mindset: fight a guerrilla like a guerrilla."[40]

Naval and Air Aspects

The Indian Navy conducted a variety of operations during the almost three-year deployment of the IPKF, including covert operations with submarines and armed patrols by front-line warships. More than 400,000 troops, 8,000 vehicles, and 100,000 tons of equipment were ferried to and from Kankesanturai and Trincomalee. The navy provided gunfire support and carried out 152 interceptions on the high seas, resulting in seventy militant boats being destroyed. The MARCOS conducted more than fifty special operations and cut their operational teeth in Sri Lanka.[41] The navy operated largely as a single-service entity and was constrained by the lack of political and strategic guidance on the use of maritime power in counterinsurgency and counterterrorism operations. The use of frigates to provide naval gunfire support was attempted, but New Delhi had not thought through the various maritime possibilities, which would have involved frequent infringement of Sri Lanka's sovereignty and territorial waters. One such possibility was Operation Jupiter, which ended up being a useful joint operational simulation.

Air operations during Operation Pawan took place under severe limitations and without adequate strategic guidance. Within the IAF itself, there was little debate and discussion on the employment of airpower at the lower end of the conflict spectrum. Like the Indian Navy, the IAF operated largely as a single-service entity, although the synergy improved as the conflict progressed. Gradually, the Indian Army was regularly and effectively supported by transport aircraft and helicopters across a range of combat operations. The various challenges included difficult jungle terrain and urban operations with restrictive rules of engagement. The mobile and fleeting nature of the targets meant that fire was largely ineffective unless enemy camps or headquarters could be discovered and engaged before they were abandoned.

Navigation, reconnaissance, and target identification and acquisition were complicated. Helicopters were compelled to fly low for target acquisition, inviting small-arms fire.[42] Several roles, such as special heliborne operations (SHBO), interdiction of the LTTE's supply and communication lines, and scout missions by Army Aviation's Cheetah and Ranjit helicopters, were tried for the first time in such an environment. Accurate intelligence has always been key for the successful execution of SHBO and the real-time targeting of fleeting targets. Even though the LTTE did not have the equipment to intercept air-to-air and air-to-ground communications, it always managed to intercept the army's communications, allowing it to stay one step ahead. This prevented many SHBO and gunship missions from achieving their aim—the University of Jaffna fiasco being a prime example.

Helicopters were inadequately equipped for night operations. There was no means of fitting searchlights onto them, which prevented the conduct of regular nighttime searching and patrolling missions. Jaguar and MiG-23 fighter aircraft flew almost sixty sorties in the reconnaissance role, but their impact in providing targeting information was minimal. Several senior army commanders have acknowledged the IAF's effectiveness, but an equal number of officers who were in the field have highlighted serious deficiencies. If numbers tell the story, the IAF flew more than 48,000 sorties on ten different types of aircraft during IPKF operations. It carried 16,000 tons of cargo and 240,000 passengers. For the IAF, it was a significant learning experience in an out-of-area contingency operation, and the helicopter and transport fleets matured significantly.[43]

EPILOGUE

The saga of one of the most protracted and brutal ethnic conflicts in the post–World War II period came to an end when Prabhakaran was finally cornered and killed on 18 May 2009. Sri Lankan forces stormed his hideout in the jungles of Mullaitivu, where the LTTE had given the mighty IPKF a lesson in counterinsurgency operations two decades earlier.

I I

Speedy Intervention in Maldives

> Operation Cactus was India's first successful strategic intervention. We got it
> right, but only with a tremendous amount of good luck.
> —Presentation by Group Captain Anant Bewoor and Brigadier S. C. Joshi,
> Defence Services Staff College, 1990

SOS

Abdullah Luthufi and Uma Maheswaran were two desperate individuals
from diverse backgrounds who ended up as coconspirators in an audacious
coup attempt in Maldives in early November 1988. A country made up
of several islands and atolls in the western Indian Ocean—or the Arabian
Sea, as it is more commonly known in India—Maldives was hardly on India's strategic radar when the crisis unfolded. Luthufi was an aide of former
Maldives president Ibrahim Nasir, who had extensive interests and invest-
ments in Sri Lanka and had previously tried to unseat the current Maldives
president, Maumoon Abdul Gayoom, who had been elected in 1978. The
1988 coup attempt prompted a decisive intervention by India. Occurring as
it did during the ongoing intervention in Sri Lanka, the Maldives operation
was another demonstration of India's desire to consolidate its position as the
preeminent power in the region.

An early confidant and lieutenant of Liberation Tigers of Tamil Eelam
(LTTE) leader Prabhakaran, Maheswaran had fallen out with him in the
mid-1980s and formed the People's Liberation Organization of Tamil Eelam
(PLOTE), another Sri Lankan rebel group. Maheswaran was soon identified
by India's intelligence agencies as more approachable than Prabhakaran.
Prabhakaran eventually overpowered all other aspirants to the leadership of
the Tamil secessionist struggle and systematically eliminated them between
1986 and 1989. Why Maheswaran would spearhead the Maldives coup was
a matter of much speculation. He may have been attracted by the promise
of a bounty of several million US dollars or the assurance of a haven and
arms-smuggling outpost. Or it is possible that he just wanted to escape from
Prabhakaran. What is known, however, is that the plot was hatched in Sri
Lanka, where Luthufi reportedly owned a farm. It was executed with a bra-
vado that almost paid rich dividends.

186

Group Captain Anant Bewoor was the commanding officer of Forty-Fourth Squadron at Agra, which was equipped with the IL-76 heavy-lift transport aircraft. He would play a pivotal role in the subsequent operation and recollects that Delhi first heard about the coup from the Indian High Commission in Male on the morning on 3 November 1988. The call was received by his brother-in-law, Kuldip Sahdev, the joint secretary in charge of the Maldives Desk in the Ministry of External Affairs.[1] Another call followed an hour later to say that more than a hundred rebels had taken over many vital installations.[2] Soon it was confirmed that President Gayoom was in a safe house and had appealed to India and other countries, including Pakistan and the United States, for immediate assistance.

Without any further intelligence input, the prime minister's office in New Delhi swung into action. It instructed the Indian Army and Indian Air Force (IAF) headquarters (HQ) to start planning for an operation in Maldives. A joint meeting was held in the army operations room, where it was determined that India must intervene. Brigadier V. P. Malik, the assistant director-general of military operations, remembers being startled by Prime Minister Rajiv Gandhi's knee-jerk reaction. The prime minister directed his newly appointed minister of state for home affairs, P. Chidambaram, to send the National Security Guard (NSG) to Maldives immediately. By then, Air Marshal Suri, vice chief of the air staff, had been alerted by his army counterpart, Lieutenant General Rodrigues, that the IAF should be ready to send a parachute battalion for a joint operation in Maldives. Therefore, when Chidambaram asked Suri to position an IL-76 in Delhi to transport the NSG, the latter indicated that he was already committed to a joint army–air force operation.

General V. N. Sharma, the army chief, convinced the prime minister that the parachute brigade was better suited than the NSG to carry out the operation. Gandhi relented on the NSG option, but not before impatiently asking Chidambaram whether the NSG had already flown out.[3] According to reliable sources, an An-12 from the Aviation Research Centre—controlled by the Home Ministry—was already airborne with the NSG commandos on a course for Male but had to abort the mission when it realized it did not have enough fuel to get there.

By 7:30 a.m., the IAF had alerted its strategic airlift assets at Agra to be ready for departure by 1:00 p.m. Around 10:30 a.m., Indian Army HQ alerted its Fiftieth (Independent) Parachute Brigade in Agra to be ready for an impending operation. However, field commanders on the ground had no idea how the operation was to be executed. By a stroke of luck, the Indian high commissioner to Maldives, Ajay Banerjee, was in Delhi at the time. He helped in the initial stages of planning, and his presence during the first briefing in Agra proved invaluable and prevented a disaster in the making. But Banerjee had not expected to be accompanying the lead intervention force to Male in the first IL-76 aircraft.

INITIAL PLANNING: OPERATION CACTUS

Back in Delhi, the planners could not even lay their hands on an operational map of Maldives, let alone a schematic diagram of the various airfields on the islands. They had no option but to use tourist maps to locate beach-heads, drop zones, and vital installations. The first idea to be floated was a company-sized parachute drop, followed by an air-landed operation to deploy the rest of the parachute brigade. A small drop zone was identified on the southeastern edge of Male, and Brigadier Vivek Sapatnekar, a former commander of Fiftieth (Independent) Parachute Brigade, was asked to examine its feasibility. Sapatnekar immediately ruled out that option, on grounds that he would lose 60 percent of his force during the drop because the prevailing winds would hinder a pinpoint landing on the small drop zone.[4]

After hectic discussions involving the directorate of military operations at Indian Army HQ and the operations directorate at IAF HQ, an air-landed operation at Hulule airfield emerged as the best option, given the circumstances. It was code-named Operation Cactus. The shifted then to Agra, the operational hub where the Indian Army's only parachute brigade was colocated with the IAF's strategic airlift assets. Chandigarh and Agra have always been the IAF's two largest air bases. The former is entrusted with air maintenance operations in the northern sectors of Jammu and Kashmir, Siachen, and Ladakh, and the latter has emerged as a hub for strategic airlifts for overseas tasks and airborne and air-landed operations in conjunction with the parachute brigade.

Brigadier Farouk Bulsara was the commander of Fiftieth Parachute Brigade. He had three parachute battalions—Third, Sixth, and Seventh—as well as an artillery regiment (Seventeenth Parachute Field Regiment) to provide fire support when the need arose. He chose Sixth Parachute Battalion (Para) as his lead battalion, with Third Para as backup. With only two companies readily available, Bulsara placed one company of Third Para under Colonel Joshi's command as part of what the paratroopers call a "spearhead battalion." Chosen to lead that company was Major Navkiran Ghei.[5]

At 7:30 a.m. on 3 November 1988, Bewoor received broad directions to keep three IL-76 aircraft at operational readiness. By 10:00 a.m., Bewoor had seen news about the coup in Maldives on television, and he was confident that their destination would be Male, possibly via Trivandrum (now Thiruvananthapuram). He speculated whether his load would be the

NSG, the parachute brigade, or the infantry brigade based at Agra, but he did not pick up the phone and ask Bulsara whether something was indeed cooking. He informed his officers of an impending operation at 10:00 a.m., and Bulsara ordered his units to be ready for possible overseas deployment by 11:00 a.m. None of the commanding officers knew where the crisis was, and Bewoor had not yet been told that he would be transporting Fiftieth Parachute Brigade. In hindsight, they all appreciated that secrecy was important, but surely there could have been a better way to alert the forces as soon as the decision was made to launch the operation. Bulsara by then had a clearer picture of the situation. Somewhere between 200 and 500 mercenaries had taken control of the TV and radio stations, telephone exchange, and other installations in Male. They were supposedly armed with machine guns, rocket-propelled grenades, and surface-to-air missiles.[6]

By 12:30 p.m., Bulsara had his entire spearhead battalion, minus the company from Third Para, ready for a paradrop or air-landed operation at Male. The Agra base had only seventy D5 parachutes, leaving Joshi with a smaller force than required. They were armed with Sten carbines, as these were the only personal weapons that could be used with the D5 parachutes. Two companies of Sixth Para were already at the airfield by 1:30 p.m., but there had still been no communication among Bewoor, Bulsara, and Joshi about the operation.

GETTING THEIR ACT TOGETHER

At 3:30 p.m. the paradrop option was discussed again and ruled out during the first combined briefing at Agra with the team from Delhi in attendance. Bewoor recalls that the alternative plan was to drop paratroopers at a drop zone in the southeast or southwest corner of Male. If this was not feasible, the drop would be at Hulule airfield. However, no one had assessed the drop zones' suitability to receive paratroopers.[7] Around 4:00 p.m. there was some clarity about the task, as it was confirmed that Hulule airfield had not yet been taken over by the mercenaries. It was finally decided to air-land Sixth Para and elements of Third Para at Hulule airfield. As the Hulule plan was being discussed, Ambassador Banerjee noticed, to his horror, that the schematic line diagram displayed in the briefing room was not Hulule airfield but Gan airfield, almost 400 miles south of Hulule on the southern tip of the Maldives archipelago. Banerjee quickly pulled out a beautiful tourist map that included a detailed photograph of Hulule International Airport and gave it to Bewoor. From then on, this became the main "intelligence resource" for the task force.

By then, the entire parachute battalion—including the company from Third Para—had arrived at the airfield. The three IL-76s had not yet been loaded, as there was no clarity about the loading sequence. The loading of the aircraft finally commenced, with heated arguments between the loadmasters and the parachute brigade, and was completed by 5:30 p.m. for a 6:00 p.m. takeoff. Bewoor and Ghei reflected on the chaos of the moment. "I had no opportunity to discuss the plan with Bulsara or Joshi," Bewoor lamented. They finally had their discussion somewhere between Bhopal and Hyderabad at 25,000 feet.[8] Ghei added, "The overemphasis on secrecy deprived troops of preparation time. We even had to prime our grenades during the flight, contrary to all safety norms. All briefings were done during the flight on A4-sized black-and-white photocopies of the tourist map of Male provided by Banerjee."[9]

The spearhead battalion was asked to establish a main and diversionary beachhead at Male by requisitioning local boats; meanwhile, the rest of the force would establish blocking and defensive positions around the airfield. The Male force would be split into two elements—one would extricate President Gayoom from the safe house, and the second would round up the mercenaries. To maintain secrecy, the flight plan had to indicate a destination within the Indian mainland. Air traffic control stations along the way were instructed not to query the two aircraft about their intended destination. However, twenty-five minutes after the two IL-76s took off from Agra, the British Broadcasting Corporation (BBC) reported that Indian troops were on their way to Male—so much for secrecy. The rebels' failure to react to this security lapse by taking over Hulule airfield says a lot about their poor situational and combat awareness.

As the IL-76s cleared Indian airspace and chased the setting sun into the Arabian Sea, Bewoor and his copilot readied for a night landing at Hulule. They were given a password that would indicate the airfield was safe. The second aircraft stayed close, using its navigation lights to stay in formation. The only navigation aid at Hulule was a beacon. After almost three and a half hours of flying, Bewoor spoke into his radio. "This is Friendly One, do you have a message for me?" With relief, the panicky air traffic controller at Hulule blurted out the password, "Hudia, Hudia, Hudia!" They were cleared to land.[10]

HULULE AND MALE HAPPENINGS

Reassured that the airfield was in friendly hands, Bewoor reduced the throttle on the four giant engines and went into a gentle descent. He was relieved when the runway lights came on for ten seconds during his final approach, as it allowed him to align the aircraft with the centerline. When he was 100 meters from the ground, he asked the tower to turn on the

Map 9.
Operation
Cactus: Layout
of Male

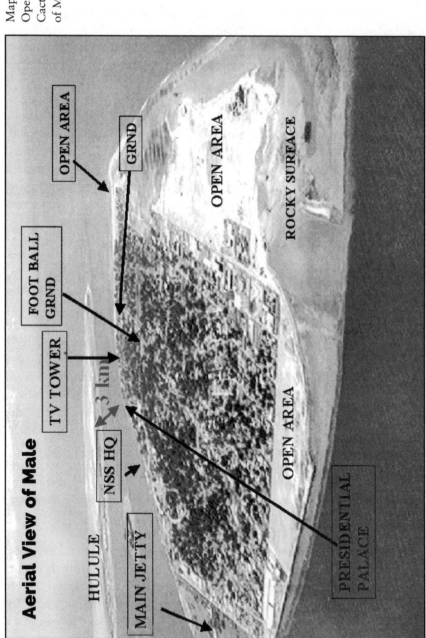

Aerial View of Male

OPEN AREA

GRND

OPEN AREA

ROCKY SURFACE

FOOT BALL GRND

TV TOWER

3 km

NSS HQ

HULULE

MAIN JETTY

OPEN AREA

PRESIDENTIAL PALACE

runway lights again. It was 9:42 p.m. when the wheels touched down. The lights of Male seemed too close for comfort, and Bewoor hoped there would be no interference while the paratroopers were exiting the aircraft and the stores were off-loaded. Encountering no opposition, Bewoor cleared the second aircraft—which was circling over Hulule at 5,000 feet—to land. As it did so, it narrowly missed a few paratroopers crossing the runway. To his dismay, Bewoor saw that the paratroopers had exited the aircraft without off-loading the cargo, which took another forty minutes—hardly a template for rapid deployment.

The paratroopers secured the primary beachhead at Male by midnight, with boats requisitioned from the luxurious Kurumba Resort. A second-ary beachhead was secured by a platoon from Third Para. Encountering no resistance on Male, Joshi and his team headed straight to the safe house to secure President Gayoom. At the same time, the other teams conducted mopping-up operations that involved cordon-and-search drills. There was some shooting that resulted in a few rebel casualties. President Gayoom was secured by 2:15 a.m. and spoke to Rajiv Gandhi at 4:15 a.m.

Ghei and his company from Third Para had taken up defensive and block-ing positions around the western approaches to Hulule airfield, which was separated from Male by a water channel barely a mile wide. At this point, the leaders of the rebel force understood that they could not withstand a multipronged assault by crack Indian troops and decided to flee on any an-chored ship they could seize. Ghei was the first to spot a ship slowly making its way out of the Male anchorage. He immediately radioed the brigade's Major Vinod Bhatia for further instructions. There was a brief lull as Bhatia gathered information about the ship. Then Ghei received a frantic call from him saying, "Fire, Fire, Fire!" All hell broke loose as the paratroopers started shooting at the ship's silhouette with their rifles and carbines. Realizing the ineffectiveness of this fire, Ghei reacted swiftly and called on his rocket-launcher team, which fired a few 84mm explosive rounds at the ship. The team ran along the beach parallel to the ship, firing two more rockets before it glided out of range. The soldiers were certain they had scored at least one hit.[11] The impact of this action would emerge later during the pursuit of the hijacked ship MV *Progress Light* by the Indian Navy warships INS *Betwa* and INS *Godavari*.

By dawn, the remainder of Third and Sixth Paras had been landed by Bewoor's squadron, which flew an additional three sorties during the night. Third Para was assigned the task of clearing Male. The remaining rebels surrendered by midday when they realized they had been left high and dry by their leaders, who were by now on the high seas and sailing toward an unknown destination. Ghei described the mopping-up operations on 4 November: "Searching houses in a foreign land where the loyalties of the locals were unknown to us was a scary proposition. Good discipline prevailed throughout despite the stress and sleep deprivation. There were several foreign tourists in Maldives during the operation, and the entire operation unfolded in front of them. Many of them appreciated the discipline, efficiency, and behavior of the paratroopers."[12] Sixth Para would stay in Maldives for an entire year at the request of President Gayoom.

A CAPTAIN'S ORDEAL

Captain Jayadevan had recently joined the Maldivian state shipping company as captain of MV *Progress Light*, a 4,000-ton cargo carrier that mainly plied the waters between Maldives and Singapore via ports in India and Sri Lanka. The ship had arrived in Male from Singapore on 2 November 1988 with a cargo of speedboats and other items for the various island resorts. It lay anchored offshore, as there were no berths available at the time. Transshipment to Male was in progress, and most of the Maldivian crew members had gone ashore, leaving Jayadevan, his engineer, and a skeleton crew on board. Jayadevan heard some gunfire that night, but by the morning of 3 November, there was continuous firing across the harbor. He tried to reach his crew members by walkie-talkie but failed to make contact. Jayadevan heard about the coup through the BBC at around 10:00 a.m. and braced himself for a long wait to learn the whereabouts and fate of his crew, who were holed up in their homes.

The exact sequence of events is hazy in Jayadevan's mind after thirty years, but it was sometime after sundown when he saw the silhouettes of aircraft landing at Hulule airport. Soon thereafter, he heard and then saw a speedboat with about fourteen people on board going past MV *Progress Light*. The boat suddenly swerved toward his ship and drew alongside, and the occupants quickly boarded the ship. They seemed to be aware that *Progress Light* had not yet off-loaded its cargo and still had enough rations and other food items on board to sustain a longish voyage. The group included men armed with AK-47s and accompanied by four hostages, whose identity Jayadevan could not immediately ascertain. He later found out that they included the Maldivian transport minister and his Swiss-German wife.

The armed men rushed to the bridge, where they apprehended Jayadevan, his engineer, and the few crew members left on board. They were all herded into the dining room. The leader of the terrorists then summoned Jayadevan to take stock of the situation. The rebel leader made it clear that if Jayadevan tried to escape, he would be executed, along with the other crew members. A few more speedboats approached the ship, and soon there were seventy to eighty rebels on board. The leader of the group told Jayadevan to start the engine and head out of port. Jayadevan objected, pointing out the difficulties of negotiating the channels in the dark and the high probability of running aground on the coral reefs. His concerns were dismissed with the threat of dire consequences if he disobeyed.[13]

Jayadevan understood that he had to take the risk if he wanted to survive. As he sailed out of the harbor, he heard a commotion on the airfield, and then *Progress Light* came under fire. His best guess was that the Indian troops had realized the rebels were attempting to flee. Jayadevan clearly remembers machine gun fire and bullets flying around the bridge but does not recall his ship taking a rocket hit. He admits he could be wrong, but his ship was certainly not listing and did not experience any control problems. Ghei, however, insists that the ship was finally intercepted only because his team's rocket hits forced it to slow down. Unfortunately, there is no way to corroborate this because *Progress Light* was later sunk by the Indian Navy. Having skillfully navigated out of Male harbor and onto the high seas in pitch darkness, Jayadevan was first instructed to sail for Sumatra. Then, after some negotiations between the rebels and the Sri Lankan government, he was told to head for the west coast of Sri Lanka. After a day's sailing, Jayadevan realized that he was being tailed by two Indian Navy ships.

WARSHIPS ON THE PROWL

The ships trailing *Progress Light* were INS *Godavari*, commanded by Captain S. V. Gopalchari, and INS *Betwa*—a training ship based at the port of Cochin (now Kochi)—with Captain H. A. Gokhale in command. There is much similarity in the narratives offered by Gokhale, Gopalchari, and Jayadevan about the prolonged cat-and-mouse game played on the high seas as the Indian warships attempted to force the rebels to surrender without resorting to offensive action. Once the Indian government learned of possible negotiations between the rebels and the Sri Lankan government, it was hesitant to get involved. Then came an intelligence report that the Sri Lankans had no intention of negotiating and were planning to sink the ship with all its occupants, most of whom were Tamil rebels from PLOTE. This forced the Indian government to contemplate taking action before the ship entered Sri Lankan territorial waters. Having commenced the intervention, Rajiv Gandhi was loath to cede the initiative to the Sri Lankans, who were already giving him a hard time over the Indian Peacekeeping Force issue.[14]

The Indian Navy's participation in Operation Cactus commenced at 4:20 p.m. on 3 November 1988 when *Betwa*—an air defense frigate of 1950s vintage—sailed out of Cochin harbor. It was first asked to maintain a naval presence in the waters around Maldives following the coup.[15] By early the next morning, Gokhale had been alerted that *Progress Light* was now a fugitive ship, headed for either Sri Lanka or one of the Southeast Asian countries. He was directed to intercept the rebel-laden ship but did not have radar contact yet. Gokhale determined that it would not be long before a US Navy ship moved into the area, and thanks to coordinates provided by a US Navy helicopter, he achieved visual detection of the hostage ship at around 2:45 a.m. on 5 November.

Despite repeated warnings from the shadowing *Betwa*, *Progress Light* continued toward Sri Lanka. *Godavari*—one of the Indian Navy's newest frigates—joined the fray later that evening. It had picked up Indian and Maldivian hostage negotiators from Colombo, who failed to broker a deal, despite concerted attempts to do so. The drama on the high seas entered its last phase on the evening of 6 November. To Jayadevan's horror, two hostages were executed on the bridge right in front of him, and their bodies were thrown overboard.[16]

That was the last straw for Gopalchari and Gokhale. Despite the lack of clear instructions from New Delhi, both naval ships commenced firing on *Progress Light* in the wee hours of 7 November. The firing—first with small-caliber weapons and then with medium guns—caused significant damage to *Progress Light* and inflicted casualties among the rebels, who were foolishly attempting to make a stand rather than surrendering. According to Jayadevan, the transport minister was hit in the leg, and small fires broke out on the ship. Realizing that the rebel leader was preoccupied with organizing his men, Jayadevan ushered his engineer and crew members and the two remaining hostages (the Maldivian minister and his wife) to a dingy. They floated toward *Betwa,* which picked them up. The rebels eventually surrendered, and naval commandos from *Godavari* boarded the severely damaged *Progress Light* to search for survivors. Jayadevan had to identify his crew members killed in the firefight, who were laid out with dead rebels. Then a volley from *Godavari* sank *Progress Light*. The next day Jayadevan was asked to confirm that some floating debris was indeed part of his ship.[17]

Per President Gayoom's request, all the hijackers and crew members were first taken to Maldives. Jayadevan and his Indian crew members were separated from the Maldivian crew and taken to a guest house. The injured minister was airlifted to Pune via Trivandrum for medical treatment. Jayadevan was questioned by Indian and Maldivian interrogators, who were trying to ascertain whether he was complicit in the whole operation. He was repeatedly asked why the rebels had boarded his ship when there were larger and more modern ships at anchor. Jayadevan suggested that his cargo of speedboats might have been appealing to the rebels, and they might have learned this information from the Maldivian crew members who had gone ashore. It was also possible that the rebels thought the Indian crew would be better at navigating the Indian Ocean.

After satisfying the intelligence agencies that he and his crew had merely been pawns in this game, Jayadevan was permitted to return home, much to the relief of his wife and children. Once he was safely back in Chennai, Jayadevan was surprised to receive a call from Home Minister P. V. Narasimha Rao. The minister complimented him for his conduct and poise throughout the ordeal but also advised him not to comment about the incident or speak to the press about what had happened on the high seas. Jayadevan refused to speak to anyone about these events until he finally agreed to be interviewed for this book. He believes the Indian government wanted to cover up details of the hostage executions, the sinking of *Progress Light*, and the number of rebels who died in the shelling. Jayadevan kept his cool throughout the ordeal and did nothing rash to endanger the lives of his crew. His biggest regret is that he lost some of his men during the gun battle. Reflecting on his experience with the Indian Navy, Jayadevan noted that *Godavari*'s maneuvering and procedures were sound, but *Betwa* was too old and should not have been assigned to the operation. He also recalled the understandably cold treatment he and his crew received from *Betwa*'s crew.[18]

BOUQUETS AND BRICKBATS

From a strategic perspective, the Maldives intervention was a resounding success. A floundering but legitimately elected government in India's backyard was restored to power after it was unable to defend itself against a ragtag bunch of mercenaries. The speed of strategic decision making was good, even though the operational planning process was fragmented. There was good leadership and initiative at all levels.

In hindsight, it was a risky operation because there was little tactical intelligence about the mercenaries and their weapons, such as whether they had rocket launchers that could potentially cause serious damage to the Indian military forces. The paratroopers were organized and accomplished their mission, despite the hazardous distribution of grenades and ammunition, the last-minute briefings over the Indian Ocean, and the use of tourist maps as direction finders and locators. There were numerous planning niggles and operational glitches, and luck ultimately played a significant role in the operation's success. The initial planning process was chaotic, and operational units were not in the informational loop until late in the day. Compatibility of equipment and weapons was a major concern because the parachute brigade did not have the right kind of parachutes or rifles for an airdrop.

The lack of actionable intelligence was not the result of a capability gap. Intelligence was lacking because, at the strategic level, Maldives was nowhere on India's intelligence horizon, given its preoccupation with Sri Lanka, Pakistan, and China. Operation Brasstacks, Operation Falcon, and Operation Pawan had stretched the intelligence agencies to their limit. From a naval perspective, the absence of sophisticated navigation aids on *Betwa* hampered the search for the rebel ship. However, the decisiveness of Captains Gopalchari and Gokhale in taking offensive action was praiseworthy. There were many things that could have gone wrong had the rebels been smarter, more zealous, and better organized. There is no end to such "what-if" scenarios. The IAF's strategic airlift concept of operations emerged from Operation Cactus, and the IL-76 proved to be a reliable platform.

THIRTY YEARS ON

Three decades later, Bewoor reflects that the lack of bloodshed and Indian casualties may leave the impression that the operation was nothing to write home about. But such operations are generally either stunning successes or dismal failures. The Entebbe rescue by Israel and the American fiasco in Iran are good examples of success and failure, respectively.[19]

Nearly thirty years after India first intervened in Maldives, the island nation was once again beset by worrisome internal instability. It sought military intervention by India in February 2018 after a widespread crackdown by President Abdulla Yameen, which included taking former president Gayoom into custody.[20] Further alarming the Indians was Yameen's clear strategic tilt toward China, possibly encouraging a Chinese presence to stave off any threat to his government. The Modi government speedily readied the Indian Army's Parachute Brigade, which was flown into Bangalore, along with the IAF's new fleet of C-130 J aircraft, and instructed it to await further orders. In the meantime, India's intelligence agencies and military operatives carried out a reconnaissance of Male. However, the operation was called off once Yameen understood that India would not tolerate any needless overt interference in its own sphere of influence.[21]

12

Jammu and Kashmir Erupts

> The terrain inside Kashmir was ideally suited for guerrilla and sabotage action. In addition, our frontier tribesmen have for centuries found India an attractive hunting ground.
>
> —Major General Akbar Khan, *Raiders in Kashmir*

EARLY KASHMIR RUMBLINGS

The oppressive rule of the Hindu ruler of the princely state of Jammu and Kashmir (J&K), Maharaja Hari Singh, gave rise to two narratives in the decades immediately preceding partition. The first narrative emerged from the Kashmir Valley, where Sheikh Abdullah and his group of moderate Kashmiri nationalists started a movement with aspirations similar to those of the Indian National Congress. The difference was that the Indian National Congress sought freedom from colonial rule, and Sheikh Abdullah sought freedom from the oppression of Maharaja Hari Singh.[1] The second narrative was a more aggressive expression of Kashmiri angst from south of the Pir Panjal Range, which separates the valley from the plains. There, Sardar Abdul Qayyum Khan, a former soldier in the Engineer Corps of the British Indian Army, brought together disaffected Muslims from the Poonch region and attempted to overthrow Maharaja Hari Singh.

The Islamist foundation of the secessionist movement in Kashmir was laid by the Pakistan-based radical group Jamaat-e-Islami, which had strong roots in the Poonch region. (It would take India more than seven decades to react to the fissiparous influence of this organization, which was finally banned in February 2019.) To further the two-nation theory of Muhammad Ali Jinnah (Pakistan's first prime minister), which sought to divide the subcontinent based on religion, an infiltration operation was executed by the Pakistan Army in 1947–1948 called Operation Gulmarg. It was poorly executed and thwarted by the spirited and professional Indian military response before it could expand into an insurrection.[2] It was a two-tier game plan. When the first tier—the planned insurrection—failed, the second tier was operationalized, with the Pakistan Army joining the battle to support the armed raiders of Jamaat-e-Islami. Although Jamaat-e-Islami was already an influential group, it had not yet sowed the seeds of religious bigotry in the valley. Once the raiders were beaten back and the planned insurgency fizzled out, the 1947–1948 contest turned into a conventional military conflict.

Consequently, Jinnah argued that Kashmir—with its predominantly Muslim population—rightfully should have joined Pakistan. Indian prime minister Jawaharlal Nehru and home minister Sardar Patel did not agree. In an eminently readable and objective article, Simon Jones articulates Nehru's reasons why J&K should have remained with India, stating that Kashmir's diversity meant that its existence was essential to the ideology of a secular state.[3] Nehru seemed rather confused about Pakistan in the aftermath of this conflict. However, he claimed to understand Pakistan's strategy on Kashmir when he argued, "The invasion of Kashmir is not an accidental affair resulting from the fanaticism or exuberance of the tribesmen, but a well-organized business with the backing of the state." He conceded that India had to deal with a nation carrying out an informal war, but a war nevertheless.[4]

And yet, despite his deep understanding of the geopolitics of the area, Nehru did little to alter the strategic landscape in the Kashmir Valley. He could have done that by ensuring good governance, strengthening political structures, and bolstering them with a robust intelligence and military setup to counter secessionist tendencies and aspirations. In the autumn of 1948 Nehru approached the United Nations (UN) and requested a cease-fire, trying to portray Pakistan as the aggressor. However, the United States and United Kingdom supported Pakistan's assertion that Kashmir was a contested area. Nehru thus lost an opportunity to restore the status quo in the valley. This would cost India dearly in the decades ahead.

Jamaat-e-Islami grew stronger in the region following Pakistan's occupation of part of Kashmir in the aftermath of the UN-brokered cease-fire in January 1949. Sheikh Abdullah and his love-hate relationship with Nehru also dominated the political landscape, and the sheikh's association with separatists worried India's intelligence agencies and Patel. Patel urged Nehru to adopt a consistent but hard-line policy toward those who either propagated *Azadi* (freedom) or sought Pakistan's assistance for a separatist movement. Unfortunately, Patel's death in December 1950 left India's Kashmir policy entirely in Nehru's hands. The prime minister was rather altruistically obsessed with restoring peace in the state of his ethnic origin at any cost. This meant that he was willing to turn a blind eye toward the fissures and cracks emerging within Kashmir's polity. Praveen Swami—who was the first to use the term "informal war"—makes some very astute observations regarding the slow deterioration of the security situation in J&K in the 1950s and 1960s. He writes that J&K's accession by India was challenged not only politically and diplomatically but also militarily. J&K was thus "a zone of continued warfare—low grade warfare, it is true, but warfare none the less."[5]

Sheikh Abdullah's arrest in 1953—for alleged secessionist and anti-national activities—followed by the installation of a pro–Congress Party state government in J&K, ushered in a period of uncertain calm. It also paved the way for the establishment of a Pakistan-directed grid of covert actors to undermine the societal fabric of J&K. These covert cells were trained in acts of subversion and coercion. They had two objectives: to create fear by causing public inconvenience and disruption through bomb blasts and acts of sabotage against symbols of the state, and to instill fear in the minority Hindu population and polarize the communities further.

In April 1964—still reeling from India's 1962 defeat at the hands of China—Nehru decided to release Sheikh Abdullah on the advice of his cabinet. The idea was to wean the sheikh away from separatism. Abdullah agreed to act as an interlocutor on Kashmir between Nehru and Pakistan's military dictator, Ayub Khan. However, a secret report by the US Central Intelligence Agency (CIA) shed light on Abdullah's real intentions, stating that, since his release, his actions suggested that although he knew he had a strong hand in dealing with Delhi, he was not yet ready to play it out. "He does not believe that the Kashmir question is settled and neither does New Delhi," stated the report, "but its public position is that the accession is final and irrevocable."[6] Unfortunately, Nehru's death on 27 May 1964 changed the situation. It gave Zulfiqar Ali Bhutto, Pakistan's foreign minister, an opportunity to speak informally with Sheikh Abdullah while flying to Delhi to attend Nehru's funeral. The sheikh was returning from Rawalpindi, where he had convinced Ayub to meet with Nehru and find a lasting solution to the Kashmir problem. According to Swami, the plan to establish a network of covert operators gathered steam after Nehru's death.[7] Bhutto was emboldened to tell Ayub that he had the sheikh's support. They decided to orchestrate a widespread people's rebellion in Kashmir and began to plan Operation Gibraltar.[8]

THE FAILURE OF OPERATION GIBRALTAR

The Pakistan Army thought it could force a military solution in Kashmir, especially after India's defeat by China in 1962. Operation Gibraltar was orchestrated by Pakistan's Foreign Office, along with Inter-Services Intelligence (ISI) and the commander of Twelfth Division, Major General Akhtar Malik. The strategy was similar to the one used in 1947–1948, the difference being the existence of a robust follow-on operation designated Operation Grand Slam, which involved a plan to cut off J&K from the rest of India. While the first operation was immediately thwarted by an alert Indian Army in J&K, the second almost succeeded, but for a slight operational pause that allowed the Indian Army and Indian Air Force to conduct a spirited rearguard action.[9]

Brigadier Pranadhar Gaur, who served in J&K, makes an interesting observation about the absence of any radical zeal within the Pakistan Army of the 1960s and the reluctance of Pakistan's president Ayub Khan to make Kashmir central to the India–Pakistan rivalry.[10] One of the president's close confidants, Major General Shaukat Riza, wrote that Ayub was "not a wild-eyed revolutionary crazed by dreams of reshaping the world. He was a realist and in his cabinet meetings had emphasized that the security of Pakistan was not to be jeopardized for the sake of Kashmir." Ayub knew that fighting in Kashmir would escalate to a war between India and Pakistan—a war that Pakistan could not win without foreign help.[11] Those were prophetic observations indeed.

It is commonly believed that Zulfiqar Ali Bhutto played the Kashmir card to convince a large number of Pakistani generals that the time was ripe to force a solution. Bhutto's opening gambit may have failed, but that only spurred him to find new methods to drive latent Kashmiri nationalism and Islamic fervor. Despite his broadly secular leanings, Ayub dabbled in jihadi ideology. He was influenced by Aslam Siddiqui, one of his pro-jihad aides. In his book *Pakistan Seeks Security*, Siddiqui argues that covert warriors and irregular warfare are elements of jihad that need to be nurtured for difficult times. He also suggests that these players can best be exploited if they are nurtured outside the "system."[12] In her seminal work on the Pakistan Army, C. Christine Fair traces the influence of Jamaat-e-Islami to the late 1950s.[13]

PAKISTAN'S ISLAMIC REVIVAL

The aftermath of the 1965 war with India saw Pakistan's army junta floundering. It was left to the mercurial Bhutto to drive Pakistan's political agenda. He wanted to transform Pakistan's engagement with the Islamic world and ensure that Kashmir remained central to the India–Pakistan strategic discourse. An alert and resilient Indian intelligence network in J&K—led by police officer Surendra Nath—was smashing the remnants of the Pakistan-sponsored covert cells, but this was not enough to extinguish the embers of Kashmiri nationalism. Sheikh Abdullah's stance in his quest to regain leadership in Kashmir also remained ambivalent. Had Nath's early reports on J&K been heeded by Delhi—first by Lal Bahadur Shastri and then by Indira Gandhi—Pakistan's covert war strategy might have faltered in its infancy. Unfortunately, these reports are still shrouded in secrecy.

President Ayub Khan's persistent belief that the "Kashmir cause" was not furthering Pakistan's national interests did not go down well with the rest of the Pakistani establishment. He was forced to agree to an elaborate plan to conduct a covert war in J&K. The strategy was to keep the pot boiling while maintaining the conflict at a level just short of war. Such a strategy was clearly designed to exploit the established norm of "deterrence with restraint and responsibility," which was the cornerstone of India's national security policy. Concurrently, Bhutto built close relations with other Islamic countries and created an Islamic narrative for Kashmir that would create multiple pressure points for India in the international environment. This led to Pakistan forging close ties with the United Arab Emirates, Saudi Arabia, Iran, Turkey, and Indonesia.[14] Sadly, India failed to work on counternarratives and remained cocooned in the smug discourse of constitutional sovereignty and territorial integrity.

The strategic consequences of the 1971 war with Pakistan—and their impact on the trajectory of any future conflict in Kashmir—were profound.[15] They signaled a departure from the existing discourse in the minds of the Pakistani military establishment, which was reeling from a humiliating military defeat. Indira Gandhi's ill-timed magnanimity—failing to resolve the Kashmir issue in the Shimla Agreement, when India held all the cards—was a blunder that still haunts India today. In its moment of triumph, India neither considered the evolving situation in Kashmir nor reflected on how warfare might change in the years ahead. The Indian military was sidelined in the discussions following the 1971 war and prior to the Shimla summit. This meant that Indian negotiators failed to leverage the impact of holding 93,000 prisoners of war and let Pakistan off the hook by not insisting on a cartographic and noninterference commitment. This provided an opening for the Pakistan military, its intelligence agencies, and jihadi forces to avenge the humiliation of 1971. They planned to do this by waging a constantly evolving covert war and inciting the people of Kashmir to rise against the Indian state.

COVERT WAR UNFOLDS

The covert war that is currently manifesting in multiple forms in J&K was largely the brainchild of the late Pakistani military dictator General Zia-ul-Haq.[16] He came to power in a 1977 military coup that overthrew the civilian government of Zulfiqar Ali Bhutto. Bhutto had elevated Zia to army chief barely a year earlier because he was perceived as a subservient general who would be amenable to taking orders from a civilian government. Little did Bhutto realize that the "pliant" general would soon send him to the gallows.

Zia also set in motion the Islamization of the Pakistan Army by introducing a Quranic concept of war.[17] These became the key drivers of the covert war strategy to "bleed India by a thousand cuts"—a phrase adapted from Mao's tested strategy of "death by a thousand cuts."[18]

The defeat of the Russians in Afghanistan in the mid-1980s made J&K a soft target for jihadis, who received active support from Zia. This is a rather simplistic summary of the origins of what has been a troublesome secessionist movement for India. Since the late 1980s, the covert war has been one phase in a constant struggle of narratives in J&K, beginning in the days preceding partition. While India chose to develop as a secular, multiethnic, and multicultural democracy, Pakistan emerged as a theocratic Islamic state where there is constant jousting for political power.

One of India's biggest strategic challenges has been to combat Pakistan's two-level strategy of subverting India and forcing the secession of J&K. This strategy is prominently discussed in various writings about the fractured relationship between these two nations.[19] Gaur analyzes the evolution of this strategy from a practitioner-scholar's perspective.[20] Swami offers an academically robust and brilliant piece of investigative writing.[21] US-based Sumit Ganguly is one of the most prolific writers on the fractured India–Pakistan relationship.[22] Also serving as invaluable resources on J&K were the field commanders who led formations in the Kashmir Valley during this period, including Lieutenant Generals M. A. Zaki, R. K. Nanavatty, J. R. Mukherjee, K. Nagaraj, S. A. Hasnain, D. S. Hooda, and Ravi Thodge and General Bipin Rawat.

Rise of the Jammu and Kashmir Liberation Front

Swami suggests that Pakistan-trained Kashmiri jihadis became common after the establishment of the Al-Fatah master cell in the mid-1960s. It was led by Ghulam Rasool Zahgir, a clerk who recruited radicalized students from Kashmir University in Srinagar. Al-Fatah carried out the first recorded killings of security personnel and vandalized and desecrated places of worship to whip up communal passions.[23] The Al-Fatah cell expanded over the next few years, bolstering its cadres with educated youths who focused on the twin pillars of the covert war—political activism and military action. During their numerous trips to Pakistan across the porous border, its cadres were trained in political subterfuge, military intelligence, and war fighting with weapons, explosives, and bombs.[24] The movement fizzled out by early 1971, just as it was ready to expand its activities. This was due to the Pakistani government's reluctance to continue to support it and the sudden alertness of India's intelligence agencies, which smashed Al-Fatah.

The National Liberation Front (NLF) was set up in the mid-1960s by Maqbool Butt, a maverick student leader. The group floundered after the 1971 hijacking of an Indian plane to Lahore. Butt was arrested and sentenced to death by India. This led to the emergence of UK-based Amanullah Khan and the NLF's transformation into the Kashmir-oriented Jammu and Kashmir Liberation Front (JKLF). This group offered the first real military challenge to the Indian state in the early 1980s. Initially set up in London, it operated out of Muzzafarabad, the capital of Pakistan-occupied Kashmir (PoK).[25] The choice of this location was symbolic: the tribal *lashkars* had launched the first attack on Kashmir in October 1947 from Muzzafarabad.[26]

The JKLF drew blood in 1984 by kidnapping and executing an Indian diplomat in Birmingham, England, an act that was immediately followed by Butt's execution in India. Britain's expulsion of many JKLF cadres—including Amanullah Khan—led to its expansion in PoK. Many Pakistani youths crossed over into PoK to be trained in the basics of infiltration and weapons handling. The 1987 election in J&K was a watershed event in which the National Conference Party and the Congress Party alliance came to power after a highly fractured and reportedly rigged mandate. Several JKLF leaders—such as Yasin Malik and Javed Mir, who had campaigned for Jamaat-e-Islami and backed the Muslim United Front—were disillusioned by the widespread fraud and became even more committed to the secessionist agenda.[27]

Disappointed by his failed election foray and attempts to join the mainstream was fiery student leader Syed Salahuddin. He would later emerge as the leader of Hizbul Mujahideen and head of the Kashmir-focused terrorist umbrella organization called the United Jihad Council.[28] The state descended into a spiral of violence marked by confrontations between separatists and security forces. The increasingly politically astute population sat on the fence watching. A combination of poor governance and effective mobilization of cadres by the secessionists proved to be the tipping point for the insurgency to escalate into a full-blown covert war. The JKLF was largely secular and drew inspiration from the Palestine Liberation Organization (PLO), and its cadres were committed to the idea of *Azadi*. General Zia was preoccupied at the time with the covert war in Afghanistan, but this did not prevent him from sending the ISI into the Kashmir Valley to work alongside the JKLF. Well versed in the art of covert war and black operations, the ISI had honed its skills under the CIA in Afghanistan. It was ready to expand its operations into J&K.

Operation Topac

Personally, General Zia was rankled by the defeat at the hands of India in 1971. Nationally, getting even with India was at the heart of all Pakistani politico-military strategy. Zia represented the new face of the Pakistan Army, which increasingly viewed Islam as the glue binding the army and the nation. Realizing that India was growing more powerful, Zia decided to wage a sophisticated covert war and complemented it with a strategy of internal radicalization. He already had insight into the response mechanisms of India's security forces through his support of Bhindranwale's Sikh secessionist forces in the early 1980s.[29] However, Zia did not live to see his plans fructify. On 17 August 1988 he perished in a suspicious airplane crash, along with many of his generals, the ISI chief, and the US ambassador to Pakistan. But Zia's vision had a self-sustaining momentum. Many believe that the radicalization of the Pakistan Army rapidly followed the gradual radicalization of Pakistani society. Soon, the Pakistanis' visceral hatred for the Indian Army morphed into a desire to wage jihad against the nation of India and its mostly Hindu citizens.

In 1975 one of Zia's trusted lieutenants, Brigadier S. K. Malik, wrote a seminal treatise on the Quranic concept of war that was reprinted in India in 1986 and widely read. It highlighted the relationship between Islam and jihad and recommended that Pakistan's armed forces embrace Islamic tenets. This was a doctrinal departure from the purely Western way of war fighting. Zia endorsed Malik's philosophy and beliefs and shared his zeal for jihad. Together, they believed that jihad was the collective responsibility of the Muslim *ummah* (the whole Muslim community) and was not restricted to soldiers. Zia emphasized that an Islamic military professional must have a "godly character." He wholeheartedly backed Malik's Quranic concept of war as the only type of war an Islamic state could wage.[30]

Zia's sustained alteration of Pakistan's military ethos and structure also had an impact on its civil society. There was an increase in the number of Deobandi clerics and madrasas across Pakistan during Zia's rule. This radicalization of Pakistan ought to have alarmed the Indian strategic establishment. Joseph C. Myers, a US Army lieutenant colonel and senior adviser at the US Air Command and Staff College, offers insights into the successful and rapid Islamization of the Pakistan Army through the 1980s. He argues that radical Muslims are more likely to adapt to and execute an asymmetric approach to war. "With respect to global jihad terrorism, as the events of 9/11 so vividly demonstrated, there are those who believe in and will exercise the tenets of the Quranic concept of war."[31]

Operation Topac first came to public notice in 1989, when *Indian Defence Review* published an article by Major General Afsar Karim.[32] Written as part truth and part fiction, the article was clearly based on leaks from Indian intelligence sources in Pakistan. It was an ingenuous attempt to sensitize the Indian political establishment and military to the ominous nature of Pakistan's designs. Operation Topac (also called Tupac, after a Peruvian prince) slowly took shape under the guidance of ISI chief Major General Akhtar Abdur Rehman.[33] It got an indirect boost from the Russian invasion of Afghanistan when a myopic CIA-led initiative gave Pakistan billions of dollars in arms and military equipment and critical intelligence in the 1980s. The United States wanted to build the military capability of the Afghan mujahideen to support their armed struggle against the Russians. But the aid also empowered Pakistan's ISI.[34]

What the Americans did not anticipate was that after the Russian defeat in Afghanistan, all this new war-waging capability would be redirected toward J&K. However, its direct impact on India in the form of a formal covert war in J&K took a decade to evolve. In April 1988 Zia outlined the framework of Pakistan's strategy at a top-level meeting attended by loyal corps commanders, ISI leadership, and elements of the Afghan and Kashmiri mujahideen. Making a conscious attempt to steer clear of Pakistan's mistakes in 1947–1948 and 1965, Zia directed the first phase of the strategy at supporting widespread infiltration, subversion, shock, and attacks on military strongpoints. The aim was to spur a people's revolt against the Indian government and initiate the gradual disintegration of peace in J&K.

The second phase of Zia's plan envisioned Pakistan taking control of Kashmir and setting right the historical aberration of partition. Zia described the Kashmiri people as "simpleminded folk" who nonetheless possessed "a few qualities" that Pakistan could exploit, such as being good at "political intrigue." "If we provide [a Kashmiri person] means through which he can best utilize these qualities, he will deliver the goods."[35] Although several Western commentators believe that Operation Topac was a figment of the Indian Army's imagination, there is much evidence of a well-orchestrated political-jihadi-military plan to undermine India's security, with Kashmir as the prize. Sean Winchell, a prolific writer on the ISI, believes that it was perfectly positioned at the time to assume the lead role in Zia's Kashmir strategy. He argues that, "since Partition, no political force within Pakistan has driven the nation's domestic and international political agenda as has its army" and, more specifically, the ISI. He corroborates the existence of such an operation, stating that in addition to supporting Afghan mujahideen fighters, "the ISI began to assist the Kashmiri separatists in their effort to make Kashmir a part of Pakistan. In 1988, as part of that support, then-president Zia created Operation Tupac [Topac]."[36]

According to the South Asia Terrorism Portal, 1988 marks the formal beginning of the externally abetted covert war in J&K. That year, there were 391 incidents and twenty-nine civilian fatalities; one terrorist and one member of the Indian security forces were also killed.[37] At the time, India's external intelligence agencies and the Indian Army were preoccupied with the Sri Lankan quagmire. Its internal intelligence agencies were handicapped by a coalition government that paid no heed to the warnings of veteran intelligence experts. On 6 September 2019 Ajit Doval—India's current national security adviser—confirmed to the media that there was indeed a paper on "Operation Topac that had emerged or leaked in 1988–89."[38] Reflecting on why Pakistan was forced to seriously rethink its Kashmir strategy, Simon Jones writes:

> India never once went to war specifically to retain control over the state. Its actions have always been defensive with respect to its national integrity. This indicates that while India is unwilling to lose more territory, it is content to live with the status quo. Besides this, the Indian military has proven its dominance in the field beyond a doubt and can weather almost anything that the Pakistan government throws at it, short of nuclear weapons.[39]

Collapse of the JKLF

Following the commencement of Operation Topac, the Kashmir Valley became a fertile recruiting ground for the JKLF. It expanded in the urban areas around Srinagar, building up an *Azadi* euphoria that thrived because of the state government's complete abdication of control. Rajiv Gandhi and the coalition government of V. P. Singh were equally responsible for India's weak-kneed Kashmir policy in the late 1980s. A comprehensive analysis of the rise and fall of the JKLF and the corresponding rise in the number of incidents during 1989–1992 is highly revealing.[40] Had the J&K state government under Dr. Farooq Abdullah taken serious note of the collusion between the ISI and JKLF, the insurgency might have been crushed before it expanded into a covert war.

The JKLF fragmented in 1990 after its first military commander, Ishfaq Majeed Wani, was neutralized in an encounter with security forces.[41] Thereafter, the JKLF could not reorganize itself militarily to face the Indian Army, which by 1991 had put together an effective counterinsurgency grid. Consequently, many J&K-based JKLF cadres escaped into PoK and joined the pro-Pakistan jihadi forces that were preparing to stoke widespread rebellion in the Kashmir Valley.[42] The ISI's decision to stop providing funds and logistics support to the JKLF hastened its collapse, and it ceased to be an effective force by the mid-1990s. Some prominent former JKLF cadres, such as Yasin Malik, tried to join the political mainstream as part of the All Party Hurriyat Conference. Amanullah Khan's dream of an independent Kashmir finally evaporated in 1996 when all remnants of the JKLF's militant wing were systematically eliminated by Indian security forces.

THE REAL JIHAD

In his book *Shadow War*, Arif Jamal writes about the ISI's role in stoking the rebellion in Kashmir. He posits that a meeting between Zia and a prominent Jamaat-e-Islami leader in 1980 laid the foundation for the "new covert war" in J&K. In addition, he believes that Zia convinced the CIA that its money was being used to train jihadi fighters in Afghanistan, when the real objective was to unleash the mujahideen in Kashmir. Jamal portrays the Kashmir secessionist movement as a by-product of Kashmiri angst and dissent exploited by the ISI.[43] It was then given a jihadi focus by Jamaat-e-Islami. Later, Zia and the larger Pakistani security establishment adopted the movement as an effective and low-cost tool for containing India. However, the only groups that Jamal designates as proxies of the ISI are the JKLF and Hizbul Mujahideen. He conveniently ignores the emerging Pakistan-based groups that included foreign fighters, such as Harkat-ul-Ansar, Harkat-ul-Mujahideen, Jaish-e-Mohammad, and Lashkar-e-Taiba. These groups emerged as viable alternatives to the milder Kashmir-based groups, with whom the ISI was fast losing patience. However, in a later book, Jamal acknowledges the predominant role of Lashkar-e-Taiba in leading the ISI-sponsored jihad in J&K.[44]

Rise of Hizbul Mujahideen

Zia was skeptical of the Kashmiri aspirations for independence that motivated the JKLF and its leader Amanullah Khan. However, he played along as the JKLF sporadically attacked state police forces and government buildings from 1984 to 1988, without taking on the might of the Indian Army. But the JKLF's nonjihadist attitude and belief in *Kashmiriyat* (Kashmir for Kashmiris) did not endear it to pro-secessionist groups such as Jamaat-e-Islami, which equated the fight for Kashmiri independence or secession with jihad. Under the fiery Syed Salahuddin, Hizbul Mujahideen (HM) became the first Kashmiri secessionist group. Salahuddin became disillusioned with mainstream politics in J&K after the rigged 1987 elections catapulted Dr. Farooq Abdullah to power and derailed his own political ambitions. He took up arms under the umbrella of the powerful Jamaat-e-Islami. Exploiting the ISI's growing impatience with the JKLF's focus on *Kashmiriyat*, he rallied thousands of disgruntled youths to follow suit. Concurrently, he bolstered the military capability of his outfit with weapons the CIA had supplied to Pakistan for the jihad in Afghanistan.

Through much of 1988 and 1989, the Kashmir Valley witnessed numerous ISI-organized strikes and rallies. These gradually progressed into attacks on government establishments. The ISI reportedly spent more than 100 crores a year to train and radicalize fighters and subvert individuals and institutions in Kashmir. Sophisticated weapons such as assault and sniper rifles, explosives, and rocket launchers enabled terrorists to attack Indian security forces.[45] As the valley entered the turbulent 1990s, HM became the first heavily armed ISI-sponsored jihadi group to engage the Indian Army in frontal firefights. However, HM soon fell out of favor with the ISI because of its largely Kashmiri flavor. Frequent fratricidal infighting made matters worse for the indigenous terrorist groups and eroded their capacity to mount a serious challenge to the Indian Army.[46] The stage was thus set for the entry of mercenary, battle-hardened, highly radicalized and violent groups such as Harkat-ul-Ansar, Harkat-ul-Mujahideen, and Lashkar-e-Taiba.[47] These groups contained a mix of mujahideen fighters who hailed from diverse regions such as Chechnya, Sudan, Yemen, and Afghanistan, complemented by highly radicalized Kashmiri youth. Older and disgruntled members of various Kashmiri secessionist and terrorist groups acted as local guides for these groups. Indian security forces soon realized that they had a serious fight on their hands.

Entry of Lashkar-e-Taiba and Jaish-e-Mohammad

Every new proxy network that sprang up in J&K was proof of the ISI's messianic zeal and the Indian government's inability to convert military successes into political outcomes. As the Indian security forces gained ascendancy over HM in the mid-1990s, the ISI unleashed Harkat-ul-Ansar (HuA) and Harkat-ul-Mujahideen (HuM) into the valley. These groups elicited Western censure following the kidnapping of six tourists, five of whom were killed, in July 1995 by HuA.[48] Next came Lashkar-e-Taiba (LeT) and Jaish-e-Mohammad (JeM), with the former working as the ISI's principal proxy. Under Hafiz Saeed, LeT emerged as the linchpin of the jihad in J&K for over a decade, even though it was labeled a terrorist organization by the United States.[49] India began to warn the global community of the need to take collective action against these two groups from the late 1990s onward. However, the world took note only after the Mumbai attacks of 2008, in which 139 Indians and 26 foreigners—including several European, Israeli, and American citizens—were killed.

Markaz-ud-Dawa-wal-Irshad, a Salafist jihadi organization, had emerged in Saudi Arabia in the 1980s and gained military momentum during the Afghanistan jihad. At the time, Hafiz Saeed was a lecturer in Islamic studies at a university in Lahore. He was recruited into the group and used his skills to incite terror in Kunar province of Afghanistan. Inspired by Saeed's incendiary oratory, LeT fighters led by Zaki-ur-Rehman Lakvi were radicalized and trained to take on the might of the Indian Army. On 25 January 1990 LeT claimed that it had killed four unarmed Indian Air Force pilots in Srinagar. However, the evidence gathered since then points to the active involvement of the JKLF and its leader Yasin Malik in planning and executing the attack.[50] Originally planned for the previous October, the attack had to be postponed for operational reasons.[51] LeT thereafter expanded its operations, engaging in prolonged encounters with the Indian Army from 1990 to 1994. LeT fighters kept platoons engaged for hours while others slipped through cordons and spread out in the valley.

Lieutenant General Rostum Nanavatty was a major general commanding Nineteenth Infantry Division at Baramulla during this period. He recollects that for the first time, his units noticed a fanatical streak among the terrorists. They appeared to be willing to die fighting and were even engaging the army in close and unarmed combat.[52] After studying LeT's tactics, Nanavatty informed all units engaged in counterinfiltration, counterinsurgency, and counterterrorism operations about the five conclusions he had reached: (1) LeT was the ISI's favorite proxy tool in the covert war in J&K; (2) it would not be long before LeT expanded its operations; (3) LeT had organizational, theological, and financial support; (4) because LeT was not targeting Westerners in J&K and was not expanding its networks elsewhere, India would have to deal with LeT by itself; and (5) LeT was willing to execute *fidayeen* attacks, which differed significantly from suicide attacks. Nanavatty explained the difference: "*Fidayeen* attacks involved fighting to the death and avoiding capture by trained fighters, while suicide attacks merely involved blowing oneself up by indoctrinated but untrained fighters."[53]

LeT operations progressed from encounters with security forces to direct attacks on civilians from the Hindu and Sikh communities. The group was emboldened by its initial successes, and its terrorist base swelled with increased funding from the ISI. It attacked the Red Fort in December 2000 and the Indian Parliament in Delhi exactly a year later. These attacks nearly sparked a war between India and Pakistan in 2002. LeT continued its terrorism spree by attacking the Akshardham temple in Gandhinagar, Gujarat, in 2002, killing thirty-three people. The group allegedly provided active support to the Dawood Ibrahim gang for the Mumbai blasts of 2003.[54] Facing heat from security forces in J&K prior to the 2003 cease-fire, LeT diversified its repertoire. It began to support indigenous jihadi groups and banned Islamist organizations such as Indian Mujahideen and Students Islamic Party of India. LeT's free run gradually slowed down after the notional censure by the United States and Pakistan in the aftermath of 9/11. LeT morphed into Jamaat-ud-Dawa in 2002 and continued to wage a covert war until it was proscribed by the United Nations after the 2008 Mumbai attacks.

In recent times, the one jihadi who has inflicted the most damage on innocent civilians and Indian security forces in J&K is Masood Azhar, the head of JeM. Azhar started out as a preacher in the Deobandi-dominated madrassas of Bahawalpur and Karachi and rose to become a fully indoctrinated Wahhabi jihadi. Endowed with fiery oratory skills, Azhar (along with Hafiz Sayeed) was identified by the ISI as someone who could energize the floundering HM-led insurgency in Kashmir.[55] It was in this milieu that HuA—whose core cadres comprised veterans of the Afghan jihad and ISI-trained Punjabi jihadis—emerged as a concurrent military threat to Indian security forces in the early 1990s. Supporting them were Kashmiri youths who had been indoctrinated by Azhar and his band of terrorist preachers and trained in the camps that sprang up all along the line of control in PoK.

Masood Azhar first entered Kashmir via New Delhi in early 1994. He had been sent there to rein in his military commander, known as Afghani, who had escalated the fight with Indian security forces to levels that made the ISI uncomfortable. Azhar's task was to recalibrate the conflict to levels that would enable the ISI to orchestrate the proxy war as planned. Azhar, Afghani, and other HuA terrorists were captured by the Indian Army in late 1994, interrogated, and interned in different Indian jails.[56] Colonel Pavan Nair, a staff officer at Fifteenth Corps headquarters at the time, recalls numerous occasions when he saw a meek Azhar sitting outside the office of Brigadier Arjun Ray, waiting to be interviewed about the jihadi network in the valley.[57]

An analysis of the fatalities in J&K in the years after Azhar's capture indicates that the jihad movement had acquired self-sustaining momentum.[58] This was due to the ISI's efforts and Azhar's ability to galvanize large numbers of Kashmiri youths to cross the line of control. His three attempts to escape from Jammu's central jail reinforced his aura among the jihadis. Azhar was released following the hijacking of Indian Airlines flight IC804 in January 2000. Encouraged by the ISI and the Taliban—which was keen on establishing a presence in J&K—Azhar launched his own outfit, JeM. UN reports indicate that Azhar was supported by none other than Osama bin Laden. This allowed him to emerge at the head of the pack of jihadis in Kashmir.[59] Azhar was furious when JeM was portrayed as playing second fiddle to LeT during the attack on the Indian Parliament in December 2001. He urged the ISI to assign an exclusive JeM team to attack an Indian Army camp. The attack happened at Kaluchak, near Jammu, in July 2002. Thirty-one people were killed—three army personnel; eighteen family members of army personnel, including several children; and ten civilians.[60]

A combination of geopolitical factors limited JeM's activity to the Kashmir Valley. These included the 2003 cease-fire across the line of control, the ISI's preoccupation with Afghanistan, LeT's designation as a global terrorist group after the 2008 Mumbai attacks, and the reconfiguration of Kashmir-centric jihadi groups. However, recent US pressure on LeT and Chinese intransigence about censuring Azhar have given JeM free rein in Kashmir and a platform for expanding its network in Punjab. The massive expansion of JeM's headquarters in Bahawalpur, Pakistan, is proof that the Pakistani government has turned a blind eye to Azhar's status as the pivot of terror in J&K.

Despite the setback after the Indian Army's surgical strikes on JeM camps following the 2016 Uri suicide attacks, the political vacuum in J&K has given Azhar a respite from the relentless operations by India's security forces. The Pulwama attack in February 2019—which was undertaken to avenge the death of Azhar's nephew, who was neutralized by security forces in November 2017—highlights the extent to which Azhar continues to be on India's "most wanted" list. Both these attacks and their consequences are covered in chapter 18. For now, the narrative moves on to the late 1980s, when the Indian Army moved into the J&K hinterland in strength to tackle the chameleon-like ISI-led covert war that had morphed into jihadi terrorism.

Naga insurgents undergoing training in southern China led by Muivah.

Publicity and propaganda photograph of Chairman Mao recovered
from captured Naga rebels.

Joint operations in Mizoram: Indian Air Force pilots of 110th Helicopter Unit (Mi-4) with army colleagues flying out captured Mizo insurgents for interrogation, 1967.

Bhindranwale's fighters monitoring the Indian Army buildup from the towers on the periphery of the Golden Temple complex.

Brigadier Nanavatty with his troops at Gyong La.

Troops at lunch after completion of their training at the Siachen Battle School.

Panoramic aerial view of the glacier.

Always on time and over target: An-32s from Forty-Eighth Squadron on a mission over a drop zone on the glacier.

Chinese and Indian soldiers arguing at Nathu La, September 1967.

Major General J. M. Singh and Lieutenant General Narahari with officers of Fifth Mountain Division surveying the operational area north of Tawang, September 1986.

Major General J. M. Singh enjoying a cuppa with Gorkha troops.

Liberation Tigers of Tamil Eelam (LTTE) cadres captured by the Sri Lanka Navy and handed over to the Indian Peacekeeping Force (IPKF). They would later swallow cyanide pills when they learned the IPKF would hand them back to Sri Lankan security forces.

Routine vehicle search in Jaffna by an Indian Army patrol.

Captured Liberation Tigers of Tamil Eelam (LTTE) flag with an intimidating caption.

Cache of weapons recovered from the Liberation Tigers of Tamil Eelam (LTTE).

Indian Air Force attack helicopter pilots with paracommandos of First Parachute Battalion (Special Forces) prior to a joint operation in Mullaitivu.

Indian Navy aircraft carrier INS *Viraat* with a full complement of aircraft and troops from Seventh Garhwal Rifles during Operation Jupiter.

Troops aboard INS *Viraat* practicing an assault with Sea King helicopters.

Brigadier Bulsara (*left*) and Group Captain Bewoor (*right*) engaged in the final planning for Operation Cactus at Agra.

Kargil 1999: Convoys lined up on the national highway in the Dras–Kargil Sector.

Typical infantry assault with rifles, light machine guns, and rocket launchers.

Pilots and engineers from 129th Helicopter Unit at Srinagar prior to the first missions against Tiger Hill in late May 1999.

Officers and troops of Eighteenth Garhwal after capturing one of the heights in the Tololing Sector.

Painting of the Mirage-2000 attack on Tiger Hill by Deb Gohain.

General Malik and Air Chief Marshal Tipnis inspecting a captured medium machine gun, surrounded by commanders and troops, after a successful assault.

Indian medics of Sixtieth Parachute Field Ambulance attending to a wounded soldier from Twenty-Seventh Commonwealth Brigade during the Korean War (1950–1953).

Indian Air Force Canberra bombers from Fifth Squadron at Kamina airfield as part of United Nations operations in the Congo (1961–1963).

Securing an Mi-35 attack helicopter during approaching bad weather in the Democratic Republic of Congo.

Indian naval frigate INS *Teg* escorting a Maersk cargo freighter in the international transit corridor.

THE COMPANY

They called themselves "The Company," and they were feared by Hizbul Mujahideen and Lashkar-e-Taiba: Colonel Gurdeep Bains (*front row, second from left*) and officers of Second Parachute Battalion (Special Forces).

Mingling with the enemy and fighting alongside the Indian Army's Special Forces: the Indian Navy's Marine Commandos (MARCOS) in North Kashmir.

Indian Air Force Garud Special Forces in central Kashmir, October 2017.

India's current chief of defense staff General Bipin Rawat (*left; then a major general*) interacting with deployed troops on the line of control during his tenure as commander of the Baramulla-based Nineteenth Division.

Winning hearts and minds: Major General Rawat meeting citizens and elders in Baramulla.

Indian Air Force Mirage with a Spice 2000 bomb used against the Jaish-e-Mohammad terrorist camp at Balakot on 26 February 2019.

Reinforcing eastern Ladakh to counter Chinese aggression. The Indian Air Force's C-17 fleet lined up at Leh after airlifting Indian Army T-72 tanks into Ladakh.

Prime Minister Narendra Modi exhorting officers and men of the Indian Army and Indian Air Force to stand firm in Ladakh, 3 July 2020.

13

The Indian Army Responds

ISI is our first line of defense and stands out as the best intelligence agency in the world.

—Prime Minister Imran Khan of Pakistan, *Economic Times*

STRATEGIZING AFTER PUNJAB

Punjab was India's first brush with terrorism. Terrorism differs from insurgency in that the perpetrators coerce noncombatants instead of seeking popular support for a cause. A largely urban and semiurban phenomenon in India, it has similarities with organized crime.[1] The character of terrorism in Jammu and Kashmir (J&K) changed beginning in the late 1980s, morphing into externally abetted communal terrorism. This was not a surprise to Indian intelligence agencies. Intelligence officers such as Surendra Nath, who had extensive experience in J&K between the 1960s and 1980s, had recommended a judicious mix of force and good governance to ensure that the indigenous terrorism led by the Jammu and Kashmir Liberation Front (JKLF) and Hizbul Mujahideen (HM) was not hijacked by Pakistan-based jihadis led by Lashkar-e-Taiba (LeT) and Harkat-ul-Ansar (HuA).[2] Not helping matters was the weak and delusionary leadership in New Delhi, starting with Prime Minister V. P. Singh's coalition government, which had little stomach for using force as an enabler of statecraft and allowed Kashmir to drift for much of the late 1980s and early 1990s. They let the situation fester until there was no choice but to deploy the Indian Army in strength in counterinfiltration and counterterrorism roles in the early 1990s.

The absence of any official strategic and operational analysis of terrorism in Punjab during the 1980s and early 1990s has resulted in the fading of some important lessons. Consequently, the impact of the Punjab experience on the contours of terrorism and the proxy war in J&K rarely figures in current discussions. A deeper examination of the Kashmir crisis by Pravin Swami reveals its linkages with the Punjab secessionist movement in the 1980s and early 1990s. It escalated the covert war in J&K from a mere irritant for India's security forces to a siege from within.[3] Hamish Telford, a Canadian professor of political science, is a keen analyst of counterterrorism operations in Punjab and J&K. He observes that India's current counterterrorism strategy in J&K is much like the one its security forces followed in Punjab, and any evolution has come through trial and error.[4] Although he may be right to some extent, the evolution of India's counterterrorism strategy has also been a flexible process driven by experiential learning.

The lessons of the Naga insurgency and the experience of the Indian Peacekeeping Force in Sri Lanka are studied at India's counterinsurgency school in Vairangte in Mizoram. This analysis is also being undertaken at the battle schools set up in Fifteenth and Sixteenth Corps, which are actively involved in counterinfiltration and counterterrorism operations in J&K. Army intellectuals have contributed immensely to the evolution of the counterinfiltration and counterterrorism strategy that exists today. Adding value to the discourse are academics such as Rajesh Rajagopalan who have written extensively on these issues.[5] Even in the early 1990s, when the Indian Army's divisions were deployed along the line of control, there was adequate clarity on the emerging templates of terrorism and the unfolding covert war in J&K. Rostum Nanavatty has often argued against the temptation to brand all conflict in J&K as terrorism because of the terror attacks against the minority Hindu population. Instead, it has conformed more closely to a calibrated Pakistan-supported covert war, with Pakistan using terrorism as an instrument of state policy to "destabilize and diminish India."[6] Several journalists such as Shekhar Gupta and Nitin Gokhale have indirectly enhanced our understanding of counterterrorism over the years thanks to their extensive sojourns in the battlegrounds of J&K, northeastern India, and Sri Lanka.

India's Kashmir strategy has been largely bereft of continuity and strategic vision. It has invariably evolved from the government's personality-centric attempts to initiate a meaningful political process. The failure of this process has generally led the center to blame the state government for the deteriorating law-and-order situation and the subversion of the political process. Following the state government's inability to manage the security landscape, the center has attempted to bring the situation under control by deploying the military and armed paramilitary forces with adequate constitutional provisions. Some of these provisions that merit attention are Article 356 of the Armed Forces Special Powers Act (1956), the National Security Act (1980), the Unlawful Activities Prevention Act (1967), and the lesser known Terrorist Affected Areas (Special Courts) Ordinance (1984) and Armed Forces (J&K) Special Powers Act (1990).[7]

Large forces have often been deployed in the affected areas to fight a battle of attrition. These forces were expected to spread out and confine the infiltration or terrorism to a few areas and prevent its spread. Once the force had consolidated its hold, it turned its attention to the leadership of the movement, offering both the leaders and their followers an opportunity to abandon their cause. This strategic model is a coercive one employed by the state to psychologically exhaust the terrorist-secessionists. It highlights the physical futility of continuing the fight. In J&K, this has been the longest and most exhausting phase for both the security forces and the terrorist-secessionists, and even more so for the common people. In this battle of attrition, there are moments when both the hunter and the hunted lose focus and resort to the indiscriminate use of force. This leads to collateral damage, human rights abuses, and diminished public support for either the terrorist-secessionists or the security forces. The media's entry into the fray makes matters worse in this information age. Over the years, the Indian Army has complemented this strategy with embedded intelligence-driven operations by its Special Forces. These operations have been particularly effective in the systematic elimination of the leadership of jihadi networks.

The last phase of the strategy is the stabilization and conflict-resolution phase and a reintroduction of the political process. This is always the most difficult stage in conflicts of this nature. In Punjab, this resolution took place gradually over three elections (1985, 1992, and 1997). Despite four elections (1996, 2002, 2008, and 2014) in J&K, the covert war has escalated since the late 1980s. Assessing the fault lines in India's counterinfiltration and counterterrorism strategies in J&K over the years, Lieutenant General Syed Ata Hasnain, commander of the Srinagar-based Fifteenth Corps between 2010 and 2012, laments the absence of a whole-government approach and continuity whenever there has been a stabilization phase after extensive kinetic operations. Defining the centers of gravity in J&K has been a source of debate within the Indian Army. Hasnain argues that these have alternated between the people of Kashmir and the terrorist leadership, and important as these groups are, he believes a more important center of gravity emerged as the secessionist movement gained steam in the mid-1990s. He identifies this as the ideology of *Azadi*, or freedom, which occupied the minds of radical elements in the secessionist movement, and he regrets that this was never adequately addressed.[8] This would prove costly for India, as the secessionist movement has transformed since 2008 into a hybrid war led by jihadis and the Pakistani deep state. Instead, India has largely taken the direct kinetic route to defeating terrorism in J&K. A better way might have been a more flexible, indirect approach that "separates the fish from the water," as suggested by John Nagl in his seminal work *Learning to Eat Soup with a Knife*.[9]

BOILING OVER

Despite the ominous warnings delivered in 1983–1984 by Lieutenant General Chibber, commander of the Indian Army's Northern Command, India was unable to control events in J&K in the mid and late 1980s. India had deluded itself into thinking that Kashmir would sort itself out, given that Pakistan was too preoccupied with Afghanistan to stoke the secessionist movement. Chibber insisted that it was time for the Indian Army to consider the socioeconomic, religious, and ethnic diversity of J&K and recognize its vulnerability to fissiparous forces from across the line of control. From this emerged the first strands of India's "winning hearts and minds" strategy. Chibber directed a study group to write an easily digestible narrative titled *Soldiers' Role in Jammu and Kashmir* and exhorted his officers to disseminate it widely.[10] Hasnain participated in this exercise as commander of a Garhwal Rifles battalion in the Poonch Sector and in the battle school at Naushera in late 1983.[11] Chibber's prescient understanding led him to believe that the Indian Army should not be perceived as an occupation force by the people of J&K in the years ahead.

Jagmohan, who twice served as governor of J&K between 1984 and 1990, sensed an ominous change in the state's security landscape. He wrote to Rajiv Gandhi in early 1990: "In August 1988, after analyzing the current and undercurrents, I had summed up the position thus: The drumbeaters of parochialism and fundamentalism are working overtime. Subversion is on the increase. The shadows of events from across the border are lengthening. Lethal weapons have come in. More may be on the way." In April 1989 he had desperately pleaded for immediate action: "The situation is fast deteriorating. It has almost reached a point of no return." Jagmohan reported that "things have truly fallen apart."[12] There was political instability and apathy at both the center and the state level, along with a mass mobilization of the educated populace and increasing penetration of Kashmiri civil society by radical elements from Jamaat-e-Islami and Pakistan's Inter-Services Intelligence (ISI).

As a result, it was impossible for the Indian Army to stem the rot that had set in. It was clear that the Indian Army, initially serving as a border protection force along the line of control, was spread too thinly to prevent the large-scale infiltration of local terrorists from training camps in Pakistan-occupied Kashmir (PoK) and foreign terrorists. The time was ripe for Zia's successors in the Pakistan Army to operationalize his Quranic concept of war. Systematically following Zia's first operational tenet, they directed well-trained subversive elements to avoid confronting the Indian Army and to test their combat skills against police and paramilitary forces. An analysis of attacks in 1989–1991 corroborates this strategy.[13] There was free movement on the roads of J&K, and there was no way to seal the highly porous line of control that stretched to the demarcated international border. Those were the days of conventional conflict, and routine patrols were undertaken to prevent infiltration across the line of control. Artillery engagements were rare, and opposing post commanders regularly exchanged memos, pleasantries, and sweets.

The Indian Army knew that young people were crossing over into PoK, but inadequate forces and the absence of an obstacle prevented it from plugging all infiltration routes. Brigadier R served in 2009 as a battalion commander in a sector in north Kashmir that was known to be one of Pakistan's favorite infiltration spots. Among his many tasks was to mingle with the people, establish a rapport with the elders, and convince them to counsel the youth not to take up arms. He described one such meeting with a Gujjar (hill tribesman) in his seventies. The man had set up the rendezvous at a desolate place so as not to be seen interacting with the officer. The old man spoke at length about his role in the ongoing secessionist movement and revealed that he had been one of the first guides recruited by the ISI to lead disgruntled Kashmiri youths into PoK in the early 1980s. He then volunteered to acquaint the battalion with the numerous infiltration routes he had traversed as a guide, noting his disillusionment with the movement and the ISI's exploitation of Gujjars, who had historically used grazing grounds astride the line of control.[14]

The years 1989 and 1990 were scarred by sporadic violence and a marked rise in the number of fatalities suffered by security forces.[15] There was a complete absence of law and order under Farooq Abdullah, who had come to power as chief minister after a dubious election.[16] His government failed to stop the pogrom unleashed by Jamaat-e-Islami–led gangs that forced more than 200,000 Hindus to flee their homes in the winter of 1989 and seek refuge in Jammu and other Indian cities. This compelled Delhi to call on the army to restore normalcy in J&K.

Lieutenant General M. A. Zaki—a distinguished infantry officer from the Maratha Regiment and the recipient of an award for gallantry in the 1971 war—took over command of Fifteenth Corps in Srinagar in October 1989. The Ministry of Defense reckoned that the appointment of a Muslim officer would send a powerful message to both the common people and the secessionists that a secular India was serious about reining in the separatists. However, Zaki could do little to stop the persecution of the Hindus and their exodus in the winter of 1989–1990. Lamenting the heavily filtered flow of intelligence from Delhi, Zaki is highly critical of intelligence bureau chief A. S. Dulat. He alleges that he received no detailed intelligence briefings by

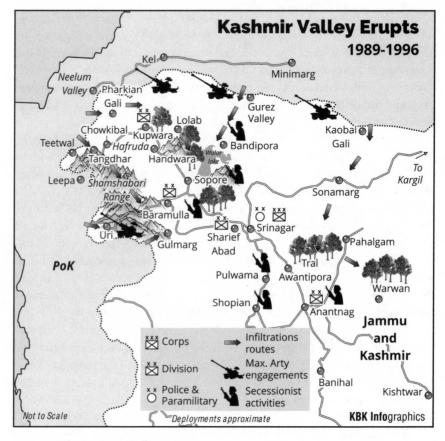

Map 10. The Kashmir Valley Erupts

either civilian or military intelligence agencies before taking over Fifteenth Corps. There seemed to be no urgency in Delhi about the deteriorating situation in J&K, and he was told that "there is no real problem in J&K."[17] By the time Zaki assumed command in Srinagar, the JKLF had already moved to the next phase of the insurrection. The key objectives during this phase were to disrupt infrastructure and various lines of communication. Targets included the Jawahar tunnel across the Banihal Pass and key points on the Jammu–Srinagar highway.

On 9 December 1989 Rubaiyya Sayeed, daughter of Indian home minister Mufti Mohammed Sayeed, was kidnapped by a group of JKLF terrorists led by Yasin Malik. This was Zaki's first major challenge. J&K police did not apprise him of the situation until 8:00 p.m.—nearly nine hours after she was abducted. Zaki knew that by then, the kidnappers would be well outside the limited security dragnet in place in and around Srinagar. The delay was apparently because back-channel negotiations were taking place among the kidnappers, the Indian government, and Farooq Abdullah. It is believed that Abdullah initially took a strong stand against negotiating with the kidnappers, but his political rival Mufti Sayeed convinced New Delhi to negotiate his daughter's release. She was eventually exchanged for jailed JKLF terrorists. This outcome gave a clear indication to secessionist forces that India was unprepared for a covert war in J&K. This incident also spelled the end for Farooq Abdullah's beleaguered government. This eventually forced Delhi to declare president's rule in J&K and to call on the army to restore normalcy there. General Krishna Rao resigned as governor of J&K, and Prime Minister V. P. Singh's coalition government reappointed Jagmohan as his successor.

COMING TO GRIPS

The Indian Army stepped in immediately, without the necessary resources. Nineteenth Infantry Division—one of the three divisions under Fifteenth Corps—was the only infantry division deployed in the valley, with its head-quarters (HQ) in Baramulla. It was primarily configured for deployment along the line of control in a border protection role, so it was now expected to add counterinfiltration and counterterrorism to its mission. Zaki was desperately short of troops to create an effective internal security grid in northern Kashmir. Completing his force were two army battalions for counter-terrorism operations in the capital city of Srinagar and a mix of armed paramilitary and police forces. Considering the vast expanse of its area of deployment from the Banihal Pass to eastern Ladakh, Fifteenth Corps was clearly undermanned and ill equipped for counterterrorism and counterin-filtration duties. Following attacks on army camps and convoys, Zaki requi-sitioned additional troops and deployed his air defense regiment as convoy protection, in addition to establishing a counterinfiltration grid. Given the prevailing inertia, Zaki can be considered the first orchestrator of active counterinfiltration and counterterrorism operations in J&K.

The JKLF increased its attacks on soft targets, killing the vice chancellor of Kashmir University and his aide in March 1990. The encounters became more protracted and included the looting of banks and the destruction of public infrastructure, such as bridges. The JKLF's chief military commander, Ashfaq Wani, was neutralized by security forces on 30 March 1990. According to Zaki, Wani accidently blew himself up with a grenade during the engagement and did not go down fighting, as claimed by the JKLF.[18] In view of the deteriorating security situation, Zaki persuaded Indian Army HQ to move Twenty-Eighth Infantry Division back to northern Kashmir from Ladakh and deployed it in the Kupwara region. He assigned one brigade from the newly inducted Eighth Mountain Division to bolster the counterterrorist operations in Pulwama and the Tral forest areas of southern Kashmir. This caused significant attrition among the JKLF and other terrorist groups in the Kashmir Valley. But it was still not enough to plug all the infiltration routes—despite the three layers of defense along major ingress routes.

By the end of 1990, there were two infantry divisions deployed along the line of control from Uri in the west to Dras in the east. Complementing them in the Budgam, Pulwama, Anantnag, and Tral Sectors of southern Kashmir was Eighth Mountain Division. In addition, there were three battalions in the city of Srinagar, along with the armed police force. This totaled 80,000 to 100,000 personnel in J&K at the time. The major routes of infiltration were down the Shamshabari Range through Gulmarg and Sonamarg, from the south across the Pir Panjal Range, and through narrow valleys in the Gurez, Naushehra, Machhil, Neelum, and Tangdhar Sectors. The towns of Kupwara, Sopore, and Baramulla emerged as safe havens for the terrorists, who were actively supported by the locals in these semiurban areas. Srinagar continued to be the intellectual hub of secessionist activity, despite a heavy security presence.

Zaki recollects that the troops had no respite, with a cycle of three days in action followed by a one-day recuperation period. Many of the initial army operations were unsuccessful because of the lack of an effective military-intelligence grid and network of informers. One such operation was mounted after intelligence reports from Delhi indicated that hundreds of infiltrators had taken over the Shamshabari Range and were waiting for an opportune moment to come down into the valley. Responding to this input, Zaki sent two battalions on a futile search that found no infiltrators. In response to Zaki's pleas for a dedicated intelligence unit, General V. N. Sharma assigned one from Sri Lanka to Fifteenth Corps. Despite the lack of intelligence, the number of terrorists killed rose dramatically in 1991, indicating the firm resolve of the security forces.[19]

Zaki recalls meeting three young travelers from Maharashtra who were cycling in Kashmir. They told him, "Sir, there are a lot of problems—the clocks everywhere are set to Pakistan Standard Time and we are often told that the next time we came, we would need a Pakistan visa." Zaki confirms that thousands of misguided Kashmiri youths crossed the line of control in 1988–1989 to be trained in camps set up at Muzzafarabad, Chakoti, and Kel. They subsequently infiltrated into the valley, mainly as armed porters; a few had received specialized training from the ISI in handling weapons and explosives, among other battle skills. They would set up arms caches at various places as part of a supply network. The crossings were tracked with information from various sources cultivated by Zaki. One of them was an ex-army officer who had been posted with Zaki in Nineteenth Infantry Division but was now setting up an India Tourism Development Corporation hotel in the valley. Zaki soon realized that the terrorists were far more numerous than estimated in routine intelligence briefings. He learned that thousands of cheap fur-lined boots and jackets were being bought in local markets in the autumn of 1989.[20]

Responding to a credible tip-off that a convoy of a hundred mules accompanied by armed terrorists and porters was making its way across the Shamshabari Range, Zaki ordered an infantry brigade into action. Surrounded and given the chance to surrender, the group chose to fight, and they were all killed—more than seventy in all. Huge amounts of arms and ammunition were recovered from hidden caches in the area as such encounters and intercepts became more frequent. Another major encounter followed a tip from a young paratrooper who had spotted two large columns of men headed toward Sonamarg from Kaobal Gali. Zaki surrounded the area with two battalions, tactically deploying them to cut off all routes of escape. This time, 200 porters and raw recruits surrendered; only one was killed as he tried to escape. Zaki was amazed by the cache of arms, which included heavy weapons—including rocket launchers—and huge quantities of ammunition.

Another operational strategy that evolved during Zaki's tenure was targeting Pakistani bunkers and positions along the Neelum-Gurez and Machil Sectors with concentrated artillery fire. This disrupted movement along the only road from the Pakistan Army's Kel Cantonment east toward Minimarg, which was being developed as a brigade HQ opposite the Mushkoh Sector. Zaki recalls moving a battery of 105mm guns and mortars to 11,000 feet and mounting a fire assault in response to infiltration of the sector. People-centric operations was another facet of Zaki's strategy. He instituted a surrender policy that assured Kashmiri terrorists of rehabilitation. Engaging with families, he built up a network of informers and pro-government militants. New Delhi missed a trick by not engaging similarly with Kashmiri terrorists jailed across the country. Thus, when many of these terrorists were released for want of evidence, they recrossed to PoK. Pakistani flags were widely flown in the hometown of Syed Salahuddin, an impoverished village called Soibug in the Budgam district of southern Kashmir.[21] Salahuddin was arrested for antinational activities in 1990, but because the charges could not be proved, he was released later that year and crossed over into Pakistan.

In June 1991 Zaki had been corps commander for almost two years. He hoped to spend the twilight of his career at the Indian Military Academy, where he had been sent to serve as commandant. But this was not to be. The new governor of J&K, Girish "Gary" Chandra Saxena, requested Zaki's services. Saxena's predecessor, Jagmohan, had been removed from the post the previous year after taking blame for the violence that occurred following the assassination of a religious leader by HM terrorists.[22] Zaki continued in the role of adviser until 1995, when he retired following differences with then-governor General K. V. Krishna Rao.

Matters came to a head when terrorists led by the notorious Mast Gul from the Khyber Pakhtunkhwa region of Pakistan set a sacred shrine, Charar-e-Sharif, on fire in May 1995. They had slipped through the elaborate grid laid by Indian security forces and occupied the shrine for almost five months. Security forces were not permitted to move in, for fear of damaging the shrine, so they remained mute spectators for months as the terrorists consolidated their hold within.[23] According to Zaki, this was a major reverse for security forces and was the result of poor coordination among the army, paramilitary forces, and the local police. The terrorists had been allowed to dig themselves in, and political indecisiveness in New Delhi let the situation get completely out of hand. Making matters worse was the terrorists' escape through the security dragnet after setting the shrine aflame.

Prime Minister P. V. Narasimha Rao's government lost an opportunity to seize the political initiative between 1993 and 1996, when the Indian Army was going hammer and tongs at the secessionist movement. To address the root of the problem, Zaki suggested comprehensive de-radicalization initiatives and institutional interaction with the families of youths who had crossed the line of control. He blames the ostrich-like attitude of bureaucrats and politicians, who refused to listen to the military at crucial junctures in the crisis. When Mast Gul returned to Pakistan after desecrating the shrine, he was hailed as a hero and a freedom fighter. No one better exemplifies the perception that "one man's terrorist is another man's freedom fighter." Mast Gul was branded a terrorist by the Pakistani state after masterminding the Peshawar attacks in February 2014.[24]

SECURING NORTH KASHMIR

Major General Nanavatty assumed command of Nineteenth Infantry Division in Baramulla in June 1993, just as HM was losing momentum in its fight against a buoyant Indian Army and the ISI had turned to HuA, LeT, and Harkat-ul-Mujahideen to intensify their attacks in the valley. The four brigades in his division were broadly responsible for the areas around Uri, Baramulla, Rafiabad, and Naugam. Twenty-Eighth Infantry Division covered Kupwara, Sopore, and the Shamshabari Range, while Eighth Mountain Division was responsible for southern portions of the Kashmir Valley, which broadly comprised the Anantnag, Budgam, Bandipora,

Pulwama, and Tral Sectors. Nanavatty's strategy of clearing Baramulla of all pockets of terrorists was much like the one adopted by the British in Northern Ireland. Self-contained detachments would maintain a sustained presence in the town of Baramulla—both south and north of the Jhelum River—by occupying abandoned and derelict buildings. This differed from the strategy in nearby Sopore, where Twenty-Eighth Infantry Division was attempting to take control street by street and house by house.

The peculiarity of Baramulla was that Old Baramulla, north of the Jhelum River, was a hotbed of secession and radicalism, while the area south of the river was controllable. However, Nanavatty recollects that within three months, a battalion had restored a modicum of normalcy in Baramulla without any untoward incidents. The battalion even set up a health care clinic that was well received by the locals. There was a gradual rebuilding of trust. Nanavatty also remembers that by late 1993, the influx of foreign terrorists had reached alarming proportions. These fighters of Pakistani, Chechen, and Arab origin had been trained by al-Qaeda and the Taliban, and they posed a significant military challenge to the Indian Army. The foreigners used the forests of Rafiabad, Hafruda, and Handwara to create caches and hideouts and then emerged to engage Indian Army patrols. It was a time of experimentation for the Indian Army as well, as it strained to meet this challenge despite the experience gained in Sri Lanka.

One of these experimental operational strategies was to exploit the fractured opposition by undertaking "pseudo gang" operations.[25] This strategy was first employed by the Rhodesian Army against antiapartheid militant groups in South Africa. According to Lawrence Cline, "Pseudo operations, in which government forces and guerrilla defectors portray themselves as insurgent units, have been a very successful technique used in several counterinsurgency campaigns. Pseudo teams have provided critical human intelligence and other support to these operations. These operations, although of considerable value, also have raised several concerns. Their use in offensive missions and psychological operations campaigns has, at times, been counterproductive."[26]

Volunteers from the Indian Army were tasked to create pseudo groups with the help of surrendered terrorists-turned-informers. These groups gathered intelligence about other outfits, fraternized with them, and even joined them on operations to win their trust; then, at an opportune moment, the pseudo groups captured or liquidated the terrorists. The volunteers were tactically and physically proficient. They wore local civilian attire, grew beards, spoke the local dialect, and performed *namaz* (Muslim prayers) five times a day. The hardest part was establishing contact with the foreign terrorists and gaining their confidence. The former terrorists in these pseudo gangs often exceeded their job descriptions and engaged in petty crime. This incurred the wrath of villagers, who stopped providing information. There was also competition for honors, kills, and awards among the pseudo gangs, which diluted their effectiveness.

A few gruesome losses led to a significant downscaling of such operations by the mid-1990s. Nanavatty argues that although these operations were initially effective, the Indian Army did not approach them scientifically or with a long-term perspective. According to him, such operations should have been run by the Special Forces, which by then had obtained covert warfare experience in Sri Lanka. As the Indian Army tightened its grip over Baramulla, Kupwara, and Sopore, Srinagar emerged as the new hot spot and intellectual hub for secessionist and terrorist operations. The army had not yet taken over operational control of this urban epicenter of secession. The army leadership's inability to convince the chief minister or Delhi to dismantle the emerging secessionist networks in Srinagar proved to be a major blunder.

HARDENING STANCE AND WINDOW FOR STABILIZATION

Colonel Pavan Nair, who served in Fifteenth Corps HQ between 1994 and 1996, recollects that by then, the Rashtriya Rifles had emerged as the main counterterrorism force in J&K:

> Those were challenging times, with three or four IED [improvised explosive device] blasts every day. One such blast killed the brigade commander of the Uri-based Twelfth Infantry Brigade. Electronic devices recovered during raids and from IEDs revealed Pakistani ordnance factory markings. The gloves were completely off, as nobody really knew how many terrorists had crossed over. Grenade attacks and firing were commonplace in Srinagar, and bullets often ricocheted off roofs in the cantonment. In response, Twenty-Eighth Infantry Division was hitting the Pakistan Army in the Neelum-Gurez Sectors with rocket launchers, antiaircraft guns, and medium artillery.[27]

Feeling the heat from the sustained kinetic operations in North Kashmir, separatists and jihadis searched for fresh pastures to extend the covert war. South Kashmir and areas south of the Pir Panjal Range emerged as new hot spots. Lieutenant General Pattabhiraman, a former vice chief of army staff, commanded Thirty-Third Infantry Brigade in the Jammu region in the early 1990s. He recalls that infiltrations had significantly increased in the Poonch and Rajouri Sectors of the Jammu region, resulting in a large terrorist presence in Doda and Kishtwar. However, the strategy adopted by the infiltrating jihadis had changed; they had started targeting communities, hamlets, and villages with Hindu populations. General Hooda, commander of the Indian Army's Northern Command in recent times, refers to this period as the "expansion of the arc of instability" in J&K.[28] The tightening of the counterterrorism grid in the Kashmir Valley had resulted in the opening of an effective second front by the ISI and the jihadis. Pattabhiraman notes that an escalation of terrorism in the areas of Rajouri, Poonch, Doda, and Kishtwar in the mid-1990s proved to be an effective smokescreen for what was unfolding in Kargil.[29]

Syed Salahuddin made one last attempt to return to the Kashmir Valley in 1994. He spoke to the Indian Army about alternative alignments and support, but these discussions proved fruitless. Salahuddin succumbed to immense pressure from the ISI, made his way back across the line of control to PoK, and set up the United Jihad Council as a figurehead and puppet of the ISI. Meanwhile, the Rashtriya Rifles had amalgamated well into the counterterrorism grid, and by 1996, the pipeline of foreign terrorists had dried up. This forced the ISI to work on a fresh strategy, propelling LeT to the vanguard of the jihad movement in Kashmir. Northern Command assessed that the military had done its job and it was time for the state and New Delhi to take over. Unfortunately, two years of political instability between 1996 and 1998 saw two ineffective prime ministers—H. D. Deve Gowda and I. K. Gujral—squander the operational gains of the preceding five years. This allowed the ISI and LeT to tighten its grip over the secessionist struggle in J&K.

Understandably, the newly elected (1998) Bharatiya Janata Party government under Atal Bihari Vajpayee wanted some time to consolidate its position before initiating any comprehensive dialogue with the people of Kashmir. Making matters worse for Vajpayee was the controversy over the acquisition of land to build better facilities for Hindu pilgrims at the sacred Amarnath shrine. This move to build shelters and toilets sparked a politically motivated dispute that led to the collapse of the Congress–People's Democratic Party coalition government in J&K. The initiation of a fresh political process distracted both the army and New Delhi as the window for conflict resolution closed when Pervez Musharraf assumed command of the Pakistan Army in 1998.[30] He provided fresh impetus to secessionist terrorism in the valley, particularly in South Kashmir and the Jammu region. He did this while hatching a sinister plan in Kargil to undermine the ongoing peace process initiated by Indian prime minister Atal Bihari Vajpayee and Pakistani prime minister Nawaz Sharif.

I4

Surprise and Riposte in Kargil

> Come October, we shall walk in to Siachen to mop up the dead bodies of hundreds of Indians left hungry, out in the cold.
> —Briefing by Lieutenant General Mahmud Ahmad, Pakistan Army,
> to senior Pakistan Air Force officers, Rawalpindi, 12 May 1999,
> quoted in Tufail, "Kargil Conflict and the Pakistan Air Force"

GETTING EVEN WITH INDIA

At the strategic level, the Kargil Conflict of 1999 was caused by the insecurity of the Pakistani deep state (meaning the Pakistan Army and its jihadi affiliates). Threatened by the very real prospect of successful peace talks between Prime Ministers Vajpayee and Sharif, the Pakistan Army sought to destabilize the subcontinent with an operation it thought would be covered by a nuclear umbrella. Both countries had demonstrated a nuclear weapons capability in the preceding year, but the leadership of the Pakistan Army thought it had the upper hand in the nuclear coercion game. Consequently, the Pakistanis thought they could extract significant gains by surreptitiously occupying Indian territory in the Kargil Sector.

At the operational level, the Pakistan Army needed to get even with India after its stunning capitulation in 1971. The preemptive occupation of the Saltoro Ridge by the Indian Army in 1984, as well as the aggressive local action by successive Indian commanders of the Siachen Brigade, created tremendous pressure on the Force Command Northern Areas (FCNA) to redeem the Pakistan Army's honor. Surprisingly, the impact of the Indian occupation of Saltoro Ridge on the operational events that unfolded between 1985 and 1999 was not adequately war-gamed in India. There was still an obsession with large-scale exercises such as Exercise Brasstacks and other massive maneuver exercises conducted in Rajasthan and Punjab. The concept of "limited war" had not yet been thought about in detail. Brigadier Devinder Singh, who played a pivotal role in the Kargil Conflict as commander of Seventieth Infantry Brigade, took part in a war game conducted by the Indian Army's Fifteenth Corps in early 1999. Role-playing an enemy commander, he correctly assessed that he could easily capture several heights in the Mushkoh Sector, but that assessment was rejected by the corps commander and the army commander.[1] They would eat humble pie months later when the same heights fell to the infiltrating Pakistan forces.

It is widely believed that Pakistan's Kargil Plan was discussed as early as 1987—when Zia was the military dictator—but was shot down as too risky and untenable by Pakistan's foreign minister, Yakub Khan.[2] It resurfaced in 1998 when General Jehangir Karamat was chief of army staff but was derailed for similar reasons.[3] It is highly likely that Pervez Musharraf saw the plan as an opportunity to make history. Colonel Vivek Chadha, an Indian Army scholar who has tracked Musharraf's career, suggests that Musharraf's close association with the Special Service Group (SSG) was the operational catalyst for the Kargil Plan.[4] Musharraf's extensive operational experience in the area included a stint as commander of 323rd Infantry Brigade in 1986–1987. The desire for payback increased each time his brigade failed to convert its assaults on Indian positions on Saltoro Ridge into tangible operational successes.[5] For example, he planned a major attack on Bilafond La that was repulsed by a battalion of the Gorkha Rifles (see chapter 6). He was later responsible for the ruthless military suppression of a Shia uprising in the area, which earned him the name "Butcher of Baltistan."[6] His operational experience in the area led him to believe that the chances of success were high.[7]

Some Pakistani analysts tend to downplay the importance of the Kargil Conflict and argue that it was merely a tactical counter to the Indian Army's pressure on Pakistan's Tenth Corps in the Neelum, Gurez, and Kel Sectors.[8] Whatever the motivation, the plan to infiltrate and occupy dominating heights to threaten the Srinagar–Kargil–Leh Highway was a bold one that depended on speed, surprise, and psychological supremacy. It was underpinned by the conviction that India would offer a tepid response and by the high probability that international opinion would drive a negotiated settlement to Pakistan's advantage in a nuclear-charged environment. Musharraf read the West well and was encouraged by the widespread opinion in the Clinton administration that even a limited conflict in the subcontinent could lead to a nuclear face-off. This, he believed, would force the Americans to intervene, thereby offering Pakistan significant geopolitical space to maneuver toward its primary objective of bringing Kashmir back into international focus.

THE BATTLEGROUND

Srinagar–Kargil–Leh National Highway 1A (NH-1A) winds its way up the Great Himalayan and Zanskar Ranges and enters the Mushkoh Valley subsector at Kaobali Gali through the Zojila Pass. This marked the western limits of the undermanned Third Infantry Division's area of responsibility at the time. On paper, it had four brigades defending an area that extended from Kaobali Gali in the west to Daulat Beg Oldie in the east and all the way to Demchok in southeastern Ladakh.

In charge of the entire Kargil Sector was Third Infantry Division's 121st Infantry Brigade, with four infantry battalions and its headquarters (HQ) located at Kargil. It was deployed along with the Ladakh Scouts across the large area between Mushkoh and Batalik. Seventieth Infantry Brigade—which was assigned the Batalik subsector—had two battalions in the Central Sector of the Siachen Glacier that were under the command of the Siachen Brigade on a three-month rotational basis; the rest of its battalions were on counterterrorism duties in the Kashmir Valley. The third brigade—114th Infantry Brigade—had seconded one of its battalions to the Siachen Brigade to man the Northern Glacier Sector on a three-month rotational basis. The fourth brigade was 102nd Infantry Brigade, with one battalion each assigned to the Northern, Central, and Southern Sectors of Siachen; a fourth battalion was assigned to an area called Subsector West (SSW).

With the exception of 102nd Infantry Brigade, Third Infantry Division's brigades were barely sufficient to even hold ground. Colonel Kuldip Mehta was posted at division HQ in February 1999 and had a ringside view of events at the tactical and operational levels. He reckons that the disposition of troops was barely sufficient to "establish contact with the enemy, let alone hold ground and contain further expansion."[9] This was validated in subsequent weeks when patrols barely made contact with several likely enemy positions—the red dots on Kuldip's map that sprang up in the following weeks.

As NH-1A descends from Zojila to Matayan along what can roughly be called the Mushkoh subsector, the distance between the line of control and the highway is over twenty kilometers. From Matayan, the road climbs to Dras. Along with Kaksar and Kargil farther east, Dras is located closest to the line of control. About fifty kilometers east of Dras is the critical Kaksar subsector, which acts as a pivot for operations in the entire region. Domination of this subsector is essential to convert any success in Dras and Mushkoh into decisive operational outcomes. Batalik (121st Infantry Brigade) and Turtuk (SSW of 102nd Infantry Brigade) are the easternmost subsectors. Although the distance between the line of control and NH-1A is greatest in these areas, their importance lies in their proximity to the Siachen Glacier—a vulnerability that has been overplayed at times.

The Indians had dominated this area since the late 1980s. Any inroads would strengthen the communication lines between Skardu and Gultari, which served as Pakistan's main gateway to the Siachen Glacier. However, there was a small vulnerability in the Indian defenses in the region between

Tyakshi, on the western edge of the Siachen Brigade's area of responsibility, and Chorbat La, on the eastern edge of the Kargil Brigade's area of responsibility. Indian posts there were vacated during the winter, for two main reasons. First, there was inadequate high-altitude equipment and limited logistics support. Second and more disturbing was the incorrect assessment that because Pakistan faced similar problems, it would not attempt anything audacious in this area, especially given its tenuous position in Siachen. Brigadier Prakash Katoch, commander of the Siachen Brigade from 1997 to 1999, recalls cautioning Third Infantry Division about neglecting SSW and Batalik whenever the Siachen Brigade was asked to patrol that area.[10] Many posts in the sector were at heights between 13,000 and 18,000 feet, and reaching them involved difficult climbs from valley floors at 7,000 to 8,000 feet.[11]

AUDACIOUS INFILTRATORS

Until mid-June 1999, many Western commentators, misled by the effective Pakistani narrative, were describing the infiltrators as "Islamic guerrillas" and "Taliban fighters."[12] The truth dawned on them only after the Indian Army displayed the identity cards of several dead soldiers that clearly indicated they were members of the Northern Light Infantry (NLI), a paramilitary force under the operational control of the Pakistan Army.[13] As casualties mounted during the conflict, the NLI was reinforced by troops from the Bajaur and Chitral Scouts from Pakistan's Frontier Corps. Most of these battalions were distributed among the FCNA's three brigades: 323rd Infantry Brigade deployed in Dansam, Eightieth Infantry Brigade at Minimarg, and Sixty-Second Infantry Brigade at Skardu. An additional brigade at Kel (Thirty-Second Brigade) made up the eastern flank of the division-sized force along the Neelum and Gurez subsectors.

It is widely believed that Sixty-Second Infantry Brigade was entrusted with operations in the Kaksar and Batalik subsectors, while Eightieth Infantry Brigade was assigned to make inroads into the Mushkoh and Dras subsectors. Reinforced by a couple of battalions from the other brigades, the intruding force comprised approximately seven to eight battalions, or 5,500 to 6,000 front-line troops.[14] These troops were spread over fifty posts, with logistics hubs for each valley manned by a reserve force from defending battalions of almost twice the strength. Overall, it was a force of 10,000 to 15,000 personnel. Pakistani historian Nasim Zehra claims that about 140 posts were established, indicating the possibility of two additional battalions. These were likely inducted following the success of the initial infiltration.[15]

Small, cohesive groups of twenty to forty soldiers from these units sporadically patrolled snowbound areas along the line of control. They seized strategically important high points from which they later attacked the Indians with mortar fire and medium-range artillery fire. The combat zone was approximately 150 to 160 kilometers long and was divided into multiple subsectors by the FCNA. The subsectors allotted to the various infiltrating battalions were Tiger Hill and Mushkoh, Dras, Tololing, Kaksar, Batalik, Chorbat La, and Turtok. Most of the officers who led NLI battalions during the Kargil Conflict were from other regiments and included Punjabis, Mohajirs, and Pathans. This ensured that no demographic group felt it had been singled out to execute what was clearly a hazardous operation.

THE OVERCONFIDENT GENERALS

Musharraf had built up an excellent operational reputation over the years. A founding member of the SSG, he had a band of loyal generals across the sectarian divide, and they ensured that the Kargil operation, code-named Operation Koh Paima by the Pakistan Army, was planned in complete secrecy. In Rawalpindi, the plan was orchestrated by Musharraf's chief of general staff, Lieutenant General Muhammad Aziz Khan, along with Lieutenant General Mahmud Ahmad. It was executed by Major General Javed Hassan, commander of the FCNA. Brigadier Nusrat Sial was in tactical command of Sixty-Second Infantry Brigade.

Aziz Khan's strident anti-India beliefs and Islamic leanings—along with his experience as a brigade commander in Siachen—made him perfectly suited to this role. He and Musharraf no doubt possessed the greatest knowledge of the terrain and the operational requirements. Mahmud Ahmad, an artillery officer, was a regimental colleague of Musharraf and an Islamic hard-liner. Musharraf brought him in specifically to command Tenth Corps at Rawalpindi. He later executed the coup that overthrew Nawaz Sharif in October 1999. Ikram Sehgal, a retired Pakistan Army officer and a defense analyst, describes Ahmad as "a professional soldier with a good reputation."[16] Shaukat Qadir, another Pakistani analyst, describes him as "sharp, intelligent and arrogant" and notes that he was not religious "until he discovered the force of Islam late in his life." At that point, according to Qadir, Ahmad "became dangerous in the way that anyone can become if they believe they are incapable of doing wrong."[17] Ahmad was without a doubt the principal orchestrator of the Kargil operations.

Javed Hassan provided a connection to the FCNA and was the operation's intellectual pivot. According to Praveen Swami, Hassan believed that the Indian military was driven by "the incorrigible militarism of the Hindus." "For those that are weak," Hassan said, "the Hindu is exploitative and domineering."[18] Christine Fair offers instructive insights into Hassan's

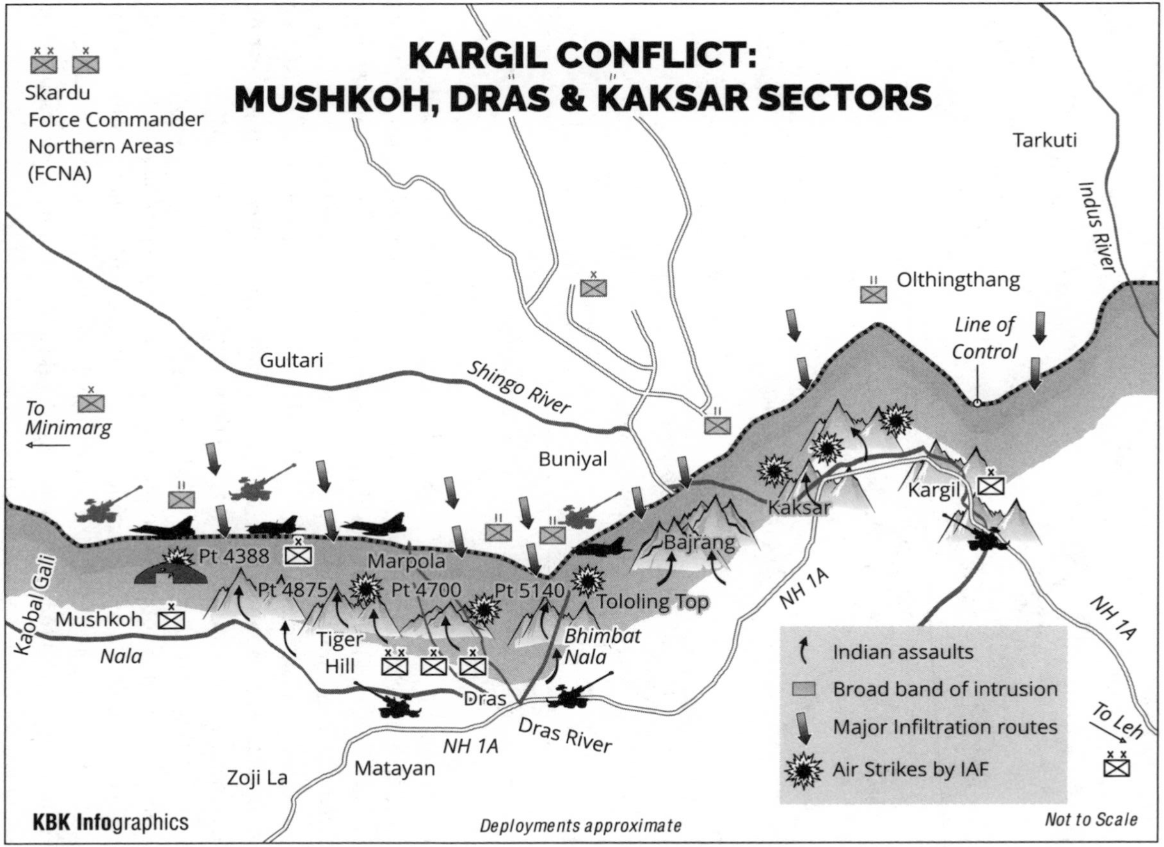

Map 11. Kargil War Zone: Mushkoh, Dras, and Kaksar Sectors

KARGIL CONFLICT:
MUSHKOH, DRAS & KAKSAR SECTORS

Skardu
Force Commander
Northern Areas
(FCNA)

Tarkuti

Indus River

Olthingthang

Line of Control

Kargil

Kaksar

NH 1A

To Leh

Legend:
- Indian assaults
- Broad band of intrusion
- Major Infiltration routes
- Air Strikes by IAF

Not to Scale

Bajrang

Tololing Top

Bhimbat Nala

Dras River

Buniyal

Pt 5140

Shingo River

Dras

NH 1A

Matayan

Marpola

Pt 4700

Tiger Hill

Zoji La

Gultari

Pt 4875

Pt 4388

Mushkoh Nala

To Minimarg

Kaobal Gali

Deployments approximate

KBK Infographics

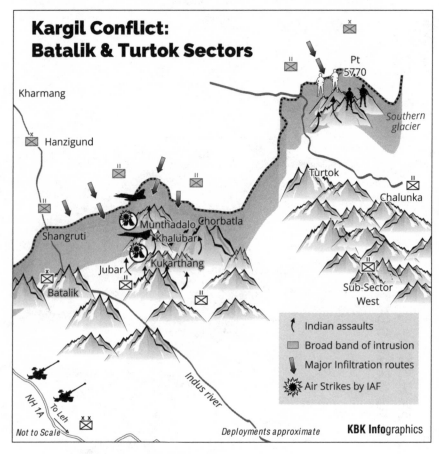

**Kargil Conflict:
Batalik & Turtok Sectors**

Kharmang

Hanzigund

Pt
5770

Southern
glacier

Tùrtok

Chalunka

Munthadalo Chorbatla

Shangruti

Khalubar

Kukarthang

Jubar

Batalik

Sub-Sector
West

↑ Indian assaults

▢ Broad band of intrusion

⬇ Major Infiltration routes

💥 Air Strikes by IAF

Indus river

NH 1A

To Leh

Not to Scale

Deployments approximate

KBK Infographics

Map 12. Kargil War Zone: Batalik and Turtok Sectors

operational orientation through a dissection of his "infamous account of
India's numerous shortcomings" in his book *India: A Study in Profile.* Written in 1990 when Hassan was on the faculty of Quetta, the Pakistan Army's
Command and Staff College, the book highlights several infirmities in India's
strategic psyche, including its "dismal absence of any popular resistance
against foreign domination" and its "hopeless performance in protecting
its own freedom and sovereignty." The results of Hassan's research seemed
to offer Pakistan "two starkly different but equally dire choices as regards
India: Either she acquiesces to the designs of Indian hegemony or she stands
up to the challenge; which would mean as an ultimate military conflict provoked by the stronger military power."[19] Clearly, there was a belief—albeit a
delusionary one in the upper echelons of Pakistan's military leadership—that
India would wilt in the face of this operation.

THE TENTATIVE BUT RESILIENT DEFENDERS

At the strategic and policy levels, Indian prime minister Vajpayee was convinced that there was a clear opportunity to normalize relations with Pakistan. This belief stemmed from the attitude expressed by the civilian government in Islamabad, led by Prime Minister Nawaz Sharif. Vajpayee's major strategic error in the run-up to the Kargil Conflict was to overlook the fact that the Pakistan Army was not on board for any peace initiative. Although a large segment of the Bharatiya Janata Party—including the home minister, Lal Krishan Advani—favored a more hawkish Pakistan strategy, they deferred to Vajpayee. However, to infer that Vajpayee simply read Pakistan wrong would be to dismiss a complex mind-set that cut across the political spectrum, particularly for a generation of India's leaders with an emotional connection to the memory of an undivided subcontinent and a lingering belief that an enduring peace with Pakistan was possible.

At the forefront of India's military response was India's chief of army staff, General V. P. Malik. A highly experienced infantryman, he had completed several successful field commands and had had a ringside seat at the Sumdorong Chu, Sri Lanka, and Maldives operations as part of the army's military operations directorate. He needed some time to come to grips with the enormity of the situation, as he was away on an official trip to Poland and Czechoslovakia when it morphed into a crisis. There has been much criticism of his decision to take that trip, but given the information available, he was likely confident that the Northern Army commander, Lieutenant General H. M. Khanna, could deal with the "intrusion." Khanna's role finds little place in either the analytical or the journalistic discourse related to the conflict. Malik's major challenge was to concurrently direct army operations and orchestrate joint operations. He immediately and easily took charge of the former upon his return, but the latter proved to be a challenge.

Lieutenant General Krishan Pal, commander of Fifteenth Corps, was preoccupied with the secessionist movement in Jammu and Kashmir (J&K) and his acrimonious relationship with Chief Minister Farooq Abdullah. His leadership during the conflict has been widely criticized for its lack of foresight and its stagnant counterterrorism mind-set. Major General Mohinder Puri, commander of Eighth Mountain Division, speedily moved his division from Kashmir to Dras. It was under his leadership that three Indian Army brigades fought some of the most important battles of the conflict. His book *Kargil: Turning the Tide* is a detailed week-to-week account of operations conducted by Eighth Mountain Division.[20]

Air Chief Marshal A. Y. Tipnis, a seasoned fighter pilot and the team leader during the early evaluation of the Mirage-2000, was India's chief of air staff at the time. He suggests that the Indian Air Force (IAF) was left out of the operational loop in the early weeks after the intrusions were detected.[21] Consequently, he was under immense pressure to employ offensive airpower without the necessary intelligence. This led to the IAF taking too many risks during the early days of the conflict, before recalibrating its tactics. Leading the IAF in battle was Air Marshal Vinod Patney, commander of Western Air Command and a decorated airman with extensive battle experience in the 1965 and 1971 wars against Pakistan. Based on initial intelligence, Patney was confident that his resources would suffice to fight a limited air campaign. The high-altitude bombing campaign took some time to evolve, but his aggressive tactics contributed significantly to the NLI's capitulation.[22] During the chaotic initial days, the task of managing the aerial element of joint operations between Western Air Command and the army's Northern Command fell to the soft-spoken and amiable Air Vice Marshal "Nana" Menon, the air officer commanding the J&K area. Menon did a tremendous job, orchestrating air efforts of all kinds and smoothing ruffled feathers as he flitted from Srinagar to Avantipur, where several IAF squadrons were based, and to Udhampur, HQ of Northern Army Command. He was the ideal foil to Patney in the field.

OPERATIONAL DISPOSITION

The line of control in the Kargil Sector on the Indian side was undermanned, with Indian posts vacated in the winter months to strengthen the counterinfiltration and counterterrorism deployment in J&K.[23] On the Pakistani side, however, three brigades were gearing up for the intrusions. The force ratios were completely unsustainable once it became clear that India had to go on the offensive. Brigadier Surinder Singh, commander of 121st Infantry Brigade, had to use augmented battalions that were rushed up from the valley during the first attacks on Tiger Hill. This was in the second week of May, once the intrusions were officially declared.[24]

At the commencement of conflict, the IAF fleet broadly comprised two MiG-21, two MiG-27/MiG-23 BN, two Jaguar, and two Mi-17 squadrons for offensive operations. There were also two MiG-29, one MiG-21, and one MiG-23 MF squadrons for air defense missions. Both of the IAF's Mirage-2000 squadrons would later be inducted for offensive operations, reconnaissance, and air defense duties as the conflict progressed. With a Canberra and a MiG-25 also available for operational and strategic reconnaissance, the IAF had sufficient aerial platforms to execute an integrated offensive battle plan. However, training for high-altitude bombing of this kind had never been anticipated in any air force, there was a shortage of bombs for delivery against targets at high altitude, and self-protection electronic warfare suites for attacking aircraft and armed helicopters (mainly infrared flares) were inadequate. The IAF would pay dearly for these shortcomings during the initial stages of the conflict.

EARLY WARNINGS

"Oh God! This has been a colossal intelligence failure." That was the opinion of India's revered strategic guru K. Subrahmanyam when he visited Leh as head of the Kargil Review Committee.[25] Despite the claims of various intelligence agencies that they had warned the government about the intrusion, there was no clear, integrated picture of what was happening. Senior journalists, Research and Analysis Wing operatives, and diplomats have indicated that intelligence about hectic military activity in Skardu and stray reports of unusual military activity in the Kargil and Batalik Sectors had been available since the previous winter.[26] However, General Malik is emphatic that the initial "fog of war and our inability to identify the intruders for some length of time cost us heavily." He attributes this to "major weakness in our intelligence system."[27]

Although India's civilian and military intelligence agencies have been blaming each other for the fiasco ever since, there is sufficient evidence that it was a collective failure. There was no consolidated strategic, operational, and tactical intelligence to give the political leadership a "stereoscopic mosaic" of the situation. This explains the lack of initial political direction for a response to the intrusion.

At the operational level, local military commanders had been voicing concerns about the thinning of troops in the area from mid-1998 onward. But these apprehensions had repeatedly been brushed aside by both Khanna and Pal.[28] Ahluwalia was an air commodore at the time and was commanding the important high-altitude air base at Leh. He recalls that in early May 1999 he was at the airfield to receive Defense Minister George Fernandes, who was on one of his many morale-boosting trips to the Siachen Glacier. Waiting along with him, as is customary during such visits, were Pal and Major General Budhwar, commander of Third Infantry Division. The overstretched division had recently been stripped of the critical Seventieth Infantry Brigade in Batalik, after an operational assessment in 1998 had suggested that 121st Infantry Brigade could take on the responsibility of patrolling that "relatively benign part" of the line of control. Ahluwalia recollects that the two generals discussed the multiple intrusions between themselves but underplayed their magnitude and seriousness. Even more surprising was that his offer to help with aerial reconnaissance had not been accepted.[29] Had the IAF and Aviation Research Center assets been employed for operational and strategic reconnaissance even at this stage, the scale of the incursions would have been revealed.

Even the Pakistan Air Force (PAF) was not officially informed about the operation until 12 May 1999. Writing in his widely read and professionally acclaimed blog *Aeronaut*, Kaiser Tufail—an accomplished PAF fighter pilot—claims that India's few covert operatives should have picked up the hectic activity in Skardu, as "troops in battle gear were to be seen all over the city." He "wonders how Indian intelligence agencies failed to read any such signs" many weeks before the operation unfolded.[30]

The PAF got its first detailed briefing from Mahmud Ahmad, and Tufail recollects that during that briefing, Ahmad broke the news that a limited operation had started two days earlier. He claimed it was nothing more than a "protective maneuver" to foreclose any further mischief by the local Indian formations, which had been a nuisance in the Neelum Valley. He then elaborated that a few vacant Indian posts had been occupied on peaks across the line of control overlooking the Dras–Kargil road. These would serve as observation posts for directing artillery fire with greater accuracy. Artillery firepower, Ahmad added, would be provided by a couple of field guns that had been transported to the heights piecemeal by helicopter and reassembled over the winter. He also suggested that the Indian Army had failed to detect this activity. The target was a vulnerable section of the Dras–Kargil road, the crucial lifeline of the Leh–Siachen Sector. Ahmad's hope was that this stratagem would isolate and choke the Indian Army in that vital sector for up to a month, after which the monsoons would prevent vehicular movement and airlifts due to landslides and other environmental factors. Demonstrating an obsession with getting even with India, Ahmad said, "Come October, we shall walk in to Siachen to mop up the dead bodies of hundreds of Indians left hungry, out in the cold."[31] This provides insight into his operational mind-set and the smug conviction that his strategy of surprise and firepower would be sufficient to stun the Indians.

COMPLETE SURPRISE

The creeping infiltration across the line of control in the Mushkoh, Dras, Kaksar, and Batalik subsectors commenced as early as October 1998 and was completed by May 1999.[32] According to the Pakistanis, it took so long because there were a surprising number of heights to take over. This resulted in a scramble for additional resources to sustain these posts. There is evidence of some firefights in the Turtuk Sector during the last week of April 1999. These went unreported by the Indian Army and were downplayed as localized intrusions. However, the Pakistan Army intended them to deflect attention from the major intrusions that had taken place farther west.

The first sightings of intruders in nonmilitary clothing were reported in the Batalik Sector on 3 May by a group of shepherds. This was on the Jubar Ridge,[33] which would later see some of the fiercest fighting of the Kargil Conflict. Following reports of multiple sightings, Third Infantry Battalion of the Punjab Regiment promptly dispatched four patrols to the area over the next four days. The first two patrols detected a few intruders on ridge-lines; the next two suffered casualties when they closed in on the intruders and engaged them. This raised some alarm in Third Infantry Division and Fifteenth Corps HQs. Between 6 and 14 May, machine gun fire was directed at Cheetah helicopters on surveillance operations, and there were reports of widespread incursions and sightings in all sectors. However, no action was taken beyond sending two battalions from Seventieth Infantry Brigade from the Kashmir Valley to the Batalik Sector. The FCNA had clearly succeeded in deceiving the Indian commanders into believing that the intruders were a "mujahideen force" and that their focus was in the Batalik and Turtok Sectors.

In early May 1999 Colonel Ghei received orders to head from Agra to Leh with his Seventh Parachute Battalion. He was immediately summoned to Kargil to join Budhwar in strategizing on the response to these early encounters. Ghei recalls troops huddled along the highway from Leh to Kargil, awaiting orders. There was complete chaos in 121st Brigade's sector, with all three battalions (Fourth Battalion of the Jat Regiment, Sixteenth Battalion of the Grenadiers Regiment, and Third Battalion of the Punjab Regiment) unprepared for what was unfolding. Ghei was asked to plan an assault on an enemy-occupied post at 16,500 feet in the Batalik Sector with just one artillery fire unit for support. He pointed out that this would be suicidal but added that his unit would attempt it if ordered to do so. Better sense prevailed, and the plan was abandoned. Along with two other commanding officers from First and Sixth Parachute Battalions, Ghei was then summoned to Srinagar to plan a three-battalion assault on Gultari, a major Pakistan Army base across the line of control. However, the plan was aborted when Vajpayee banned operations across the line of control once India officially declared war on 26 May.[34]

On 10 May Pakistani 105mm guns destroyed a large ammunition dump in Kargil, jolting the Indian Army into action.[35] This was followed by further setbacks between 14 and 17 May in the Kaksar Sector.[36] Pakistani guns continued to harass movement on NH-1A until they were silenced a few weeks later by an Indian counterbombardment. Lieutenant Saurabh Kalia of Fourth Jat was leading a five-man patrol on 14 May near the Bajrang post in the Kaksar Sector. His men came under heavy fire from the vacated post, which had been occupied by about thirty soldiers of the NLI. Unable to withdraw and out of ammunition, the Indians were surrounded and captured. They would be held captive for three weeks, tortured, and eventually decapitated.[37] Led by Lieutenant Amit Bharadwaj, a rescue team of thirty attempted a frontal assault on Bajrang on 17 May. However, they were forced to withdraw under fire from well-fortified positions, and Bharadwaj and a *havildar* were killed in action. Repeated attempts to retrieve their bodies failed until the post was finally overrun by another unit in late June. The strength and preparedness of the intruders had been underestimated. Sadly, Bharadwaj's courage under fire would go unrecognized in the aftermath of the larger fiasco that was unfolding.[38]

CRANKING A RESPONSE

Stung by the initial losses and clearly losing faith in Pal and Budhwar, General Malik took over operations upon his return. Left with no choice but to undertake large-scale operations, Indian Army HQ finally declared the commencement of Operation Vijay on 23 May and moved additional formations into the area. Although Malik grasped the situation, he chose to initiate a risky response with widespread and direct infantry assaults. He made this decision because "there was immense pressure from the top" and the perception that "something needed to be done immediately."[39]

The 121st Infantry Brigade was now confined to the Mushkoh, Dras, and Kaksar subsectors and reinforced by Seventieth Infantry Brigade, which was responsible for the Batalik subsector. Over the next two weeks, Fifty-Sixth Infantry Brigade took over Dras, and Seventy-Ninth Infantry moved into Mushkoh.[40] First Battalion of the Naga Regiment and Eighth Battalion of the Sikh Regiment were the first battalions of Fifty-Sixth Brigade to be moved up, with little acclimatization. They were temporarily placed under the command of 121st Brigade. They were followed in quick succession by Eighteenth Battalion of the Grenadier Regiment, Eighteenth Battalion of the Garhwal Rifles, Second Battalion of the Rajputana Rifles, and Thirteenth Battalion of the Jammu and Kashmir Rifles. Last to be inducted was 192nd Infantry Brigade. Gradually, a new command structure emerged as Eighth Mountain Division HQ was moved into the Dras and Mushkoh Sectors under General Puri and took over major operations from Third Division. Malik had commanded Eighth Mountain Division in the early 1990s and was confident that it was best suited for the task. Three regiments from its integral artillery brigade were also moved up to provide the missing fire support that had severely hampered the initial assaults.

John Gill—a former faculty member at National Defense University in Washington, DC, and a prolific writer on the Indian military—says that Malik outlined three key operational tasks for Operation Vijay: clearing the Tololing and Tiger Hill complexes, which were the closest infiltrations to the NH-1A; clearing the heights around the Jubar Ridge in the Batalik subsector, which had the potential to threaten the logistics lines to Siachen; and isolating the Turtok and SSW area from the Kargil battle.[41] Fifty-Sixth and 192nd Infantry Brigades in Dras and Seventieth Infantry Brigade in Batalik would perform creditably in the weeks ahead.

North of the windswept Dras War Memorial—where the mercury can dip to −50 degrees Celsius in winter—is an imposing ridgeline called the Tololing complex. Apart from Tololing Top, the other prominent feature on the ridge is its northern edge, known as Point 5140. Two other prominent heights—Hump and Knoll—made up the main Pakistani posts. These heights, captured by the NLI, offered a commanding view of NH-1A on a clear day. Located 5,000 meters west of the Tololing complex is Tiger Hill. The ridgeline between Tololing complex and Tiger Hill was also occupied by the intruders. Point 4875 is about two kilometers southwest of Tiger Hill, and it, along with Rocky Knob and India Gate, constitutes the Tiger Hill complex. This too was occupied by the Pakistanis. The recapture of both the Tololing and Tiger Hill complexes was critical to the success of the Indian operation.

Confronted with the sudden unfolding of a threatening tactical situation, Brigadier Surinder Singh was under immense pressure. However, the division and corps commanders were still under the illusion that this was nothing but a series of intrusions that could be tackled immediately. Surinder Singh first ordered First Naga to capture Tololing and Point 5140. Then, on 18 May, he told Eighth Sikh that "there are a few mujahideen on top, go throw them off." (The "top" he was referring to was Tiger Hill, which, along with Tololing, would remain a thorn in the Indian Army's side for more than six weeks.)[42] Eighth Sikh commenced operations that very night and was soon joined by some troops from First Naga. Both units took heavy casualties over the next few days. Their repeated attempts at frontal assaults were beaten back by enemy mortars and 105mm guns. Once it was determined that both complexes were heavily defended, the Nagas and Sikhs aborted their attack and dug defenses on the lower slopes to regroup before their next assault. More than 140 men from these two units were lost during the initial assault. After these reverses, Fifty-Sixth Infantry Brigade was moved to Dras, and Eighteenth Grenadiers relocated from the Kashmir Valley and started operations without any acclimatization.[43] Eighteenth Garhwal Rifles followed shortly.

Colonel (later Major General) Samir Chakravorty, the commanding officer of Eighteenth Garhwal Rifles, insisted on at least a week's acclimatization before being pushed into battle, and this stood his men in good stead in the weeks ahead. Surinder Singh was desperate by now and told the Grenadiers to "just go up and bring them down by their neck."[44] As the two initial assault units dug in around Tiger Hill and Tololing, Eighteenth Grenadiers and the remainder of First Naga prepared to attack the latter. The battle for Tololing commenced on 22 May, and despite initial reports that the enemy positions were well manned, the assault commenced without adequate artillery fire support. Here too, the Nagas and Grenadiers became sitting ducks for the well-entrenched Pakistanis as the Indians struggled to make progress over the next few days.

PRELIMINARY AIR OPERATIONS

Air Marshal "Nana" Menon recollects that the army's first formal request for armed helicopter support came on 12 May, after a Cheetah was shot at from Tololing Top in the Dras Sector.[45] The Indian Army could provide neither target coordinates nor information about the kind of air defense weapons the enemy had. The IAF wanted greater clarity before committing the slow-moving armed helicopters into operations at unfamiliar altitudes.[46] By the time General Malik returned from his overseas trip, the operational picture had become quite clear: the Indian Army was faced with an infiltration by two oversized brigades in prepared defenses at over a hundred locations across a front of more than a hundred kilometers. Even by conservative estimates, the Indians would need a minimum of six brigades supported by heavy artillery and airpower if they wanted to evict the intruders before the snows arrived. However, disagreements between the army and air force over committing armed helicopters persisted and led to some animosity between Malik and Tipnis.[47] Tipnis finally relented, but only after Vajpayee approved the use of offensive airpower with the stringent restriction not to cross the line of control. During these discussions, Foreign Minister Jaswant Singh— a former army officer himself—continued to oppose the widespread use of airpower, terming it escalatory.[48]

Was the IAF caught napping about the type of conflict it was dealing with? Had it adequately gamed and trained for offensive operations at high altitudes? Why were no joint exercises conducted with the army to address such contingencies? Air Marshal Patney admits that he was taken by surprise when—at 3:00 p.m. on 25 May—the air chief told him to commence Operation Safed Sagar, the code name for offensive air operations during the Kargil Conflict. Shackled by the prime minister's directive not to cross the line of control during aerial attacks, Patney's main battle plan in the sector had to be reworked. The original plan had revolved around interdicting Pakistani lines of communication and supplies across the line of control. Patney was also constrained by the lack of actionable and accurate target intelligence, which is essential for hitting targets in proximity to one's own troops. However, he contests the proposition that his force suffered from a lack of high-altitude expertise and maintains that its flexibility allowed it to quickly recalibrate its missions after the initial setbacks.[49]

Between 5 and 15 May the Indian Army kept the IAF completely out of the loop and merely demanded helicopter support. Therefore, when the time came to develop an operational plan, it took some time for the IAF to undertake the reconnaissance missions required to identify targets. Between 15 and 21 May Mi-17s attempting to carry out visual reconnaissance were shot at and damaged. Jaguars obtained long-range oblique photographs that provided some target details, while MiG-21s performed photo reconnaissance with scanty intelligence. This was followed up with a mission using a Canberra bomber modified with powerful cameras, as this was the only platform available for long-range tactical recce. On 21 May an IAF Canberra was damaged by Chinese-built Anza shoulder-fired missiles. The pilot, Squadron Leader Alagaraja Perumal, somehow managed to fly the damaged aircraft back to Srinagar.[50] MiG-25 strategic reconnaissance aircraft were also used extremely effectively during the later stages of the conflict and facilitated several accurate attacks by Mirage-2000s.[51]

The attack on the Tiger Hill complex began on 26 May with Mi-17 armed helicopters, complemented by MiG-21s, MiG-23s, and MiG-27s. It is largely unknown that MiG-27s from Ninth Squadron and MiG-21s from Fifty-First Squadron were among the first over the target areas in the Tiger Hill and Tololing complexes, respectively. Wing Commander Sameer Joshi (then a flight lieutenant) clearly recollects the attack profiles on Tololing and notes that the pilots "scared the daylights out of themselves" while carrying out pull-up rocket and gun attacks against hazily reported targets that were supposed to be concealed *Sangars*, or rock-based defenses.[52] The aircraft were met with antiaircraft fire and shoulder-fired missiles from the mountaintops. The IAF reacted quickly, transitioning from attack to information gathering through reconnaissance, which would aid subsequent aerial attacks and infantry assaults. The main problem faced by the ad hoc Strike and Air Defense Planning Cell at Srinagar air base was the complete mismatch in methodologies for fixing target locations between the air force and the army.[53]

Several air force officers highlighted senior army leaders' lack of understanding of airpower capabilities at high altitudes during the early days of the conflict. Given the heavy losses the army was suffering, its leadership wanted offensive airpower over the peaks immediately. In such a combat milieu, the IAF was unable to explain the importance of obtaining target information before committing fighter assets. There appeared to be a dissonance in operational synergy between the two services in May. However, Patney disagrees and suggests that the IAF demonstrated a high degree of flexibility in a complex battlefield milieu.[54]

MiG-21s from Seventeenth Squadron flew photo reconnaissance missions to add to the information brought back by the Canberra. Using this intelligence, Patney decided to target locations around Tiger Hill and Tololing. After confirming the presence of snow tents and bunkers at both locations, strikes commenced, carried out by MiG-27s and MiG-23s of Ninth and 221st Squadrons and MiG-21s of 108th Squadron. MiG-21s from Seventeenth Squadron also pitched in with bomb-damage assessment missions. During the initial days, the IAF used rockets, guns, and iron bombs, and attacks were carried out by flying low over the crest tops and then pulling up to deliver weapons in a dive. As a result, the attacking aircraft remained within range of antiaircraft guns, Stingers, and Anzas for the entire duration of their attack. They had only an inadequate protective shower of infrared flares, and the IAF was soon suffering losses.

Air attacks were halted temporarily on 28 May after the loss of two fighters and a helicopter. The first to go down was a MiG-27 piloted by Flight Lieutenant Kambampati Nachiketa Rao from Ninth Squadron, which suffered engine failure after attacking the Muntha Dalo logistics camp in the Batalik subsector. After executing a successful rocket attack, Nachiketa went in for a gun pass and experienced an engine surge, followed by engine failure. Ejecting in Pakistani-held territory, he was taken prisoner and held for several days before being repatriated.

Air Chief Marshal Birender "Tony" Singh Dhanoa was the commanding officer of Seventeenth Squadron during the Kargil Conflict. His tenure during this period of uncertainty, tragedy, and achievement under tremendous odds holds a special place in his heart. Arriving at Srinagar on 21 May, he realized that morale was low after Perumal's Canberra got shot up. In a brainstorming session with his squadron, they came up with a standard procedure for coping with a missile hit at those altitudes: stay with the aircraft and try to glide into a valley, rather than eject over the jagged peaks. Little did they realize that days later, one of them would be hit by a missile.[55]

It was difficult to identify specific targets around Tiger Hill in the first week of aerial operations. Dhanoa recollects that the commanding officer of 129th Helicopter Unit went up for an aerial reconnaissance with the second in command of Eighth Sikh, which had assaulted Tiger Hill a few days earlier. Unfortunately, the second in command could not identify any targets for the IAF pilots, despite the earlier assault, as they were well concealed and blended into the rocky terrain.

Dhanoa clearly recalls the loss of his flight commander, Squadron Leader Ajay Ahuja, on 27 May. Ahuja was waiting at the takeoff point with his number 2, Flying Officer Reddy, for a reconnaissance mission when he heard that Nachiketa had been shot down. The leader of the MiG-27 formation radioed Nachiketa's coordinates and wanted someone to ascertain whether he had ejected safely. Ahuja and Reddy flew to the area, descending lower and lower to try to locate the crash site. Reddy's fuel level became dangerously low, so Ahuja continued the search alone. This was not standard wartime procedure, and Ahuja paid the price for staying too long over the ejection area. He was targeted and shot down by a Stinger-class portable air defense system. He did not eject immediately but stuck to the procedure established by the squadron. Ahuja succeeded in identifying a valley and glided into it, but unfortunately, it was on the other side of the line of control. Eventually ejecting safely, he was captured. Unlike Nachiketa, however, Ahuja was brutally beaten and killed. It was a rude awakening for the IAF. It now understood that the intruders were no pushovers; they were well-trained, ruthless troops who were prepared for aerial attacks.

The next day, 28 May, Tololing was attacked by four Mi-17 armed helicopters led by Wing Commander Sinha, the commanding officer of 129th Helicopter Unit. Sinha was familiar with the target, having attacked it the previous day. When one of the main aircraft in the formation developed technical problems prior to mission takeoff, a standby from 152nd Helicopter Unit took its place at the last minute. It turned out to be the only aircraft in the formation without infrared flares. Third in the attack sequence, it was shot down after the preceding aircraft managed to evade hits from several Stinger-class missiles, thanks to its infrared flares.[56] Major General Alok Deb, commanding a field regiment, was positioned near Dras and witnessed the Mi-17 attack, which he characterized as an effective use of firepower.[57] Despite the tactical soundness, all these mishaps merit serious reflection. Two decades later, Patney accepts that there were costly errors in judgment. Ahuja and Sinha were the only IAF recipients of the Vir Chakra, India's third highest wartime gallantry award.

Air Chief Marshal Major—one of the most experienced helicopter pilots in the IAF—was asked to assess the effectiveness of the ongoing offensive helicopter operations. After flying a couple of sorties and observing the flight path of approaching helicopters in a benign area, he realized that the noise level in the valleys and mountaintops made the helicopters easy to spot, and they could subsequently be shot down by surface-to-air missiles and air defense guns. He therefore recommended strikes only at dusk, dawn, or night, accompanied by a heavy artillery barrage in the area to mask the sound of the helicopters.[58]

The Pakistani intruders and their missile fire surprised the IAF.[59] One squadron commander recollects that in the first week, they went in blind in terms of intelligence about the presence of Stingers on the hilltops, and they paid the penalty.[60] The IAF eventually abandoned all low-level attacks and stuck to medium-level attacks, where the aircraft could pull out and largely stay out of range of the Stingers. Conventional bombs dropped by MiG-21s, MiG-23s, and MiG-27s had limited effect during the initial days. Some had delayed fuses, so when the bombs bounced off rocky hillsides and bunkers and exploded some distance away, they caused shock but not enough damage. When instantaneous impact fuses were substituted, the effects improved significantly. When aerial operations resumed, the Mirage-2000s made a big impact with 250-kilogram Spanish bombs and 1,000-pound bombs, the latter being fitted with kits that converted them into precision bombs.[61]

Eighteenth Grenadiers suffered the heaviest losses, losing Major Rajesh Adhikari and five others in close combat around Tololing Top on 28 May. Caught in a vicious crossfire while attempting to recover the bodies of Adhikari and his fallen comrades on 2 June, the unit's second in command, Lieutenant Colonel Visvanathan, was also killed. The army's top brass subsequently called a halt to such suicidal and knee-jerk assaults.[62] The second wave of attacks on Tiger Hill, Tololing, and the other objectives cost the Indians dearly. The Indian Army lost fifty-six men killed and more than a hundred injured. The IAF lost three aircraft and five crew members. It was clearly time to reflect, regroup, and come up with a fresh operational plan.

15

A Costly Victory

In tactics as in strategy, superiority of numbers is the most common element in victory.

—Carl von Clausewitz, *On War*

FRESH THINKING

Hedging against a possible intervention by the Pakistan Air Force that never came, Air Marshal Patney added Seventh Squadron (Mirage-2000s) and Fifth and Fourteenth Squadrons (Jaguars) to his initial attacking force. A detachment of First Squadron (Mirage-2000s) was also inducted to provide air defense cover. There was now more firepower to assault the other important heights on and around Tiger Hill and the Tololing Ridge—such as Point 5140 and Point 4700. Risky visual attacks were replaced by those utilizing the Global Positioning System (GPS) and inertial navigation. Instead of rockets and guns, 250-kilogram, 500-kilogram, and 1,000-pound bombs were used. Some of these were mated with Indian fuses and Israeli "Litening" targeting pods on Jaguar and Mirage aircraft.[1] The aerial attacks against entrenched defenses on the hilltops continued, with increasing physical and psychological degradation of targets due to improved delivery accuracy. The Indian Air Force (IAF) also identified larger targets, which, if attacked with greater weapon loads, could decisively assist the ongoing assaults. To achieve this objective, reconnaissance platforms were tasked with locating logistics hubs that were supporting the troops on the hilltops.

The Mirage-2000 was the best option to lead a high-altitude bombing campaign because of its precision. The challenge was how best to integrate the Litening pod and hastily modified 1,000-pound bombs with the Paveway-II guidance kits strapped to the front and rear of the bombs.[2] Air Marshal Raghunath "Namby" Nambiar was part of the first group of flight lieutenants in the Mirage-2000 fleet. A tech-savvy and passionate test pilot, he was an integral part of upgrades on the Mirage-2000. Associated with the Litening project from 1996, Nambiar recalls that the Israeli pod was chosen over the French "Damocles" and British "TIAD" pods because it was much cheaper, at US$25 million for six pods.

Patney also considered night bombing to keep psychological pressure on the enemy.[3] He was supported by Dhanoa, whose squadron did a trial in late June at Toshe Maidan—a high-altitude firing range—dropping four bombs with fair results. "Attacks by night were conducted from lower altitudes of about one kilometer above target level and commenced a few nights before the assault on Tiger Hill. It entailed flying below the crest level if need be, but since the mountains were snow covered and it was a moon phase, everything was brilliantly lit," recalls Dhanoa.[4]

GUNNERS MAKE AN IMPACT

As the battle progressed, the 105mm guns and howitzers supporting the infiltrators caused significant attrition among the Indians. It became clear that counterbombardment was essential if the Indians were to gain the upper hand. Silencing enemy guns and putting pressure on the infiltrators by relentless firing through the day and night became a critical operation. In mid-May 121st Infantry Brigade was being supported by one artillery regiment with about sixty light mortars, 105mm guns, and a few howitzers. While the mortars had a range of four to six kilometers, the guns had a maximum range of ten to sixteen kilometers. By mid-June, the artillery brigade of Eighth Mountain Division added to the firepower with three field regiments equipped with 105mm guns and one light regiment with 120mm mortars. A regiment with the formidable 155mm Bofors gun was also brought in from the Kashmir Valley. Pakistan had not factored this gun into its assessment of the Indian response. There were now more than 150 guns with ranges from ten to thirty-five kilometers spread out across the three sectors. By late June, Grad B rocket launchers and the Pinaka multibarrel rocket launcher system were inducted for field trials. By the end of June, there were approximately six regiments with more than 200 guns spread across all sectors.[5] These guns, in combination with sustained pressure from repeated aerial bombardment, would cause tremendous attrition and psychological degradation and would contribute significantly to the enemy's eventual capitulation.

Mohinder Puri's combined ground assault was to be accompanied by relentless aerial and artillery bombardment, followed by sustained infantry assaults. Gunners called this a "100-gun fire assault" during the later stages of the conflict. Colonel (later Major General) Alok Deb, who commanded one of the artillery regiments in the conflict, orchestrated fire plans in the Dras Sector, coordinating with the air force and infantry units as troops closed in on enemy positions. The unorthodox use of the Bofors gun for direct firing was among several bold initiatives in the employment of firepower, turning the tide in India's favor.

TOLOLING FALLS

Before the psychological impact of airpower and artillery manifested it-self, the attacking Indian infantry battalions faced stiff resistance from a determined adversary. According to John Gill, "the NLI [Northern Light Infantry] troops demonstrated great skill in siting their positions and great tenacity in holding out against repeated attacks, often literally to the last bul-let and last man."[6] It was time for the Indian Army to make a decisive move. The first concerted attack on Tololing had taken a heavy toll on Eighteenth Grenadiers and First Naga, and it was time for fresh legs to consolidate those limited gains. On 1 June Second Rajputana Rifles was moved to Dras from Jammu and Kashmir (J&K). Camping at Draupadi Kund a few kilome-ters short of Dras, the battalion acclimatized for a few days while receiving all the information required to execute its task. It then gradually moved up to the launchpads created by Eighteenth Grenadiers. Led by Major Vivek Gupta, it managed to climb to within 600 meters of Tololing Top before commencing its final assault at 9:00 on the night of 12 June.[7] When Gupta was killed in the assault, a young artillery officer, Captain M. K. Singh, continued the attack. Tololing Top fell on the morning of 13 June after an all-night operation that left eleven dead and more than fifty injured.

Years later, the commanding officer of Second Rajputana Rifles, Colonel Ravindranath recalled with sadness that although the operation changed an adverse situation in India's favor, it came at an enormous cost of human life. The battalion launched another ferocious and successful attack on 29 June on another height called Three Pimples, in which nine soldiers were killed.[8] A young lieutenant wrote about the final battle for Tololing in a letter to his friend: "[Our] orders were explicit—Tololing had to be taken at all cost. We took the objective but the price my company paid was a heavy one. My leading section was wiped out, everyone either dead or injured. The rest of my platoon was in tatters. Going to battle was a terrible and frightening experience."[9]

After Seventeenth Squadron lost its flight commander, Dhanoa led the mission once air operations recommenced and dropped the squadron's first bombs since the 1971 war. The target was Point 5140, a key height in the Tololing complex. Dhanoa's formation was part of an eighteen-aircraft strike over Tololing that set the tone for subsequent medium-altitude bombing. Bomb damage assessment sorties filmed huge black impact spots, but there was still room for improvement in accuracy. Facing resistance from some elements at IAF headquarters (HQ), Patney asked the squadrons to come up with something quickly, which they did. The 221st Squadron devised an improvised bombing profile that allowed aircraft to stay outside the range of

Stingers by using GPS to calculate weapon throw distances and improve final accuracy. This new strategy allowed them to remain at almost 30,000 feet but still bomb with reasonable accuracy.[10] Between 3 and 13 June the IAF flew approximately 125 sorties. One of the most effective strikes was carried out on the ridge leading to Point 5140 on the morning of 13 June after the fall of Tololing Top, to ensure that the gains accrued by Second Rajputana Rifles were consolidated.

The Indians continued to have faith in diplomacy, even as the fighting intensified. Sartaj Aziz, the foreign minister of Pakistan, arrived for talks in Delhi on 12 June. The final phase of the battle for Tololing coincided with the unsuccessful discussions between Aziz and his Indian counterpart, Jaswant Singh. As joint combat operations in Kargil entered a third week with no decisive tactical victories, both the army and air force chiefs were seriously contemplating asking the government's permission to open another front. Otherwise, they thought it would be impossible to recover the lost heights before the fighting season ended.[11] Prepared for escalation, the IAF issued preliminary orders to Ninth and Seventeenth Squadrons to strike Skardu and other targets in Pakistan-occupied Kashmir on 13 June. Stray reports in the media regarding this escalatory move were corroborated by participants in the mission from both squadrons.[12]

It was during these seesaw battles of attrition around Tololing that Thirteenth Battalion of the Jammu and Kashmir Rifles captured the imagination of the country with its courage and dogged persistence. Having arrived in the area only on 6 June, the battalion had hardly acclimatized when it was pitched into battle. Its mission was to relieve an exhausted Second Rajputana Rifles and consolidate the capture of Tololing by taking all the surrounding heights still in enemy hands. Captain Vikram Batra led this assault as it advanced along Tololing Ridge and captured Point 5140. The unit was then pulled back for a period of recuperation before its next assault around Tiger Hill.[13] The battles around Tololing Ridge marked a reversal of fortunes and the gradual ascendancy of the Indian Army over the Pakistan Army.

THE STORY OF EIGHTEENTH GARHWAL RIFLES

While the stories of Second Rajputana Rifles and Thirteenth J&K Rifles have been widely narrated in the media, other battalions performed equally creditably but stayed out of the limelight. Eighteenth Garhwal Rifles was one such unit. Mohinder Puri acknowledged the battalion's contribution after it captured Point 4700, writing that it displayed "exceptional valor and dogged determination" to "overcome initial setbacks with competence and professionalism."[14] The battalion had been operating in the Lolab Valley of southern Kashmir at a significantly lower altitude, and after a week's acclimatization, it was inducted into battle. It was early June, and Eighteenth Grenadiers had dug in a few hundred meters below its objective of Tololing Top, creating a base for the final assault. Eighteenth Garhwal Rifles was initially directed to secure Tololing Top, but that task was reassigned to Second Rajputana Rifles. The Garhwalis were instead ordered to assault the formidable Point 5140 from the east through the Bhimbat Nala (rivulet). Thirteenth J&K Rifles would simultaneously attack it from the south and First Naga from the west. A multipronged attack was considered essential to keep the enemy guessing, but it was fraught with danger as the attackers were vulnerable to fire from multiple enemy locations on the ridge. Climbing slowly up a seven-kilometer stretch, Eighteenth Garhwal Rifles came under constant fire from all the heights to the west but managed to avoid too many casualties. This was the same route attempted, unsuccessfully, by First Naga two weeks earlier, leading Colonel Chakravorty, the commanding officer of Eighteenth Garhwal Rifles, to term his mission a "reinforcement of failure." Between 12 and 15 June the battalion was beaten back from Point 5140, but after a couple of firefights, the enemy vacated the feature. By 17 June, the Indians occupied Point 5140.

Eighteenth Garhwal Rifles returned to base and, after a few days of recuperation, was assigned another tricky set of heights northwest of Tololing, including Point 4700. This was an equally tough proposition, and by the time the unit captured the heights, it had been fighting for more than three weeks and had lost fifteen men killed and another fifty-five injured. Chakravorty is one of the few senior commanders who has consistently been critical of how the Indian Army went into battle. He remains cynical about the "guts and glory" stories told later and believes it is time to confront the several shades of gray that emerged from those tough days.[15]

Despite the numerous bombing sorties by the IAF between 3 and 15 June against targets in the Tololing complex, the impact on the defenders was largely psychological, according to Chakravorty. As the troops closed in, it was natural for air strikes to decrease because of the proximity of friendly forces. The artillery started to become effective just before the final assault on Tololing, once all the regiments had arrived. Despite six shells landing perilously close to his troops' position on one occasion, Chakravorty notes that there were minimal losses to friendly fire owing to the excellent coordination of firepower. Deb was coordinating the guns at the time and initially dismissed the shelling as enemy fire, but after a quick check, he ordered his guns to hold their fire immediately.[16]

When incoming units in Kargil came face-to-face with casualties from the units they were replacing, "there was fear and doubt that they may be next," recalled Chakravorty. It was a leadership challenge, but he notes that "good leadership can isolate the outside pressures, concentrate on the task at hand, and fight battles as trained and rehearsed." He posits, "The margin between our victory in Kargil and having to accept a suboptimal outcome that left several posts in Pakistan's hands was wafer thin."[17] This is a fair assessment because, if the attacks on Tololing had failed, the Indians might have opened multiple fronts. This would have alarmed the Americans, who would have left no stone unturned to broker a cease-fire before the Indians recaptured all the Kargil heights.

The IAF also had leadership problems at the tactical level. Both Dhanoa and Nambiar recalled the gloom and despondency that descended on Srinagar and Avantipur when the Canberra was shot at on 21 May and when the IAF lost three aircraft in quick succession a week later. Menon found that morale in the squadrons depended on the dynamism of the squadron commander and his willingness to go into battle, and some tough decisions had to be made to raise mission effectiveness. Wing Commander K. T. Sebastien, who had recently commanded a MiG-29 squadron, observed the action from the Strike Planning Cell at Srinagar. He called the two MiG-21 squadrons (Seventeenth and 108th) the most "dynamic and proactive of the strike squadrons." Both squadrons had an unusually large number of young and relatively inexperienced pilots who benefited immensely from their commanding officers, "who led from the front."[18] Leo Murray, a British military analyst and former soldier, observes that "if the conditions are right then almost any man will fight, change those conditions and almost everybody will stop fighting," and "training and experience set the psychological backdrop for a battle."[19]

GROUND BATTLES AND AIRPOWER IN BATALIK

The Batalik subsector made up the eastern edge of the Kargil Sector and had some of the most inaccessible and logistically challenging operational areas. During the mid-1990s, Seventieth Brigade was deployed at Chumathang, with a focus on Siachen and not on Batalik. However, as the proxy war in J&K intensified, the brigade was pulled out. Two of its battalions were deployed for counterinsurgency operations in the Kashmir Valley, and two remained in Ladakh for rotational deployment on the Siachen Glacier. In a routine move in late 1998, brigade HQ moved back to Chumathang, leaving the two battalions in the valley. Thus, it was left to the overstretched Third Punjab from 121st Brigade to patrol Batalik. This was a huge tactical mistake that was fully exploited by Brigadier Sial, commander of Pakistan's Sixty-Second Infantry Brigade. The significance of this sector in the run-up to operations is significant. It is highly probable that Musharraf wanted the infiltration to be detected in this sector first, to draw significant Indian forces eastward into the region. He hoped that this would allow the more critical intrusions in the Mushkoh, Dras, and Kaksar Sectors to consolidate, causing significant harassment along the Srinagar–Leh highway. This would force the Indians to negotiate a cease-fire from a positional disadvantage.

Musharraf chose Fifth NLI and Eighth NLI for the operation and set up two large logistics hubs at Munthadalo and Kukarthang. These gradually expanded as the operation progressed. It was only after the first Canberra recce missions and the subsequent tactical recce missions by MiG-21s that the extent of the intrusion emerged. The NLI had occupied four ridges, of which Jubar, Khalubar, and Kukarthang were the most critical. In response, Third Infantry Division moved the HQ of Seventieth Infantry Brigade to Batalik and deployed the maximum number of battalions there because of the vast area that had to be covered, compared with other sectors. With some overlap and rotation, close to ten battalions were inducted into the area, with four battalions in operation at any given time. While First Battalion of the Bihar Regiment carried out most of the operations during the early days, First Battalion of Eleventh Gorkha Rifles fought the most successful battles in the closing stages of the conflict, taking over multiple ridgelines. Lieutenant Manoj Pandey from the latter unit was the sole recipient of the Param Vir Chakra in that sector during the battle for Khalubar Ridge.

As the war progressed, the need for IAF support in the Batalik Sector increased. To meet this need, it committed significant reconnaissance efforts to identifying the major logistics hubs that sustained Pakistani posts in the area. One such hub was the Munthadalo logistics camp, which had grown from eight to ten fabricated tents to fifty to sixty igloo tents by mid-June. Following a dummy run in a trainer with Litening pods to locate the camp, on 17 June six Mirages of Seventh Squadron dropped thirty-six 250-kilogram bombs on Munthadalo—one of the most impactful air attacks of the campaign.[20] The sprawling hub was razed. This effectively choked off supplies to the Batalik and Kaksar Sectors, thereby sealing the fate of all the Pakistani posts there.[21] This strike was followed closely by MiG-27 strikes at Kukarthang, which turned out to be a fuel supply dump; it was seen smoking for days. General Malik acknowledges the impact of airpower in the Batalik Sector and reckons that IAF pilots would not have been able to carry out their attacks without crossing the line of control. A senior Mirage-2000 pilot admits that this happened several times, particularly during air defense escort missions.

TIGER HILL AND MUSHKOH

Following the capture of the Tololing complex, Puri shifted his focus westward to Point 4875 in the Mushkoh area and the formidable Tiger Hill. Thirteenth J&K Rifles captured Point 4875 on the morning of 3 July after a punishing climb and brutal close combat. Batra was killed in action by enemy artillery fire during the battle and was posthumously awarded the Param Vir Chakra.[22] Puri had sequenced the assault on Tiger Hill a day after the one on Point 4875 to confuse the enemy. The Pakistanis on the Tiger Hill complex withstood a continuous assault for more than a month, despite "food and ammunition shortages and India's nerve-wracking air power."[23]

From 23 June onward, Mirages targeted key nodes and bunkers on Tiger Hill. The first mission by Wing Commander Nambiar and Flight Lieutenant Monish was hampered by clouds that obscured the Litening pod's field of view, and it had to be aborted. However, over the next two days, they managed to score direct hits on bunkers and a communications node. Images of enemy soldiers running were captured by the Litening pods. An Aviation Research Center long-range photography mission, followed by a MiG-25 recce, located a hangar-like structure (probably Nissan huts) at Point 4388. Situated behind and to the west of Tiger Hill, it served as a forward logistics and helicopter base. Between 5 and 9 July Mirage-2000s from Seventh Squadron were again in the thick of the action as they flew two missions that destroyed the hangar and then carried out a reconnaissance mission to check the damage.

For Puri, Point 4875 was a greater priority than Tiger Hill, given the former's closer proximity to NH-1A.[24] Also, because of the sheer physical challenges of assaulting Tiger Hill, it would be the last major post to fall. Puri assigned Eighteenth Grenadiers the task of delivering the final blow, with Eighth Sikh in support. They reclaimed Tiger Hill on 4 July after several personal acts of courage in extremely bitter close combat. These included the exploits of grenadier Yogendra Singh Yadav, who was part of the lead assault team and is one of the two surviving recipients of the Param Vir Chakra from the Kargil Conflict, along with rifleman Sanjay Kumar from Thirteenth J&K Rifles. By 8 July, the entire Tiger Hill complex had been taken over by Indian troops. On 9 July Pakistan commenced negotiations for a cease-fire, farcically holding on to the lie that it had convinced the mujahideen to withdraw.[25]

THE SILENT SERVICE PITCHES IN

Although the Indian Navy did not participate directly in the Kargil Conflict, the aggressive deployment of a combined task force of its Western and Eastern Fleets in the northern Arabian Sea reflected its coercive intent and readiness to interdict Pakistani shipping and naval assets. Vice Admiral Madhavendra Singh (later admiral and chief of naval staff) was the commander in chief of Western Naval Command and modestly recounts the impact of deploying India's vastly superior naval forces. This posed a significant threat and had the potential to choke the Makaran coast, considered by many to be Pakistan's soft underbelly. In an operation code-named Talwar, Madhavendra deployed his submarines and warships as far forward as feasible. He knew this deployment would inevitably be picked up by US satellites and could result in pressure on Pakistan at the strategic level to pull back from Kargil.[26] In the final analysis, this may have created doubt in the minds of Pakistan's security planners about India's willingness to expand the conflict and when that would happen, and the Indian Navy was in an effective position to commence a naval blockade of Karachi and choke its sea lines of communications.

LESSONS FROM KARGIL

Notwithstanding all the subsequent criticism in Pakistan and the Indian narrative that Musharraf's Kargil operation was a misadventure, the first reaction of the Indian strategic establishment was a muted acceptance of the element of surprise. A body of experts led by India's strategic guru K. Subrahmanyam assessed that "strategic surprise comes from actions that are not anticipated by the adversary. Surprise was achieved by Pakistan by carrying out an operation considered unviable and irrational."[27] Peter Lavoy offers the most objective and comprehensive Western analysis of the conflict. He writes, "Kargil dispelled the common notion that nuclear-armed states cannot fight one another." The only other instance was the Ussuri River clashes between China and the Soviet Union in 1969.[28] Lavoy was proved right two decades later in 2019, when India and Pakistan engaged in a short but sharp armed face-off. There were air strikes and aerial battles, but only a muted escalation rhetoric and nuclear bluff from the Pakistani military establishment.[29]

Military historians such as John Gill argue that Kargil was somewhere in the "gray zone" between low-intensity conflict and all-out war. Pakistan nearly convinced the global media that its army was not involved in the conflict, and even Indian correspondents writing for Western media seemed to believe that the intrusion was the handiwork of "militants and jihadis."[30] In line with the Indian propensity to downplay the impact of conflicts, Vajpayee described it as a "war-like situation."[31] However, it is best described as a limited high-intensity conflict—"limited" because it happened within a confined geographic space and time frame, and not all the tools of war fighting were employed by either side; and "high intensity" because of the ferocity of combat and the use of heavy artillery and airpower. The Indian armed forces are comfortable with this term because of the growing possibility of such contingencies unfolding along a stressed line of actual control with China.

Incredibly, Pakistan thought that by not supporting its troops with airpower, logistics, or casualty evacuation operations, it could convince the world that the intruders were jihadis. India wanted to seize the moral high ground in the conflict by concentrating on the violation of territorial sovereignty and resisting the temptation to expand the conflict. Despite Western concerns, Pakistan never came close to exercising the nuclear option. The operation was always considered expendable and did not violate any of Pakistan's nuclear red lines, which primarily concerned significant enemy gains in Punjab and Sind.[32] Had India expanded the conflict, the outcome may well have been different.

US president Bill Clinton and national security adviser Sandy Berger were condescending about the Indians' and Pakistanis' ability to comprehend red lines and the limits of deterrence. After extensive discussions with Prime Minister Nawaz Sharif in Washington, DC, in early July, they were convinced that the two countries had never been closer to a nuclear conflict than they were in 1999.[33] Aggravating the Americans' concerns was Sharif's apparent ignorance of what his army chief was up to, in both the operational and nuclear domains.[34] However, they erred in placing India in the same category as Pakistan and did not publicly acknowledge that Vajpayee's decision not to permit his military to cross the line of control meant that he understood red lines. To be fair to Clinton, though, he did acknowledge that Vajpayee had taken a "risk for peace" by going to Lahore before the outbreak of the conflict.[35] Lavoy is also critical of the American media's propensity to see "lurking around every corner of this India–Pakistan crisis a validation of their arguments about nuclear instability in South Asia and, more generally, the perils of nuclear proliferation."[36]

WHY PAKISTAN STUMBLED

What made Pakistan take the calculated risk of occupying Indian territory in Kargil? Two decades down the road, there can be no denying that the initial plan was audacious and sought to exploit the strategic slowness of a large democracy like India. Had the infiltration succeeded and had Pakistan managed to hold on to even a few heights, General Musharraf would have been a hero.[37] However, in his book *In the Line of Fire*, Musharraf has all but disowned the operation, despite being its principal orchestrator. His reluctance to write about some of the major battles in the Kargil Conflict and to highlight conspicuous acts of gallantry reveals his unwillingness to claim ownership of the conflict and to identify himself as the leader who put his men in the line of fire.[38]

Flawed planning led to a string of oversights and failures by Pakistan. The wider military and diplomatic ramifications were not accounted for. Pakistan also failed to correctly predict the response of a powerful enemy, and the absence of political guidance and objectives led field commanders to needlessly expand the operation's scope to unmanageable levels. History shows that possession of high ground does not always translate into an operational advantage in defense, especially when the attacker has a preponderance of firepower at his disposal. When this firepower is supplemented by airpower, the advantage becomes overwhelming. This was seen in Greece in 1941, when Germany's Fifth Geibrigs Division overran the seemingly impregnable Metaxis Line at 6,000 to 8,000 feet with Stuka dive-bombers.[39] The final nail in the coffin for Musharraf's Kargil misadventure was his failure to sustain communication and supply lines as the battle progressed. Had he read Clausewitz more carefully, he might not have made this mistake. According to Clausewitz, "The second crisis most commonly occurs at the end of a victorious campaign when lines of communications have begun to be overstretched. This is especially true when the war is conducted in a thinly populated and possibly hostile country."[40]

If there was any positive takeaway from the Pakistani perspective, it was the performance of the NLI. Despite being abandoned in the closing stages of the conflict and mortified by Pakistan's refusal to accept the bodies of their fallen comrades, the men of the NLI fought on. As Nasim Zehra writes, "many were confronted with tough dilemmas of whether, as lone survivors, to vacate the post or fight on."[41] After Kargil, the NLI was upgraded from a paramilitary force to regular infantry.

POLITICO-STRATEGIC ISSUES

Was the tremendous loss of life worth it, or was Kargil a Pyrrhic victory for India? Yet again, India missed an opportunity to leverage its tactical victories into long-term operational and strategic gains. Notwithstanding combat fatigue, the political push for early conflict termination, and the desire to come across as a responsible and restrained power, the line of control should have been made more defensible in the Kargil Sector by consolidating the gains in Batalik and north of the Tiger Hill and Tololing complexes. The Kargil Review Committee had no mandate to assess the quality of India's strategic responses. It steered clear of assessing the effectiveness of strategic national leadership and commented only on operational issues. Even so, many of the committee's recommendations were prescient and reformative.[42]

Preoccupied with his efforts to lead a historic peace dialogue with Sharif, Vajpayee was handicapped by the lack of a firm threat assessment that could have convinced him early on of Pakistan's sinister motives. His defense minister, Fernandes, was focused more on consolidating the gains in Siachen, managing the counterterrorism campaign in J&K, and building a strategic consciousness of the security threat posed by a resurgent China. He could have raised an alarm about the Kargil intrusions only if he had received a clear and decisive threat assessment from the Indian Army and the intelligence community, but he received no such intelligence. At the strategic level, the cabinet committee on security did little to validate the reports of hectic military activity in the Skardu and Kargil Sectors—an oversight that either escaped the notice of the review committee or was deliberately ignored.

To deny that there was an intelligence failure—as J. N. Dixit has tried to do in his writings—is as fallacious as General Malik's assertion that India's armed forces had little or no warning of the intrusion.[43] The mudslinging and accusations that flew thick and fast in the years following the Kargil Conflict only increased the lack of synergy in the upper echelons of India's national security apparatus. This takes the sheen away from the adaptable war-fighting capabilities displayed by the Indian Army and IAF at the unit level during the conflict. Malik takes ownership for India's military response and provides a fairly accurate operational account in his book *From Surprise to Victory*. However, he attributes the Indian Army's initial response mainly to the suboptimal intelligence provided by India's civilian intelligence agencies.[44] Similarly, the IAF leadership has never acknowledged that it was not adequately prepared for a limited conflict and a high-altitude offensive air campaign in the mountains that had never been attempted before.

INDIAN ARMY REFLECTIONS

At the operational level, could the Indian Army have insisted on better intelligence, rather than hoping that the sheer size of its force would be adequate to evict the entrenched and acclimatized NLI troops? When an anxious Indira Gandhi asked Manekshaw to move into Bangladesh in early 1971, he told the government that he needed more time to initiate operations.[45] Had this history been forgotten so soon? On the one hand, time was a critical factor because the Kargil–Dras–Leh highway—the lifeline to Ladakh—was under threat, and it had to be secured quickly. The destruction of the ammunition depot at Kargil on 10 May probably precipitated the hasty response. On the other hand, in hindsight, a measured induction of troops and extensive use of artillery and airpower before committing ground forces might have allowed the Indian army to reoccupy the heights just as swiftly but with significantly fewer casualties. It was a tough choice for Malik, and he chose the former.

Artillery played a big role in the Kargil Conflict. The progressive Indian artillery assault degraded the NLI's physical and psychological capacity to withstand multiple infantry assaults. Likening the impact of India's firepower to a sledgehammer, Zehra highlights the devastating effect of 100 to 120 guns being fired simultaneously. Though many Indian artillery officers would argue that the 105mm guns performed as effectively as the Bofors, Zehra conveys the Pakistanis' awe of the Bofors gun, writing that "it spread terror amongst the defenders and had a devastating effect in the destruction of enemy bunkers."[46] Its maximum range of thirty kilometers—enhanced a bit by the rarefied atmosphere at high altitudes—enabled deep strikes on the enemy's gun positions, administrative installations, ammunition dumps, and headquarters.

AIRPOWER OUTCOMES

The escalatory nature of airpower was at odds with India's counterterrorism strategy of restraint. There was dissonance within the Cabinet Committee on Security on the doctrinal use of airpower, with Foreign Minister Jaswant Singh emerging as an important voice against its use. It was initially unclear whether these incursions were nothing more than jihadi infiltrations, so the hesitation to commit offensive airpower resources to the fight was understandable. In retrospect, though, airpower contributed significantly to conflict termination, and a golden opportunity to pave the way for truly integrated operations in mountainous terrain was lost. Although the IAF's effectiveness in providing close support during assaults was both appreciated and criticized by several senior army commanders, very little has been said about the sequencing of ground operations, which gave the IAF little time to decisively exert its influence.

Like the Indian Army, the IAF took some unnecessary risks in the early days of the air war and paid a heavy price. It also took the time to visualize operations in the mountains at unusually high altitudes with limited and localized objectives. It wanted to take the war to the enemy by hitting strategic targets in enemy territory without being fettered by the constraints of fighting in one's own territory. The Indian government's refusal to allow the IAF to cross the line of control meant that India could occupy the moral high ground, but it prevented the IAF from operating to its full potential. Summarizing the broad lessons learned by the IAF, Patney observed that it had "prepared for a different kind of war," and "the learning curve was steep." He added emphatically, "Today, if Kargil were to be repeated, our combined strategy should be to allow the IAF to first clean out the hilltops with sighting assistance from the army," which would reduce army casualties.[47]

SUBOPTIMAL JOINTMANSHIP

The military objectives of the Indian Army reflected a conventional mindset—it looked to fight a high-altitude battle on its own.[48] Had the objective been to simply evict the intruders with the application of integrated combat power, airpower could have been included in the strategy from the outset. The operational sequencing may have turned out quite differently, and perhaps the intruders could have been evicted with fewer casualties.

Artillery played a dominant role in providing fire support during Operation Vijay, and vital time was lost because of artillery guns' mobility constraints in such terrain. Airpower could have helped in that situation, as it is capable of both area and precision firepower.[49] With better targeting intelligence and technology at its disposal, the IAF might have been able to provide battlefield air strikes with handheld laser designators, better communication sets, and well-trained forward air controllers. Much of the appreciation of the IAF's role in Kargil has been cosmetic, and there has been much uninformed criticism of the leadership's reluctance to commit helicopters to the fight.[50] However, Zehra highlights the impact of Indian airpower, writing that it "psychologically hit the Pakistani troops," who felt "unnerved and terrorized by it."[51] Kaiser Tufail, another respected analyst, reckons that "though the Indians had been surprised, the IAF supplemented and filled in where the artillery could not be positioned." He argues that "clearly the Army-Air Joint Operations had a synergistic effect in evicting the intruders."[52] Patney highlights the close coordination of firepower and points out that there were no losses due to friendly fire from the air throughout the conflict.[53] Although the synergy between the Indian Army and the IAF has improved significantly since 1999, leveraging the competencies of offensive airpower in high-altitude conflict continues to trouble military planners at all levels.

IN HINDSIGHT

While Malik, Puri, Tipnis, and Patney had to think on their feet, a historian has the luxury of reflecting with the benefit of hindsight. An integrated plan launched simultaneously as a single operation rather than separately would have highlighted the strengths of the two services and compensated for their individual deficiencies. The initial strategy should have been to apprise the government of the intrusion as soon as it was detected and ask for the authority to employ the full range of combat power against the intruders. The IAF could have committed its entire range of reconnaissance resources to find and fix enemy locations within the operational restrictions laid down by the government without worrying about escalation. This could have been followed by a concerted shaping of the battlefield by offensive airpower and artillery as infantry units acclimatized for assault operations. Attacks on concealed positions on the heights, along with a systematic targeting of logistics hubs, would have significantly depleted the intruders' fighting potential. Finally, infantry assaults would have cleaned up the heights with fewer casualties, as the enemy would have been demoralized by the sustained punishment meted out by artillery and airpower.

The flip side to this sequenced and calibrated plan was that its prolonged execution could have subjected India to immense international pressure to negotiate a cease-fire. Consequently, there was a good possibility that India would have had to settle for a cease-fire with the Pakistan Army still holding on to several heights. The plan would have succeeded only if the government held firm until the stated military objectives had been achieved. In the circumstances—particularly in a nuclear-charged environment—the Americans would have been breathing down Vajpayee's neck sooner rather than later.

Two decades after Kargil, it is important to determine whether the Indian Army and IAF are now better prepared, both doctrinally and operationally, for another Kargil-like situation.[54] Kargil was a highly unconventional conflict because the operating environment was significantly different from that experienced during joint operations anywhere in the world. Existing and established doctrines and tactics had to be replaced with new and untried ones.[55] In the final analysis, although the outcome was determined by the dogged infantry, which moved up the slopes and wore down the NLI in a classic campaign of attrition, flexibility and ingenuity came into play as airpower and artillery were used innovatively and decisively. Reflecting on the conflict, Patney—one of the few commanders on either side to be in the thick of action in 1965, 1971, and 1999—remarked that the "Pakistani military leadership was brash and overconfident, and they had forgotten the lessons of 1965 and 1971. On the other hand, even after being surprised, we applied common sense, were more resilient, thought instinctively, grabbed the initiative, and sustained it."[56]

16

Hybrid War in Jammu and Kashmir

The Government of India has no policy about a possible solution to the Kashmir issue but hopes that as long as the issue is kept out of international attention and the insurgency and terrorism are contained through attrition, the problem will go away.

—K. Subrahmanyam, "A Proactive Kashmir Policy"

VALLEY IGNITED

Major General Harsha Kakar, a security analyst, has attempted to simplify the nuances of the current nature of conflict in Jammu and Kashmir (J&K). He argues that it reflects several features of hybrid war in its various hues. Offering a homegrown perspective on hybrid war, he classifies it as "an all-encompassing term which goes beyond destroying an enemy's military capabilities. . . . It remains below the threshold of an all-out war and continues during peace and war."[1] In that respect, the secessionist and terrorist violence in the Kashmir Valley and Jammu region while the Kargil Conflict was raging can be considered the onset of hybrid war in J&K.

Reflecting on operations in J&K during the Kargil Conflict and its aftermath, Lieutenant General J. R. Mukherjee, a highly respected counterinsurgency expert and chief of staff and commander of the Srinagar-based Fifteenth Corps headquarters (HQ) between July 1999 and December 2001, argues that the existing narratives on the Kargil and post-Kargil operations have been incomplete. His view is that, "besides cutting off Ladakh and Siachen, Pakistan's larger game-plan was also to 'set the whole of Kashmir on fire,' by exploiting the large-scale side stepping of resources from Kashmir and Jammu to Ladakh, to deal with the Pakistani intrusions." This created gaps and voids along the line of control and the counterinfiltration grid, which allowed Pakistan to infiltrate more than 3,000 terrorists into Kashmir and Sixteenth Corps' zone (Doda, Kishtwar, Poonch, and Rajouri Sectors) during the summer of 1999. Reflecting on the violence, he explained that although Fifteenth Corps suffered heavy losses on the counterinfiltration and counterterrorism grids, it also killed more than 2,000 terrorists, including several Pakistani regulars. Suicide attacks by highly radicalized Pakistan-trained terrorists and shallow cross-border strikes by both sides were quite normal and were managed at the operational level. Mukherjee also emphasized that the senior Indian Army leadership was involved in exploring options to combat the very sophisticated covert war being waged by Pakistan. This included his own engagement in psychological operations to cause local Kashmiri insurgent and terrorist groups such as Hizbul Mujahideen (HM) to doubt the sustainability of their operations.[2]

These efforts by Fifteenth Corps coincided with attempts by the Vajpayee government in Delhi to put forth a peace initiative. The Indian prime minister involved the Farooq Abdullah government in Srinagar and moderate elements within HM, such as Abdul Majeed Dar. Delhi announced the non-initiation of combat operations from October 2000 to March 2001, but this did not mean there was no violence. The initiative was a failure and was called off in June 2001. Nearly 500 civilians, 635 terrorists, and 285 security personnel lost their lives between October 2000 and June 2001 in violence that spanned the full spectrum of conflict.[3]

Division commanders, including Rostum Nanavatty, had urged Fifteenth Corps HQ to deploy the Indian Army in Srinagar, which was emerging as the intellectual hub of the secessionist movement. However, until 1999, the Indian Army avoided sending infantry units to Srinagar City in deference to political considerations. Around the same time Mukherjee was at the helm in Fifteenth Corps, Colonel Ranjan Kumar (R. K.) Singh, who later retired as a brigadier, was in command of Fourth Battalion of the Kumaon Regiment, one of the Indian Army's most decorated battalions. It was located about thirty kilometers from Srinagar and was rushed into the city's iconic Badami Bagh Cantonement in November 1999 following a Lashkar-e-Taiba (LeT) suicide attack that killed the army's public relations officer and several others. Fourth Kumaon was soon followed into Srinagar by Third Infantry Battalion of the Garhwal Rifles. Together they set up an elaborate urban counterterrorism grid that would, over the next two years, effectively combat LeT. Noting that this was a time of great concern for commanding officers, Singh does not remember anyone in his unit sleeping for more than a few hours at a stretch for almost two years.

There were several close shaves, including the sheer horror of being cornered in the narrow lanes of Srinagar with a twenty-man patrol as kerosene oil was poured on the unsuspecting Kumaonis by a LeT team on the rooftops. Singh instinctively ordered his men to remove their bulletproof vests, cover their heads, and make a run for it as bullets started to rain down. Luckily for the Kumaonis, they timed their exit perfectly and got away with minimal injuries. Fighting fire with fire was commonplace in those days, and the Kumaonis launched an operation the very next day to eliminate the

LeT group responsible for the previous night's ambush. Commenting on the reckless and fanatical zeal of LeT in the early 1990s, Singh reckons that most of the suicide bombers or *fidayeen* were heavily into drugs. During an operation in which his unit eliminated four of the five terrorists it was after, Singh recollects being led to the fifth by a trail of vials and syringes containing Calmpose (a sedative). When the terrorist was finally cornered, he had a pistol in his hand but was shaking too hard to squeeze the trigger.[4] The debilitating impact of the army's absence from Srinagar was evident.

A COMMANDING OFFICER'S TALE

The Second Battalion, Parachute (Special Forces) Regiment, was blooded in combat during one of the most violent phases of the proxy war in J&K post Kargil, having been moved into the valley to replace Ninth Battalion. Within months of assuming command of Second Battalion, Colonel Gurdeep Bains was surprised to hear that it was being pulled out of J&K. He wrote to the army commander (Nanavatty), explaining that the unit needed more combat experience to consolidate its new role. The army commander agreed, and Second Battalion continued to operate independently in seek-and-destroy and deep-ambush missions or as part of a larger force. The unit added significant value during the high-intensity counterterrorism operations in the valley.[5]

However, Bains still thought his battalion was performing below the high expectations he had for it. In 2001, even though the battalion had eliminated twenty-one terrorists and recovered sizable quantities of arms, ammunition, and equipment, its casualties were inordinately heavy, as it had lost four soldiers killed and nine injured. "I bear responsibility for these setbacks and have instituted remedial measures," Bains wrote in a letter to his battalion's officers after intensifying the unit's training regimen. He concluded by adding, "I hope that the rigorous training carried out will manifest itself in good results."[6]

Second Battalion was assigned to Fifteenth Corps and deployed with Nineteenth and Twenty-Eighth Infantry Divisions. The unit spent its first year with Kilo Force in North Kashmir before joining Victor Force in South Kashmir, where it notched up a stupendous tally of terrorist kills by December 2002. The unit also participated in special missions with Sixth Mountain Division and First Corps during Operation Parakram. Bains recollects that during the peak of activity in the summer and autumn of 2002, as many as six or seven teams would be engaged in operations at multiple locations. This diffused and dispersed concept of operations demanded exceptional decision-making skills and a team dynamic that developed as the unit gained battle experience. Victor Force found the battalion's performance "exemplary."[7] In three years under Bains's command, Second Battalion neutralized eighty-three terrorists but lost seven men killed and seventeen wounded.[8] These casualties still haunt him, and he sometimes wakes up at night wondering what he could have done to save them.[9]

In October 2002, soon after local elections were held in J&K, there were reports of widespread disturbances in certain areas. One such area was the Warwan Valley. Situated in the upper reaches of the Himalayas at around 7,000 feet, Warwan is bounded by the Kashmir Valley on one side and Ladakh on the other. It remains completely cut off from the rest of the world for seven months of the year.[10] The valley was within Victor Force's area of responsibility. Second Battalion's C Team and a section of the Indian Navy's Marine Commandos (MARCOS) were inducted into the Warwan Valley, along with some J&K police and other army units. A week later, they were withdrawn to indicate to the locals and the terrorists that district authorities believed there had been a return to normalcy. However, C Team and the MARCOS moved into the adjoining hills of the Kishtwar Range, where they established hideouts and continued to observe developments in the valley. Three days later, they noticed suspicious activity. In a swift operation at daybreak, three terrorists were neutralized, with no loss of civilians or friendly forces.[11] MARCOS are now considered an integral part of the Special Forces deployment in the valley. Admiral Arun Prakash recalls that they blended into the environment perfectly—unshaven, speaking the local dialect, and wearing traditional robes—and "the army had a lot of faith in them."[12]

In another intelligence-driven operation, a joint seek-and-destroy mission commenced in Durapur village at 10:00 a.m. on 30 December 2002 with a battalion of Rashtriya Rifles and a unit from the J&K police's special operations group. A team from Second Battalion joined the encounter at midday, by which time several terrorists had spread out in the village. In a well-coordinated operation, a total of eight terrorists were killed over an eighteen-hour period, with minimal collateral damage and casualties.[13] Bains attributed this success to the ability to operate in small teams and blend into a hostile environment. He recognized the importance of leveraging the collective strengths and capabilities of the diverse security forces operating in the area.[14]

EXPANDING THE ARC OF TERROR

Surankote is a small town in the Poonch Sector, southwest of the Pir Panjal Range. The Poonch River flows through the town, and it is flanked by

Map 13. Expanded Zone of Conflict in Jammu and Kashmir (J&K)

the Hil Kaka subsidiary range, where Gujjar and Bakarwal tribesmen graze their livestock in the summer. Like Sopore in the 1980s, Surankote and the adjoining hills of Hil Kaka had become a haven for terrorists. From there, they would fan out into the Jammu region and take the covert war deep into what Pakistan's Inter-Services Intelligence (ISI) termed "enemy territory." Constantly searching for fresh areas to expand its covert activities, Pakistan revived the traditional infiltration routes in the Poonch area to consolidate forces in the area. Led by LeT, Jaish-e-Mohammad (JeM), and Al-Badr, the brazen terrorists felt secure enough to play cricket with the locals in Surankote. For almost four years, the Surankote area remained a haven for terrorists south of the Pir Panjal, until Romeo Force of the Rashtriya Rifles was finally directed to clear Surankote–Hil Kaka.

Romeo Force was commanded by Major General H. S. Lidder. After some discussion with the army chief, Lieutenant General Nanavatty chose Sixty-Third Infantry Brigade to undertake the operation. He was allotted teams from First, Ninth, and Tenth Parachute Battalions (Special Forces) for this operation.[15] Nanavatty had suggested Operation Rat's Nest as the code name for the operation, but Lidder chose the more dramatic Operation Sarp Vinash (destroy the snake). In April and May 2003 Mi-26s and Mi-17s were employed to build helipads at key locations, lifting bulldozers and construction machinery onto hilltops. Employing more than three battalions, Romeo Force inflicted significant casualties on the terrorists, recovered large caches of arms from the many abandoned Gujjar dwellings on the hillsides, and cut off most routes of escape. Though the number of kills claimed by the Indian Army were questioned and contested by the media,[16] what mattered to Nanavatty was that Surankote had been cleaned up, and since then, there have been no problems in the area.[17]

Lieutenant General D. S. Hooda, who commanded a brigade in the Uri Sector, Sixteenth Corps in Nagrota, and the Northern Army from 2014 to 2016, has spent a lifetime in J&K. He confirmed that a massive infiltration into the Poonch and Rajouri Sectors was part of the ISI's strategy of "spreading the arc of terrorism" into the areas south of the Pir Panjal Range.[18] Thana Mandi, Poonch, and Rajouri were the main infiltration routes for terrorists, and the hills of Doda and Kishtwar emerged as safe havens. The Gujjar and Bakarwal communities have played an important role in counterterrorist operations in the Jammu region. Gujjars raise cattle and have semipermanent settlements, while Bakarwals raise sheep and are largely nomads. In winter, both communities concentrate around Reasi, Udhampur, and the lower reaches of the Pir Panjal Range. In summer, they cross the range into the Kashmir Valley in search of grazing grounds. The more adventurous even cross the Zoji La Pass into the Kargil and Batalik Sectors. Along the way, they have been exploited in various ways by the residents of the valley. Thus, there is no love lost between these communities and the Kashmiris. They have also been exploited by the terrorists, who take their cattle, sheep, and women and kill anyone suspected of acting as informers for the Indian Army. In Hooda's opinion, not enough credit has been given to these two communities in the fight against terrorism in the Jammu region. He notes that Romeo Force used some Gujjars as guides and porters during Operation Sarp Vinash. According to Hooda, Village Defense Committees (VDCs) were established following the massacre of Hindus in remote villages in the Poonch and Rajouri regions. Although the initial VDCs were manned predominantly by Hindus, several all-Muslim VDCs sprang up in the area, particularly in the Surankote and Hil Kaka regions. There is even an all-female VDC, indicating women's proactive role in the counterterrorist campaign. The concept of community-specific VDCs is now being discouraged, as it tends to polarize communities.

HEAT, CEASE-FIRE, AND A FENCE

Quasiofficial figures reveal the hit taken by the Pakistan Army and the jihadis prior to the 2003 cease-fire. From 1 January 2000 to 15 October 2002 (roughly corresponding to the period from the cessation of the Kargil Conflict to the end of Operation Parakram), Indian artillery and mortars firing across the line of control caused 700 fatalities to the Pakistan Army and its associated border management forces. Retaliatory fire caused about 140 fatalities on the Indian side. Approximately 230,000 mortar rounds and 102,000 artillery shells were fired by the Pakistan Army, and the Indian Army responded with 270,000 mortars and 133,000 artillery shells. Small-team engagements around the line of control were widespread and caused approximately 130 fatalities among both Pakistani regulars and mujahids; fatalities on the Indian side were much lower, at just under fifty. The most telling statistic from this period is that the number of terrorists killed per encounter went up from 1.7 to 2.3.[19]

Pakistan offered a comprehensive cease-fire in November 2003 after feeling the heat from sustained Indian military action and diplomatic pressure following the attack on the Indian Parliament by ISI-trained LeT terrorists in December 2001. India accepted the offer, but it was never formalized into a binding agreement because of India's insistence that it be linked to Pakistan's commitment to stop supporting the Kashmiri secessionist struggle and using terrorism against India. The lull in relentless operations allowed General N. C. Vij, the army chief, to push through his ambitious project of fencing almost the entire 700 kilometers of the line of control—which runs from what the Indian Army calls Zero Point in the Akhnoor Sector to the edge of the Gurez Sector in the Mushkoh Valley. The anti-infiltration obstacle system (i.e., the fence) required 300 tons of steel per kilometer and was completed in early 2005 at a cost of over 1,150 crores. It took 25,000 Indian Army soldiers eighteen months to build it. The fence made infiltration extremely difficult until the ISI developed tactics to overcome it.

Lieutenant General Hasnain was commanding Twelfth Infantry Brigade in Uri at the time and remembers General Vij's insistence that the fence be a continuous obstacle, despite local commanders' protests that this was an impossible task, given the terrain. Vij visited Hasnain's brigade HQ every twenty days to get an update on the progress of the fence. Hasnain said, "Much credit for the fence must go to Vij. His strategic vision cannot be faulted, as between 2004 and 2007, the combination of the cease-fire and the fence had impacted the mathematics of the infiltration and significantly reduced the number of cease-fire violations."[20]

The double-layered fence is twelve feet high and about twelve feet wide. It is made up of coils of concertina wire strung between rows of pickets and is electrified at places. Unlike the one built by the Israelis to control the infiltration of terrorists from Palestine,[21] this fence has not come under a lot of international scrutiny, as it follows the alignment of the line of control and is well within Indian territory. There was also surprisingly little opposition from the Pakistanis, as it suited Musharraf's "dovish" strategy to try to control anti-India terrorist groups. No obstacle can prevent movement without surveillance, so the Indian Army has deployed motion sensors, thermal imaging devices, and night-vision equipment.[22] It has also divided the cease-fire zone into grids so that officers can be held accountable for movement in designated areas.

Amy Waldman, writing in the *New York Times*, quoted Umar Farooq, a pro-*Azadi* (freedom) Kashmiri political leader. "People who want to come and are determined to come, they will come. They have routes and maps, and they will use them. It's a waste of money," he said. Farooq thought it would be better to pursue a political settlement. Waldman also quoted senior Indian military officials, who said they had seen "tentativeness" among the terrorists and believed "the fence has allowed the army to foil many crossing attempts." Although terrorists in Pakistan say the fence has made "crossing the ceasefire line riskier," they claim they have "enough men and ammunition already inside Kashmir to sustain the insurgency for years."[23]

Hooda knows the fence intimately. In the Jammu region, it has been relatively easy to manage the two-layered fence and install surveillance devices. The fence has not collapsed in the winter under the weight of the snow, except in some areas of the Poonch Sector. However, farther north in the valley, the fence practically disappears in the upper reaches of the Tangdhar, Neelum, and Gurez Sectors, and repairs must be made every year in May. This is a herculean task, as sand, cement, and wire are needed to repair and rebuild many kilometers of damaged fence. Though he was a skeptic when it was being built, Hooda acknowledges that the fence has done its job and is a serious obstacle for infiltrators.[24]

FORCE LEVELS AND MILITARY CIVIC ACTION

The constant movement of security forces in and out of J&K since the early 1990s has led to intense speculation about their profile and strength. There was a time in the 1980s when Fifteenth Corps in Srinagar had only one oversized division (Nineteenth Infantry Division), a couple of additional brigades, and a few Border Security Force battalions. This added up to around 35,000 troops to defend the line of control in the Kashmir region. However, in 2002—after a decade of violence and heightened infiltration—the number of counterinfiltration forces along the line of control had almost doubled to 50,000 to 60,000 troops. South of the Pir Panjal Range in the Jammu region, the Indian Army had three infantry divisions under Sixteenth Corps, with an extra division moving in when required. This four-division counterinfiltration and counterterrorist force had a total strength of 100,000 to 110,000 troops.

Third Corps in the northeast and Sixteenth Corps in the Jammu region are the Indian Army's largest corps, and they reflect India's security focus and concerns. Including the J&K police, there were more than 400,000 security personnel deployed in J&K in the 2000s. Ajai Shukla has estimated that this figure might have been closer to 470,000 in 2018. The latest figures endorsed by the Indian Army point to a smaller force.[25] However, Pakistan puts the number at 1 million.[26] These figures do not include the Indian Army and Indo-Tibetan Border Police deployments in Ladakh.

India's armed forces, particularly the Indian Army and the Indian Air Force (IAF), have constantly been engaged in civic action in remote areas of the country since independence. Major examples include in the aftermath of partition, in the months after the cessation of 1947–1948 hostilities with Pakistan, in Nagaland and Mizoram during the peak years of the insurgencies, and during natural disasters across the country. The Indian Navy has effectively contributed to every humanitarian assistance and disaster relief operation in the maritime domain since independence.

In 1998 the Indian Army launched a civic action program in J&K called Operation Sadhbhavna. While most commanders acknowledge the utility of military civic programs in remote areas, others, such as retired lieutenant general Rakesh Sharma, think the Indian Army committed excessive resources to this operation. Hooda, however, argues that initiatives such as the army goodwill schools and health care centers have had a positive impact, particularly in the rural areas of J&K, where there is a heavy army presence but hardly any civil administration or police. He recalls meeting a group of parents who requested that the army take back a school that had been handed over to the civil administration. Another high-impact initiative was setting up youth clubs in hotbeds of secessionist activity—such as Anantnag and Shopian—because of their potential for de-radicalization. However, Hooda agrees that getting into infrastructure projects, such as constructing small hydroelectric projects, is a mistake because they are not sustainable unless they are run by the civil administration. Overall, Hooda thinks military civic action must be used in a measured manner without diluting the core responsibilities of the military.[27]

THE LOST YEARS: 2003-2012

The earthquake that ravaged J&K and large portions of Pakistan-occupied Kashmir (PoK) in October 2005 could have been a turning point had the Manmohan Singh government moved decisively to win over the people of Kashmir. The speed with which the Indian Army and the IAF swung into action for relief operations was in stark contrast to the lukewarm response to the calamity in PoK. The districts of Uri and Tangdhar were hardest hit on the Indian side, and they were rehabilitated in no time. However, people living in Muzaffarabad in PoK languished for months amidst the destruction. The Srinagar–Muzaffarabad bus service—started as a confidence-building measure—had allowed the locals to compare development in J&K with that in PoK. Soon, many of those who had crossed the border in 1989–1990 as teenagers realized that it was time to go back. Now in their mid-thirties, they had married locals and had become disillusioned with the jihadi movement. However, after the initial amnesty offered to about a hundred hard-core terrorists, the initiative fizzled in 2007, following resistance from hard-liners within the Indian Army and the intelligence agencies. Hooda thinks this may have been a lost opportunity.

General Bipin Rawat, then a brigadier, commanded a Rashtriya Rifles sector (akin to a standard infantry brigade, but reconfigured for counterinsurgency and counterterrorist operations) in the Sopore Sector of North Kashmir as part of Kilo Force between 2006 and 2008. He recollects that although the 2003 cease-fire of was holding, the fence-based counterinfiltration grid had not stabilized in his sector, and infiltration was continuing. This was because the thickly forested bowl-shaped Lolab Valley immediately south of the Shamshabari Range was an ideal postinfiltration staging point for infiltrators before they climbed over the only ridge separating Lolab from Sopore. Then they could join the locals in buses and other vehicles running on the solitary road connecting Sopore with Kupwara. Among the successes that Rawat recollects are the operations his units conducted within and on the fringes of the Lolab and Handwara forests. They often had the help of former terrorists who penetrated the HM terror gangs and acted as double agents. They provided Rawat with critical information that led to several successful encounters. These operatives were extricated from the jihadi groups after a few operations, and not one of them was compromised during Rawat's tenure. A few of them were recruited into the territorial army battalions of the Regiment of Jammu and Kashmir Light Infantry and are still serving.[28]

Hasnain's first attempt to seriously influence the intellectual dimension of the covert war against the Indian state was during his tenure as division commander in Baramulla in 2008. Attempting to bridge the cultural, social, and religious divide, symposiums were held for *maulvis* of different sects and met with some success. But such ideas could not be sustained because of an inherent resistance to digress from the more visible kinetic attempts to tackle the problem. Hasnain pursued the idea and delved deeper into Islam during his next assignment as head of the Junior Command Wing of the Army War College. Since then, Hasnain has been at the forefront of a healthy debate within the Indian Army on the importance of targeting the intellectual dimension of the *Azadi* movement in J&K.

Prime Minister Manmohan Singh was an idealist and an internationalist like his predecessor, Vajpayee. He too believed in taking the path of reconciliation in India–Pakistan relations. The five expert groups he set up in 2006 to address the various facets of the Kashmir imbroglio made several useful recommendations that were never implemented.[29] However, it seemed that his parleys with President Musharraf to explore outside-the-box solutions for the Kashmir conflict were headed in the right direction. Analyzing the situation prior to the Mumbai attacks of November 2008, Hooda notes that there was a steep decline in the number of deaths due to terrorism and insurgency—from more than 4,000 in 2001 to fewer than 1,000 in 2007. This, along with the rapid progress of the Manmohan–Musharraf discussions, led the ISI to derail any nascent peace initiatives.

The Indian security establishment was preoccupied with the widespread protests in Kashmir over innocuous issues such as the transfer of a hundred acres of land around the sacred Hindu shrine at Amarnath for the construction of temporary shelters for pilgrims. Initiated by environmentalists and exploited by secessionists, who linked it to a dilution of their autonomy, the protests in May and June 2008 resulted in the governor's resignation and the fall of the elected coalition government led by Ghulam Nabi Azad of the Congress Party.[30] This led to the first manifestation of a people's movement called *Chalo* (let's go). Chalo Muzzafarabad was the first of many such slogans that sparked a gradual spike in violence in J&K.[31] With Delhi now focused on Kashmir, the field was open for LeT to plan attacks in India. The Mumbai terror attacks were followed by the souring of India–Pakistan relations, Western pressure on Musharraf to dismantle terror networks in Pakistan, and a deterioration in the security situation in Kashmir.

While terrorist attacks and infiltrations decreased following the Mumbai attacks, civilian protests and mass mobilizations commenced in earnest as an evolving "strategy of the weak." These presented the Indian Army with a new threat—stone-pelting and mass mob protests designed to provoke a fierce response. The year 2010 was a violent one, with 112 deaths, including both protesters and security forces. Meanwhile, Hasnain was firmly ensconced as commander of the army's third strike corps, Twenty-First Corps, until he was asked to move to Srinagar in September by the army chief, General V. K. Singh. This was the challenge Hasnain was waiting for. He reckoned that by the end of 2010, the agitation had reached an inflection point wherein fatigue had set in among the populace. Education had suffered, the apple crop had wasted away, and tourism had reached an all-time low. The separatist leaders had to make a decisive move if they wanted to spark an uprising.

Syed Shah Geelani, the pro-Pakistan leader of the All Party Huriyat Conference,[32] appealed to the people to surround military camps and raised "Chalo UN" and "Chalo Baramulla" calls to paralyze the civil administration. This is when Lieutenant General Marwah, Hasnain's predecessor as corps commander, put out a stern warning that if the military camps were threatened, the army would retaliate decisively. The issue was discussed at the Unified Command in Srinagar, and clear instructions and guidelines were passed on to the police, Rashtriya Rifles, and army units to stamp out what was threatening to become a major rebellion. While the J&K police and Rashtriya Rifles managed to control the mobs of stone throwers, soldiers from the regular army battalions were often unnerved by them. Had it not been for the restraint demonstrated by young officers, there might have been several cases of retaliatory firing by outnumbered troops. Hasnain remembers several instances of young, unarmed officers confronting the mobs, urging them to return to their homes, and even daring the protesters to target them. As always, they rose to the occasion with alacrity and fearlessness.[33]

Retired lieutenant general Ravi Thodge was commanding Kilo Force in northern Kashmir as a major general under Hasnain. He recollects that when his troops were cornered by a huge mob, they were compelled to open fire, killing two in the crowd. When he made it clear to the protesters that the soldiers would fire in self-defense, the intensity of the agitation fell off in his area. Worried by the trend toward violence, Manmohan Singh sent a group of civilian interlocutors to the valley in late 2010. It was led by senior journalist Dileep Padgaonkar and included academic and author Radha Kumar and academic–turned–civil servant M. M. Ansari. The group's principal mandate was to study the situation and initiate a dialogue with various stakeholders. Thodge recalls that the civilian group was clueless about military matters, underestimated the potential of the ISI, and downplayed the growing menace of the mobs. Thodge tried to explain counterterrorism operations to the group and pointed out the ominous signs that Kashmiri youths were being brainwashed to believe that *Azadi* was right around the corner. The group asked questions such as, "Why don't you identify the terrorists before opening fire?" Clearly, they were unaware of the restraint shown by the Indian Army during cordon-and-search operations, during which the army often took casualties, thus yielding the initiative to the terrorists. Thodge told the interlocutors that no heavy weapons or airpower were used in such operations and that the Indian Army was probably the most restrained counterterrorism force in the world. Kilo Force had several successes in 2011 after government agencies began providing intelligence on LeT and JeM. These operations were particularly effective in the Gurez Sector, where Kilo Force experienced several successes during Thodge's tenure. It was clear from this experience that operations driven by intelligence and technology would be the way forward.[34]

In the mind games that followed, the separatists wilted, and there appeared to be an opportunity for Hasnain to apply a healing touch to a tired but angry and sullen local population. The years 2011 and 2012 were relatively quiet, with Hasnain building on the good work done by his predecessors Lieutenant Generals Vinayak Patankar and Nirbhay Sharma, who had started several citizen outreach programs. Apart from exhorting his troops to understand the cultural terrain and institute citizen-friendly initiatives, such as rescheduling disruptive military convoys through populated areas, he was clear that there would be no letup along the line of control and in the targeting of terrorist leadership, particularly in North Kashmir. New Delhi and the Indian Army were impatient, however, and wanted a speedy conversion of the stabilization phase into a conflict resolution phase. This prevented the detection of the separatist movement's migration from North to South Kashmir.

What slipped under Srinagar's and New Delhi's radar was the emergence of a new crop of local terrorist leadership in 2012, made up of heavily radicalized youths who had seen nothing but violence while growing up in the valley. Exploiting a protective local population and creating a Robin Hood–like reputation with a fanatic jihadi fervor, South Kashmir's locally recruited terrorists soon made it the epicenter of the separatist movement. When asked whether there was an element of overreach in his version of the "winning hearts and minds" strategy and whether he had unrealistic expectations of achieving any meaningful politico-strategic outcomes from his initiatives, Hasnain was candid. He emphatically maintained that he had correctly identified the center of gravity within the secessionist movement. He also reckoned that there was a lack of institutional continuity and an understanding that the stabilization phase in Kashmir would take a few more years before a push for conflict resolution would be feasible. Hasnain believes this resulted in a reversal of the gains made between 2010 and 2012. He admitted, however, that he may have built unrealistic expectations of what could be achieved in his limited two-year tenure as commander of Fifteenth Corps.[35]

ESCALATION

Hooda was the commander of Sixteenth Corps by 2012, when there was little terrorist activity south of the Pir Panjal Range. This was because local support had dried up and some headway was being made in the political process. Total killings were at an all-time low of 107, and tourism was showing signs of revival. Senior commanders of the security forces told the Omar Abdullah government in J&K that the time was right to improve state-driven governance, pursue de-radicalization initiatives, and restore law and order. However, both the state and the center failed to exploit the window, leaving room for the ISI to keep the Kashmir pot boiling.

Nawaz Sharif returned as prime minister of Pakistan in June 2013 and wanted to revisit the India–Pakistan peace process. This was when the General Kayani–led Pakistan Army decided to up the ante in the Jammu region by embedding its border teams with SSG commandos. First an Indian soldier was captured during a cross-border operation by the Pakistanis and beheaded. Then a police station was raided and stripped of hundreds of weapons. This was followed by a hit on Sixteenth Armored Regiment of the Indian Army at Samba by LeT. Outfits such as LeT and JeM were desperate for action after almost five years of forced restraint following the Mumbai attacks. As infiltrations rose, there were massive exchanges of fire across the line of control. This led to a meeting between the director-generals of military operations of both armies in December 2013, where de-escalation was discussed.

Taking over as Northern Army commander in June 2014, Hooda was immediately confronted with a massive flood-relief operation in J&K. The Indian Army and IAF performed well, but subsequent relief, rehabilitation, and reconstruction initiatives were suboptimal, causing a great deal of dissatisfaction with the newly elected Mehbooba Mufti J&K government. The winter of 2015 was a restive one because, as Hooda had cautioned New Delhi, there was anger and radicalization in the valley. He suggested a flexible response that included the possibility of a cease-fire. Concurrently, in a change of strategy, the ISI scaled down infiltrations. It used the terrorists mainly to conduct strikes against military bases and as handlers for the radicalized and disenchanted Kashmiri youths who were joining HM in droves. Designated a local commander, Burhan Wani soon emerged as the poster boy of the new wave. Wani was finally cornered by security forces in Kokernag in July 2016 and refused several opportunities to surrender. According to Hooda, even though the operation had been an intelligence-driven one, no one knew that Wani was holed up in that location. A policeman was injured in the firefight, and two HM terrorists were killed, one of whom was Wani.

The turnout at his funeral and the ripple effect across the valley surprised everyone and heralded a second wave of stone-throwing protests.

The Indian security establishment had dismissed the 2010 protests as a one-time expression of angst, but that was not the case in 2016. Hooda was surprised at the scale of the uprising; it was far more widespread than those in 2009–2010, which had been restricted to urban areas. "As local recruitment rose, women joined the protests and helped trapped terrorists escape cordons," he said. Shopian and Bandipora emerged as hotbeds of protest in southern and northeastern Kashmir, and Kupwara in northern Kashmir saw mass protests. Mobs in Kupwara tried to set the military hospital on fire, and there was looting of police armories. Hooda added, "Equally worrisome was the radicalization, which saw families divided on the mosques they visited to offer prayers.[36] Eleven-year-olds were getting radicalized in Salafist/Wahhabi mosques and joining street mobs."[37]

GARUDS IN ACTION

The Garud Forces were formed in 2004 as the IAF's Special Forces unit. To gain experience, they were initially embedded in small numbers in units of the Indian Army's Special Forces in Kashmir. However, this proved to be of little operational value. They were not involved in any major intelligence-driven operation because of their inexperience. It took the IAF almost a decade to convince the Ministry of Defense and Indian Army HQ that the Garuds were capable of participating in operations. Following this, two large teams of Garuds were sent on a six-month tour of the central Kashmiri district of Bandipora, along with the Rashtriya Rifles.

The squadron leader, identified here only as R, was assigned command of an element of Garuds in February 2017 and led his team into the valley in July 2017. They were fully supported by the IAF with the best weapons, clothing, and night-vision and communication devices. The teams plunged into active operations after two weeks of rigorous training at Fifteenth Corps' battle school at Khrew. They were then assigned to Hajun, a densely populated town of 35,000 inhabitants on the banks of the Jhelum River. Hajun had emerged as a den of secessionist activity, and the Garuds soon discovered that it was easy for the town to mobilize a stone-throwing mob of up to 10,000 people. R recalls that women hid stones in their *phirens* (gowns) and distributed them to the boys and men, who would throw them at security forces. R was injured and needed stitches on his left shoulder and right hand.

R soon developed a feel for the situation and recognized the importance of intelligence-driven operations. Northern and central Kashmir were largely

LeT dominated, while JeM controlled southern Kashmir. HM was, for the most part, a spent force; its local members had become a liability because of their poor fighting skills, and they were being eliminated in large numbers by security forces. When cornered, HM terrorists called up family members to rally a crowd and facilitate their escape. This was a different kind of warfare and required great restraint, skill, and patience.

The first major operation in which R and his team participated took place at Rakh Hajun—a hamlet of about ten houses north of Hajun. The J&K police confirmed the presence of eight to ten LeT terrorists in the hamlet. A dense cordon was laid by three Special Forces teams from the Garuds, Ninth Parachute Battalion, and a Rashtriya Rifles battalion. The Garuds were the blocking force to the rear, where the terrorists were expected to try to break through the cordon and make a run for the apple orchards. The operation commenced at around 9:00 p.m. on 10 October 2017, and it took more than twelve hours for the teams to close in on the target house. When the terrorists finally made a run for it, they encountered the Garuds. Two militants were shot down immediately, and another was severely injured in a firefight that lasted no more than three or four minutes. The Garuds also lost two men during this operation—their first casualties.

Afterward, there was talk that the Garuds might be reassigned to a quieter sector. R asked his sector commander to have faith in the team and give the Garuds an opportunity to avenge the loss of their comrades. What followed was a month of painstaking intelligence collection with the active assistance of the J&K police. This involved the continuous tracking of one terrorist's communications by the intelligence agencies and J&K police. His location was finally identified as Chandargeer village, seven kilometers from the town of Manasbal. A dangerous physical recce of the town confirmed these findings.

On 17 November 2017 there were reports of heightened activity in the town and announcements from the mosque that the local people must rise in response to any provocation by the Indian Army. Learning from their previous encounter, the terrorists had chosen a haven next to a mosque, and they were not expecting the army to attack by day. The Garuds and Rashtriya Rifles drove into the town at around 3:00 p.m. and parked undetected next to a sawmill. The terrorists would be resting at this time of day, having completed their midday prayers and eaten lunch. What R did not know, however, was that the top LeT leadership in J&K was in the targeted house, with several other cadres waiting at other locations in the village. It was later determined that the group could have been planning a major strike. The area was cordoned by the Rashtriya Rifles' modest but heavily armed blocking force, and R's Garuds were covering the rear exit.

A few hours later, the trapped terrorists rushed out the rear exit, firing their AK-47s. Some were shot down immediately, while the others took cover in a ditch and started lobbing grenades. R had two grenades ready and responded with an accurate throw. Luckily for him, one of the grenades thrown at him hit a tree some distance away, and another was deflected back at the terrorists. Corporal Nirala of the Garuds charged at the remaining terrorists but was fatally shot in the head. When the six dead terrorists were identified, it became clear that the Garuds had scored a major success. Four of the slain terrorists were relatives or confidants of LeT chief Hafiz Sayeed and Zakiur Rehman Lakhvi, mastermind of the Mumbai attacks. R and his slain comrades were awarded gallantry medals. This operation established the Garuds as a trained force that could be called on in multiple situations.

FIGHTING FAIRLY

A comparison of the number of terrorists, security forces, and civilians killed in encounters during counterterrorist and counterinfiltration operations in J&K over a ten-year period shows that the Indian Army is extremely restrained and mindful of collateral damage and has taken unusually heavy casualties itself. Admiral Arun Prakash has called for a better understanding of the dilemmas the military faces when it is asked to participate in internal security operations. Writing in *Indian Express*, he notes that most insurgencies rooted in alienation and socioeconomic factors are aggravated by political venality and apathy. After the serial failure of the elected government, civil administration, and police, an area is declared "disturbed." The Armed Forces Special Powers Act (AFSPA) is then invoked, and the military is asked to restore order. "Even when the army restores relative peace and normalcy, the local police and administration repeatedly fail to resume their normal functioning," Prakash laments. "The prolonged imposition of the AFSPA is therefore a fig leaf used by successive governments to hide egregious failures of governance. The governments knew that deployment of the army without the AFSPA would be illegal and that any orders issued would constitute 'unlawful commands.'" Prakash goes on to say that "soldiers, being human, do make mistakes and violations of human rights have occurred from time to time. But the army as a highly-disciplined body is acutely conscious that violation of human rights is a crime that sullies the organization's good name." He insists that "strict and comprehensive codes of conduct have been laid down by the army's leadership and drastic punishments are meted out where infringements are proved."[38]

With regard to the Indian Army's human rights record in Kashmir, Hooda claims that 95 percent of the allegations made by human rights activists are false and that the Indian Army has a record of fair investigation and punishment for those found guilty.[39] Statistics provided by the Indian Army as of 2019 reveal that of the 1,053 allegations received from J&K by the army's human rights cell, 1,030 were investigated and 999 were found to be baseless. In the cases of the thirty-one allegations found to be true, seventy personnel were subjected to punishments that included dismissal from service and imprisonment. Compensation was awarded in eighteen cases. Twenty-three cases are still under investigation.[40]

UNDERSTANDING PAKISTAN'S KASHMIR STRATEGY

Is Pakistan's strategy in Kashmir trapped by history, driven by revenge, and propelled by radicalization? Is the crisis in its present form a security dilemma for both India and Pakistan, or is India preventing a revisionist and greedy Pakistan from severing Kashmir from India?[41] From the Indian perspective, there is no security dilemma. If Pakistan stopped fomenting covert war in the state, India could manage the internal dynamics at play there. What has compelled Pakistan to embark on its futile attempt to force the secession of J&K? One reason is an unresolved agenda from partition, which, according to Sumit Ganguly, has converted Pakistan into a "predatory and greedy state."[42] Another is the Pakistan Army's deeply ingrained compulsion to get even with India for its humiliating defeat in 1971. Encouraging the common people of Pakistan to fear India is the only way to sustain the myth that only the Pakistan Army can "save" Pakistan from being gobbled up by a predatory India. A third reason is the radicalization of large sections of Pakistani society, as well as the Pakistan Army and the ISI. This has given traction to the desire to see Kashmir become part of an "Islamic republic."

Aided by poor governance by successive state governments, J&K has become a testing ground for new, disruptive, and low-cost jihadi strategies of radical Sunni Islam from Rawalpindi and Islamabad.[43] Driven by jihadists like Masood Azhar and Hafiz Saeed—and supported by secessionist elements in J&K such as the All Party Hurriyat Conference—these strategies seek to fuse the traditional methodologies of covert war with the more nebulous strategies involving proxies and hybrid tools. They seek to exploit social media and the cyberdomain and foment public unrest that spirals into violence and tests the state's resilience to the limit. A senior army officer recalls that in the 1970s and 1980s, the Indian Army had a very friendly image in the Kashmir Valley:

> The Indian Army did not correctly read the signs of the changed profile of visits across the line of control over the years. Earlier, travelers from India to PoK

on a fourteen-day visa would return within three days, lamenting on the state of affairs across the line of control. However, in the late 1980s, the number of youths who overstayed in PoK increased. These youths would return after three or four weeks, radicalized and having received limited arms training. They had been sent back with the message "we will contact you and the weapons will reach you."[44]

The same officer pointed out that from 2010 onward, the separatists started to attract younger worshippers to more radicalized discourses in new foreign mosques, even as the elders continued to attend traditional family mosques. Religious teachers in these "youthful" mosques were forced, under pressure of the gun, to read a passage to their congregations before commencing traditional prayers. That passage began: "We are Muslims and the Quran says that there is no way Hindus and Muslims can live together." However, Muslim preachers have confirmed that the Quran does not say this. The rest of the passage quoted inflammatory portions of rhetorical speeches that punctured the moderate argument against *Azadi* and made false allegations that Muslims in eastern India were being deported to Bangladesh. The preliminary sermon concluded by saying: "If we join India, all Muslims will be pushed out." This led to the proposition that Muslim youth in Kashmir have a choice: fight for independence or join Pakistan. Clearly acknowledging that India is a powerful country, the sermon cited the example of David and Goliath and concluded that jihad is the only way forward. Indoctrination of women also commenced after 2005 and peaked around 2010. Virulent separatists such as Asiya Andrabi—leader of Dukhtaran-e-Millat (daughters of the nation)—engaged with women, telling them that the best form of governance is a caliphate and that it is sacrilegious to vote.[45]

PRACTITIONERS REFLECT ON CONFLICT RESOLUTION IN J&K

After taking over as army chief in 1997, General Malik sought to disengage from counterterrorism operations after almost seven years of relentless activity. He suggested to Chief Minister Farooq Abdullah that it was time for the army to return to its primary task in a phased manner. This prompted a panicky call from Abdullah to Prime Minister Inder Gujral, who tentatively asked Malik to remain engaged. Malik's assessment is that Abdullah was not confident that he could oversee the return of normalcy through governance and maintain law and order with only the state police and other assigned paramilitary forces.[46]

Relentlessly targeting the jihadi and militant leadership in the Kashmir

Valley and adjoining regions of Kishtwar and Doda in the summer of 2001, Nanavatty was also thinking about peace. He drafted a holistic and all-encompassing document entitled *Jammu and Kashmir (J&K): Strategy for Conflict Resolution* (which he updated in 2003). The clarity, constancy, boldness, and contemporary relevance of his arguments seem particularly prescient today, especially after the abrogation of Articles 370 and 35A of the Constitution by the Modi government.[47] Nanavatty and his team submitted the strategy document to Indian Army HQ, and copies were later sent to many senior government officials, including Home Minister L. K. Advani, Home Secretary N. N. Vohra, and Foreign Minister Jaswant Singh. Jaswant Singh discussed the document with Nanavatty, but the rest showed little interest in it.

Recalling his interactions with Abdullah, Nanavatty describes him as an opportunistic politician who wore his patriotism on his sleeve and was unwilling to deal with core issues. Nanavatty tried to discuss three core issues with Abdullah: dealing with Pakistan, addressing the aspirations of the Kashmiri people, and acknowledging that J&K was being held hostage by agitating Kashmiri Muslims. Abdullah responded by telling Nanavatty to discuss the matter with the chief secretary of the state. Nanavatty could never hold Abdullah's attention, and he was never consistent. "I used to urge him to initiate an intellectual discussion on Kashmir on the lines of the highly popular debates on Palestine that Tim Sebastien of the British Broadcasting Corporation (BBC) would host in Doha, but he would not listen," Nanavatty recalled.[48] Nanavatty's assessment proved correct, as in the year ahead, Abdullah would urge the government to engage with the pro-Pakistan Hurriyat People's Conference—particularly when he and his son Omar were out of power.

The opening argument of Nanavatty's strategy document is that the internal conflict in J&K is as much a consequence of the people's alienation, poor governance, and lack of development and employment as it is a by-product of Pakistan's covert war and support for terrorism. The strategy's aim is to restore normalcy in the state so that democratic institutions, including those responsible for law and order, can function unimpeded. Its key points are:

1. Persuade, dissuade, and, if necessary, deter Pakistan from pursuing its strategy of covert war and support for terrorism in J&K.
2. Seek a peaceful resolution of the conflict within the framework of the Constitution of India.
3. Fulfill the legitimate political and economic aspirations of the state.
4. Ensure the sanctity of the line of control, the actual ground position line (AGPL), and the international border in J&K.

5. Suppress and neutralize all terrorist groups.
6. Prevent the spread of conflict to the unaffected areas of Ladakh and Jammu.
7. Synergize the functioning of the central and state governments and the various instruments of government within the state.
8. Improve administration and governance within the state.
9. Mold public opinion in support of a peaceful resolution of conflict.

By April 2003, Vajpayee had initiated peace talks with Pakistan and had created a special group to engage all stakeholders in J&K. Voicing the frustration of every corps and army commander who has served in J&K since the early 1990s, Nanavatty urged the special group to consider his strategy document. Even though the army had not been asked to comment on political, diplomatic, social, and economic matters, Nanavatty felt "compelled to do so with the hope of stimulating an informed debate that could lead to a blueprint for a strategy. Any failure to address the issue holistically will condemn security forces to manage the conflict at great cost," he warned.[49]

A serving lieutenant colonel notes the metamorphosis of the brutal proxy war of yesteryear into the sophisticated hybrid war of today. Reflecting on the challenges he is likely to face during counterterrorism operations in J&K, he observes, "they are blurred and span multiple domains. It is time we countered the hybrid threat with a hybrid response." About holistic strategies, he says, "it is time for the armed forces and the government to undertake planned campaigns to target the youth by engaging with them, educating them, and empowering them with opportunities." Comparing the threat to a hydra, he notes that if it is not eliminated, it "will resurface again."[50]

17

Under the United Nations Flag

India's commitment to peacekeeping is strong and will grow.
—Prime Minister Modi, "Full Text of Statement by
PM Modi at UN Peacekeeping Summit"

EARLY YEARS: IMPACT IN KOREA

The face-off on the Korean peninsula in the early 1950s was the first major post–World War II confrontation between communist North Korea and South Korea, which was emerging as a key ally of the United States. The alliance was critical for the United States' quest to stem the surge of communism in East Asia. The North Koreans carried out an offensive across the thirty-eighth parallel in June 1950 and overran Seoul. A US-led United Nations (UN) force—backed by Security Council Resolution 83—came to the assistance of the South Koreans in September. Under General Douglas MacArthur, the UN force first outflanked the North Koreans with an audacious amphibious landing at Incheon on 15 September 1950 and then pushed the North Koreans north of the thirty-eighth parallel. The UN force did not stop there; it continued its advance toward the Yalu River, which for the Chinese was a "red line" that threatened China's sovereignty. Mao committed almost 3 million troops, and the People's Liberation Army (PLA) pushed the UN force back across the thirty-eighth parallel.[1] General MacArthur had underestimated the Chinese resolve, and after a bitter war of attrition that lasted more than two years, the UN-sponsored armistice was signed in July 1953, with active Indian participation.[2] This effectively—but not officially—ended the war and created a demilitarized zone.

India has never received enough credit for being one of the key drivers of the Korean armistice in 1953. Jairam Ramesh—a prominent Indian intellectual and a minister in Prime Minister Manmohan Singh's cabinet between 2010 and 2014—set the record straight in an article published in the prominent Indian newspaper the *Hindu*. He explains that Nehru and his ambassador in China, K. M. Pannikar, used their good relationship with Mao to convince China to come to the negotiating table, paving the way for a cessation of hostilities. Among other Indian initiatives was the formation of the Neutral Nations Repatriation Commission (NNRC) to monitor the repatriation of about 150,000 prisoners of war—the bulk of them being Chinese and North Korean, many of whom did not want to return to their countries.[3] The commission was composed of representatives from five neutral nations: Sweden, Switzerland, Poland, Czechoslovakia, and India. Its primary mandate was to take custody of all prisoners and coordinate their repatriation.[4]

Lieutenant General K. S. Thimayya from India was chosen chairman of the commission. Supporting the NNRC was a brigade-sized Indian force called Custodian Force India, commanded by Major General S. P. P. Thorat. This was independent India's first foray into the realm of peacekeeping. Despite facing stiff opposition from the South Korean government, Custodian Force India carried out the process of interviewing and repatriating prisoners with professionalism.[5] Thimayya's deft handling of the situation was praised by everyone, including US president Dwight Eisenhower, who lauded the mission as a difficult and delicate job well done. According to Ramesh, Thimayya was considered a hero at the end of the NNRC's tenure in February 1954. He was feted both at home and abroad for courageously executing a thankless task.[6]

The honor of being the first unit deployed overseas for UN peacekeeping operations rests with Sixtieth Parachute Field Ambulance, led by Lieutenant Colonel A. G. Rangaraj. It was initially attached to US Eighth Army in November 1950 as it retreated from North Korea, and then it was transferred to the British Commonwealth Brigade as a medical evacuation unit. Its 346 men included four combat surgeons, two anesthesiologists, and a dentist. When the Chinese swarmed over UN lines in November 1950, the unit had to evacuate its position but had no transport and was reluctant to abandon its medical equipment. Stumbling upon an ancient steam locomotive, the men filled its boilers with water, loaded the train with equipment, and chugged across the last bridge south before it was blown. Rangaraj later said it would have been a great pity to leave all that first-class equipment behind. "We would have been of little use without it, and could not afford to lose it," he remarked.[7] The Indian medics stuck with the troops during the horrific rearguard fighting that winter and refused to abandon the wounded.

On 23 March 1951 a dozen medics from the unit parachuted behind the lines into Munsan-ni, along with 4,000 US troops. It was the second-biggest airborne operation of the war: Operation Tomahawk. A US commander recalled that he was immediately struck by the efficiency of the Indians. "That small unit, adapted for an airborne role, carried out 103 operations," and "probably fifty of those operated on owed their lives to those men." He wrote, "In freezing conditions, with the wounded lying in the open, the

Indian medics dug trenches to shelter them and covered them with parachute silk to keep them warm."[8]

The men of Sixtieth Parachute Field Ambulance fought alongside Canadian and Australian troops of the British Commonwealth Brigade in April 1951, and Canadian veterans acknowledged them in their accounts of the Battle of Kapyong.[9] Following more fierce fighting in September 1951, the unit treated 448 casualties over six days, and a month later it evacuated another 150 wounded while under fire. Sixtieth Parachute Field Ambulance received many decorations from its own country as well as from South Korea, the UN, and the United States, including a unit citation from MacArthur. Rangaraj was awarded the Maha Vir Chakra, India's second highest wartime gallantry award, on 10 March 1955.[10] India issued a postage stamp to honor the unit's heroism. In all, it conducted 2,300 field medical operations and trained several Korean doctors and nurses. Without taking anything away from Nehru, Krishna Menon, Thimayya, or Thorat, the real Indian heroes of the Korean War were the men of Sixtieth Parachute Field Ambulance. Rangaraj and his band of paratrooper-medics braved two years of fierce fighting and the icy Korean winter to save thousands of lives.

JOINT OPERATIONS IN CONGO

Congo gained independence from Belgian colonial rule on 30 June 1960. However, within seven months, the country was plunged into chaos when its first president, Patrice Lumumba, was assassinated by Belgian mercenaries. The assassination had been orchestrated by the United States because Congo appeared to be gravitating toward the USSR. This opened multiple fissures in the fabric of the young state.[11] The trouble had begun in Katanga, in the southeastern part of Congo bordering the British colony of Northern Rhodesia (now Zambia), almost 2,400 kilometers away from the capital Kinshasa. Belgian and South African mercenaries were unwilling to give up this mineral-rich province. Supported by Northern Rhodesia and led by Michael "Mad Mike" Hoare, the mercenaries propped up a rebel leader, Moise Tshombe, who declared himself president of the breakaway state of Katanga on 11 July 1960.[12] The secession set in motion a chain of events that led to the assassination of Lumumba and a civil war that lasted four years.

On 14 July 1960 the Organization des Nations Unies au Congo (ONUC) was launched after UN Security Council Resolution 143 was passed. A UN peacekeeping force under the command of a Swedish general, with 4,000 troops from Tunisia and five other African states, arrived in August. Despite overseeing the withdrawal of Belgian troops from most of Congo, the UN peacekeepers were shackled by a weak mandate that abjured the use of force. Even as the civil war intensified, it took almost a year for the UN to authorize the unrestricted use of force against the Katanga rebels. At various stages during this unstable period, the crisis took on the characteristics of an anticolonial struggle. It became a war of secession between the province of Katanga and the UN force, which eventually managed to disarm the rebels and restore some semblance of normalcy.[13]

India played a pivotal role in this transformation. The fiercest fighting during the UN peacekeeping operations involved an Indian contingent that suffered heavy casualties. The ONUC mandate was subsequently expanded to include maintaining Congo's territorial integrity and political independence, preventing a civil war, and ensuring the removal of all mercenaries and foreign military, paramilitary, and advisory personnel not under UN command. With about 20,000 personnel, the ONUC contributed significantly to the eventual reunification of Congo. Reflecting the importance India attached to its participation in UN peacekeeping operations, Major General Rikhye was pulled out of a critical command assignment in Ladakh to become military adviser to UN Secretary-General Dag Hammarskjöld. He would continue in this role until the end of ONUC operations in 1964. Hammarskjöld was killed in a mysterious airplane crash not long after Rikhye joined him. Investigations into the crash are still ongoing. A recent report in the *New York Times* suggests that the plane might have been brought down by "colonial-era mining interests, perhaps backed by Western intelligence agencies," and executed by "South African or Belgian mercenaries."[14]

The Katanga rebels immediately violated a two-month cease-fire, and repeated attacks on UN peacekeepers followed. This prompted acting UN secretary-general U Thant to direct the peacekeepers to use maximum force against the rebels. Security Council Resolution 169 of 24 November 1961 ratified this decision. However, Tshombe ordered attacks on UN peacekeepers at Elizabethville airfield to prevent them from advancing on Elizabethville (renamed Lubumbashi in 1966)—the largest city and capital of Katanga province.

In November 1960 the Indian Air Force (IAF) had sent C-119 Packet transport aircraft from Twelfth Squadron in support of the UN peacekeepers. The aircraft were directed to assist with logistics operations between the capital of Leopoldville (later renamed Kinshasa) and ONUC headquarters (HQ) at Elizabethville. The Indian brigade was under the command of Brigadier K. A. S. Raja and based in Katanga. Supporting this ground force initially were fighter, bomber, and transport aircraft from the Canadian Air Force based at Kamina airfield. In early October 1961 six IAF Canberra aircraft from Fifth Squadron commanded by Wing Commander A. I. K. Suares arrived at Kamina. By then, fighting had intensified, and the Katanga rebels had inflicted some casualties on the UN peacekeepers.

During a hostage rescue mission in late November 1961, Major Ajit Singh of Third Battalion of First Gorkha Rifles was the first Indian officer to be killed. On 5 December 1961 the same Gorkha Rifles battalion attacked a Katangese roadblock between rebel HQ in Elizabethville and ONUC HQ at Elizabethville airfield. A platoon from the same battalion attempted to reinforce the attack but ran into opposition.[15] The rebel position was manned by about ninety men, whereas the Indian peacekeepers, led by Captain Gurbachan Singh Salaria, numbered only sixteen soldiers. Despite being outnumbered, the Gorkhas overwhelmed the enemy. The rebels fled, leaving behind more than forty casualties. Captain Salaria was shot in the neck but continued to fight until he succumbed to his injuries. The ONUC HQ, however, was saved from encirclement. Salaria became the fifth recipient of the Param Vir Chakra, India's highest military award for courage in war. He remains the most decorated Indian to serve in a UN peacekeeping operation.

Fighting was intense the next day, too. Lance Naik Ram Bahadur singlehandedly charged a rebel machine gun post, killing nine rebels before succumbing to his injuries. Ram Bahadur was posthumously awarded the Maha Vir Chakra (the second highest wartime gallantry award). From July 1960 to June 1964, the Indians suffered a total of 147 casualties, including 39 peacekeepers killed in action. This was the largest number of casualties any Indian peacekeeping contingent has suffered in almost six decades of UN peacekeeping operations.

Authorized to use only their 20mm cannons—despite their capacity to carry 2,000 kilograms of bombs—the Canberra bombers began strafing missions against rebel troop positions around the town of Kolwezi and the air base there.[16] Sensing that Indian troops were close to capturing Elizabethville, the air effort shifted to support the ground battle.[17] On 9 December Raja briefed Suares on the various targets in and around Elizabethville that had to be engaged from the air by IAF Canberras.[18] Later that day, Flight Lieutenant Dushyant Singh and Squadron Leader Charanjit Singh attacked a post office in the heart of Elizabethville that was serving as rebel HQ.

The Canberra squadron, which played a critical role in the Indian brigade's battle for Elizabethville, continued limited offensive and recce operations for the next few months. By 18 December, the city was under UN control. In mid-1962 Raja handed over command of the Indian brigade to Brigadier Noronha, and Major General Diwan Prem Chand arrived from Gaza to take over command of the UN peacekeeping forces in Katanga. Fifth Squadron also saw a change in command and crew as it shifted its base to Leopoldville. A detachment operated out of Kamina whenever the need for photo and visual reconnaissance arose.[19] There was some action involving the Indian brigade and Ethiopian troops in late 1962, and the last vestiges of rebel resistance crumbled by mid-1963. The ONUC was finally dissolved six months later in 1964. Nearly four decades later, Indian peacekeepers returned as part of the United Nations Organization Mission in the Democratic Republic of Congo.

AFTER THE COLD WAR

United Nations peacekeeping operations underwent significant changes in the years after the collapse of the Soviet Union, as new security challenges emerged around the world. Nationalism, anticolonialism, and ideological differences were the principal drivers of most of the conflicts that necessitated UN intervention during the Cold War. This changed in the 1990s and beyond, as conflicts became mostly ethno-religious, laced with regional power struggles and stray protests against economic exploitation. The primary objectives of UN peacekeeping operations during the Cold War era were to restore political stability and reconcile warring parties. However, the current UN mandate is based on a concept called "responsibility to protect," or R2P. Its goal is to prevent genocide and mass killings in fractured and weak countries. This shift was spurred by the Rwandan genocide and the ethno-religious strife in the Balkans in the 1990s.

Although the outcomes of the peacekeeping initiatives in these emerging hot spots were suboptimal, India contributed significantly to these missions. Lieutenant General Satish Nambiar was appointed commander of the United Nations Protection Force for Yugoslavia in 1992, as part of India's increased contribution to peacekeeping efforts. This was just one element of a larger strategy to expand India's influence and achieve its medium-term objective of securing a permanent seat on an expanded UN Security Council. However, the mission in Yugoslavia struggled to heal the deep fractures in the Balkans. Bringing the Serbs and the Croats—the region's two largest ethnic communities—to the negotiating table proved to be a bridge too far. According to Nambiar, the reasons for this failure included a weak mandate, inadequate manpower, and halfhearted support from the various European and Western stakeholders in the region, including the United States and United Kingdom.[20]

MUSCULAR PEACEKEEPING IN SIERRA LEONE

India deployed peacekeeping forces in Sierra Leone (1999) and Somalia (2003) that included sizable army and air force contingents. It was in Sierra Leone that the Indians engaged in serious combat with rebel forces. India had previously participated in UN peacekeeping operations in Rwanda, where

UN deployment had been delayed and ineffective in preventing mass killings or separating warring factions. The rising presence of warlords, mercenaries, and mineral bounty hunters in Africa had changed the rules of engagement, and the UN was not prepared to take on this new dynamic. The changing character of war and conflict demanded adjustments in peacekeeping and peace enforcement. Failing to learn from the suboptimal experience in the Balkans, the intervention in Sierra Leone quickly exposed the irrelevance of existing peacekeeping procedures and mandates.

The United Nations Mission in Sierra Leone was authorized in October 1999 by Security Council Resolution 1270. Its mandate was to implement the Lome Agreement, which had brought the legitimately elected government of President Ahmad Tejan Kabbah and two rebel groups to the negotiating table after two years of fierce civil war. However, when militia from the main rebel force, the Revolutionary United Front (RUF), made a run for the capital of Freetown, the UN sensed that the country was headed for a bloodbath and had no option but to intervene. Major General Vijay Jetley from India was appointed the first commander of the UN Mission in Sierra Leone, with a Nigerian officer as his deputy. The force initially had 6,000 troops from Nigeria, India, Kenya, and Ghana and was later complemented by British troops. This was woefully inadequate for any kind of robust peacekeeping. By May 2000, the rebel forces were testing the peacekeepers' resolve in Makeni and Magburarka, which was rebel territory. On 7 May 2000 two IAF Mi-8s carried out a daring operation under heavy firing by RUF rebels to rescue Kenyan troops and UN observers who were being held hostage in Makeni.[21]

The RUF began to disrupt UN camps and escalated the confrontation by taking peacekeepers hostage at Kailahun and Makeni. The hostages included a large complement of Indian and Zambian soldiers and UN military observers. Bolstered by the presence of British troops in Freetown, and aided by their Chinook helicopters, Jetley launched Operation Khukri in July 2000 to rescue the hostages. The 3,000 Indian troops in Sierra Leone were from the Gorkha Rifles, the Mechanized Infantry Regiment, and the Special Forces. There was also an IAF unit with eight Mi-8 and three Mi-35 helicopters. Indian HQ was at Daru, and the main deployment was at Kailahun. The IAF contingent was commanded by Group Captain B. S. Siwach and operated out of Hastings, near Freetown. The Indian battalion group was assisted by troops from Ghana and Kenyan and caused much attrition among the RUF. The hostages in Kailahun staged a fighting breakout and linked up with the forces advancing on Kailahun from Daru.

Although Operation Khukri was successful at the tactical level, a hard look reveals that it was a reactive operation that failed to retain ground. The

UN Mission in Sierra Leone had neither the troops nor the will to seize the initiative and dominate the RUF. In May 2000 the Indian battalion group was split and deployed in two locations in eastern Sierra Leone. The Kenyan battalion in the north had been attacked and overrun by the RUF, and the Nigerian forces were not yet fully deployed. The local population had lost trust in the UN mission, and since the UN contingents were not mandated to fight, there was very little that Jetley could do. Soon, the weaknesses of the UN military system in terms of force, training, capabilities, intelligence, and surveillance mechanisms became apparent. The hostage crisis dealt a severe blow to the UN's reputation and confused the transition between peacekeeping and peace enforcement.

Adding to the confusion were the British troops under the command of Major General David Richards, who was appalled at the RUF's brutality and perplexed by the inaction of the UN Mission in Sierra Leone. Richards argued with Jetley over his reluctance to respond strongly to the rebels' brutality and his decision not to expand the mandate from peacekeeping to enforcement. Richards was also quite scathing about the UN force's unwillingness to fight, despite being attacked and challenged.[22] Jetley questioned Richards's moralistic approach, pointing out that British troops had generally not been part of UN peacekeeping operations in Africa, unlike the Indians, who better understood the concept of restraint.

However, the British did play a role in defending Freetown and the Lungi airport against the RUF. They also made substantial contributions to stabilizing Sierra Leone, even after the UN mission was disbanded in 2005. This was among the few successful long-term interventions of recent times.[23] Jetley has not been given enough credit for initiating the turnaround in July 2000 and freeing the hostages. Instead, Jetley's differences with his Nigerian deputy and his accusations that Nigeria tried to undermine the success of the mission have been highlighted in most Western narratives on events in Sierra Leone. American academic David Ucko writes that "even the successful Operation Khukri envisaged UN forces falling back to secure positions rather than seize RUF territory around Kailahun."[24] Among the few positives was that, for the first time in nearly four decades, the Indian Army and IAF operated jointly under the UN flag in a sustained operation involving large forces. From May to September 2000 IAF helicopters flew about a hundred sorties, including offensive missions, armed reconnaissance, insertion and extrication of troops, casualty evacuation, and logistics support. Troops of the Gorkha Rifles made considerable headway in limiting the RUF's recruitment of child soldiers in the areas under their jurisdiction.

Two months after Operation Khukri, Jetley was recalled to New Delhi. It is likely that this move was initiated to register India's protest against regional bullying and the undermining of its leadership. Matters were complicated by the fact that UN Secretary-General Kofi Annan was West African. He tended to side with the Nigerians when Jetley accused them, and proxies from neighboring Liberia, of colluding with the RUF and engaging in illegal diamond mining. Soon thereafter, much to the surprise of the UN, India gradually pulled its entire force out of Sierra Leone.[25] India was just recovering from the Kargil Conflict, and the Vajpayee government was in no mood to suffer needless casualties in a foreign land. The decision was also influenced by the security crisis following the attack on the Indian Parliament by Lashkar-e-Taiba (LeT) terrorists in December 2000. The Indian experience in Sierra Leone led to a heated debate in Parliament over committing Indian troops to UN peacekeeping operations in distant lands where India had little or no strategic interest. Responding to British criticism of Jetley's leadership, Brigadier Anil Raman— who was a captain with the Indian contingent in Sierra Leone and took part in planning operations during the siege of Kailahun—dismissed British accounts as inaccurate. "The British general was speaking rather expansively," Raman said, 'without a realistic appreciation of the situation on ground.'"[26]

CONTINUED PRESENCE IN CONGO

After the departure of UN peacekeepers in 1965, Congo endured three decades of misery under dictator Mobutu Sese Seko. He first changed the country's name to Zaire and then to the Democratic Republic of Congo (DRC) in 1971. Seko ruled the second largest African nation until May 1997, when a coalition of neighboring countries led by Rwanda and Uganda overthrew him. The fragile nation continued in chaos as ethnic conflict and greedy neighbors undermined the authority of President Laurent Kabila's newly formed government in Kinshasa. The epicenter of the conflict was in eastern Congo, with its ethnic divides and huge mineral deposits. Although the intervention succeeded in ousting Seko, Kabila remained a puppet of the foreign regimes that put him in power.

To increase his own domestic support, Kabila began to turn against his foreign allies and expelled all foreign forces from the DRC on 26 July 1998. The Second Congo War began almost immediately, taking the form of a Hutu insurgency in Rwanda's western provinces that was supported by extremist Hutu elements in eastern DRC.[27] Unable to effectively fight the insurgents, DRC sought a coalition with Uganda and Burundi to quell the rebellion. In August 1998 two brigades of the DRC Army rebelled against the government and formed groups that worked closely with neighboring countries. The Second Congo War eventually involved nine African countries, as well as approximately twenty armed groups.

Map 14. UN Peacekeeping Operations in Congo

The UN had a series of unsuccessful peacekeeping initiatives in the Balkans, Rwanda, and Somalia in the 1990s. However, its first African secretary-general, Kofi Annan, redefined its role as the world's conscience.[28] Peacekeeping norms were amended, and the concepts of protection of civilians and R2P were introduced. The UN intervened to ensure that the Second Congo War did not escalate and result in the kind of genocide that had rocked Rwanda in 1994. Mandated by Security Council Resolution 1279, the United Nations Organization Mission in the DRC was set up to oversee the July 1999 Lusaka cease-fire between the DRC and five neighboring countries—Angola, Namibia, Rwanda, Uganda, and Zimbabwe. Despite these initiatives, the war and its aftermath caused millions of deaths, principally because of disease and starvation. It has become the deadliest conflict in the post–World War II era.[29]

In 2003, after four years of negotiations, the Vajpayee government decided

Map 15. UN Peacekeeping Operations in Sierra Leone

to send a large Indian brigade with a strong IAF contingent to support UN operations in the DRC. Air Vice Marshal Rajesh Isser wrote about his experiences commanding the Mi-17 squadron during this operation in his book *Peacekeeping and Protection of Civilians: The Indian Air Force in Congo*.[30] He recollects that IAF chief Krishnaswamy assured the contingent that it would get everything it needed from the IAF, but "heads would roll" if the mission did not fare well.[31] The Indian brigade set up its HQ in the town of Goma, and battalions were deployed at Goma, Beni, Ituri, and Bukavu. Five Mi-17 helicopters were based at Goma, and four Mi-25 attack helicopters were positioned at Bunia in North Kivu, with an additional support unit at Kindu. The aviation contingent was expanded in 2005 with the induction of upgraded Mi-17s and Mi-35 attack helicopters at Bukavu in South Kivu.[32] A division HQ was set up at Kisangani to ensure close control of operational forces.

In June 2005 reports of a massacre in Ituri province, about 100 kilometers north of Bunia, led to a special operation. IAF Mi-17s and Mi-35s executed a risky mission to land Pakistani troops in the area. This required a high-speed approach, a low hover, and a quick exit. The operation was successful, and the UN mission sent a strong message that it would not hesitate to take military action. Only later did Isser realize that the Pakistani troops belonged to none other than the Northern Light Infantry. They had been the Indians' enemy at Kargil, but now they were comrades. UN peacekeeping makes for strange bedfellows.[33]

Brigadier (now General) Rawat was the most senior Indian Army officer in eastern DRC between August 2008 and August 2009, and he led the military action that was largely responsible for the March 2009 cease-fire.[34] He explained the complicated relationships among the peacekeepers, the Rwanda-supported and Tutsi-dominated rebel group National Congress for the Defense of the People (CNDP), the pro-government and Hutu-dominated rebel group Democratic Forces for the Liberation of Rwanda (FDLR), and the government's Armed Forces of the Democratic Republic of Congo (FARDC). There were several occasions when firepower in the form of mortars, rocket launchers, and attack helicopters had to be used to protect civilians from rebel attacks. Rawat argued that these actions were essential to coerce rival factions to accept a cease-fire. In 2008 the Indian brigade and its aviation contingent were deployed in the DRC's North Kivu province, along the border with Rwanda and Uganda, where most of the action was taking place. The Indian brigade was part of a division that included a Nepali brigade in Ituri, a Pakistani brigade in South Kivu, and a brigade from Ghana.

Soon after Rawat took command, he sensed that a major operation was right around the corner. His forward locations reported that the CNDP was massing forces barely two kilometers from the border. The FARDC was flying large stocks of ammunition into Goma airfield, which was just a few kilometers from Indian HQ. Rawat ordered the Indian battalions to start digging trenches and preparing defenses for what he envisaged as serious operations. Another issue was that while the CNDP was able to communicate with Indian troops in English, the FARDC and FDLR spoke only French and had to rely on an interpreter at Indian brigade HQ. This led to a feeling that the Indians were partial to the CNDP, so the FARDC and FDLR thought it might be time to take matters into their own hands.

As fighting intensified, Rawat had to deploy Mi-35 attack helicopters to destroy the CNDP's advancing tanks. It was quite clear to Rawat and the Senegalese UN force commander, Lieutenant General Babacar Gaye, that the CNDP needed to be cut down if there was to be a cease-fire. Serious differences surfaced when they sought formal clearance to increase military action against the CNDP from the senior representative of the security general, the de facto head of the UN mission. Gaye resigned in September 2008 after the senior representative refused to authorize attacks against the CNDP. His departure meant that Rawat had to take over as force commander, which the Pakistani-led brigade in South Kivu found unacceptable, even though the other brigade commanders from Nepal and Ghana did not object.

Eight UN battalions created a ten-kilometer buffer zone between the warring forces. There were no roads to support the thin deployment, and the forces had to be supported by air. Mi-17 helicopters from the IAF and the Bangladesh Air Force sustained the battalions. In late October 2008 a Spanish general was appointed force commander. He too insisted on the extensive use of firepower and airpower, and by December, he had resigned because of differences with the senior representative of the security general. The UN found it difficult to find a replacement and asked Gaye to reassume command on 15 December. The border town of Goma became the focus of attention around Christmas because it was understood that CNDP forces intended to loot the town to pay its cadres. Then they planned to retreat into Rwanda. However, this time around, Gaye authorized the unrestricted use of firepower against the CNDP.

Prior to embarking on offensive operations, Rawat wanted to study the situation. He sought an audience with the CNDP commander, who called himself General Bosco Ntganda. Ntganda was short of stature and wore a hat with stars and "Bosco" embossed on it. During that meeting, which Rawat describes as "quite an experience," he offered Ntganda US$10,000 to distribute among his men in return for calling off the assault on Goma. Rawat warned, "As we speak, my men have gone around your area and if you advance further, we will have no option but to bring down fire on you."[35] Ntganda did not comply. By 16 December, more than 2,000 CNDP troops had lined up across Goma. Rawat ordered his battalions to fire warning and illumination rounds the moment the CNDP force started to advance. When the CNDP force got to within 500 meters of the Indian line, it came under mortar and machine gun fire. Soon the CNDP troops broke ranks, and all of them, including Ntganda, turned around and fled. After this incident, CNDP commander Laurent Nkunda was arrested, as the peace process gained momentum.

The IAF operated in the DRC from 2003 to 2011, making it the longest-serving air contingent in any UN peacekeeping operation worldwide. It has won many accolades for its ability to switch between peacekeeping and enforcement operations.[36] The IAF's impact inspired Isser to write that the DRC rebels were "afraid of only two things in the world—God and the IAF attack helicopter."[37] Group Captain Navkaranjit Singh Dhillon was the IAF contingent commander at Goma from 2007 to 2008 and worked alongside Rawat for three months. He recollects that Mi-35 helicopters destroyed CNDP tanks and several armored vehicles during some of the critical joint operations. The Indian aviation contingent was organized quite loosely, with assets regularly being swapped among the three locations at Goma, Bukavu, and Bunia to ensure that the Indian battalions had aviation support across the extended front defended by the Indian brigade.

The UN mission's name was changed in 2010 to United Nations Organization and Stabilization Mission in the Democratic Republic of Congo, to reflect the addition of a stabilization phase, in the hope that peace would follow. In July 2010 Lieutenant General Chander Prakash was appointed force commander to take the peace process forward. A fragile peace prevailed, with ex-rebels from the CNDP and FDLR continuing activities in their areas of domination with minimal interference from either the UN mission or the Congolese government. With Nkunda in UN custody, the CNDP was amalgamated into the FARDC under the cease-fire guidelines. Threatened with imminent capture in early 2012, Bosco Ntganda broke away from the CNDP and formed the violent M23 group. In November 2012 M23 captured Goma, with assistance from Rwandan forces. They faced only token resistance from UN forces, who withdrew from the city after failing to stall the advance, despite the assistance of IAF Mi-35 helicopters. The UN forces' inability to stop the raiders before they could mingle with local population was widely criticized. Chander Prakash received most of the flak. However, M23 withdrew eleven days later, after hectic diplomatic parleys. There has been much debate on UN peacekeeping operations in the DRC since then. The recent formation of an intervention brigade is believed to be the result of the 2012 experience.

ANTIPIRACY OPERATIONS

In 2008 the UN Security Council authorized the use of force against pirates off the coast of Somalia when a Saudi supertanker ship was hijacked in November. The previous month, a Hong Kong–based tanker with a large Indian crew had been hijacked in the same area, creating immense pressure on the Indian government to send the Indian Navy on an antipiracy mission in the area. INS *Tabar*, a Russian-built frigate, became the first Indian Navy warship deployed in the Gulf of Aden. Commanded by Captain P. K. Banerjee, *Tabar* struck fear in the hearts of the pirates with its immediate offensive action in early November. *Tabar* had just returned to Mumbai from the Persian Gulf on the eve of Diwali in late October 2008. It was ordered to deploy in the Gulf of Aden on the morning of 29 October, with only a day to prepare. The operation was not under the UN umbrella, and this was a new experience for India's armed forces. "We deployed independently," Banerjee said, "but in close cooperation with the US and other European navies in a common cause to ensure safety of seafarers transiting the piracy-infested waters."[38]

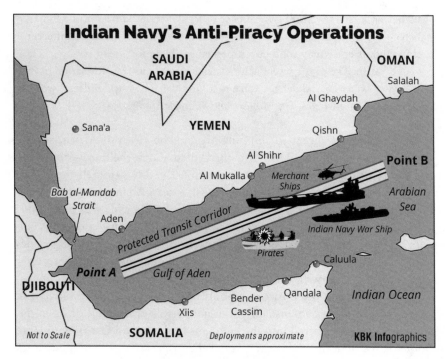

Map 16. The Indian Navy's Antipiracy Operations

On 11 November there was a distress call from the merchant ship *Jag Arnav*, which was operating under the Indian flag and had an all-Indian crew. *Tabar*'s helicopter chased the pirate skiffs away and escorted *Jag Arnav* out of troubled waters.[39] On 18 November *Tabar* detected a suspicious vessel that matched the description of a known pirate mother ship. When it was threatened by the pirate vessel, *Tabar* fired at it and set it ablaze. This stern warning to the pirates set the template for future operations. *Tabar* was replaced on antipiracy duties by INS *Mysore*, a new destroyer. The latter recovered a huge cache of arms and ammunition and captured twenty-four Somali and Yemeni pirates. This action had legal implications because no government was willing to take custody of the pirates. Only after intense negotiations between the Indian and Yemeni governments did the latter accept custody of the pirates.[40] Reacting to the Indian initiative, the Kenyan newspaper *Daily Nation* wrote:

> This incident is one of the many decisive actions that the Indian Navy has come to be reputed for in the fight against piracy in the lawless Somalia waters. Most foreign navies patrolling that coast have been reluctant to detain suspected pirates because of uncertainties over where they would face trial, since Soma-

lia has no effective central government or legal system. However, the Indian Navy—the fifth-largest in the world—has shown that it is cut from different cloth and its entry may soon deal a permanent blow to Somali piracy in the Gulf of Aden. The navy's recent achievements attest to its transformation from a "brown-water coastal defense force to a formidable blue-water fleet," wrote David Scott in the *Journal of Military and Strategic Studies.*[41]

Recognizing the threat to shipping around the Horn of Africa, several global navies—including those from the United States, the European Union, and the North Atlantic Treaty Organization (NATO)—joined the Indian Navy's initiative in deploying antipiracy task forces. An international transit corridor 500 nautical miles long and 20 nautical miles wide was established in the Gulf of Aden. Merchant vessels were advised to transit along this corridor under escort. Secure communications protocols allow patrolling navies to operate safely. The Indian Navy established a deployment pattern after a few patrol cycles, with critical inputs from Banerjee and other captains. After initially using the port of Djibouti, the navy switched to Salalah in Oman. To avoid these intense international patrols in the Gulf of Aden, pirate groups have ventured into the high seas of the Indian Ocean with large mother ships that allow them to extend their operations to shipping lanes around Seychelles, Maldives, and Lakshadweep.

Responding to these threats, the Indian Navy launched Operation Island Watch, which succeeded in sinking a couple of stolen Thai trawlers in the seas west of Lakshadweep. The navy also captured several pirates and seized huge caches of arms. These trawlers had been hijacked by pirates off the Somali coast, equipped with motorized skiffs, and converted to mother ships. They were then used to attack unsuspecting merchant vessels in the Indian Ocean. The antipiracy operation closest to India's west coast was conducted about 700 kilometers from the southern port of Kochi on 11 March 2011. A pirate mother ship called *Vega* was sunk by the Indian Navy, and more than sixty pirates were arrested and turned over to the Mumbai police.[42] This resulted in an antipiracy bill being proposed in the Indian Parliament.

As the world rallied against piracy, the number of attacks fell from 237 in 2011 to 75 in 2012.[43] It had dropped to fewer than ten in 2015, and the global naval presence started to wind down in the wake of the diminished threat. However, an uptrend has been detected since 2017.[44] In March 2017 Somali pirates hijacked a Comoros-flagged oil tanker, marking the first seizure of a large commercial vessel since 2012. They later released the vessel when it turned out to be a Somali charter. On 1 April 2017 the Indian dhow *Al Kausar*, with eleven crew members, was hijacked off the island of Socotra and taken to the port of Hobyo. An Indian Navy ship deployed in the area was diverted to the east coast of Somalia to monitor the situation. Negotiations between the owner and the hijackers resulted in the dhow being released eleven days later.

Since 2017 the Indian Navy has transitioned to a new philosophy of mission-based deployments across the Indian Ocean. Drawing on the lessons learned from antipiracy operations, it has chosen to maintain a near-permanent presence in certain geographic areas and choke points. The warships deployed in these areas are fully prepared to respond to all contingencies, while being perfectly placed to monitor all other forces operating in the region. These mission-based deployments have paid rich dividends.

The Indian Navy had been operating with foreign navies for several decades before the commencement of antipiracy operations. However, this was the first prolonged operational exposure for Indian ships in a diffused multilateral environment. The exposure significantly enhanced its standard operating procedures in actual scenarios. The Indian Navy is the only one that maintains a continuous escort cycle in the international transit corridor during the monsoon season. Regular deployments in the Gulf of Aden have enhanced its situational awareness in the western Arabian Sea and allowed it to gain substantial operational information and intelligence. There is also a deeper understanding of the PLA Navy after these deployments. There is little doubt that the Indian Navy has emerged as a navy of significant capabilities, and it has become a coveted maritime partner in the Indian Ocean and Indo-Pacific regions. Thanks to the unbroken patrol by seventy Indian Navy ships in the Gulf of Aden over the last ten years, no merchant ship under its protection has ever been captured by pirates.

INDIAN LEGACY

India has a history of being a willing participant in UN peacekeeping and peace enforcement operations since their inception. It has participated in forty-nine UN peacekeeping operations and has been the largest contributor of troops, with more than 240,000 personnel deployed so far. There have been fifteen Indian force commanders and two military advisers.[45] India has also suffered the largest number of battle casualties, with 168 killed in action. Its contingents have been fair, restrained, and responsible while conducting operations in diverse lands and strife-torn communities. It is unknown whether India will be able to strategically leverage its contributions to become a permanent member of the UN Security Council. However, despite diverse internal and external security challenges, India is unlikely to dilute its commitment to peacekeeping.

18

Operations Other than War along the Western Front

[Sundarji] brought a new line of thinking to the Indian military establishment with his systems-management-scenario approach.
—Chidanand Rajghata, "The Country's Foreign and Military Policies Need to Be Disciplined"

DOCTRINAL EVALUATION OR MUSCLE FLEXING?

Thirty-Fifth Squadron was the only electronic warfare squadron in the Indian Air Force (IAF) in 1986. It was equipped with the Canberra bomber–cum–recce aircraft and MiG-21s that had been modified to carry Swedish electronic warfare pods. In the winter of 1986 the entire squadron was moved to two forward air bases—Ambala in the Haryana and Punjab Sector, and Nal near the town of Bikaner in Rajasthan—and it spent two months escorting Jaguars and MiG-27s on simulated strikes as part of Exercise Brasstacks. These exercises were part of an operational plan orchestrated by General Sundarji, India's army chief. On occasion, they even crossed a few kilometers over the border to check the alertness of Pakistan's air defense network. The moment the radar warning receivers beeped or a warning was received over the radio, the entire formation would turn back. The game of cat and mouse continued for two months before all forces were de-inducted.

Several of those Jaguar missions were led by Flight Lieutenant (now Air Chief Marshal and IAF chief) "Chotu" Bhadauria from Fourteenth Squadron. As probably the youngest leader of large missions during that period, he was someone young IAF fighter pilots looked up to. He was crisp in his briefings and cool in the air, and he always struck his targets. Several new mission profiles emerged during these exercises as the IAF grappled with the danger posed by the Pakistan's Crotale surface-to-air missile system. Among them was a toss bombing profile by Jaguars, MiG-23s, and MiG-27s that involved a steep climb to 15,000 feet, with a weapon release during the climb and a sharp break downward with high g-forces to stay outside the Crotale's range. Unable to keep up with the Jaguars and MiG-27s because of their heavy configuration with pods, MiG-21s from Thirty-Fifth Squadron would stay low, skirt the target, and rendezvous with the formation at a preplanned point, gazing skyward to pick up their buddies and head back to base. For the pilots and navigators of Thirty-Fifth Squadron, it was just another case of intensive training in near warlike conditions. The absence of any detailed briefings about what was really going on gave rise to much speculation and discussion in the crew room, focused on whether war was indeed right around the corner.[1]

When Sundarji took over as army chief in 1986, he had several ideas for strengthening deterrence in the subcontinent. He was also convinced that a strong, modern, well-trained military was essential if India was to emerge as a powerful nation. However, except for a brief face-off in the Rann of Kutchh during the prelude to the 1965 war, Sundarji did not have much combat experience. He made up for that with his varied operational assignments and powerful intellect. Given his ideas about maneuver warfare and nuclear war fighting, Sundarji thought he was well prepared to spearhead the Indian Army's transition into a potent fighting force. Lieutenant General Pattabhiraman served in the military operations directorate as a major during the tumultuous period when Sundarji was chief. He describes Brasstacks as an exercise undertaken when mistrust between India and Pakistan was at its peak. Pattabhiraman also recalls that Sundarji was close to Minister of State for Defense Arun Singh, who was a keen student of contemporary military affairs. The two of them advised Rajiv Gandhi on all matters related to national security—the nuclear dimension, maneuver warfare, and expanding India's influence in its strategic neighborhood.[2]

BRASSTACKS, TRIDENT, AND HAMMERHEAD

Lieutenant General Shamsher "Shammi" Mehta, who headed the Western Command during the second half of Operation Parakram, was Sundarji's military adviser for much of the latter's tenure as chief. Sundarji was looking to develop capability with an eye toward the future. Mehta said, "Training this capability and exercising it was a logical progression in Sundarji's mind, and if it did send a signal to an adversary, did it not meet the demands of deterrence?" He added, "Incorporating all three dimensions of conflict (land, air, and maritime) was also merely putting doctrine into practice and taking forward what he had initiated in Exercise Digvijay when he was the Western Army commander. Analysts and so-called experts have read too much into the whole thing. Exercise Brasstacks and Exercise Trident were not any brazen muscle-flexing or expression of intent to go to war."[3]

An ardent proponent of maneuver and mechanized warfare as the sword arm of conventional warfare in the plains, Sundarji was influenced by the

US Army's *FM 100-5* (air-land battle concept) and the Russian operational maneuver groups. He created the Mechanized Infantry Regiment based on some of the most accomplished battalions of the acclaimed infantry regiments.[4] He also converted some standard infantry divisions into Reorganized Army Plains Infantry Divisions (RAPIDs). When the RAPIDs were grouped with armored divisions equipped with the recently inducted T-72 tank, the Indian Army had a mobile offensive element with the potential to make deep inroads into the desert-dominated terrain of Pakistan's Punjab and Sindh provinces opposite the Indian states of Rajasthan and Gujarat. Sundarji strengthened the RAPID formations by embedding an armored brigade, and he was impatient to test the RAPIDs' capability, despite the volatile security situation in the subcontinent. This led to Exercise Brasstacks, which was undertaken to translate this reorganization into actual capability.

Sundarji planned Exercise Brasstacks as a massive air-land exercise conducted in three phases over several months, culminating with a concentration of forces in the Rajasthan Sector.[5] Skeptics, however, claim that Sundarji had little time for the air force and considered it his maneuver arm in the third dimension.[6] The exercise involved two strike corps (First and Second Corps) executing a main and subsidiary thrust with speed and surprise. It was carried out in the Rajasthan and Gujarat Sectors to determine whether large formations could cover good distances at night against moderate opposition. This raised alarm bells in Rawalpindi and Washington, and the Pakistan Army responded by moving its offensive formations toward India's vulnerable areas in Punjab and Jammu.

Lieutenant General Praveen Bakshi was then a major and a tank squadron commander in Skinner's Horse, a T-72 tank regiment. Deployed for months in the desert during both Exercise Digvijay and Exercise Brasstacks, he corroborates the conservative view that Sundarji had no intention of going to war. He says that although Seventh Cavalry was the first unit to convert to the T-72 tanks, Skinner's Horse was the first to be deployed during Exercise Digvijay. Seventh Cavalry then joined Skinner's Horse in Exercise Brasstacks. They easily covered sixty to seventy kilometers in one night, and Bakshi recalls traveling 800 kilometers on tracks. Despite pushing the T-72 to its limits, there were no breakdowns. The tank's only drawback was the lack of effective night-vision devices.[7] Exercise Brasstacks consisted of long maneuvers in the open desert and simulated isolation and capture of small townships while engaging in tank battles. According to Bakshi, they never loaded ammunition into the tanks, so there was little chance of going to war. "We wouldn't have flogged the tanks so much if we had to cross the border," he said. "It was more of posturing and preparing ourselves for the future, as also sending a strong message across to the adversary of our overwhelming strength with modernized equipment like T-72 tanks and infantry combat vehicles."[8]

Riding on the long-standing Indian aspiration of recovering lost territories in Pakistan-occupied Kashmir (PoK), Sundarji also had Gilgit and Skardu in his sights. Some hawkish analysts such as Ravi Rikhye believe that Exercise Brasstacks was a smokescreen to obscure Sundarji's focus on the northern areas of Gilgit and Skardu. He was also ready to validate offensive operations in the mountains and other sectors of Jammu and Kashmir (J&K) with Exercise Trident.[9] It is not entirely correct to suggest this was Sundarji's plan because it originated in the minds of the commanders who executed Operation Meghdoot. Brigadier V. K. Channa, who led a force that assaulted Saltoro Ridge in April 1984, had wanted to press down the western slopes of the ridge. According to Channa, pushing through the Bilafond Glacier to capture the town of Gayari—a virtual gateway to the glacier and the site of a Pakistan Army battalion headquarters (HQ)—was essential if India wanted to recapture Skardu and restore historical boundaries. However, his plan was shot down at higher levels.

Exercise Trident, though feasible, ran the risk of logistical overreach. The advance into PoK via the Burzil Pass was entrusted to Nineteenth Infantry Division, while the main thrust from the Kargil Sector was to be executed by Twenty-Eighth Infantry Division and Third Mountain Division. These divisions were already acclimatized and waiting in the Ladakh Sector. Sixth Mountain Division was flown in from Bareilly to replace Third Mountain Division in the defensive role in the Ladakh Sector, and the IAF flew more than seventy sorties into Leh from various bases in central India.[10] There are varying perspectives about the rationale for all these moves. Mehta claims there was no political directive to go to war, and in the absence of such guidance, Sundarji would not be so foolish as to take his country to war. General V. N. Sharma—who succeeded Sundarji as army chief—was the chief umpire for Exercise Brasstacks. He confirms that there was no plan to go across the border and considers the Pakistani mobilization the natural fallout of a volatile situation. He reckons that Sundarji and Arun Singh wanted to convince Rajiv Gandhi to adopt a harder posture toward Pakistan and China.

In the summer of 1987 Sundarji decided to resolve the Siachen Glacier imbroglio militarily, once and for all. He asked the parachute brigade commander, Brigadier Sapatnekar, to plan an ambitious airborne operation at Khapalu, some sixty kilometers across the line of control.[11] Code-named Operation Hammerhead, the plan was to sever the Pakistani lines of communication to the Siachen Glacier. The paratroopers would then join up with advancing formations from Chalunkha before capturing key hubs such as Dansam and Gayari. The plan was bold, but Sapatnekar found it to be rather impractical and risky and cited three main issues. First, the brigade's parachutes were not designed for high-altitude landings. This could endanger the paratroopers in the landing phase, as the rates of descent would be significantly faster than what they were accustomed to. Second, it was not possible to adhere to Sundarji's time frame for linking up with the ground formation. The paratroopers would therefore be vulnerable to a concentrated enemy riposte, which could include air strikes by Pakistan's newly inducted F-16s. Third, the IAF could not undertake a simultaneous two-battalion drop because most of its An-32 and IL-76 aircraft were committed to Operation Pawan in Sri Lanka. This would mean a secondary drop without the benefit of surprise, leaving it vulnerable to interception.

The plan was dropped because of the huge risks and because Sundarji, nearing the end of his tenure as army chief, could hardly afford another setback. Sapatnekar concurs with Sundarji's belief in the huge payoffs of airborne and heliborne operations, but he notes that there was a wide gap between the concept and its conversion into an implementable and practical plan insofar as Operation Hammerhead was concerned.[12]

Mehta defends Sundarji, saying that Exercise Brasstacks, Exercise Trident, Exercise Chequerboard, Operation Falcon, and Operation Hammerhead were all expressions of Sundarji's desire to push the limits of deterrence and dissuasion. "His purpose really was the achievement of strategic objectives without having to fight a war," said Mehta. "If you see the geographical span, it covers the entire length of contested frontiers and all the army commands. They were all moves on the same chess board. Let's give him credit for having a perspective and communicating it to his commanders. However, a visionary does not have the wherewithal to ensure that his successors follow through."[13] Sundarji's critics question the overall effectiveness of his attempt to change the Indian Army's mind-set and the conduct of operational art and its impact on deterring India's traditional adversaries.[14] A fair analysis would be that it yielded mixed results. Although it enhanced deterrence along the line of control with Pakistan and the line of actual control with China, it also hastened the buildup of Chinese military capability on the Tibetan plateau and forced Pakistan to evolve new, low-cost military strategies.

ALERTING AMERICA

Generally dismissive of Indian strategic thinking and India's Cold War leanings toward the USSR, the United States was forced to take note of General Sundarji's muscular military posturing and attempts to infuse fresh thinking into the Indian Army. Adding to this concern was Sundarji's interest in nuclear war fighting, expressed through his writings while posted at the Army War College.[15] Thus far, India's and Pakistan's nuclear ambitions had been seen only as a danger to stability in South Asia, but now a new possibility had emerged: India's rise as a regional hegemon. Interestingly, despite the geopolitical hostility, the United States saw value in testing the waters in the realm of defense cooperation. India's light combat aircraft program received a major fillip when the United States cleared the export of the General Electric GE-404 jet engine to power the aircraft.[16]

Exercise Brasstacks was the first time the United States considered acting as a neutral interlocutor in the emerging India–Pakistan crisis. Among the reasons for this change was the realization that Pakistan was not the reliable ally it had been in the past, and it had been less than transparent about its nuclear weapons program. Chari, Cheema, and Cohen argue, "Brasstacks was a 'typical' cold war crisis for the United States. While no vital American interests were engaged, larger, global concerns were present: containment and non-proliferation." They conclude that "Brasstacks had no immediate impact on U.S.-Pakistan relations because the two countries were so closely intertwined in Afghanistan."[17] Although the exercise delayed normalization of relations between the United States and India, it hastened introduction of the concept of confidence-building measures into the subcontinent.

While the Indians were certain that the exercise was merely a validation of emerging operational thinking, the Americans saw it as a crisis that "had the potential to trigger a conflict as much by accident and misperception as per design."[18] Bruce Riedel confirms the American perception of escalation associated with Brasstacks: "Whatever India's motives—and they were clearly muddled—the deployment in January 1987 of two armored divisions, one mechanized division, and six infantry divisions along the border with lots of supporting air power prompted a major Pakistani response."[19]

ATLANTIQUE DOWN

It was 10 August 1999, a normal day at the air force station in Naliya, a marshy region in Kutchh, Gujarat.[20] Forty-Fifth Squadron (Flying Daggers) had just returned from deployment in the Kargil Conflict, and the station was busy preparing for the visit of Air Chief Marshal A. Y. Tipnis. Flying Officer Sanjeev "Nanu" Narayanen was asked to head to the operational readiness platform and relieve the number 2 pilot at around 11:00 a.m. Little did he realize that his life was about to change forever. Narayanen prepared his aircraft and greeted Squadron Leader "Bandy" Bundela, who would be number 1 on the mission. The tannoy—a secure buzzer between the platform and the controlling radar unit—startled the two men when it indicated the presence of an unidentified aircraft close to the border. It was in the hostile area, and a "scramble" was imminent.

Bundela and Narayanen were put on Standby 2—a state of readiness that raises the alert level and has pilots start their engines and await takeoff. The call "Scramble, scramble, scramble" was their signal to taxi down the runway and take off with maximum afterburners. Bundela took off a minute before Narayanen, but the latter was the first to pick up the intruder on his Almaz radar at about forty kilometers—surprisingly good for the "ancient" Russian airborne radar. Soon thereafter, Bundela picked up the intruder visually, identifying it first as a slow-moving transport aircraft but then confirming that it was the highly capable Atlantique maritime reconnaissance aircraft of the Pakistan Navy. The IAF pilots were surprised when the Atlantique turned toward them. Bundela maneuvered to stay on the Atlantique's port side and draw the intruder's attention through standard radio and visual procedures. Narayanen stayed high and behind his leader in visual contact, protecting Bundela's tail from possible Pakistan Air Force (PAF) interceptors.

Not getting any response from the Atlantique, Bundela received clearance from ground control to fire his R-60 missile. The missile hit the port engine of the Atlantique and sent it down in a trail of smoke. The pair of MiG-21s immediately returned to the base for debriefing. It was only after landing that Narayanen realized the enormity of what had happened. Reports came in from border patrols that an aircraft had gone down near the marshy border of Kutchh, with no survivors. News reports later pegged the toll at five officers and eleven sailors. Reflecting on these events twenty years later, Narayanen writes, "While there is no remorse on a job done in the line of duty, one can't but help call the incident an unfortunate one for the lives lost on board the Atlantique. If it indeed was a probing mission, it was a foolhardy move just a few weeks after cessation of hostilities. If the aircraft had crossed over inadvertently, then it was a costly mistake."[21]

OPERATION KABADDI

The withdrawal of the cease-fire in June 2001 allowed concerted counterterrorist operations by the Indian Army's Northern Command. It wanted Indian Army HQ to lift restrictions on the use of mortars and artillery for direct fire on Pakistani posts. In a briefing to the army chief, General Padmanabhan, in mid-2001, Nanavatty said it was time to clearly articulate and adopt a punitive policy to respond to all violations of the line of control, including those by jihadis. The action could be taken by any of the three services, and it should be proportionate and retain the element of surprise by choosing the

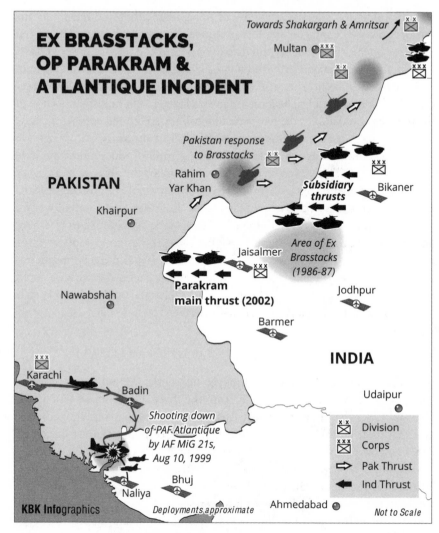

Map 17. Operations Other than War along the Western Front

time and place of application. Approved in principle by the army chief, but subject to final political clearance, preparations for Operation Kabaddi were initiated in autumn 2001, with the aim of redefining and redrawing the line of control as part of the Indian Army's offensive strategy in J&K. The plans included attacks to take out enemy posts and capture and hold ground for a limited duration. Forces were earmarked to be drawn from command and corps reserves without upsetting the counterinfiltration grid.[22] Operational training also commenced in pursuit of this operational objective.

Responding to collective ideas about straightening out and redefining the line of control by capturing shallow objectives, the chief agreed that it offered immense operational benefits and displayed aggression toward the adversary. If the action threatened northern Punjab, which is the heartland of Pakistan, and provided some northern protection for India's vulnerable Chhamb Sector, it had the potential to be a major game changer.[23] In hindsight, although the plan was bold and fit the template of a calibrated limited conflict in J&K, there may have been an element of overreach in Nanavatty's proposal. He thought he could change the rules of the game and introduce a new punitive paradigm in J&K. However, he may have overlooked the absence of a trigger to convince the Vajpayee government to adopt an offensive posture in J&K. Then 9/11 happened. US president George W. Bush declared a global war on terror, and the window for coercive action closed. With Musharraf drawn into supporting the United States in Afghanistan, things got complicated for India. Operation Kabaddi never saw the light of day, and the entire operational scenario on the line of control and the western border with Pakistan had to be reassessed following the deadly suicide attack on the Indian Parliament by Lashkar-e-Taiba (LeT) on 13 December 2001.

MOBILIZING FOR OPERATION PARAKRAM

After the attack on Parliament, Vajpayee instructed the military to formulate a response and asked for input from the three service chiefs. Air Chief Marshal "Kichcha" Krishnaswamy was the first to respond and immediately indicated that he was ready for either a limited response against targets in PoK or a conventional response across multiple sectors in J&K, Punjab, and Rajasthan.[24] While the former was eminently doable with the right intelligence, the latter had an element of overreach, even though several IAF planners thought the PAF was at a lower state of readiness than the IAF. The naval chief, Admiral Sushil Kumar, agreed. Understandably, the army chief, General Padmanabhan, took some time to formulate his response. Consulting with his army commanders, he decided that a full mobilization of the Indian Army was required to respond to a strong multisectoral Pakistani reaction to air and naval strikes. This effectively squashed any element of surprise and closed the window for India to calibrate the escalation by exploring limited options.

By the third week of December, India's armed forces had commenced mobilizing for operations across the entire international border and line of control with Pakistan. While the offensive plans for Western and Southern Army Commands were largely the same as those practiced during Brasstacks, with minor variations, Northern Command was tasked with executing an ambitious offensive in the general area south of the Pir Panjal Range. A hastily assembled offensive corps comprising two divisions from the east and an additional division from the reserves was placed under the command of Lieutenant General V. K. Jetley. Nanavatty asked for time to prepare his corps-sized offensive. Major General (later Lieutenant General) Nagaraj, who subsequently commanded South Western Army Command, was closely involved with the planning and remembers that "there were several valid reasons why a decisive offensive was almost impossible, given the lack of cohesion among the formations and inadequate medium-range artillery support."[25] Offering a realistic assessment, Nanavatty still maintains that it was the wrong way to go to war. He knew exactly what was in store for him, as it had been just over two years since he had moved his corps HQ from the east to J&K during the Kargil Conflict, in anticipation of hostilities escalating. He said, "In Northern Command, we were conducting counterterrorism, counterinfiltration, and conventional defensive operations. I was now given three ad hoc divisions which had not operated together to create a strike formation." Nanavatty pleaded, "I need time to ready my forces. If you want to start elsewhere, I will be ready in a couple of months."[26]

In the author's assessment, India's strategic establishment missed a trick or two by going ahead with a full mobilization of the armed forces for Operation Parakram. It was quite clear that, despite the limited success in Kargil, the concept of a limited war under the nuclear umbrella had not yet been formalized. In hindsight, given that Northern Command had limited brigade-sized offensive plans ready for multiple sectors, it is surprising that neither Nanavatty nor Padmanabhan thought of selectively putting Kabaddi into play and integrating the IAF into those plans, since the air chief had indicated he was ready to hit targets in PoK, assuming he had the necessary intelligence. This could have been an immediate punitive response to the attack on Parliament, without infringing on any of the red lines that could have triggered a nuclear response by Pakistan. That would have been India's best option for a limited response. Instead, the army commanders were asked to disengage from regular operations and reshape everything. Queried about this possibility two decades later, Nanavatty pondered and said, "I had never thought about it then, but in hindsight, yes, that was a possibility."[27]

The broad mobilization plan was sequenced to support an immediate offensive option in Northern Command in the areas south of the Pir Panjal Range. Western Command was to focus on making gains in the North Punjab Sector, complemented by the entire panoply of offensive air operations. Most of the gains were anticipated to be in the Rajasthan Sector, where the IAF would support deep incursions by two of the Indian Army's strike corps. If war had broken out, one possible outcome would have been an attrition-based scenario with heavy casualties on both sides. Major General (later Lieutenant General) Panag, who had taken over First Armored Division, observed that while the going might have been tough in the northern sectors, the armored divisions in the Rajasthan Sector could have made deep inroads toward the first obstacle, the Nara Canal.

Though acknowledging very candidly that several of his contemporaries believed it was his reluctance to rush into battle that stalled Operation Parakram, Nanavatty is firm in his assessment that it was "an incorrect way of going to war and in my heart of hearts, I am glad we did not go to war." Reflecting further, he said, "My inputs may have been among the several issues that confronted Paddy [General Padmanabhan], but had it been the principal contributory factor, I am sure he would have told me."[28] Nagaraj concurs with Nanavatty on this issue and recalls the extensive briefings in Indian Army HQ that he and Nanavatty gave, with Jetley in attendance.

On 14 May 2002 Jaish-e-Mohammad (JeM) terrorists carried out *fidayeen* attacks in Kaluchak near Jammu, striking a bus and a military camp where family members were present. Thirty-one were killed and forty-seven injured in these attacks.[29] This was the second trigger that almost led to war between India and Pakistan, with a spectrum of leadership clamoring for retributive action. Hooda recollects that the Indian Army commenced moving First Corps northward to supplement Second Corps in the Shakargarh Sector, even as Padmanabhan waited for the order from the government to commence hostilities. The Pakistan Army had moved all its formations into battle positions, so the Indians had no room for surprise. It is possible that, when faced with the prospect of a battle of attrition, Vajpayee realized the futility of going to war. It is believed that large armored formations from Second Corps under Lieutenant General Kapil Vij moved into dangerously provocative offensive positions in northern Rajasthan in February 2002 and were detected by US satellites. This alarmed both Washington, DC, and Islamabad. Surprisingly, Vij resigned and has not spoken publicly since then, even though many feel it is time for the truth to come out. Mehta, who took over as Western Army commander toward the closing phases of Operation Parakram, argues that only Padmanabhan knew how close they were to going to war. About Vij, he said, "We will never know whether Vij suffered because he was an aggressive commander or whether he was the fall guy for a mistake made by a subordinate commander."[30]

JOINTNESS AND SYNERGY

Airpower has often been used for coercion in less-than-war situations, but it is not widely known that India also employed airpower as a tool of forceful persuasion during Operation Parakram. In a written reply to Parliament in November 2002—four months after the incident in question—Defense Minister George Fernandes categorically stated that IAF fighters had been used to evict intruders from Point 3260 (about 10,000 feet) in the Machil and Neelum-Gurez Sectors in late July 2002. This sector includes the Kishenganga River, the beautiful Neelum Valley, and a series of ridges that run almost parallel to the line of control. The Special Service Group (SSG), in tandem with jihadis, reportedly launched an operation from the town of Kel in PoK, a Pakistan Army cantonment, to occupy positions on a ridgeline about 800 meters inside Indian territory. This would have allowed a continuous observation of Indian positions in an area where Pakistan has always been vulnerable. In an operation reminiscent of the methodology used by Pakistan during the Kargil Conflict, vantage points were occupied stealthily in the darkness, and temporary bunkers were built to shelter the troops. However, Fifteenth Corps detected the intrusion in late July 2002 and decided that a firm response was called for.

Lieutenant General Vinayak Patankar, the commander of Fifteenth Corps, ordered a brigade from the Kupwara-based Twenty-Eighth Infantry Division to evict the intruders. Not wanting to repeat the mistakes of Kargil, Northern Command convinced Delhi of the perils of acting in haste, and an operation was planned to use airpower before launching an infantry assault. Air Marshal Menon got a call from Indian Army HQ in early July 2002 about stray intrusions in the Kel area that needed to be repulsed with airpower. Air Marshal Adi Ghandhi, the commander in chief of Western Air Command, received the same intelligence from Nanavatty. Realizing that Patankar was under tremendous pressure from Indian Army HQ to evict the intruders, Nanavatty chose to bring in airpower before committing to a ground assault. Getting a green light from Air Chief Marshal Krishnaswamy, Ghandhi moved four Mirage-2000s to Adampur from Gwalior in late July. Wing Commander Rajesh Kumar, the commander of Seventh Squadron, was given a set of coordinates the following day for a dummy run. The squadron conducted a simulated strike based on those coordinates and was then given the actual ones. The next day, four Mirage-2000s armed with a combination of conventional and laser-guided bombs attacked the position and destroyed the bunkers, resulting in the immediate withdrawal of the SSG and the jihadis.[31]

Intercepted enemy communications revealed that the intruders suffered several casualties, but these figures were never released or corroborated by the Indian Army.[32] A mopping-up operation by the Indian Army later that evening and the next day reported that there were no intruders at the location. Other locations had also been vacated in anticipation of further air strikes. It is important to highlight that the limited application of airpower in a localized action in high-altitude terrain reinforced airpower's utility for coercion, as it proved to be decisive, forceful, legitimate, and nonescalatory.

US PERSPECTIVES AND INTERLOCUTERS

Strobe Talbott, President Bill Clinton's deputy secretary of state and a close friend of Jaswant Singh, India's foreign minister, emerged in the post-Kargil era as a key US interlocutor in crisis situations involving India and Pakistan. Clearly acknowledging Musharraf's complicity in the ongoing infiltration of jihadis into India after the 9/11 attacks, he writes of US concerns upon receiving intelligence reports that India was readying its nuclear arsenal to respond to a possible first strike by Pakistan. Talbott attaches great significance to the visit of his successor, Richard Armitage, to Islamabad to diffuse the crisis following the "nuclear alarm" as Operation Parakram was escalating toward possible war.[33]

Chari, Cheema, and Cohen offer a critique of the US response after Operation Parakram and argue that "the United States again played an ambiguous role, being uncertain as to which side to come down on." They also call out Washington's unwillingness to mount a long-term strategy of regional conflict resolution. Washington, they reckon, "was interested in crisis management, not in conflict prevention or resolution."[34] Clearly, the crisis of 2001–2002 came at the wrong time for the United States to choose between India and Pakistan as its long-term strategic partner in South Asia. Though a preference had clearly emerged in the aftermath of the Kargil crisis, Pakistan remained a critical ally in the ongoing war on terror in Afghanistan.

INDIA'S PROACTIVE DOCTRINE

Even though the Kargil Conflict ended without any talk of nuclear options, every operational or doctrinal recalibration by India's armed forces since then has been viewed by Western military analysts with some alarm. They see India as wanting to upset the military balance in the subcontinent, "leading to a breakdown of deterrence which could have serious consequences, including the potential use of nuclear weapons."[35] The "cold start doctrine" was one such tweaking of existing operational concepts.

Discussions about improving the Indian Army's mobilization schedule commenced after Operation Parakram was aborted in late 2002. It gained traction during General Nirmal Vij's tenure as India's army chief. As part of the operational logistics directorate, Hooda found nothing overtly aggressive about the strategy. He considered it a much-needed logistics and mobility recalibration to cater to the emerging paradigms of limited conflict in which the more powerful of two adversaries (in this case, India) sought to claim its legitimate advantage. The strategy mainly involved moving offensive formations to fresh locations in the desert sector, where India sought to create any asymmetry that would strengthen deterrence rather than weaken it.

There was also a move to regroup armored elements belonging the defensive, or pivot, corps into battle groups that could launch an initial offensive. This could shape the wide desert spaces for further exploitation by India's strike corps. The cooling of tensions along the line of actual control with China in 2003 also allowed the Indian army to create dual-task divisions that relied on the IAF's growing air mobility capability to move large units from the east to the western desert. This move was intended to free elements of the pivot corps to supplement ongoing offensive operations, based on their familiarity with the terrain. Washington, DC, believed that improved synergy between the Indian Army and the IAF would allow India to make decisive thrusts in the deserts of Sind and trigger Pakistan's nuclear red lines. With parallel naval strategies, the proactive doctrine appeared to have all the elements of an offensive strategy in place.

Hooda argues that despite having good synergy with the IAF in terms of air mobility, there was still much work to be done to ensure that the IAF's offensive capabilities blended seamlessly into this process. Despite a clear doctrinal shift in 2012, only in the last few years has the IAF truly embraced parallel operations.[36] Several Western narratives on the cold start doctrine were heavily influenced by the desire to "protect" Pakistan and ensure that it remained on the front lines of the global war on terror. The doctrine also offered an excuse for the West to remain engaged in the "potentially catastrophic" India–Pakistan rivalry, despite strong assertions from India that there was no room for external players.[37] Not helping India's cause has been the lack of Indian narratives on the proactive doctrine in Washington and London. This is in contrast to the effective Pakistani counternarratives by retired and serving military officers and military scholars, whose writings are quite prolific and whose presence at seminars is noticeable.[38]

AN EYE FOR AN EYE ACROSS THE LINE OF CONTROL

In July 2011 the Indian Army's Twenty-Eighth Infantry Division suffered six casualties as two battalions switched duties at a post on one of the ridgelines north of Kupwara. These casualties were different from those caused by routine firing or an artillery barrage—the Pakistanis' attack was brutal and premeditated, and two Indian soldiers were decapitated.[39] This act called for an immediate retaliatory response. Resisting the urge to strike back immediately, division commander Major General Samir Chakravorty sought permission from the Northern Army commander, Lieutenant General K. T. Parnaik, to explore options for retaliatory strikes after surveillance and reconnaissance of potential targets. Seven intrusive reconnaissance missions were conducted between the towns of Kel and Neelum in PoK, and a target was identified about a kilometer across the line of control. Two days before the Eid holiday, Indian commandos ambushed two parties of four Pakistanis each. The Indian troops killed the enemies with improvised explosive devices, grenades, and gunfire. It was a typical revenge operation.

On 18 September 2016 four JeM terrorists stormed a camp of Twelfth Brigade in Uri, killing eighteen and wounding more than twenty soldiers.[40] It put the Indian Army under tremendous pressure, as commanding officers asked the leadership how long they would be expected to sit back and do nothing. Lieutenant General Hooda, the Northern Army commander, notes that in the autumn of 2015, his HQ had brainstormed a few such contingencies and concluded that two of the Special Forces units involved in counterterrorism operations had to be pulled out and trained for cross-border raids. He recalls, "A fair amount of preparatory work had already been done by the time the Uri attack happened. Once the political decision was taken, it took us no more than ten days to launch five cross-border strikes across the line of control—two of them in northern Kashmir and three opposite the Poonch-Rajouri Sector." These camps were chosen because they were within ten kilometers of the line of control and had been identified as terrorist launchpads. The prospect of Pakistan Army posts being near these terrorist camps was not ruled out. Therefore, "it was decided to carry out fire assaults to minimize the risks and ensure no casualties."[41]

The strikes took place between 1:00 and 6:00 a.m. on 29 September 2016 and were monitored by Hooda via live streaming from unmanned aerial vehicles. There were a number risks inherent in this operation. For one, more than a hundred Special Forces troops were involved, which meant that the enemy would be alerted, and the troops would be in danger as they returned after executing the attacks. Another was the lack of actionable intelligence on one of the targets. But rather than aborting the attack—which would have disappointed the troops who had trained hard for the mission—Hooda approved the plan, based on the report of a surveillance team, even though just one casualty would have diluted the mission's effectiveness.

The near simultaneous fire assault inflicted heavy casualties on the camps, killing as many as seventy to seventy-five terrorists and their handlers during the stealthy operation.[42] Hooda's estimate of eighty casualties was based on radio intercepts and an assessment by the commanders of the two units, both of which had earlier operational experience in the sector. Pakistan denied that

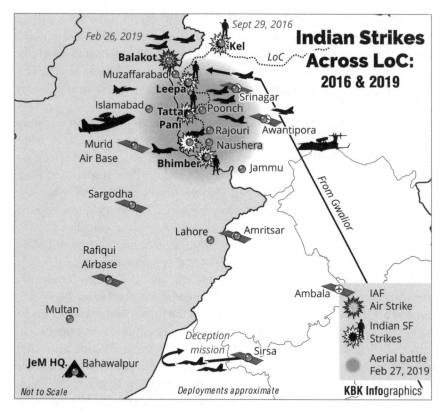

Map 18. Proactive Operations across the Line of Control (LoC)

the strikes took place, and India felt no need to provide evidence of the camps' destruction. Even so, there was a quiet sense of confidence within the Indian Army that punitive strikes would no longer be taboo as a standard response to terrorist attacks. Unconfirmed reports suggest that "revenge strikes" were conducted the previous night too. Soldiers from the unit that suffered losses in the Uri attack reportedly crossed over with "pathfinder" support from the Special Forces and neutralized several terrorists at a launchpad.[43] Nineteen personnel from the two Special Forces units were given gallantry awards, including a Kirti Chakra (the second highest gallantry award for peacetime operations) for the major who led one of the strikes.[44]

PEELING THE MASK AT BALAKOT

On 14 February 2019 a Central Reserve Police Force convoy was attacked along the Jammu–Srinagar highway at Pulwama by a JeM suicide bomber, killing forty-four security personnel. That event changed the trajectory of India's response mechanisms. The Indian strategic establishment realized that—after its response to the 2016 Uri terror attacks—Pakistan would be ready for any kind of surface retaliation following the Pulwama attack. This meant that air and naval strikes against nonmilitary targets were the only viable option.

The three service chiefs had met a few weeks earlier to brainstorm joint operational responses to various contingencies. So there was clarity when Prime Minister Modi asked them to respond with an air strike after consultations with the national security adviser and the defense minister. A senior government official—who had also been present in 2008, when the Manmohan Singh government had contemplated a military response after the Mumbai terrorist attack—was struck by the chiefs' confidence and the alacrity with which they responded to Modi's "free hand" to plan India's punitive response.[45] This time around, there was no hesitation.

In Rawat's estimation, the Indian Army was only 75 percent ready, but the adversary was at less than 50 percent readiness. The Indian Navy was not worried because the asymmetry between the Indian and Pakistani navies was enormous.[46] As for the IAF, Dhanoa possessed excellent operational acumen.[47] It did not take his team long to put together a viable plan after national security adviser Ajit Doval provided reliable targeting intelligence about an active JeM training camp in the remote province of Khyber Pakhtunkhwa. The training camp was located at Juba Top near the town of Balakot, about sixty kilometers north of the Pakistan Army's cantonment town of Abbottabad. Credible intelligence confirmed the presence of hundreds of terrorists in training, as well as senior cadres, trainers, and commanders.

Dhanoa was confident the IAF could respond to the challenge of escalation after the massive Exercise Gaganshakti in 2018, which had created an operational plan for ten days of high-intensity combat. Assisting him in implementing the operational plan were the director-general of air operations and the commanders in chief of Western and Central Air Commands. Dhanoa's confidence would be vindicated in part, but several shortfalls in the IAF's performance would also become apparent.

AIR STRIKE

Early on the morning of 25 February 2019 Squadron Leader A from Ninth Squadron returned from a rehearsal sortie with no idea of what the actual target would be. Only at around 8:00 p.m. did he learn that he was part of a large formation from the Mirage fleet that would be striking a nonmilitary terrorist target in Pakistan. After a comprehensive briefing at 10:00 p.m.,

Air Commodore W, a Mirage pilot with combat experience in Kargil, gave the team a pep talk. "This is what you have trained for and now it is time to deliver," he told them. The group then split up and headed to their respective squadrons. They would not meet again until they landed at the designated recovery base after the mission.[48]

The air force station at Gwalior hummed like a hornets' nest in the wee hours of the morning of 26 February 2019. While the ground crew was busy strapping air-to-ground weapons and air-to-air missiles on the Mirage-2000s, the commanding officers of the three Mirage squadrons in Gwalior—First, Seventh, and Ninth Squadrons—were going through their individual briefings, contingency plans, and escape drills. They knew there was no possibility of rescue if anyone ejected in enemy territory.

The target was Juba Top, and the strike force comprised twelve Mirage-2000 aircraft, each of which was armed with a single Spice 2000 bomb and a few of the older Crystal Maze bombs to ensure a threefold overkill factor. Escorting them were several upgraded Mirage-2000s with MICA beyond visual range (BVR) missiles—the best weapon the IAF had to counter the potent AIM-120 advanced medium-range air-to-air missiles carried by PAF F-16s. Squadron Leader A recollects that the MICA BVR missiles on the tarmac were the most intimidating sight he had ever seen. Four Su-30 MKI aircraft from Fifteenth Squadron joined the Mirages for additional air defense protection, while a diversionary group of Jaguars and Su-30s headed south toward Bahawalpur in Pakistan—JeM HQ—to draw away PAF air defense fighters and the Airborne Warning and Control System (AWACS) orbiting near the PAF air base in Murid.

The weather over the target area prompted a rethink and the consideration of a delay. However, the IAF leadership's decision to proceed was vindicated by the Spice 2000's ability to gather adequate details despite the cloud cover and strike the target accurately. Demonstrating reach and precision while maintaining complete radio silence, the fuel-efficient Mirages flew more than 1,300 kilometers one way with an aerial refueling. They used the mountains to mask their entry into PoK airspace and dropped five Spice 2000 bombs with unerring accuracy onto selected buildings that housed terrorists. Contrary to reports that the PAF had been caught napping, a post-strike IAF review claimed that several pairs of PAF interceptor aircraft had been scrambled but failed to intercept the Mirages, or they had been drawn away by the decoys headed toward Bahawalpur. The decoys turned back short of the international border, giving the Mirages a free run to the north.

The lack of any clear evidence of the destruction caused by the Spice 2000 bombs does not trouble either the IAF or the Indian government. Communication intercepts between top JeM leaders about a strike on their facility, as well as the Pakistanis' reluctance to allow foreign journalists access to the site as late as April, only reinforce the Indians' poststrike assessment. Sources who wish to remain anonymous confirm that recent satellite forays over the area indicate an increased sulfur content around the Juba Top camp, suggesting that large numbers of hurriedly buried bodies are decomposing.

To better understand the Juba Top air strike, it is important to explain how the Spice 2000 bomb works. The 1,000-kilogram Spice 2000 glide bomb used by the IAF has an explosive charge of merely 60 to 80 kilograms. Planting this charge against the door of a building or strapping it around a suicide bomber would produce a very different result than using it in a penetrative weapon. The casing that surrounds the explosive in the Spice 2000 bomb weighs more than 900 kilograms. The bomb does not detonate instantaneously on impact, such as on the roof of a building. It has a time-delay fuse that allows it to penetrate through concrete before detonating. Informed sources indicate that the time delay is just long enough to cause detonation after minimal penetration, preventing an excessive upheaval effect. The primary shock wave of the explosion is first transmitted to the casing, which fragments and disperses at velocities ranging from 1.3 to 1.8 kilometers per second (approximately 5,000 to 7,000 kilometers per hour). In effect, the lack of damage to surrounding structures can be attributed to this configuration. The result is similar to the release of pressure in a large room—which merely blasts open the windows and doors.

Vipin Narang, an associate professor at the Massachusetts Institute of Technology, has been a vocal supporter of the larger strategic narrative that India should have exploited after the Balakot strikes, but he is critical of the ensuing tactical and operational narratives. Nevertheless, he said, "Let analysts like me say whatever, who cares? Though I maintained from day one that the resolve to hit mainland Pakistan was the game changer. The rest is noise."[49]

PAKISTAN RESPONDS: OPERATION SWIFT RETORT

Expecting an immediate riposte, the IAF's air defense radar and combat air patrols were on high alert. The PAF attempted to catch the IAF by surprise with a raid in broad daylight the following day. Although this had succeeded in 1965 and 1971, this time around, it failed. However, the PAF still managed to catch the IAF out of phase during the recycling of its air defense assets. India's sole AWACS had been pulled east of its normal patrolling position, which meant that the IAF's "eye in the sky" was not available when the PAF planes approached. Thanks to an alert fighter controller, Squadron Leader Minty Agarwal, two airborne pairs of Sukhoi and Mirage aircraft were vectored (directed on radar) to the incoming PAF aircraft. Agarwal controlled multiple pairs of interceptors, including MiG-21 Bisons that were scrambled from Srinagar.[50] This was one of largest aerial battles in a less-than-war situation in recent times, and the details presented here are based on bits and pieces of information that have been made available by the IAF in its efforts to combat Pakistan's fake narrative.[51]

The PAF aircraft were JF-17 and Mirage-III aircraft armed with H4 weapons,[52] and their target was the Indian Army's Naushera brigade. In addition, F-16s armed with AIM-120s and targeting pods were intended to keep the IAF's Mirage-2000s and Su-30s engaged while the other aircraft delivered their weapon loads. An analysis of the rules of engagement followed during the maneuver reveals that both forces stayed on their own side of the line of control. In this cat-and-mouse aerial combat, both sides attempted to get a shot at the target from a distance while trying to avoid getting shot themselves.

The IAF aircraft could not take shots because of the weapon range advantage enjoyed by the PAF's F-16s. This meant that if the IAF fighters wanted to attempt a BVR launch, they had to fly into the range of the AIM-120s. Despite their advantage, the F-16s were surprised by the IAF's sophisticated and synergized tactics. Monitored radio calls provide ample evidence that four or five AIM-120s were launched by the F-16s but missed their targets due to either electronic countermeasures or a combination of timely offensive and defensive maneuvering by the IAF aircraft. The Avenger formation from the IAF's Su-30 fleet surprised the PAF with its synchronized and excellent maneuvering, during both the offensive mission on 26 February and the air defense response the following day. The IAF chief later remarked that if he had fielded the Rafale aircraft armed with Meteor BVR missiles, the outcome of the aerial engagement would have been very different.

Meanwhile, radio transmissions intercepted by the Indian Army revealed that several H4 weapons had been launched by the JF-17s and Mirage-IIIs but had missed their targets because faulty digital elevation maps had been fed into the weapons computer. Realizing that the Sukhois and Mirages needed support, Agarwal scrambled four MiG-21 Bison aircraft from Srinagar. This is where Wing Commander Abhinandan Varthaman entered the fray. First to arrive in the area where the Sukhois had been battling the F-16s, Varthaman came into the fight from above. He locked on to an F-16 that had sneaked close to the target area, possibly to film the damage from just across the line of control. No aircraft had yet crossed it.

As Varthaman approached the line of control at top speed, Agarwal ordered him to "go cold," which means "turn around." However, his aircraft was equipped with an old radio set (which should have been replaced years ago), and he missed the instruction, possibly because the PAF was jamming communications. Varthaman fired a shot at the receding F-16, taking it down. Seconds later, as he initiated a turn to get back home, Varthaman was shot down, probably by another F-16. Ejecting a few kilometers inside enemy territory, he attempted to escape from the pursuing locals and Pakistan Army personnel and make it back to India across a rivulet. The locals caught up with him first, and he was lucky not to be lynched. The Pakistan Army quickly arrived on the scene and took him into custody. After much drama and media attention, he was repatriated to India a few days later, having conducted himself with courage and dignity while in captivity.[53] Varthaman soon returned to active duty and was awarded a Vir Chakra for "courageously engaging the enemy aircraft package with utter disregard to his personal safety" and "displaying exceptional air combat acumen."[54] Agarwal and five Mirage and Su-30 pilots were also recognized for their distinguished service.

LESSONS FROM BALAKOT

Notwithstanding the political rhetoric and hyperbole that followed these attacks, Pakistan got the message: India would no longer depend on diplomacy to expose Pakistani machinations; it would take suitable punitive action. No country—not even Pakistan's ally China—criticized the Indian air strikes, which were considered preventive strikes against nonmilitary targets in an established terrorist camp.

An objective analysis of the operation and tactics reveals both positives and negatives. The preventive air strikes were planned in utmost secrecy and executed with finesse and surprise, but there were also a few hiccups that diluted the overall impact of the strikes and denied the Indians real-time information on target destruction. The synergy between the armed forces was good, and the army chief understood the importance of surprise; he held back and closely monitored the surface movement of large ground formations until the attack was over. The IAF's air defense response kept at bay a potent and numerically superior adversary. However, the orchestration of air defense resources could have been better in terms of the speed of recycling airborne air defense fighters.

The downing of an IAF Mi-17 by friendly fire reportedly unsettled the air defense network in J&K.[55] The Su-30s and Mirage-2000s acquitted themselves well; they did not allow the F-16s to maneuver into launch ranges, even though the PAF planes' BVR missiles outranged the Indian missiles by about 20 percent. The MiG-21 Bisons acted as classic disrupters. The flurry of emergency acquisitions of critical weapons by the IAF in the months following Balakot indicates that there will be no letup in building the capability for coercive deterrence.[56]

DETERRING A SEEMINGLY IRRATIONAL ADVERSARY

Pakistan's irrational strategic behavior along India's western borders—influenced in no small measure by jihadi and Salafi and Wahhabi extremism—is apparent across the political and military spectrum.[57] Adding to the confusion are the few rational segments in Pakistan's beleaguered diplomatic corps and civil society that harbor hope of a rapprochement with India. However, it is possible that a rational Pakistan is trying to appear irrational to plant a seed of doubt in its principal adversary. Even if a cease-fire is restored along the line of control, what guarantee does India have that the Pakistan Army will honor it? Pakistan's army chief, General Qamar Javed Bajwa, has clearly indicated that he thinks it is wise to segregate the "good terrorist from the bad one," thereby endorsing terrorism as a strategy for Pakistan.[58] Will Pakistan abandon its obsession with the secession of Kashmir in the irrational expectation of getting even with India for 1971, Siachen, and Kargil? Will India's political establishment engage with the Pakistan Army to gauge whether it is serious about restoring peace along the line of control? These are just some of the questions that loom large over the continued India–Pakistan imbroglio.

19

Stress along the Line of Actual Control

The overarching reality seems to be that both India and China have been subtly but profoundly influenced by the possibility that the other side might use military force.

—John Garver, *Protracted Contest: Sino-Indian Rivalry in the Twentieth Century*

DETERRENCE AND PROBING

Following the Sumdorong Chu face-off in 1986–1987, Beijing realized that India would be no pushover in any type of conflict. Consequently, both sides felt the need to implement some kind of recessed deterrence mechanism. They decided on an agreement to control escalation along the line of actual control (LAC) in 1993. Much of the credit for this move must go to Prime Minister Narasimha Rao, who first created a political consensus in India and then signaled to the Chinese that India was willing to negotiate the first bilateral agreement since the 1962 war.[1] The agreement, called Maintenance of Peace and Tranquility along the Line of Actual Control, outlined the procedures to be followed during periodic high-level military contacts and put in place several confidence-building measures for maintaining the status quo. Among these were prior notice of military exercises in areas close to the LAC and the establishment of a ten-kilometer no-fly zone for fighter aircraft along the LAC. These measures worked well and led to the pullback of some forces from the LAC. However, in the absence of a clearly delineated border, neither side let its guard down. Both countries considered this delineation of the LAC an essential first step toward settling the boundary issue. Clarity on the LAC reduces the risk of accidental conflicts by removing the reason to cross it. It also sets the stage for final settlement of the boundary question. Joint working groups, interlocutors, and special representatives have made slow progress, however, despite the signing of a Border Defense Cooperation Agreement (BDCA) in 2013 during Prime Minister Manmohan Singh's visit to Beijing.[2] This agreement, which is a slight variation of the 1993

340

agreement, is valuable only as a deterrent because it offers no road map for conflict resolution.

The power asymmetry between China and India widened rapidly in the first decade of the twenty-first century. It was only a matter of time before China—under an assertive Xi Jinping—tested Indian resolve in two sectors. In 2013 People's Liberation Army (PLA) forces first intruded into and then set up camp for a week in the Depsang plains of northern Ladakh, close to the Indian advance landing ground at Daulat Beg Oldi. A year later, even as Xi was exchanging pleasantries with recently elected Prime Minister Narendra Modi during a state visit to India, PLA and Indian troops were engaged in pushing and shoving at Chumar in eastern Ladakh. Both Depsang and Chumar had been the sites of fierce battles in 1962, and the Chinese wanted to remind the Indians of their focus on these disputed enclaves. The PLA's attention soon shifted eastward as it carried out probing intrusions in areas of Arunachal Pradesh. The Indian Army calls these areas Fishtail 1 and Fishtail 2 because on their appearance on maps. China then went for a big push in Doklam that led to a two-month standoff in 2017.

DEPSANG AND CHUMAR FACE-OFFS

Located a few kilometers southeast of the Daulat Beg Oldie airfield and the Chip Chap region, the Depsang plains are part of an area known in the Indian Army as Subsector North. It is flanked by the Sasoma Range to the west, the Karakoram Range to the north, and the Kun Lun Range to the east. It is part of a huge area that has been defended by a single Indian infantry brigade for a long time. But Indian Army deployments in the area have depended on the trajectory of the insurgency in Jammu & Kashmir (J&K). After the Depsang face-off, the Indian Army enhanced its troop strength in the region and seriously considered deploying tanks in the area. However, a metaled road to support operations remains a work in progress.

Lieutenant General Vinod Bhatia, a former director-general of military operations, explained the technicalities of maintaining a presence in the several disputed areas in eastern Ladakh.[3] The PLA routinely conducted four or five vehicular patrols a month, but their total monthly stay in the area was only fifteen to twenty hours because the trip from their nearest camp took about four hours. India was constrained by the lack of roads into the region and conducted six-day foot patrols twice a month. This irritated the Chinese immensely, as they construed it as a prolonged presence in a disputed area. On the morning of 15 April 2013 an officer from the Ladakh Scouts, on a routine helicopter surveillance and observation sortie, spotted something abnormal in the Raki Nala area on the desolate Depsang plains, well inside the Indian Army's domain. A closer look confirmed that the PLA had erected four or five tents overnight, with the clear intention of staying put.

The Indian Army had only one platoon in the area at the time. Within forty-eight hours, additional troops were called in from acclimatized infantry battalions, Ladakh Scouts, and Indo-Tibetan Border Police. They quickly set up camp opposite the PLA camp, and troops were deployed as a physical barrier to prevent any further intrusion. The overarching message from Indian Army headquarters (HQ) to the officers and troops was "no blinking and no brinkmanship." There was much pushing and shoving during the three-week face-off before a series of flag meetings between the two brigade commanders and higher-level diplomatic parleys diffused the situation.[4] Interestingly, the intrusion took place weeks before Chinese premier Li Keqiang's visit to India.[5]

Bhatia recollects that national security adviser Shiv Shankar Menon was supportive throughout the crisis, even though he had often advised against adopting a hawkish approach to border management. Bhatia is also convinced that it is risky to have insufficient troops in large spaces such as the Depsang plains and Subsector North. Nanavatty offers a contrarian perspective, arguing that many posts and locations in eastern Ladakh were indefensible. Describing the strategy in the early 2000s as a policing strategy and not a defensive line, he invoked Fredrick the Great, who said, "You defend everywhere and you defend nowhere." Cautioning against mirroring the Chinese in every respect, he was against the strategy of "fingering or needling," which was being propounded by some commanders on both sides.[6]

Bhatia characterizes the PLA as a rule-based force that largely follows the templates of patrolling laid out in various border agreements, a proposition that would be seriously tested in 2020 when the PLA made several major transgressions across the LAC (see the afterword). He has studied the behavior of PLA commanders, particularly in Tibet, and discounts the view, held by several Indian commanders, that local PLA commanders flex their muscles periodically.[7] However, he acknowledges that, despite exercising restraint and responsibility, patrols from both sides have often transgressed the limits of penetration. He attributes this to the desire to acquire updated situational awareness of the LAC in the absence of roads and tracks, which he justifies as being necessary at times.

The Chumar incident of April and May 2014, barely a few months after the signing of the BDCA, was an exercise in coercive signaling and posturing from the Chinese. Chumar is in southern Ladakh and west of the prominent frontier outpost of Demchok. The disputed area southwest of it has a vehicular track that links it to both the Indian and the Chinese sides. Chumar was constantly visited by Chinese motorized (and even horseback) patrols, and Indian patrols established a post near the disputed area of the LAC on a plateau called 30R. Matters came to head when the Chinese brought in construction vehicles with the intent to extend their track beyond 30R. This move was followed by rapid troop inductions on both sides. Human chains of several hundred infantry soldiers and personnel from the Indo-Tibetan Border Police blocked a prominent river crossing and the adjoining plateau where the PLA wanted to build a road. The Chinese even landed helicopters on the plateau for resupply. This prompted Hooda, who was the Northern Army commander at the time, to ask the Indian Air Force (IAF) to send Mi-17s with supplies. In a lighter vein, he recollects some supplies falling on the Chinese side, and the PLA troops were seen enjoying Indian chocolates.

A significant and unreported de-escalatory event occurred when a PLA officer who had fallen off the plateau was rescued by the Indians. He was treated for his injuries and immediately sent back. This cooled local nerves and ended the sixteen-day face-off. Media reports of the PLA demolishing Indian bunkers were unsubstantiated. However, the Chinese clearly intended to establish themselves on the plateau southwest of Chumar and signal their disagreement with the contours of the LAC in the area. Based on his understanding of China's strategic behavior, Hooda is certain that the operation had the blessings of top leadership, as part of China's periodic probing of disputed areas along the LAC. The face-off demanded extreme operational restraint from local Indian brigade commanders, who had to ensure that junior commanders refrained from making reactive tactical decisions. Instead, Northern Command sought continual updates from the field and urged caution at all times.[8] Eastern Ladakh continues to simmer, and as recently as May 2020, Pangang Tso Lake and the Galwan Valley emerged as the scene of a clash between PLA border guards and the Indian Army that involved stone throwing and resulted in injuries on both sides. As always, the incident was downplayed by both sides following a meeting between sector commanders.[9]

STRESS IN ARUNACHAL PRADESH

The LAC in Arunachal Pradesh stretches for almost 1,000 kilometers, which makes it impossible for the Tezpur-based Fourth Corps to defend the whole region. Therefore, eastern Arunachal Pradesh has been segregated from the Tawang (Kameng) Sector. The area is now under Fifty-Sixth Mountain Division and Second Infantry Division, forming part of an expanded Third Corps zone. Along with Subsector North in Ladakh, eastern Arunachal Pradesh has the poorest infrastructure and roads. Advanced landing grounds at Mechuka, Tuting, and Walong are the lifelines of the region.

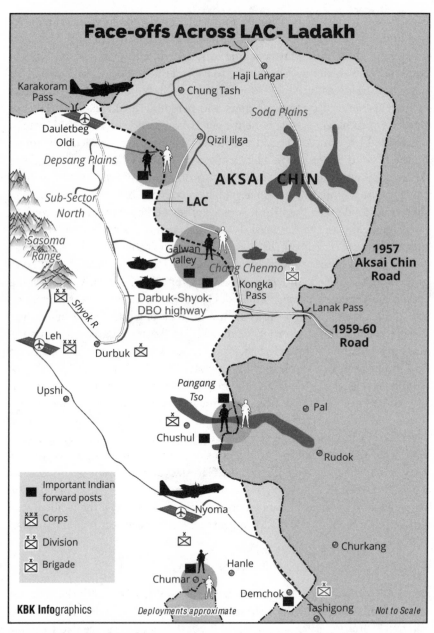

Map 19. Stress in Ladakh along the Line of Actual Control (LAC) with China

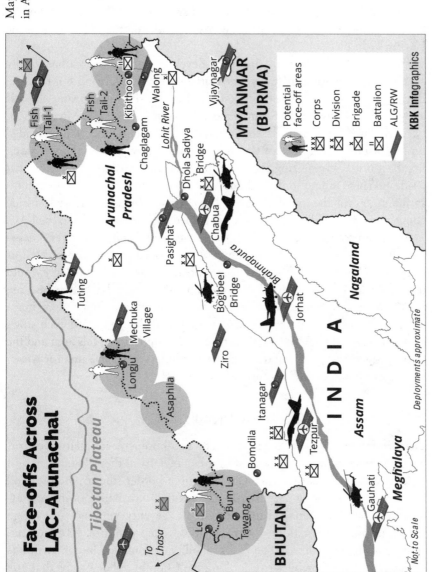

Map 20. Conflict Potential
in Arunachal Pradesh

**Face-offs Across
LAC-Arunachal**

Tibetan Plateau

To
Lhasa

*Arunachal
Pradesh*

Fish
Tail-1

Fish
Tail-2

Kibithoo

Walong

Chaglagam

Lohit River

Vijaynagar

**MYANMAR
(BURMA)**

Dhola Sadiya
Bridge

Chabua

Pasighat

Tuting

Mechuka
Village

Longju

Asaphila

Ziro

Bogibeel
Bridge

Jorhat

Brahmaputra

Itanagar

Bomdila

Tezpur

I N D I A

Assam

Nagaland

Bum La

Tawang

Le

BHUTAN

Gauhati

Meghalaya

Deployments approximate

Not to Scale

| | Potential
face-off areas |
| --- | --- |
| xxx ⊠ | Corps |
| xx ⊠ | Division |
| x ⊠ | Brigade |
| = ⊠ | Battalion |
| | ALG/RW |

KBK Infographics

Soon after the Doklam crisis, China and India accused each other of violating the LAC around Longju and the areas west of it called Asaphila, a place of religious significance for locals living near the border town of Taksing. India also accused the Chinese of unduly provocative road-building activity one kilometer inside the LAC in the area close to Tuting. The Chinese, in turn, alleged that India damaged the road equipment left behind during the winter. There is constant jousting in the areas north of the village of Chaglagam (Fishtail 1 and Fishtail 2). These are historically disputed areas because of poor demarcation.[10] In September 2019 a local politician claimed that the Chinese had built a bridge across a rivulet on the Indian side of the LAC in Fishtail 1.[11]

The pace of infrastructure and road development in the area has visibly accelerated over the last few years, with several roads being built by the Border Roads Organization. The construction of sixty-one strategic roads along the borders with China and Pakistan has been hastened.[12] In addition, two bridges have been built: the nine-kilometer-long Dhola Sadiya bridge on the eastern extremities of the Brahmaputra and the five-kilometer-long Bogibeel bridge connecting the town of Dibrugarh with eastern Arunachal Pradesh. These are not only lifelines for civilians but also critical communication nodes for the Indian Army. What remains now is to ensure last-mile connectivity by building a network of metaled roads that run up to the LAC.

An Indian commander recollects the farcical and benign—but very real—face-offs in the Fishtail region. They usually started with a group of ten or fifteen PLA border guards intruding into areas claimed by India. They would unfold their tripod stools and sit around for the whole day before heading back to their camp at night. The Indians would respond in a similar manner. Finally, a border patrol meeting would be called to record each side's protests. Given the significant infrastructural asymmetry in this area and the PLA's propensity to continuously probe the Indian defensive line for weaknesses, this could be the next area of concern.[13]

THE DOKLAM CRISIS

The Chumbi Valley is a dagger-shaped, 100-kilometer-long sliver of traversable but mountainous terrain that emerges from the Tibetan town of Yatung and connects the India–China–Bhutan border (the trijunction) and the 100-kilometer-long Siliguri corridor leading into Bangladesh. Any attacking force that managed to penetrate the seventy kilometers of tough Indian terrain after making it through this valley would have a free run across the Siliguri plains.[14] The PLA's inability to dominate Indian positions on the mountain ridgelines overlooking the Chumbi Valley means that any

Chinese attempt to cut off the Siliguri corridor would be a risky one. Any advance would be covered by Indian fire from tactically superior positions overlooking the valley.

Tactically, therefore, the Chumbi Valley has the potential to become a killing ground for the PLA. This has been the operational conundrum facing PLA commanders for decades, and it led them to encroach onto the Dolam plateau and attempt to dominate the Jampheri Ridge south of Batang La Pass, marking the trijunction. The PLA's continued attempts to gain tactical advantage have been foiled by the Indian Army, which, along with a strong IAF deployment, is well positioned to deter the Chinese in the region. For ease of understanding, the events of 2017 are commonly referred to as the Doklam crisis, as the Bhutanese and Indians call the area around the Dolam plateau Doklam, while the Chinese call it Donglang.

In the summer of 2017 India's Thirty-Third Corps and the PLA had a face-off on the Dolam plateau in southwestern Bhutan that lasted for seventy-three days. It was a continuation of the periodic and worrisome encounters that had taken place across the LAC since India and China went to war in October 1962.[15] Much has been written about the crisis and its aftermath.[16] The Dolam plateau lies south of the highest point on the crest line (Merung La) and the mountain pass of Batang La. China's claim to the plateau rests on an agreement signed with Britain in 1910 that settled the Sikkim and Tibet boundary; Bhutan was not a signatory. It marked Mount Gyomochen as the point of the trijunction, but it was later confirmed cartographically that Merung La and not Mount Gyomochen was the highest point in the watershed. Therefore, India thought the trijunction should be at that point.[17]

Over the years, both India and China acknowledged that the Dolam plateau was disputed territory, even though maps showed it as part of Bhutan. The Chinese had been actively eyeing the area since 2007 and had constructed a track that facilitated regular visits to the plateau by PLA border patrols. They were always met by Indian patrols, which rebuffed the PLA after the usual arguments and symbolic pushing or shoving. They justified their actions based on the treaty of 2012, which clearly stated that the status quo could not be altered by any side unilaterally.

The Indian Army's Eastern Command was aware of China's desire to occupy Jampheri Ridge, and plans were in place to thwart any such misadventure. Therefore, in June 2017, when the Indian Army noticed seventeen pieces of heavy road construction equipment being moved toward the center of the Dolam plateau, it knew the PLA's goal was to occupy Jampheri Ridge. The objective was to build a road from the Dolam plateau to Jampheri Ridge, thus effectively claiming it as Chinese territory. This ridge would afford the PLA good visibility over the Chumbi Valley and parts of the Sili-

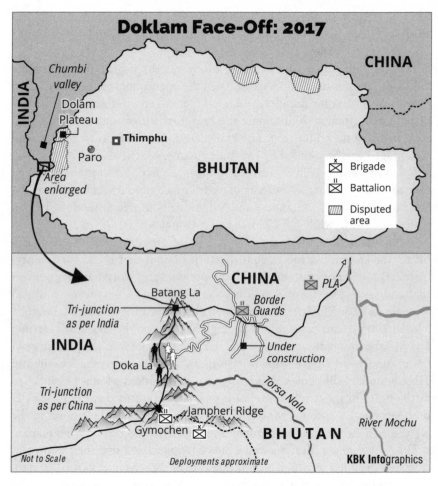

Map 21. The Doklam Crisis

guri corridor. Since this move had been anticipated by the Indian Army, it responded quickly.

CRANKING A RESPONSE

Lieutenant General Praveen Bakshi, the Eastern Army commander at the time, understood Chinese articulation and posturing in the area. Chinese general Zhao Zongqui had visited Kolkata in December 2016 to meet with Bakshi. There had been much bonhomie, but also an element of sizing each other up. Both commanders affirmed their adherence to the BDCA but also expressed concerns about the other's moves in their respective areas of interest. A large PLA delegation visited Kolkata in February 2017.[18] Soon thereafter, field commanders started to report a significant increase in patrolling and face-offs in Sikkim—especially in the hitherto relatively quiet northern plateau of Sikkim, eastern Arunachal Pradesh, and western Kameng.

Bakshi suggests that there was an emerging mind-set within the Indian strategic and intelligence communities that the Daulat Beg Oldi and Depsang areas in eastern Ladakh and Chumar were more important to the Chinese due to their proximity to the China–Pakistan economic corridor. They assumed that the Chinese now wanted to use Arunachal Pradesh only as strategic leverage. The first signs of Chinese intent emerged toward the end of May 2017, when the PLA asked the Indian Army to demolish two old unoccupied bunkers on the Indian side of the border near the Dolam plateau. The Indians did not comply. The PLA waited a week and then demolished one bunker on 8 June, warning that it would destroy the second one too. On the morning of 16 June Bakshi got a call from the commander of Thirty-Third Corps, Lieutenant General Sanjay Jha, alerting him that a PLA column was heading toward the Dolam plateau with heavy road construction equipment. Following standard practice, Bakshi reported the matter to the army chief.

Bakshi initiated standard protocols to obtain permission from Indian Army HQ to intervene and prevent the PLA from laying a road toward Jampheri Ridge, as this would have adverse operational implications for India. He received a call in the evening from New Delhi, telling him, "You are free to act as deemed appropriate." Bakshi immediately directed Jha to stop the PLA from building the road, even if this involved crossing the India–Bhutan border. Operational parameters were laid down, while giving full freedom to the troops and formations in contact to execute the task at hand. Defending that stretch of the LAC was a brigade commanded by Brigadier Gambhir Singh. Gambhir's men crossed the border immediately and ordered the PLA troops to halt all construction activity. He set up a continuous blocking position on the plateau in front of the construction equipment, rotating his troops to ensure that they remained fresh and would not crack under pressure. Initially, Gambhir assigned 250 men to this position, but soon this number increased to 450. The men were replaced every two hours because of weather conditions. The Indian troops were fully acclimatized, which greatly facilitated the task. In the meantime, Bakshi had ordered a media ban.

On 26 June 2017 the Chinese Foreign and Defense Ministries issued a press release stating that India had invaded China's territory. Beijing's anti-India newspaper *Global Times* made not-so-veiled threats to India to back off.[19] The Chinese followed up by suspending the Mansarover Yatra, a traditional Hindu pilgrimage to a sacred lake in Tibet, and moving troops closer to the Bhutan border from Yatung, a division HQ. However, they were outnumbered throughout the standoff. By early July, diplomatic efforts kicked in, and a gradual downsizing of troops on the Dolam plateau took place. China initially demanded an Indian withdrawal, but India refused. Finally, after much negotiation, both sides simultaneously withdrew to their previous positions.

There has been some criticism from strategic commentators, including Lieutenant General Prakash Menon, that India has not contested the PLA's ongoing construction of tracks leading to Jampheri Ridge from farther east. Menon argues that by staying quiet about this continued buildup, India runs the risk of a swift PLA move toward Jampheri Ridge should the Chinese plan another incursion.[20] Bakshi responded by pointing out that the topography favors India, as all tracks currently being built by the PLA must traverse down to the Torsa Nala (a small rivulet) or go around it and then wind up to Jampheri Ridge, making it tactically unsound to assault the ridge from that direction. Many officers who have served in the area concur with this assessment. Therefore, there is little chance of the PLA occupying Jampheri Ridge.

In Bakshi's opinion, there has been too much hype around the Doklam incident, as well as the forward stationing of PLA troops in certain areas along the LAC. He dismisses it as window dressing because of the tremendous tactical advantage enjoyed by Indian troops in this area. In fact, he sees the PLA's forward deployment as a tacit admission by the Chinese of their vulnerability, given India's growing military capabilities. Even so, he believes it is time for India to ramp up the use of technology and limited mechanized warfare assets—such as light tanks and infantry combat vehicles that can be easily deployed at high altitudes—along with unmanned aerial vehicles, airpower, and strategic road building.

The demarche Bhutan issued to China in July 2018 to restore the status quo and stop building roads immediately gave the initiative to India and allowed it to occupy the moral high ground.[21] Citing Chinese ambiguity, Bakshi argues that this may well have been a misadventure by a local military commander who did not expect a strong military response from India. This view is contested by several military analysts, who note Xi's viselike grip on the PLA. However, the assessment after the face-off commenced was that it was toned down after seeing the Indian reaction.[22] Reconciliatory talks between Modi and Xi at Wuhan have been criticized by some as a case of backing down, as the military response was not followed by robust deterrence. However, the episode clearly reveals that neither India nor China is ready to change the nature of deterrence along the LAC. Both nations are more concerned about the possibility of peace and tranquility being shattered inadvertently by troops in contact—something that must be avoided at all costs.[23] It is India's turn to "bide its time," as Deng advised China to do in the 1980s.[24]

NO WAR, NO PEACE

The "Army Tour" allows groups from the national security program conducted by the National Defence College to visit operational areas. These include a corps zone near the LAC, the line of control, and the border with Pakistan in the Punjab, Rajasthan, and Kutchh Sectors. The purpose of the trip is to give the one hundred participants, including twenty-five from friendly foreign countries, an opportunity to witness the Indian Army's continuing large-scale deployment along India's stressed borders and frontiers. The trip also showcases the role of the IAF and provides insight into why India's armed forces are always on a high state of operational readiness. On such trips, it is easy to understand the prevailing situation of "no war, no peace" that prevails in J&K and the northeastern states of Sikkim, Arunachal Pradesh, Nagaland, and Manipur.

Dimapur—a bustling and crowded frontier town at the Nagaland–Assam border—serves as the HQ of Third Corps, the Indian Army's largest. Its area of responsibility includes much of lower Assam, some parts of northern Assam, two-thirds of the state of Arunachal Pradesh, the "hot" states of Nagaland and Manipur, and the peaceful states of Mizoram and Tripura. The corps has multiple responsibilities, but in recent years its most important has been ensuring deterrence along the LAC with China. It must also deal with insurgencies, which involve ethnic and tribal complexities ranging from the still-festering Naga problem to the violent Manipuri internecine conflict to the residual embers of the Assamese dissent. Last, the corps must maintain vigilance along the international borders, even with friendly countries such as Myanmar and Bangladesh, owing to the challenges of illegal immigration, human trafficking, and drug running, among others.

Located at the northeastern edge of Third Corps' zone is the Lohit Valley, which lies close to the junction of India, China, and Myanmar. The Tsangpo River in southern Tibet takes a sharp turn southward and becomes the Brahmaputra in northeastern Assam at the mouth of the Lohit Valley. The Lohit River is the easternmost of the Brahmaputra's tributaries, and it flows down from the watershed between India and China. It is close to Parashuram Kund, a holy spot where warrior-ascetic Parashuram performed penance in search of military prowess. North of the Lohit Valley is an area patrolled by a brigade belonging to Second Infantry Division. Located here are the border outposts of Walong and Kibithoo, which saw fierce fighting during the 1962 war. The Battle of Walong remains one of the few bright spots for India in the otherwise dismal story of 1962. It is the sector where the Sikh and Kumaon Regiments, supported by IAF Otters and Mi-4s, launched counterattacks on the advancing Chinese. After suffering heavy casualties, the Chinese radioed their headquarters that they had entered the "tiger's lair."[25]

From the northern part of the valley, one can clearly see the built-up Chinese areas through a gap in the ridgeline. The battalion commander from the Sikh Light Infantry who briefed the National Defence College group was confident and aware of his responsibilities in the sector. He was clear that 1962 would not be repeated and that, should he be forced to fight a defensive battle, he would do so from advantageously located and well-stocked positions that had fire support. "I know how to fight my battle, and I will not wait for directions from brigade," he said.

Transport aircraft and helicopters are important for sustaining operations in the region, as a convoy from the closest major railhead of Tinsukia or the airport at Dibrugarh would take at least three days to reach Kibithoo in good weather and a week in inclement weather. There are two IAF Mi-17 squadrons at Mohanbari to serve the Lohit Valley. For larger loads, the brand-new advance landing ground at Walong can now receive the C-17 heavy-lift aircraft. There are seven advance landing grounds in Arunachal Pradesh—Mechuka, Tuting, and Walong constitute the forward tier, while Itanagar, Ziro, Pasighat, and Vijaynagar form the rear chain of connectivity to Myanmar and the adjoining states.[26]

The 132nd Helicopter Unit at Air Force Station Chabua is a busy one. Whenever there is clear weather in the Lohit Valley, helicopters are packed with multiple loads—rations, barrels of K-oil, a rare bag of mail, and much more. According to the unit's flight commander, the Lohit Valley is one of the broader valleys, and it is quite an experience to see the pristine beauty of the pine forests and green grazing grounds overlooking the gushing torrent of the Lohit River as one flies into Kibithoo. Once the commander at Kibithoo completed his briefing on a sand model overlooking the LAC, a wreath was laid at the war memorial. Then, after grabbing a handful of *Shakarpara* (an indigenous energy snack that Indian soldiers love) and a glass of steaming *chai*, it was time to heed the urgent request of the captain of the Mi-17, who was anxiously looking at the dark rain clouds approaching.

As the group boarded the helicopter, an earnest-looking young Sikh soldier joined them. Shyly grinning, he sprang to attention and sought permission to get a lift to his hometown in Punjab in time for his wedding. He would be there two days ahead of schedule, he said, and wanted to surprise his fiancée. Such are the daily tales from the east. The enduring image as the Mi-17's rotor blades picked up speed was a group of officers, led by their commander, waving as if to say, "Tell them about us, and more importantly, tell them not to worry!"

STANDING FIRM

Deterrence by denial accompanied by diplomacy has long been the Indian response to China-related national security challenges. However, there have been some expressions of proactivity from India, such as at Nathu La, Sumdorong Chu, Depsang, and Doklam. Since 1993, deterring China has been a work in progress. However, fear is no longer the primary driver of strategy. A deeper analysis of some of India's decisions vis-à-vis China reveals an apprehension of the consequences, which is exactly what China seeks.[27] It also forces India to revisit some of its strategic aspirations and alter its decision-making process rather frequently. This does not reflect India's growing power, and it must realize that Doklam-style incursions are low-cost Chinese strategies to coerce adversaries by staying below the threshold of deterrence by punishment.

Deterrence by denial must include a clear communication of India's core security concerns and a statement that disruption of the mutually accepted peace and tranquility along the LAC will exact a mutual cost unless a comprehensive political settlement is reached. More important, India's neighborhood policy is the key to limiting Chinese influence in South Asia through robust economic and military engagement. Concurrently, India must continue to enhance its strategy of deterrence by deepening the security dimension of its relationship with partners such as Vietnam, Japan, the United States, France, and Australia. The last few decades have seen some convergence between diplomacy and hard power within India's strategic establishment, and one hopes that this will continue.

Ambiguity may have been the hallmark of Chinese strategy in the Deng Xiaoping and Hu Jintao eras, but contemporary Chinese strategy is not just about Sun Tzu, Wei Chi, or Confucius. Xi Jinping has shown that China has learned from Russia and the West and is ready to take on the world in an overtly aggressive manner. India needs to demonstrate a consistent and robust policy of deterrence by denial, acquire dissuasive capabilities of various kinds, and practice sophisticated diplomacy in its relationship with China. Given the adversarial and competitive profile of the India–China relationship, it is remarkable that despite the huge military buildup on both sides, not a shot has been fired across the LAC since 1967.

The Indian Army has almost five divisions deployed across the LAC in the Eastern Sector, as the superb Chinese infrastructure on the Tibetan plateau allows the PLA to speedily deploy reinforcements in the event of conflict. In Ladakh, however, it has only recently beefed up its deployment on the LAC to almost an entire division, including an armored brigade.[28] The IAF enjoys a significant advantage over the PLA Air Force when it comes to the number of bases, quality of platforms, and aerial capabilities around Tibet, but the overwhelming superiority of the PLA Rocket Forces has the potential to neutralize this advantage in a first strike against IAF bases using a variety of surface-to-surface missiles. This vulnerability could prove decisive during the early stages of any future limited conflict.[29] The establishment of a mountain strike corps to launch offensives into the region has been put on hold by the Modi government. Instead, it has proposed the formation of leaner integrated battle groups from internal resources.

Both sides have engaged in posturing and periodic incursions, testing the other's patience. According to unofficial Indian figures for 2013, Chinese troops violated the LAC on more than 200 occasions, while the Chinese claim a similar number of Indian incursions. Most of these were unreported. A recent report from the Observer Research Foundation mentions only thirty reported incidents of incursions and face-offs from 2003 to 2014.[30] The absence of firefights means that these incursions remain on the periphery of the national consciousness in both countries. While such face-offs have led to hectic diplomatic parleys and subsequent de-escalation, a few have involved protracted physical jostling that kept local commanders on tenterhooks. Ensuring that these incursions do not lead to firefights requires great restraint and professionalism on both sides.

RESOLUTION?

L. M. H. Ling is a professor of international affairs at the New School in New York City and offers an interesting perspective on the mood swings that afflict the security dimension of the India–China relationship. She identifies four cyclical phases of the relationship: "dangerous mood swings, stunted growth, alienation and systemic neurosis."[31] Citing a line of treatment that may seem strange to military minds, she draws on the ancient Indian and Chinese therapies of *Ayurveda* and *Zhongyi* to suggest that a systemic transformation of the relationship through balance has immense potential to reduce the trust deficit.[32] She argues that India and China need to evaluate their respective outlooks and move away from their inflexible and egoistic positions on the border dispute.

For India, a bipartisan political consensus is needed to revisit the parliamentary resolution on regaining all lost territories. China needs to negotiate with India based on clear cartographic templates and revive some of the quid pro quo proposals floated by Chou En-lai and Deng Xiaoping, such as formalizing a swap whereby India recognizes Aksai Chin as an integral part of Tibet in exchange for China's acceptance of Arunachal Pradesh as an integral part of the Indian Union. Any deal would also have to stabilize the China–Bhutan boundary situation so that it does not pose a security threat to India. Once this is achieved, the demarcation, delineation, and ratification of all disputed enclaves in all sectors can be accomplished through a mutual spirit of give-and-take. China last showed geopolitical sagacity in 1960, when it formally delineated its boundary with Myanmar. It needs to do the same if it is serious about demilitarizing 4,000 kilometers of its shared boundaries with India and Bhutan.

In 2003 an unambiguously worded media release from the Ministry of External Affairs put the entire boundary question in perspective, stating that the 1962 Parliament resolution on regaining every square inch of "lost" territory from China was no longer relevant. The statement went on to say: "Parliaments are sovereign bodies and reflect the political sense of the times, rather than a mere commitment to past resolutions. Any final settlement of the boundary dispute with China will have to be based on a broad agreement within the Indian political class. As negotiations move forward, the cries of 'sell-out' will be heard with greater vehemence than ever before." However, it acknowledges that "persuading the Indian public to accept a recasting of the Indian territorial map that many generations have grown up with is not going to be easy" and warns that "while the new Chinese leadership appears amenable to a productive political dialogue, India should be fully prepared for the unexpected."[33] Whether a post–COVID-19 world will offer some hope for a negotiated settlement is something that needs to be carefully considered by both countries.

20

India's Nuclear Conundrum

> We aim to have enough to strike back.
> —Brajesh Mishra, India's national security adviser, quoted in Vipin Narang,
> *Nuclear Strategy in the Modern Era*

Military historians during the post–World War II era have generally stayed away from nuclear issues, as nuclear strategy emerged as the focus of the new genre of strategic studies. Nuclear war was the possible nightmarish consequence of a breakdown of deterrence during the Cold War. Consequently, several theories of international relations developed, and political scientists and strategic studies experts wrote extensively about nuclear dynamics over the past five decades. Though India has always claimed that its nuclear weapons program aimed to deter China, Pakistan's concurrent and clandestine development of nuclear weapons to deter India contributed in no small measure to the continued geopolitical instability in South Asia. This instability attracted the attention of the United States, which saw (and still sees) itself as an interlocutor in ensuring that the long-standing dispute over Kashmir did not boil over into a nuclear conflict.

There is much robust writing on India's nuclear journey from strategic scholars, particularly in the United States and India, and this brief examination of India's quest to become a responsible nuclear weapons state draws heavily from a cross section of them.[1] Over the years, the Indian armed forces have been minority stakeholders in the development of India's nuclear weapons and the associated draft nuclear doctrine. The emergence of a parallel strategic enclave in the 1950s and 1960s dominated by civilian scientists and strongly supported by successive governments in New Delhi indicated a clear line of thinking that a nuclear weapon, if developed, would be a political weapon.[2] A glimpse into India's journey will help Western readers understand its rise as a leading power through a wide-angle lens that goes beyond traditional military history.

THE PEACEFUL NUCLEAR EXPLOSION

India's interest in harnessing nuclear energy for peaceful purposes commenced in the 1950s with the setting up of the Atomic Energy Commission and the commissioning of India's first nuclear reactor, Apsara, with help from the United Kingdom. It was, however, the Chinese nuclear test in 1964 that propelled India on the path to a "peaceful nuclear explosion," a process considered to be the first step toward developing nuclear weapons.

The death of Prime Minister Jawaharlal Nehru in 1964, the India–Pakistan war of 1965, political instability between 1966 and 1970, and the 1971 India–Pakistan war left this aspiration in cold storage for almost a decade. Prime Minister Indira Gandhi emerged as the prima donna on the Indian political scene after the 1971 war, and she gave the go-ahead for the peaceful nuclear explosion only when challenged by a political opposition that was gathering strength. In the interim, India emerged as a staunch opponent of the Non-Proliferation Treaty, refusing to sign it in 1968. The treaty was finally signed by 46 countries in 1970, and since then, it has been adopted by 190 states.[3] Among those countries that have either not signed the treaty or withdrawn from it are India, Israel, Iran, and Pakistan, all of which aspired to develop nuclear weapons.

India's underground nuclear test, code-named Smiling Buddha, was conducted at Pokharan in the Rajasthan Desert on 18 May 1974. Postexplosion briefings indicated that it had an explosive yield of twelve to fifteen kilotons, on a par with the weapon dropped over Hiroshima. Subsequent interviews with Indian nuclear scientists and Western analysis put the figure slightly lower. The decision to conduct the nuclear test was made in great secrecy, with only the prime minister and top civilian scientists from the strategic enclave in the know. George Perkovich pithily describes the broader objectives of the nuclear test, also called Pokharan-I: "Thus, the decision seemed based on intuition, bureaucratic and technological momentum, and the personal, enigmatic calculations of a beleaguered prime minister under the influence of trusted nuclear scientists. It was to be a marker of standing and power for a nation with high aspirations suffering diminishing respect."[4]

Over the next five years, India's peaceful nuclear explosion was not accompanied by an articulated doctrinal road map or a demonstrated ability to convert to nuclear weapons. Political instability, continued sanctions, and the absence of a bipartisan consensus on the necessity of possessing a nuclear arsenal were among the reasons for this inertia. Perkovich notes that American diplomacy (and coercion in the form of sanctions) contributed significantly to India's restraint.[5] Pakistan's accelerated progress toward nuclear tests in the late 1970s, US sanctions following the hanging of Zulfiqar Ali Bhutto in 1979, and growing talk of an "Islamic bomb" forced India to refocus on its nuclear weapons program. After Pakistan carried out its first subcritical tests in 1983, an alarmed Prime Minister Indira Gandhi explored multiple options to either neutralize Pakistan's emerging nuclear threat or accelerate

India's nuclear weapons program. Unfortunately, her assassination in 1984 delayed India's program, despite support emanating from India's strategic establishment. K. Subrahmanyam, a bureaucrat with exceptional intellect, and General K. Sundarji, the cerebral army chief, emerged as fresh voices that talked and wrote about nuclear strategy and doctrine.

UPPING THE ANTE

China's active assistance to Pakistan's nuclear weapons program in the 1980s jolted India into action. During his tenure as commandant at the Indian Army's College of Combat, Sundarji was among the first senior military officers to write about nuclear war fighting.[6] He took this thought process to New Delhi when he became chief of army staff in 1986. Meanwhile, Subrahmanyam sensitized policy makers about the need to frame a policy for the use of nuclear weapons before India's nuclear arsenal became operational. His four preliminary imperatives still lie at the heart of India's nuclear doctrine: no first use (NFU), credible minimum deterrence, civilian control, and commitment to disarmament.[7]

At the height of Exercise Brasstacks in 1987, tensions ran high between India and Pakistan, and the latter threatened to use nuclear weapons for the first time, albeit in an oblique manner. In an interview with Indian journalist Kuldip Nayyar, Dr. A. Q. Khan, revered in Pakistan as the father of the Islamic bomb, threatened to drop a nuclear bomb should India try to start a war with Pakistan. Several US think tanks and scholars assess that this led to a crisis and "accelerated the nuclear programs of both states."[8]

New Delhi was alarmed by Pakistan's nuclear saber rattling, and Pakistan's likely possession of nuclear weapons allowed it to expand the low-cost proxy war in Jammu and Kashmir (J&K). Several Western analysts term this the "crisis of 1990."[9] Subrahmanyam, however, calls it a "noncrisis" and notes that journalists such as Seymour Hersh and academics such as George Perkovich read too much into the mid-1990 visit to Islamabad by Robert Gates, the US deputy national security adviser. Absent any visit to India or discussion with Indian leaders, Subrahmanyam finds it hard to buy Washington's story that India and Pakistan were going to war in 1990. Both India and Pakistan may have made plans to strike each other's nuclear facilities. Pakistan had not demobilized after Exercise Zarb-e-Momin, its response to Brasstacks, and India had moved large formations into J&K to tackle the expanding covert war. To the West, this appeared to be precise preparations for war. Still, in the India–Pakistan context, it was posturing of different kinds, triggered by Pakistan's overt display of nuclear prowess.

PRESSING THE TRIGGER

Before being ousted from power in 1989, Prime Minister Rajiv Gandhi had given shape and direction to India's nuclear weapons program. His nuclear weapons committee, made up of the "strategic enclave" and trusted confidants, was capable of cobbling together a few low-yield weapons and their delivery systems. Prime Minister Narasimha Rao had closely monitored and supported the nuclear weapons program through the years as a senior member of Rajiv Gandhi's cabinet, and in late 1995 he gave the go-ahead for a series of nuclear tests that would herald India's formal entry into the nuclear weapons club. US satellites picked up unusual activity around the proposed test site, and a concerned President Bill Clinton convinced Rao to call off the tests just a few days before the planned date. Caught between US arm-twisting and the advice of his scientific advisers, which included V. S. Arunachalam, A. P. J. Abdul Kalam, R. Chidambaram, and P. K. Iyengar, Rao postponed the tests. Twice in the following year (1996), Rao came close to testing but balked in the face of relentless US pressure and other domestic compulsions.[10]

Rao's successors in a short-lived coalition government, I. K. Gujral and H. D. Devegowda, were unmitigated disasters. However, the strategic enclave comprising the Atomic Energy Commission, the Defence Research and Development Organisation, and the Indian Space Research Organization maintained the momentum of the nuclear weapons program. Atal Behari Vajpayee, leader of the right-wing Bharatiya Janata Party and prime minister of India from 1998 to 2003, was a strong advocate and supporter of India's nuclear weapons aspirations throughout his long political career. Barely two months after he was elected prime minister, India conducted five weapons-grade nuclear tests between 11 and 13 May 1998. Code-named Operation Shakti (power), these tests involved a high-yield thermonuclear device, a medium-yield fission device, and three subkiloton devices.[11]

Indian analysts, including Subrahmanyam, claimed that Pakistan had acquired the capability to develop six to twelve low-yield nuclear weapons with active assistance from China and North Korea between 1987 and 1990. Pakistan chose to couch this development in a shroud of secrecy and ambiguity, for fear of being labeled a "rogue" nuclear state by the West. Therefore, it is not surprising that two weeks after India openly declared its nuclear ambitions, Pakistan followed suit with a series of tests in late May. The gloves were finally off. From a US perspective, as the nuclear watchdog in the region, it had a serious problem on its hands.

A combination of triggers could have led to the 1998 tests. India's nuclear and civilian-scientist strategic enclave had been working assiduously to match India's nuclear weapon with likely warheads and delivery systems since the mid-1980s. India's delivery platforms expanded from fighter-bombers such as the Jaguar and Mirage that could carry a rudimentary low-yield bomb to the short-range and road-mobile Prithvi short-range ballistic missile (SRBM) and the Agni-II intermediate-range ballistic missile (IRBM). The former had a range of 150 kilometers and was inducted into the Indian Army in 1994, and the latter was successfully launched in April 1999. However, A. P. J. Abdul Kalam, director of the Integrated Guided Missile Project and future president of the Republic of India, assured Prime Minister Vajpayee in 1998 that India would soon possess an IRBM that could carry a thermonuclear weapon. From a threat perspective, the successful test of the Ghauri IRBM with a range of 700 to 1,000 kilometers on 6 April 1998 meant that Pakistan had overtaken India in the race for delivery platforms. India had to test if it hoped to catch up.

THE UNITED STATES REACTS

Having successfully stalled India's nuclear program for three years, the Clinton administration was surprised by the Indian tests. There was a complete intelligence blackout, and the Indians managed to evade the prying eyes of US satellites.[12] The strategic rapprochement between India and the United States initiated by President George H. W. Bush in 1991 and taken forward by President Clinton came to a grinding halt. Imposing a slew of sanctions on India, the Clinton administration came down hard on Pakistan as well. However, with the nuclear genie out of the bottle, the best it could hope to do was maintain stability in South Asia. American authors tend to assign too much importance to the US role in ensuring nuclear security in the subcontinent, but the United States remained actively engaged in the decades after 1998. Writing dramatically in his book *Avoiding Armageddon*, Bruce Riedel declares, "From 1990 to 2000 India and Pakistan lurched from crisis to crisis, fighting one small war (Kargil) and almost going to war several times. In each crisis, Washington would be a key player, keeping the worst—nuclear war in South Asia—from happening."[13]

During the Kargil Conflict, negotiations broke down during Pakistan foreign minister Sartaj Aziz's visit to New Delhi in mid-June 1999, marking US entry as an interlocutor (see chapter 15). As the Indian Army and Air Force pounded the Northern Light Infantry positions into submission, worried State Department officials in Washington alerted President Clinton to the possibility of a nuclear showdown. They did so based on a general lack of knowledge regarding Pakistan's nuclear threshold rather than a careful examination of whether India had crossed any red lines or Pakistan had taken concrete steps toward the imminent use of nuclear weapons. Unfortunately, the Pakistan Army's Special Plans Division, which controlled Pakistan's nuclear forces and nuclear doctrine, had not yet clearly enunciated which red lines would prompt Pakistan to resort to nuclear war. It was this ambiguity that led the Americans to assume that if the Indians gained ground beyond a certain point, Pakistan might play the nuclear card, which it perceived as a "weapon of the weak" and not a "weapon of last resort."[14]

American analysts and writers often overplay the coercive impact of President Clinton's stern message to Pakistan prime minister Nawaz Sharif during the latter's quick visit to Washington in early July. While Musharaff denies the existence of a nuclear contingency plan should Kargil go awry, Jaswant Singh, the Indian foreign minister and principal liaison with Washington, reckoned that Pakistan had not yet fully operationalized its nuclear arsenal. Consequently, any movement of delivery platforms or other components allegedly picked up by US intelligence was mainly a smokescreen that India did not take seriously. In the final analysis, although Clinton's stern message to Sharif and the earlier visit to Islamabad by General Anthony Zinni, commander of US Central Command, had an impact on the withdrawal of Pakistani troops from Kargil, the Indians would have thrown them off anyway.

Kargil demonstrated the availability of a window for the conduct of conventional conflict in the escalatory matrix of the India–Pakistan adversarial relationship, but the United States continued to see South Asia as the second most combustible nuclear hot spot in the world, after the Korean peninsula. The United States was preoccupied with its global war on terror, and Operation Enduring Freedom, with Pakistan as a front-line ally, was in full swing. The crisis of 2001–2002 after the Lashkar-e-Taiba (LeT) suicide attack on India's Parliament was a most unwelcome event for the United States. Making matters more delicate was that President George W. Bush had initiated steps to establish a robust strategic partnership with India.

The crisis of 2001–2002 was the closest India and Pakistan have come to a nuclear exchange resulting from the failure of conventional deterrence or escalation control (see chapter 18 for a detailed examination of Operation Parakram). Testing of IRBMs by both sides and the launch of the Brahmos cruise missile by India complicated matters. The movement of tactical surface-to-surface missiles closer to the border by both countries and their incessantly provocative rhetoric convinced the international community that South Asia was a nuclear flashpoint.[15] US involvement and mediation in this crisis followed the same trajectory as earlier. This time around, though, the mediation process was effectively handled at a lower level and introduced confidence-building measures into the deterrence process.

Since 2003, the India–Pakistan nuclear conundrum has revolved around three themes. The first is the Pakistan Army's willingness to use tactical nuclear weapons to blunt the growing conventional asymmetry between the two armed forces and shrink the envelope for conventional conflict. The second is India's consistent nuclear doctrine, which eschews first use and has allowed it to emerge as a responsible nuclear weapons state. The third theme is the one that causes the greatest concern in the United States and, to a lesser extent, in India because the latter anticipated this turn of events in the 1990s after Pakistan's deep state intensified the proxy war in J&K. It revolves around the realization that Pakistan's nuclear posture, combined with the increasing radicalization of its army and society, sounds an ominous warning in Washington that a former ally is turning rogue. This development, as well as the close nuclear relationship Pakistan has forged with China, North Korea, and Iran, leaves the United States no option but to be worried.

SIMPLIFYING INDIA'S NUCLEAR DOCTRINE

India's draft nuclear doctrine was made public by the National Security Advisory Board in August 1999, just a year after India's nuclear tests in May 1998. In its original form, the document was as explicit as it could be, considering that India's strategic establishment was treading new ground. India's posturing was consistent with its original thinking (after the 1974 nuclear test) insofar as focusing its nuclear weapons program on developing minimum credible nuclear deterrence vis-à-vis China and not Pakistan. Merely an aspirational articulation of India's nuclear ambitions, the draft received some criticism for its lack of widespread political backing and the absence of a follow-up document that made it official government policy.[16] Ashley Tellis reckons that the evolution of India's nuclear posture over the years included several alternatives, ranging from "renouncing the nuclear option" to possessing a "ready arsenal." Along the way, it explored options for "limited arms control," "no operational nuclear forces," and the possibility of an "operational nuclear force in months."[17] Between 1974 and 1987, while the civilian-scientists leading the strategic enclave advocated the speedy weaponization of India's nuclear capability, the prevailing political, economic, regional, and internal security dynamics prevented this from happening.

However, the emerging strategic discourse in India led by Subrahmanyam and Sundarji in the operational backdrop of Exercise Brasstacks resulted in provocative statements from Pakistan about its nuclear aspirations. India had no option but to seriously contemplate acquiring nuclear weapons. Thus, from 1987 to 1998, it can be extrapolated that India concurrently postured its abhorrence for nuclear weapons on the global stage while quietly pursuing whatever steps were necessary to build a recessed nuclear deterrent.[18] Writing in the *Times of India* in June 1988, Subrahmanyam alerted the world to the transfer of Chinese IRBMs (CSS-2 missiles) to Pakistan and the possibility (though unconfirmed) that Pakistan had already tested a nuclear weapon.[19] Adding to India's concern was the reported basing of Chinese medium-range missiles and IRBMs in Tibet.[20] The 1998 tests and the testing of the Agni-II the following year were part of this strategy. From then on, India's nuclear posture has steadily grown, and since 2003 it has had its own Strategic Forces Command. It has stable nuclear command authority and an arsenal comprising a nuclear delivery triad (air, surface, and subsurface) with suitable warheads and command-and-control systems.

According to Subrahmanyam, two fundamental principles guided India's nuclear doctrine: "India will not be discriminated against and treated as a nation with lesser privileges than some others. The second is that while India favors total elimination of nuclear weapons and missiles, its security warrants developing technological capabilities and keeping options open."[21] Speaking at the release of India's draft nuclear doctrine on 17 August 1999, Brajesh Mishra, India's national security adviser, offered some clarity. He indicated that the doctrine was "aimed at providing us the autonomy of exercising strategic choices in the best interests of our country without fear or coercion in a nuclearized environment." Minimum but credible deterrence was the watchword of India's nuclear doctrine. Its other cardinal principles were NFU, unconditional guarantees to states that do not have nuclear weapons, and complete civilian control under the overarching Indian policy of restraint and responsibility.[22]

This chapter does not discuss the fine print of India's draft nuclear doctrine, but two doctrinal shifts over the last few years are worth mentioning: the change from "assured retaliation" to "assured massive retaliation," which emerged in 2003, and the recently suggested ambiguity of India's NFU doctrine. Defense Minister Manohar Parrikar recommended in November 2016 that NFU should not be explicitly stated in the doctrine and that India must have the flexibility to choose its response.[23] Though his comments were later described as opinion, they reflect the feeling that NFU is not congruent with India's growing power potential. Vipin Narang, an associate professor at the Massachusetts Institute of Technology and the author of a definitive book titled *Nuclear Strategy in the Modern Era*, indicates that there is an emerging debate in India about its nuclear targeting philosophy and the ambiguity of NFU.[24]

Narang draws on pronouncements from a recent book by Shivshankar Menon, India's former national security adviser, to posit that India may be reconsidering its policy of NFU against other nuclear weapons states. Menon writes, "Circumstances are conceivable in which India might find it useful to strike first, for instance, against an NWS [nuclear weapons state] that had declared it would certainly use its weapons, and if India were certain that adversary's launch was imminent. But India's present public nuclear doctrine is silent on this scenario." On the targeting philosophy, Narang argues that there could be a shift from countervalue (meaning cities) to counterforce (nuclear assets). He offers this argument based on another clear articulation by Menon, who argues that should Pakistan open an exchange with tactical nuclear weapons against Indian forces that have crossed Pakistan's nuclear red lines, "India would hardly risk giving Pakistan the chance to carry out a massive nuclear strike after the Indian response to Pakistan using tactical nuclear weapons. In other words, Pakistan's tactical nuclear weapon use would effectively free India to undertake a comprehensive first strike against Pakistan." More explicitly, this would entail an Indian nuclear strike against Pakistan's nuclear assets and command-and-control structure. In the final analysis, Menon succinctly encapsulates India's nuclear posture as one that is strategically bold and tactically cautious.[25] When one adds ambiguity to that position, it reflects India's flexibility and willingness to explore new boundaries of deterrence in South Asia while continuing to stress its core tenets of nuclear restraint such as NFU.

ARSENALS AND ADVERSARIES

Nuclear warheads, delivery platforms, and command-and-control systems are the three essential components of a nuclear arsenal. When India conducted its first nuclear test in 1974, it possessed only a few crude nuclear bombs that could be delivered by Jaguar fighter-bombers and the Mirage-2000 aircraft. However, when the Integrated Guided Missile Project was created as a hybrid entity with expertise from the Indian Space Research Organisation and the Defence Research and Development Organisation, India's nuclear weapons program gathered some steam.

India's land-based delivery arsenal consists mainly of Prithvi SRBMs and Agni IRBMs. These were operationalized soon after the Pokharan-II tests in 1998. As of 2018, India's land-based delivery arsenal consisted of approximately twenty-four Prithvi-II launchers with a range of 350 kilometers; sixty Agni-I, -II, and -III IRBMs with ranges of 700 to 3,200 kilometers; and a small number of Agni-IV and -V launchers with ranges of 3,500 to 5,000 kilometers. Recent news reports indicate that the Agni-V is operational and can carry a 1,200-kilogram warhead and strike targets in the Chinese hinterland, making it a credible deterrent. The induction of the land-attack cruise missile Nirbhay, which has a range of 1,000 kilometers, is a significant addition to India's nuclear arsenal. The aerial delivery component comprises the Jaguar, the Mirage-2000, and the recently upgraded Su-30 MKI; the latter can launch the Brahmos cruise missile, which can possibly be modified to carry a nuclear warhead. Despite claims that entire squadrons of Jaguars and Mirages can carry nuclear bombs, it is more likely that only a few of these aircraft have been modified for the nuclear role. The successful induction of the Dhanush (a maritime variant of the Prithvi) ship-launched surface-to-surface missile and the operational mating of the K-15 Sagarika submarine-launched ballistic missile (with a range of 700 kilometers) with the indigenously designed and manufactured Arihant class of nuclear-propelled ballistic-missile submarine completes the nuclear triad. It also validates a second-strike capability with high chances of survivability.[26] INS *Arihant* conducted its first operational patrol in 2018, and the second in the class, INS *Arighat*, is ready for operational induction. Yogesh Joshi reckons that "unless India deploys an SSBN [nuclear-propelled ballistic-missile submarine] fleet carrying missiles of intercontinental range, its deterrent vis-à-vis China will lack credibility."[27] India is currently thought to possess approximately 150 warheads with yields varying from subkiloton to twelve and forty kilotons. The development of the Agni-VI, with launch ranges exceeding 6,000 kilometers, and the K-4 submarine-launched ballistic missile, with a range of 3,5000 kilometers, would finally cap India's nuclear arsenal in a post-COVID-19 world.[28] India's triservice Strategic Forces Command is the custodian of India's nuclear arsenal. At the same time, command and control rests with a civilian-controlled (apex political leadership plus selected scientists) National Command Authority.

China's nuclear posture emerged under the overhang of the dual nuclear threat posed by the United States and USSR. Its nuclear doctrine is based on NFU and minimum credible deterrence vis-à-vis the United States. Its force structure, therefore, is based on intercontinental ballistic missiles (ICBMs) to deter the United States and a modest number of SRBMs and IRBMs to counter any threat emerging from Taiwan and India. With almost 260 launchers of various kinds across the nuclear triad and 320 warheads with yields ranging from a few hundred to a few thousand kilotons, China's arsenal dwarfs India's nuclear forces.[29] However, the absence of any kind of nuclear posturing between the two countries lends some stability to the relationship. Barring the movement of People's Liberation Army Rocket Force launchers onto the Tibetan plateau, and with the presence of Indian launchers in areas where it is possible to strike a few Chinese targets in the hinterland, there is some confidence about the maintenance of stable nuclear deterrence.

Pakistan's nuclear force structure presents an immediate threat to India, considering the shroud of secrecy around its growth. Pakistan has violated all international norms of nonproliferation by engaging in dubious deals with China and North Korea. Its less-than-transparent collusive development of missile and warhead capability with China is accompanied by reasonably cogent strategizing by Pakistan's Special Plans Division. Pakistan's nuclear forces are on a par with India's in the short- and medium-range launcher categories, with a significant focus on tactical nuclear weapons. The impact of tactical nuclear weapons on the India–Pakistan nuclear conundrum is well analyzed by Frank O'Donnell and Debolina Ghoshal in their recent article in *Nonproliferation Review*.[30]

Pakistan's nuclear strategy and nuclear force structure seek to blunt India's growing advantage in conventional war-fighting capabilities and its fast-developing nuclear triad. The strategy aims to exploit India's NFU doctrine by initiating or threatening to launch a highly localized nuclear strike using tactical nuclear weapons should Indian forces cross any nuclear red lines following the commencement of a conventional conflict, be it limited or widespread. This strategy was articulated for the first time by General Khalid Kidwai, former chief of Pakistan's Special Plans Division, in the hope that Indian restraint and immediate international (meaning US) pressure would hold back the "assured and massive retaliation" at the heart of India's response mechanism. Regarded by several Indian strategic analysts as a "nuclear bluff," this statement nevertheless infused an element of circumspection and doubt in the minds of Indian security planners for a while. Once that doubt emerged, it limited the availability of a window to conduct conventional punitive operations following a "black swan" event, such as a Pakistan-sponsored terrorist attack similar to the Mumbai attacks. It took two decades for India to think through this strategy, even though the Kargil Conflict took place under a nuclear overhang. The Modi government, it seems, has solved this puzzle.

According to the Stockholm International Peace Research Institute, Pakistan possesses 150 to 160 nuclear warheads and an almost equal number of delivery platforms ranging from the Nasr and Ghaznavi SRBMs to the Ghauri and Shaheen classes of medium-range ballistic missiles, with ranges between 300 and 2,750 kilometers.[31] The latest family of Babur cruise missiles offers the potential for both land and sea-launched options. They were reverse-engineered from unexploded Tomahawk cruise missiles recovered in Afghanistan during Operation Enduring Freedom. Pakistan's entire arsenal of missiles has been reverse-engineered from a continuous flow of North Korean and Chinese designs over the years, from the North Korean Nodong missile to the Chinese M-9 and M-11 missiles of late 1980s vintage.[32] Its aerial delivery platforms consist primarily of F-16 fighter-bombers, and it is believed the JF-17 has now been modified to carry nuclear bombs to replace the aging Mirage-Vs. The nuclear situation in South Asia is delicate but not as alarming as Western analysts paint it. There is an element of ambiguity and unpredictability in Pakistan's nuclear posture, and there is also a hint of uncertainty whether nuclear weapons could fall into the hands of jihadis. However, the fact that the Pakistan Army controls these weapons offers some degree of stability, as long as the Special Plans Division continues to be a professionally run command-and-control authority. India, in contrast, is now seen by the world as a responsible quasiofficial nuclear weapons state after signing the 123 Agreement with the United States. This agreement ends the three-decades-long denial of technology to India and ends India's nuclear isolation. It also opens the door to civil nuclear cooperation between India and the rest of the world.[33] From a US perspective, the India–Pakistan nuclear conundrum will continue to interest analysts and generate much debate on nuclear policy, strategy, and force structures.

Afterword
The GAP Crisis

The face-off between India and China that commenced on 5 May 2020 in several areas of eastern Ladakh, including the Depsang Plains, the Galwan Valley, and across the northern and southern banks of the Pangang Tso Lake (called the Galwan and Pangang Tso crisis and referred to here as the GAP crisis), continues as both countries try to negotiate a face-saving settlement. The escalatory trajectory of this conflict, which involved more than 300 troops from both sides and resulted in violent clashes between Indian troops and People's Liberation Army (PLA) troops in the Galwan Valley on the night of 15 June, is a cause for serious concern. These clashes were preceded by several minor scuffles at several points along the line of actual control (LAC), the most prominent ones occurring at Pangang Tso on 5–6 May and at Naku La on 9 May. Until that time, the last firefight between India and China had taken place in November 1975, when a patrol of the Assam Rifles was ambushed by PLA border guards in the Tulung La Sector of Sikkim and four Indian troops were killed.[1] However, since the clashes at Nathu La and Chola in 1967, the two countries have never been closer to a major localized firefight than they are now. It is therefore appropriate to ponder the causes and consequences of the current face-off, which is more complex than any of those highlighted in chapter 19.

CHINA'S RATIONALE AND THE CONSEQUENCES OF ITS ACTIONS

Preliminary analyses point to China's growing irritation with the change in the configuration of the erstwhile state of Jammu and Kashmir (J&K), specifically, the creation of Ladakh as a separate union territory. Another trigger is thought to be the imminent completion of the Darbuk–Shyok–Daulat Beg Oldie road fifteen years after construction commenced. The road significantly adds to the defensive potential of the northern subsector in eastern Ladakh and reduces China's traditional operational advantage in that area. A third trigger could be a desire to get even with India for preempting Chinese attempts to creep forward at the India–China–Bhutan trijunction at Doklam in 2017. Given these perceived threatening moves by India, China—

which has historically been obsessed with stability on its periphery, to the point of paranoia—is now worried about the security of the segment of its ambitious Belt Road Initiative that runs close to the LAC in eastern Ladakh. Using this as sufficient justification to change the operational narrative in areas close to the LAC where it felt threatened, the PLA commenced its current operation. The Galwan Valley and the Gogra Post area of the Hot Springs Sector are two such areas that were given special attention by the Chinese during the most recent face-offs.

The PLA has also significantly increased its presence and fortifications in the disputed areas of the LAC, particularly along Pangang Tso Lake between finger 4 and finger 8 (clearly identifiable fingerlike protrusions into the lake that have been used as claim lines by both India and China). Speculative and uncorroborated transgressions by the PLA across China's own claim lines have been reported in the strategically important Depsang Plains, close to the Indian advance landing ground of Daulat Beg Oldie (DBO).[2] How one views these transgressions depends on how one views both countries' assessments of the undemarcated LAC and the status and ownership of the disputed areas where both sides have patrolled over the years but refrained from establishing a permanent presence.

The difference between previous and current disputes is that, by setting up camps and semipermanent structures close to or across its claim lines, the PLA has violated established border protocols and tried to change the status quo. By doing so, China has directly threatened the sanctity of the LAC and India's territorial sovereignty. This operational strategy has succeeded in both rattling and provoking the Indians, but not to the point of their accepting the change. Any action that results in skirmishes or a limited conflict is not favorable for Beijing, as it would lead to significant casualties and a loss of face for Xi Jinping. Western assessments of the crisis have been measured but critical of China for its disproportionate response and paranoia over the recent constitutional changes involving J&K. However, they have also been critical of India's response mechanisms and have pointed out the difficult challenge of restoring the status quo in a highly asymmetric operational environment.[3]

Both Indian and Chinese forces suffered grievous casualties after the Galwan encounter during the night of 15 June, which resembled a savage medieval fight with clubs, sticks, and metal rods rather than a twenty-first-century firefight with precision weapons. It is estimated that total casualties on both sides (killed and injured) could exceed one hundred, including two commanding officers, one from each side. Colonel Santosh Babu, commanding officer of the Sixteenth Battalion of the Bihar Regiment, led from the front as he tried to convince the PLA troops to dismantle an observation post on the Indian side of the LAC. When they refused, he ordered that the post be demolished. After Babu was ambushed and killed in action, the infuriated Bihari troops, assisted by soldiers from the Punjab Regiment and an artillery regiment, mounted a spirited revenge operation that lasted more than two hours and accounted for most of the deaths. The icy Galwan River proved to be unforgiving and deadly as several Indian and Chinese soldiers who were engaged in hand-to-hand combat tumbled off the steep ledges and into the freezing waters.[4]

The last time the PLA suffered large casualties was during the war against Vietnam in 1979. The Indian Army, in contrast, has suffered casualties in a variety of duels across the line of control and Saltoro Ridge, during Operation Pawan in Sri Lanka, and during counterinfiltration-counterterrorism operations in J&K and the northeast. This offers insight into each side's ability to absorb the psychological impact of battle casualties, and PLA commanders are surely considering this factor as they evaluate various options. While military commanders search for ways to initiate disengagement and de-escalation, the international community is hoping for a political settlement led by Prime Minister Modi and President Xi Jinping. At worst, India and China may be heading for a limited conflict in which the exchange ratios in every domain puncture the carefully devised Chinese narrative of military modernization. For the Indians, a limited conflict could derail the fragile economy and slow down India's attempt to attain status as a world power. Assessing the impact of the clashes, Brahma Chellaney—a professed China hawk and one of the few consistent critics of India's China policy, irrespective of the government in power—argues on Twitter that while the clashes at Pangang Tso and Nakula were a "draw," the outcome of the Galwan clash was a "humiliation for China."[5]

INDIA STRIKES BACK

Resisting strident calls from diverse domestic constituencies to respond immediately to PLA provocations, the Indian Army, supported by the Indian Air Force (IAF), steadily built up its forces over the next two months. In a deliberate, stealthy, and well-planned operation, the Indian Army moved to occupy several tactical heights on the northern and southern banks of Pangang Tso Lake on the night of 29–30 August. Executed by a mix of specialized units made up of Special Forces and well-acclimatized regular troops, the operation, code-named Snow Leopard, rattled the PLA and offered the Indians adequate maneuver space to negotiate disengagement and de-escalation. Apart from surprising the PLA, the action demonstrated that India was prepared to respond to Chinese aggression at a time and place of its own choosing.[6]

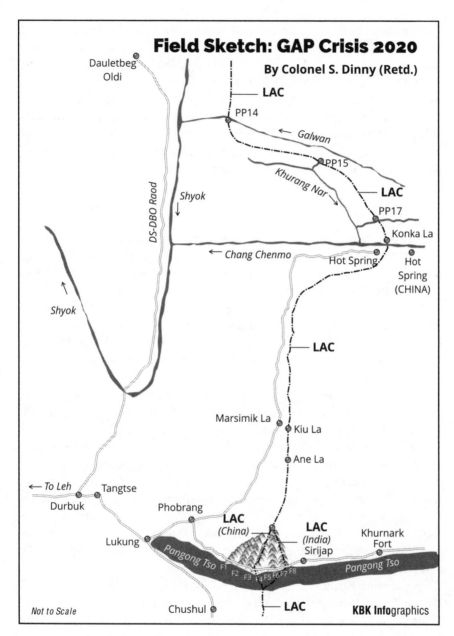

Field Sketch: GAP Crisis 2020

By Colonel S. Dinny (Retd.)

Dauletbeg Oldi

LAC

PP14

Galwan

Khurang Nar

PP15

LAC

Shyok

PP17

Konka La

Chang Chenmo

Hot Spring

Hot Spring (CHINA)

DS-DBO Raod

Shyok

LAC

Marsimik La

Kiu La

Ane La

To Leh

Tangtse

Durbuk

Phobrang

LAC (China)

LAC (India) Sirijap

Khurnark Fort

Lukung

Pangong Tso

F1

F2

F3 F4 F5 F6 F7 F8

Pangong Tso

Not to Scale

Chushul

LAC

KBK Infographics

Map 22. Field Sketch of the 2020 GAP Crisis

Flying activity by both the IAF and the PLA Air Force has increased, and reports indicate that the Hotan airfield in southern Xinjiang has seen the deployment of large numbers of J-7 and J-11 fighter aircraft, along with other supporting platforms.[7] Similarly, IAF operations in Ladakh have increased exponentially in an area that had been a no-go for several decades, owing to the ongoing confidence-building measures that restricted air activity on both sides. Fighters (newly inducted Rafales, Mirage-2000s, Su-30 MKIs, and MiG-29s) and helicopters (Apaches and Chinooks) have been undergoing complicated operational and acclimatization drills.

SPECULATION ABOUT THE PROSPECTS FOR PEACE

Despite several marathon meetings between senior military commanders and a joint statement announcing disengagement and de-escalation following a meeting between the foreign ministers of the two countries, the PLA has continued to build up its forces all the way to the northern extent of the LAC marked by the Depsang Plains, in the area around Daulat Beg Oldie. There may have been a few token withdrawals from several locations, according to Chinese Foreign Ministry spokesperson Wang Wenbin,[8] but it is quite likely that tens of thousands of troops with artillery and tanks have been left behind.

Though several strategic commentators have pointed out gaps in intelligence gathering and assessments prior to the crisis,[9] it is too early to evaluate these claims. Tara Kartha, a former director in the National Security Council secretariat, has mounted a spirited defense of the strategic and operational intelligence-gathering process.[10] It is quite evident that the Indians got their act together quickly, as Operation Snow Leopard was the result of excellent intelligence that alerted them to the movement of PLA units toward the heights the Indians eventually occupied. Whatever the facts are, these face-offs must be followed by serious introspection and a bolstering of the combined intelligence-gathering process along the LAC if the ghosts of 1962 and Kargil are not to appear again.

As the winter of 2020–2021 approaches, dilemmas abound for India's strategic establishment. The Indian military continues to demonstrate an ability to reassure its citizens that it is ready to meet any contingency imposed by the Chinese. This, however, is not likely to result in a return to the pre–May 2020 status quo unless India is prepared to show coercive intent. In other words, the smaller and weaker India must consider harder options, including the threat of force to convince the Chinese to return to pre-May dispositions. Options to consider include launching combined assaults on selected Chinese positions that seriously threaten Indian sovereignty, causing attrition with surprise and firepower, even though this runs the risk of escalation. However, it is unlikely that India will initiate a conflict unless the Chinese push further. For hawks, this means reversing India's attitude of diffidence and reactiveness, which it has been comfortable with for decades, with three exceptions: the Nathu La skirmish, the occupation of Saltoro Ridge, and the envelopment of PLA positions in the Sumdorong Chu Valley and the robust response at Doklam. Notwithstanding all its talk of economic posturing, India may not have the economic muscle or the diplomatic heft to reverse the negative fallout of the GAP crisis. War is always the last option, and a series of localized skirmishes along the LAC could be costly for both nations. However, the language of power and coercive posturing is the only strategic language the Chinese will take seriously.[11]

Two intellectual opinions expressed in the media necessitate some deep introspection within India's strategic community, particularly the politico-diplomatic and military-intelligence structures. The first is a recent piece in the *New York Times* that quotes Tian Feilong, a front-line Chinese scholar addressing primarily Western liberal constituencies: "Back when I was weak, I had to totally play by your rules. Now I am strong and I have the confidence, so why can't I lay down my own rules and values and ideas?"[12] Similar views have emerged over the past few years from a group of uncompromisingly antiliberal and pro-authoritarian Chinese intellectuals who have been called "statists." Essentially, Tian is invoking an old Thucydidean principle called the Melian dialogue that emerged during the Peloponnesian War prior to Athens' siege of the island of Melios: the strong will do what they can, and the weak will suffer what they must.

The second opinion comes from India's foreign minister, Dr. S. Jaishanker. During an interview with the *Times of India*, he argued, "Reaching an equilibrium with China is not going to be easy. We will be tested and we must stand our ground."[13] He also asserts that the state of the border and the future of bilateral ties cannot be separated. India may be slowly realizing the suboptimal outcomes that have accrued from its existing China policy. As the current crisis in Ladakh continues, India may finally be coming to grips with a possible fait accompli and the new status quo the Chinese are offering. Will it be a case of the Melian dialogue playing all over again, or is it time for India to emerge from its cocoon of postindependence diffidence?

STRATEGIC ISSUES

India's reluctance over the years to proactively use force against belligerent adversaries, despite having the means to do so, can be perplexing to some. It is easy to understand why India has been circumspect and wary of China, given the growing power differential, particularly on the Tibetan plateau and in the maritime domain. India's unwillingness to follow through with sustained punitive action in response to Pakistan's repeated provocations on multiple subconventional fronts has been frustrating. Several times in the troubled 1980s and 1990s and during the first decade of the twenty-first century, India's political establishment contemplated embarking on what Jonathan Renshon terms a "preventive war" against Pakistan.[14] It is believed that India considered preemptive aerial strikes against Pakistan's nuclear facilities in the early 1980s. It also contemplated large-scale attacks in multiple sectors to counter Pakistan's support for the proxy war in J&K in the late 1980s and early 1990s, as well as aerial strikes on Pakistani targets across the line of control during the Kargil Conflict. Offensives in J&K and massive armored attacks in the Desert Sector, accompanied by air strikes, were debated during Operation Parakram in the aftermath of the 2002 attack on Parliament.

In his book *Why Leaders Choose War*, Renshon—an American political scientist—suggests that among Britain, France, the United States, Israel, and India, only India does not subscribe to the idea of preventive war as a solution to actual or perceived security threats. This draws attention to the larger question of whether India has been diffident or wise when it comes to waging war in modern times. Renshon's list of preventive war factors broadly considers a declining power differential, sustained hostility and rigidity of thought that lead to conflict, and opportunities to engage in preventive military action.[15] He has mainly used the India–Pakistan template to prove his hypothesis and has identified India as a country that has not resorted to preventive military action, despite all supporting factors. However, between 1982 and 2002, India did in fact undertake two significant military actions that could be characterized as preventive limited military action. The first was the swift occupation of Saltoro Ridge in April 1984—which was both preventive and preemptive, as the Pakistanis were a few days away from doing so themselves. The second was the Indian Peacekeeping Force's intervention in Sri Lanka in 1987. Although the primary aim there was to broker peace between the Liberation Tigers of Tamil Eelam and the Sri Lankan government, Rajiv Gandhi and his strategic advisory team also perceived this as an opportunity to cement India's strategic position along its southern flank and prevent the entry of external players. Operation Pawan was an operational failure, but it did send a message to the rest of the world that India would not hesitate to engage in limited preventive military action to further its national interests. Operation Pawan infused an element of circumspection into India's strategic establishment in terms of the effectiveness of preemptive and preventive military action in a nuclear neighborhood—particularly against Pakistan, which was inclined to indulge in brinkmanship after the heady success of its Inter-Services Intelligence in Afghanistan.

Like several liberal democracies, India has struggled to cope with the changing character of war in the twenty-first century. It was slow to understand the complexities of hybrid warfare and its effectiveness when the situation in J&K remained volatile despite the overwhelming presence of the Indian Army. India has been more successful than many Western countries in combating radical and extremist Islam, but it has failed to capitalize on this success because of poor governance in border states such as J&K.

Do India's recent actions indicate a shift in deterrence and security strategies away from the propensity for restraint in the use of force over the last three decades? Has India's threshold for considering punitive action as a regular response to security provocations been lowered, particularly against Pakistan? Has India finally broken free from the shackles of the 1962 defeat at the hands of China and emerged as a power that is willing to contest Chinese hegemony in Asia? India's rise as a power of consequence has much to do with its economic and demographic potential. Its resolute, responsible, and restrained use of force as an instrument of statecraft has played an equally important role in this rise, despite periods of diffidence and excessive caution. Political probabilities and aims have generally determined military outcomes—such as the timing of the cessation of the Kargil Conflict or the Indian Peacekeeping Force's withdrawal from Sri Lanka. These decisions may not have gone down well with the military leadership, but they have generally been consistent with the rather cautious attitude of India's postcolonial political establishment toward the use of force.

Suboptimal civil-military relations and the lack of political interest in military strategy have resulted in a lack of congruence among policy, strategy, and doctrinal planners in the areas of national security and the study of war and conflict. The need for wide-ranging reform and remedial measures within the Indian military has often been articulated by Prime Minister Modi, but there has been a lack of political continuity in the Ministry of Defense to ensure a top-down approach to military reform. The appointment of Rajnath Singh, a senior confidant of the prime minister, as defense minister augurs well, provided there is continuity until 2024, when general elections are scheduled in India. The recent appointment of a chief of defense staff by the government and the impending restructuring of the military can only be a step in the right direction.

Recalibrating its relationships with its adversaries can help India define the extent to which it is willing to be pushed by them. India has demonstrated a growing willingness to move from reactive to proactive deterrence, but it is too early to assess whether it will be able to walk the talk, given the capability deficit that exists across the national security architecture. "Willing and capable" is a phrase that is commonly used in contemporary strategic debates. "Willing" implies intent, resolve, and a risk-taking propensity, while "capable" signifies the capacity to employ all elements of statecraft from a focused national security perspective to deter an irrational adversary. Is India emerging as a "willing and capable" state with respect to security challenges?

The disruptive impact of the COVID-19 pandemic is likely to impede efforts to build India's military capability over the next five years, and the maxim "do more with less" may well be the clarion call from the prime minister. While there may be fewer instances of traditional conflict in the next few years, the Indian military will have to find the ways and means to wield the traditional sharp end of the sword whenever called on to do so. Concurrently, it will need to build intellectual capital, evolve strategies, and train its forces to cope with the new ways of war. Domains as diverse as space, cyberspace, social media, internal security, and military diplomacy will no longer be considered peripheral. India's military must remain a critical instrument of statecraft as the nation continues its march toward becoming a world power.

It was difficult to strike a balance between seeking the truth and telling a credible story within the parameters of the Official Secrets Act. Some will argue that there is far too much advocacy in this book. However, I hope this advocacy has been accompanied by the right amount of introspection, respect, transparency, and criticism, making for a balanced piece of work. If you have come this far, thank you for reading about and understanding India's armed forces. If this book succeeds in reaching a wide readership, I will consider it mission accomplished.

Appendix
Serving and Retired Officers Formally Interviewed, Informally Spoken to, or Corresponded With

Brigadier Xerxes Adrianwalla
Commander Vinayak Agashe
Air Vice Marshal H. S. Ahluwalia
Colonel Gurdeep Bains
Lieutenant General Praveen Bakshi
Commodore P. K. Banerjee
Group Captain Anant Bewoor
Lieutenant General Vinod Bhatia
Major General Samir Chakravorty
Captain Prakash Chandavarkar
Air Marshal V. R. Chaudhuri
Wing Commander Rajiv Chauhan
Colonel Navdeep Cheema
Major General Alok Deb
Air Chief Marshal B. S. Dhanoa
Major General H. Dharmarajan
Air Marshal N. J. S. Dhillon
Air Vice Marshal M. Fernandez
Lieutenant General N. S. Ghei
Colonel R. Hariharan
Lieutenant General S. A. Hasnain
Lieutenant General D. S. Hooda
Air Vice Marshal Rajesh Isser
Colonel A. Jairam
Captain Jayadevan
Major General Gajendra Joshi
Group Captain Unni Kartha
Lieutenant General P. C. Katoch
Commodore Srikant Kesnur
Brigadier V. M. B. Krishnan

Air Chief Marshal S. Krishnaswamy
Air Marshal C. Hari Kumar
Major General Devinder Kumar
Group Captain K. P. S. Lamba
Air Chief Marshal F. H. Major
Wing Commander R. Malhotra
General V. P. Malik
Air Marshal Teshter Master
Air Marshal R. D. Mathur
Lieutenant General Shamsher Mehta
Air Marshal N. Menon
Air Commodore Shashank Mishra
Lieutenant General J. R. Mukherjee
Lieutenant General K. Nagaraj
Commodore Arjun Nair
Air Marshal R. Nambiar
Lieutenant General R. K. Nanavatty
Lieutenant General S. L. Narasimhan
Group Captain Sanjeev Narayenan
Brigadier Ravi Palsokar
Air Marshal Vinod Patney
Lieutenant General S. Pattabhiraman
Admiral Arun Prakash
Lieutenant Colonel T. P. Rajkumar
Major General A. K. Ramesh
General Bipin Rawat
Brigadier Vivek Sapatnekar
Wing Commander K. T. Sebastian
General V. N. Sharma
Wing Commander Dushyant Singh
Major General Gurbirpal Singh
Lieutenant General J. M. Singh
Lieutenant General K. H. Singh
Admiral Madhavendra Singh
Air Commodore Tejinder Singh
Colonel Vijayant Singh
Group Captain Raju Srinivasan
Air Chief Marshal A. Y. Tipnis
Group Captain S. Tokekar
Lieutenant General M. H. Zaki

The author is also deeply grateful to former defense secretary Shri Sanjay Mitra for his candid views on several vital issues. More than fifty other officers and men of various ranks and ages shared their perspectives on the operations in which they participated but requested anonymity. These include several officers from the Indian Army's Special Forces, the Marine Commandos (MARCOS) of the Indian Navy, and pilots from the squadrons that participated in the Kargil Conflict and the Balakot strikes. My deepest gratitude goes out to them.

NOTES

Introduction

1. Arjun Subramaniam, *India's Wars: A Military History 1947–1971* (Annapolis, MD: US Naval Institute Press, 2017).

2. Subramaniam, *India's Wars*, 369–370.

3. Lawrence Freedman, ed., *War* (Oxford: Oxford University Press, 1994), 8.

Chapter 1. Chameleon Wars

1. My comfort with the term "limited war" was prompted by a thought-provoking talk by Professor Dan Stoker, US Naval Postgraduate School, during the Changing Character of War program at Oxford on 23 January 2018. The talk was provocatively titled "How to Think about Limited War (without Limiting Your Thinking)."

2. A detailed practitioner's perspective on the contours of twenty-first-century warfare is available in Thomas X. Hammes, *The Sling and the Stone: On War in the 21st Century* (St. Paul, MN: Zenith Press, 2006), introduction, ch. 1.

3. This is my personal geomilitary perspective, arrived at after extensive discussions over the years with both Indian and Western military leaders and security experts involved in internal armed conflicts across the globe.

4. Hew Strachan, *The Direction of War: Contemporary Strategy in Historical Perspective* (Cambridge: Cambridge University Press, 2013), 82–83.

5. See chapter 8 for a detailed examination of the Nathu La crisis and firefight.

6. For a detailed examination of this conflict, see Arjun Subramaniam, *India's Wars: A Military History 1947–1971* (Annapolis, MD: US Naval Institute Press, 2017), chs. 8–12.

7. Subramaniam, *India's Wars*, 251.

8. Subramaniam, *India's Wars*, 326.

9. Subramaniam, *India's Wars*, 427.

10. This is the broad methodology followed by India's armed forces in operational formations and war colleges.

11. For an excellent analysis, see Douglas W. Skinner, "Air-Land Battle Doctrine," Center for Naval Analyses, September 1988, http://www.dtic.mil/dtic/tr/fulltext/u2/a202888.pdf.

12. A good monograph on sequential military operations is Major Richard Dixon, *Operational Sequencing: The Tension between Simultaneous and Sequential Operations* (Fort Leavenworth, KS: School of Advanced Military Studies, US Army Command and Staff College, 1994), http://www.dtic.mil/dtic/tr/fulltext/u2/a284087.pdf.

13. Parallel operations have emerged as a dominant concept of conventional war

fighting due to airpower's greater ability to influence joint operations. See proposition 6 in Phillip S. Meilinger, "Ten Propositions Regarding Airpower," Air Force History and Museums Program, 1995, https://www.airuniversity.af.edu/Portals/10/ASPJ/journals/Chronicles/meil.pdf.

14. These impressions are based on Sundarji's writings, study group sessions with him during the Forty-Ninth Staff Course at Wellington, and exhaustive interviews with Lieutenant General Shamsher Mehta, who was on Sundarji's staff when the latter was army chief.

15. Jasjit Singh, *Air Power in Joint Operations* (New Delhi: Knowledge World, 2003).

16. For clarity on EBO, see Meilinger, "Ten Propositions Regarding Airpower."

17. See Benjamin Lambeth, "American and NATO Airpower Applied: From Deny Flight to Inherent Resolve," in *Airpower Applied: US, NATO and Israeli Combat Experience*, ed. John Andreas Olsen (Annapolis, MD: Naval Institute Press, 2017), 124–216.

18. Prakash Menon, *The Strategy Trap: India and Pakistan under the Nuclear Shadow* (New Delhi: Wisdom Tree, 2018), 176–177.

19. Hammes, *Sling and the Stone*, 5–29.

20. Integrated Headquarters of Ministry of Defense (Army), *Doctrine for Sub-conventional Operations* (December 2006), 65.

21. *Doctrine for Sub-conventional Operations*, 65.

22. *Doctrine for Sub-conventional Operations*, 65.

23. Indian Ministry of Defense, *Joint Services Glossary of Military Terms* (Delhi, 2003), 119.

24. *Doctrine for Sub-conventional Operations*, 66. Also see Russell D. Howard and Reid L. Sawyer, *Terrorism and Counterterrorism: Understanding the New Security Environment; Readings and Interpretations*, 3rd ed. (New York: McGraw-Hill, 2009), 26.

25. Praveen Swami, "Failed Threats and Flawed Fences: India's Military Responses to Pakistan's Proxy War," *India Review* 3, 2 (April 2004): 147.

26. A black swan event is an unpredictable occurrence that goes beyond normal expectations and has potentially severe consequences. Black swan events are characterized by their extreme rarity and severe impact and the widespread insistence that they were obvious in hindsight.

27. Parvez Hoodbhoy, "Views from Pakistan: 'Bleed India with a Thousand Cuts' Policy Is in Shambles," *Open*, 13 October 2016, http://www.openthemagazine.com/article/views-from-pakistan/bleed-india-with-a-thousand-cuts-policy-is-in-a-shambles.

28. H. P. S. Sidhu, "Understanding Hybrid Warfare and Developing a Response" (paper presented at National Defence College, 5 May 2016, published in *Understanding Strategy*, a collection of seminar papers with limited distribution).

29. Frank Hoffman, "Conflict in the 21st Century: The Rise of Hybrid Wars" (Potomac Institute for Policy Studies, December 2007).

30. David Kilcullen, *The Accidental Guerrilla* (London: Hurst, 2009), 25.

31. Qiao Liang and Wang Xiangsui, *Unrestricted Warfare* (Beijing: PLA Literature and Arts Publishing House, 1999).

32. Kilcullen, *Accidental Guerrilla*, 3.

33. H. R. McMaster, former national security adviser in the Trump administration, quoted in Patrick Radden Keefe, "McMaster and Commander," *New Yorker*, 30 April 2018, 36–49.

34. John Boyd, "Patterns of Conflict" (presentations at Marine Corps Staff College, Quantico, VA, 2015 and 2018), https://thestrategybridge.org/the-bridge /2015/11/16/uploading-john-boyd?rq=Boyd and https://thestrategybridge.org /the-bridge/2018/3/22/john-boyd-on-clausewitz-dont-fall-in-love-with-your -mental-model. Although he never wrote a book, Boyd's impact on contemporary warfighting has been phenomenal. See http://www.projectwhitehorse.com/pdfs/boyd /patterns%20of%20conflict.pdf.

35. This was before Nagaland was granted statehood.

36. Rostum K. Nanavatty, *Internal Armed Conflict in India* (New Delhi: Pentagon Press, 2013), 65–69. Also see Armed Forces (Jammu and Kashmir) Special Powers Act, 1990, https://www.mha.gov.in/sites/default/files/The%20Armed%20Forces%20 %28Jammu%20and%20Kashmir%29%20Special%20Powers%20Act%2C%20 1990_0.pdf.

37. Vivek Chadha, ed., *Armed Forces Special Powers Act: The Debate* (New Delhi: Lancer, 2013), 10–21.

38. Sanjoy Hazarika, *Strangers No More* (New Delhi: Aleph, 2018), x–xi.

39. Nikhil Raymond Puri, "Assessing Disturbance in Jammu and Kashmir's 'Disturbed Areas,'" ORF Issue Brief 104, September 2015, https://www.orfonline.org /wp-content/uploads/2015/12/ORFIssueBrief104.pdf.

40. Nanavatty, *Internal Armed Conflict*, xvii.

41. Carl von Clausewitz, *On War*, ed. and trans. Michael Howard and Peter Paret (Princeton, NJ: Princeton University Press, 1976), 594. See Book 8 on "Scale of the Military Objective and of the Effort to Be Made."

Chapter 2. India's Military Renaissance

1. Arjun Subramaniam, *India's Wars: A Military History 1947–1971* (Annapolis, MD: US Naval Institute Press, 2017), 401–406.

2. Based on several interviews and conversations with Lieutenant General Shamsher Mehta between 2013 and 2019.

3. International Institute of Strategic Studies, *Military Balance* 73, 1 (1973): 45–58, https://doi.org/10.1080/04597227308459833. The annual *Military Balance* series of consolidated reports and analyses from the International Institute of Strategic Studies in London analyzes military capability from a global perspective. All comparisons with the situation at the end of the 1970s have been made by referring to volume 79 of the same series, https://doi.org/10.1080/04597227908459894.

4. Mehta interview.

5. *Military Balance* 73.

6. *Military Balance* 73.

7. G. M. Hiranandani, *Transition to Eminence: The Indian Navy 1976–1990* (New Delhi: Lancer Publishers, 2004), 27 (tabular compilation of various warships).

8. Subramaniam, *India's Wars,* 415–417.

9. The story of the HF-24 is well narrated by Sushant Singh, "In Fact: Before the LCA, India Had Its Own Fighter—Marut," *Indian Express,* 8 July 2016, https://indianexpress.com/article/explained/tejas-hf-24-marut-tejas-combat-aircraft-indian-air-force-2894021/.

10. *Military Balance* 73, 79.

11. Interview with Air Marshal Patney, 6 August 2018.

12. *Military Balance* 81, 90.

13. Amit Gupta, "Determining India's Force Structure and Military Doctrine: I Want My MiG," *Asian Survey* 35, 5 (May 1995): 441–458, https://www.jstor.org/stable/2645747?seq=1.

14. Gupta, "Determining India's Force Structure."

15. Interview with Lieutenant General Pattabhiraman (retired), former vice chief of the Indian Army, 15 March 2017.

16. Selig Harrison and K. Subrahmanyam, eds., *Superpower Rivalry in the Indian Ocean: Indian and American Views* (New York: Oxford University Press, 1989); Raja Menon, *Maritime Strategy and Continental Wars* (London: Frank Cass, 1998).

17. *Military Balance* 80, 81, 90. Also see Gupta, "Determining India's Force Structure."

18. For a perceptive piece on Subrahmanyam's legacy and his contribution to contemporary Indian strategic thought, see Anit Mukherjee, "K. Subrahmanyam and Indian Strategic Thought," *Strategic Analysis* 35, 4 (July 2011): 710–713.

19. Interviews with Air Marshal Patney, 2 June 2013 and 6 August 2018.

20. *Military Balance* 91, 98, 100.

21. Based on my personal recollection of getting Romanian engines for MiG-21s in my squadron in the 1990s.

22. "Army's Elite Counterinsurgency Unit Rashtriya Rifles Celebrates 25 Years," accessed 15 February 2017, https://economictimes.indiatimes.com/news/defense/armys-elite-counter-insurgency-unit-rashtriya-rifles-turns-25-tomorrow/articleshow/49171891.cms?from=mdr.

23. "New Army Chief for Debate on Security," *Hindustan Times,* 1 July 1993.

24. "New Army Chief Suggests Restructuring to Fight Militancy," *Financial Express,* 1 July 1993.

25. George Fernandes, "Examining the Concept of National Security." in *General B. C. Joshi Memorial Lectures on National Security*, ed. Gautam Sen (Pune, India: University of Pune Press, 2006), 54–55.

26. Patney interview, 6 August 2018.

27. John F. Burns, "India's New Defense Chief Sees Chinese Military Threat," *New York Times,* 5 May 1998, https://www.nytimes.com/1998/05/05/world/india-s-new-defense-chief-sees-chinese-military-threat.html.

28. *Military Balance*, 2001.

29. *Military Balance* comparison, 2016.

30. "Army Inducts Three Artillery Guns Including US M777 Howitzers," *Times of India,* 9 November 2018, https://timesofindia.indiatimes.com/india/k9-vajra-m777 -howitzers-to-be-inducted-today-sitharaman-to-attend-event/articleshow/66552262 .cms.

31. For a succinct evaluation of the PLA Navy, see Christopher Yung, "China's Evolving Naval Force Structure: Beyond Sino-US Rivalry," *China Brief* 18, 9, accessed 12 November 2017, https://jamestown.org/program/chinas-evolving-naval -force-structure-beyond-sino-us-rivalry/.

32. Arjun Subramaniam, "Closing the Gap: A Doctrinal & Capability Appraisal of the IAF and PLAAF," in *Defence Primer: An Indian Military in Transformation,* ed. Pushan Das and Harsh V. Pant (New Delhi: ORF, 2018), https://www.orfonline .org/contributors/arjun-subramaniam/.

Chapter 3. The Naga Rebellion

1. For a detailed profile of Bob Khathing, see H. Bhuban Singh, *Major Bob Khath-ing: The Profile of a Nationalist Manipuri Naga* (Manipur, India: P. Haoban Publishers, 1992). The book is largely out of print but is available at the library in the Assam Rifles Regimental Centre.

2. Singh, *Major Bob Khathing.*

3. Vikram Singh, *Spitfire in the Sun* (New Delhi: Ambi Knowledge Resources, 2017), 75–76.

4. Archives at Assam Rifles Regimental Centre.

5. Singh, *Spitfire,* 75–76.

6. Singh, *Spitfire,* 75–76.

7. R. D. Palsokar, *Forever in Operations, a Success Story: A Historical Record of the 8th Mountain Division in Counterinsurgency in Nagaland and Manipur, and in the 1971 Indo-Pak Conflict* (Pune, India: HQ Eighth Mountain Division, 1991), 26.

8. J. R. Mukherjee, *An Insider's Experience of Insurgency in India's North-East* (London: Anthem Press, 2005), 27.

9. Associated Press, "Angami Phizo, 83, Fought for Secession in North Indian State," *New York Times,* 4 May 1990, https://www.nytimes.com/1990/05/04/obitu aries/angami-phizo-83-fought-for-secession-in-north-india-state.html.

10. "Revolt in the Hills," *Time,* 16 April 1956, 33.

11. For a succinct review of the origin of the Naga people and their migration into the hills of northeastern India, see Y. D. Gundevia, *War and Peace in Nagaland* (New Delhi: Palit & Palit, 1975), 1–6.

12. Gundevia, *War and Peace in Nagaland,* 29–51.

13. Gundevia, *War and Peace in Nagaland,* 42.

14. Gundevia, *War and Peace in Nagaland,* 42.

15. Nirmal Nibedon, *Nagaland: The Night of the Guerrillas* (New Delhi: Lancer, 1978), 20–25.

16. Singh, *Major Bob Khathing.*

17. Nibedon, *Nagaland*, 29.

18. Nibedon, *Nagaland*, 32–35. This work also includes the gist of the dialogue between the NNC and Mahatma Gandhi.

19. Phizo was first arrested by the Indian government in 1949 for delivering inflammatory speeches against India.

20. Sanjoy Hazarika, *Strangers No More* (New Delhi: Aleph, 2018), 54.

21. Nibedon, *Nagaland*, 63.

22. Palsokar, *Forever in Operations*, 26.

23. Nibedon, *Nagaland*, 63.

24. Palsokar, *Forever in Operations*, 30.

25. Palsokar, *Forever in Operations*, 31.

26. For a detailed profile of Lieutenant Colonel Chitnis, see https://www.honour point.in/profile/lieutenant-colonel-jagannath-raoji-chitnis-ac/.

27. Harish Chandola, *The Naga Story: First Armed Struggle in India* (New Delhi: Chicken Neck, 2012), 57–62.

28. Palsokar, *Forever in Operations*, 35.

29. Palsokar, *Forever in Operations*, 35–36. Also see Nibedon, *Nagaland*, 90–91.

30. Email correspondence with Wing Commander Chandrashekhar Misra. Also see http://www.bharat-rakshak.com/IAF/Database/Aircraft/HJ-233, an Indian website that tracks all units of the three armed forces; this link highlights the Dakota aircraft.

31. From the diaries of Forty-Third Squadron.

32. Email correspondence with IAF veterans and airpower historians.

33. Email correspondence with Air Marshal Bharat Kumar, the IAF's foremost historian, 11 November 2018. Samir Chopra, an airpower historian and professor at New York University, recalls seeing entries in his father's logbook of live strafing missions in the early 1960s from Tezpur; email correspondence, 10 November 2018.

34. D. K. Palit, *The Sentinels of the North-East* (New Delhi: Palit & Palit, 1984), 224.

35. Extracts from the operational record books of Twenty-Ninth Squadron for the period October–December 1961, compiled by Flying Officer Bhavnani and sent to the author by Polly Singh.

36. This verification was possible thanks to the efforts by Group Captain Sartaj Singh from the Historical Cell at the College of Air Warfare and Group Captain Unni Kartha, who served for many years in the region.

37. *Bashas* are portable dwellings made of bamboo and reed and found throughout northeastern India.

38. Operational record book of Twenty-Ninth Squadron for the quarter ending 31 December 1961, 1–3.

39. Operational record book of Twenty-Ninth Squadron for the quarter ending 31 December 1961, 1–3.

40. For a brief mention of air operations against Naga insurgents in the early 1960s, see S. P. Sinha, "CI Operations in the Northeast," *Indian Defence Review* 21, 2 (April–June 2006), http://www.indiandefencereview.com/spotlights/c-i-operations

-in-the-northeast/0/. Also see http://vayu-sena.tripod.com/other-coin-offensive
-fighter-ops-ne.html, a website related to military aviation in India.

41. Subir Bhaumick, *Troubled Periphery: India's Troubled North-East* (New
Delhi: Sage, 2009), 44–47.

42. The Battle of Walong was one of the few sectoral battles in NEFA in which
the Indian Army gave the People's Liberation Army a bloody nose in the 1962 war,
before being overwhelmed by sheer numerical superiority. For a detailed overview
of the battle, see Arjun Subramaniam, *India's Wars: A Military History 1947–1971*
(Annapolis, MD: US Naval Institute Press, 2017), 245–246.

43. Rostum Nanavatty, diaries and interviews, 14 February and 13 March 2017,
8 and 9 August 2018.

44. For a detailed narrative of the Goa operations, see Subramaniam, *India's Wars,*
180–194.

45. Palsokar, *Forever in Operations.*

46. For a detailed analysis of external actors' threat to stability in northeastern
India since the early years of the Naga insurgency, see S. P. Sinha, "Northeast: The
Threat Posed by External Actors," *Indian Defence Review,* 14 February 2016, http://
www.indiandefencereview.com/spotlights/northeast-the-external-dimension/.

Chapter 4. Joint Operations in Mizoram and Nagaland

1. J. R. Mukherjee, *An Insider's Experience of Insurgency in India's North-East*
(London: Anthem Press, 2005), 49.

2. Ali Ahmed, "Mizo Hills: Revisiting the Early Phase," http://www.claws.in/im
ages/journals_doc/1607757556_AliAhmed.pdf. This article is by far the best analysis
of the Mizo insurgency from a politico-military perspective.

3. Sushil Kumar Sharma, "Lessons from Mizoram Insurgency and Peace Accord
1986," Vivekananda International Foundation, June 2016, https://www.vifindia
.org/sites/default/files/lessons-from-mizoram-insurgency-and-peace-accord-1986
.pdf.

4. Interview with Lieutenant General Mathew Thomas, 12 November 2014.

5. Email exchanges with IAF History Yahoo group, following my request for
personal accounts of IAF veterans who participated in extensive aerial operations in
the northeast in the 1960s.

6. Email from the late Air Marshal Teshter Master, IAF Yahoo group.

7. Anand Ranganathan, "A Brief History of Mizoram: From the Aizwal Bombing
to the Peace Accord," https://www.newslaundry.com/2015/08/06/a-brief-history-of-
-mizoram-from-the-aizawl-bombing-to-the-mizo-accord.

8. Email from Air Marshal Bharat Kumar, IAF Yahoo group.

9. Times News Network, "Silent Rally Echoes Mizo Pain of '66 IAF Attacks," *Times
of India,* 5 March 2011, https://timesofindia.indiatimes.com/city/guwahati/Silent
-rally-echoes-Mizo-pain-of-66-IAF-attacks/articleshow/7636603.cms?referral=PM.

10. Conversation with Colonel Vivek Chadha, 11 April 2020.

11. J. V. Hluna and Rini Tochhwang, *The Mizo Uprising: Assam Assembly De-*

bates on the Mizo Movement 1966–1971 (Newcastle, UK: Cambridge Scholars Publishing, 2012), xix.

12. Rinchen Norbu Wangchuk, "Mizo Peace Accord: The Intriguing Story behind India's Most Enduring Peace Initiative," 2 July 2018, https://www.thebetterindia.com/148387/mizo-peace-accord-laldenga-rajiv-gandhi/.

13. Mukherjee, *Insider's Experience*, 52.

14. Group Captain Anil Bendre, personal account of an incident in Nagaland on 20 May 1974, in Air Vice Marshal Ahluwalia, email to author, 29 September 2018.

15. *Citizen's Voice*, 18 December 1969, 1.

16. Nishit Dholabhai, "70-Plus and Still Going Strong in BSF," *Telegraph*, 9 May 2004, https://www.telegraphindia.com/states/north-east/70-plus-and-still-going-strong-in-bsf-septuagenarian-naga-sentinels-continue-in-service-thanks-to-fudged-age/cid/1557309.

17. Interview with General Narasimhan, Coimbatore, India, 15 February 2017.

18. Sushil Sharma, *The Complexity Called Manipur: Perceptions and Reality* (New Delhi: Viva Books, 2019).

19. Interview with Rostum Nanavatty, Dehra Dun, India, August 2018.

20. Nanavatty interview.

21. Nanavatty interview.

22. Patricia Mukhim, "A Deal at Last," *Hindu*, 28 March 2019, https://www.thehindu.com/opinion/op-ed/a-deal-at-last/article26656012.ece.

23. Interview with General Bipin Rawat, Chief of Army Staff, 21 April and 7 July 2019.

24. Rawat interviews.

25. For a gripping people-centric narrative of this operation, see Shiv Aroor and Rahul Singh, *India's Most Fearless: True Stories of Modern Military Heroes* (New Delhi: Penguin Random House, 2017), 37–64.

26. Times News Network, "7 Medals for Special Forces Team that Hit Myanmar Camps," *Times of India*, 15 August 2015, https://timesofindia.indiatimes.com/india/7-medals-for-Special-Forces-team-that-hit-Myanmar-camps/articleshow/48490051.cms.

27. "Terror Camps on India–Myanmar Border Destroyed," *Economic Times*, 15 March 2019, https://economictimes.indiatimes.com/news/defence/terror-camps-on-india-myanmar-border-destroy ed/articleshow/68432469.cms.

28. "Terror Camps on India–Myanmar Border Destroyed."

29. Rawat interviews.

30. For a poignant description of the arrival of Phizo's body at the Dimapur airfield on 11 May 1990, see Pieter Steyn, *Zapuphizo: Voice of the Nagas* (London: Kegan Paul, 2002), 159–163.

31. Samudra Gupta Kashyap and Praveen Swami, "Explained: Everything You Wanted to Know about the Naga Insurgency," *Indian Express*, 4 August 2015, https://indianexpress.com/article/india/india-others/everything-you-need-to-know-about-nagaland-insurgency-and-the-efforts-to-solve/.

32. Kashyap and Swami, "Explained."

33. Interview with Lieutenant General Hooda, Panchkula, Chandigarh, India, 20 July 2019.

34. Kashyap and Swami, "Explained."

35. D. K. Palit, *The Sentinels of the North-East* (New Delhi: Palit & Palit, 1984).

36. Shekhar Gupta, YouTube video, https://www.youtube.com/watch?v=CcI4 NOsmw4I.

37. Namrata Goswami, "India's Counterinsurgency Experience: The 'Trust and Nurture' Strategy," *Small Wars and Insurgencies* 20, 1 (2009), https://doi.org /10.1080/09592310802573475.

38. Bibhu Prasad Routray, "China's New Game in India's Northeast," 4 July 2017, http://mantraya.org/analysis-chinas-new-game-in-indias-northeast/.

39. Sanjeev Hazarika, "Genesis of Naga Imbroglio, Status of Underground Groups, Prevailing Situation, Prognosis and Army Activities," *Infantry Journal* 20, 1 (April 2009): 31–34.

Chapter 5. Operation Blue Star: Ours Is Not to Question Why

1. Lieutenant General S. K. Sinha, *A Soldier Recalls* (New Delhi: Lancer Publishers, 1992), 278–280.

2. The Damdami Taksal was the fountainhead of Sikh fundamentalism and the nerve center of antigovernment extremism in the late 1970s and 1980s. Over the years, particularly in recent times, it has reinvented itself as a moderate center of Sikh religious teaching.

3. The Nirankaris are a secular, spiritual sect unaffiliated with any religion, and they deny that the Sikhs have any authority over them. See "Who Are the Nirankaris," *Indian Express*, 18 November 2018, https://indianexpress.com/article /who-is/who-are-nirankaris/.

4. Sinha, *Soldier Recalls*, 290.

5. Harminder Kaur, *Blue Star over Amritsar* (New Delhi: Ajanta Publications, 1990), 117–118.

6. Mark Tully and Satish Jacob, *Amritsar: Mrs Gandhi's Last Battle* (New Delhi: Rupa, 1985), 10–14.

7. R. K. Chopra, "Internal Security Environment in India" (thesis, National Defence College, 1988).

8. "Suspected Sikh Extremists Slay Editor," https://www.upi.com/Archives/1984 /05/12/Suspected-Sikh-extremists-slay-editor/3839453182400/.

9. Michael Kaufman, "Sikh Separatists Hijack Indian Jetliner to Pakistan," *New York Times,* 30 September 1981, https://www.nytimes.com/1981/09/30/world/sikh -separatists-hijack-indian-jetliner-to-pakistan.html.

10. For an excellent overview, see Rajshri Jetly, "The Khalistan Movement in India: The Interplay of Politics and State Power," *International Review of Modern Sociology* 34, 1 (Spring 2008): 61–75, https://www.jstor.org/stable/41421658?seq=1.

11. Pravin Swami, *India, Pakistan and the Secret Jihad* (New Delhi: Routledge, 2007), 147.

12. Data sheets of annual fatalities caused by terrorist-related violence, 1981–2019, South Asia Terrorism Portal, https://satp.org/satporgtp/countries/india/states/Punjab/data_sheets/annual_casualties.htm.

13. K. S. Brar, *Operation Blue Star: The True Story* (New Delhi: UBS Publishers, 1993), 33–39.

14. Mark Tully, "Operation Blue Star: How an Indian Army Raid on the Golden Temple Ended in Disaster," *Telegraph*, 6 June 2014, https://www.telegraph.co.uk/news/worldnews/asia/india/10881115/Operation-Blue-Star-How-an-Indian-army-raid-on-the-Golden-Temple-ended-in-disaster.html.

15. For a detailed description of SFF involvement in Operation Blue Star, see Claude Arpi, "Special Frontier Force and Operation Blue Star," January 2014, http://claudearpi.blogspot.com/2014/01/special-frontiers-forces-and-operation.html.

16. Brar, *Operation Blue Star*, 88.

17. Interview with Lieutenant General Prakash Katoch, 13 May 2019.

18. Arjun Subramaniam, *India's Wars: A Military History 1947–1971* (Annapolis, MD: US Naval Institute Press, 2017), 355–357.

19. Tully and Jacob, *Amritsar*, 88–89.

20. Tully and Jacob, *Amritsar*, 88–89.

21. Brar, *Operation Blue Star,* 100–115; Katoch interview.

22. Brar, *Operation Blue Star*, 100–115.

23. Katoch interview.

24. Based on personal conversations over the years.

25. Brar, *Operation Blue Star*, 124. Also see Kaur, *Blue Star over Amritsar*, 46–48.

26. Interview with General Bipin Rawat, chief of the army staff, 21 April 2019.

27. Email correspondence with General Ghei.

28. Rashi Lal, "When LU Became Ground Zero for PAC Revolt," *Times of India*, Lucknow ed., 1 June 2018, https://timesofindia.indiatimes.com/city/lucknow/when-lu-became-ground-zero-for-pac-revolt/articleshow/64417667.cms.

29. "The Secret behind Operation Blue Star: Britain's Dilemma Explained," *ET Online*, 13 June 2018, https://economictimes.indiatimes.com/news/et-explains/the-secret-behind-operation-blue-star-britains-dilemma-explained/articleshow/64569757.cms?from=mdr.

30. Katoch interview.

31. "Golden Temple Attack: UK Advised India but Impact Limited," BBC, 7 June 1984, https://www.bbc.com/news/uk-26027631.

32. Tully and Jacob, *Amritsar*, 194. Also see Kaur, *Blue Star over Amritsar*, 49.

33. Mary Anne Weaver, "Sikh Mutiny Spreads in Indian Army," *Christian Science Monitor*, 12 June 1984, https://www.csmonitor.com/1984/0612/061237.html#:~:text=A%20third%20mutiny%20by%20Sikh,the%20Indian%20Ministry%20of%20Defense.&text=On%20Sunday%2C%20in%20a%20crack,general%2C%20was%20shot%20and%20killed.

34. Apurba Kundu, "The Indian Armed Forces' Sikh and Non-Sikh Officers' Opinions of Operation Blue Star," *Pacific Affairs* 67, 1 (Spring 1994): 46–69, https://www.jstor.org/stable/2760119?seq=1.

35. Kundu, "Indian Armed Forces' Sikh and Non-Sikh Officers' Opinions."

36. Sumit Mitra, "Rajiv–Longowal Accord: Mathew Commission Delivers an Unexpected Anti-Climax," *India Today*, 15 February 1986, https://www.indiatoday.in/magazine/cover-story/story/19860215-rajiv-longowal-accord-mathew-commission-delivers-an-unexpected-anti-climax-800593-1986-02-15.

37. Suman Dubey, "Shiv Sena Militarily Gears Itself to Protect Hinduism and Hindu Interests in Punjab," *India Today*, 15 April 1986, https://www.indiatoday.in/magazine/cover-story/story/19860415-shiv-sena-militantly-gears-itself-to-protect-hinduism-and-hindu-interests-in-punjab-80075-1986-04-15#ssologin=1#source=magazine.

38. Swami, *India, Pakistan*, 47.

39. Suman Dubey, "Punjab under Savage Siege," *India Today*, 15 April 1986, https://www.indiatoday.in/magazine/cover-story/story/19860415-punjab-under-savage-siege-as-terrorist-killings-hindu-sikh-friction-wound-the-state-800791-1986-04-15.

40. Chopra, "Internal Security Environment."

41. For a detailed narrative of Gill's tenure as DGP in Punjab and his efforts to stamp out terrorism there, see K. P. S. Gill, ed., *Terror Containment: Perspectives on India's Internal Security* (New Delhi: Gyan Publishing House, 2001), 23–83.

42. Gobind Thukral, "Extremists, AISSF Leaders Once Again Use Golden Temple as an Occasional Hideout," *India Today*, 15 May 1986, https://www.indiatoday.in/magazine/indiascope/story/19860515-extremists-aissf-leaders-once-again-use-golden-temple-as-an-occasional-hideout-800876-1986-05-15.

43. For a detailed narration of Operation Black Thunder, see Ved Marwah, *Uncivil Wars: Pathology of Terrorism in India* (New Delhi: Indus, 1995), 188–200.

44. Marwah, *Uncivil Wars*, 188–200.

45. A. Suryaprakash, "The President Corrects Some Historical Facts, Gives Narasimha Rao His Due," 4 May 2016, https://www.vifindia.org/article/2016/may/04/the-president-corrects-some-historical-facts-gives-narasimha-rao-his-due.

Chapter 6. Siachen: An Icy Battleground

1. Harish Kapadia, *The Siachen Glacier: A Historical Review* (102nd Infantry Brigade, 2011), 1. This booklet was specially written for the officers and men who serve on the glacier.

2. Giotto Dainelli, "My Expedition in the Eastern Karakoram: 1930," *Himalayan Journal* 4 (1932), https://www.himalayanclub.org/hj/04/4/my-expedition-in-the-eastern-karakoram/. This article (which was also published in the *Royal Geographical Journal*) was attached to a letter written by Harish Kapadia to Nanavatty when he was Northern Army commander, following the discovery of an old stone from Dainelli's expedition by Captain Nitin Shreshtha, an officer from the Seventh Battalion, Eleventh Gorkha Rifles.

3. Grid NJ 9842 represents an area on the map, not a point.

4. Interview with Rostum Nanavatty, 13 March 2017.

5. Kapadia, *Siachen Glacier*, 5–6.

6. Omer Farook Zain, "Siachen Conflict: Discordant in Pakistan-India Reconciliation," *Pakistan Horizon* 59, 2 (April 2006): 73–82, https://www.jstor.org/stable/41394127?seq=1.

7. Translated from Sanskrit, Meghdoot is the messenger of the clouds.

8. M. L. Chibber, "Siachen—The Untold Story," *Indian Defence Review*, January 1990, 146–152.

9. The Cheetal is a reengineered version of the Cheetah, optimized by Hindustan Aeronautics Limited in 2002 for better high-altitude performance. All three variants are offshoots of the French Alloutte light helicopter.

10. M. Bahadur, "The Buildup to Operation Meghdoot," 10 December 2017, http://www.bharat-rakshak.com/IAF/history/siachen/1046-meghdoot.html.

11. Kevin Fedarko, "The Coldest War," updated 22 April 2012, https://www.wesjones.com/coldest.htm.

12. Chibber, "Siachen," 149. Also see Zain, "Siachen Conflict," 79.

13. Based on multiple conversations with Indian and Pakistani veterans who have served on the glacier.

14. Telephone interview and email correspondence with Group Captain Rohit Rai, 10–17 June 2020.

15. The best operational account of the initial assault is in Nitin Gokhale's *Beyond NJ 9842: The Siachen Saga* (New Delhi: Bloomsbury, 2014). For a review of the book, see *Strategic Analysis* 39, 1 (2015): 97–99.

16. Interviews with Sanjay Kulkarni by Nitin Gokhale, http://www.abplive.in/blog/meet-the-man-who-planted-the-first-indian-flag-on-siachen.

17. Syed Ishfaq Ali, *Fangs of Ice* (Rawalpindi, Pakistan: Pak America Commercial, 1991), 24.

18. Ali, *Fangs of Ice*, 29–30.

19. Zain, "Siachen Conflict," 79.

20. Kumar FLB was moved east of the Siachen Glacier in 2001–2002—onto terra firma instead of glacial ice—and was converted into an advanced base camp for mountaineering expeditions. It has the potential to be converted into a scientific research station in the future.

21. Interview with Lieutenant General Ghei, National Defence College, New Delhi, 12 October 2016.

22. Raj Mehta, "Bravery beyond Comparison: Hony Captain Bana Singh, PVC," *Scholar Warrior* (Autumn 2013): 132–136, https://archive.claws.in/images/journals_doc/20-Bravery%20Beyond%20Comparison%20-%20Hony%20Capt%20Bana%20Singh%2C%20PVC.pdf.

23. Onkar Singh, "True Valour," *Illustrated Weekly of India*, 28 March 1988, 38–39 (from Nanavatty's personal documents).

24. Ali, *Fangs of Ice,* 56–68.

25. Mehta, "Bravery beyond Comparison," 135.

26. Ali, *Fangs of Ice,* 56–68.

27. Ali, *Fangs of Ice,* 67.

28. Singh, "True Valour," 38.

29. Nanavatty interviews, 2017–2018.

30. Nanavatty interviews and email correspondence, 18 November 2019.

31. Nanavatty interviews.

32. All these posts have been named by the Indian Army, but because they are still manned, their names are represented by letters.

33. Nanavatty interviews.

34. In army parlance, Point 6400 (pronounced "six-four-zero-zero") refers to an unnamed height that measures 6,400 meters.

35. Ali, *Fangs of Ice*, 87–117.

36. Ali, *Fangs of Ice*, 87–117. Force Command Northern Areas is a division-sized force deployed in Gilgit and Baltistan, including the Siachen Glacier.

37. Nanavatty interviews and compilation of operational reports from various sources.

38. Nanavatty interviews.

39. Nanavatty diaries.

40. Telephone interview with Captain Vijayant, 10 August 2019.

41. For a second Pakistani perspective, see S. M. H. Y. Naqvi, "The Battle of Chumik," *Pakistan Army Journal* 30, 4 (December 1989), available at the library of the Defence Services Staff College, Wellington, India.

42. Fedarko, "Coldest War."

43. Email exchange with Nanavatty, 18 November 2019.

44. Information on Bofors sent via email from Lieutenant General Ahuja, 10 October 2019. See chapter 2 for further details.

45. Interview with Brigadier V. K. Sharma, National Defence College, New Delhi, May 2017.

46. Edward W. Desmond, "War on High Ground," *Time*, 17 July 1989, 8.

47. These figures are mainly representative and may not be accurate. They are based on a discussion with Nanavatty on the modalities of artillery engagements on the glacier.

48. Interview with Brigadier Ramesh, National Defence College, New Delhi, May 2017.

49. Nanavatty interviews.

Chapter 7. Flyboys over the Glacier

1. Interviews and email correspondence with Air Commodore Shashank Mishra, October 2016–March 2017.

2. Mishra interviews and email correspondence.

3. From the squadron diary of 114th Helicopter Unit.

4. Mishra email correspondence.

5. Air Vice Marshal Manmohan Bahadur, "In 1990, There Was Another Daring Rescue of an IAF Helicopter from Siachen Glacier," *Print*, 28 December 2018, https://theprint.in/opinion/in-1990-there-was-another-daring-rescue-of-an-iaf-heli copter-from-siachen-glacier/170068/.

6. "Siachen Glacier: Roll of Honour," http://www.bharat-rakshak.com/IAF/Personnel/Martyrs/198-4-99-Siachen.html.

7. Interviews with Group Captain Harpal Ahluwalia.

8. Ahluwalia interviews.

9. Email correspondence with Group Captain K. S. Lamba.

10. Conversation with pilots of Forty-Eighth Squadron at Chandigarh, India.

11. Arjun Subramaniam, *India's Wars: A Military History 1947–1971* (Annapolis, MD: US Naval Institute Press, 2017), 8.

12. From multiple conversations with pilots from the MiG-23 MF squadrons, correlated with log entries.

13. Prakash Katoch, "Tryst with Deceit," *Outlook*, 23 April 2012, https://www.outlookindia.com/website/story/tryst-with-deceit/280653.

14. Email correspondence and telephone conversation with Air Chief Marshal Fali Major.

15. Telephone conversation with Colonel A. Jayaram, 15 July 2019.

16. Jayaram conversation.

17. These were the Grenadiers, Gorkhas, Rajputs, Jats, Dogras, Mahars, Marathas, and Jammu and Kashmir Rifles, among others. Mishra email correspondence.

18. Interviews with Brigadier V. M. B. Krishnan, 2016.

19. Interviews with Rostum Nanavatty.

20. Interview with Subedar Major Satheesan, Madras Regimental Centre, Wellington, India, 21 April 2016.

21. Rostum Nanavatty, presentation to cadets of the Rashtriya Indian Military College, Dehra Dun, India, 16 October 1992, from Nanavatty diaries.

22. Nanavatty diaries.

23. "869 Soldiers Have Died in Siachen since 1984," 13 July 2018, https://economictimes.indiatimes.com/news/defence/869-indian-soldiers-have-died-in-siachen-since-1984/articleshow/50138852.cms?from=mdr.

24. "Siachen: 879 Deaths and Still Counting," *Indian Express*, 11 February 2016, http://indianexpress.com/article/india/india-news-india/siachen-avalanche-hanuman-thappa/.

25. "Avalanche Traps 135 People Near Siachen," *Tribune*, 7 April 2012, https://tribune.com.pk/story/361097/avalanche-traps-over-100-pakistani-soldiers-report/.

26. Anna Orton, *India's Borderland Dispute: China, Pakistan, Bangladesh, Nepal* (New Delhi: Epitome Books, 2010), 96–98.

27. Interview with Lieutenant General Prakash Katoch, 13 May 2019.

28. Shyam Saran, *How India Sees the World* (New Delhi: Juggernaut, 2017), 90–92.

29. "When M. K. Narayanan Stalled the Siachen Deal," 7 September 2017, http://www.dnaindia.com/india/report-when-mk-narayanan-stalled-siachen-deal-2543556.

30. A. Linsbauer, H. Frey, W. Haeberli, H. Machguth, M. Azam, and S. Allen, "Modelling Glacier-Bed Overdeepenings and Possible Future Lakes for the Glaciers in the Himalaya Karakoram Region," *Annals of Glaciology* 57, 71 (2016): 119–130, https://www.cambridge.org/core/journals/annals-of-glaciology/article

/modelling-glacierbed-overdeepenings-and-possible-future-lakes-for-the-glaciers-in
-the-himalayakarakoram-region/C18FD61BBB68E27ECCF5657074A8246A.

31. Karan Kharb, "Why China and Pakistan Want Demilitarization of Siachen," *Indian Defence Review*, 19 May 2014, http://www.indiandefencereview.com/news /why-china-and-pakistan-want-demilitarization-of-siachen/.

32. Nanavatty interviews.

33. Interview with Lieutenant General Hooda, 20 July 2019.

34. Javed Hassan, "The Fight for Siachen," *Express Tribune*, 22 April 2012, https://tribune.com.pk/story/368394/the-fight-for-siachen/.

35. Vinayak Bhat, "Fresh Provocation: China Building a 36 km-Long Road in Strategic J&K Valley Near Siachen," *Print*, 15 January 2018, https://theprint.in/se curity/china-building-a-36-km-long-road-valley-siachen/28812/.

36. Nanavatty diaries and interviews.

37. Omer Farook Zain, "Siachen Conflict: Discordant in Pakistan-India Reconciliation," *Pakistan Horizon* 59, 2 (April 2006): 82, https://www.jstor.org /stable/41394127?seq=1.

Chapter 8. Standing Up to the Dragon

1. Anit Mukherjee, *The Absent Dialogue: Politicians, Bureaucrats and the Military in India* (New Delhi: Oxford University Press, 2019), 66–67.

2. For a brilliant account of the buildup to the battles at Nathu La and Cho La, see Probal Dasgupta, *Watershed 1967: India's Forgotten Victory over China* (New Delhi: Juggernaut, 2019), 51–81.

3. See Inder Malhotra, "Indian Tonic at Nathu La," *Guardian*, 18 September 1967, 8.

4. Dasgupta, *Watershed 1967*, 100.

5. Sheru Thapliyal, "Nathu La and Cho La Clashes of 1967: How the Indian Army Dealt with Chinese Trouble," *Indian Defence Review*, 22 September 2014, http://www.indiandefencereview.com/when-chinese-were-given-a-bloody-nose/.

6. Thapliyal, "Nathu La and Cho La Clashes."

7. P. K. Roy, "The Scene of the Incident," *Baltimore Sun*, 17 September 1967, 12.

8. Interview with Vivek Sapatnekar, December 2012. Also see Dasgupta, *Watershed 1967*, 139–138.

9. Joseph Lelyveld, "India: New Troubles," *New York Times*, 17 September 1967.

10. "PM Hopes Firing Is Local Affair," *Times of India*, 2 October 1967.

11. Tanvi Madan, "How the US Viewed the 1967 Sikkim Skirmishes between India and China," *Print*, 13 September 2017, https://theprint.in/2017/09/13/how -the-us-viewed-the-1967-sikkim-skirmishes-between-india-and-china/.

12. Arunachal Pradesh was declared the twenty-fourth state of India in February 1987.

13. For a detailed account of the Battle of Namka Chu in October 1962, see Arjun Subramaniam, *India's Wars: A Military History 1947–1971* (Annapolis, MD: US Naval Institute Press, 2017), 232–234.

14. For a short journalistic overview of the crisis, see Claude Arpi, "The Sumdorong Chu Incident: A Strong Indian Stance," *Indian Defence Review*, 4 May 2013, www.indiandefencereview.com/the-sumdorong-chu-incident-a-strong-indian -stand/.

15. Email correspondence with J. M. Singh, 15 June 2019.

16. Singh email correspondence.

17. Singh email correspondence.

18. Forward air controllers are normally young air force officers deployed with forward army formations to control and direct fighters and helicopters during offensive missions over the tactical battle area.

19. Interview with General V. N. Sharma, 21 August 2019.

20. Singh email correspondence; telephone conversations with J. M. Singh, July– December 2019.

21. Email correspondence with Wing Commander Raju Srinivasan, 15 June 2019.

22. Email correspondence with Air Chief Marshal Fali Major, June 2019.

23. Singh email correspondence.

24. Singh email correspondence.

25. Email correspondence with Lieutenant General Ahuja, 10 October 2019; conversations with Lieutenant General V. K. Ahluwalia, 14 October 2019.

26. Singh email correspondence.

27. Singh email correspondence.

28. "Rajiv Gandhi's 1988 Visit Broke Ice between India and China: Chinese Diplomat," *Hindustan Times*, 13 October 2017, https://www.hindustantimes.com/india -news/rajiv-gandhi-s-1988-visit-broke-ice-between-india-and-china-chinese-diplo mat/story-JiQdkXFbI5jcNsE7c6pGoJ.html.

29. Subramaniam, *India's Wars*, 220–224.

30. Singh email correspondence.

31. Amit Gupta, "Determining India's Force Structure and Military Doctrine: I Want My MiG," *Asian Survey* 35, 5 (May 1995): 441–458, https://www.jstor.org /stable/2645747?seq=1.

Chapter 9. Peacekeeping in Sri Lanka: Was India Prepared?

1. Sunil Dasgupta, "Why Terrorism Fails While Insurgencies Can Sometimes Succeed," Brookings Op-ed, 4 January 2002, https://www.brookings.edu/opinions /why-terrorism-fails-while-insurgencies-can-sometimes-succeed/. See chapter 1 for an explanation of the difference between an insurgent and a terrorist.

2. John M. Senaveratna, *The Story of the Sinhalese from the Most Ancient Times up to the End of the Mahavansa or Great Dynasty* (New Delhi: Asian Educational Services, 1997), 7–20.

3. Channa Wickremesekara, *The Tamil Separatist War in Sri Lanka* (Oxford: Routledge, 2016), 6–9.

4. V. S. Sambandan, "A Promise of Identity," *Frontline* 20, 5 (1 March 2014), http://www.frontline.in/static/html/fl2005/stories/20030314000805700.htm.

5. Shankar Bhaduri and Afsar Karim, *The Sri Lankan Crisis* (New Delhi: Lancer, 1990), 7–15. Also see Wickremesekara, *Tamil Separatist War*, 31–34.

6. "Airgram A-97 from the Embassy in Sri Lanka to the Department of State," 23 November 1976, https://history.state.gov/historicaldocuments/frus1969-76ve08/d102.

7. J. N. Dixit, *Assignment Colombo* (New Delhi: Konark Publishers, 1998), 12.

8. Rohan Gunaratna, *Indian Intervention in Sri Lanka* (Colombo, Sri Lanka: Gunaratne Offset, 1993), 135–136. Also see Wickremesekara, *Tamil Separatist War*, 11–13.

9. M. R. Narayanswamy, *Inside an Elusive Mind: Prabhakaran* (New Delhi: Konark Publishers, 2003), 3–9.

10. Shekhar Gupta, "Such a Long Lankan Journey," *Indian Express*, 11 September 2013, http://indianexpress.com/article/opinion/columns/such-a-long-lankan-journey/.

11. Wickremesekara, *Tamil Separatist War*, 36–37.

12. Wickremesekara, *Tamil Separatist War*, 39–42

13. Gupta, "Such a Long Lankan Journey."

14. "The Largest LTTE Training Camp Was Located at Kolathur," *Hindu*, 28 August 2014, https://www.thehindu.com/news/national/tamil-nadu/the-largest-ltte-training-camp-was-located-at-kolathur/article6357629.ece.

15. Narayanswamy, *Inside an Elusive Mind*, 94.

16. David Brewster, "An Indian Sphere of Influence in the Indian Ocean?" *Security Challenges* 6, 3 (Spring 2010): 15, https://www.jstor.org/stable/26459796?seq=1#metadata_info_tab_contents. Also see James R. Holmes and Toshi Yoshihara, "India's 'Monroe Doctrine' and Asia's Maritime Future," *Strategic Analysis* 32, 6 (November 2008): 997–1011, https://www.tandfonline.com/doi/abs/10.1080/09700160802404539.

17. Barbara Crossete, "Sri Lanka Air Force Raids Tamil Guerrilla Bases," *New York Times*, 23 April 1987, https://www.nytimes.com/1987/04/23/world/sri-lanka-air-force-raids-tamil-guerrilla-bases.html.

18. Narayanswamy, *Inside an Elusive Mind*, 149.

19. Crossete, "Sri Lanka Air Force."

20. Email exchange and telephone conversation with Commander Vinayak Agashe (retired), 6 April 2020.

21. Interview and conversation with Arun Prakash, 6 April 2020.

22. Agashe conversation.

23. For a detailed Sri Lankan perspective on Operation Liberation, see Cyril Ranatunga, *Adventurous Journey: From Peace to War, Insurgency to Terrorism* (Colombo, Sri Lanka: Vijitha Yapa Publications, 2009).

24. Gunaratna, *Indian Intervention*, iii.

25. Dixit, *Assignment Colombo*, 326–350.

26. For a detailed account of Operation Poomalai, see Bharat Kumar, *Operation Pawan: Role of Airpower with IPKF* (New Delhi: Manohar, 2015), 54–66.

27. Dilip Bobb, "Sri Lanka: Tackling the Tigers," *India Today*, 30 June 1987,

http://indiatoday.intoday.in/story/indias-decision-to-airdrop-supplies-over-jaffna
-opens-up-a-diplomatic-pandora-box/1/337218.html. Also see Dixit, *Assignment Colombo*, 100–109.

28. Interview with Air Vice Marshal H. S. Ahluwalia, 7 September 2016.

29. Indo–Sri Lanka Accord, https://peacemaker.un.org/sites/peacemaker.un.org
/files/IN%20LK_870729_Indo-Lanka%20Accord.pdf.

30. Information from a reliable anonymous source.

31. Interviews with Brigadier R. R. Palsokar and Brigadier Sapatnekar, Pune, January 2013.

32. Dixit, *Assignment Colombo*, 156.

33. Palsokar interview.

34. Interview with Rostum Nanavatty, 14 February 2017.

35. Interview with General V. P. Malik, 31 January 2020.

36. There was no mention of any impending operations in the operational record book of Seventh Squadron.

37. Interview with Major General Bhaduria. His unit was among the first inducted into Jaffna.

38. Interview with Arun Prakash, Naval War College, 30 October 2016.

39. Email correspondence between Admiral Arun Prakash and Rear Admiral Kapil Gupta, 17 October 2019.

40. Harkirat Singh, *Intervention in Sri Lanka: The IPKF Experience Retold* (New Delhi: Manohar, 2007), 30–34.

41. Arjun Subramaniam, *India's Wars: A Military History 1947–1971* (Annapolis, MD: US Naval Institute Press, 2017), 411–412.

42. Singh, *Intervention in Sri Lanka*, 33.

43. Singh, *Intervention in Sri Lanka*, 28–33.

44. Kumar, *Operation Pawan*, 79.

45. G. M. Hiranandani, *Transition to Eminence: The Indian Navy 1976–1990* (New Delhi: Lancer Publishers, 2004), 192–194.

46. Depinder Singh, *The IPKF in Sri Lanka* (New Delhi: Trishul Publications, 1992), 43.

47. Interview with X, the anonymous covert operative.

48. Singh, *Intervention in Sri Lanka*, 47. Also see M. R. Narayanswamy, *Tigers of Lanka: From Boys to Guerrillas* (Colombo, Sri Lanka: Vijitha Yapa Publications, 1994), 252–254.

49. Vellupilla Pirabakaran, "On the Indo–Sri Lanka Accord," 4 August 1987, http://tamilnation.co/ltte/vp/87suthumalai.htm.

50. Interview with Colonel R. Hariharan, http://www.internationallawjournal
oflondon.com/interview-with-indian-peacekeeping-forces-intelligence-corps-chief
-col.-hariharan.html.

51. Gupta, "Such a Long Lankan Journey." For an equally insightful look into the activities of R&AW, see Shekhar Gupta, "The Espionage Game," *India Today*, 31 December 1993, http://indiatoday.intoday.in/story/the-espionage-game/1/303572.html.

52. Hariharan interview.

53. Singh, *IPKF in Sri Lanka*, 59.

54. Kumar, *Operation Pawan*, 88.

55. Nanavatty interview. He was privy to these conversations during his short stint with the IPKF.

56. S. Murari, *The Prabhakaran Saga: The Rise and Fall of an Eelam Warrior* (New Delhi: Sage, 2012), 39–41.

57. Gunaratna, *Indian Intervention*, 235–236.

58. Interview with Lieutenant General Pattabhiraman, 13 December 2016.

Chapter 10. Into the Tiger's Lair

1. Joanne Richards, "An Institutional History of the Liberation Tigers Tamil of Eelam," CCDP Working Paper 10, November 2014, http://repository.graduateinsti tute.ch/record/292651/files/CCDP-Working-Paper-10-LTTE-1.pdf.

2. Shekhar Gupta, "India's Blackhawk Down: Incompetence and Heroism in a Commando Raid," *Print*, 14 October 2018, https://theprint.in/opinion/indias-black hawk-down-incompetence-heroism-in-a-commando-raid-gone-wrong-at-jaffna-univ /134316/.

3. Harkirat Singh, *Intervention in Sri Lanka: The IPKF Experience Retold* (New Delhi: Manohar, 2007), 174–176.

4. For a detailed account of myriad facets of the Jaffna battle, see Shekhar Gupta, "In Rush to Vanquish," *India Today*, 13 January 1988; Shekhar Gupta, "Uncovering the War," *Indian Express*, 13 September 2013, http:/indianexpress.com/article/news -archive/print/uncovering-the-war/; Dilip Bobb, "A Bloodied Accord," *India Today*, 15 November 1987, http://indiatoday.intoday.in/story/after-16-days=of-bloody-fight ing-ipkf-finally-captures-ltte-stronghold-jaffna/1/337703.

5. Gupta, "In Rush to Vanquish."

6. Bobb, "Bloodied Accord."

7. Jagan Pillarisetti, "Descent into Danger," 7 March 2015, https://swarajyamag .com/politics/descent-into-danger-the-jaffna-university-helidrop.

8. Pillarisetti, "Descent into Danger."

9. A lungi is a garment worn by men in southern India and Sri Lanka. It is wrapped around the waist, much like a sarong.

10. S. C. Sardeshpande, *Assignment Jaffna* (New Delhi: Lancer, 1992), 46–47.

11. R. R. Palsokar, *Ours Not to Reason Why* (Pune, India: Sunidhi Publishers, 2017). My narration of the trials and tribulations of Seventh Brigade is a fusion of my understanding of Palsokar's narrative, several email exchanges and conversations with him, and conversations with many who served in the brigade or supported it.

12. Telephone interview with Brigadier Xerxes Adrianwalla, 29 November 2019, and email correspondence, 13 November 2019.

13. Palsokar, *Ours Not to Reason Why*, 106–107.

14. Email correspondence with Palsokar.

15. Email correspondence and interviews with Palsokar and others.

16. Bharat Kumar, *Operation Pawan: Role of Airpower with IPKF* (New Delhi: Manohar, 2015), 148–159.

17. Unni Kartha, "Stroll through the Killing Fields of Sri Lanka," 31 October 2018, http://cyclicstories.blogspot.com/2018/.

18. Several conversations with Group Captain Rajnish Malhotra (retired).

19. Interview with Rostum Nanavatty, 14 February 2017.

20. Off-the-record conversations with officers currently serving in the Indian Army who wish to remain anonymous.

21. Off-the-record conversations.

22. Telephone interview and email exchange with Colonel Hariharan, 9 September 2019.

23. Interview with Lieutenant General Katoch, 13 May 2019.

24. Katoch interview.

25. Nanavatty interview.

26. Email correspondence with Captain Chandavarkar, 16 July 2019. Also see G. M. Hiranandani, *Transition to Eminence: The Indian Navy 1976–1990* (New Delhi: Lancer Publishers, 2004), 241–242.

27. From the Fifty-Seventh Division's operational diaries. Also see Rohan Gunaratna, *Indian Intervention in Sri Lanka* (Colombo, Sri Lanka: Gunaratne Offset, 1993), 258.

28. Anita Pratap, "Sri Lanka: IPKF Gains Public Acceptance in Batticaloa," *India Today*, 15 June 1988, https://www.indiatoday.in/magazine/neighbours/story/19880615-sri-lanka-ipkf-gains-public-acceptance-in-batticaloa-797341-1988-06-15.

29. Shyam Tekwani, "Sri Lanka Voters Back United National Party but Peace Remains Elusive," *India Today*, 15 March 1989, https://www.indiatoday.in/magazine/neighbours/story/19890315-sri-lanka-voters-back-united-national-party-but-peace-remains-elusive-815847-1989-03-15.

30. Gunaratna, *Indian Intervention*, 259.

31. Interview with General V. N. Sharma, 21 August 2019.

32. Sharma interview.

33. Telephone conversation with Admiral Madhavendra Singh, 2 May 2020.

34. Hiranandani, *Transition to Eminence*, 195; Sharma interview.

35. Ashoke Mehta, "Tackling the Tigers," 1999, http://www.india-seminar.com/1999/479/479%20mehta.htm. Also see "Revisiting Interventionism: India's Peacekeeping Force in Sri Lanka," Brookings India, 5 May 2019, https://www.brookings.edu/events/revisiting-interventionism-indias-peacekeeping-force-in-sri-lanka/.

36. David Brewster, "An Indian Sphere of Influence in the Indian Ocean?" *Security Challenges* 6, 3 (Spring 2010): 15, https://www.jstor.org/stable/26459796?seq=1#metadata_info_tab_contents.

37. Email correspondence with Hariharan, 19 September 2019.

38. Interview with X.

39. Nanavatty interviews.

40. Mehta, "Tackling the Tigers."

41. Hiranandani, *Transition to Eminence*, 196.

42. Hiranandani, *Transition to Eminence*, 196.

43. Arjun Subramaniam, "The Use of Air Power in Sri Lanka: Operation Pawan and Beyond," *Air Power Journal* 3, 3 (July–September 2008): 15–35, http://capsindia .org/files/documents/Air-Power-Jul-Sep-08-Inside.pdf.

Chapter 11. Speedy Intervention in Maldives

1. Conversation with Group Captain Anant Bewoor, March 2020.

2. Sushant Singh, *Mission Overseas: Daring Operations by the Indian Military* (New Delhi: Juggernaut, 2017), 18–20.

3. Interview with General V. P. Malik, 31 January 2020.

4. Group Captain Anant Bewoor and Brigadier S. C. Joshi, presentation at Defence Services Staff College, 1990; several conversations with Bewoor.

5. Email correspondence with Lieutenant General Navkiran Singh Ghei, 9 June 2019.

6. Telephone conversation with Bewoor.

7. Presentation by Bewoor and Joshi.

8. Presentation by Bewoor and Joshi.

9. Ghei email correspondence.

10. Presentation by Bewoor and Joshi.

11. Ghei email correspondence.

12. Ghei email correspondence.

13. Interview with Captain Jayadevan, 2 and 4 June 2019.

14. Anonymous sources.

15. H. A. Gokhale, "Operation Cactus: A Naval Perspective" (presentation at Defence Services Staff College, 1990).

16. Jayadevan interview.

17. Jayadevan interview.

18. Jayadevan interview.

19. Bewoor papers, briefings, and conversations.

20. Nayanima Basu and Amiti Sen, "India Mulls Intervention as Maldives Crisis Deepens," *Hindu Business Line*, 6 February 2018, https://www.thehindubusiness line.com/news/world/india-mulls-intervention-as-maldives-crisis-deepens/article 22670700.ece.

21. Input from a retired senior IAF officer who was involved in the operation and has requested anonymity.

Chapter 12. Jammu and Kashmir Erupts

1. Sheikh Abdullah, *Flames of Chinar*, trans. Khushwant Singh (New Delhi: Viking, 1993).

2. Arjun Subramaniam, *India's Wars: A Military History 1947–1971* (Annapolis, MD: US Naval Institute Press, 2017), 121–131.

3. Simon Jones, "India, Pakistan and Counterinsurgency Operations in Jammu and Kashmir," *Small Wars and Insurgencies* 19, 1 (March 2008): 4, https://www.tandfonline.com/doi/abs/10.1080/09592310801905736.

4. C. Dasgupta, *War and Diplomacy in Kashmir: 1947–1948* (New Delhi: Sage Publications, 2002), 102.

5. Pravin Swami, *India, Pakistan and the Secret Jihad* (New Delhi: Routledge, 2007), 46.

6. "Sheikh Abdullah and the Kashmir Issue," declassified CIA report, 18 April 1964, https://www.cia.gov/library/readingroom/docs/DOC_0000283431.pdf.

7. Swami, *India, Pakistan*, 53–55.

8. Subramaniam, *India's Wars*, 275–282.

9. Subramaniam, *India's Wars*, 261–335.

10. Pranadhar Gaur, "Use of Force in Regional Conflicts: A Study of Pakistan's Two-Level Strategy in Kashmir since 1987" (Ph.D. diss., Jawaharlal Nehru University, 2000), http://shodhganga.inflibnet.ac.in/handle/10603/15150?mode=full.

11. Gaur, "Use of Force in Regional Conflicts," 78; Shaukat Riza, *The Pakistan Army War 1965* (Lahore, Pakistan: Wajid Ali's, 1984), 20.

12. Hussain Haqqani, *India vs Pakistan: Why Can't We Just Be Friends* (New Delhi: Juggernaut, 2016), 115–116. Also see Aslam Siddiqui, *Pakistan Seeks Security* (Lahore, Pakistan: Longman Green, 1960), 67.

13. C. Christine Fair, *Fighting to the End: The Pakistan Army's Way of War* (New Delhi: Oxford University Press, 2014), 101.

14. Gaur, "Use of Force in Regional Conflicts," 105–107.

15. Subramaniam, *India's Wars*, 423–438.

16. Fair, *Fighting to the End*, 81–82. Fair covers Zia's theological impact on the Pakistan Army in chapter 4, "The Army's Defense of Pakistan's Ideological Frontiers."

17. S. K. Malik, *The Quranic Concept of War* (New Delhi: Himalayan Books, 1986). For an excellent review of this book, see Gurmeet Kanwal, "Misinterpreting the Quran to Justify Jihad," Center for Land and Warfare Studies Issue Brief 13, 2009, https://www.claws.in/static/IB13_Misinterpreting-the-Quran-to-Justify-Jihad.pdf.

18. Zia's derivative subconventional strategy against India bore a striking similarity to Mao's guerrilla war-fighting strategy.

19. Fair, *Fighting to the End*, 40–65. Fair's chapter 3, "Born an Insecure State," offers insights into the origins of Pakistan's deep sense of insecurity vis-à-vis India.

20. Gaur, "Use of Force in Regional Conflicts."

21. Swami, *India, Pakistan*.

22. Of the numerous books written by Sumit Ganguly, I found *Conflict Unending: India-Pakistan Tensions since 1947* (New York: Columbia University Press, 2002) and *Deadly Impasse: Indo-Pakistan Relations at the Dawn of a New Century* (Cambridge: Cambridge University Press, 2016) to be most instructive.

23. Swami, *India, Pakistan*, 78–85.

24. Swami, *India, Pakistan*, 78–85.

25. Swami, *India, Pakistan*, 125–130.

26. Subramaniam, *India's Wars*, 119.

27. Swami, *India, Pakistan*, 158–160.

28. "Who Is Syed Salahuddin, and Why Is He Designated as a 'Global Terrorist'?" *Hindu*, 27 June 2017, https://www.thehindu.com/news/national/who-is-syed-sala huddin-and-what-is-a-global-terrorist/article19154173.ece.

29. Ved Marwah, *Uncivil Wars: Pathology of Terrorism in India* (New Delhi: Indus, 1995), 166–175.

30. Marwah, *Uncivil Wars*, 166–175.

31. Joseph C. Myers, "The Quranic Concept of War," *Parameters* (Winter 2006–2007), http://insct.syr.edu/wp-content/uploads/2013/03/MyersJoseph.Quranic-Con cept-of-War.pdf.

32. Afsar Karim, "Operation Topac," *Indian Defence Review*, July 1989.

33. Karim, "Operation Topac," 35–48.

34. Sean P. Winchell, "Pakistan's ISI: The Invisible Government," *International Journal of Intelligence and Counter Intelligence* 16, 3 (Fall 2003): 374, https://www .tandfonline.com/doi/abs/10.1080/713830449.

35. Gaur, "Use of Force in Regional Conflicts," ch. 5.

36. Winchell, "Pakistan's ISI," 374, 379.

37. Fatalities due to terrorist violence, 1988–2017, South Asia Terrorism Portal, http://www.satp.org/satporgtp/countries/india/states/jandk/data_sheets/annual_casu alties.htm.

38. "Ajit Doval Says Not One Bullet Fired in Kashmir in the Past Month, a Record since 1988," *Print*, 6 September 2019, https://theprint.in/india/ajit-doval-says-not -one-bullet-fired-in-kashmir-in-the-past-month-a-record-since-1988/288279/.

39. Jones, "India, Pakistan and Counterinsurgency Operations," 7.

40. Paul Staniland, "Organizing Insurgency: Networks, Resources and Rebellion in South Asia," *International Security* 37, 1 (Summer 2012): 142–177, https://www .jstor.org/stable/23280407?seq=1; South Asia Terrorism Portal. Staniland's article offers an excellent overview of all the major terrorist networks and groups in J&K.

41. Siddhartha Gigoo, "In Search of Stories Lost," https://www.livemint.com/Lei sure/AIQpbcotgcNTeiGf71zFoI/In-search-of-stories-lost.html. Gigoo wrote this story twenty-six years after being forced to leave his home as part of the pogrom unleashed on Kashmiri Hindus by radical Kashmiri separatists led by Jamaat-e-Islami.

42. For a detailed account of this period, see Manoj Joshi, *The Lost Rebellion: Kashmir in the Nineties* (New Delhi: Penguin, 1999). Also see Pravin Swami, "Terrorism in Jammu and Kashmir in Theory and Practice," *India Review* 2, 3 (2003): 55–58.

43. Arif Jamal, *Shadow War* (New York: Melville Publishing, 2009), 109.

44. Arif Jamal, *Call for Transnational Jihad: Lashkar-e-Tayyaba (1985–2014)* (New Delhi: Kautilya Books, 2015), 92–119.

45. Winchell, "Pakistan's ISI," 380.

46. Staniland, "Organizing Insurgency," 167. Also see Swami, "Terrorism in Jammu and Kashmir," 58–59.

47. Jones, "India, Pakistan and Counterinsurgency Operations," 9–10.

48. Praveen Swami, "Remains of Another Day," *Frontline* 17, 2 (22 January 2000), https://frontline.thehindu.com/static/html/fl1702/17020100.htm.

49. For a list of terrorist organizations declared by the United States, see https://www.state.gov/j/ct/rls/other/des/123085.htm.

50. Rahul Pandita, "Beyond Balakot," *Open Magazine*, 28 February 2019, https://openthemagazine.com/cover-stories/beyond-balakot/.

51. C. Christine Fair, *In Their Words: Understanding Lashkar-e-Tayyaba* (New Delhi: Oxford University Press, 2019), 77; Indian Air Force archives and operational diary at the air force station in Srinagar.

52. Interviews with Lieutenant General Rostum Nanavatty, 14 February 2017, 8 and 9 August 2019.

53. Nanavatty interviews.

54. A detailed overview of major terrorist attacks in India prior to 2008 is available in Gurmeet Kanwal and N. Manoharan, eds., *India's War on Terror* (New Delhi: KW Publishers, 2010), 283–296.

55. Adrian Levy and Cathy-Scott Clark, *The Meadow: Kashmir, Where the Terror Began* (New Delhi: HarperCollins, 2012), 31–57. The best profile of Masood Azhar is in the chapter titled "A Father's Woes."

56. Shujaat Bukhari, "From a Calm Moulvi to a Dreaded Militant," *Hindu*, 17 October 2001, https://www.thehindu.com/thehindu/2001/10/17/stories/02170003.htm.

57. Interview with Colonel Pavan Nair, Pune, India, 30 March 2019.

58. South Asia Terrorism Portal.

59. United Nations Security Council, Jaish-i-Mohammed, https://www.un.org/securitycouncil/sanctions/1267/aq_sanctions_list/summaries/entity/jaish-i-mohammed.

60. "Kaluchak Massacre, 14 May 2002," press release, Indian Ministry of External Affairs, https://mea.gov.in/in-focus-article.htm?18990/Kaluchak+Massacre+14+May+2002.

Chapter 13. The Indian Army Responds

1. Interview with Rostum Nanavatty, 8 August 2019. Many of Nanavatty's briefings and letters to his commanders attempted to differentiate insurgency and terrorism.

2. Interview with Lieutenant General M. A. Zaki, Hyderabad, India, 1 July 2019.

3. Pravin Swami, *India, Pakistan and the Secret Jihad* (New Delhi: Routledge, 2007), 145–149.

4. Hamish Telford, "Counterinsurgency in India: Observations from Punjab and Kashmir," *Journal of Conflict Studies* 21, 1 (Spring 2001), https://journals.lib.unb.ca/index.php/JCS/article/view/4293.

5. Rajesh Rajagopalan, *Fighting Like a Guerrilla* (New Delhi: Routledge, 2008); Rostum K. Nanavatty, *Internal Armed Conflict in India* (New Delhi: Pentagon Press, 2013).

6. Nanavatty interview.

7. Kaushik Adhikary, "Combating Terrorism in 21st Century: The Legal and Institutional Responses with Special Reference to Indian Security Laws" (thesis, University of Calcutta, 2017), ch. 5, https://shodhganga.inflibnet.ac.in/handle/10603/172205.

8. Skype interview with Lieutenant General Syed Ata Hasnain, 6 April 2020.

9. John A. Nagl, *Learning to Eat Soup with a Knife: Counterinsurgency Lessons from Malaya and Vietnam* (Chicago: University of Chicago Press, 2005), 28.

10. HQ Northern Command Study Group, *Soldiers' Role in Jammu and Kashmir* (New Delhi: HQ Northern Command, 1984).

11. Hasnain interview.

12. Letter from Jagmohan to Rajiv Gandhi, April 1990, http://www.newindianexpress.com/nation/2019/aug/17/potatoes-one-day-the-pope-the-next-2020117.html.

13. Pranadhar Gaur, "Use of Force in Regional Conflicts: A Study of Pakistan's Two-Level Strategy in Kashmir since 1987" (Ph.D. diss., Jawaharlal Nehru University, 2000), 287, http://shodhganga.inflibnet.ac.in/handle/10603/15150?mode=full.

14. Interview with Brigadier R (who requested anonymity).

15. Swami, *India, Pakistan*, 175.

16. Jagmohan, *My Frozen Turbulence in Kashmir* (Bombay: Allied Publishers, 1991), 162–165. Also see Inderjit Badhwar, "Rising Unpopularity Threatens Kashmir Accord," *India Today*, 15 September 1987, https://www.indiatoday.in/magazine/special-report/story/19870915-rising-unpopularity-threatens-kashmir-accord-799268-1987-09-15.

17. Zaki interview.

18. "Ashfaq Majeed Wani Remembered," *Greater Kashmir*, 5 July 2019, https://www.greaterkashmir.com/news/kashmir/ashfaq-majeed-wani-remembered/.

19. Swami, *India, Pakistan*, 175.

20. Zaki interview.

21. For a detailed profile of Salahuddin, see Hakim Irfan Rashid, "Syed Salahuddin: Tale of a Preacher Turned Terror Chief," *Economic Times*, 14 July 2018, https://economictimes.indiatimes.com/news/defence/syed-salahuddin-tale-of-a-preacher-turned-terror-chief/articleshow/59343807.cms?from=mdr.

22. Pankaj Pachauri, "Mirwaiz Fiasco Sparks off a Change in Guard in Kashmir," *India Today*, 15 June 1990, https://www.indiatoday.in/magazine/indiascope/story/19900615-mirwaiz-fiasco-sparks-off-a-change-of-guard-in-kashmir-812692-1990-06.

23. Bilal Handoo, "Charar after Mast Gul," *Kashmir Life*, 17 May 2016, https://kashmirlife.net/charar-after-mast-gul-issue-09-vol-08-105467/.

24. "Mast Gul, a Freedom Fighter Turned Terrorist Attacks Peshawar," *News*, 7 February 2014, https://www.thenews.com.pk/archive/print/636032-mast-gul,-a-freedom-fighter-turned-terrorist-attacks-peshawar.

25. Lawrence E. Cline, "Pseudo Operations in Counterinsurgency: Lessons from Other Countries" (SSI Monograph, US Army War College, 2005), https://www.globalsecurity.org/military/library/report/2005/ssi_cline.pdf. The paper does not cover operations conducted by the Indian Army because these were never publicized. Also

see Paul Staniland, "Organizing Insurgency: Networks, Resources and Rebellion in South Asia," *International Security* 37, 1 (Summer 2012), https://www.jstor.org/stable/23280407?seq=1.

26. Cline, "Pseudo Operations in Counterinsurgency."

27. Interview with Colonel Pavan Nair, 30 March 2019.

28. Interview with Lieutenant General Hooda, 20 July 2019.

29. Interview with Lieutenant General Pattabhiraman, 13 December 2016.

30. Hasnain interview.

Chapter 14. Surprise and Riposte in Kargil

1. Telephone conversation with Major General Alok Deb, 22 November 2019.

2. Vivek Chadha, *Low Intensity Conflicts in South Asia: An Analysis* (Delhi: Sage, 2005), 141. Also see Shaukat Qadir, "An Analysis of the Kargil Conflict 1999," *RUSI Journal* 147, 2 (2002): 24–30, https://doi.org/10.1080/03071840208446752.

3. Owen Bennet Jones, *Pakistan: Eye of the Storm* (New Haven, CT: Yale University Press, 2002), 94–96.

4. Chadha, *Low Intensity Conflicts*, 141.

5. Many of the Indian officers interviewed have acknowledged the professional capabilities and raw courage of the SSG.

6. Ajai Sahni, "Area of Darkness," *Outlook*, 18 September 2009, https://www.outlookindia.com/website/story/an-area-of-darkness/261931.

7. Chadha, *Low Intensity Conflicts*, 141. Also see Alok Bansal, "Gilgit-Baltistan: The Roots of Political Alienation," *Strategic Analysis* 32, 1 (January 2008): 84.

8. Zafar Iqbal Cheema, "The Strategic Concept of the Kargil Conflict," in *Asymmetric Warfare in South Asia*, ed. Peter Lavoy (New York: Cambridge University Press, 2009).

9. Telephone conversation with Colonel Kuldip Mehta, 15 August 2019.

10. Interview with Lieutenant General Katoch, 13 May 2019.

11. This overview of the Indians' area of operation is based on personal visits to the region and discussions with several Indian Army officers who served there.

12. Rahul Bedi, "Intel Failures Made Indian Attacks in Kashmir Inevitable," *Jane's Intelligence Review* 11, 6 (June 1999).

13. Rohit Saran, Harinder Baweja, and Raj Chengappa, "Kargil Conflict Shows Signs of Intensifying as India Gains, Pakistan Remains Resilient," *India Today*, 5 July 1999, https://www.indiatoday.in/magazine/cover-story/story/19990705-kargil-conflict-shows-signs-of-intensifying-as-india-gains-pakistan-remains-resilient-824618-1999-07-05.

14. Nasim Zehra, *From Kargil to the Coup* (Lahore, Pakistan: Sang-e-Meel Publications, 2018), 96–97.

15. Zehra, *From Kargil to the Coup*, 100.

16. Ikram Sehgal, "Choosing Merit over Friendship," Media Monitors Network, 9 October 2001, https://www.mediamonitors.net/perspectives/choosing-merit-over-friendship/.

17. Qadir, "Analysis of Kargil Conflict."

18. Praveen Swami, "General Kayani's Quiet Coup," *Hindu*, 3 August 2010, http://www.thehindu.com/todays-paper/tp-opinion/General-Kayanis-quiet-coup /article16117389.ece.

19. C. Christine Fair, *Fighting to the End: The Pakistan Army's Way of War* (New Delhi: Oxford University Press, 2014), 163–164. Fair devotes an entire chapter to how the Pakistan Army perceives India through multiple lenses.

20. Mohinder Puri, *Kargil: Turning the Tide* (New Delhi: Lancer, 2016).

21. Conversation with Subroto Park, former air chief at Western Air Command, 16 July 2019, after an airpower seminar to commemorate the twentieth anniversary of the Kargil Conflict.

22. Interview with Air Marshal Vinod Patney, 6 August 2018.

23. Kargil Review Committee, *From Surprise to Reckoning* (New Delhi: Sage Publications, 1999), 85–86. Also see John Gill, "Military Operations in the Kargil Conflict," in Lavoy, *Asymmetric Warfare in South Asia*, 101.

24. General V. P. Malik, "The Capture of Tiger Hill: A First-hand Account," Indian Ministry of Defense Media Center, 26 July 2002, http://mea.gov.in/articles -in-indian-media.htm?dtl/14805/The+capture+of+Tiger+Hill+a+firsthand+acco unt.

25. Mehta conversation.

26. See J. N. Dixit, *India-Pakistan: In War and Peace* (London: Routledge, 2002); Praveen Swami, "Skeletons in the Generals' Cupboards," *Hindu*, 10 August 2009, http://www.thehindu.com/todays-paper/tp-opinion/Skeletons-in-the-Generalsrsquo -cupboards/article16530736.ece; B. Raman, "Should We Believe Gen Malik," Rediff, 5 May 2006, http://m.rediff.com/news/1999/jul/16akd.htm.

27. V. P. Malik, *India's Military Conflicts and Diplomacy* (New Delhi: HarperCollins, 2019), 120.

28. Swami, "Skeletons."

29. Interview with Ahluwalia, 21 February 2019.

30. Kaiser Tufail, "Kargil Conflict and the Pakistan Air Force," *Aeronaut*, 28 January 2009, http://kaiser-aeronaut.blogspot.co.uk/2009/01/.

31. Tufail, "Kargil Conflict."

32. Zehra, *From Kargil*, 101

33. Praveen Swami, "The Kargil War: Preliminary Explorations," South Asia Terrorism Portal and Institute for Conflict Management, 2001, http://www.satp.org /satporgtp/publication/faultlines/volume2/Fault2-SwamiF.htm.

34. Interview with Lieutenant General Ghei, Chandigarh, 19 July 2019.

35. Gill, "Military Operations."

36. Rahul Bedi, "Paying to Keep the High Ground," *Jane's Intelligence Review* 11, 10 (October 1999).

37. V. P. Malik, *From Surprise to Victory* (New Delhi: HarperCollins, 2006), 209.

38. Josy Joseph, "Three Battalions Ignored as the Nation Honours Martyrs of Kargil," Rediff, 25 July 2000, https://www.rediff.com/news/2000/jul/25kargil.htm.

39. Interview with General V. P. Malik, 31 January 2020.

40. See Gill, "Military Operations"; Malik, *From Surprise to Victory*; Zehra, *From Kargil.*

41. Gill, "Military Operations."

42. Gill, "Military Operations."

43. Sumit Walia, "Head Hunters in Kargil-Naga Regiment," *Indian Defence Review*, 28 July 2017, http://www.indiandefencereview.com/spotlights/head-hunters -in-kargil-naga-regiment/.

44. "Tololing Peak: The Battle that Probably Changed the Course of the Kargil War," *India Today*, 5 July 1999, https://www.indiatoday.in/magazine/cover-story /story/19990705-tololing-peak-the-battle-that-probably-changed-the-course-of-kar gil-war-824608-1999-07-05.

45. Interview with Air Marshal "Nana" Menon, Bangalore, India, 21 January 2019. Also see Benjamin Lambeth, "Air Power at 18,000: The Indian Air Force in the Kargil War" (Carnegie Endowment for International Peace, 20 September 2012). Lambeth's monograph is an authoritative document that was written after extensive research conducted during two visits to India.

46. Patney interview.

47. Conversation with Air Chief Marshal Tipnis.

48. Malik interview.

49. Patney interview.

50. Lambeth, "Air Power"; official records and Kargil diaries, IAF history cell, Air HQ New Delhi. Also see Squadron Leader Alagaraj Perumal, "Missile Strike," 12 June 2017, http://www.bharat-rakshak.com/IAF/history/kargil/1060-perumal.html.

51. Conversation with Group Captain Tokekar, an active participant in the conflict as part of Seventh Squadron.

52. Email correspondence with Wing Commander Sameer Joshi, 15 October 2019.

53. Tokekar conversation.

54. Telephone conversation with Patney, 25 November 2019.

55. Interview with Air Chief Marshal Dhanoa, 27 June 2019.

56. Air Commodore Sinha's narration is in the squadron diary of 129th Helicopter Unit.

57. Vivek Chadha, "Artillery in Op Vijay: Perspective of a Commanding Officer," 28 June 2019, https://www.youtube.com/watch?v=6V_XiMHyPo8. Also see Alok Deb, "Artillery in Operation Vijay: Perspective of a Commanding Officer," in *Surprise, Strategy and Vijay—20 Years of Kargil and Beyond*, ed. V. K. Ahluwalia and Narjit Singh (New Delhi: Pentagon Press, 2019), 77–85.

58. Email correspondence with Air Chief Marshal Major.

59. Marcus P. Acosta, "The Kargil Conflict: Waging War in the Himalayas," *Small Wars and Insurgencies* 18, 3 (2007): 397–415, https://doi.org/10.1080 /09592310701674325.

60. IAF squadron commander who requested anonymity.

61. Conversations with Bhanoji Rao, a weapons expert, and Mirage pilots who dropped the Spanish bombs, 12 October 2019.

62. L. N. Subramanian, "A Ridge Too Far: Battle for Tololing," 12 October 2006,

http://www.bharat-rakshak.com/ARMY/history/kargil/307-battle-for-tololing.html?
tmpl=component&print=1&layout=default&page=.

Chapter 15. A Costly Victory

1. Benjamin Lambeth, "Air Power at 18,000: The Indian Air Force in the Kargil War" (Carnegie Endowment for International Peace, 20 September 2012).

2. See Lambeth, "Airpower at 18,000."

3. Interview with Air Marshal Patney, 6 August 2018.

4. Interview with Air Chief Marshal Dhanoa, 29 June 2019.

5. John Gill, "Military Operations in the Kargil Conflict," in *Asymmetric Warfare in South Asia*, ed. Peter Lavoy (New York: Cambridge University Press, 2009), 113; interview with Major General Alok Deb, 15 September 2019.

6. Gill, "Military Operations," 120.

7. A dramatic description of the assault by Havildar Digendra Singh is available on YouTube, https://www.youtube.com/watch?v=qzkm-yWXmdc. Also see the account by Colonel Ravindranath, "Victory in Kargil War: Lessons Learnt at Great Human Cost," 26 July 2015, https://www.thequint.com/news/india/victory-in-kargil-war -lessons-learnt-at-great-human-cost.

8. Ravindranath, "Victory in Kargil War."

9. Diksha Dwivedi, *Letters from Kargil* (New Delhi: Juggernaut, 2017).

10. Dhanoa interview.

11. Interview with General V. P. Malik, 31 January 2020.

12. Vishnu Shome, "In Kargil War, India Was Minutes away from Bombing Pak Bases," 19 July 2016, https://www.ndtv.com/india-news/exclusive-in-kargil-war-india -was-minutes-away-from-bombing-pak-bases-1433345.

13. Mohinder Puri, *Kargil: Turning the Tide* (New Delhi: Lancer, 2016), 78.

14. Puri, *Kargil*, 87.

15. Several personal interviews and conversations with Chakravorty between July 2019 and March 2020.

16. Chakravorty interviews; email correspondence with Alok Deb, 19 February 2019.

17. Chakravorty interviews.

18. Conversation with Wing Commander K. T. Sebastian (retired), 4 May 2020.

19. Leo Murray, *War Games: The Psychology of Combat* (Mumbai: Jaico Publishing, 2019).

20. Conversations and interview with Air Marshal Nambiar; conversations with Wing Commander Anupam Banerjee.

21. Nambiar conversations and interview; Banerjee conversations; telephone conversations with Group Captain Tokekar, who participated in both missions as a flight lieutenant.

22. Nishtha Gupta, "10 Heroes India Will Always Be Proud Of,' *India Today*, 26 July 2019, https://www.indiatoday.in/india/story/10-kargil-heroes-india-will-always -be-proud-of-1574014-2019-07-26.

23. Nasim Zehra, *From Kargil to the Coup* (Lahore, Pakistan: Sang-e-Meel Publications, 2018), 230.

24. Puri, *Kargil*, 90–95. Also see V. P. Malik, *From Surprise to Victory* (New Delhi: HarperCollins, 2006), 169–175; Harinder Baweja, "Kargil War: Army Took over a Month Planning to Recapture Tiger Hill in Dras Sector," *India Today*, 19 July 1999, https://www.indiatoday.in/magazine/cover-story/story/19990719-kargil -war-army-took-over-a-months-planning-to-recapture-tiger-hill-in-drass-sector -824832-1999-07-19.

25. Malik, *From Surprise to Victory*, 263.

26. Interview with Admiral Madhavendra Singh, 2 May 2020.

27. Kargil Review Committee, *From Surprise to Reckoning* (New Delhi: Sage Publications, 1999), 160.

28. Introduction to *Asymmetric Warfare in South Asia*, ed. Peter Lavoy (New York: Cambridge University Press, 2009).

29. Sushant Sareen, "Balakot Air Strikes: The End of the Madman Theory," *ORF Commentary*, 5 March 2019, https://www.orfonline.org/research/balakot-air-strikes -the-end-of-the-madman-theory-48730/.

30. Rahul Bedi, "Paying to Keep the High Ground," *Jane's Intelligence Review* 11, 10 (October 1999).

31. Gill, "Military Operations."

32. Peter Lavoy, "A Conversation with Gen Khalid Kidwai," Carnegie International Nuclear Policy Conference, 23 March 2015, https://carnegieendowment.org/files /03-230315carnegieKIDWAI.pdf.

33. Strobe Talbott, "The Day a Nuclear Conflict Was Averted,' *Yale Global Online*, 13 September 2004, https://yaleglobal.yale.edu/content/day-nuclear-conflict-was -averted.

34. Strobe Talbott, *Engaging India: Diplomacy, Democracy, and the Bomb* (Washington, DC: Brookings Institution Press, 2006), 154–169.

35. Talbott, *Engaging India*.

36. Lavoy, *Asymmetric Warfare*, 4.

37. Lavoy, *Asymmetric Warfare*, 4.

38. Pervez Musharraf, *In the Line of Fire* (New York: Free Press, 2006).

39. Arjun Subramaniam, "Kargil Revisited: Air Operations in a High-Altitude Conflict," *CLAWS Journal* (Summer 2008): 183–195.

40. Carl von Clausewitz, *On War*, ed. and trans. Michael Howard and Peter Paret (Princeton, NJ: Princeton University Press, 1976), 340.

41. Zehra, *From Kargil*, 219–220.

42. Kargil Review Committee, *From Surprise to Reckoning*, 252–264.

43. J. N. Dixit, *India-Pakistan: In War and Peace* (London: Routledge, 2002). Praveen Swami largely goes along with Dixit's hypothesis in his writings, blaming the Indian Army for gross dereliction of duty.

44. Malik, *From Surprise to Victory*, 85–112.

45. Subramaniam, "Kargil Revisited," 191.

46. Zehra, *From Kargil*, 215.

47. Patney interview.

48. Vinod Anand, "India's Military Response to the Kargil Aggression," *Strategic Analysis* 23 (October 1999): 56.

49. Marcus Acosta, "High Altitude Warfare: The Kargil Conflict and the Future" (thesis, Naval Postgraduate School, Monterey, CA, 2003), 18–45, https://calhoun .nps.edu/handle/10945/1043.

50. Mohan Bhandari, "Kargil Controversy: Army Trashed IAF Perspective," *Indian Defense Review* 25 (April–June 2010), http://www.indiandefensereview.com /spotlights/kargil-controversy-army-trashes-iaf-perspective/.

51. Zehra, *From Kargil*, 232.

52. Kaiser Tufail, "Kargil Conflict and Pakistan Air Force," *Aeronaut*, 28 January 2009, http://kaiser-aeronaut.blogspot.com/2009/01/kargil-conflict-and-pakistan-air -force.html.

53. Telephone conversation with Patney, 25 November 2019.

54. Subramaniam, "Kargil Revisited," 194.

55. Ved Shenag, "The IAF in the Kargil Operations—1999," *Bharat Rakshak*, 16 October 2009, http://bharat-rakshak.com/IAF/History/Kargil/1055-VedShenag.html.

56. Patney interview.

Chapter 16. Hybrid War in Jammu and Kashmir

1. Harsha Kakar, "Has Pakistan Started Losing the Hybrid War in Kashmir," Raisina Debates, *ORF Online*, 2018, https://www.orfonline.org/expert-speak/has -pakistan-started-losing-hybrid-war-kashmir-46027/.

2. Extensive email correspondence with Lieutenant General John Ranjan Mukher-jee (retired), August 2019.

3. Rajesh Ahuja, "Looking Back, the Ceasefire in Kashmir in 2000 Saw More Violence but Lasted Longer," *Hindustan Times*, 17 June 2018, https://www.hindu stantimes.com/india-news/looking-back-the-ceasefire-in-2000-saw-more-violence -but-was-longer/story-eD1BIfi109TFgopG.

4. Extensive conversation with Brigadier R. K. Singh (retired), Dehra Dun, India, 11 and 12 March 2019.

5. Email correspondence with Colonel Gurdeep Bains, October 2018.

6. Letter from Bains to his battalion, 11 December 2001.

7. Letter from Victor Force to Indian Army HQ, 28 May 2002.

8. Letter from Bains to his battalion, 23 April 2003.

9. Email correspondence with Gurdeep Bains.

10. Firdaus Tak, "Warwan Valley: A Hidden Beauty," *Greater Kashmir*, 24 July 2012, https://www.greaterkashmir.com/news/news/warwan-valley-a-hidden -beauty/125718.html.

11. Personal papers of Bains.

12. Interview with Arun Prakash, 30 October 2016.

13. Personal papers of Bains.

14. Interview with Gurdeep Bains, Bangalore, India, 10 February 2019.

15. Interviews with Rostum Nanavatty, 8 and 9 August 2018.

16. Praveen Swami, "Hype and the Folly," *Frontline* 20, 13 (20 June 2013), https://frontline.thehindu.com/static/html/fl2013/stories/20030704007300400.htm.

17. Nanavatty interviews.

18. Interview with Lieutenant General Hooda, 20 July 2019.

19. Nanavatty interviews and diaries.

20. Interview with Syed Ata Hasnain, 6 April 2020. Also see Happymon Jacob, *Line on Fire: Ceasefire Violations and India-Pakistan Escalation Dynamics* (New Delhi: Oxford University Press, 2019), table 4.2, https://doi.org/10.1093 /oso/9780199489893.001.0001.

21. Amy Waldman, "India and Pakistan: Good Fences Make Good Neighbours," *New York Times*, 4 July 2004, https://www.nytimes.com/2004/07/04/world/india -and-pakistan-good-fences-make-good-neighbors.html.

22. Waldman, "India and Pakistan."

23. Waldman, "India and Pakistan."

24. Hooda interview.

25. Snehesh Alex Phillip, "What Imran Khan Says Is 9 Lakh Soldiers in Kashmir Is Actually 3.43 Lakh Only," *Print*, 12 November 2019, https://theprint.in /defense/what-imran-khan-says-is-9-lakh-soldiers-in-kashmir-is-actually-3-43-lakh -only/319442/. For an earlier report, see Ajai Shukla, "India Has 700,000 Troops in Kashmir? False !!!" Rediff, 17 July 2018, https://www.rediff.com/news/column /india-has-700000-troops-in-kashmir-false/20180717.htm.

26. "India Has Deployed More than 1 Million Troops in Held Kashmir: Foreign Office," Dawn, 30 November 2016, https://www.dawn.com/news/1299621/india-has -deployed-more-than-1-million-troops-in-held-kashmir-foreign-office.

27. Based on discussions with Nanavatty, Hooda, and Rakesh Sharma.

28. Interview with General Bipin Rawat, 21 April 2019.

29. Harsha Kakar, "Pace the Key for Interlocutor Success," *ORF Online*, 20 October 2017, https://www.orfonline.org/expert-speak/pace-key-interlocutors-success -kashmir/. Also see G. Parthasarathy and Radha Kumar, *Frameworks for a Kashmir Settlement* (New Delhi: Delhi Policy Group, 2006).

30. "Chronology of Amarnath Land Row," *Times of India*, 6 August 2008, https://timesofindia.indiatimes.com/india/Chronology-of-Amarnath-land-row/ar ticleshow/3331566.cms.

31. Hasnain interview.

32. The Huriyat, as it is known, is a twenty-six-member alliance of separatist parties that was formed in 1993 with enduring support from the Pakistani deep state.

33. Hasnain interview.

34. Discussion with Lieutenant General Ravi Thodge during one of the Rawat interviews.

35. Hasnain interview.

36. See Aarti Tikoo Singh, "Here's How Schools of Faith, Mobiles Are Radicalising Kashmir," *Times of India*, 9 July 2017, https://timesofindia.indiatimes.com/india /how-mosques-and-mobiles-are-radicalising-kashmir/articleshow/59507200.cms.

37. Hooda interview.

38. Arun Prakash, "Who Defends the Defenders," *Indian Express*, 22 August 2018, https://indianexpress.com/article/opinion/columns/independence-day-afspa-indian-soldiers-miliatry-army-act-ministry-of-defense-5318222/.

39. Question-and-answer session during a talk by Hooda at Ashoka University, 18 September 2019.

40. Handling of human rights violations by the Indian Army's human rights cell, annexure 1, https://indianarmy.nic.in/Site/FormTemplete/frmTempSimple.aspx?MnId=xc6s3otnoaeLSkagPIPQRg==&ParentID=HyPoMmCZnmSA9FT9WPkFlw==.

41. Sumit Ganguly, *Deadly Impasse: Indo-Pakistan Relations at the Dawn of a New Century* (Cambridge: Cambridge University Press, 2016), 1–2.

42. Ganguly, *Deadly Impasse*, 19.

43. Ganguly, *Deadly Impasse*, 19.

44. Interview with a senior officer in the Indian Army who requested anonymity.

45. Interview with anonymous senior officer. Also see Ananya Bharadwaj, "Asiya Andrabi: Kashmir's First Separatist Who Also Dreamt of Marrying a Mujahid," *Print*, 10 December 2018, https://theprint.in/india/governance/asiya-andrabi-kashmirs-first-woman-separatist-who-also-dreamt-of-marrying-a-mujahid/160138/.

46. Interview with General Malik, 31 January 2020.

47. Sushant Sareen, "Pakistan Punched by Article 370 Move," *ORF Online*, 9 August 2019, https://www.orfonline.org/research/pakistan-punched-by-indias-article-370-move-54261/.

48. Nanavatty interviews.

49. Nanavatty interviews.

50. Conversation and email correspondence with an infantry officer currently posted in J&K who requested anonymity.

Chapter 17. Under the United Nations Flag

1. Odd Arne Westad, *The Cold War: A World History* (New Delhi: Penguin Books, 2017), 159–182.

2. Robert Barnes, "Between the Blocs: India, the United Nations and Ending the Korean War," *Journal of Korean Studies* 18, 2 (Fall 2013): 263–286, https://doi.org/10.1353/jks.2013.0022.

3. "Agreement on Prisoners of War (Official UN Documents)," *American Journal of International Law* 47, 4 (October 1953), https://www.jstor.org/stable/2213914.

4. Jairam Ramesh, "India's Role in Ending the Korean War," *Hindu*, 3 May 2018, www.thehindu.com/opinion/op-ed/india's-role-in-ending-the-korean-war/article23750989.ece.

5. Kim Chan Wahn, "The Role of India in the Korean War," *International Area Review* 13, 2 (Summer 2010): 22–24, https://journals.sagepub.com/doi/abs/10.1177/223386591001300202?journalCode=iasa.

6. Ramesh, "India's Role."

7. War diary of Sixtieth Parachute Field Ambulance.

8. Battle accounts from the US Army recovered from the war diary of Sixtieth Parachute Field Ambulance.

9. "Canadians in Korea," https://www.veterans.gc.ca/eng/remembrance/history /korean-war/valour-remembered.

10. From the archives of the Indian Army's parachute regimental training center, Bangalore.

11. Georges Nzongola-Ntalja, "Patrice Lumumba: The Most Important Assassination of the 20th Century," *Guardian*, 17 January 2011, https://www.theguardian .com/global-development/poverty-matters/2011/jan/17/patrice-lumumba-50th-anni versary-assassination.

12. A. Walter Dorn and David J. H. Bell, "Intelligence and Peacekeeping: The UN Operation in the Congo, 1960–64," *International Peacekeeping* 2, 1 (Spring 1995): 11–33. Also see Robert D. McFadden, "Mad Mike Hoare, Irish Mercenary Leader in Africa, Dies at 100," *New York Times*, 3 February 2020, https://www.nytimes .com/2020/02/03/obituaries/mike-hoare-dies.html.

13. Dorn and Bell, "Intelligence and Peacekeeping."

14. Rick Gladstone and Mike Ives, "UN Report Bolsters Theory that Hammarskjold Plane Was Downed," *New York Times*, 8 October 2019, https://www.nytimes .com/2019/10/08/world/africa/dag-hammarskjold.html.

15. "Elizabethville Fighting Rages as Plan Found," *Desert Sun*, 5 December 1961, https://cdnc.ucr.edu/cgi-bin/cdnc?a=d&d=DS19611205.2.10&e=-en-20-1 -txt-txIN-1.

16. K. K. Sharma, "Congo: First African War and Indian Soldiers (1960–64)," https://www.academia.edu/32888328/congo_first_african_war_and_indian_sol diers_1960-64_.doc.

17. K. S. Nair, *Ganesha's Flyboys: The IAF in Congo* (Hyderabad, India: Anveshan Enterprises, 2012).

18. Nair, *Ganesha's Flyboys*.

19. A. S. Ahluwalia, *Airborne to Chairborne: Memoirs of a War Veteran Aviator-Lawyer of the Indian Air Force* (Bloomington, IN: Xlibris, 2012), 189.

20. Satish Nambiar, "An Indian General Recalls How the World Failed Srebnica Years Ago," *Wire*, 12 July 2015, https://thewire.in/external-affairs/an-indian-general -recalls-how-the-world-failed-srebrenica-20-years-ago.

21. "IAF Contingent 2000 to UNAMSIL," http://indianairforce.nic.in/content /sierra-leone.

22. Chris McGreal, "What's the Point of Peacekeepers When They Do Not Keep the Peace?" *Guardian*, 17 September 2015, https://www.theguardian.com /world/2015/sep/17/un-united-nations-peacekeepers-rwanda-bosnia.

23. David H. Ucko, "Can Limited Intervention Work: Lessons from Britain's Success Story in Sierra Leone," *Journal of Strategic Studies* 39, 5–6 (December 2015): 847–877, https://www.tandfonline.com/doi/abs/10.1080/01402390.2015 .1110695.

24. Ucko, "Can Limited Intervention Work."

25. Colum Lynch, "India to Withdraw Large UN Force from Sierra Leone,"

Washington Post, 21 September 2000, https://www.washingtonpost.com/archive /politics/2000/09/21/india-to-withdraw-large-un-force-from-sierra-leone/33c46528 –678d-4014-b8b2-8aa299a3658b/?utm_term=.e2dfe7d4c37f.

26. Email correspondence with Brigadier Anil Raman.

27. Timothy Longman, "The Complex Reasons for Rwanda's Engagement in Congo," in *The African Stakes of the Congo War*, ed. John F. Clark (New York: Palgrave Macmillan, 2002), 131–132.

28. Christopher Bangert, "Kofi Annan, Who Redefined the UN, Dies at 80," *New York Times*, 18 August 2018, https://www.nytimes.com/2018/08/18/obituaries/kofi -annan-dead.html.

29. Upsala Conflict Data Programme, http://ucdp.uu.se/#/exploratory.

30. Rajesh Isser, *Peacekeeping and Protection of Civilians: The Indian Air Force in Congo* (New Delhi: KW Publishers, 2012).

31. Email correspondence with Air Vice Marshal Rajesh Isser.

32. Isser, *Peacekeeping and Protection*, 73–84.

33. Isser, *Peacekeeping and Protection*, 73–84.

34. Interview with General Rawat, 7 July 2019.

35. Rawat interview.

36. Isser, *Peacekeeping and Protection*, 78.

37. Isser, *Peacekeeping and Protection*, 90.

38. Interview with Commodore P. K. Banerjee.

39. "Navy Saves Vessel in Pirate Channel," *Telegraph*, 11 November 2008, https:// www.telegraphindia.com/india/navy-saves-vessel-in-pirate-channel/cid/524854.

40. Patrick Mutahi, "India Plays Globo Cop of Somali Coast as Western Navies Play Safe," *Daily Nation*, 18 December 2008, https://www.nation.co.ke/news /africa/1066-504022-7e1nn7z/index.html.

41. Mutahi, "India Plays Globo Cop."

42. Press Information Bureau, India Ministry of Defense, "Indian Navy Nabs 61 Pirates and Rescues 13 Crew, Neutralizes Pirate Mother Vessel Vega 5," 14 March 2011, http://pib.nic.in/newsite/PrintRelease.aspx?relid=70909.

43. "2012 Annual IMB Piracy Report," https://www.scribd.com/document /305029896/2012-Annual-Imb-Piracy-Report.

44. "ICC IMB Piracy and Armed Robbery against Ships: 2017 Annual Report." https://www.icc-ccs.org/reports/2017-Annual-IMB-Piracy-Report.pdf.

45. "India and United Nations: Peacekeeping and Peace Building," https://www .pminewyork.gov.in/pdf/menu/submenu_455847884.pdf.

Chapter 18. Operations Other than War along the Western Front

1. The author was part of the deployment and operations with Thirty-Fifth Squadron during Exercise Brasstacks.

2. Interview with Lieutenant General Pattabhiraman, Wellington, India.

3. Interview with Lieutenant General Shamsher Mehta, Pune, India.

4. For a brief history and organization of the Mechanized Infantry Regiment of the

Indian Army, see https://indianarmy.nic.in/Site/FormTemplete/frmTempSimple.aspx?
MnId=yZlkklVdHhGdbYlCE+KXUw==&ParentID=+ngVrzsh95uOjf39RLAeIg==.

5. Mehta interview.

6. Ravi Rikhye, *The War that Never Was: The Story of India's Strategic Failures* (New Delhi: Prism Paperbacks, 1988), 34–40.

7. Email correspondence with Lieutenant General Praveen Bakshi.

8. Bakshi correspondence.

9. Rikhye, *War that Never Was*, 209–211.

10. Rikhye, *War that Never Was*, 192–204. The author also recalls hectic activity at Bareilly airfield during this period.

11. Conversations with Brigadier Sapatnekar and Brigadier Palsokar, December 2012.

12. Sapatnekar conversation.

13. Mehta interview.

14. Interview with General V. N. Sharma, 21 August 2019.

15. When he was commandant of the Army War College, Sundarji published the proceedings of a seminar on nuclear issues. This catapulted him to the forefront of the Indian military's attempt to become a major stakeholder in the emerging domain of nuclear strategy. See Ali Ahmed, "In Tribute: Recalling the 'Sundarji Doctrine,'" *USI Journal of India*, January–March 2008, https://usiofindia.org/publication/usi -journal/in-tribute-recalling-thesundarji-doctrine-2/.

16. Srinath Raghavan, *Fierce Enigmas: A History of the United States in South Asia* (New York: Basic Books, 2018), 341.

17. P. R. Chari, Pervaiz Iqbal Cheema, and Stephen P. Cohen, *Four Crises and a Peace Process: American Engagement in South Asia* (Washington, DC: Brook- ings Institution Press, 2007), 73–79. For a detailed overview of the American per- spectives on Exercise Brasstacks, see the chapter titled "The Brasstacks Crisis of 1986–87."

18. Chari, Cheema, and Cohen, *Four Crises*, 73–79.

19. Bruce Riedel, *Avoiding Armageddon: America, India and Pakistan to the Brink and Back* (Washington, DC: Brookings Institution Press, 2013).

20. The following detailed account comes via email from Group Captain Sanjeev Narayanen, 6 September 2019.

21. Narayanen email.

22. Narayanen email. Also see Happymon Jacob, *Line on Fire: Ceasefire Viola- tions and India-Pakistan Escalation Dynamics* (New Delhi: Oxford University Press, 2019), 1–6.

23. Interview with Rostum Nanavatty, 8 and 9 August 2018.

24. Conversation with Air Chief Marshal Krishnaswamy at a reception at Air House, New Delhi, October 2019.

25. Telephone interview with Lieutenant General Nagaraj, 15 May 2020.

26. Nanavatty interview.

27. Telephone conversation with Nanavatty, 25 April 2020.

28. Nanavatty conversation.

29. Press release from Ministry of External Affairs, 14 May 2002, https://mea.gov.in/in-focus-article.htm?18990/Kaluchak+Massacre+14+May+2002.

30. Mehta interview.

31. The entire operation has been reconstructed based on conversations with Lieutenant General Nanavatty, Air Marshal Menon, and Air Marshal Rajesh Kumar. Also see Arjun Subramaniam, "From Kargil to Parakram: A Lesson in Forceful Persuasion," *Hindu*, 27 July 2012, https://www.thehindu.com/opinion/op-ed/from-kargil-to-parakram-a-lesson-in-forceful-persuasion/article3687855.ece.

32. Input from one of the key planners of the operation who was posted in Western Air Command.

33. Strobe Talbott, *Engaging India: Diplomacy, Democracy, and the Bomb* (Washington, DC: Brookings Institution Press, 2006), 214–215.

34. Chari, Cheema, and Cohen, *Four Crises*, 183.

35. Walter C. Ladwig III, "A Cold Start for Hot Wars," *International Security* 32, 3 (Winter 2007): 158–190, https://www.belfercenter.org/sites/default/files/files/publication/IS3203_pp158-190.pdf.

36. For a clear understanding of parallel operations, see *Basic Doctrine of the Indian Air Force* (New Delhi: Air HQ, 2012), 11. This document is the first unclassified and publicly distributed doctrine of the IAF.

37. Ladwig, "Cold Start."

38. This is the impression the author got during various interactions at think tanks in Washington and London during a sabbatical in 2017 and 2018.

39. Interview with Major General S. K. Chakravorty, 20 September 2019.

40. Manjeet Singh Negi, "Uri Attack: An Inside Account of How It Happened," *India Today*, 18 September 2016, https://www.indiatoday.in/india/story/uri-attack-inside-story-pashtun-map-pakistani-ammunition-jash-e-mohammed-341761-2016-09-18.

41. Interview with Lieutenant General Hooda, 20 July 2019; Chakravorty interview.

42. Nitin Gokhale, "The Inside Story of India's 2016 Surgical Strikes," *Diplomat*, 23 September 2017, https://thediplomat.com/2017/09/the-inside-story-of-indias-2016-surgical-strikes/. Also see Hooda interview.

43. Conversation with a serving officer who wishes to remain anonymous.

44. Press Trust of India (PTI) report, *Economic Times*, 11 July 2018, https://economictimes.indiatimes.com/news/defence/heroes-of-surgical-strike-honoured-with-gallantry-medals/articleshow/56782741.cms?from=mdr.

45. Conversation with a senior government official who wishes to remain anonymous, 7 August 2019.

46. Interview with General Rawat, 7 July 2019. Also see International Institute of Strategic Studies, *IISS Military Balance Report 2019*, ch. 6, Asia, https://doi.org/10.1080/04597222.2018.1561032. This report highlights the stark asymmetry between the Indian Navy and the Pakistan Navy.

47. A personal assessment shared by many in the IAF.

48. Anonymous sources.

49. Twitter exchange with Professor Vipin Narang.

50. "I Witnessed Wing Commander Abhinandan Shooting Down Pak's F-16 Aircraft: Squadron Leader Minty Agarwal," *India Today*, 15 August 2019, https://www.indiatoday.in/india/story/i-witnessed-wing-commander-abhinandan -varthaman-shooting-down-pakistan-f-16-aircraft-squadron-leader-minty-agarwal -1581180-2019-08-15.

51. Short media briefings by IAF public relations office.

52. "Why Is Pakistan Being Secretive about JF-17's Recent 'Smart Weapon' Test," 14 March 2019, https://www.theweek.in/news/world/2019/03/14/pakistan-secretive -smart-weapon.html.

53. The narrative of the Balakot strike and the aerial engagement the next day has been deconstructed based on a combination of unclassified information provided by the IAF public relations office during the crisis, several articles by experts in the open media, open source intelligence, random conversations with IAF leaders and participants in the mission, and the author's consolidated analysis that is reflected in two analytical pieces. See Arjun Subramaniam, "Balakot and After: IAF Demonstrates Full Spectrum Capability," *First Post*, https://www.firstpost.com/world/balakot-and-after-iaf-demonstrates-full-spectrum-capability-6236391.html; Arjun Subramaniam, "The Indian Air Force, Subconventional Operations and Balakot: A Practitioner's Perspective," ORF Issue Brief 294 (May 2019), https://www.orfonline.org/research/the-indian -air-force-sub-conventional-operations-and-balakot-a-practitioners-perspective-50761/.

54. Shiv Aroor, "Revealed: Wing Commander Abhinandan's Elusive Vir Chakra Citation," 29 January 2020, https://www.livefistdefence.com/2020/01/revealed-wing -commander-abhinandans-elusive-vir-chakra-citation.html.

55. Manjeet Singh Negi, "Indian Air Force Probe Finds Friendly Fire Caused February 27 Budgam Chopper Crash, 5 Officers in Dock," *India Today*, 23 August 2019, https://www.indiatoday.in/india/story/indian-air-force-budgam-chopper-crash -friendly-fire-officers-guilty-1590764-2019-08-23.

56. Manjeet Singh Negi, "Indian Air Force Signs Rs 1500 Crore Deal with Russia for R-27 Air-to-Air Missile," *India Today*, 29 July 2019, https://www.india today.in/india/story/indian-air-force-r-27-air-to-air-missiles-russia-defense-deal -1574898-2019-07-29.

57. Arjun Subramaniam, "Raising Costs for Infiltration without Abandoning India's Core Principles of Restraint," *Print*, 16 March 2018, https://theprint .in/opinion/raising-costs-infiltration-without-abandoning-indias-core-principles -restraint/41752/.

58. Harsha Kakar, "Pakistan's 'Good' and 'Bad' Terrorists," Raisina Debates, *ORF Online*, 8 March 2018, https://www.orfonline.org/expert-speak/pakistan-good -bad-terrorists/.

Chapter 19. Stress along the Line of Actual Control

1. Shivshankar Menon, *Choices: Inside the Making of India's Foreign Policy* (New Delhi: Penguin Random House, 2016), 26–29.

2. Press Information Bureau, Government of India, Prime Minister's Office, "Border Defense Cooperation Agreement between India and China," 23 October 2013, https://pib.gov.in/newsite/PrintRelease.aspx?relid=100178.

3. Interview with Lieutenant General Vinod Bhatia, 2 August 2019.

4. For a detailed academic paper that assesses the strategic dimension of the Depsang crisis, see Manoj Joshi, "Depsang Incursion: Decoding Chinese Signal," *ORF Online*, 14 May 2013, https://www.orfonline.org/research/depsang-incursion-decoding-the-chinese-signal/.

5. "Chinese Incursion of April 2013 in Depsang, Ladakh," Takshashila Issue Brief, May 2013, http://takshashila.org.in/wp-content/uploads/2013/05/TIB-ChineseIncursions2013-May2013.pdf.

6. Interview with Lieutenant General Rostum Nanavatty, 9 August 2018.

7. Bhatia interview.

8. Interview and telephone conversations with Lieutenant General Hooda.

9. Rajat Pandit, "Several Soldiers Injured in Clashes in Ladakh & Sikkim as Border Tensions Flare up between India and China," *Times of India*, 11 May 2020, https://timesofindia.indiatimes.com/india/several-soldiers-injured-in-two-clashes-between-indian-chinese-troops-along-the-border/articleshow/75660665.cms.

10. "China Objects to India's Transgression in Arunachal Pradesh, India Says It's Our Land," *Outlook*, 8 April 2018, https://www.outlookindia.com/website/story/china-objects-to-indias-transgression-in-arunachal-pradesh-india-says-its-our-la/310746.

11. Pawan Bali, "BJP MP Alleges Chinese Intrusion in AP's 'Fishtail,'" *Asian Age*, 5 September 2019, https://www.asianage.com/india/all-india/050919/bjp-mp-alleges-china-intrusion-in-aps-fish-tail.html.

12. Manjeet Singh Negi, "India Building 61 Strategic Roads along Pakistan, China Border," *India Today*, 15 July 2019, https://www.indiatoday.in/india/story/india-building-61-strategic-roads-along-pakistan-china-borders-1569516-2019-07-15.

13. Interview with General Rawat, 8 July 2019.

14. H. S. Panag, "India-China Standoff: What Is Happening in the Chumbi Valley?" 8 July 2017, https://www.newslaundry.com/2017/07/08/panag-india-china-sikkim-bhutan.

15. Interview with Lieutenant General Praveen Bakshi, Chandigarh, India, 20 July 2019.

16. The most detailed Indian analysis of the Doklam crisis is a document from the Takshashila Institution, a multidisciplinary and bipartisan Indian think tank based in Bangalore. See Anirudh Kanisetti and Prakash Menon, "Takshashila Discussion Document: The Doklam Imbroglio," September 2018, https://takshashila.org.in/takshashila-discussion-document-the-doklam-imbroglio/. For a Chinese perspective on Doklam, see Liu Lin, "India-China Doklam Standoff: A Chinese Perspective," *Diplomat*, 27 July 2017, https://thediplomat.com/2017/07/india-china-doklam-standoff-a-chinese-perspective/.

17. Kanisetti and Menon, "Doklam Imbroglio."

18. "To Boost Ties, Chinese Army Delegation Visits Indian Army's Eastern Com-

mand in Kolkata," *Hindustan Times*, 24 February 2017, https://www.hindustan
times.com/india-news/to-boost-ties-chinese-army-delegation-visits-indian-army-s
-eastern-command-in-kolkata/story-Oa1RqC1Iu3LazyPNhA5rFL.html.

19. Shen Yi, "China Prevails in Doklam Standoff but India Attempts to Distort
Public Opinion," *Global Times*, 3 September 2017, http://www.globaltimes.cn/con
tent/1064491.shtml.

20. Prakash Menon, "Stand up against China," *Pragati*, 20 April 2018, https://
www.thinkpragati.com/opinion/4291/stand-up-against-china/.

21. "Construction of Roads by China a Violation of Pacts: Bhutan," *Times of India*,
13 July 2018, https://economictimes.indiatimes.com/news/defense/construction-of
-road-by-china-direct-violation-bhutan/articleshow/59376510.cms?from=mdr.

22. Bakshi interview.

23. Arjun Subramaniam, "For Modi and Xi, Not Achieving Much at Wuhan May
Be the Best Thing," *Print*, 5 May 2018, https://theprint.in/opinion/for-modi-and-xi
-not-achieving-much-in-wuhan-may-be-the-best-outcome/55393/.

24. Interview with former Australian prime minister Kevin Rudd, "Emperor Xi's
China Is Done Biding Its Time," 3 March 2018, https://www.belfercenter.org/publi
cation/emperor-xis-china-done-biding-its-time.

25. Extract from transcripts at the Walong War Memorial.

26. Deepshika Hooda, "IAF to Have Seven Operational Advanced Landing Grounds in Arunachal Pradesh in a Month," *Economic Times*, 13 July 2018,
https://economictimes.indiatimes.com/news/defense/iaf-to-have-7-operational-ad
vanced-landing-grounds-in-arunachal-pradesh-in-a-month/articleshow/49809013
.cms?from=mdr.

27. The Wuhan meeting between Modi and Xi following the Doklam incident is
one such instance.

28. Dinakar Peri, "Third Regiment of T-72 Tanks to Be Moved to Ladakh Soon,"
Hindu, 19 July 2016, https://www.thehindu.com/news/national/Third-regiment-of-T
-72-tanks-to-be-moved-to-Ladakh-soon/article14497629.ece. A recent assessment of
force levels by the Belfer Center at Harvard University's Kennedy School of Government is instructive. See Frank O'Donnell and Alex Bollfrass, "The Strategic Postures
of China and India: A Visual Guide," Project on Managing the Atom, Belfer Center for Science and International Affairs, https://www.belfercenter.org/publication
/strategic-postures-china-and-india-visual-guide.

29. Iskander Rehman, "Hard Men in a Hard Environment: Indian Special Operators along the Border with China," January 2017, https://warontherocks.com/2017/01
/hard-men-in-a-hard-environment-indian-special-operators-along-the-border-with
-china/. Also see Arjun Subramaniam, "Closing the Gap: A Doctrinal and Capability
Appraisal of the IAF and PLAAF," in *Defence Primer: An Indian Military in Transformation*, ed. Pushan Das and Harsh V. Pant (New Delhi: ORF, 2018), 35–43.

30. Mihir Bhonsale, "Understanding Sino-Indian Border Issues: An Analysis
of Incidents Reported in the Indian Media," ORF Occasional Paper, 12 February
2018, https://www.orfonline.org/research/understanding-sino-indian-border-issues
-an-analysis-of-incidents-reported-in-the-indian-media/.

31. L. M. H. Ling, "Border Pathology," in L. M. H. Ling, Adriana Erthal Abdenur, Payal Banerjee, Nimmi Kurian, Mahendra P. Lama and Li Bo, *India China: Rethinking Borders and Security* (Ann Arbor: University of Michigan Press, 2018), 123.

32. Ling, "Border Pathology," 122.

33. Media Center, Ministry of External Affairs, "Settling the Border Question," 3 July 2003, https://www.mea.gov.in/articles-in-indian-media.htm?dtl/13537/Settling +the+China+border.

Chapter 20. India's Nuclear Conundrum

1. For the most comprehensive and holistic examination of India's emergence as a nuclear weapons state, see Ashley J. Tellis, *India's Emerging Nuclear Posture: Between Recessed Deterrence and Ready Arsenal* (New Delhi: Oxford University Press, 2001), https://www.rand.org/pubs/monograph_reports/MR1127.html. Also see George Perkovich, *India's Nuclear Bomb: The Impact on Global Proliferation* (Berkeley: University of California Press, 1999).

2. Tellis, *India's Emerging Nuclear Posture*, 89–91. Also see Itty Abraham, "India's 'Strategic Enclave': Civilian Scientists and Military Technologies," *Armed Forces and Society* 18, 2 (January 1992), Worldwide Political Science Abstracts 231, https://journals.sagepub.com/doi/abs/10.1177/0095327X9201800205.

3. A timeline of the Non-Proliferation Treaty is available at https://www.arms control.org/factsheets/Timeline-of-the-Treaty-on-the-Non-Proliferation-of-Nuclear -Weapons-NPT.

4. Perkovich, *India's Nuclear Bomb*, 178. Perkovich's chapter 7 ("India Explodes a 'Peaceful' Nuclear Device") gives an excellent overview of India's peaceful nuclear explosion.

5. Perkovich, *India's Nuclear Bomb*, 183–187.

6. Kumar Sundaram and M. V. Ramana, "India and the Policy of No First Use of Nuclear Weapons," *Journal for Peace and Nuclear Disarmament* 1, 1 (2018): 153–154, https://www.tandfonline.com/doi/pdf/10.1080/25751654.2018.1438737 ?needAccess=true.

7. K. Subrahmanyam, *Shedding Shibboleths: India's Evolving Strategic Outlook* (New Delhi: Wordsmiths, 2005), 143.

8. P. R. Chari, Pervaiz Iqbal Cheema, and Stephen P. Cohen, *Four Crises and a Peace Process: American Engagement in South Asia* (Washington, DC: Brookings Institution Press, 2007), 39.

9. Apart from Chari, Cheema, and Cohen (*Four Crises*), almost every other India watcher in the United States likened the nuclear posturing between India and Pakistan in the early 1990s to a crisis, much to the chagrin of the Indians.

10. Vinay Sitapati, *Half Lion: How PV Narasimha Rao Transformed India* (New Delhi: Penguin, 2016), 282–295.

11. Perkovich, *India's Nuclear Bomb*, 181–183.

12. Bruce Riedel, *Avoiding Armageddon: America, India and Pakistan to the Brink and Back* (Washington, DC: Brookings Institution Press, 2013), 121

13. Riedel, *Avoiding Armageddon*, 105.

14. An alarmist perspective is offered by Chari, Cheema, and Cohen, *Four Crises*, 121–128. V. P. Malik offers an Indian view in *From Surprise to Victory* (New Delhi: HarperCollins, 2006), 272–280.

15. Chari, Cheema, and Cohen, *Four Crises*, 173–175, 179.

16. Tellis, *India's Emerging Nuclear Posture*, 252–257.

17. Tellis, *India's Emerging Nuclear Posture*, 199, fig. 1.

18. Tellis, *India's Emerging Nuclear Posture*, 199, fig. 1.

19. K. Subrahmanyam, "Indo-Pak Nuclear Stand-off: A Challenge and an Opportunity," *Times of India*, 6 June 1988, 8.

20. Narendra Gupta, "Nuclear Missiles in Tibet," *Times of India,* 24 March 1988, 8.

21. Subrahmanyam, *Shedding Shibboleths*, 143.

22. Prakash Menon, *The Strategy Trap: India and Pakistan under the Nuclear Shadow* (New Delhi: Wisdom Tree, 2018), 234–235; for the entire text of India's draft nuclear doctrine, see appendix A, 227–233. Also see https://www.armscontrol .org/act/1999–07/indias-draft-nuclear-doctrine.

23. Vishnu Som (with input from Reuters), "Defence Minister Manohar Parrikar's Nuclear Remark Stressed as 'Personal Opinion,'" 10 November 2016, https://www .ndtv.com/india-news/defence-minister-manohar-parrikars-nuclear-remark-stressed -as-personal-opinion-1623952.

24. Vipin Narang, presentation, Fletcher School of Law and Diplomacy, 20 November 2018.

25. Shivshankar Menon, *Choices: Inside the Making of India's Foreign Policy* (New Delhi: Penguin Random House, 2016), 123.

26. A comprehensive overview of India's nuclear forces is offered by Hans M. Kristensen and Matt Korda, "Indian Nuclear Forces," *Bulletin of the Atomic Scientists* 74, 6 (2018): 361–366, https://www.tandfonline.com/doi/full/10.1080/009634 02.2018.1533162.

27. Yogesh Joshi, "Samudra: India's Convoluted Path to Undersea Nuclear Weapons," *Non-Proliferation Review* 26, 5–6 (2019): 82, https://www.tandfonline.com /doi/abs/10.1080/10736700.2020.1720243.

28. Rajat Pandit, "More Nuclear Warheads with Pak, but India Unfazed," *Times of India*, 16 June 2020, 1, https://timesofindia.indiatimes.com/india/pakistan-re mains-ahead-in-nuclear-warheads-but-india-confident-of-its-deterrence-capability /articleshow/76381003.cms. The report is based on the latest assessment of the Stockholm International Peace Research Institute, June 2019, https://www.sipri.org /yearbook/2019/06.

29. A detailed overview of China's nuclear capability is offered by Hans M. Kristensen and Matt Korda, "Chinese Nuclear Forces," *Bulletin of the Atomic Scientists* 75, 4 (2019): 171–178, https://www.tandfonline.com/doi/pdf/10.1080/00963402.2 019.1628511?needAccess=true. Also see Stockholm International Peace Research Institute, June 2019.

30. Frank O'Donnell and Debolina Ghoshal, "Managing Indian Deterrence: Pres-

sures on Credible Minimum Deterrence and Nuclear Policy Options," *Non-Proliferation Review,* https://www.tandfonline.com/doi/full/10.1080/10736700.2019.1565187.

31. Stockholm International Peace Research Institute, "Modernization of World Nuclear Forces Continues Despite Overall Decrease in Number of Warheads: New SIPRI Yearbook Out Now," 17 June 2019, https://www.sipri.org/media/press-release/2019/modernization-world-nuclear-forces-continues-despite-overall-decrease-number-warheads-new-sipri.

32. Menon, *Strategy Trap,* 58–66.

33. India Ministry of External Affairs, "Frequently Asked Questions on the India–US Agreement for Co-operation Concerning Peaceful Uses of Nuclear Energy," https://mea.gov.in/Uploads/PublicationDocs/19149_Frequently_Asked_Questions_01-11-2008.pdf.

Afterword: The GAP Crisis

1. Ananth Krishnan, "Forgotten in Fog of War, the Last Firing on the India-China Border," *Hindu,* 14 June 2020, https://www.thehindu.com/news/national/forgotten-in-fog-of-war-the-last-firing-on-the-india-china-border/article31827344.ece.

2. Rahul Shrivastava, "How Much of Indian Land Is Occupied by China? As Centre, Congress Trade Barbs, the Truth Lies in Parliament Records," *India Today,* 23 June 2020, https://www.indiatoday.in/india/story/how-much-of-indian-land-in-ladakh-is-occupied-by-china-1691859-2020-06-23.

3. Vipin Narang and Christopher Clary, "India's Pangong Pickle: New Delhi's Options after Its Clash with China," *War on the Rocks,* 2 July 2020, https://warontherocks.com/2020/07/indias-pangong-pickle-new-delhis-options-after-its-clash-with-china/.

4. Shiv Aroor, "3 Separate Brawls, Outsider Chinese Troops & More: Most Detailed Account of the Brutal Galwan Battle," *India Today,* 21 June 2020, https://www.indiatoday.in/india/story/3-separate-brawls-outsider-chinese-troops-more-most-detailed-account-of-the-brutal-june-15-galwan-battle-1691185-2020-06-21.

5. Brahma Chellaney, Twitter, @Chellany, 25 June 2020, https://twitter.com/Chellaney/status/1276156416269713418.

6. "Know What the Indian Army's Operation Snow Leopard Is," *Daily Hunt,* 17 September 2020, https://m.dailyhunt.in/news/india/english/ampinity+news-epaper-amptnw/know+what+the+indian+army+s+operation+snow+leopard+is-newsid-n215482156. Also see Gaurav Sawant, "Op Snow Leopard: Inside Story of How Army Reclaimed Heights in Eastern Ladakh," *India Today,* 16 September 2020, https://www.indiatoday.in/india/story/snow-leopard-inside-story-army-reclaimed-heights-ladakh-exclusive-1722311-2020-09-16.

7. Vinayak Bhat, "A Peek at China's Aerial Preparedness along the Ladakh Borders," *India Today,* 20 July 2020, https://www.indiatoday.in/india/story/a-peek-at-china-s-aerial-preparedness-along-the-ladakh-borders-1702508-2020-07-20.

8. Shubhajit Roy, "Ahead of Military Talks, China Claims Troops Have Disengaged at Most Sites," *Indian Express,* 29 July 2020, 1–2.

9. Air Vice Marshal Manmohan Bahadur, "Indian Intelligence Failure Again? Heroism at Galwan Must Lead to Reforms," *Print*, 23 June 2020, https://theprint .in/opinion/indian-intelligence-failure-again-heroism-at-galwan-must-lead-to-re forms/446865/.

10. Tara Kartha, "Calling LAC Conflict 'Intelligence Failure' Is Lazy. It Ignores India's Real Problem," *Print*, 26 June 2020, https://theprint.in/author/tara-kartha/.

11. Arjun Subramaniam, "Can Counter-Coercion Work against a Belligerent China?" *ORF Online*, https://www.orfonline.org/expert-speak/can-counter-coercion -work-belligerent-china/.

12. Chris Buckley, "Clean up This Mess: The Chinese Thinkers behind Xi's Hard Line," *New York Times*, 12 August 2020.

13. Indrani Bagchi, "China Shouldn't View Us through US Lens. That Would Be a Great Disservice, Says S Jaishankar," *Times of India*, 2 August 2020, https://timesof india.indiatimes.com/india/china-shouldnt-view-us-through-us-lens-that-would-be -a-great-disservice-says-s-jaishankar/articleshow/77307398.cms.

14. Jonathan Renshon, *Why Leaders Choose War* (New York: Praeger Security International, 2006).

15. Renshon, *Why Leaders Choose War*, 149.

BIBLIOGRAPHY

Abdullah, Sheikh. *Flames of the Chinar*. Trans. Khushwant Singh. New Delhi: Viking, 1993.

Abraham, Itty. "India's 'Strategic Enclave': Civilian Scientists and Military Technologies." *Armed Forces and Society* 18, 2 (January 1992). Worldwide Political Science Abstracts. https://journals.sagepub.com/doi/abs/10.1177/0095327X9201800205.

Acosta, Marcus. "High Altitude Warfare: The Kargil Conflict and the Future." Thesis, Naval Postgraduate School, Monterey, CA, 2003. https://calhoun.nps.edu/handle/10945/1043.

————. "The Kargil Conflict: Waging War in the Himalayas." *Small Wars and Insurgencies* 18, 3 (2007): 97–415. https://www.tandfonline.com/doi/abs/10.1080/09592310701674325?journalCode=fswi20.

Adhikary, Kaushik. "Combating Terrorism in 21st Century: The Legal and Institutional Responses with Special Reference to Indian Security Laws." Thesis, University of Calcutta, 2017. https://shodhganga.inflibnet.ac.in/handle/10603/172205.

"Agreement on Prisoners of War (Official UN Documents)." *American Journal of International Law* 47, 4 (October 1953). https://www.jstor.org/stable/2213914.

Ahluwalia, A. S. *Airborne to Chairborne: Memoirs of a War Veteran Aviator-Lawyer of the Indian Air Force*. Bloomington, IN: Xlibris, 2012.

Ahmed, Ali. "In Tribute: Recalling the 'Sundarji Doctrine.'" *USI Journal of India*, January–March 2008. https://usiofindia.org/publication/usi-journal/in-tribute-recalling-thesundarji-doctrine-2/.

————. "Mizo Hills: Revisiting the Early Phase." http://www.claws.in/images/journals_doc/1607757556_AliAhmed.pdf.

Ahuja, Rajesh. "Looking Back, the Ceasefire in Kashmir in 2000 Saw More Violence but Lasted Longer." *Hindustan Times*, 17 June 2018. https://www.hindustantimes.com/india-news/looking-back-the-ceasefire-in-2000-saw-more-violence-but-was-longer/story-eD1BIfi109TFgopG.

"Airgram A-97 from the Embassy in Sri Lanka to the Department of State." 23 November 1976. https://history.state.gov/historicaldocuments/frus1969-76ve08/d102.

"Ajit Doval Says Not One Bullet Fired in Kashmir in the Past Month, a Record since 1988." *Print*, 6 September 2019. https://theprint.in/india/ajit-doval-says-not-one-bullet-fired-in-kashmir-in-the-past-month-a-record-since-1988/288279/.

Ali, Syed Ishfaq. *Fangs of Ice*. Rawalpindi, Pakistan: Pak America Commercial, 1991.

Anand, Vinod. "India's Military Response to the Kargil Aggression." *Strategic Analysis* 23 (October 1999).

Aroor, Shiv. "Revealed: Wing Commander Abhinandan's Elusive Vir Chakra Citation." 29 January 2020. https://www.livefistdefence.com/2020/01/revealed-wing-commander-abhinandans-elusive-vir-chakra-citation.html.

————. "3 Separate Brawls, Outsider Chinese Troops & More: Most Detailed Account of the Brutal Galwan Battle." *India Today*, 21 June 2020. https://www.indiatoday.in/india/story/3-separate-brawls-outsider-chinese-troops-more-most-detailed-account-of-the-brutal-june-15-galwan-battle-1691185-2020-06-21.

Aroor, Shiv, and Rahul Singh. *India's Most Fearless: True Stories of Modern Military Heroes*. New Delhi: Penguin Random House, 2017.

Arpi, Claude. "Special Frontier Force and Operation Blue Star." http://claudearpi.blogspot.com/2014/01/special-frontiers-forces-and-operation.html.

————. "The Sumdorong Chu Incident: A Strong Indian Stance." *Indian Defence Review*, 4 May 2013. www.indiandefencereview.com/the-sumdorong-chu-incident-a-strong-indian-stand/.

"Ashfaq Majeed Wani Remembered." *Greater Kashmir*, 5 July 2019. https://www.greaterkashmir.com/news/kashmir/ashfaq-majeed-wani-remembered/.

Associated Press. "Angami Phizo, 83, Fought for Secession in North Indian State." *New York Times*, 4 May 1990. https://www.nytimes.com/1990/05/04/obituaries/angami-phizo-83-fought-for-secession-in-north-india-state.html.

"Avalanche Traps 135 People Near Siachen." *Tribune*, 7 April 2012. https://tribune.com.pk/story/361097/avalanche-traps-over-100-pakistani-soldiers-report/.

Bagchi, Indrani. "China Shouldn't View Us through US Lens. That Would Be a Great Disservice, Says S Jaishankar," *Times of India*, 2 August 2020, https://timesofindia.indiatimes.com/india/china-shouldnt-view-us-through-us-lens-that-would-be-a-great-disservice-says-s-jaishankar/articleshow/77307398.cms.

Bahadur, Air Vice Marshal Manmohan. "In 1990, There Was Another Daring Rescue of an IAF Helicopter from Siachen Glacier." *Print*, 28 December 2018. https://theprint.in/opinion/in-1990-there-was-another-daring-rescue-of-an-iaf-helicopter-from-siachen-glacier/170068/.

————. "Indian Intelligence Failure Again? Heroism at Galwan Must Lead to Reforms." *Print*, 23 June 2020. https://theprint.in/opinion/indian-intelligence-failure-again-heroism-at-galwan-must-lead-to-reforms/446865/.

Bahadur, M. "The Buildup to Operation Meghdoot." 10 December 2017. http://www.bharat-rakshak.com/IAF/history/siachen/1046-meghdoot.html.

Bali, Pawan. "BJP MP Alleges Chinese Intrusion in AP's 'Fishtail.'" *Asian Age*, 5 September 2019. https://www.asianage.com/india/all-india/050919/bjp-mp-alleges-china-intrusion-in-aps-fish-tail.html.

Bangert, Christopher. "Kofi Annan, Who Redefined the UN, Dies at 80." *New York Times*, 18 August 2018. https://www.nytimes.com/2018/08/18/obituaries/kofi-annan-dead.html.

Bansal, Alok. "Gilgit-Baltistan: The Roots of Political Alienation." *Strategic Analysis* 32, 1 (January 2008). https://www.tandfonline.com/doi/full/10.1080/09700160801886355.

Barnes, Robert. "Between the Blocs: India, the United Nations and Ending the Korean War." *Journal of Korean Studies* 18, 2 (Fall 2013): 263–286. https://doi.org/10.1353/jks.2013.0022.

Basic Doctrine of the Indian Air Force. New Delhi: Air HQ, 2012.

Basu, Nayanima, and Amiti Sen. "India Mulls Intervention as Maldives Crisis Deepens." *Hindu Business Line*, 6 February 2018. https://www.thehindubusinessline.com/news/world/india-mulls-intervention-as-maldives-crisis-deepens/article22670700.ece.

Baweja, Harinder. "Kargil War: Army Took over a Month Planning to Recapture Tiger Hill in Dras Sector." *India Today*, 19 July 1999. https://www.indiatoday.in/magazine/cover-story/story/19990719-kargil-war-army-took-over-a-months-planning-to-recapture-tiger-hill-in-drass-sector-824832-1999-07-19.

Bedi, Rahul. "Intel Failures Made Indian Attacks in Kashmir Inevitable." *Jane's Intelligence Review* 11, 6 (June 1999).

———. "Paying to Keep the High Ground." *Jane's Intelligence Review* 11, 10 (October 1999).

Bhaduri, Shankar, and Afsar Karim. *The Sri Lankan Crisis*. New Delhi: Lancer, 1990.

Bhandari, Mohan. "Kargil Controversy: Army Trashed IAF Perspective." *Indian Defense Review* 25 (April–June 2010). http://www.indiandefensereview.com/spotlights/kargil-controversy-army-trashes-iaf-perspective/.

Bharadwaj, Anaya. "Asiya Andrabi: Kashmir's First Separatist Who Also Dreamt of Marrying a Mujahid." *Print*, 10 December 2018. https://theprint.in/india/governance/asiya-andrabi-kashmirs-first-woman-separatist-who-also-dreamt-of-marrying-a-mujahid/160138/.

Bhat, Vinayak. "Fresh Provocation: China Building a 36 km-Long Road in Strategic J&K Valley Near Siachen." *Print*, 15 January 2018. https://theprint.in/security/china-building-a-36-km-long-road-valley-siachen/28812/.

———. "A Peek at China's Aerial Preparedness along the Ladakh Borders." *India Today*, 20 July 2020. https://www.indiatoday.in/india/story/a-peek-at-china-s-aerial-preparedness-along-the-ladakh-borders-1702508-2020-07-20.

Bhaumick, Subir. *Troubled Periphery: India's Troubled North-East*. New Delhi: Sage, 2009.

Bhonsale, Mihir. "Understanding Sino-Indian Border Issues: An Analysis of Incidents Reported in the Indian Media." ORF Occasional Paper, 12 February 2018. https://www.orfonline.org/research/understanding-sino-indian-border-issues-an-analysis-of-incidents-reported-in-the-indian-media/.

Bobb, Dilip. "A Bloodied Accord." *India Today*, 15 November 1987. http://indiatoday.intoday.in/story/after-16-days=of-bloody-fighting-ipkf-finally-captures-ltte-stronghold-jaffna/1/337703.

———. "Sri Lanka: Tackling the Tigers." *India Today*, 30 June 1987. http://indiatoday.intoday.in/story/indias-decision-to-airdrop-supplies-over-jaffna-opens-up-a-diplomatic-pandora-box/1/337218.html.

Boyd, John. "Patterns of Conflict." Presentations at Marine Corps Staff College, Quantico, VA, 2015 and 2018. https://thestrategybridge.org/the-bridge/2015/11/16/uploading-john-boyd?rq=Boyd and https://thestrategybridge.org/the-bridge/2018/3/22/john-boyd-on-clausewitz-dont-fall-in-love-with-your-mental-model.

Brar, K. S. *Operation Blue Star: The True Story*. New Delhi: UBS Publishers, 1993.

Brewster, David. "An Indian Sphere of Influence in the Indian Ocean?" *Security Challenges* 6, 3 (Spring 2010): 15. https://www.jstor.org/stable/26459796 ?seq=1#metadata_info_tab_contents.

Brodie, Bernard. "A Guide to the Reading of *On War*." In *On War* by Carl Von Clausewitz, ed. and trans. Michael Howard and Peter Paret. Princeton, NJ: Princeton University Press, 1976.

Buckley, Chris. "Clean up This Mess: The Chinese Thinkers behind Xi's Hard Line." *New York Times*, 12 August 2020.

Bukhari, Shujaat. "From a Calm Moulvi to a Dreaded Militant." *Hindu*, 17 October 2001. https://www.thehindu.com/thehindu/2001/10/17/stories/02170003.htm.

Burns, John F. "India's New Defense Chief Sees Chinese Military Threat." *New York Times*, 5 May 1998. https://www.nytimes.com/1998/05/05/world/india-s -new-defense-chief-sees-chinese-military-threat.html.

Chadha, Vivek. "Artillery in Op Vijay: Perspective of a Commanding Officer." You Tube, 28 June 2019. https://www.youtube.com/watch?v=6V_XiMHyP08.

———. *Low Intensity Conflicts in South Asia: An Analysis*. Delhi: Sage, 2005.

———, ed. *Armed Forces Special Powers Act: The Debate*. New Delhi: Lancer, 2013.

Chandola, Harish. *The Naga Story: First Armed Struggle in India*. New Delhi: Chicken Neck, 2012.

Chari, P. R., Pervaiz Iqbal Cheema, and Stephen P. Cohen. *Four Crises and a Peace Process: American Engagement in South Asia*. Washington, DC: Brookings Institution Press, 2007.

Cheema, Zafar Iqbal. "The Strategic Concept of the Kargil Conflict." In *Asymmetric Warfare in South Asia*, ed. Peter Lavoy. New York: Cambridge University Press, 2009.

Chibber, M. L. "Siachen—The Untold Story." *Indian Defence Review*, January 1990.

"China Objects to India's Transgression in Arunachal Pradesh, India Says It's Our Land." *Outlook*, 8 April 2018. https://www.outlookindia.com/website /story/china-objects-to-indias-transgression-in-arunachal-pradesh-india-says-its -our-la/310746.

"Chinese Incursion of April 2013 in Depsang, Ladakh." Takshashila Issue Brief, May 2013. http://takshashila.org.in/wp-content/uploads/2013/05/TIB-ChineseIn cursions2013-May2013.pdf.

Chopra, R. K. "Internal Security Environment in India." Thesis, National Defence College, 1988.

"Chronology of Amarnath Land Row." *Times of India*, 6 August 2008. https:// timesofindia.indiatimes.com/india/Chronology-of-Amarnath-land-row/article show/3331566.cms.

Clausewitz, Carl von. *On War*, ed. and trans. Michael Howard and Peter Paret. Princeton, NJ: Princeton University Press, 1976.

Cline, Lawrence E. "Pseudo Operations in Counterinsurgency: Lessons from Other Countries." SSI Monograph, US Army War College, 2005. https://www.globalse curity.org/military/library/report/2005/ssi_cline.pdf.

"Construction of Roads by China a Violation of Pacts: Bhutan." *Times of India*, 13 July 2018. https://economictimes.indiatimes.com/news/defense/construction -of-road-by-china-direct-violation-bhutan/articleshow/59376510.cms?from=mdr.

Crossette, Barbara. "Abducted Woman Freed in Kashmir." *New York Times*, 14 December 1989. https://www.nytimes.com/1989/12/14/world/abducted-woman -freed-in-kashmir.html.

———. "Sri Lanka Air Force Raids Tamil Guerrilla Bases." *New York Times*, 23 April 1987. https://www.nytimes.com/1987/04/23/world/sri-lanka-air-force-raids -tamil-guerrilla-bases.html.

Dainelli, Giotto. "My Expedition in the Eastern Karakoram: 1930." *Himalayan Journal* 4 (1932). https://www.himalayanclub.org/hj/04/4/my-expedition-in-the -eastern-karakoram/.

Dasgupta, C. *War and Diplomacy in Kashmir: 1947–1948*. New Delhi: Sage Publications, 2002.

Dasgupta, Probal. *Watershed 1967: India's Forgotten Victory over China*. New Delhi: Juggernaut, 2019.

Dasgupta, Sunil. "Why Terrorism Fails While Insurgencies Can Sometimes Succeed." Brookings Op-ed, 4 January 2002. https://www.brookings.edu/opinions/why-ter rorism-fails-while-insurgencies-can-sometimes-succeed/.

Deb, Alok. "Artillery in Operation Vijay: Perspective of a Commanding Officer." In *Surprise, Strategy and Vijay—20 Years of Kargil and Beyond*, ed. V. K. Ahluwalia and Narjit Singh. New Delhi: Pentagon Press, 2019.

Desmond, Edward W. "War on High Ground." *Time*, 17 July 1989.

Dholabhai, Nishit. "70-Plus and Still Going Strong in BSF." *Telegraph*, 9 May 2004. https://www.telegraphindia.com/states/north-east/70-plus-and-still-going-strong -in-bsf-septuagenarian-naga-sentinels-continue-in-service-thanks-to-fudged-age /cid/1557309.

Dixit, J. N. *Assignment Colombo*. New Delhi: Konark Publishers, 1998.

———. *India-Pakistan: In War and Peace*. London: Routledge, 2002.

Dixon, Richard. *Operational Sequencing: The Tension between Simultaneous and Sequential Operations*. Fort Leavenworth, KS: School of Advanced Military Studies, US Army Command and Staff College, 1994. http://www.dtic.mil/dtic/tr/fulltext /u2/a284087.pdf.

Dorn, A. Walter, and David J. H. Bell. "Intelligence and Peacekeeping: The UN Operation in the Congo, 1960–64." *International Peacekeeping* 2, 1 (Spring 1995).

Dubey, Suman. "Shiv Sena Militarily Gears Itself to Protect Hinduism and Hindu Interests in Punjab." *India Today*, 15 April 1986. https://www .indiatoday.in/magazine/cover-story/story/19860415-shiv-sena-militantly-gears -itself-to-protect-hinduism-and-hindu-interests-in-punjab-800756-1986-04-15#ss ologin=1#source=magazine.

Dwivedi, Diksha. *Letters from Kargil*. New Delhi: Juggernaut, 2017.

"869 Soldiers Have Died in Siachen since 1984." *Economic Times*, 13 July 2018. https://economictimes.indiatimes.com/news/defence/869-indian-soldiers-have -died-in-siachen-since-1984/articleshow/50138852.cms?from=mdr.

"Elizabethville Fighting Rages as Plan Found." *Desert Sun*, 5 December 1961. https:// cdnc.ucr.edu/cgi-bin/cdnc?a=d&d=DS19611205.2.10&e=-en-20-1-txt-txIN-1.

"Emperor Xi's China Is Done Biding Its Time." Belfer Center, 3 March 2018. https:// www.belfercenter.org/publication/emperor-xis-china-done-biding-its-time.

Fair, C. Christine. *Fighting to the End: The Pakistan Army's Way of War.* New Delhi: Oxford University Press, 2014.

———. *In Their Own Words: Understanding Lashkar-e-Tayyaba.* London: Hurst Publishers, 2018. New Delhi: Oxford University Press, 2019.

Fedarko, Kevin. "The Coldest War." Updated 22 April 2012. https://www.wesjones.com/coldest.htm.

Fernandes, George. "Examining the Concept of National Security." In *General B. C. Joshi Memorial Lectures on National Security*, ed. Gautam Sen. Pune, India: University of Pune Press, 2006.

Freedman, Lawrence, ed. *War.* Oxford: Oxford University Press, 1994.

"Full Text of Statement by PM Modi at UN Peacekeeping Summit." *Times of India*, 29 September 2015. https://timesofindia.indiatimes.com/india/Full-text-of-statement-by-PM-Modi-at-UN-Peacekeeping-Summit/articleshow/49145092.cms.

Ganguly, Sumit. *Conflict Unending: India-Pakistan Tensions since 1947.* New York: Columbia University Press, 2002.

———. *Deadly Impasse: Indo-Pakistan Relations at the Dawn of a New Century.* Cambridge: Cambridge University Press, 2016.

Garver, John. *Protracted Contest: Sino-Indian Rivalry in the Twentieth Century.* Seattle: University of Washington Press, 2002.

Gaur, Pranadhar. "Use of Force in Regional Conflicts: A Study of Pakistan's Two-Level Strategy in Kashmir since 1987." Ph.D. diss., Jawaharlal Nehru University, 2000. http://shodhganga.inflibnet.ac.in/handle/10603/15150?mode=full.

Gigoo, Siddhartha. "In Search of Stories Lost." 19 December 2015. https://www.livemint.com/Leisure/AIQpbcotgcNTeiGf7lzFoI/In-search-of-stories-lost.html.

Gill, John. "Military Operations in the Kargil Conflict." In *Asymmetric Warfare in South Asia*, ed. Peter Lavoy. New York: Cambridge University Press, 2009.

Gill, K. P. S., ed. *Terror Containment: Perspectives on India's Internal Security.* New Delhi: Gyan Publishing House, 2001.

Gladstone, Rick, and Mike Ives. "UN Report Bolsters Theory that Hammarskjold Plane Was Downed." *New York Times*, 8 October 2019. https://www.nytimes.com/2019/10/08/world/africa/dag-hammarskjold.html.

Gokhale, H. A. "Operation Cactus: A Naval Perspective." Presentation, Defence Services Staff College, 1990.

Gokhale, Nitin. *Beyond NJ 9842: The Siachen Saga.* New Delhi: Bloomsbury, 2014.

———. "The Inside Story of India's 2016 Surgical Strikes." *Diplomat*, 23 September 2017. https://thediplomat.com/2017/09/the-inside-story-of-indias-2016-surgical-strikes/.

"Golden Temple Attack: UK Advised India but Impact Limited." BBC, 7 June 2014. https://www.bbc.com/news/uk-26027631.

Goswami, Namrata. "India's Counterinsurgency Experience: The 'Trust and Nurture' Strategy." *Small Wars and Insurgencies* 20, 1 (2009). https://doi.org/10.1080/09592310802573475.

Gunaratna, Rohan. *Indian Intervention in Sri Lanka.* Colombo, Sri Lanka: Gunaratne Offset, 1993.

Gundevia, Y. D. *War and Peace in Nagaland.* New Delhi: Palit & Palit, 1975.

Gupta, Amit. "Determining India's Force Structure and Military Doctrine: I Want My MiG." *Asian Survey* 35, 5 (May 1995). https://www.jstor.org /stable/2645747?seq=1.

Gupta, Nishtha. "10 Heroes India Will Always Be Proud Of." *India Today*, 26 July 2019. https://www.indiatoday.in/india/story/10-kargil-heroes-india-will-always -be-proud-of-1574014-2019-07-26.

Gupta, Shekhar. "The Espionage Game." *India Today*, 31 December 1993. http:// indiatoday.intoday.in/story/the-espionage-game/1/303572.html.

———. "India's Blackhawk Down: Incompetence and Heroism in a Commando Raid." *Print*, 14 October 2018. https://theprint.in/opinion/indias-blackhawk -down-incompetence-heroism-in-a-commando-raid-gone-wrong-at-jaffna-univ /134316/.

———. "In Rush to Vanquish." *India Today*, 13 January 1988.

———. "Such a Long Lankan Journey." *Indian Express*, 11 September 2013. http:// indianexpress.com/article/opinion/columns/such-a-long-lankan-journey/.

———. "Uncovering the War." *Indian Express*, 13 September 2013. http:/indianex press.com/article/news-archive/print/uncovering-the-war/.

Hammes, Thomas X. *The Sling and the Stone: On War in the 21st Century.* St. Paul, MN: Zenith Press, 2006.

Handoo, Bilal. "Charar after Mast Gul." *Kashmir Life*, 17 May 2016. https://kash mirlife.net/charar-after-mast-gul-issue-09-vol-08-105467/.

Haqqani, Hussain. *India vs Pakistan: Why Can't We Just Be Friends.* New Delhi: Juggernaut, 2016.

Harrison, Selig, and K. Subrahmanyam, eds. *Superpower Rivalry in the Indian Ocean: Indian and American Views.* New York: Oxford University Press, 1989.

Hassan, Javed. "The Fight for Siachen." *Express Tribune*, 22 April 2012. https:// tribune.com.pk/story/368394/the-fight-for-siachen/.

Hazarika, Sanjeev. "Genesis of Naga Imbroglio, Status of Underground Groups, Prevailing Situation, Prognosis and Army Activities." *Infantry Journal* 20, 1 (April 2009): 31–34

Hazarika, Sanjoy. *Strangers No More.* New Delhi: Aleph, 2018.

Hiranandani, G. M. *Transition to Eminence: The Indian Navy 1976–1990.* New Delhi: Lancer Publishers, 2004.

Hluna, J. V., and Rini Tochhwang. *The Mizo Uprising: Assam Assembly Debates on the Mizo Movement 1966–1971.* Newcastle, UK: Cambridge Scholars Publishing, 2012.

Hoffman, Frank. "Conflict in the 21st Century: The Rise of Hybrid Wars." Potomac Institute for Policy Studies, December 2007.

Holmes, James R., and Toshi Yoshihara. "India's 'Monroe Doctrine' and Asia's Maritime Future." *Strategic Analysis* 32, 6 (November 2008): 997–1011. https://www .tandfonline.com/doi/abs/10.1080/09700160802404539.

Hooda, Deepshika. "IAF to Have Seven Operational Advanced Landing Grounds in Arunachal Pradesh in a Month." *Economic Times*, 13 July 2018. https://economic times.indiatimes.com/news/defense/iaf-to-have-7-operational-advanced-landing -grounds-in-arunachal-pradesh-in-a-month/articleshow/49809013.cms?from=mdr.

Hoodbhoy, Parvez. "Views from Pakistan: 'Bleed India with a Thousand Cuts' Policy Is in Shambles." *Open*, 13 October 2016. http://www.openthemagazine .com/article/views-from-pakistan/bleed-india-with-a-thousand-cuts-policy-is-in-a -shambles.

Howard, Russell D., and Reid L. Sawyer. *Terrorism and Counterterrorism: Understanding the New Security Environment; Readings and Interpretations.* 3rd ed. New York: McGraw-Hill, 2009. https://www.tandfonline.com/doi/abs /10.1080/09700169908455030.

HQ Northern Command Study Group. *Soldiers' Role in Jammu and Kashmir.* New Delhi: HQ Northern Command, 1984.

"IAF Contingent 2000 to UNAMSIL." https://indianairforce.nic.in/content/sierra -leone.

"ICC IMB Piracy and Armed Robbery against Ships: 2017 Annual Report." https:// www.icc-ccs.org/reports/2017-Annual-IMB-Piracy-Report.pdf.

"India and United Nations: Peacekeeping and Peace Building." https://www .pminewyork.gov.in/pdf/menu/submenu__1260383365.pdf.

"India Has Deployed More than 1 Million Troops in Held Kashmir: Foreign Office." *Dawn*, 30 November 2016. https://www.dawn.com/news/1299621/india-has-de ployed-more-than-1-million-troops-in-held-kashmir-foreign-office.

Indian Ministry of Defense. *Joint Services Glossary of Military Terms.* Delhi, 2003.

Indo–Sri Lanka Accord. https://peacemaker.un.org/sites/peacemaker.un.org/files /IN%20LK_870729_Indo-Lanka%20Accord.pdf.

Integrated Headquarters of Ministry of Defense (Army). *Doctrine for Sub-conventional Operations*, December 2006.

International Institute of Strategic Studies. *IISS Military Balance Report 2019.* https://doi.org/10.1080/04597222.2018.1561032.

———. *Military Balance* 73, 1 (1973). https://doi.org/10.1080/04597227308459833.

Isser, Rajesh. *Peacekeeping and Protection of Civilians: The Indian Air Force in Congo.* New Delhi: KW Publishers, 2012.

"I Witnessed Wing Commander Abhinandan Shooting Down Pak's F-16 Aircraft: Squadron Leader Minty Agarwal." *India Today*, 15 August 2019. https:// www.indiatoday.in/india/story/i-witnessed-wing-commander-abhinandan-var thaman-shooting-down-pakistan-f-16-aircraft-squadron-leader-minty-agarwal -1581180-2019-08-15.

Jacob, Happymon. *Line on Fire: Ceasefire Violations and India-Pakistan Escalation Dynamics.* New Delhi: Oxford University Press, 2019.

Jagmohan. *My Frozen Turbulence in Kashmir.* Bombay: Allied Publishers, 1991.

Jamal, Arif. *Call for Transnational Jihad: Lashkar-e-Tayyaba (1985–2014).* New Delhi: Kautilya Books, 2015.

———. *Shadow War.* New York: Melville Publishing, 2009.

Jetly, Rajshri. "The Khalistan Movement in India: The Interplay of Politics and State Power." *International Review of Modern Sociology* 34, 1 (Spring 2008). https:// www.jstor.org/stable/41421658?seq=1.

Jones, Owen Bennet. *Pakistan: Eye of the Storm.* New Haven, CT: Yale University Press, 2002.

Jones, Simon. "India, Pakistan and Counterinsurgency Operations in Jammu and Kashmir." *Small Wars and Insurgencies* 19 (March 2008). https://www.tandfon line.com/doi/abs/10.1080/09592310801905736.

Joseph, Josy. "Three Battalions Ignored as the Nation Honours Martyrs of Kargil." Rediff, 25 July 2000. https://www.rediff.com/news/2000/jul/25kargil.htm.

Joshi, Manoj. "Depsang Incursion: Decoding Chinese Signal." *ORF Online*, 14 May 2013. https://www.orfonline.org/research/depsang-incursion-decoding-the -chinese-signal/.

———. *The Lost Rebellion: Kashmir in the Nineties.* New Delhi: Penguin, 1999.

Joshi, Yogesh. "Samudra: India's Convoluted Path to Undersea Nuclear Weapons." *Non-Proliferation Review* 26, 5–6 (2019). https://www.tandfonline.com/doi/abs /10.1080/10736700.2020.1720243.

Kakar, Harsha. "Has Pakistan Started Losing the Hybrid War in Kashmir." Raisina Debates, *ORF Online*, 2018. https://www.orfonline.org/expert-speak/has-paki stan-started-losing-hybrid-war-kashmir-46027/.

———. "Pace the Key for Interlocutor Success." *ORF Online*, 20 October 2017. https://www.orfonline.org/expert-speak/pace-key-interlocutors-success-kashmir/.

———. "Pakistan's 'Good' and 'Bad' Terrorists." Raisina Debates, *ORF Online*, 8 March 2018. https://www.orfonline.org/expert-speak/pakistan-good-bad-terror ists/

"Kaluchak Massacre, 14 May 2002." Press release, Ministry of External Affairs. https:// mea.gov.in/in-focus-article.htm?18990/Kaluchak+Massacre+14+May+2002.

Kanisetti, Anirudh, and Prakash Menon. "Takshashila Discussion Document: The Doklam Imbroglio." Takshashila Institution, September 2018. https://takshashila .org.in/takshashila-discussion-document-the-doklam-imbroglio/.

Kanwal, Gurmeet. "Misinterpreting the Quran to Justify Jihad." Center for Land and Warfare Studies Issue Brief13, 2009. https://www.claws.in/static/IB13_Misin terpreting-the-Quran-to-Justify-Jihad.pdf.

Kanwal, Gurmeet, and N. Manoharan, eds. *India's War on Terror.* New Delhi: KW Publishers, 2010.

Kapadia, Harish. *The Siachen Glacier: A Historical Review.* 102nd Infantry Brigade, 2011.

Kargil Review Committee. *From Surprise to Reckoning.* New Delhi: Sage Publica- tions, 1999.

Karim, Afsar. "Operation Topac." *Indian Defence Review*, July 1989.

Kartha, Tara. "Calling LAC Conflict 'Intelligence Failure' Is Lazy. It Ignores India's Real Problem." *Print*, 26 June 2020. https://theprint.in/author/tara-kartha/.

Kartha, Unni. "Stroll through the Killing Fields of Sri Lanka." 31 October 2018. http://cyclicstories.blogspot.com/2018/.

Kashyap, Samudra Gupta, and Praveen Swami. "Explained: Everything You Wanted to Know about the Naga Insurgency." *Indian Express*, 4 August 2015. https:// indianexpress.com/article/india/india-others/everything-you-need-to-know-about -nagaland-insurgency-and-the-efforts-to-solve/.

Katoch, Prakash. "Tryst with Deceit." *Outlook*, 23 April 2012. https://www.outlook india.com/website/story/tryst-with-deceit/280653.

Kaufman, Michael. "Sikh Separatists Hijack Indian Jetliner to Pakistan." *New York Times*, 30 September 1981. https://www.nytimes.com/1981/09/30/world/sikh -separatists-hijack-indian-jetliner-to-pakistan.html.

Kaur, Harminder. *Blue Star over Amritsar*. New Delhi: Ajanta Publications, 1990.

Keefe, Patrick Radden. "McMaster and Commander." *New Yorker*, 30 April 2018.

Kharb, Karan. "Why China and Pakistan Want Demilitarization of Siachen." *Indian Defence Review*, 19 May 2014. http://www.indiandefencereview.com/news/why -china-and-pakistan-want-demilitarization-of-siachen/.

Kilcullen, David. *The Accidental Guerrilla*. London: Hurst, 2009.

"Know What the Indian Army's Operation Snow Leopard Is." *Daily Hunt*, 17 September 2020. https://m.dailyhunt.in/news/india/english/ampinity+news-epa per-amptnw/know+what+the+indian+army+s+operation+snow+leopard+is-new sid-n215482156.

Krishnan, Ananth. "Forgotten in Fog of War, the Last Firing on the India-China Border." *Hindu*, 14 June 2020. https://www.thehindu.com/news/national/forgotten -in-fog-of-war-the-last-firing-on-the-india-china-border/article31827344.ece.

Kristensen, Hans M., and Matt Korda. "Chinese Nuclear Forces." *Bulletin of the Atomic Scientists* 75, 4 (2019): 171–178. https://www.tandfonline.com/doi/pdf /10.1080/00963402.2019.1628511?needAccess=true.

———. "Indian Nuclear Forces." *Bulletin of the Atomic Scientists* 74, 6 (2018): 361–366. https://www.tandfonline.com/doi/full/10.1080/00963402.2018.15331 62.

Kumar, Bharat. *Operation Pawan: Role of Airpower with IPKF*. New Delhi: Manohar, 2015.

Kundu, Apurba. "The Indian Armed Forces' Sikh and Non-Sikh Officers' Opinions of Operation Bluestar." *Pacific Affairs* 67, 1 (Spring 1994). https://www.jstor.org /stable/2760119?seq=1.

Ladwig, Walter C., III. "A Cold Start for Hot Wars." *International Security* 32, 3 (Winter 2007). https://www.belfercenter.org/sites/default/files/files/publication /IS3203_pp158-190.pdf.

Lal, Rashi. "When LU Became Ground Zero for PAC Revolt." *Times of India*, Lucknow ed., 1 June 2018. https://timesofindia.indiatimes.com/city/lucknow/when-lu -became-ground-zero-for-pac-revolt/articleshow/64417667.cms.

Lambeth, Benjamin. "Air Power at 18,000: The Indian Air Force in the Kargil War." Carnegie Endowment for International Peace, 20 September 2012.

———. "American and NATO Airpower Applied: From Deny Flight to Inherent Resolve." In *Airpower Applied: US, NATO and Israeli Combat Experience*, ed. John Andreas Olsen. Annapolis, MD: Naval Institute Press, 2017.

"The Largest LTTE Training Camp Was Located at Kolathur." *Hindu*, 28 August 2014. https://www.thehindu.com/news/national/tamil-nadu/the-largest-ltte-train ing-camp-was-located-at-kolathur/article6357629.ece.

Lavoy, Peter. "A Conversation with Gen Khalid Kidwai." Carnegie International Nuclear Policy Conference, 23 March 2015. https://carnegieendowment.org /files/03-230315carnegieKIDWAI.pdf.

———, ed. *Asymmetric Warfare in South Asia.* New York: Cambridge University Press, 2009.

Lelyveld, Joseph. "India: New Troubles." *New York Times*, 17 September 1967.

Levy, Adrian, and Cathy-Scott Clark. *The Meadow: Kashmir, Where the Terror Began.* New Delhi: HarperCollins, 2012.

Liang, Qiao, and Wang Xiangsui. *Unrestricted Warfare.* Beijing: PLA Literature and Arts Publishing House, 1999.

Lin, Liu. "India-China Doklam Standoff: A Chinese Perspective." *Diplomat*, 27 July 2017. https://thediplomat.com/2017/07/india-china-doklam-standoff-a-chinese-perspective/.

Ling, L. M. H. "Border Pathology." In L. M. H. Ling, Adriana Erthal Abdenur, Payal Banerjee, Nimmi Kurian, Mahendra P. Lama, and Li Bo, *India China: Rethinking Borders and Security.* Ann Arbor: University of Michigan Press, 2018.

Linsbauer, A., H. Frey, W. Haeberli, H. Machguth, M. Azam, and S. Allen. "Modelling Glacier-Bed Overdeepenings and Possible Future Lakes for the Glaciers in the Himalaya Karakoram Region." *Annals of Glaciology* 57, 71 (2016). https://www.cambridge.org/core/journals/annals-of-glaciology/article/modelling-glacierbed-overdeepenings-and-possible-future-lakes-for-the-glaciers-in-the-himalayakarakoram-region/C18FD61BBB68E27ECCF5657074A8246A.

Longman, Timothy. "The Complex Reasons for Rwanda's Engagement in Congo." In *The African Stakes of the Congo War*, ed. John F. Clark. New York: Palgrave Macmillan, 2002.

Lynch, Colum. "India to Withdraw Large UN Force from Sierra Leone." *Washington Post*, 21 September 2000. https://www.washingtonpost.com/archive/politics/2000/09/21/india-to-withdraw-large-un-force-from-sierra-leone/33c46528-678d-4014-b8b2-8aa299a3658b/?utm_term=.e2dfe7d4c37f.

Madan, Tanvi. "How the US Viewed the 1967 Sikkim Skirmishes between India and China." *Print*, 13 September 2017. https://theprint.in/2017/09/13/how-the-us-viewed-the-1967-sikkim-skirmishes-between-india-and-china/.

Malhotra, Inder. "Indian Tonic at Nathu La." *Guardian*, 18 September 1967.

Malik, S. K. *The Quranic Concept of War.* New Delhi: Himalayan Books, 1986.

Malik, V. P. "The Capture of Tiger Hill: A First-hand Account." Indian Ministry of Defense Media Center, 26 July 2002. http://mea.gov.in/articles-in-indian-media.htm?dtl/14805/The+capture+of+Tiger+Hill+a+firsthand+account.

———. *From Surprise to Victory.* New Delhi: HarperCollins, 2006.

———. *India's Military Conflicts and Diplomacy.* New Delhi: HarperCollins, 2019.

Mankekar, D. R. *On the Slippery Slope in Nagaland.* Bombay: Manaktalas, 1967.

Marwah, Ved. *Uncivil Wars: Pathology of Terrorism in India.* New Delhi: Indus, 1995.

"Mast Gul, a Freedom Fighter Turned Terrorist Attacks Peshawar." *News*, 7 February 2014. https://www.thenews.com.pk/archive/print/636032-mast-gul,-a-freedom-fighter-turned-terrorist-attacks-peshawar.

McFadden, Robert D. "Mad Mike Hoare, Irish Mercenary Leader in Africa, Dies at 100." *New York Times*, 3 February 2020. https://www.nytimes.com/2020/02/03/obituaries/mike-hoare-dies.html.

McGreal, Chris. "What's the Point of Peacekeepers When They Do Not Keep the Peace?" *Guardian*, 17 September 2015. https://www.theguardian.com /world/2015/sep/17/un-united-nations-peacekeepers-rwanda-bosnia.

Media Center, Ministry of External Affairs. "Settling the Border Question." 3 July 2003. https://www.mea.gov.in/articles-in-indian-media.htm?dtl/13537 /Settling+the+China+border.

Mehta, Ashoke. "Tackling the Tigers." http://www.india-seminar.com/1999/479/479 %20mehta.htm.

Mehta, Raj. "Bravery beyond Comparison: Hony Captain Bana Singh, PVC." *Scholar Warrior* (Autumn 2013). https://archive.claws.in/images/journals_doc/20 -Bravery%20Beyond%20Comparison%20-%20Hony%20Capt%20Bana%20 Singh%2C%20PVC.pdf.

Meilinger, Phillip S. "Ten Propositions Regarding Airpower." Air Force History and Museums Program, 1995. https://www.airuniversity.af.edu/Portals/10/ASPJ/jour nals/Chronicles/meil.pdf.

Menon, Prakash. "Stand up against China." *Pragati*, 20 April 2018. https://www .thinkpragati.com/opinion/4291/stand-up-against-china/.

———. *The Strategy Trap: India and Pakistan under the Nuclear Shadow.* New Delhi: Wisdom Tree, 2018.

Menon, Raja. *Maritime Strategy and Continental Wars.* London: Frank Cass, 1998.

Menon, Shivshankar. *Choices: Inside the Making of India's Foreign Policy.* New Delhi: Penguin Random House, 2016.

Mitra, Sumit. "Rajiv–Longowal Accord: Mathew Commission Delivers an Unexpected Anti-Climax." *India Today*, 15 February 1986. https://www.indiatoday .in/magazine/cover-story/story/19860215-rajiv-longowal-accord-mathew-commis sion-delivers-an-unexpected-anti-climax-800593-1986-02-15.

Mukherjee, Anit. *The Absent Dialogue: Politicians, Bureaucrats and the Military in India.* New Delhi: Oxford University Press, 2019.

———. "K. Subrahmanyam and Indian Strategic Thought." *Strategic Analysis* 35, 4 (July 2011). https://www.tandfonline.com/doi/abs/10.1080/09700161.2011.57 6111.

Mukherjee, J. R. *An Insider's Experience of Insurgency in India's North-East.* London: Anthem Press, 2005.

Mukhim, Patricia. "A Deal at Last." *Hindu*, 28 March 2019. https://www.thehindu .com/opinion/op-ed/a-deal-at-last/article26656012.ece.

Murari, S. *The Prabhakaran Saga: The Rise and Fall of an Eelam Warrior.* New Delhi: Sage, 2012.

Murray, Leo. *War Games: The Psychology of Combat.* Mumbai: Jaico Publishing, 2019.

Musharraf, Pervez. *In the Line of Fire.* New York: Free Press, 2006.

Mutahi, Patrick. "India Plays Globo Cop of Somali Coast as Western Navies Play Safe." *Daily Nation*, 18 December 2008. https://www.nation.co.ke/news /africa/1066-504022-7e1nn7z/index.html.

Myers, Joseph C. "The Quranic Concept of War." *Parameters* (Winter 2006–2007).

http://insct.syr.edu/wp-content/uploads/2013/03/MyersJoseph.Quranic-Concept -of-War.pdf.

Nagl, John A. *Learning to Eat Soup with a Knife: Counterinsurgency Lessons from Malaya and Vietnam*. Chicago: University of Chicago Press, 2005.

Nair, K. S. *Ganesha's Flyboys: The IAF in Congo*. Hyderabad, India: Anveshan Enterprises, 2012.

Nambiar, Satish. "An Indian General Recalls How the World Failed Srebnica Years Ago." *Wire*, 12 July 2015. https://thewire.in/external-affairs/an-indian-general -recalls-how-the-world-failed-srebrenica-20-years-ago.

Nanavatty, Rostum K. *Internal Armed Conflict in India*. New Delhi: Pentagon Press, 2013.

Naqvi, S. M. H. Y. "The Battle of Chumik." *Pakistan Army Journal* 30, 4 (December 1989). Available at the library of the Defence Services Staff College, Wellington, India.

Narang, Vipin. *Nuclear Strategy in the Modern Era*. Princeton, NJ: Princeton University Press, 2014.

Narang, Vipin, and Christopher Clary. "India's Pangong Pickle: New Delhi's Options after Its Clash with China." *War on the Rocks*, 2 July 2020. https:// warontherocks.com/2020/07/indias-pangong-pickle-new-delhis-options-after-its -clash-with-china/.

Narayanswamy, M. R. *Inside an Elusive Mind: Prabhakaran*. New Delhi: Konark Publishers, 2003.

———. *Tigers of Lanka: From Boys to Guerrillas*. Colombo, Sri Lanka: Vijitha Yapa Publications, 1994.

"Navy Saves Vessel in Pirate Channel." *Telegraph*, 11 November 2008. https://www .telegraphindia.com/india/navy-saves-vessel-in-pirate-channel/cid/524854.

Negi, Manjeet Singh. "India Building 61 Strategic Roads along Pakistan, China Border." *India Today*, 15 July 2019. https://www.indiatoday.in/india/story/india -building-61-strategic-roads-along-pakistan-china-borders-1569516-2019-07-15.

———. "Indian Air Force Probe Finds Friendly Fire Caused February 27 Budgam Chopper Crash, 5 Officers in Dock." *India Today*, 23 August 2019. https://www .indiatoday.in/india/story/indian-air-force-budgam-chopper-crash-friendly-fire -officers-guilty-1590764-2019-08-23.

———. "Indian Air Force Signs Rs 1500 Crore Deal with Russia for R-27 Air-to- Air Missile." *India Today*, 29 July 2019. https://www.indiatoday.in/india/story /indian-air-force-r-27-air-to-air-missiles-russia-defense-deal-1574898-2019-07-29.

———. "Uri Attack: An Inside Account of How It Happened." *India Today*, 18 September 2016. https://www.indiatoday.in/india/story/uri-attack-inside-story -pashtun-map-pakistani-ammunition-jash-e-mohammed-341761-2016-09-18.

"New Army Chief for Debate on Security." *Hindustan Times*, 1 July 1993.

"New Army Chief Suggests Restructuring to Fight Militancy." *Financial Express*, 1 July 1993.

Nibedon, Nirmal. *Nagaland: The Night of the Guerrillas*. New Delhi: Lancer, 1978.

Nzongola-Ntalja, Georges. "Patrice Lumumba: The Most Important Assassination

of the 20th Century." *Guardian*, 17 January 2011. https://www.theguardian.com
/global-development/poverty-matters/2011/jan/17/patrice-lumumba-50th-anniver
sary-assassination.

O'Donnell, Frank, and Alex Bollfrass. "The Strategic Postures of China and India:
A Visual Guide." Project on Managing the Atom, Belfer Center for Science and
International Affairs, Kennedy School of Government, Harvard University, March
2020. https://www.belfercenter.org/publication/strategic-postures-china-and-in
dia-visual-guide.

O'Donnell, Frank, and Debolina Ghoshal. "Managing Indian Deterrence: Pressures
on Credible Minimum Deterrence and Nuclear Policy Options." *Non-Proliferation Review*, February 2019. https://www.tandfonline.com/doi/full/10.1080/1073
6700.2019.1565187.

Pachauri, Pankaj. "Mirwaiz Fiasco Sparks off a Change in Guard in Kashmir."
India Today, 15 June 1990. https://www.indiatoday.in/magazine/indiascope
/story/19900615-mirwaiz-fiasco-sparks-off-a-change-of-guard-in-kashmir
-812692-1990-06.

Palit, D. K. *The Sentinels of the North-East*. New Delhi: Palit & Palit, 1984.

Palsokar, R. D. *Forever in Operations, a Success Story: A Historical Record of the
8th Mountain Division in Counterinsurgency in Nagaland and Manipur, and in
the 1971 Indo-Pak Conflict*. Pune, India: HQ Eighth Mountain Division, 1991.

Palsokar, R. R. *Ours Not to Reason Why*. Pune, India: Sunidhi Publishers, 2017.

Panag, H. S. "India-China Standoff: What Is Happening in the Chumbi Valley?" 8
July 2017. https://www.newslaundry.com/2017/07/08/panag-india-china-sikkim
-bhutan.

Pandit, Rajat. "More Nuclear Warheads with Pak, but India Unfazed." *Times of
India*, 16 June 2020. https://timesofindia.indiatimes.com/india/pakistan-remains
-ahead-in-nuclear-warheads-but-india-confident-of-its-deterrence-capability/ar
ticleshow/76381003.cms.

———. "Several Soldiers Injured in Clashes in Ladakh & Sikkim as Border Tensions
Flare up between India and China." *Times of India*, 11 May 2020. https://times
ofindia.indiatimes.com/india/several-soldiers-injured-in-two-clashes-between-in
dian-chinese-troops-along-the-border/articleshow/75660665.cms.

Pandita, Rahul. "Beyond Balakot." *Open*, 28 February 2019. https://openthemaga
zine.com/cover-stories/beyond-balakot/.

Parthasarathy, G., and Radha Kumar. *Frameworks for a Kashmir Settlement*. New
Delhi: Delhi Policy Group, 2006.

Peri, Dinakar. "Third Regiment of T-72 Tanks to Be Moved to Ladakh Soon."
Hindu, 19 July 2016. https://www.thehindu.com/news/national/Third-regiment
-of-T-72-tanks-to-be-moved-to-Ladakh-soon/article14497629.ece.

Perkovich, George. *India's Nuclear Bomb: The Impact on Global Proliferation*.
Berkeley: University of California Press, 1999.

Perumal, Alagaraj. "Missile Strike." 12 June 2017. http://www.bharat-rakshak.com
/IAF/history/kargil/1060-perumal.html.

Phillip, Snehesh Alex. "What Imran Khan Says Is 9 Lakh Soldiers in Kashmir Is
Actually 3.43 Lakh Only." *Print*, 12 November 2019. https://theprint.in/de

fense/what-imran-khan-says-is-9-lakh-soldiers-in-kashmir-is-actually-3-43-lakh
-only/319442/.

Pillarisetti, Jagan. "Descent into Danger." 7 March 2015. https://swarajyamag.com
/politics/descent-into-danger-the-jaffna-university-helidrop.

Pirabakaran, Vellupilla. "On the Indo–Sri Lanka Accord." 4 August 1987. http://
tamilnation.co/ltte/vp/87suthumalai.htm.

"PM Hopes Firing Is Local Affair." *Times of India*, 2 October 1967.

Prakash, Arun. "Who Defends the Defenders." *Indian Express*, 22 August 2018.
https://indianexpress.com/article/opinion/columns/independence-day-afspa-in
dian-soldiers-miliatry-army-act-ministry-of-defence-5318222/.

Pratap, Anita. "Sri Lanka: IPKF Gains Public Acceptance in Batticaloa." *India Today*,
15 June 1988. https://www.indiatoday.in/magazine/neighbours/story/19880615
-sri-lanka-ipkf-gains-public-acceptance-in-batticaloa-797341-1988-06-15.

Press Information Bureau, Government of India, Prime Minister's Office. "Border
Defense Cooperation Agreement between India and China." 23 October 2013.
https://pib.gov.in/newsite/PrintRelease.aspx?relid=100178.

———. "Indian Navy Nabs 61 Pirates and Rescues 13 Crew, Neutralizes Pirate
Mother Vessel Vega 5." 14 March 2011. http://pib.nic.in/newsite/PrintRelease
.aspx?relid=70909.

Press Trust of India. PTI report. *Economic Times*, 11 July 2018. https://economic
times.indiatimes.com/news/defence/heroes-of-surgical-strike-honoured-with-gal
lantry-medals/articleshow/56782741.cms?from=mdr.

Puri, Mohinder. *Kargil: Turning the Tide*. New Delhi: Lancer, 2016.

Puri, Nikhil Raymond. "Assessing Disturbance in Jammu and Kashmir's 'Disturbed
Areas.'" ORF Issue Brief 104, September 2015. https://www.orfonline.org/wp
-content/uploads/2015/12/ORFIssueBrief104.pdf.

Qadir, Shaukat. "An Analysis of the Kargil Conflict 1999." *RUSI Journal* 147, 2
(2002): 24–30. https://doi.org/10.1080/03071840208446752.

Raghavan, Srinath. *Fierce Enigmas: A History of the United States in South Asia*.
New York: Basic Books, 2018.

"Rajiv Gandhi's 1988 Visit Broke Ice between India and China: Chinese Diplomat."
Hindustan Times, 13 October 2017. https://www.hindustantimes.com/india-news
/rajiv-gandhi-s-1988-visit-broke-ice-between-india-and-china-chinese-diplomat
/story-JiQdkXFbI5jcNsE7c6pGoJ.html.

Raman, B. "Should We Believe Gen Malik." Rediff, 5 May 2006. http://m.rediff
.com/news/1999/jul/16akd.htm.

Ramesh, Jairam. "India's Role in Ending the Korean War." *Hindu*, 3 May 2018.
www.thehindu.com/opinion/op-ed/india's-role-in-ending-the-korean-war/arti
cle23750989.ece.

Ranatunga, Cyril. *Adventurous Journey: From Peace to War, Insurgency to Terrorism*. Colombo, Sri Lanka: Vijitha Yapa Publications, 2009.

Ranganathan, Anand. "A Brief History of Mizoram: From the Aizwal Bombing to
the Peace Accord." https://www.newslaundry.com/2015/08/06/a-brief-history-of
-mizoram-from-the-aizawl-bombing-to-the-mizo-accord.

Rashid, Hakim Irfan. "Syed Salahuddin: Tale of a Preacher Turned Terror

Chief." *Economic Times*, 14 July 2018. https://economictimes.indiatimes.com /news/defence/syed-salahuddin-tale-of-a-preacher-turned-terror-chief/article show/59343807.cms?from=mdr.

Ravindranath, Colonel. "Victory in Kargil War: Lessons Learnt at Great Human Cost." 26 July 2015. https://www.thequint.com/news/india/victory-in-kargil-war -lessons-learnt-at-great-human-cost.

Rehman, Iskander. "Hard Men in a Hard Environment: Indian Special Operators along the Border with China." *War on the Rocks*, January 2017. https://waron therocks.com/2017/01/hard-men-in-a-hard-environment-indian-special-operators -along-the-border-with-china/.

Renshon, Jonathan. *Why Leaders Choose War.* New York: Praeger Security International, 2006.

"Revisiting Interventionism: India's Peacekeeping Force in Sri Lanka." Brookings India, 5 May 2019. https://www.brookings.edu/events/revisiting-interventionism -indias-peacekeeping-force-in-sri-lanka/.

"Revolt in the Hills." *Time*, 16 April 1956.

Richards, Joanne. "An Institutional History of the Liberation Tigers Tamil of Eelam." CCDP Working Paper 10, November 2014. http://repository.graduateinstitute.ch /record/292651/files/CCDP-Working-Paper-10-LTTE-1.pdf.

Riedel, Bruce. *Avoiding Armageddon: America, India and Pakistan to the Brink and Back.* Washington, DC: Brookings Institution Press, 2013.

Rikhye, Ravi. *The War that Never Was: The Story of India's Strategic Failures.* New Delhi: Prism Paperbacks, 1988.

"Rising Unpopularity Threatens Kashmir Accord." *India Today*, 15 September 1987. https://www.indiatoday.in/magazine/special-report/story/19870915-rising-unpop ularity-threatens-kashmir-accord-799268-1987-09-15.

Riza, Shaukat. *The Pakistan Army War 1965.* Lahore, Pakistan: Wajid Ali's, 1984.

Roy, P. K. "The Scene of the Incident." *Baltimore Sun*, 17 September 1967.

Roy, Shubhajit. "Ahead of Military Talks, China Claims Troops Have Disengaged at Most Sites." *Indian Express*, 29 July 2020.

Sahni, Ajai. "Area of Darkness." *Outlook*, 18 September 2009. https://www.outlook india.com/website/story/an-area-of-darkness/261931.

Sambandan, V. S. "A Promise of Identity." *Frontline* 20, 5 (1 March 2014). http:// www.frontline.in/static/html/fl2005/stories/20030314000805700.htm.

Saran, Rohit, Harinder Baweja, and Raj Chengappa. "Kargil Conflict Shows Signs of Intensifying as India Gains, Pakistan Remains Resilient." *India Today*, 5 July 1999. https://www.indiatoday.in/magazine/cover-story/story/19990705 -kargil-conflict-shows-signs-of-intensifying-as-india-gains-pakistan-remains-resil ient-824618-1999-07-05.

Sardeshpande, S. C. *Assignment Jaffna.* New Delhi: Lancer, 1992.

Sareen, Sushant. "Balakot Air Strikes: The End of the Madman Theory." *ORF Online*, 5 March 2019. https://www.orfonline.org/research/balakot-air-strikes-the -end-of-the-madman-theory-48730/.

———. "Pakistan Punched by Article 370 Move." *ORF Online*, 9 August

2019. https://www.orfonline.org/research/pakistan-punched-by-indias-article-370-move-54261/.

Sawant, Gaurav. "Op Snow Leopard: Inside Story of How Army Reclaimed Heights in Eastern Ladakh." *India Today*, 16 September 2020. https://www.indiatoday.in/india/story/snow-leopard-inside-story-army-reclaimed-heights-ladakh-exclusive-1722311-2020-09-16.

"The Secret behind Operation Blue Star: Britain's Dilemma Explained." *ET Online*, 13 June 2018. https://economictimes.indiatimes.com/news/et-explains/the-secret-behind-operation-blue-star-britains-dilemma-explained/articleshow/64569757.cms?from=mdr.

Sehgal, Ikram. "Choosing Merit over Friendship." Media Monitors Network, 9 October 2001. https://www.mediamonitors.net/perspectives/choosing-merit-over-friendship/.

Senaveratna, John M. *The Story of the Sinhalese from the Most Ancient Times up to the End of the Mahavansa or Great Dynasty.* New Delhi: Asian Educational Services, 1997.

Sharma, K. K. "Congo: First African War and Indian Soldiers (1960–64)." https://www.academia.edu/32888328/congo_first_african_war_and_indian_soldiers_1960-64_.doc.

Sharma, Sushil. *The Complexity Called Manipur: Perceptions and Reality.* New Delhi: Viva Books, 2019.

Sharma, Sushil Kumar. "Lessons from Mizoram Insurgency and Peace Accord 1986." Vivekananda International Foundation, June 2016. https://www.vifindia.org/sites/default/files/lessons-from-mizoram-insurgency-and-peace-accord-1986.pdf.

"Sheikh Abdullah and the Kashmir Issue." Declassified CIA report, 18 April 1964. https://www.cia.gov/library/readingroom/docs/DOC_0000283431.pdf.

Shenag, Ved. "The IAF in the Kargil Operations—1999." *Bharat Rakshak*, 16 October 2009. http://bharat-rakshak.com/IAF/History/Kargil/1055-VedShenag.html.

Shome, Vishnu. "In Kargil War, India Was Minutes away from Bombing Pak Bases." 19 July 2016. https://www.ndtv.com/india-news/exclusive-in-kargil-war-india-was-minutes-away-from-bombing-pak-bases-1433345.

Shrivastava, Rahul. "How Much of Indian Land Is Occupied by China? As Centre, Congress Trade Barbs, the Truth Lies in Parliament Records." *India Today*, 23 June 2020. https://www.indiatoday.in/india/story/how-much-of-indian-land-in-ladakh-is-occupied-by-china-1691859-2020-06-23.

Shukla, Ajai. "India Has 700,000 Troops in Kashmir? False!!!" Rediff, 17 July 2018. https://www.rediff.com/news/column/india-has-700000-troops-in-kashmir-false/20180717.htm.

"Siachen: 879 Deaths and Still Counting." *Indian Express*, 11 February 2016. http://indianexpress.com/article/india/india-news-india/siachen-avalanche-hanuman-thappa/.

"Siachen Glacier: Roll of Honour." http://www.bharat-rakshak.com/IAF/Personnel/Martyrs/198-4-99-Siachen.html.

Siddiqui, Aslam. *Pakistan Seeks Security.* Lahore, Pakistan: Longman Green, 1960.

Sidhu, H. P. S. "Understanding Hybrid Warfare and Developing a Response." Paper presented at the National Defense College, 5 May 2016. Published in *Understanding Strategy*, a collection of seminar papers with limited distribution.

Sidhu, W. P. S. "Tenuous Lifeline." *India Today*, 31 May 1992.

Singh, Aarti Tikoo. "Here's How Schools of Faith, Mobiles Are Radicalising Kashmir." *Times of India*, 9 July 2017. https://timesofindia.indiatimes.com/india/how-mosques-and-mobiles-are-radicalising-kashmir/articleshow/59507200.cms.

Singh, Depinder. *The IPKF in Sri Lanka*. New Delhi: Trishul Publications, 1992.

Singh, Harkirat. *Intervention in Sri Lanka: The IPKF Experience Retold,* New Delhi: Manohar, 2007.

Singh, H. Bhuban. *Major Bob Khathing: The Profile of a Nationalist Manipuri Naga*. Manipur, India: P. Haoban Publishers, 1992.

Singh, Jasjit. *Air Power in Joint Operations*. New Delhi: Knowledge World, 2003.

Singh, Onkar. "True Valour." *Illustrated Weekly of India*, 28 March 1988.

Singh, Sushant. "In Fact: Before the LCA, India Had Its Own Fighter—Marut." *Indian Express*, 8 July 2016. https://indianexpress.com/article/explained/tejas-hf-24-marut-tejas-combat-aircraft-indian-air-force-2894021/.

———. *Mission Overseas: Daring Operations by the Indian Military*. New Delhi: Juggernaut, 2017.

Singh, Vikram. *Spitfire in the Sun*. New Delhi: Ambi Knowledge Resources, 2017.

Sinha, Lieutenant General S. K. *A Soldier Recalls*. New Delhi: Lancer Publishers, 1992.

Sinha, S. P. "CI Operations in the Northeast." *Indian Defence Review* 21, 2 (April–June 2006). http://www.indiandefencereview.com/spotlights/c-i-operations-in-the-northeast/0/.

——— "Northeast: The Threat Posed by External Actors." *Indian Defence Review*, 14 February 2016. http://www.indiandefencereview.com/spotlights/northeast-the-external-dimension/.

Sitapati, Vinay. *Half Lion: How PV Narasimha Rao Transformed India*. New Delhi: Penguin, 2016.

Skinner, Douglas W. "Air-Land Battle Doctrine." Center for Naval Analyses, September 1988. https://apps.dtic.mil/sti/pdfs/ADA202888.pdf.

South Asia Terrorism Portal. http://www.satp.org/satporgtp/countries/india/states/jandk/data_sheets/annual_casualties.htm.

Staniland, Paul. "Organizing Insurgency: Networks, Resources and Rebellion in South Asia." *International Security* 37, 1 (Summer 2012). https://www.jstor.org/stable/23280407?seq=1.

Steyn, Pieter. *Zapuphizo: Voice of the Nagas*. London: Kegan Paul, 2002.

Strachan, Hew. *The Direction of War: Contemporary Strategy in Historical Perspective*. Cambridge: Cambridge University Press, 2013.

Subrahmanyam, K. "Indo-Pak Nuclear Stand-off: A Challenge and an Opportunity." *Times of India*, 6 June 1988.

———. "A Proactive Kashmir Policy." *Economic Times*, 7 September 1988.

———. *Security in a Changing World*. New Delhi: D. K. Publishers, 1990.

———. *Shedding Shibboleths: India's Evolving Strategic Outlook.* New Delhi: Wordsmiths, 2005.

Subramaniam, Arjun. "Balakot and After: IAF Demonstrates Full Spectrum Capability." *First Post*, 11 March 2019. https://www.firstpost.com/world/balakot-and-after-iaf-demonstrates-full-spectrum-capability-6236391.html.

———. "Can Counter-Coercion Work against a Belligerent China?" *ORF Online.* https://www.orfonline.org/expert-speak/can-counter-coercion-work-belligerent-china/.

———. "Closing the Gap: A Doctrinal and Capability Appraisal of the IAF and PLAAF." In *Defence Primer: An Indian Military in Transformation*, ed. Pushan Das and Harsh V. Pant. New Delhi: ORF, 2018. https://www.orfonline.org/contributors/arjun-subramaniam/.

———. "For Modi and Xi, Not Achieving Much at Wuhan May Be the Best Thing." *Print*, 5 May 2018. https://theprint.in/opinion/for-modi-and-xi-not-achieving-much-in-wuhan-may-be-the-best-outcome/55393/.

———. "From Kargil to Parakram: A Lesson in Forceful Persuasion." *Hindu*, 27 July 2012. https://www.thehindu.com/opinion/op-ed/from-kargil-to-parakram-a-lesson-in-forceful-persuasion/article3687855.ece.

———. "The Indian Air Force, Subconventional Operations and Balakot: A Practitioner's Perspective." ORF Issue Brief 294 (May 2019). https://www.orfonline.org/research/the-indian-air-force-sub-conventional-operations-and-balakot-a-practitioners-perspective-50761/.

———. *India's Wars: A Military History 1947–1971.* Annapolis, MD: US Naval Institute Press, 2017.

———. "Kargil Revisited: Air Operations in a High-Altitude Conflict." *CLAWS Journal* (Summer 2008). https://archive.claws.in/images/journals_doc/464654525_ASubramanian.pdf.

———. "Raising Costs for Infiltration without Abandoning India's Core Principles of Restraint." *Print*, 16 March 2018. https://theprint.in/opinion/raising-costs-infiltration-without-abandoning-indias-core-principles-restraint/41752/.

———. "The Use of Air Power in Sri Lanka: Operation Pawan and Beyond." *Air Power Journal* 3, 3 (July–September 2008). http://capsindia.org/files/documents/Air-Power-Jul-Sep-08-Inside.pdf.

Subramanian, L. N. "A Ridge Too Far: Battle for Tololing." 12 October 2006. http://www.bharat-rakshak.com/ARMY/history/kargil/307-battle-for-tololing.html?tmpl=component&print=1&layout=default&page=.

Sundaram, Kumar, and M. V. Ramana. "India and the Policy of No First Use of Nuclear Weapons." *Journal for Peace and Nuclear Disarmament* 1, 1 (2018). https://www.tandfonline.com/doi/pdf/10.1080/25751654.2018.1438737?needAccess=true.

Suryaprakash, A. "The President Corrects Some Historical Facts, Gives Narasimha Rao His Due." 4 May 2016. https://www.vifindia.org/article/2016/may/04/the-president-corrects-some-historical-facts-gives-narasimha-rao-his-due.

"Suspected Sikh Extremists Slay Editor." 12 May 1984. https://www.upi.com/Archives/1984/05/12/Suspected-Sikh-extremists-slay-editor/3839453182400/.

Swami, Praveen. "Failed Threats and Flawed Fences: India's Military Responses to Pakistan's Proxy War." *India Review* 3, 2 (April 2004).

———. "General Kayani's Quiet Coup." *Hindu*, 3 August 2010. http://www .thehindu.com/todays-paper/tp-opinion/General-Kayanis-quiet-coup/arti cle16117389.ece.

———. "Hype and the Folly." *Frontline* 20, 13 (20 June 2013). https://frontline .thehindu.com/static/html/fl2013/stories/20030704007300400.htm.

———. "The Kargil War: Preliminary Explorations." South Asia Terrorism Portal and Institute for Conflict Management, 2001. http://www.satp.org/satporgtp/pub lication/faultlines/volume2/Fault2-SwamiF.htm.

———. "Remains of Another Day." *Frontline* 17, 2 (22 January 2000). https://front line.thehindu.com/static/html/fl1702/17020100.htm.

———. "Skeletons in the Generals' Cupboards." *Hindu*, 10 August 2009. http:// www.thehindu.com/todays-paper/tp-opinion/Skeletons-in-the-Generalsrsquo -cupboards/article16530736.ece.

Swami, Pravin. *India, Pakistan and the Secret Jihad*. New Delhi: Routledge, 2007.

———. "Terrorism in Jammu and Kashmir in Theory and Practice." *India Review* 2 (2003).

Tak, Firdaus. "Warwan Valley: A Hidden Beauty." *Greater Kashmir*, 24 July 2012. https://www.greaterkashmir.com/news/news/warwan-valley-a-hidden -beauty/125718.html.

Talbott, Strobe. "The Day a Nuclear Conflict Was Averted." *Yale Global Online*, 13 September 2004. https://yaleglobal.yale.edu/content/day-nuclear-conflict-was -averted.

———. *Engaging India: Diplomacy, Democracy, and the Bomb*. Washington, DC: Brookings Institution Press, 2006.

Tekwani, Shyam. "Sri Lanka Voters Back United National Party but Peace Remains Elusive." *India Today*, 15 March 1989. https://www.indiatoday.in/magazine/neigh bours/story/19890315-sri-lanka-voters-back-united-national-party-but-peace-re mains-elusive-815847-1989-03-15.

Telford, Hamish. "Counterinsurgency in India: Observations from Punjab and Kash- mir." *Journal of Conflict Studies* 21, 1 (Spring 2001). https://journals.lib.unb.ca /index.php/JCS/article/view/4293.

Tellis, Ashley J. *India's Emerging Nuclear Posture: Between Recessed Deterrent and Ready Arsenal*. New Delhi: Oxford University Press, 2001.

"Terror Camps on India–Myanmar Border Destroyed." *Economic Times*, 15 March 2019. https://economictimes.indiatimes.com/news/defence/terror-camps-on-india -myanmar-border-destroy ed/articleshow/68432469.cms.

Thapliyal, Sheru. "Nathu La and Cho La Clashes of 1967: How the Indian Army Dealt with Chinese Trouble." *Indian Defence Review*, 22 September 2014. http:// www.indiandefencereview.com/when-chinese-were-given-a-bloody-nose/.

Thukral, Gobind. "Extremists, AISSF Leaders Once Again Use Golden Temple as an Occasional Hideout." *India Today*, 15 May 1986. https://www.indiatoday .in/magazine/indiascope/story/19860515-extremists-aissf-leaders-once-again-use -golden-temple-as-an-occasional-hideout-800876-1986-05-15.

Times News Network. "7 Medals for Special Forces Team that Hit Myanmar Camps." *Times of India*, 15 August 2015. https://timesofindia.indiatimes.com/india/7-med als-for-Special-Forces-team-that-hit-Myanmar-camps/articleshow/48490051.cms.

———. "Silent Rally Echoes Mizo Pain of '66 IAF Attacks," *Times of India*, 5 March 2011. https://timesofindia.indiatimes.com/city/guwahati/Silent-rally-echoes-Mizo -pain-of-66-IAF-attacks/articleshow/7636603.cms?referral=PM.

"To Boost Ties, Chinese Army Delegation Visits Indian Army's Eastern Command in Kolkata." *Hindustan Times*, 24 February 2017. https://www.hindustantimes.com /india-news/to-boost-ties-chinese-army-delegation-visits-indian-army-s-eastern -command-in-kolkata/story-Oa1RqC1Iu3LazyPNhA5rFL.html.

"Tololing Peak: The Battle that Probably Changed the Course of the Kargil War." *India Today*, 5 July 1999. https://www.indiatoday.in/magazine/cover-story /story/19990705-tololing-peak-the-battle-that-probably-changed-the-course-of -kargil-war-824608-1999-07-05.

Tufail, Kaiser. "Kargil Conflict and the Pakistan Air Force." *Aeronaut*, 28 January 2009. http://kaiser-aeronaut.blogspot.co.uk/2009/01/.

Tully, Mark. "Operation Blue Star: How an Indian Army Raid on the Golden Temple Ended in Disaster." *Telegraph*, 6 June 2014. https://www.telegraph.co.uk/news /worldnews/asia/india/10881115/Operation-Blue-Star-How-an-Indian-army-raid -on-the-Golden-Temple-ended-in-disaster.html.

Tully, Mark, and Satish Jacob. *Amritsar: Mrs. Gandhi's Last Battle*. New Delhi: Rupa, 1985.

"2012 Annual IMB Piracy Report." https://www.scribd.com/document/305029896 /2012-Annual-Imb-Piracy-Report.

Ucko, David H. "Can Limited Intervention Work: Lessons from Britain's Success Story in Sierra Leone." *Journal of Strategic Studies* 39, 5–6 (December 2015). https://www.tandfonline.com/doi/abs/10.1080/01402390.2015.1110695.

Upsala Conflict Data Programme. http://ucdp.uu.se/#/exploratory.

Wahn, Kim Chan. "The Role of India in the Korean War." *International Area Review* 13, 2 (Summer 2010). https://journals.sagepub.com/doi/abs/10.1177/2233865910 01300202?journalCode=iasa.

Waldman, Amy. "India and Pakistan: Good Fences Make Good Neighbours." *New York Times*, 4 July 2004. https://www.nytimes.com/2004/07/04/world/india-and -pakistan-good-fences-make-good-neighbors.html.

Walia, Sumit. "Head Hunters in Kargil-Naga Regiment." *Indian Defence Review*, 21 July 2019. http://www.indiandefencereview.com/spotlights/head-hunters-in-kargil -naga-regiment/.

Wangchuk, Rinchen Norbu. "Mizo Peace Accord: The Intriguing Story behind In-dia's Most Enduring Peace Initiative." 2 July 2018. https://www.thebetterindia .com/148387/mizo-peace-accord-laldenga-rajiv-gandhi/.

Westad, Odd Arne. *The Cold War: A World History*. New Delhi: Penguin Books, 2017.

"When M. K. Narayanan Stalled the Siachen Deal." 7 September 2017. http://www .dnaindia.com/india/report-when-mk-narayanan-stalled-siachen-deal-2543556.

"Who Are the Nirankaris." *Indian Express*, 18 November 2018. https://indianex press.com/article/who-is/who-are-nirankaris/.

"Who Is Syed Salahuddin, and Why Is He Designated as a 'Global Terrorist'?" *Hindu*, 27 June 2017. https://www.thehindu.com/news/national/who-is-syed-sa lahuddin-and-what-is-a-global-terrorist/article19154173.ece.

Wickremesekara, Channa. *The Tamil Separatist War in Sri Lanka*. Oxford: Rout-ledge, 2016.

Winchell, Sean P. "Pakistan's ISI: The Invisible Government." *International Journal of Intelligence and Counter Intelligence* 16, 3 (Fall 2003). https://www.tandfon line.com/doi/abs/10.1080/713830449.

Yi, Shen. "China Prevails in Doklam Standoff but India Attempts to Distort Pub-lic Opinion." *Global Times*, 3 September 2017. http://www.globaltimes.cn/con tent/1064491.shtml.

Yung, Christopher. "China's Evolving Naval Force Structure: Beyond Sino-US Ri-valry." *China Brief* 18, 9. Accessed 12 November 2017. https://jamestown.org /program/chinas-evolving-naval-force-structure-beyond-sino-us-rivalry/.

Zain, Omer Farook. "Siachen Conflict: Discordant in Pakistan-India Rec-onciliation." *Pakistan Horizon* 59, 2 (April 2006). https://www.jstor.org /stable/41394127?seq=1.

Zehra, Nasim. *From Kargil to the Coup*. Lahore, Pakistan: Sang-e-Meel Publications, 2018.

PHOTO CREDITS

All photographs are nonproprietary, unpaid for, and part of the author's personal collection. The author is grateful to the following organizations and individuals that helped build this collection for use in this book:

Indian Ministry of Defense, Photo Division
Indian Army
Indian Air Force
Artillery School
218th Medium Regiment
Seventh Squadron
Forty-Eighth Squadron
114th Helicopter Unit
129th Helicopter Unit
Indian Air Force Garud Flight
General Bipin Rawat
Admiral Madhavendra Singh
Lieutenant General R. K. Nanavatty
Major General Samir Chakravorty
Air Vice Marshal Vikram Singh
Commodore P. K. Banerjee
Colonel G. S. Bains
Marine Commandos (MARCOS) Archives
Sixtieth Parachute Field Regiment
Wing Commander Ramji
Wing Commander Dushyant Dahiya
Group Captain A. G. Bewoor
Wing Commander Samtani
Lieutenant General J. M. Singh
Probal Dasgupta
Group Captain Deb Gohain

INDEX